THE TRADITION OF EVERLASTING BÖN

The Library of Tibetan Classics is a special series being developed by the Institute of Tibetan Classics aimed at making key classical Tibetan texts part of the global literary and intellectual heritage. Eventually comprising thirty-two large volumes, the collection will contain over two hundred distinct texts by more than a hundred of the best-known authors. These texts have been selected in consultation with the preeminent lineage holders of all the schools and other senior Tibetan scholars to represent the Tibetan literary tradition as a whole. The works included in the series span more than a millennium and cover the vast expanse of classical Tibetan knowledge—from the core teachings of the specific schools to such diverse fields as ethics, philosophy, linguistics, medicine, astronomy and astrology, folklore, and historiography.

The Tradition of Everlasting Bön
Five Key Texts on Scripture, Tantra, and the Great Perfection

Bön is commonly recognized as the pre-Buddhist religion of Tibet. According to the most established tradition, Everlasting Bön, or Yungdrung Bön, evolved on the basis of the teachings of Shenrab Miwoché in the Kingdom of Zhangzhung, which some historians locate in the western region of Tibet. The exact date of Shenrab is still a matter of speculation and the dates suggested vary from sometime during the sixth century CE to as far back as the late Neolithic period (7000–5000 BCE). Since the arrival of Buddhism in Tibet, Bön has undergone great transformation in all aspects, including its philosophy, doctrinal teachings, and meditative practices. The present volume contains five central texts of the Everlasting Bön school, each representing an important aspect of the tradition. The first text is by Drogön Azha Lodrö Gyaltsen (1198–1263) and presents the grounds and paths of the Greater Vehicle of the Bön tradition. This text represents the philosophical ideology of Bön teachings based on the scriptures contained in the Bön canon. The second text is a short root tantra attributed to revealed teachings from Kuntu Zangpo, the personification of the unconditioned absolute. The third text is a commentary on this root tantra attributed to Drenpa Namkha (fl. eighth century), a Bönpo sage contemporary with Padmasambhava. This commentary is part of a larger body of texts collectively known as the canon of commentaries. The fourth text was written by Nyamé Sherab Gyaltsen (1356–1415) and presents a general exposition of the tantric system according to Yungdrung Bön. The final text is by Drutön Gyalwa Yungdrung (1242–90) and pertains to the oral instructions on the meditation practices of Bön, especially on the cycle of practices associated with experiencing the nature of the mind, generally known as the Great Perfection systems. All five texts have been selected for inclusion in *The Library of Tibetan Classics* by the late H. H. Menri Trizin Rinpoché, Lungtok Tenpai Nyima (1927–2017), who was the thirty-third abbot of Menri Monastery, the central institution of the Yungdrung Bön school.

THE LIBRARY OF TIBETAN CLASSICS • VOLUME 9
Thupten Jinpa, General Editor

THE TRADITION OF EVERLASTING BÖN

Five Key Texts on Scripture, Tantra, and the Great Perfection

Translated by J. F. Marc des Jardins

in association with the Institute of Tibetan Classics

Wisdom Publications
132 Perry Street
New York, NY 10014 USA
wisdomexperience.org

Library of Congress Cataloging-in-Publication Data
Names: Des Jardins, J. F. Marc, 1958– translator.
Title: The tradition of everlasting bön: five key texts on scripture, tantra, and the great
    perfection / translated by J.F. Marc des Jardins.
Description: First edition. | Somerville: Wisdom Publications, 2023. |
    Series: Library of Tibetan classics; 9 | Includes bibliographical references and index.
Identifiers: LCCN 2022047051 (print) | LCCN 2022047052 (ebook) |
    ISBN 9780861714483 (hardcover) | ISBN 9781614298793 (ebook)
Subjects: LCSH: Bon (Tibetan religion)—Doctrines.
Classification: LCC BQ7965 .T833 2023 (print) | LCC BQ7965 (ebook) |
    DDC 299.5/4—dc23/eng/20221026
LC record available at https://lccn.loc.gov/2022047051
LC ebook record available at https://lccn.loc.gov/2022047052

ISBN 978-0-86171-448-3   ebook ISBN 978-1-61429-879-3

27 26 25 24 23
5 4 3 2 1

Cover and interior design by Gopa & Ted2, Inc. Cover typeset by Tony Lulek. Interior
typeset by PerfecType.

Message from the Dalai Lama

THE LAST TWO MILLENNIA witnessed a tremendous proliferation of cultural and literary development in Tibet, the Land of Snows. Moreover, owing to the inestimable contributions made by Tibet's early spiritual kings, numerous Tibetan translators, and many great Indian paṇḍitas over a period of so many centuries, the teachings of the Buddha and the scholastic tradition of ancient India's Nālandā monastic university became firmly rooted in Tibet. As evidenced from the historical writings, this flowering of Buddhist tradition in the country brought about the fulfillment of the deep spiritual aspirations of countless sentient beings. In particular, it contributed to the inner peace and tranquility of the peoples of Tibet, Outer Mongolia—a country historically suffused with Tibetan Buddhism and its culture—the Tuva and Kalmuk regions in present-day Russia, the outer regions of mainland China, and the entire trans-Himalayan areas on the southern side, including Bhutan, Sikkim, Ladakh, Kinnaur, and Spiti. Today this tradition of Buddhism has the potential to make significant contributions to the welfare of the entire human family. I have no doubt that, when combined with the methods and insights of modern science, the Tibetan Buddhist cultural heritage and knowledge will help foster a more enlightened and compassionate human society, a humanity that is at peace with itself, with fellow sentient beings, and with the natural world at large.

It is for this reason I am delighted that the Institute of Tibetan Classics in Montreal, Canada, is compiling a thirty-two-volume series containing the works of many great Tibetan teachers, philosophers, scholars, and practitioners representing all major Tibetan schools and traditions. These important writings will be critically edited and annotated and will then be published in modern book format in a reference collection called *The Library of Tibetan Classics*, with the translations into other major languages to follow later. While expressing my heartfelt commendation for this noble project, I pray and hope that *The Library of Tibetan Classics* will not only make these important Tibetan treatises accessible to scholars of Tibetan studies but will also create a new opportunity for younger Tibetans to study and take interest in their own rich and profound culture. It is my sincere hope that through the series' translations into other languages, millions of fellow citizens of the wider human family will also be able to share in the joy of engaging with Tibet's classical literary heritage, textual riches that have been such a great source of joy and inspiration to me personally for so long.

The Dalai Lama
The Buddhist monk Tenzin Gyatso

Special Acknowledgments

THE INSTITUTE OF TIBETAN CLASSICS expresses its deep gratitude to the Ing Foundation for its generous support of the entire cost of translating this important volume. The Ing Foundation's long-standing patronage of the Institute of Tibetan Classics has enabled the institute to support the translation of multiple volumes from *The Library of Tibetan Classics*. We are deeply grateful to the foundation for offering us the opportunity to share many of the important texts of the Tibetan tradition with wider international readership, making these works truly part of the global literary, knowledge, and spiritual heritage.

Publisher's Acknowledgment

THE PUBLISHER WISHES TO extend a heartfelt thanks to the following people who have contributed substantially to the publication of *The Library of Tibetan Classics*:

Pat Gruber and the Patricia and Peter Gruber Foundation
The Hershey Family Foundation
The Ing Foundation

We also extend deep appreciation to our other subscribing benefactors:

Anonymous, dedicated to Buddhas within
Anonymous, in honor of Dzongsar Khyentse Rinpoche
Anonymous, in honor of Geshe Tenzin Dorje
Anonymous, in memory of K. J. Manel De Silva—may she realize the truth
Anonymous, in memory of Gene Smith
Dr. Patrick Bangert
Nilda Venegas Bernal
Serje Samlo Khentul Lhundub Choden and his Dharma friends
Nicholas Cope
Kushok Lobsang Dhamchöe
Diep Thi Thoai
Tenzin Dorjee

Richard Farris
Gaden Samten Ling, Canada
Evgeniy Gavrilov & Tatiana Fotina
Petar Gesovic
Great Vow Zen Monastery
Ginger Gregory
the Grohmann family, Taiwan
Gyaltsen Lobsang Jamyang (WeiJie) and Pema Looi
Rick Meeker Hayman
Steven D. Hearst
Jana & Mahi Hummel
Curt and Alice Jones
Julie LaValle Jones
Heidi Kaiter
Paul, Trisha, Rachel, and Daniel Kane
Land of Medicine Buddha
Dennis Leksander

Diane & Joseph Lucas
Elizabeth Mettling
Russ Miyashiro
Kestrel Montague
the Nalanda Institute, Olympia, WA
Craig T. Neyman
Kristin A. Ohlson
Arnold Possick
Magdalene Camilla Frank Prest
Quek Heng Bee, Ong Siok Ngow,
    and family
Randall-Gonzales Family
    Foundation
Erick Rinner
Andrew Rittenour
Dombon Roig Family
Jonathan and Diana Rose
the Sharchitsang family

Nirbhay N. Singh
Wee Kee Tan
Tibetisches Zentrum e.V. Hamburg
Richard Toft
Alissa KieuNgoc Tran
Timothy Trompeter
Tsadra Foundation
the Vahagn Setian Charitable
    Foundation
Ellyse Adele Vitiello
Jampa (Alicia H.) Vogel
Nicholas C. Weeks II
Mr. and Mrs. Richard and Carol
    Weingarten
Claudia Wellnitz
Bob White
Kevin Michael White, MD
Eve and Jeff Wild

and the other donors who wish to remain anonymous.

Contents

PART 5. THE PRACTICE MANUAL OF THE REVELATORY TRADITION OF THE GREAT PERFECTION FROM ZHANGZHUNG
Drutön Gyalwa Yungdrung (1242–90)

General Editor's Preface

THE WORKS in this volume of *The Library of Tibetan Classics*, chosen by His Holiness the late Menri Trizin Rinpoché and now made available to English-speaking readers, bring to the world in a powerful way the depth and richness of the Bön tradition. The antiquity of the Tibetan people's relationship with Bön can be detected in the Tibetan word *Bö* (spelled *Bod*), the very name Tibetans use to refer to Tibet. In one interpretation at least, the word *Bö* derives from the word *Bön,* suggesting that the land derived its name from its native religion. So, as a Tibetan and as the editor of this series, it is a source of both pride and satisfaction to include in the series a special volume featuring the profound Bön tradition.

Two primary objectives have driven the creation and development of *The Library of Tibetan Classics*. The first aim is to help revitalize the appreciation and the study of the Tibetan classical heritage within Tibetan-speaking communities worldwide. The younger generation in particular struggle with the tension between traditional Tibetan culture and the realities of modern consumerism. To this end, efforts have been made to develop a comprehensive yet manageable body of texts, one that features the works of Tibet's best-known authors and covers the gamut of classical Tibetan knowledge. The second objective of *The Library of Tibetan Classics* is to help make these texts part of a global literary and intellectual heritage. In this regard, we have tried to make the English translation reader-friendly and, as much as possible, keep the body of the text free of unnecessary scholarly apparatus, which can intimidate general readers. For specialists who wish to compare the translation with the Tibetan original, page references of the critical edition of the Tibetan text are provided in brackets.

The texts in this thirty-two-volume series span more than a millennium—from the development of the Tibetan script in the seventh century to the first part of the twentieth century, when Tibetan society and culture first encountered industrial modernity. The volumes are thematically organized and cover many of the categories of classical Tibetan knowledge—from the teachings specific to each Tibetan school to the classical works on philosophy, psychology, and phenomenology. The first category includes teachings of the Kadam, Nyingma, Sakya, Kagyü, Geluk, and Jonang schools, of miscellaneous Buddhist lineages, and of the Bön school. Texts in these volumes have been largely selected by senior lineage holders of the individual schools. Texts in the other categories have been selected primarily in recognition of the historical reality of the individual disciplines. For example, in the field of epistemology, works from the Sakya and Geluk schools have been selected, while the volume on buddha nature features the writings of Butön Rinchen Drup and various Kagyü masters. Where fields are of more common interest, such as the three codes or the bodhisattva ideal, efforts have been made to represent the perspectives of all four major Tibetan Buddhist schools. *The Library of Tibetan Classics* can function as a comprehensive library of the Tibetan literary heritage for libraries, educational and cultural institutions, and interested individuals.

It has been a profound honor for me to be part of this important translation project. I wish first of all to express my deep personal gratitude to His Holiness the Dalai Lama for always being such a profound source of inspiration and being an exemplary representative of the Tibetan tradition in the world. I would like to take this opportunity to also express my deep gratitude to His Holiness the late Menri Trizin Rinpoché for advising me on the selection of these important texts for the volume. I must also thank the translator of our volume, J. F. Marc des Jardins, a fellow Montrealer, for rendering these texts in English with such clarity and precision. Marc's introductory essay is a gem illuminating the volume, helping the modern reader navigate the complex history of Bön, including its long and interwoven philosophical and doctrinal relationship with the Buddhism that came to be the dominant faith of the land.

To the following individuals and organizations, I owe my sincere thanks: to Wisdom Publications, especially David Kittelstrom for his long-time stewardship of the series and Mary Petrusewicz for carefully editing the volume; to Phuntsok Nyima and Nyima Kunkhyab for their help with editing the original Tibetan volume on which this translation is based; to BDRC (Buddhist Digital Resource Center) for providing unrestricted access to its comprehensive digital Tibetan texts during the editing of the Tibetan texts; and to my wife Sophie Boyer Langri for taking on the numerous administrative chores that are part of a project such as this.

Finally, I would like to express my deepest gratitude to the Ing Foundation for its long-standing patronage of the Institute of Tibetan Classics. The entire cost of this translation project has been supported through the foundation's generous grant to the Institute, and the foundation's support also enables me to continue to devote the time and attention necessary for ensuring the success of the thirty-two-volume *Library of Tibetan Classics* project.

Thupten Jinpa
Montreal, 2023

Translator's Introduction

The Everlasting Bön Tradition

The texts comprising this volume are key representatives of the Tibetan religious tradition known as Yungdrung Bön (*g.yung drung bon*), or Everlasting Bön. This school is presently the most prominent among the traditions in Tibet that portray themselves as heirs to the pre-Buddhist religious practices known under the generic title of Bön. Therefore, Everlasting Bön is an indigenous movement that can be traced at least to the beginning of the eleventh century when Shenchen Lüga (996–1035)[1] discovered a cache of non-Buddhist texts in 1017 and began to transmit their practices to a host of disciples. The discovery in 913 of the collection of scriptures titled the *Hundred Thousand Verses on the Water Spirits* (*Klu 'bum*) supports earlier beginnings or, at least, definite traces of ancestry. This collection contains many elements that characterize Bön as we know it today as well as myths and their associated practices from the imperial period (seventh–ninth centuries).[2]

The word *Bön* was used initially as a generic name for disparate systems of cultic and religious practices and beliefs that were current through the introduction of Buddhism in Tibet in the reign of Songtsen Gampo (604–649/50). For Buddhist apologists, the term Bön became synonymous with all non-Buddhist competing religious practices. Identifying the latter referent with exactitude remains a difficult task. Early documents from Dunhuang indicate some purposes for which these rites were conducted. They mention royal funerary practices[3] and other forms of funerals (*shid, rman, mdad*), healing liturgies, calling for good fortune (*g.yang*), divination (*mo, phya*), diagnosis of inauspicious occurrences (*dpyad*), ritual strategies for counteracting baleful influences, ransom rites[4] (*glud*), and other miscellaneous rites (*gto*) involving different types of spirits and deities.[5] Examples of treatises on these rites still form parts of the current available literature of the Bön canon.[6]

Sources from Dunhuang mention two main classes of indigenous Tibetan priests or ritual specialists, the Bön (also named *Bönpo*) and the Shen (*gshen*). Their respective functions are not clear but there are indications that these priests used a variety of ritual techniques and means for their trade. Initially they may have been specialists in different cultic practices or part of different family and religious lineages. In some texts, the Bönpos appear to be competing with the Shen; however, in other early documents, distinctions between them seem nominal, for both were occupied with similar activities for their patrons.[7] The methods used to perform various rites were varied and involved a wide range of strategies and objectives. Indigenous priests used any appropriate ritual tool to make their trade more successful and competitive. Hence, for example, Bönpos and Shen used Buddhist spells and mantras to control the *theu* (*the'u*) *rang* and other spirits.

The composite nature of Bön is certain, particularly in Everlasting Bön, which shows the most prevalent Buddhist elements. The wide use of external methods is apparent in all available written material of this tradition from early on. After all, Bön sources themselves credit widely different geographical regions as the sources of their different practices. These regions include China, India, Gilgit (*bru sha*), Zhangzhung, Tazik (*stag zig*), and others.

Today, Bön is represented in the majority by members of the Everlasting Bön school, whereas other schools, such as New Bön (*bon gsar ma*), Sipé Bön (*srid pa'i bon*), Leu Bön (*le'u bon*), and others are now found mostly in the periphery areas of the Tibetan cultural world such as Nepal, Sikkim, North-Western Yunnan, Western Gansu, Inner Mongolia, the neighboring Karakoram range, Gilgit, and other connected areas. The lineages of these ritualists are disappearing due to the growing ban on blood sacrifices that many of them still perform, as well as changing cultural practices and geographical environments due to immigration, modernization, and climate change. Given these conditions, some have opted for adapting their practices to current realities. For example, the Yolmo (also Hyolmo) shamans, whose ritual activities stem directly from the type of Bön represented in some of the oldest scriptures of the Bön canon, recently joined forces with the Bön monastery of Triten Norbutsé in Kathmandu and adjusted to Everlasting Bön doctrines. These Yolmo shamans stopped performing blood sacrifices and began using ritual cakes (*gtor ma*) instead, while still maintaining their characteristic spirit-possession rites.[8]

The Foundation of Yungdrung Bön

A key moment for this lineage is the foundation of Yeru Bensakha[9] by Dru Namkha Yungdrung in 1072. For the following 314 years, this establishment became the main center of learning for Bönpo lamas. From the start, it was the nexus from which many key lineages spread. The meditation lineages of Atri (*A khrid*), the Zhangzhung Oral Transmission from Zhangzhung (*zhang zhung snyan rgyud*), and the Great Perfection (*rdzogs chen*) were all at some point transmitted from its eminent masters. This religious center orchestrated its activities in four colleges created for the study of philosophy (*mtshan nyid*), the tantras (*gsang sngags*), and monastic vows (*sdom gtsang*), the latter considered by contemporary historians to be a new trend among Bönpos of the twelfth century. Bönpo masters have established hereditary lineages from early on and there is ample evidence that celibacy was not a strict norm.[10] Since many meditation lineage holders, including our three authors, spent some time there, Yeru Bensakha must have devoted part of its curriculum to meditation training and practice despite not having a college dedicated to this per se.

Yeru Bensakha was built on the northern bank of the Tsangpo River in Central Tibet. It is important to note that by 1240, when Mongol troops invaded Tibet and established control of the region, this Bön center in par-ticular was surrounded by no less than nineteen Buddhist establishments. At least fourteen of these were representatives of the Kadam tradition, which was in full expansion at that time and specialized in the study of Buddhist logic and philosophy.[11] This might help us to understand the presence of Buddhist elements in Everlasting Bön teachings and writings. This school of Bön entirely espouses Buddhist soteriological and ontological worldviews. It reinterpreted these in its own "indigenous" ways, adopting many cultural elements from surrounding Indian, Chinese, Mongolian, and possibly Cen-tral Asian cultures. Its scriptures, teachings, and practices are vast and com-plex and have not yet been fully investigated.[12] Therefore, one should be very careful to not adopt a reductionist stance or a simplistic definition that moves toward generic typologies such as shamanism, Buddhist heterodoxy, or plagiarism.

Buddhist dogma and philosophy are most prevalent in Yungdrung Bön. It is not known exactly when Buddhist dogma and philosophy were first adopted. There are clear indications that this occurred early on, possibly as early as the time of Azha Lodrö in the thirteenth century. Bönpo lamas intent on philosophical studies often spent time in Buddhist centers of learning, where they studied logic, Madhyamaka, the Perfection of Wisdom literature, and other subjects. Upon graduation, they would go to Menri Monastery and later to Yungdrung Ling (f. 1834) or other satellite institutions to perfect their knowledge of Bön. Sherab Gyaltsen (1356–1415), the founder of Menri, is reported to have studied Buddhist philosophy with the famed Sakya master Rongtön Sheja Kunrik (1367–1449) before starting his teaching career at Yeru Bensakha in 1386.

By the time our first author, Azha Lodrö Gyaltsen, became the eighth abbot of Yeru Bensakha[13] sometime in the mid-thirteenth century, Yungdrung Bön already had in its curriculum of studies well over a hundred scriptures, including several well-developed Tantric corpora. The standardization of indigenous cults rearranged into tantric pantheons with uniform ritual templates was well underway. This continued until the last century, when charismatic Bönpo lamas such as Kundröl Drakpa (b. 1700), Sangyé Lingpa (1705–35), Sangnak Lingpa (b. 1864), Tashi Gyaltsen (1859–1933/35), and others further developed the curriculum of practices. For instance, they added prayers, sections, and sometimes introduced new versions to older tantric cycles and other aspects of Bön in general.[14] However, it is fair to mention here that Bönpos consider their traditions to consist in practices that preexisted even the Yarlung dynasty (c. 600–c. 842).

The emic view of Bön credits its manifestation on Earth to the enlightened being Tönpa Shenrab Miwoché (*mi bo che*, lit. "the great important man," *gshen rab*, "the excellent priest" who is the "teacher," *ston pa*). The earliest hagiographies of Shenrab, the *Collected Discourse* (*Mdo 'dus*) and the *Eye of the Needle* (*Gzer mig*), can be dated to the tenth–eleventh centuries, as they are mentioned in the writings of three Bönpo lamas of the eleventh–twelfth centuries.[15] Both are cited extensively in the texts presented in this volume. The *Collected Discourse*[16] is the first life story of Shenrab for the Yungdrung Bön movement. It is the most concise of the three extant hagiographies available. Critical studies of this scripture show how the account partly reappropriates themes from the life of the Buddha in its earliest Tibetan version, the *Gyacher Rölpa*,[17] and from the Buddhist Jātaka tales. It also recontextualizes Chinese myths with uniquely Tibetan content.

With the middle-length *Eye of the Needle*, the narrative becomes more Tibetan despite using a variety of events from previous lives of Śākyamuni. Shenrab's life begins in heaven, where he studied the teachings of Bön, after which he undertook reincarnations and manifestations on Earth and elsewhere and transmitted the teachings through various feats. Here Shenrab is no longer just a saint but also a mediator between non-humans and denizens of this plane of existence.[18] This Bön scripture must have been important and widespread, since research indicates that it might have served as the basic template from which the life of Padmasambhava was constructed.[19]

However, it was not until the last and voluminous hagiography, the *Stainless Splendor* (*Gzi brjid*), delivered to Loden Nyingpo (b. 1360)[20] sometime during the fourteenth century, that Shenrab becomes the initiator of the twelve rituals (*cho ga bcu gnyis*), now a universal feature of Bön rites.[21] In the context of the Bön tantras devoted to tutelary deities and protectors, Shenrab became the single source of all transmissions and manifestations of Bön, a cosmic principle, emanating himself through avatars such as Sangwa Düpa, Takla Mebar, and other ancient masters.

Through the lens of Everlasting Bön, the teacher Shenrab is seen as the epitome of realization and is made a historical personage. Dates are forwarded (2021 celebrated his 18,039th birthday)[22] and conflicting locations of fabled lands and fallen kingdoms, such as the Kingdom of Zhangzhung and its province of Tazik (*stag zig*, lit. "the land of tigers and leopards"), continue to puzzle scholars. However, many of these Bön traditions are solidly attested from the tenth century onward, and there are clear indications that various cultic systems having direct affinities, if not direct transmission links, were extant before and during the Yarlung dynasty. For instance, from this historical period, five early Bönpo clans, still enduring today, are traditionally linked to religious specializations in Bön. These are the Zhu, early specialists on funerary rites; the Mushen (*dmu gshen*),[23] credited as direct descendants of Shenrab and holding the lineage of the Magyü Tantra; the Dru (*bru*), who came early to Tibet from Drusha[24] (*bru sha*, i.e., Gilgit) and were early exponents of philosophy; the Pa (*spa*), who were masters of the tantric teachings; and the Me'u (*rme'u*), to whom are credited several scholarly studies. Bönpos over the centuries established new hereditary lineages with prestigious families. An example is the Khyung clan that is linked to the famous treasure-text discoverer from Nyakrong, Sangnak Lingpa (b. 1864), whose Walkhyung (*dbal khyung*) Monastery in the 1980s was the discovery site of the last complete set of the Bön canon. Other now prominent families are the Japhur (*bya phur*), the Böngya (*bon brgya*), and so on.[25] Most are now using religious materials that were either produced or edited by hierarchs of the Everlasting Bön school, to which they add their own lineage particularities.

The Categories of Teachings

Over the centuries, Everlasting Bön organized its teachings, practices, and corpora of scriptures and commentaries. It has pursued a curriculum of training involving philosophical studies and debates that are largely congruent with what slowly became the norm in leading Buddhist schools in Tibet. The general categories of its corpora consist of scriptures (*mdo*), the tantras, and meditation practices.

THE SCRIPTURAL SYSTEM OF LEARNING

Scriptural studies that convey the teachings of Shenrab consist in philosophical studies rather than close readings of the scriptures. In fact, scriptures might be recited ritually but are seldom studied without available commentaries. The commentaries consist in expositions of the path and its stages (*sa lam*) that lead to ultimate enlightenment. All nine major commentaries that are studied are concerned with the path and its stages. One of the most important is certainly the *Magical Key to the Precious Gradual Path and Grounds of the Greater Vehicle* by Azha Lodrö Gyaltsen, the first text presented in this volume.[26] These philosophical studies include logic and metaphysical categories very much of the Abhidharma genre of Buddhist literature. Its treatises, such as those of Azha Lodrö Gyaltsen, comment on Bön scriptures that are neither classified as tantric nor concerned with meditation practice techniques. Some of the treatises considered central to this part of the tradition are the *Treasury of the World*, the *Eye of the Needle*, the collection of the *Minute Scriptures*, the *Scripture of the Eight Realms* (*Khams brgyad*, the Bön version of the *Perfection of Wisdom Scripture in One Hundred Thousand Lines, Śatasāhasrikāprajñāpāramitā*), the *Hundred Thousand Verses on the Summit of Awareness* (*Rig pa'i rtse mo'i 'bum*, or *Rtse 'bum*), the *Compendium on the Spreading*, the middle-length version of the *Great Realms Scripture*, the *Collection of the Rising of the Nine Suns*, the *White Hundred Thousand Water-Spirits*, and so forth.

The scriptural curriculum constitutes the outer vehicle of the teachings of Everlasting Bön.

THE TANTRIC SYSTEMS

The tantric teachings constitute the second part of the path of Bön. The general concept is to bring forth some transformation in oneself and the world around oneself through the agency of the tantric pantheon. For this reason, it is often referred to as the path of transformation (*bsgyur lam*). These are part of the inner/insider (*nang*) or esoteric teachings. The pantheon is quite varied and points to the many sources that influenced this Tibetan religion. Everlasting Bön tantric traditions harnessed local gods and demons (*lha 'dre*) and turned them into organized cultic systems using in part Indian tantric templates. For instance, the Bön deities that appear to specialize in subjugating indigenous demons (*'dre*), such as the the'u rang (*the'u rang*), the nyen (*gnyan*), the masang (*gnyan, ma sang*), the gyalsen (*rgyal bsen*), and others, are the gekhö (*ge khod*),[27] a class of 360 gods based on Mount Tisé (aka Kailash). Their leader is the All-Piercing Gekhö, to whom a corpus of ritual manuals is devoted.[28] His ritual compendium contains several fumigation (*bsang*) and lustration (*khrus*) rites to remedy various types of pollution. Gekhö is a local deity associated with a particular region, such as Zhangzhung and Mount Kailash. Through the agency of the pandits of Everlasting Bön, he has become the main character at the center of his own tantric universe. Hence Gekhö represents a complete cycle of practices for spiritual attainment. He stands in the middle of his court surrounded by 360 other *gekhö* and attending spirits. His abode on this plane of existence is the stony castle of Mount Kailash overlooking the former Zhangzhung kingdom that was, according to Bön history, annexed by the thirty-eighth king of the Yarlung dynasty, Trisong Detsen (r. 756– c. 797). In Everlasting Bön, Gekhö now represents the embodiment of the enlightened qualities of Shenrab, and his demonifuge activities are salvific. He brings down the transforming influences of the enlightened ones of the three times and purifies the negative karma of all sentient beings. His priests and adepts propitiate him in order to help attain sapience as well as to protect and assist their patrons in their mundane pursuits.

The tantric cycles are numerous in Bön, but most are now to be found in the canonical material of either the Bön scriptural collection (K) or the commentarial corpus (T). Some of the most important tantric cycles are mentioned in the commentary of Sherab Gyaltsen in the tantric section of this volume—part 4, the *Magic Key That Disentangles the Secret Meaning*. It suffices to say here that the following are the main texts representing the tantric tradition at the beginning of the fifteenth century:

> *The Secret Capable Sen-Demoness* (*Gsang ba bsen thub*)
> *The Father Tantra That Is the Lore of the Cuckoo of Awareness*
>   (*Pha rgyud rig pa khu byug*)

> *The Three Tantras of the Enlightened Mother Tantra (Ma rgyud*
>   *sangs rgyas rgyud gsum)*
> *The Six Tantras of the Wrathful Ones (Khro bo rgyud drug)*
> *The cycles of the Tantras of Phur pa (Phur pa rgyud skor)*
> *The Blazing Fire of Tagla (lit. Tiger-God, Stag lha me 'bar)*
> *The Universal Heap That Is the Five Excellent Ones of the Citadel*
>   *(Spyi spungs gsas mkhar mchog lnga)*, and so forth.

As the commentaries on tantric practices in this volume indicate, these systems of practice involve taking on pledges, the use of mandalas, symbolic hand-gestures (*phyag rgya, mudrā*), rites for offerings, fire offerings, and so on.

THE GREAT PERFECTION SYSTEMS

The secret level on the path to enlightenment in Bön consists in meditative practices and a corpus of pith instructions and advice. Four main systems[29] are present in Bön, and they are known under the following generic names: The Revelatory Transmission from Zhangzhung (*zhang zhung snyan rgyud*), the Instructions on the A (Atri, *A khrid*),[30] the Instructions That Clear Away the Ten Thousand Limits to the Primordial (*ye khri mtha' sel*), and the Great Perfection. Each has its own particular practices and its own corpus of pith instructions, scriptures, and commentaries. However, all show common underlying principles. Their discourses follow the conceptual triple division of the base, the path, and the result, where spontaneity, non-fabrication, and the manipulation of awareness are favored over tantric forms. These four meditative systems are considered superior to all the other vehicles in Everlasting Bön. They primarily use meditation on lights, visions, dark retreat, and the cultivation of natural and non-conceptual states of awareness.

These meditative traditions are said to have been transmitted orally from one master to another. Therefore, their textual sources consist in transmitted poems, pith instructions, advice, secret instructions, and so on. These have acquired canonical status in Bön and are to be found in the fourth section of the canon, in the mind division (*sems sde*). Hence, the first of the eight volumes (K171–78) consecrated to these meditation teachings is designated as the *Four Cycles of the Oral Diffusion of the Revelatory Transmission of the Great Perfection from Zhangzhung*. As part of this tradition, the *Practice Manual of the Oral Tradition of the Great Perfection from Zhangzhung* by Dru Gyalwa Yungdrung that is translated last in this volume is its most emblematic text. The other main scriptures of the mind section are the *Nine*

Arcana and its commentary, the *Trilogy of the Proclamation of the Great Perfection*, the *White Heaven of the Great General Transmission, the Cycle That Clears Away the Ten Thousand Limits to the Primordial*, and the *Transmission of the Boundless Spreading of the Great Perfection.*

There are a number of teachings written by treasure-text revealers and pandits that have been added to the Great Perfection systems in Bön. One thinks of the voluminous material written by Shardza Tashi Gyaltsen (1859–1934) in his *Self-Arising of the Three Bodies*[31] and his other commentaries on the above-mentioned cycles.[32]

Classificatory Schemes in Everlasting Bön

Establishing an umbrella system to coordinate all the teachings and scriptures of the tradition was not only the preoccupation of the pandits of Everlasting Bön but an overarching concern for Buddhists in China and Tibet as well.[33] By the thirteenth century the vast amount of material already extant was on its way to being organized into a classificatory scheme. The division of the Bön teachings in nine vehicles was previously mentioned in the *Practice Manual* by Dru Gyalwa Yungdrung. By the fourteenth century, when Loden Nyingpo compiled the *Stainless Splendor* hagiography, he fixed this division for posterity after he had Shenrab discourse on the scale of graded practices. These are so present in the tradition that David Snellgrove, in collaboration with Lopön Tenzin Namdak, considered them representative enough to translate excerpts under the title *The Nine Ways of Bon.*

To quote Sherab Gyaltsen from the *Magic Key*, the nine ways according to the nine views of each particular vehicle are the following:

The nine views of the vehicle of self-realization are related to the nine distinctive aspects of the senses. They are:

1. The vehicle of the Shen of prediction (*phywa*)
2. The Shen of the visual world
3. The Shen of illusion
4. The Shen of existence

These are the causal vehicles. The result vehicles are:

5. The virtuous adherers
6. The great ascetics

  7. The White A
  8. The primeval Shen
  9. The Unsurpassed Moon (*zla bla med*)

Each is said to have its own view. These points can be expanded
at length. The Greater Vehicle is connected to this and consists in
acquiring the very result of finality.

The general distinguishing feature of the twofold division of these nine
ways is that the first four are considered to deal with causal activities. The
Shen of prediction consists in making prognostics on inauspicious events
such as sickness, bad luck, and so forth in order to identify their spiritual
sources. The next three classes, the Shen of the visual world, of illusion, and
of existence, are the reservoirs of ritual strategies used to counter these unfortunate events. They deal with ransom rites, controlling spirits, exorcism, subjugation, funerals, astrology, and many other methods that seek to achieve
concrete results in the mundane world. They are the four causal vehicles.

The remaining five of the nine ways are the five vehicles of results and are
religious and mystical in outlook. They bring one to the ultimate fruition
of enlightenment. They consist in the taking of lay and monastic vows (the
virtuous adherers and the great ascetics), the tantric practices of the transformation of reality (the White A), more advanced tantric practices based on
the Magyü Tantra of the Shen lineage (the Vehicle of Primeval Shen), and
finally the meditative practices (the Unsurpassed Moon, more commonly
called the Great Perfection) that bring one to full enlightenment.

Alternatively, Bönpo authors divide these practices into the four portals
and the one treasury (*sgo bzhi mdzod lnga*). Different metaphors are applied
to make sense of this classification. Hence, in this volume, the commentary
on the root tantra the *Precious Universal Gathering* entitled the *Net of Sunrays*, attributed to the eighth-century sage Drenpa Namkha, uses this classification to encompass all Bön teachings when it says:

> The circles of words consist in the four portals with the treasury
> that make five, the hierarchy of the nine vehicles, and the 84,000
> portals of Bön.

Snellgrove mentions the four portals as consisting in the teachings of the
masters (*dpon gsas*, i.e., the Great Perfection), the Black Waters/Dominion

(*chab nag*, demonifuge rites), the White Waters/Dominion (*chab dkar*, tantric rites), and the portal to the country of Phan (*'phan yul*), the place from which some of the teachings of Shenrab originated. Shenrab dispensed these teachings in the realms of the gods (*lha*), among the underground water-spirits (*klu*), the *nyen* (*gnyan*) spirits, the deities controlling the world (*sa bdag*), the *tö* (*gtod*) spirits, and then to humans.[34]

The *Eye of the Needle* provides further details and describes these teachings as precepts and pith instructions from the masters. The second portal, Black Waters/Dominion, comprises rites dealing with ransom, exorcism, funerals, and so forth. The third portal, White Waters/Dominion, is that of the tantric practices of the generation and perfection stages. The fourth, the portal to the country of Phan, consists in the teachings from the scriptures and their recitations. The fifth portal to the treasury is called the Pure Summit (*gtsang mtho thog*) where individual streams of conditioned existence are cut off and where enlightenment is reaped.[35]

Texts in This Anthology

The texts presented in this anthology were selected in consultation with the late thirty-third abbot of Menri Monastery, Lungtok Tenpai Nyima (1929–2017), the head of the Everlasting Bön school. They are ordered according to the three categories mentioned above: scriptural/philosophical studies, tantric studies, and meditative practices.

Azha Lodrö Gyaltsen

The first text, the *Magical Key to the Precious Gradual Path and Grounds of the Greater Vehicle*, is a study of the path and its stages (*sa lam*), interpreting the teachings of the scriptures. It was written by Azha Lodrö Gyaltsen, alias the Famous Azha (*mtshan ldan a zha*), also known as the Protector of Wandering Beings, Drogön (*'gro dgon*) Lodrö Gyaltsen. He was a member of the Azha clan also known as the Tuyuhun (吐谷渾), an ethnic group settled around Kokonor (Qinghai) Lake in present-day Qinghai, China. The kingdom of the Tuyuhun lasted from the middle of the third century CE until its annexation by the Tibetan king Songtsen Gampo in 634. During the Tibetan occupation, some of the Azha moved to eastern Chinese regions, while others remained under the dominion of Tibet. Lodrö Gyaltsen was born to a Bönpo family in Yorpo (*g.yor po*) in the southern province of Lhokha (*Luoka* 洛卡), the present-day Shanan prefectural city

(山南市) in Central Tibet. This region is associated with the birth of the Tibetan Yarlung dynasty and is south of Lhasa, bordering Bhutan. By the time our author was born in 1198, the Kingdom of Gugé was at its height in the western region, controlling trade from the south, and Lhokha was being developed with irrigation projects and land cultivation.

The biography of Lodrö Gyaltsen mentions several early predispositions and signs that signaled his future religious career. In 1226 when he was twenty-eight years old he took religious vows from his uncle, Dutsi Gyaltsen (fl. twelfth century), his main root guru. The latter was then the abbot of Yeru Bensakha and a direct disciple of Yorpo Mepal (1134–69),[36] the fifth lineage holder of the Atri system of meditation as well as the fifth abbot of Yeru Bensakha.[37] The three lamas not only studied in this center of learning but also sat on its abbatial seat, succeeding one another.

From his early days and throughout his career, Lodrö Gyaltsen received a great number of teachings and empowerments from treasure-text revealers, lineage-holders, and masters. The various lineages that he was part of include the tantric practices of Phurba from Lopön Mé (fl. eleventh–twelfth centuries). He received the full transmission of the teachings from the two most prominent Bönpo treasure-text revealers of his time, Pönsé Khyungö Tsal (b. 1175) and Matön Sherab Sengé (twelfth–thirteenth centuries). He received through intermediaries, taught, and transmitted major teachings from Shenchen Lüga (996–1035), Nyenthing (eleventh century), Zhotön Ngodrup (twelfth century), Lungbön Lhanyen (twelfth century), Orgom Kundul (eleventh century), and many others. These included Great Perfection practices from the four lineages together with pith instructions. He received tantric teachings, such as the *Six Tantras of the Wrathful Ones* (*Khro bo rgyud drug*) and the *Southern Treasure Text* (*Lho gter*) on the Great Perfection from the lineage of Khutsa Dawo (b. 1024).[38] He is credited with receiving teachings from masters of the past and directly from spirits in visions while following his uncle or alone during ascetic practices in the mountains of North Tibet and other places.[39] His works demonstrate such a breath of knowledge that it would be fair to say that he possibly mastered all the Bön teachings of his generation and his institution.

There are many important titles under Lodrö Gyaltsen's name.[40] Some of his most influential works are:

1. *Essence of Valid Cognition, a Compilation from All Sources on the Conceptual Mind and Suchness* (*Tshad ma snying po de kho na yid kun las*

btus pa).[41] This is a textbook on logic and valid cognition. The use of Dharmakīrti's process on reasoning and logic is quite transparent here. However, the author makes certain that this view is rendered within a Bön paradigm involving the base, the path, and the result.

2. *A Commentary on the Innermost Treasury of the World, the Scripture and Its Defining Characteristics* (*Lung mtshan nyid srid pa'i mdzod phugs kyi 'grel ba*).[42] This is also a seminal work on one of the earliest datable scriptures explaining Bön cosmology and metaphysics. The discovery of the *Innermost Treasury of the World* is attributed to Shenchen Luga, and it was part of his 1017 find. It is also the most comprehensive source for the Zhangzhung language, since most of the text is bilingual.[43] The nature of the discourse in the *Innermost Treasury of the World* mixes mythological narratives and Buddhist philosophical discussions. The commentary of Lodrö Gyaltsen focuses on the philosophical discussions that find echoes in his *Magical Key*, which takes ample quotations from the *Innermost Treasury of the World*. Lodrö Gyaltsen's text is, to my knowledge, one of the few extant commentaries on this important scripture.[44]

3. *The Ornament That Displays Wishes That Were Fulfilled, That Is the Precious Commentary on the Secret Capable Sen-Demoness, the Great Root Tantra* (*Rtsa rgyud chen po gsang ba bsen thub kyi 'grel bar rin po che yid bzhin rnam par bkod pa'i rgyan*).[45] This is probably one of the most important early commentaries on the three tantras constituting the *Universal Heap* cycle.[46] It establishes a standard in the propitiation rites of tantric deities as well as the accompanying lore, such as pledges, the stages of practice, etc. This commentary tackles the many points summarily exposed later by Sherab Gyaltsen and contained in this anthology.

4. *How to Differentiate between the Greater and the Lower Vehicle, the Above and the Below, the Key Points* (*Theg pa che chung gong 'ong rnam par 'byed pa'i gal mdo*). This text deals with practices of the Great Perfection and comments on the scripture commonly known as the *Key Points of Shari*. Lodrö Gyaltsen cites this scripture in his *Magical Key* and emphasizes the difference between the Great Perfection style of meditation practice and others based on the scriptures.[47]

5. *The Lamp That Dispels Obscurity and Clears Away Hindrances* (*Gegs sel mun sel sgron me*) is composed of pith instructions (*man ngag*) and oral directives for the practice of the Great Perfection.[48]

6. The *Magical Key to the Precious Gradual Path and the Grounds of the Greater Vehicle*, the first book translated here, is certainly one of the most widely read works by Lodrö Gyaltsen. It is a comprehensive overview of the five paths and the ten stages leading to enlightenment according to the non-tantric scriptures of Bön.

This treatise is a condensed exposé of Buddhist (named "the others" in the text) and Bön philosophies extant in thirteenth-century Tibet. Possibly because of the large inventory of concepts and ideas it covers, its specialized vocabulary and discourse is difficult to render into intelligible English. Many passages remain quite opaque despite consultation with a number of Bönpo lamas. To my knowledge, there are no commentaries available on this text. Therefore, the reader's indulgence is required and we strongly encourage the elucidation of unclear passages with the help of a competent Bönpo lama schooled in this system.

Despite these difficulties, *Magical Key* is invaluable in that it clearly depicts the path that leads to enlightenment as conceived and perpetuated in Everlasting Bön until today. Lodrö Gyaltsen discourses on the categories of the two truths. Two points of view, the conventional and the absolute, are used as skillful means to address the spiritual realizations one experiences along the five paths and the ten stages. Using Dharmakīrti's[49] principles on valid reasoning and Dignāga's[50] logical paradigm already popular in Tibet during his day, our author points to categories made by the mind when experiencing conditioned reality and how these change with the practices particular to the five paths of accumulation, application, seeing, meditation, and no-more-learning. He provides detailed analyses of the four (noble) truths that are identical to those of Buddhism and explains how, relying on them, one attains the correct and genuine realization of intrinsic unconditioned reality. To quote Lodrö Gyaltsen:

> First, meditative states of the ten grounds consist only in the realization of emptiness in the sphere of reality through the four truths on subjects that exist without being distinct. The cause resides in engaging in the apprehension of the first insight, like seeing the light of a lamp. This is proven by the scripture when it says:

The sign is the opening of the door of the path of vision in order to see without perceiving.

Throughout his treatment of the path and its stages, and after explaining the various key points of the subject, Lodrö Gyaltsen explains how they relate to the experiential aspect of the Great Perfection. This system is the basis of all Everlasting Bön philosophical doctrinal principles and is carried on through all subsequent "vehicles," such as the tantra and meditation practices. In this, views are to be trained using all possible means, whether philosophical, tantric, or meditative realization. It is the mechanism of the very apprehension of perception and its objects that need to be deconstructed. Experienced reality is composed of a collection of isolated objects in one's mind. In order to directly perceive the dynamic nature of reality that is spontaneously ever producing, one must become aware of the underlying supporting basis of reality that goes unperceived, like the translucence of a lamp. Hence, Lodrö Gyaltsen explains, saying:

> The difference in this is that in the continuum [of the path of meditation], there is application where there is no distinction in the realization of mere isolates. Engaging successfully in the continuum of vision is likened to the translucence of a lamp. In particular, subjects that are perceived as distinct are connected to all other subjects. There are distinctions in the realization of the sphere of reality that are connected to all subjects. Because realization on each ground generates no existing common particularities, it is like a lump of crystals covered with gauze. The *Eye of the Needle* (14.448.3) says:

>> Signs are systemic productions of pristine cognition that are generated and the gradual distinctions of the view.

> This saying proves it. The strength of its comprehensive reasoning is thus proven.

And again, on realizations, he says:

> . . . realizations on the ten grounds are subject based. Only the realization of the body of the absolute has no distinctiveness

because of its application with the apprehension of insight imbued with the two purities.

The realization of the body of the absolute pertains to directly seeing the vast extent of manifestations that are unconditioned in their very roots. It is the beholding of the everlasting dynamic process of reality. The absolute is not static, it is forever emitting, while its basis remains untouched through involvements in the temporary manifestations of its dynamism.

Lodrö Gyaltsen's dissertation is ambitious, for it attempts to explain everything that is included in Bön philosophy and tenets. Although it does not fail to achieve this, it seems to suffer from an overabundance of material and topics to discuss. He organizes his narrative with sections and sub-sections, but the reader easily gets lost in the increasing number of subdivisions. Thus, as the author frequently fails to name the topic to which a given section refers, one is often startled by numbers referring to an earlier subheading. The recurrent problem here is that although one can infer it within the context, the succinct manner in which the topic is addressed sometimes makes one wonder to which of the successive points numbered "three"—and there may be as many as four successive paragraphs starting with "thirdly"—the author refers. I have tried my best to provide subsection headings that do not appear in the original text. Not all these are certain, but I hope the reader will bear this in mind while going through my translation of this text.

The tantras in Bön
The next three texts in this volume pertain to the tantric path in Bön. A canonical tantric text is first presented in its entirety: The *Lore of the Root Tantra, the Precious Universal Gathering* is attributed to the manifestation of the absolute in its form of the teacher Kuntu Zangpo. His name signifies the "all-good," and in Buddhist texts his Sanskritized name is rendered as Samantabhadra. This supreme enlightened one is the personification of the unconditioned in Bön, while in Buddhism he is considered a bodhisattva. The exception to this is found in the Nyingma school, where he is a supreme buddha, an ādibuddha.

The story of the discovery of this text with its two commentaries[51] concerns the three *ācāryas*, or Buddhist monks, lost in Tibet while looking for gold. Instead, they found Bönpo treasure texts. They discovered three bags in a pillar of Samyé Monastery and took these with them. On their way back (the story does not say to where), they encountered Tibetans looking for

Buddhist treasure texts. Passing off their discovery as Buddhist texts in order to get the Tibetans' horse, the ācāryas handed over the bear-, tiger-, and leopard-skin bags containing several important Bönpo texts. In the bags, 340 texts were found, including seminal tantra texts, such as Phurpa, Gekhö, and the *Precious Universal Gathering* and its commentaries. The books eventually found their way to a certain Zegur (*gze sgur*) and were passed on to Shen Naljigur (fl. tenth century). The latter gave them to Zhang Longom Ringmo, who then transmitted them to Me'u Rok Walmo (fl. tenth–eleventh centuries), who passed them on to his son, Me'u Lhari Nyenpo (1024–91). If we follow the date of the discoveries of the ācāryas given by Gurung as 913,[52] we have a period of about 125 years between the discovery and Me'u Lhari Nyenpo's transmission. Therefore this tantra and possibly its commentary *Net of Sunrays* would date from the beginning of the tenth century at the earliest and the first quarter of the eleventh at the latest.

Our second text, the *Precious Universal Gathering*, is a short text of no more than four pages in the Tibetan original. Though concise, it contains all the elements that comprise the practice of the tantras that will be developed later. These consist in the threefold exposition of most tenets according to the principles of the base, the path, and its result. Without enumerating them, the text mentions the importance of tantric pledges, empowerments, mantra recitations, activities, views, and conduct. It further raises these in the context of the path of accumulation seen in the earlier writings, albeit with a tantric twist, and mentions the constituents of tantric rituals, such as ritual cakes, hand-seals, lineage and instruction, and the stages of generation and perfection culminating with the Great Perfection.

All these parts are further addressed in its commentary, *Net of Sunrays*, which may have been part of the original discovery described above. This commentary contains most of the original *Precious Universal Gathering*, and its writing is attributed to the eighth-century sage, Drenpa Namkha. This personage is particularly important in Bön in general for his impartial universalistic views that, according to Bönpos, demonstrate his spiritual achievements. His hagiography in eight volumes contains much material that attests to his importance in Bön as well as the growing cults that were built around his person.

During the persecution of Bön by King Trisong Detsen between 780 and 790, many Bönpos were faced with either exile or conversion. The Great Soul (*bla chen*) and the Priest of Mu (*dmu gshen*), Drenpa Namkha, realizing the futility of sectarianism between the Buddhists and the Bönpos, allegedly made the following comments:

> Buddhist and Bönpos sitting here
> believe in a religion that does not exist.
> If you desire to make the kingdom white
> and wish to attain enlightenment,
> why do you differentiate between me and you?
> Why do you make distinctions between Bön and Buddhism?
> . . .
> Firstly, the king is mighty,
> secondly, the Buddhists are jealous,
> thirdly, I have (no feelings of) partiality for anything.
> Therefore I shall be ordained.[53]

Drenpa Namkha then took up a razor and shaved his head to become a Buddhist monk. Despite this, the sage is credited with preparing for that persecution by proactively burying and hiding Bön scriptures and other material so that they could be rediscovered later during more auspicious times.

He is reported to have had two sons, Tsewang Rikzin and Pema Tongdröl. The first is credited with many mystical accomplishments that were described in three accounts of his peregrinations and feats. The two accounts still extant and containing several types of rituals and meditative practices are *Tsewang in India* (*Tshe dbang rgya gar ma*) and *Tsewang in Tibet* (*Tshe dbang bod yul ma*). The third, *Tsewang in Zhangzhung*, is lost.[54]

The second son, Pema Tongdröl (alias Yungdrung Tongdröl), is considered among Bönpos to be the same as the Buddhist Padmasambhava. This character is rather complex in Bön and the material goes beyond the introductory nature of this essay. However, suffice it to mention here that these three, the father and his sons (*yab sras gsum*), are the central figures of a contemporary movement that is relatively independent from Everlasting Bön and given the generic (if not misleading) title of "New Bön" (*bon gsar*). Proponents of this movement are quite numerous in the Tibetan cultural sphere within Chinese borders and their practices are based on treasure-text discoveries by charismatic lamas such as Kundröl Drakpa, Sangyé Lingpa, Dechen Lingpa, Sangnak Lingpa, and others.[55]

Our third text, the *Net of Sunrays: A Commentary on the Root Tantra, the Precious Universal Gathering*, is a word-by-word commentary on the *Precious Universal Gathering*. This exposé has been divided into thirteen sections dealing with the general theory of the tantric path. It provides more detail as to what the circles of deities, the recitations of the mantras, the principle of secrecy, the base, the path, and its result entail. The discussion is not technical but speculative and doctrinal, addressing how the practices are divided, their modalities, and some details on their main components. These include the families/clan of enlightened ones; the outer, inner, and secret paths of the tantras; the thirteen grounds; the four enlightened tantric activities; the tantric pledges and what they involve; key points on conduct, views, training, empowerments, formulas of concentration (i.e., mantras, recitations, and spells), seed-syllables, deities, parts of the rituals, and the paths of the knowledge-holders; and the main rationales of the different tantric systems.

The various points mentioned here are repeatedly reviewed and reexamined in this commentary and made to correspond to the general outline by Azha Lodrö Gyaltsen in his *Magical Key*. Although it is possible that this commentary antedates the Azha Lodrö Gyaltsen's writings, dating this text is particularly difficult. Was it written before or after Azha Lodrö Gyaltsen? I cannot answer that question as of now. *Net of Sunrays* is a long commentary and the material that it summarizes is quite complex. As for what precisions are needed for practice, one will find them in the fourth text in this volume.

Our fourth text, the *Magic Key That Disentangles the Secret Meaning*, was authored by the Incomparable (*mnyam med*) Sherab Gyaltsen,[56] the founder of Menri Monastery and heir to the traditions of Yeru Bensakha who systematized the school of Everlasting Bön. His contributions formed the ways of Everlasting Bön as we know it today.

Sherab Gyaltsen was born in 1356 in Tekchok (*steg cog, steg skyog,* and *steg mchog*) in Gyamorong (*rgya mo rong*), a large enclave of narrow valleys between Chinese lands to the east and the nomadic territories of Kham in the west. Chinese histories, such as the *Historical Chronicles* (*Shiji* 史记) of Sima Qian (司馬遷, 145–86 BCE), mention this region as being populated by an ethnic group called the Ranmang (冉駹). The region had been populated from early on, and by the time of Azha Lodrö Gyaltsen in the twelfth century, it was a bastion of Bön with the greatest number of datable temples and monasteries. It is difficult to ascertain how influential Yeru Bensakha was to the region. Sherab Gyaltsen took several religious vows (*bsnyen gnas, dge bsnyen,* and *gtsang gtsug*) at age nine in 1365 from Chala Yungdrung Gyaltsen and formally received the religious name that would define him, Sherab Gyaltsen. His biography mentions that he first studied with different masters from Nyakrong, Amdo, and Kham, all regions surrounding his native land. He later went to Central Tibet where he studied with different eminent Buddhist masters, including the famous Sakya master Rongtön Sheja Kunrik. Under him, he studied Buddhist systems such as the Perfection of Wisdom (*pāramitā*), epistemology (*pramāṇa*), monastic vows (*vinaya*), Buddhist philosophy (*abhidharma*), and the Middle Way (*Madhyamaka*). His knowledge of Buddhism was extensive and he became known as a great scholar (*rab 'byams pa*). It was at this time that a fated meeting with Tsongkhapa (1357–1419), the founder of the Geluk order, is said to have occurred. Scholars doubt this, however, since the meeting is recorded only in a late biography and not in the early ones.

At thirty-one he entered Yeru Bensakha and was eventually offered the abbatial seats of two monastic colleges, Utsé Karpo and Utsé Marpo, by two unnamed descendants of the Dru (*bru*) clan. He received many teachings and empowerments from renowned Bönpo masters during his early travels, and some more in Central Tibet and at Yeru Bensakha. Miraculous visions and events are reported to have happened to him during retreats and empowerment ceremonies. For instance, when he received the empowerment of Phurpa and his *cortège* of deities from Metön Kunzang Gyaltsen, he is reported to have seen his master, Metön, as the deity Takla Mebar. He saw Metön's wife and children as the gods and goddesses of the mandala.

At some point he decided to go back to Gyarong to visit his mother. Once he reached Dartsedo (*dar rtse mdo*, today Kangding City in Sichuan), he learned that Yeru Bensakha had been destroyed by a flood. It is said that his distress was so severe that he contemplated suicide. Despite that, he eventually returned to the ruins of the monastery, collected some items that were left scattered here and there, and went to practice in solitary retreat. He eventually moved closer to Darding (*dar lding*), the ancestral village of the Shen clan, and founded Menri Monastery in 1405, instituting a tradition that endures to this day. Many extraordinary events and miraculous deeds are mentioned in his biography during the period of his wanderings and the creation of Menri Monastery. He passed away amid miraculous displays in 1415 at the age of fifty-nine.

Following the fall of the Mongol Yuan dynasty (1279–1368) that dominated Tibet, the fifteenth century was a period that saw the emergence of reformers such as Tsongkhapa (Lozang Drakpa, 1357–1419) and Ngorchen Kunga Zangpo (1382–1456). Tibetan traditions rose on their own merits and no longer relied on imported authorities. Sherab Gyaltsen was one of these great luminaries. The enormous loss of Yeru Bensakha's heritage and culture must have been paramount in his mind. He therefore began to write in earnest, and his literary production eventually became central to the whole tradition of Everlasting Bön. He became a lineage-holder of much of what was considered Everlasting Bön during his own time. His writings are varied, numerous, and touch upon all important aspects of this tradition.[57] They are usually quite concise, and his writing style is sometimes very terse. However, his writings provide detailed information that enables readers to find other sources to complete their knowledge. In that, Sherab Gyaltsen was a true scholar.

The *Magic Key That Disentangles the Secret Meaning* is such a work, blending extremely numerous details with relevant information on the practice of the tantras. The main challenge to the reader of this text rests in its first part, where the author points to what constitutes the tantric systems in Bön, their central texts, the names of their cycles, and their different classes. There, the reader—as did this translator—might have difficulty distinguishing titles of scriptures and commentaries from the names of tantric cycles mentioned in passim. I have tried to identify most items; however, tantric cycles are tag names to which are grafted different texts, ritual techniques, and other elements. Since the writing of *Magic Key*, Menri pandits and masters from all over Tibet have added their own material to these various systems, and many source texts have been lost. Identifying the various elements of Sherab Gyaltsen's discourse with precision is thus quite difficult. Therefore, I beg the indulgence of readers in this matter.

I have divided *Magic Key* into two parts. Part 1 lists the sources for tantric study and practices in Bön at the time of the author. There are three main currents in this author's arrangements of the sources: the tantras of the peaceful deities, of the wrathful ones, and those of Phurpa. The main source of many of the individual cycles is the *Heap of Universality of the Precious Heavenly Citadel*. From this central system, many branches and subgroups spring. Sherab Gyaltsen lists many important titles, commentaries, and known tantric cycles.

Part 2 focuses on practical instructions or guidelines regarding the methods of practice. The discourse consists in advice on what one needs to be mindful of, such as the qualities of a good master, the necessity for the empowerments, right views, the overall place of the tantra in the scheme of the nine ways, conduct, the divine citadel (i.e., the mandala of deities), the process and stages of practice, pledges, mind, and concepts. It is a short summary of the essential elements that one needs to know in order to practice the tantric path of Bön.

Sherab Gyaltsen had several important students who continued to expand tantric commentaries and practices and elaborated on his basic guidelines through succeeding generations.[58] These scholars expanded the detailed outlines drafted in Sherab Gyaltsen's exposition of the tantras. Therefore, this contribution is a cornerstone of the edifice of Everlasting Bön tantric systems.

DRU GYALWA YUNGDRUNG AND HIS *PRACTICE MANUAL*

Gyalwa Yundrung[59] (1242–90) was a member of the Dru clan that originated in Gilgit and is recorded as being the bearer of the philosophical tradition of the *Treasury of the World* in Bön.[60] He was born in Yeru Bensakha, and this, as well as many other instances of births linked to Bön temples and monasteries, points to the non-monastic and clan-based nature of religious lineages in Bön. He was the fourth son of Drusha Sönam Gyaltsen, who was linked to Dru Namkha Yungdrung (994–1054), who received direct teachings on the *Treasury* from Shenchen Luga, the famed treasure-discoverer. These teachings were prevalent among members of this clan, and Gyalwa Yungdrung is reported to have discoursed on them at Yeru Bensakha while still young. Dru Dulwa Gyaltsen (1239–93), who was a student of Azha Lodrö Gyaltsen and holder of the lineage of Atri, gave the young Gyalwa Yungdrung his religious name as well as his monastic ordination. Under this master's tutelage, Gyalwa Yungdrung first studied the outer and inner aspects of the tantras before receiving Great Perfection instructions on the nature of the mind. After a breakthrough in his practices, he received further teachings from direct disciples of important treasure-text revealers, such as Khyungö Tsal (b. 1175).[61] He received teachings on different systems of the Great Perfection in the lineage of Lungbön Lhanyen (b. 1088)[62] from Lungbön Tashi Gyaltsen. From Matön Drangsong[63] he received the transmission of the treasure texts of Matön Sölzin (b.1092)[64] that include the *Root Tantra of the Secret Mother, Goddess Senthub.*

Gyalwa Yungdrung also received the initiation and the oral transmission of the *Revelatory Transmission from Zhangzhung* and the *Experiential Transmission (Nyams rgyud)* from two masters, Latö Tokden Depa Sherab and Zhangtön Sönam Rinchen. Few titles are credited to our author. Besides instructions on the prayer for blessings (*gsol 'debs*) to the masters of the lineage of the Atri[65] system of meditation, he is best known for his famed treatise on this tradition, which is translated here in its entirety in one volume for the first time, the *Practice Manual of the Oral Tradition of the Great Perfection from Zhangzhung.*

The *Practice Manual* is composed of twelve texts of different lengths that constitute a whole independent system of meditation practice. The first and second texts are devotional prayers to the masters of the Zhangzhung Oral Transmission from Zhangzhung that include poetic musings on the ephemeral nature of life, confession, the generation of the mind of enlightenment, going for refuge, offerings, recitation of mantras, and supplications to the long list of lineage masters of the tradition. It is a complete recitation of the preliminary practice of the system and is currently recited daily by its practitioners.

The third text is a commentary on the previous two texts and provides directives for practice that include meditations on the four ephemeralities and more (impermanence, endless wandering, loss, illness, death, etc.), methods of visualization, purification of the mind, and so forth.

In the subsequent chapters, Gyalwa Yungdrung begins his instruction on the different methods of meditation within the Zhangzhung tradition and describes proper postures, methods, timing, as well as experiences that the meditator will have. Chapter 4 focuses on the practice of dark retreat. This consists essentially in sequestering oneself in a dark room where no light enters. The practitioner will soon experience hallucinatory visions, but must focus on remaining mindful. Gyalwa Yungdrung quotes from the *Lamp* (222.2):

> Mindfulness is the spear of the mind. With it, one should stab through the shield of light visions.

And,

> The great soul Drenpa Namkha said: "The fortunate being with good karma should cut off all illusions from the rays of the sun."

One is directed to move energy through the channels using visualizations coordinated with breathing. Other practices are suggested using the open sky, controlling the body with specified postures, and so on. Some of these bodily positions have descriptive names such as the Reposing Elephant, the Crouching Ascetic, and so forth. Methods of gazing are most important in the Great Perfection systems. These involve pointing one's eyes toward different translucent objects or looking into space. This is practiced in keeping with distinctive mental attitudes and awareness. Warnings should be mentioned here. Would-be practitioners must follow the directives of an experienced master. Some practices suggest, for instance, pressing certain veins to block the flow of blood in the arteries. This should be done only with extreme caution. Our author warns the reader with repeated pleas.

> Moreover, the *Commentary on the Sun* says: These two methods above of day visions and night visions are there to effect progress. If one practices them according to their timings, whichever they are, and relies on them continually, then they may affect one's constitution and senses. One should know what to adopt and discard.

Gyalwa Yungdrung suggests alternatives here and there, such as in the following example that relates to gazing.

> If these practices are unbearable for one's constitution and senses, then one can use a piece of transparent Chinese cloth similar to dark-blue paper and follow the essential instructions. One uses a piece of blue cloth with one's head inside, following the method above on gazing.

The experiences coming from these exercises will include flows of sensations and bodily reactions. However, the goal is to have a direct experience of the unconditioned nature of the mind, a foretaste of the state of enlightenment. In order to realize this, the apprentice needs to receive guidance on what it is that needs to be recognized. One also needs to be able to assess whether what is experienced is real or false. Chapter 5 of the *Practice Manual* addresses these issues and contains many passages that echo Azha Lodrö Gyaltsen's discourses on the nature of the mind, on consciousness, and the process of apprehending reality.

> A name cannot be imputed to it, yet it does not go beyond one meaning. One can see its one essence, yet different manifestations emerge forth from it. In this one basis are contained the great particularities of happiness and suffering. Great variety arises, yet what is called "this" cannot be defined, for at some point it is hidden. It cannot be seen at all, yet everyone is connected to it. Its essence is unknown. It is all-encompassing. It is nonexistent to others, for it is beyond the mind. It is [called] the great inexpressible one.

What is sought in this system is the direct apprehension of the natural state, which is uncontrived, dynamic, and manifests continually and spontaneously.

> Thus, first, dynamism and the radiance of the pristine cognition
> of awareness do not have an agent as primary cause. They arise
> without interruption as self-manifested rays, lights, and sound.
> The radiance, which has no shade, is the factor of clarity of aware-
> ness that arises as the light that is self-illuminating awareness, like
> a rainbow. Its capacity, which is completely without roots, is the
> factor of the emptiness of awareness that arises as the sound that
> is self-sounding awareness, like an echo. Dynamism, which is
> devoid of the duality of an intrinsic essence to clarity and empti-
> ness, arises as the sound that is self-sounding awareness.

Reality is forever manifesting indiscriminately as lights, rays, and sounds. These are somewhat "translated," or made to manifest in an illusory but concrete manner, by our senses and, most of all, by the mind. Therefore, understanding the operations of the mind through these meditative experiences is considered the key to enlightenment in this tradition. Liberation is therefore a matter of practice and realization.

Once experiences come on, one treads the path using proper attitudes and focuses on clear light that is like space, transparent and clear, unimpeded by whatever may be passing through. Chapter 6 goes through this process of recognition and focus and teaches how to increase the visions triggered by these meditative exercises. A variety of angles are examined in order to help realize their ultimate functions. The path and its stages and grounds as described by Lodrö Gyaltsen are integrated within the discourse of Gyalwa Yungdrung to provide a general orientation to how they relate to the quest for enlightenment in Bön.

Chapter 7 discusses the practices of forceful purification and describes them in detail. It specifies which practices one should engage in at which level. Chapter 8 concentrates on the methods used for a direct introduction to the self-manifestation of the ultimate. Many metaphors as well as concrete exercises are used here involving gazing, hearing, seeing, and how one must consider these as pointers toward the state of realization.

How are obstacles to direct perception removed in a practical manner? This is the concern of chapter 9, which introduces the whole program of practice and its aspects. An untitled addendum contains descriptions of the calisthenic movements or yogic exercises that must be performed during retreat or during sustained practice of this system. The text was not corrected by the Tibetan editors and contains several orthographic mistakes. It describes physical bodily movements involving arms and legs, breathing, stretching, kicking, and so forth. One is reminded that in order to practice these movements, one needs to have been taught by someone conversant with them. The text consists in mnemonic notes that remind one of the movements and their sequences. I have suggested a modern source in the notes that describes these physical postures and their accompanying movements with illustrations that may help make sense of the descriptions.

Chapters 10 and 11 describe how to exercise and make use of the psychic veins or channels (*rtsa*) by circulating the energy or breath (*rlung*). Chapter 11 spreads these exercises through a seven-week program and details what is to be focused on during these seven weeks.

The *Practice Manual* concludes with an exhortation to the practitioner for good practice from Lishu Takring.[66] Tradition asserts that he was a contemporary of Drenpa Namkha in the eighth century. He is credited with having hidden the *Collected Discourse*, the shortest hagiography of Shenrab that he translated into Tibetan, in a stupa of Samyé Monastery. This was the one subsequently discovered by the three ācāryas. He is central to the Three Cycles of Propagation, which is the ancient propagation of the teachings of Bön in the realms of the gods, of the subterranean deities (*klu*), and in the realm of humans.

Lishu Takring was born a daughter to King Nyen Takpung. After performing the rite of the five supreme tantric deities,[67] she became a man. The man Lishu then spread the teachings for eighty-two years, after which he went to Tazik to seek further teachings. After intense practices and numerous miraculous feats performed over the course of seven hundred years, he translated many teachings from India, China, and Zhangzhung into Tibetan. He overpowered mystical goddesses in eight places and mastered all outer and inner phenomena. In the end, he became free from birth and death. His mind and tantric teachings are said to have been transmitted through a chain of eighteen great ascetics.[68]

* * *

I was first introduced to the text of the preliminary practices of the Zhang-zhung tradition in 1991 when visiting the Drak Yungdrungkha hermitage in Amdo Sharkhok (Songpan). It was recited there daily by those entering the practice of the Great Perfection system in the Zhangzhung tradition. There-fore, all the texts presented here are likely to have been in continual use since the thirteenth century, except for Sherab Gyaltsen's *Magic Key*, which dates from the fifteenth century. They are all presently used in the various curric-ula of Bönpo monastic and retreat centers.

Four of this collection of texts have been translated here into a West-ern language for the first time. The fifth, the *Practice Manual*, was partially translated into several European languages and here translated into English in its entirety for the first time. Thus, I hope that this volume will make a significant contribution to Tibetan studies in general and to Bön studies in particular. I hope that these translated texts will benefit scholars, students, and practitioners of Bön. I dedicate this work to past, present, and future Bön scholars and practitioners as well as to whomever it can benefit. I beg for compassionate understanding for any errors in translation that may be found.

Acknowledgments

This project was completed over a longer period than initially predicted. I would like to thank Thupten Jinpa and David Kittelstrom for their heroic patience. I would like to profusely thank Mary Petrusewicz for the very dif-ficult task of editing the whole volume. I am also much in debt to several friends, colleagues, and Bön masters for their help in making sense of diffi-cult sections of the texts presented here. I would like to particularly thank Sengé Trulku Rikzin Nyima, an exceptional scholar, if not one of the most learned Bönpo of the younger generation. He has been a constant source of support and counsel when tackling difficult passages. I am also extremely grateful for the help of the following dear friends and colleagues: Charles Ramble, Daniel Berounsky, Dan Martin, Tsering Thar, Geshe Namkha Gya'o, Geshe Nyima Choekorsang, and Henri Pavot. There are also many others too numerous to name here who contributed significantly to bringing this book to light. I would like to send them each a thousand thanks.

I would like to offer my utter gratitude to my wife, Dr. Pouneh Shabani-Jadidi, who has been with this project from its inception. She bore with me, with loving-kindness and patience, during the many stormy nights when

I could not see solutions to philosophical conundrums and the riddles of ungrammatical sentences.

I would like to dedicate this work to Rachel Labbé Desjardins (1926–2022); to Michael Bertiaux, who pointed the way; and to the late Ayung Lama (1926–97), who opened the doors of Bön to me.

Technical Note

THE TIBETAN TITLE OF the volume translated here is *G.yung drung bon gyi mdo sngags sems gsum gyi gzhung,* which means the *Fundamental Traditions on the Three [Categories] of Scriptures, Tantras, and Mind of Everlasting Bön.* This edition was prepared specifically for *The Library of Tibetan Classics.* Bracketed numbers embedded in the text refer to page numbers in the critical and annotated Tibetan edition published in New Delhi by the Institute of Tibetan Classics as volume 9 of the *Bod kyi gtsug lag gces btus* series. In preparing this translation, the Institute of Tibetan Classics edition served as the primary source, with reference also to other editions.

The titles of all texts are rendered in English, regardless of whether translations of those texts have been published in English. When those texts are available in translation, we have tried to provide the relevant information in the bibliography.

The conventions for phonetic transcription of Tibetan words are those developed by the Institute of Tibetan Classics and Wisdom Publications. They reflect approximately the pronunciation by a modern Central Tibetan; Tibetan speakers from Ladakh, Kham, or Amdo, not to mention Mongolians, might pronounce the same words quite differently. Transliterated spellings of the phoneticized Tibetan names can be found in the Table of Tibetan Transliteration at the end of the volume. Sanskrit diacritics are used throughout, except for certain terms that have entered the English language, such as Mahayana, mandala, sutra, samsara, and nirvana.

Pronunciation of Tibetan phonetics
ph and *th* are aspirated *p* and *t*, as in *pet* and *tip.*
ö is similar to the *eu* in the French *seul.*
ai is similar to the *e* in *bet.*
é is similar to the *e* in *prey.*

z is similar to the *z* in *zebra*.
zh is similar to the *g* in *genre*.

Pronunciation of Sanskrit
Palatal *ś* and retroflex *ṣ* are similar to the English unvoiced *sh*.
c is an unaspirated *ch* similar to the *ch* in *chill*.
The vowel *ṛ* is similar to the American *r* in *pretty*.
ñ is somewhat similar to the nasalized *ny* in canyon.
ṅ is similar to the *ng* in *sing* or *anger*.

PART 1

The Magical Key
to the Precious Gradual Path
and Grounds of the Greater Vehicle

By the protector of wandering beings,
Azha Lodrö Gyaltsen (1198–1263)

1. Teachings Introducing the Preliminary Practices from the Corpus on the Basis of the Mode of Being

Introductory verses

I bow at your feet benevolent master!
The sunrays of your loving-kindness pervade all spheres of heaven.
Your uncontaminated melody is a refuge from the place of misery.
Having accumulated the two stainlesses,[69] you possess all goodness.
To you, mother of the conqueror of the three times, I prostrate!

[Just like] the all-encompassing sky, the purity of your own nature is
    inexpressible.
You demonstrated the excellent path of certainty using undefiled truth.
You have overcome ignorance and opened the mouth of the mute.
To you, whose many emanations[70] guide wandering beings, I prostrate!

Your selfless wisdom on the path of the two accumulations
shines the light of realization and has set you on the path of great bliss!
Your association with the two aims[71] made you a compassionate protector.
Progressing along the stages, I prostrate to the hosts of spiritual heroes!

The strength of your purifications has made your science of the scriptures
    and reasoning extensive.
The continuous rain of nectar from Tshangpa's[72] melodious voice
removes the thirst and every evil from the three abodes.[73]
To you masters, owners of the stream, I prostrate!

By wrong dualistic clinging to ignorance and misunderstanding, one is thoroughly bound in the three-worlds system. One wanders astray aimlessly to

wrong places. In order to be set on the path to supreme great bliss, the king and his sons, the good noble ones, have delivered these fine words. With flawless certainly they fulfilled the benefit of others.

When beings express themselves in words, they speak in conjectures. Their excessive explanations that indeed do not change the meaning of the scriptures are based on childish ignorance. The significance of these instructions is profound and their understanding is difficult. Nevertheless, in order to make understanding easy for those with feeble minds, I have skillfully composed these words appropriately. This is for those fortunate ones who desire to be established in benefits and happiness. This is for those people who aim faithfully at discarding sorrow completely. It is for those who are faithfully established here, mindful of their aspiration, so that they will obtain the realization of the unsurpassed without limits. [4]

Teachings on the essential points of the traditional basic practices

Because sentient beings do not acquire the realization of the welfare of others by themselves, or they have misleading ideas or are in doubt, they are unable to journey on the path and therefore wander in cyclic existence. For that reason, having explained the path, its stations, and so forth, these explanations will lead one through the door so that one will be able to attain realization.

Whatever the teacher explained, the most important are traditions, such as the ways of the charioteers,[74] that resolve issues on the *Eight Realms* and the class of the *Hundred Thousand* scriptures, and so forth. Their meanings have been condensed here so that they may easily be understood.

Furthermore, the object of the teachings of this *Magical Key* is to demonstrate purposefully by means of [discussions on] the base, the path, and the result. On their modes, the *Eight Realms* (2.124.6) refers to the "root" as "base" and to "meditation" as the "path," saying:

The result that is the complete purity of Shenrab will be obtained.

The *Summary of the Hundred Thousand* also mentions the base and the path. On the essence of intrinsic reality, the *Compendium on the Spreading of the Essence of Suchness* (1.60.2) says:

These three [the base, the path, and the result] abide as one essential droplet (*thig le*) in the universal base.

[Furthermore, it says (1.60.2):]

One will engage and tread on the five paths.

The *Compendium on the Spreading* (1.64.6) further says:

In that way, with practice, one will acquire the state of abiding in the essence of the sky, the body of the all-knowing.

The *Eye of the Needle* (8.277.2) says:

First, what is the cause of birth? Second, what is the path of transmigration? Lastly, what are the grounds of the journey?

I will teach the main points on all of these.

The *Summary of the Hundred Thousand* is written in eight meters (*sho lo ka*) of four verses in 100,000 stanzas. On the mode of treading the path, it says:

There are eight aspects to the method to realize fruition. These consist in the sequences of empowerments, the path, and the grounds. They will be explained accordingly with words that are flawless and meaningful.

These teachings are threefold: (1) the meaning of the ground that is to be understood, (2) the stages of the path of practice, and (3) the result of the practice of the path.

The meaning of the ground

The first topic is also divided into three sections: (1) the recognition of the root and the base, (2) determining their nature, and (3) the method of the realization of what they are.

The recognition of the root and the base

The first of these is further divided into three sections: (1) to recognize self-isolates [i.e., what one recognizes as endowed conceptually with a self], (2) to separate the coarse, and (3) to summarize the root of the condensed meaning.

To recognize self-isolates

First, the *Hundred Thousand* (2.125.6) says:

> The words pronounced by Shenrab have summarized that the base and the roots of all phenomena are [to be found] completely in one's own self.

The *Eight Realms* (125.7) says:

> Thus, following the request of one with a childish mind, the teacher has summarized as such: The base and the roots of all phenomena are completely in one's own self. The words pronounced by Shenrab have recapitulated that the base and the roots of all phenomena [5] are exhaustively in one's own self; all phenomena in the circle of migration are misery; and liberation from sorrows is realized through the purification of all phenomena. If one asks: What are these? The body is afflicted by all phenomena in the cycles of migration from old age until death. From the perfection of giving to the unsurpassable until one transcends suffering, all aspects of phenomena must be purified.

If one asks: How can one summarize (1) where an intrinsic entity is, (2) its ground, and (3) its root? Others refute these three points through a system of analysis. As for us, we establish meaning through realization. That is how we dispel objections.

What are scholars asserting?

First, what are some scholars claiming?

[Argument:] "Phenomenon" (*bon*) means that it holds to its own characteristic. "Everything" means without exception within cyclic existence. The "base" is perfectly pure in itself. The "root" is the consciousness (*rnam shes*) of the universal base. "Self" is by way of exaggerating the ego as Suchness.[75] "Inherent basis" is a manner of designating inherent reality (*bon nyid*). "Aggregates" (*'dus pa*) are the collections of one's childish stream of being. The results of separating the root from the base are the collections in the stream of the great self. The two purities (*dag pa gnyis*) are said to be that of "endowment" (*ldan*) and "the wisdom of the mirror."

[Answer:] But this is not the case. Reasoning can disprove this proposition and its contradiction.

First of all, it is said that the conventional truth covers the topics from Suchness to the cycle of transmigration. The absolute truth covers the topics from suffering to transcendence. The *Compendium on the Spreading* says:

> All the roots of phenomena can be subsumed into the two truths.

Therefore, this effectively contradicts what has been said above.

Second, what if a phenomenon is holding to its very own specific character [i.e., that it is inherently existent]? The *Treasury* (137.3) responds to this, saying:

> [Individual] constituents change with the number of their aspects. It is because one grasps for specifically characterized phenomena that there are constituents.

If the universal base consisted in the roots, then there would be no base. If this [basis] is maintained, then the *Compendium on the Spreading* (3.122.2) clearly says:

> Space, intrinsic reality, and intrinsic mind: everything there is transformed into the universal base.

As for a "substantial entity," it is needlessly imputed as a separate thing. If the result of disengaging were that one becomes endowed with the two purities [of primordial essence and free from defilements] yet the aggregates of one's childish continuum of being were still there, then there would be no need to tread the path. If there were no aggregates of one's childish continuum of being, then one would have to accept what was previously stated.

The great inherent self brings about the reality of being endowed with the two purities to those who have no realization. This is because of the aggregates of one's childish continuum of being. If these two purities were said to be the aggregates of the great intrinsic self, then mere phenomena would not exist among the childish. That would be unreasonable.

The seven points of our own tradition

Second, our own tradition proceeds along these seven topics:[76] (1) the blissful ones, (2) the path, (3) suffering and transcendence, (4) the objects of the mind, (5) formulations, (6) aim, and (7) quotations from the scriptures.

The blissful ones, the path, suffering, and transcendence

Here, when one engages with the topics of the blissful ones, cyclic existence, and transcendence, [6] there is a multitude of everything. The base is abiding in the primordial, while there is no basis to the material elements. The *Hundred Thousand* says:

> The root is in the two truths.

The objects of the mind

As for the inherent self, it is intrinsic to the mind. The aggregates that are misrepresentations, these are intrinsic to the mind abiding in naturally occurring attributes. This is explained through clear demonstration. The *Compendium on the Spreading* (3.122.2) says:

> Space, intrinsic reality, and intrinsic mind, everything there transforms into the universal base
> ... the root of all phenomena is the two truths.

The Eight Realms says:

> The body that is aging and dies, this is about the conventional truth and its categorization of the cyclical world. From the perfection of giving to the unsurpassable and so on, this is about the absolute truth and its categorization of transcending suffering.

Elimination of objections

Third, is the elimination of objections section.

[Argument:] When one posits that there is no root to the universal base, this makes concrete changes to the process of transcending suffering for those caught in a childish continuum of existence, for this would also exist in the continuum of the spiritual heroes, the blissful ones.

[Answer:] While there is no change to the reality and the existence of the spiritual heroes, there is the existence of the mere seed of enlightenment, and at the moment of liberation and realization, there is no more continuation of a conditioned self in cyclic existence. It is posited that one abides and becomes liberated in primordial awareness.

Teachings on the phenomena of cyclic existence and transcendence

This second topic is divided into three sections: (1) defining characteristic, (2) the basis of the defining characteristic, and (3) definition.

(1) Defining characteristics on cyclic existence and transcendence

The position of others

First is the refutation from the **traditions of the others** [i.e., the Buddhists and others].

[Argument:] One scholarly assertion is that when someone seizes on any characteristic of a self out of everything else, this grasping brings suffering and stands in opposition to purification. This is cyclic existence.

When someone grasps onto any characteristic of a self out of everything there is, it is asserted that one transcends all sufferings through the mere purification of one's woes.

[Answer:] But it is not so. In the first case, the spiritual heroes in the seven lower grounds reincarnate again into cyclic existence. This is on account of being affected by suffering, from the seven levels of heaven until the Indestructible Citadel established on the top. The *Eye of the Needle* (14.445.7) mentions this as the "drying up of the four demonic rivers." This is when adversity is transformed by itself, where its expression is no longer eliminated as something that is "other."

As for the second point, there is no transcendence of sorrow in the lower seventh level on account of the existence of afflictions and defilements. Above the first six levels of heaven, grasping that produces suffering in the dirt of cyclic existence is transformed into transcending the obstacles to pure cognition. Concerning the second of these assertions, it is said: "There is no clearing away of the hosts of darkness and obstruction in cyclic existence."

The purification of aspects does not eradicate characteristics that are perceived as other, since there is no differentiation on the basis of characteristics. [7]

[Argument:] Again, someone made this assertion connected with suffering that, according to the scriptures, cyclic existence comes to those endowed with birth, old age, sickness, and death. And accordingly, the opposite is asserted when these are not present: this is liberation from sorrow.

[Answer:] First, while someone on the path goes through cyclic existence, one experiences temporary happiness that is not pervasive. One has to tackle suffering and be unconcerned with harm and so forth, for it has been taught that this is the way to transcend sorrow. As said above, it has been taught that transcending sorrow is to perceive the truth directly. Second, the mere truth that is manifest at that moment is very pervasive [i.e., unmistakable], whereas it is not present for someone still on the path of cyclic existence.

Our own tradition on cyclic existence and transcendence

[Argument:] Second, as for **our own tradition**, cyclic existence is connected with grasping at a self and suffering. The blissful ones that have no-self transcend sorrow.

[Answer:] But it is not so, for the *Summary of the Hundred Thousand* says:

> The very nature of cyclic existence is its inseparability from suffering. The transcending of sorrow has the defining characteristic of great bliss.

Dispelling objections

Third is dispelling objections on cyclic existence and transcending sorrow.

First, the spiritual heroes of the lower seven levels are, as a consequence, transmigrating. That is flawless. This brings about the realization of the self-lessness of suffering.

Second, the resulting bliss at the time of this realization is greatly pervasive. This is also flawless.

However, there is [still] no realization of the lack of self and there is no being endowed with great bliss.

(2) The basis of the defining characteristic on cyclic existence and transcendence

Second, the basis of the defining characteristic has three parts: (1) cause, (2) the limits of the grounds, and (3) the enumeration of its aspects.

Cause

With respect to the first, vices and virtues are both contaminated and contribute to cyclic existence. The *Summary of the Hundred Thousand* has explained that the two accumulations [of merit and wisdom] are the causes of transcendence.

The limits of the grounds

The second point is threefold.

[Argument:] First, some scholars posit this objection: Can the path of vision be generated or not? They explain that the worldly and the transcendent are separated and that through the paths of accumulation and application one transforms cyclic existence into liberation from suffering. This is done with the application of mindful recollection and so forth.

Again, some have asked: Are essence and suffering separate or not? Are the limits of the grounds [based on] seeing the truth or not seeing it? And also, is it about achieving the enlightened body, et cetera, and [practicing the perfections of] giving and so forth, or not?

[Answer:] First of all, let us counter the above and then review the explanation about worldly and transcendent realities. And then third, let us refute the double proposition above.

Negation

If one does not transcend sorrow through the application of mindful recollection and so forth, this stands in opposition to the scriptures. However, if this is the case, then it defiles the assertion of liberation from sorrow, since worldly practices would be its cause. [8]

Review according to our own tradition

Second, our tradition explains whether essence and clinging to a self are or are not separate, whether the path through the limits of the grounds can or cannot be trodden, and it also explains the natural state, the enlightened body, the practices of giving, and so on.

Dispelling of objections

Third is dispelling the objections.

[Argument:] It is explained, by those near and far, that the truth can be either perceived or not.

[Answer:] Since there is neither cyclic existence nor transcendence from sorrow, it should be understood from the duality of the worldly and the transcendent.

Enumeration of the aspects of the defining characteristic on cyclic existence and transcendence

The third point concerns the enlightened body, old age and death, and the practice of the [perfections from] giving to omniscience. This third point is explained in the *Summary of the Hundred Thousand*, which says:

> The six kinds of causes do not rest in cyclic existence, even for an instant. And so it is, from the torments of cyclic existence all the way to liberation from sorrow.

Concise meaning: the two truths

[Argument:] Third, with respect to the concise meaning, it is summarized in the two truths of cyclic existence and transcendence from sorrow in the following way:

> All phenomena of cyclic existence are summarized in the relative truth.

[Answer:] This examination does not support that analysis; therefore, it is untenable. The *Hundred Thousand Verses on the Summit of Awareness of Clear Realization* (1.129.2) says:

> Where do beings come from and where are they going? Those beings that have obstructions, they are the phenomena of cyclic existence.

And again, the *Hundred Thousand Verses on the Summit of Awareness of Clear Realization* (129.2) says:

> All phenomena that have transcended from sorrow are gathered in the absolute truth. When one scrutinizes isolated things, then they become empty of inherent existence. There are no beings anywhere and there are no obstructions. All phenomena and so forth have transcended sorrow.

[Argument:] Suppose that, from the practice of the perfection of giving to that of the perfection of mindful equanimity, these become part of the absolute truth. What if someone asks if these are complexities of the desire realm, and if relative truth is explained as part of transcendence?

[Answer:] Then someone could posit that the eighteen emptinesses[77] are simply part of the absolute. Others would then designate named objects as being in the realm of absolute truth. This is not the case!

If it were like that, then there would be contradictions all the way to the Unsurpassable. It would contradict the position that there is no inherent existence. It would go against the transmission of the means of realization and there wouldn't be any realization. There would be no realization of the absolute. That which is a subject would indeed exist. There would be an absence of fabricated objects. Yet this is asserted as true!

For these reasons, from the contradiction of emptiness all the way to the

Unsurpassable, these go against the position that there is no inherent self that is the absolute truth.

But contrary to this, abiding free from conceptualizations is the absolute. The perfection of giving and so forth, when viewed in isolation, are only conventional truth.

[Argument:] If someone asks: If the perfections of giving and so forth, when viewed in isolation, are conventional truth, then isn't this contrary to the explanations on absolute truth?

[Answer:] In this case, one generates absolute truth by using its contradictions to impute realization.

Inherent nature

The second point on inherent nature concerns the two truths [i.e., relative and absolute] and the four truths [i.e., old age, sickness, death, and transcendence] that are gathered into these three sections: [9] (1) defining characteristic, (2) divisions, and (3) precise definition.

Defining characteristic

The first is threefold: (1) refutation of others' systems, (2) establishment of our positions, and (3) dispelling objections.

Refutation of others' points on defining characteristics

[Argument:] Someone said that the established mind [i.e., the "cognitive framework," *blo ngor*] of the spiritual heroes of Everlasting Bön is separate from the established mind of the common people.

[Answer:] This definition is not it. Concerning relative truth and so forth, there is no truth that is established in childish people. If that were the case, then someone would quote a scripture, saying: "Conventional truth is a mistake. The object of activities of the minds of the pure ones is intrinsic self." If that were the case, then there would be no realization of the absolute truth in the enlightened mind of the conqueror that is free from conceptualizations. There would be no realization of the absolute through the discriminative cognition of finality. Such is not the case, as there is no essential category of analysis for [the enlightened] finality.

[Argument:] Again, what if someone asserts that this is incontrovertible? Relative truth is not all-encompassing when it concerns deceptive cognition. The *Cycles of the Nine Mirrors* says:

Conventional reality is certainly deceptive.

Furthermore, *Cycles of the Nine Mirrors* (27.4) says:

Validating conventions are overreaching conclusions. Incontrovertible inferences are themselves subsequent cognition after investigation.

[Argument:] Again, someone made this point on the scholarly allegation that an assertion becomes a mental object in the ordinary mind. Conventional object of cognition is an overreaching conclusion that is being passed on subsequently.

[Answer:] The lama, the lord of scriptures and reasoning, accepts that there is no such thing as an established ordinary mind. Both scriptures and reasoning refute this established ordinary mind. In the first case, it is contradicted by the *Very Pure Transmission* (21.172.3), which says:

A word, real or imagined, does not express transcendence.

Also, it is said faultlessly:

Are entity and its attributes beyond conceptual mind or not?

[Argument:] Can the attributes of the absolute be perceived or not?

[Answer:] In the first case [i.e., attributes of the absolute can be perceived], this thesis is mistaken. As for the second case, it comes to establishing attributes to a non-established basis.

Establishing attributes to a non-established basis

This second point is fourfold: overreaching concept, inadequate reach, unproven concept, and logical absurdity.

An overreaching concept

[Argument:] On the first point, these two terms, "conventional object of cognition" and "moon," are too broad concepts but can somehow be related to [the metaphoric image of] a golden conch.

[Answer:] Concerning the natural state [of manifest reality], this is unproven. Concerning its mode of appearing [i.e., appearances], it is said to be accurate. Thus, if it is accurate in its own mode of appearance, then it establishes that the moon and the golden conch are objects that appear in the mind. If this were untrue, then one would be aware of it as illusion; it would be a false assertion.

An inadequate reach

[Argument:] As for the second point, someone may say that the absolute truth is not pervasive when it is established as a particularity [i.e., an object in the mind]. The absolute should be clear in the mind when one is meditating.

[Answer:] As for that, what comes later is that one ponders and one's ordinary mind becomes familiar with this idea. It is similar to when one has become familiar with an object that has already been destroyed. Pristine cognition can realize the transcendence of ordinary mind. If not, then the grasping mind that meditates just becomes convoluted. It is clearly said in the *Six Transmissions* (144.1):

> Meditating versus ordinary mind, there are no doubts about the ordinary mind. [10]

Unproven

[Argument:] Third, if there is no established essence of an ordinary mind, then the ordinary mind itself can be claimed to be unreal.

[Answer:] If proven, this would change the understanding on the duality of the mental continuum. It is impossible to hold this duality together as one. The *Great Perfection* says:

> One cannot hold on to the duality of the mental continuum in sentient beings.

Logical absurdity

The fourth has to do with reversing falseness with the truth.

4. Concerning Truth

Establishment of our positions

Second, concerning **our own tradition**, the great one, Lodrö, said: "One is endowed with a mode of being."

Dispelling objections

Third, dispelling objections is threefold: no entailment, overreaching, and abandoning logical absurdity.

No entailment

[Argument:] Someone posited that when the moon is perceived as double [by an impaired vision] or as a golden conch, this does not entail them as being particularities of conventional truth.[78]

[Answer:] There is a conventional aspect to this but no truth in it.

[Argument:] If someone counters this by saying that in that case, the difference in these aspects is that the conventional truth is both correct and incorrect. There is one moon that appears [mistakenly] as double.

[Answer:] What is implied as the conventional truth here is what has been designated only by conventional imputation. That is conventional evidence. As for its necessity, it is a truth that is determined through a false and artificial understanding. Therefore, since they do not truly exist, once this is realized, then there is no more support for these to be considered as truly existing. Once one has clarified this mistake, the double manifestations of the conch and its golden color are treated as mere appearances.

Overreaching

[Argument:] Second, what is false in principle can bring about real consequences to an existing being.

[Answer:] But it is not the case. First, it [i.e., the one endowed with life] is either a false substantial entity or an isolated proposition. Second, it is not proven. For example, in order to negate the existence of a false entity or of an isolated proposition, a phenomenon that is produced must be an impermanent substantial entity. It is not an isolated object existing by itself. Therefore the substantial entity that is the object of perception is not truly established. It does not exist.

Abandoning logical absurdity

[Argument:] Third, someone said that there is something similar to a subject that is perceived.

[Answer:] This is faultless. It would be absurd to have a non-ascertainable appearance, since there is no existing true absolute. The *Arcana* (192.7) says:

> Concealed in non-manifested intrinsic reality, undivided intrinsic mind is without perceivable reference. It is like looking at the color of the sky, bright rising light.

This [the point where there is a perceived semblance of a subject] is not unlike this quotation.

The basis of defining characteristics

Second, the topic of the basis of characteristics is threefold: the truth of intrinsic nature, the truth about temporary states, and collected reasoning.

The truth of intrinsic nature

The first of the three is a specifically characterized phenomenon. [11]
    It is said:

> What is endowed with the mode of existence becomes the entailing agent.

Divisions

The second topic[79] is threefold: analysis of the grounds and stages, explanations of numbered categories, and objects of each division.

Inherent nature, unfabricated and fabricated

The first [i.e., specifically characterized phenomenon] has to do with the unfabricated and the fabricated. The first of these is the absolute. The second is the conventional. These are, respectively, transcendence and cyclic existence, the unobservable to the ordinary mind, and the observable.

Analysis of the grounds and stages

The second topic is again divided into five points: Where are the separate grounds? What are their separate essences? What are the reasons for these divisions? How are these separate objects? How many different numbered categories are there?

Where are the separate grounds?

[Argument:] First, if someone merely asserts that there is no intrinsic self, then because of the existence of the two general truths, there cannot be the absence of an intrinsic nature, otherwise there would be no reason for these two truths. If to the foolish, conventional truth consists in no inherent nature, then one would effortlessly become free. If it is not the case, then one is mistaking the existence of Suchness for categories and the two truths do not have the particularities of no inherent nature. The absolute is established through the absence of inherent nature. Yet the conventional truth is not the reverse of the absence of inherent nature in the manifested.

[Answer:] If that were so, then the reversal effected by the lack of inherent existence of conventional truth would be cleared away and said to be illusory. Therefore, this is merely the truth on [the process of] attributing [a label on a] specific characterized phenomenon.

What are their separate essences?

Second, the *Hundred Thousand* says:

> All phenomena are summarized in the two truths.

The *Eye of the Needle* (8.253.2) says:

If the two truths were similar to curds and milk, there would be
no Everlasting Bön.

The *Inner Tantra* says:

If the two truths are not established as an object of comprehension, then it is similar to comparing them to an arrow without a
target.

This was about the absolute and the conventional truths.

What are the reasons for these divisions?

[Argument:] Third, concerning the nature and extent of subject and object,
they are not truly established within the mode of an existing ordinary mind.
To the essence of ordinary mind their mode of appearance is not obstructed.
To the ordinary mind, the intrinsic enlightened mind of the conqueror
appears as something else, and in the meditative and post-meditative states,
as spiritual heroes.

[Answer:] The object of refutation is illusory and therefore it refutes
attachment to entities as truly existent. The refutation of everything depends
on the separation of the two, the unfabricated and inherent existence. It differentiates the relative and the absolute truths.

How are these separate objects?

Fourth, are these of one essence or different? If one asks if they are different
aspects of one essence, or neither one nor different, which one is it? Here
there are three possibilities:

(1) System of refutation of opponents

The **system of refutation of opponents** has these four points: entities are
one in essence, entities are different in essence, they have one essence but different aspects, and they only refute the assertion that refutes the one essence.

Entities are one in essence

[Argument:] First, some great expert said: "The essence is one, depending on whether there is realization or no realization."

[Answer:] But it is not the case. [12] The scriptures explain the differences. Reasonable as well as foolish ones conceptualize the absolute according to the perception of the conventional. They come to establish the reality of the conventional as the enlightened mind of the conqueror.

[Argument:] Is the absolute free from elaborations or not? If it were free, then the conventional would change into being free from elaboration because of the one essence. If it were not, then words, described or imagined, would explain transcendence and so forth.

[Answer:] But it is not the case; therefore it is refuted.

Entities are different in essence

[Argument:] Second, Dru Namkha Ö (fl. eleventh–twelfth centuries)[80] explained about differentiation that the concept of different essences is explained in the scriptures.

[Answer:] But it is not the case. Concerning the one essence, the scriptures explain that if one reaches beyond the conventional for the absolute using reasoning, then one degenerates into differentiation. If one does not reach to this point, then examination of the refutation will prevent one from coming to ascertain the truth. One will be able to overcome these two with certitude with the realization of the absolute and through the appearances of the characteristics of the conventional.

They have one essence but different aspects

[Argument:] Third, concerning the one-essence position, what if someone considers whether the conventional and the absolute are realized or not.

[Answer:] Then, when in the conventional there is cause for production and cessation, the absolute would also have production and cessation. That would make them impermanent! If they do not arise and cease, then as a result, they cannot be of one essence. Therefore, this one-essence assertion falls apart.

They refute the assertion that refutes the one essence

[Argument:] Fourth, following the great one, well-born scholars have followed the different-essence arguments that refute the one-essence arguments. The *Hundred Thousand* says:

> At the moment of realization, there is one essence. If there is no realization, then it is different.

Furthermore, if one's point of view is to rely on the one-essence argument, then one differentiates. If one relies merely on what is perceived, then the conventional exists while the absolute does not and there is differentiation. Seeing beyond, the absolute is realized and, as it says: "There is no more duality."

[Answer:] But it is not the case. This is not validly proven, and therefore it is refuted.

First, there is the scriptural tradition on non-duality. To realize the non-fabricated absolute as one is to be free from the multiplicity of characteristics. It is explained that there are divisions made in the non-realized ordinary mind, but this does not prove to be a negation of the one essence.

Second, after due consideration, it is illogical and completely absurd. First, by relying on a one essence of the mind, if one differentiates, then the absolute will be established from a childish delusive viewpoint because of the distinguishing mind. It is contradictory.[81] If this is accepted, then there will be release without efforts. If it is not accepted, one will rely on a faulty assertion with a differentiating mind.

[Argument:] If the one essence is posited, then are the enlightened ones and the mind of sentient beings to be relied on as being one?

[Answer:] First, if one sees it this way [i.e., as one essence], then manifest absolute itself and manifest conventional will be of one essence. If this is accepted, then there will be no freedom from elaboration. Second, if it is seen this way, then the intrinsic manifestation of the conventional is released effortlessly through the manifested absolute. [13]

[Argument:] If it is asked: Notwithstanding on which view one relies, will both manifest as one essence?

[Answer:] Mind and essence will manifest in duality and the differentiating mental continuum will corrupt the unity of essence. Second, a pot is by itself accordingly empty. This oneness and its essence are not one and this difference is endowed with conditioned changes.

What is the difference between another's negating position and our own refuting position on this oneness? The absolute is refuted in the conventional. The changes of one essence establish appearances that are devoid of inherent existence and mutate as real and true.

(2) Our own tradition on essence, differentiation, and Suchness

Second, **our own tradition** is that Suchness cannot be expressed in words, like the other [traditions,] due to the fact that there is no separation between the one essence and differentiation. Separation is inexistent. Given that there is clear realization, the *Hundred Thousand Verses on the Summit of Awareness* says:

> Just as there is no one essence, there are no others. The one essence and the non-existent others do not exist.

The *Tantra on Action* (8.212.4) says:

> The two truths and the one essence do not exist. Differentiation does not exist.

The *Hundred Thousand* further says:

> There is unity in the moment of realization. When there is no realization, there is differentiation.

In these, it is explained that if there is realization, there is the absolute. However, in the state of non-realization, there is only the conventional.

(3) Dispelling objections

Third, **dispelling objections** consists in scriptures, contradictions, disproof through reasoning, and abandoning logical absurdities.

Scriptures

The saying of the *Hundred Thousand* above is not contradicted. Therefore, it is said that realization and non-realization are, respectively, the absolute and the conventional. It is said that there are differentiations in the conventional. These are conceived as divisions in conventional expressions.

Contradictions

[Argument:] If someone says that there are no divisions in the Suchness of the absolute, what about the conventional?

[Answer:] These two exist [nominally]. As for the state of realization being the absolute and the state of non-realization as the conventional, [ultimately,] there is no division between them.

Disproof through reasoning

[Argument:] If someone were to say that it is logical that the one essence entails no differentiation of essence?

[Answer:] This assertion of non-differentiation in differentiation refutes the one essence. It is invalid to posit that there is separation in the non-differentiation of unrecognized independent entities. It makes no sense to posit that there are no divisions among inexistent and divided objects. Therefore, there is no division between the one essence and differentiation.

Abandoning logical absurdities

As for the other's thesis about our thesis on the one essence and the refutation of differentiation, it is unacceptable to ascertain the lack of divisions of differentiation. It is like the absurdity of the horns of a rabbit that does not exist. There is no support for this.

Is the ordinary mind deceived or not deceived?

[Argument:] Fifth, is the ordinary mind deceived or not deceived?

[Answer:] Concerning objects, phenomena themselves, and those endowed with phenomena [i.e., subjects], their mode of existence is not established, while [14] their mode of manifestation is unobstructed. These are ascertained.

Main points on each division

Third, the section on the main points on each division is twofold:
The first point, **meaning**, is threefold: [defining characteristics, divisions, and precise definition.]
The first, **defining characteristics**, is threefold: [tradition of the others, our own tradition, and dispelling objections.]

The tradition of the others

[Argument:] First, according to **the traditions of the others**, lama Wang-chuk,[82] lord of the scriptures and reasoning, is said to have established the final analysis through reasoning by his profound speech on the absolute that is: "There is no existing absolute." Yet this is not established by reasoning. It is gained through the study and the contemplation of rational knowledge where there is realization.

[Answer:] For followers of these mundane conventions, the absolute becomes no longer the absolute.

[Argument:] Furthermore, Dopa[83] ascertained as true the recognition of what is not illusory, what is not apparent, and what is proven through study and contemplation.

[Argument:] But it is not the case. If it were the case, then a particular object that is pointed out would be proven to be truly existent. Identifying an isolated particularity does not make it a substantial object.

[Argument:] If study and contemplation were proven as non-deceptive, then in the ordinary mind, would the absolute be manifest or not?

[Answer:] In the first case [i.e., the absolute is manifest to the mind], because it would be established as a manifest object, it would come to be a conceptual fabrication. Furthermore, once it is established by rational cognition and rationality, this would bring reality to the subject. Reasoning establishes this perception as an overreaching imputation.

In the case of the second proposition [i.e., it is not manifest to the mind], then it is a deficient proposition.

5. THE TWO TRUTHS

Our tradition

Second, it is said in our tradition: "What is endowed with empirical reality (*yin lugs*) is not proven by characteristics."

Dispelling objections

Third is dispelling objections:
  [Argument:] Someone says that there is no freedom from proliferation in the following three: defining characteristic, the object being defined, and the bearer of characteristic.[84]
  [Answer:] This is faultless. The absolute cannot be established as a self-isolate. However, the conventional is established through imputed examples. The *Arcana* (129.5) says:

> If unrealized sentient beings cannot be guided by words, it is because a cover obscures their fingers. They cannot see the sign.

Divisions

On the second point about divisions, the *Commentary on The Nine Mirrors* (27.3) says:

> When an object is not established, whatever [this non-object may be] cannot be processed by cognition [and] cannot be perceived.
> When it is not established, although it is true that it is free from division and devoid of conceptual elaboration, but for convention one wants to use an appropriate symbol [lit. "banner and sings"], then the mirror is a profound expression of the absolute. That is the absolute for the proponents of mundane conventionality.

Moreover, can words and means of expression be demonstrative of the absolute or not? Concerning this subject matter, both possibilities negate biased elaborations and negate various other aspects.

Precise definition

Third is the precise definition:
The motive [that is the basis] of the behavior of enlightened beings is the highest. Their [aim to] ultimate finality is the highest. [15] The *Enlightened Ethic of Activities* says:

> The ultimate is the highest truth. The meaning of highest truth is explained as the enlightened intent and conduct of lama Shenrab, who taught the transcendence of suffering.

Counterarguments on conventional, specifically characterized phenomena

The second point is to refute the three specifically characterized phenomena of the **tradition of the others**. This is the first of the three kinds of conventional truth.[85]

[Argument:] The lord of scriptures and reasoning asserts that conventionality in the ordinary mind is established.

[Answer:] If one posits that the noble ones in their post-attainment state still generate conceptions that are not pervasive and deceptive, then it is defiling the truth.

[Argument:] Another question is that of a learned one asking (1) if the inconceivable manifestations of wisdom beings have the ability to manifest the welfare of those with ordinary consciousness, and (2) if they can manifest emptiness through their ability to act for the welfare of those endowed with ordinary consciousness?

In general, it is said there are specifically characterized phenomena [pertaining] to the true and the false conventional truths.

[Answer:] But it is not the case. First, the virtuous ones instantly understand subtle points. A logician understands that a vase that was fabricated is impermanent. He realizes that it was made with effort and that the conventional does not truly exist. He knows it through investigation and analysis.

Second, one can accept whether one is unable to investigate and analyze or one is able to investigate and analyze. The first case [i.e., not being able] is like identifying a horse or an elephant in a dream [i.e., it cannot be ascertained]. The second case [i.e., one is able to] relates to a conventional truth that is not proven, since analysis cannot be established.

Third, the above understanding of the post-attainment states of spiritual heroes is wrong. Because they have the realization of emptiness and the illusory nature of reality, they have the ability to fulfill their function.

[Argument:] Again, Dopa has posited that the only truth in the face of consciousness is a convention.

[Answer:] Truth is merely an isolated concept with no substantial entity, a convention that does not encompass the post-attainment states of spiritual heroes.

Our tradition

Second, **our tradition** is that empirical reality manifests with characteristics.

Dispelling objections

Third is the dispelling of objections.

There is no overreaching assumption concerning the examples of the moon [perceived as] double and the golden conch. These have no empirical reality. There is still some conventionality, yet they do not truly exist.

On the second point on the basis of characteristic [i.e., empirical reality that manifests with characteristics], the *Commentary on the Nine Mirrors* (26.4) says:

From a mirror, one can either ascertain the deceptive or not.

In this, there is the correct and the inaccurate.

On the specifically characterized phenomenon

The first point of the three is on the specifically characterized phenomenon.

[Argument:] Dopa said that the consciousness of the noble ones is facing the truth when in the state of post-attainment it entails the flaw that there is no absence of differentiation between the self-isolate that is devoid of substantial reality and the basis of its characteristic.

[Answer:] Therefore it is said that what is endowed with a mode of being that manifests with characteristics is free from any type of predisposition. [16]

6. THE CORRECT AND THE INCORRECT CONVENTIONAL TRUTHS

Second, on the **essence of the basis of characteristics:** The enlightened one generates bodies with enlightened qualities. They arise manifesting as someone else engaged in the enlightened activities of primordial wisdom and the manifestations of the post-attainment states of the spiritual heroes of everlastingness.

Third, the **precise definition** of the basis of characteristics is: the correct is free from any kind of obstruction.

Second, incorrect is one of the three points on **defining characteristic:**

[Argument:] It has been said that the truth on the face of the consciousness of immature ones cannot be analyzed. Self-isolates devoid of substance have been explained with the metaphor that sound cannot be described.

[Answer:] Therefore it is said that hindrances having joined with reality are what is endowed with a mode of existence that manifests with characteristics.

Secondly, the basis of characteristics of the two types of conventional truth are: authentic and false.

Authentic conventions

The first of three points is the **basis of characteristics.**[86]

[Argument:] Dopa said: "Objects that are apprehended by mundane convention are true in the face of cognition that is not illusory."

[Answer:] However, these do not endure analysis. These objects that are apprehended are explained as words but non-substantial entities. Therefore, to the conventional ordinary mind, what is endowed with a mode of existence with manifested characteristics is not false.

False conventions

Second, regarding the **essence of the basic characteristic:**

[Argument:] Someone said that a fool barely knows the truth but has the ability to perform the function of perceiving and labeling.

[Argument:] Therefore, a perceiver and the object directly perceived are incorporated into one's awareness and the awareness that one has of the other [i.e., the object perceived]. The ordinary mind sees the points about the body and so forth, as well as its own characteristics. There is a general understanding in dependence upon concordant facts and ontological meaning. Its overall meaning is made of these conceptions.

Third, the **precise definition** is that conscious beings take every perception as a true imputation.

7. Authentic Conventional Truth and False Conventional Truth

The second point of three on **defining characteristics**:

[Argument:] Dopa considers that truth is based on a false cognition of the objective reality of the conventional world and that objective reality ultimately cannot be analyzed.

[Answer:] But it is not the case. If the two faults are perceived truly from the viewpoint of a deluded mind as characterized earlier, then they will no longer appear as false. If an entailing factor[87] is not established, then the mistake of the assumption must be ascertained through valid cognition. The mind must clear out and ascertain that the faulty object is an illusion. Then it will become impossible for faulty cognition to occur. For that reason, one must prove the delusory nature of cognition to be sure that appearing characteristics are empty.

In the case when these perceived phenomena are not real, the assertion cannot be proven. Therefore, there is no conventional truth there. [17]

The essence of the basis of characteristics

Second, concerning the essence of the basis of characteristics: When the consciousness of an object is a confused perception, as in the case of seeing two moons, a golden conch, and so forth, everything is then perceived as a dream illusion. When the objects are discordant, then the object's activity is not real in reality.

Third precise definition

The third **precise definition** of the basis of characteristics is: It is the mistaken apprehension of objects that performs an ontological ascertaining. This third definition is grasping with attachment to reality. It is inseparable from predispositions that are manifested.

Third, if one analyzes while conceptualizing, then one realizes that these have no essence and that one cannot successfully carry on analysis. This is the conventional. The *Ethics of deeds* says:

> Everyone trains in the conventional truth. This is where individuals are the objects of activity.

This is the conventional truth.

Another third point is about the existence of entailing agents in temporary conditions.

Truth on temporary conditions

Second, the truth on temporary conditions is threefold: defining characteristics, divisions, and practical definition.

Defining characteristics

[Argument:] First, a master on scriptures and reasoning said that the ordinary mind of each and every individual is established as the same as the ordinary mind of the spiritual heroes of everlastingness.

[Answer:] But it is not the case. If it were, then the truth that each and every person's inherent nature is different from the transformative aspect of the spiritual heroes would be negated. Therefore the great Lodrö proclaimed that it is the arising of entailing factors that endows a mode of being.

Divisions

The second point, divisions, is threefold: dividing boundaries, enumeration, and individual properties.

Dividing boundaries

Transcendence includes both cessation and the path, while the continuum of cyclic existence comprises suffering and universal origination.

Enumeration

The second point is fivefold. (1) The basic division has to do with the remaining items that are entailed with a specifically characterized phenomenon. Their [possible] essences are [classified along] the following four categories: (2) suffering, (3) universal origination, (4) cessation, and (5) the path.

The *Hundred Thousand* (4.504.4) says:

> Suffering is to be understood. Universal origination is to be eliminated. Cessation is to be manifested, and the path is to be meditatively cultivated.

The causal characteristics consisting in the two above [i.e., suffering and origination] are objects to be abandoned, while the two below [i.e., cessation and the path] are antidotes. Thus, these two above, the cause and results of cyclic existence, have to be differentiated as two. The cause of universal origination is suffering and its results, the object produced, and the agent of production. The cause of the path is cessation and its results, the object of realization, and the realizing agent.

Furthermore, the cause of cessation is the result of treading the true path. As *Determining the Root of the Realms* (69.372.7) says:

> The teaching on causality [18] and the teachings on the resulting sphere of reality consist in pristine cognition.

As the great Lodrö says: "If one considers the above, there are the manifest and the agent. If one considers the below, there is the object to be eliminated that is imputed in the result of the cause by merely acting on the object of the phenomenon to be eliminated."

As for the **reason for these divisions**, they are refuted, since the others do not have these divisions.

Third, cyclic existence and transcendence are separate. These two are differentiated as the cause and the result. One can ascertain them by looking at the precise enumeration of these two aspects as cause and result. Thus, one can ascertain them through the mode of engaging objects because this sickness [i.e., cyclic existence] is the cause for the teachings on elimination. The *Hundred Thousand* says:

Suffering is taught first.

The *Hundred Thousand Verses on the Water-Spirits* says:

> Universal origination was first taught so that sickness could be first eliminated.

That having been taught, sickness does not arise, and as such, it is being taught. As for cessation, it is similar to freedom from sickness.

As for the path: "It consists in acting as a skilled physician who frees one from it [i.e., sickness]." It is taught as an object of knowledge. The Great Lodrö said: "The Bön of later times is taught faithfully following the teachings from previous times."

8. THE FOUR TRUTHS

Individual points

Third, the topic on **individual points** is fourfold:

The truth of suffering

First are the three points on the truth of suffering.

First, the lord has explained its **specifically characterized phenomena** by saying: "When the causes of karma and suffering arise, their very characteristic is that there is no peace. Yet this is established in the mind of the spiritual heroes of everlastingness." This is saying that suffering is not all-encompassing.

Again, Dopa said: "In truth, karma and afflictive emotions are objects of impure minds. Spiritual heroes have not objectified the truth of suffering." This is why it is said: "The cause of karma arises when there is the essence of a self that endows a mode of existence conditioned with suffering."

The second point [on suffering] is about its two **divisions**:

It is by means of the support [i.e., the world] that the continuum of beings is gathered; and [because of this] the continuum of the spiritual heroes of everlastingness gathers as well. The *Hundred Thousand* (4.504.4) says:

Knowledge of suffering is the truth of Shenrab. To take suffering
to task is the truth of Shenrab. To be indifferent to harm is the
truth of Shenrab. To realize Suchness, the truth of Shenrab, is
that there is no self.

The essence of suffering

The divisions regarding the essence are the following four: suffering, impermanence, emptiness, and no self.
The *White Hundred Thousand Water-Spirits* (7.378.3) says: [19]

> There is no permanent suffering. There is no annihilation. There
> is impermanence, emptiness, and no self. Therefore, the mental
> continuum is afflicted, while the nature of compounded phe-
> nomena is not established in a second instance. The reality of the
> factual is empty. All are inclusively free of a self.

The third point [on the truth of suffering] is its **precise definition**: It is
that one's own mind abides in suffering and this abiding is merely and truly
a temporary condition.

The truth of universal origination

The **second** truth, universal origination, is divided into three points [i.e., dis-
cussing defining characteristics, divisions of the topic, and offering a more
precise definition]:
[Argument:] First, concerning its **defining characteristics**, the Lord says:
"There is the production of non-peaceful states, but what arises as a pure
cause is the specifically characterized phenomenon of the spiritual heroes of
everlastingness."
[Answer:] [However], a few causes and the arising of all sentient beings
are not connected.
Furthermore, Dopa said: "On the truth that there are objects in the
impure mind, these are in substance the object of suffering. However, these
co-emergent conditions are not pervasive to the activities of the objectives
of the spiritual heroes. Therefore it is true that there is a mode of being where
suffering is produced."
Second, about the **divisions of the causes of universal origination**:

given that there are four aspects to the conditions of the unrelenting process of production, the *Hundred Thousand Verses on the Water-Spirits* (7.378.3) says:

> Causes, universal origination, and production are not [truly] existent. Cessation is also non-existent. These are strong aspects produced by minor conditions.

Therefore, the generator of suffering is the cause. There is nothing at all that is not produced. That is universal production. What is swiftly produced is the unceasing process of production. The conditions that follow, these are the different aspects of conditions.

Third, the **exact definition** is that all the sufferings of one's continuum are products.

The truth of cessation

The **third** truth, cessation, is also threefold:

First, on **defining characteristics**, the Lord says: "The five aggregates come from the sphere of reality. They abide in the essence of the cessation of suffering, the defining property that establishes the mind of the spiritual heroes of everlastingness." Cessation is here made to be a particular object of definition.

Again, Dopa asserts that the object of the truth of cessation is pristine cognition that is non-conceptual. That non-conceptual pristine cognition is the subject and the object, the apprehender and the apprehended. The object and the subject are explained as the apprehended and apprehender.

Myself, Lodrö, said: "Karma and afflictions are endowed with isolated modes of being, and cessation is the annihilation of the obstructions to knowledge where these cease to be. Therefore, karma [20] and obstructions are things that are endowed with isolated modes of being.

Second, the **divisions**: From the perspective of the support and its divisions, what are the views of the greater and the smaller vehicles in terms of the stages to realization? What are their manifest characteristics? How do they differ in regard to apprehending designations?

Concerning the object to be suppressed, the four categories of cessation consist in the suppression of karma and obstructions; the cessation of the suffering of conditioning; the cessation of offenses and of the conception of true existence; and the analysis of the passing beyond sorrow [i.e., enlightenment], the emergence of the moment, and the definite arising of the basis for prosperity and happiness.

Cessation consists in stopping the essence; this is complete cessation, peace, excellence, and definite emergence. These are the four terms that definitely describe cessation.

Third, the **precise definition** concerning only this truth of cessation is to completely stop the objects to be stopped.

The truth of the path

The **fourth**, the truth of the path, is also threefold:

First, about its **defining characteristic**, the Lord says: "Shenrab's realization of the absence of self is the established cognition of the heroes of everlastingness." The accomplished mind of the hero of everlastingness is devoid of eliminating categories[88] and does not pervade the essential point of subsequent attainments.

Dopa asked: Whose mind is it that realizes the absence of self? How real are the objects of the mind?

There is no substantial composite self; therefore, one comes to understand that there is no realization in an absent self. One then accepts the realization of this truth. Thenceforth, one has reached and attained the mode of being of the realization of the absence of self.

Second, its **divisions** are twofold: the perception or the non-perception of the reality of the support.

Once the path of the essence of the self and its knowledge are achieved, there is deliverance. One has reached the city beyond sorrow. Having abandoned ignorance, the object to be discarded, one realizes without mistake what is erroneous and what is correct knowledge. Then one has come forth into the final place of certainty.

Third, its **precise definition** is: one has arrived to the city beyond sorrow. This third definition refers to the truth at the moment of abiding on the path of the heroes of everlastingness. This third is like the gathering of reasoning. It is the collecting of the teachings of the four noble truths and the two truths. Thus, cessation is the path of the absolute truth. It is conventionally referred to as the subsequent attainment of the absolute, the ultimate meditative state. The duality of the others is the conventional truth. However, this does not bear analysis.

[Argument:] In that case, one wonders if there is a need for the four noble truths or [if] they even exist.

[Answer:] These teachings exist so that using the mode [of pondering on] the four noble truths, one can enter the path of the heroes of everlastingness.

The second case concerns when [21] one wonders if these [four noble truths] exist or not, or even if both possibilities are true.[89] The second case [i.e., both possibilities exist] is that it is hard [to use this statement as a referent in order to come to] realization. Having made distinctions between these four noble truths, it is easier to understand them. One can realize these [truths] in the cause and results of cyclic existence.

The third aspect is the truth of reality itself.

9. THE MANNER OF REALIZING THE BASE

The third topic that is the manner of realization has three points: refutation of others views, proving our own tradition, and dispelling objections.

Refutation of others views

The first point consists in refuting the doctrines that are the misrepresentations of the outsiders [i.e., non-Bönpos], refuting the doctrines on the absolute truth on subject and object, and refuting the doctrines that express a unilateral decision[90] on emptiness.

Refuting the doctrines that are the outsiders' misrepresentations

First, once the son of the gods, the sage monk Sherab Ganden[91] had extinguished the impurities on the spiritual stage of the Foe Destroyer,[92] he did not take up another rebirth. It was then that false ideas were promulgated. The *Tantric Scripture That Explains the Real Stages of the Spiritual Way* (2.5) says:

> Alas, you, good old friend, conqueror with your retinue, you will
> try to fulfill your desire to satiety as long as you do not die! But
> once you die, these objects of your activities no longer truly exist.

The body is destroyed, and as a consequence it is gone in a similar way. When alive once more, what will you do about this?

If one summarizes the 360 heretical views that use this saying as support [for their views], one can condense them into two views. These two are the views to be refuted: the view that propounds the falsehood that nothing exists [i.e., nihilist] and the exaggerated view that [everything] exists [i.e., eternalist].

The first task is to formulate the arguments of the others and to refute them.

This first point of formulating the argument is threefold and starts with denigrating karma and causality.

In the *Tantric Scripture of the Way of Syllogism That Destroys the Heretics* (10.4), the conqueror of the heretics[93] says:

> The existence of a former life gives rise to the karma of influence and good fortune. That is similar to the contradictory consequence of a dying fire.

Therefore, all tangible things arise without causes. Moreover, the body arises from the power of the four elements as well as the mother and father. As for the mind that is intangible, it seemingly arises suddenly from space. One can mention the examples of thunder, hail, and thunderbolt strikes from the sky, or mushrooms that come up by themselves.

The second point is about the denigration of the results.

The *Tantric Scripture of the Way of Syllogism That Destroys the Heretics* (9.5) says:

> Someone said that the seeds, causes, and results of the great Mount Meru, the sun, and so forth, have no virtues or faults. However, despite having none of these, each still exists! These are similar to the example of seeds and their fruits.

The next life does not exist; therefore there are no consequences to virtuous or sinful actions. As a result, transmigration to higher realms from virtuous deeds or to an evil destiny due to sins does not exist. There is no birth coming from a separate and non-existent basis. Therefore, the opinion of the followers of the conqueror is: "The name of the Enlightened Shenrab does not even exist because it has never been mentioned." [22] The *Tantric Scripture of the Way of Syllogism That Destroys the Heretics* (9.1) says:

> That proven, it is impossible that there be meditation on phe-
> nomena. Even if there is, it is not possible to truly acquire
> [enlightenment].

It is said: "The knowledge of everything arises from familiarity with higher and lower reincarnations. The knowledge of everything arises from attainment despite no true existence. But it is impossible to attain while not existing."

The third point is about denigrating an essence.

[Argument:] They say: "From the realms of the gods to that of hell-beings and so forth, there are no past or future lives because these have never been seen. Therefore, it follows that body and mind are one. If there is no body, the mind will not arise because there is this continuum involving body and mind. If there is no body, then the mind will not arise. Because the body is the receptacle of the mind, without receptacle, there would be no support and the mind would not arise."

Second, their refutations: The refutation to the above is that it has no valid points. First, without past mothers, the cause for existence is not possible, since the present generation is the result of mothers giving birth. If this were not proven, your father and mother, who were previously born, as well as past mothers, would not have been born. Second, future generations of mothers would not be born. If this cause were not proven, then similarly there would be no production of sprouts from seeds in order to generate the present. Fruition of karmic results would not be proven. This explains below the conditions of the continuation of predispositions [i.e., karmic traces]. Third, on the point of something not having been previously seen: It is not proven that all individuals at all times and places have not been seen. Some may not have been seen, and you, who have not seen them, have not seen all. It is the same for things such as the birth of your father and mother that you have not seen.

It is also not proven that body and mind are substantially identical. The body is a temporary condition. On account of cause and effect, anyone can refute the negation of the mind. If there is a continuum of temporary states, then one experiences an identical substance of body and mind. In the assertion that there are the support and the supported, there is the existence of a supported. However, without an entailing factor, there is no form, and so forth. It is similar to the case of a blue vase [i.e., the entailing factor]. When it is negated as a vase, the existence of the color blue itself is not negated.

The second refutation: First, this simple knowing awareness was produced by a knowing awareness in a previous moment even though the knowing awareness of the past is gone. When it is said "to be aware of noontime," it is a similar case. That case can be negated implicitly as something that never occurred. Although a child can be made aware of an arrow, his awareness may not be able to remember it subsequently [i.e., he has no recollection] since there is no subsequent generator [i.e., the arrow is missing]. This concept is accepted and ascertained through the inference of an entailing factor, so that later, in order to see the former concept that was produced when one wishes to experience it again, it can clearly be done. If someone then posits that the production of karma is without cause, it is similar to saying that a flower was generated in the sky.

[23] Second, it is proven that a state of pure presence of mind produces later knowledge. Although an old man is conscious at the moment of death, it is proven that there is no further production of knowing awareness afterward. The proof that one knows of noontime implicitly refutes that there is no production of this awareness subsequently. Again, the knowing awareness that an old man has at the moment of death is not proven through the subsequent awareness of the one experiencing it. And since there is no subsequent result to this production of awareness, one must accept that reasoning: factors of entailment are established by inference.

The past produces because there are subsequent results. This assertion clearly demonstrates the experience of past knowledge. For that reason, this proposition is similar to the sun and its fire, where the heat of fire would not be issuing light [i.e., it is an impossible proposition].

Third, if gods and so forth are non-existent because of not being seen, then for the same reason there is no divine ruler. The body that is manifested exists because we can perceive its existence; therefore, the fact that it is both existent and non-existent as one substantial existence cannot be. The result of a mind as caused by the body cannot be established, since if the self is not identical with the body, it invalidates that they are one substance. If they were one, then there would be no cause and result. The produced and the producer are non-existent. If the support and the supported were pervasive, then there would be few scriptures. It would be similar to the horse and the elephant being of one substance [i.e., an impossible proposition].

This second refutation [i.e., the ability to know or be consciously aware of something] is twofold:

[Argument:] First, concerning recorded traditions, some assert that the enjoyment of objects such as gold, gray, and so forth, substances and qualities, karma and the world, the details of the desire world of the six realms of reincarnation and so forth, all this is done by (1) an independent single permanent self. Beings that are born, in the past and future and so forth, all these are permanent and changeless. These ocean-like manifestations, momentary happiness, sufferings, and so forth, and all deeds that follow after the pleasure between man and wife, therefore stick to the five aggregates and the inherent self that does not change over the three times. [Proponents of this] assert that these inherent selves are not numerous but do exist. They are [manifest] in the ultimate truth, (2) as agents with their resultant bodies and so forth, the five complete enjoyment bodies.

The second countering is about the absence of proof and its refutation.

[Answer:] First, there is no self and so forth in the aggregates. Consequently, the performer of the activity is empty of inherent self, and this is also true with reference to production, and again in connection to the many. External power is different from composite things that are without power. The truth about inherent existence of objects is not proven. Second, if what is permanent does not change, then it is always indestructible. This reasoning is accepted.

The assertion is flawed if the entailing factor is there at one moment and not there in a second moment. If it is there, then it will always be indestructible, which is a false assertion. If it is not there, then experience proves otherwise. [24] How can these be independent from each other? Is it that they are performing a function gradually or suddenly?

First, if an enabling cause exists without obstruction, then it impairs a gradual operation. If the cause does not exist, then there is no ability for the operation to be produced as a result, and it impairs the thesis of being independent.

Second, if this is the case (that they perform their function suddenly) and if the cause at the time of the result stops, then it cannot be permanent. If there is no obstruction, then experience clearly shows that results can be reproduced simultaneously. If this were proven, then an object that can be enjoyed could be materialized in the blink of an eye! Chronic deafness and blindness would be annihilated and their experience stopped. If not, then someone could say that this cannot be done but could be done separately at some other time. That some of these would be possible or not, in either case, would corrupt the concept of permanence.

Second, in the present state of this critique, the view that the absolute negates subject and object is a twofold negation:

First, self-awareness in the tradition of the vehicle of Shenrab posits the duality of subject and object. In this, there are continuums that are momentary tangibles with undifferentiated particles, and these transform every facet of the conventional and the ultimate truths. The mass of tangibles, form and so forth, is the conventional. The subtle atoms and the profound subtleties are in the domain of the ultimate truth.

It is asserted that the ongoing continuum of the six aggregates of knowing awareness is the conventional truth and that grasping truly for momentary subtleties constitutes the ultimate truth.

Thus, the proponents of the doctrine of no characteristics of Shenrab assert that when an object and the mind are in contact, grasping makes them inseparable, like a magnet.

Those who are proponents of the importance of inherent characteristics stress the existence of a unity in the subtle profundity of designation, such as the designations "pig" or "woman." Between the conflation of mind and object and non-conflation where they are not joined at all, consciousness will be present. They say that objects feature characteristics and that cause and result are separate, because it is in one's consciousness that subject and objects, causes and results, past and present are determined. This is how they assert their reasoning on the ultimate truth.

The second point of this refutation is in two parts:

First, the refutation of the object apprehended:

[Argument:] If there are subtle particles in the ultimate, then it logically follows that the absolute is in these parts.

[Answer:] If this is accepted, it will not withstand analysis in regard to the relative. If there are no particles, then are coarse objects compounded or not? If we look at the first [i.e., the compounded], and accept that there are arrays of particles making it, then one must also look at the second [i.e., the non-compounded] where composite particles are not compounded. Then the coarseness [i.e., the composite nature] of the relative cannot be proven.

[Argument:] An entailing factor is established through valid cognition and the asserted proof.

[Answer:] If that is accepted, then the assertion is wrong. Moreover, if there are no composite particles, and if there is no reality, [25] then this assertion is false. If there are existing entities, they can be understood as being irreducible. If the compounded and coarse object is able to perform a function, then its array of particles has been proven. If it is not able to perform a function, then the reality of its non-existence is proven.

The second refutation of the apprehending subject:

[Argument:] When one asserts that the absolute truth is sudden, is one saying that there are existing particles or not?

[Answer:] This argument is countered in the same manner as the last.

[Argument:] Moreover, the above assertion is that consciousness (*shes*) is not separated from the consciousness of the object and that becoming familiar with it will not change it. This proposition is proven with the experience of tasting and not tasting and whether it is delectable or not. That being said, it changes when there is no cognizance of the object. There is no separation between the object and consciousness.

[Answer:] If this is proposed, then it can be dispelled with the logical argument about consciousness interacting with many objects. When one reasons with the above, it is similar to the point made about a sow that is mistakenly taken by sense consciousness to be a woman. If it does not appear as such, then it contradicts the capacity of the leading variants. Then, sense consciousness is not manifested.

A third point is that the unilateral view on inherent emptiness is two-fold: the refutation of the assertion of the truthfulness of mind and knowing awareness and the refutation of the proposition of emptiness in objects.

The refutation of the assertion of the truthfulness of mind and knowing awareness

[Argument:] First, the established tradition on mind and awareness is the tradition of the vehicle of the compassionate heroes. That is the dualistic tradition that asserts that objects and consciousness are two. If that is accepted as correct in relation to the sensory spheres, then the variety of colors and shapes that are manifest to the sensory spheres are the consciousness of the sensory spheres that can be truly known. Thus, the appearances to the various consciousnesses are sensory spheres of consciousness. Then it affirms that one's consciousness is separated from one's inherent self. Some assert mistakenly about sensory spheres that colors and shapes manifest differently in the sensory spheres.

[Answer:] This assertion is false. It is falsely imagined. One cannot prove as true a vase in the sky or a rabbit's horns. This is the truth about the essence of consciousness, that these two can be ascertained as inseparable.

The second refutation is twofold:

[Argument:] First, the refutation of the "correct position" is that consciousness of form, et cetera, and the self are not one because matter and other substantial objects are derived from consciousness. When one asks about the mind being able to truly manifest matter without an entailing factor [i.e., a concept, an idea, an object, etc.], it is just that. It is like making genuine water appear where there is nothing apparent. Is the image in the ordinary mind [i.e., mental image] that is not outwardly manifest deceptive or not? If the mind is deceived, then it follows that it is a false object that is not real water. If this is accepted, then one has to deny that it is real water. If it is not deceptive to the ordinary mind but nothing is appearing, one can ask if it is a deception of real water.

[Answer:] Again, one must repeat the point on the falsity or veracity of the ordinary mind manifesting objects. If one says that it is both deceptive and true, then in this, it is deceptive and not deceptive as mentioned. [26]

The second point on the refutation of the deceptive position:

[Argument:] If one asks about happiness, suffering, and so forth even without having any realization, what are they? Also, if one asks about fire, water, and so forth, and whatever one cannot understand, and whether they exist? What are the differences between the coarse, the subtle, and the many?

[Answer:] These cases must receive similar treatment to the one case that was negating the ultimate but not negating the conventional.

The refutation of the proposition of emptiness in objects

The second point is the refutation of the assertion that the objects are inherently empty.

[Argument:] Someone belonging to the Higher Vehicle postulated that mere appearances are not established in the face of realization in conventional truth, while the reality of the ultimate truth asserts that inherent emptiness [means] that there is no self in emptiness.

[Answer:] These two conceptions of selfhood [i.e., phenomenal and individual] are established as objects of conceptual consciousness inherently empty of emptiness. Thus if these two do not exist, then there is no conceptual consciousness, and therefore appearances are real. Consequently, it is said that the truth is empty of realization.

[Argument:] Following on this refutation, are appearances and inherent emptiness one essence or many?

[Answer:] If they were like the first one [i.e., one essence], then it would change the many so that the many should appear as one. If they were like the second [i.e., many essences], then the existence of the ultimate would be false. If they were two and not one, this would really change the veracity of what appears, and inherent emptiness will not be one.

[Argument:] Again, if the absolute truth is proven as an object of conceptual consciousness, then is conscious awareness endowed with objects or not?

[Answer:] In the first case [i.e., if it is endowed with objects], then subject and object would be the consequential proof of conventional truth. The *Summary of the Hundred Thousand* explains the object as the grasped and the apprehender as the one endowed with the object. In this second point, it is then no longer proven that there is an object; therefore, it is a false claim. Moreover, the emptiness of true reality would change into inherent emptiness of ephemeral particles. Inherent Suchness would not be empty.

Proving our own tradition

Next, our own tradition is twofold: concrete reality and proof.

Concrete reality

First, having proven the modes of the two truths, if again it is correct that these are manifest as such, then this still does not support the position that there is an essence to whatever is transcendence from all illusory elaborations. Having asserted that there is no production, this transcendence is said to be primordially pure and unfathomable. Furthermore, the isolation of all the elaborations that are objects and subjects are beyond the intellect, while unceasing manifestations are mere conceptualizations of the conventional. These elaborations and their arising that are proven as really true are in fact non-existent. They exist only as dreams abiding in an illusory manner, completely pure, observed as many, but mere illusions. Moreover, in the context of the base, there are the ultimate and conventional truths. When on the path [27], there are meditative states and subsequent attainments. At the time of fruition there are the two exalted knowledges of "things as they are and all that exists."[94]

Proof

The second point is to set up premises using the scriptures and reasoning.

Proofs from the scriptures

First, the *Hundred Thousand* says:

> Inherent self is completely pure from primordial beginning.

And:

> The sphere of everlastingness is without production, enlightened.
> . . . consciousness engages free from the nine limits.

The *Outer Tantra* (21.172.4) says:

> Unborn, uninterrupted, endowed with the nature of the sky, transcending description or imagination, inexpressible.

Other sayings:

> The Bön of transcendence is inexpressible from the primordial beginning.

The *Arcana* (207.2) says:

> Conventions and forms are like illusions.

And:

> They are like the eight analogies of illusion.[95]

The *Lore of the Cuckoo of Awareness* (353.2) says:

> What face is hidden by confused appearances?

Proof by logic

The second point is proof by logic. Elaborations are similar to those on a magical mirror. They are proven to be without self by using the four great syllogisms.[96] This discussion is twofold: the cessation of completely interconnected objects, and proving the contradictory nature of conventionality.

The cessation of completely interconnected objects

The first point is threefold: the proof of the absence of inherent self-essence, the proof of the absence of inherent cause, and the proof of the absence of inherence in the results.

Establishing the absence of inherent self-essence

The first point is a proven reason, free from the one and the many,[97] that is twofold: proven evidence and proven modes [of reasoning].

Proven evidence

The first concerns a subject that is barely appearing. It is empty of substantial and true existence because it is disconnected from being a single or a manifold [i.e., composite] true being. It is like the saying: "It is illusory like a dream."

The proven modes of reasoning

The second is threefold: the subject, what is to be proven, and the mark of the evidence.

The **first** [i.e., the **subject**] has only the appearance of a substance. Alone, in single events, or in a collection of events, it is posited as having the essence of unfabricated particularities of many while being proven using common factual appearances.

The **second** [i.e., the **object to be proven**] is the object of negation that is identified and that is proven to lack inherent existence. These two are: the object to be negated and the object being proven.

The object to be negated

When one says that the object to be negated is only appearance, but appears in reality, one is unable to negate its existence. In that case, one cannot negate its lack of inherent existence and, not understanding its real nature, it is proven as a real thing. Therefore, the main point of the subject that is a substantial appearance is the substance of reality.

Furthermore, the object to be negated on the path is refuted in an indirect contradiction.

[Argument:] By establishing the lack of inherent existence of appearances, the five poisons, the three poisons, and so forth are eliminated. [28] These erroneous objects superficially obstruct the objects to be eliminated on the path. Appearances are the objects to be negated by reasoning. It is possible to stop an existing thing correctly despite the apparent reality of its true existence in the face of reasoning. Mere designation does not establish true reality. Therefore, the object to be eliminated negates the mere reality of these two: the subject as a true reality and appearances.

[Answer:] If it were so, then by keeping away the objects to be negated, non-inherent existence would not come to be established.

[Argument:] What if someone says that the object to be negated is in fact not real?

[Answer:] The non-proven absence of inherent self in the absolute has been maintained. The conventional is not pervasive. Therefore non-existence negates the illusory mental conception of existence. It is similar to the negation of the blue horns of a rabbit. It does not change the argument even if they are not blue.

The object being proven

The second point is to prove that there is no inherent existence in the subject that is the one who is endowed with phenomena (*bon can*) nor in any object (*bon*). It is implied that to prove the illusory nature of an object is to refute its non-existence. It is the objective here to completely eradicate the proof of the conventional.

[Argument:] The subject that is the one endowed with phenomena and conditioned phenomena refutes the non-existence of the negation that all mental constructs are true or false.

[Answer:] This excludes a proven absolute. The concepts of real and implicit realization give strength to the reality of freedom from the one and the many. They are, successively, inference, rational cognition, and the two truths. Therefore at the moment of engaging with the path there are inferences and rational reasoning on the path of accumulation. Using these, one's engagement with the path of accumulation transforms into the path of application and above, subsequent realization, and meditative equipoise.

The mark of evidence

Third, the topic of the mark of evidence is threefold: identifying the essence of the indication of characterized objects, determining the pervasiveness and the properties of specific characteristics, and using reasoning as evidence to ascertain the defined object.

Identifying the essential of the indication of characterized objects

First, one refutes the specific characteristics of a concept and the absence of an object that can be proven to exist. Subsequently, the proof is established with the threefold criterion of a syllogism,[98] a thesis, and its antithesis.

Determining the pervasiveness and the properties of specific characteristics

The second topic is to establish the pervasiveness and categories of specific characteristics. First, one should recognize the one and the many and the method to separate them, and then one can dispel objections.

The one and the many

First, it is unnecessary to say that untrue arguments are unable to refute the many units of the parts. If one were to do so, it would be similar to saying that there is no need for parts. Therefore, that which is "partless" and indivisible and that which is made of many [parts] make up the one and the many [elements] of reality. Using this again, heretics assert the unity of that which is without parts, the body that is made of parts, and the tangible. The self-realized Shenrab asserts the particles and the momentary. For that reason, what is a composite represents the many. [29]

The manner of becoming free

The second point is composed of establishing the essential point of the manner of becoming free and the reason behind establishing this convention.

Establishing the essential point of the manner to become free

The first point has to do with conditioned phenomena that are manifesting. There is not only one manifestation, since we can see many parts, similar to the stars. This explicit notion is contrary to that of the opponents. Alone, a direction has six parts,[99] and each part has six separate parts. If this were not proven, then the central point that is in the middle of the six directions would disappear and the composing particles of matter would not be able to manifest.

Again, one subject that is manifest is, correctly, not many, since one cannot really accurately find [just] one in many. It is similar to the sky. The reason for this saying is that unifying this multiplicity cannot be done, for there are too many aspects, and these cannot be combined [as one entity].

[Argument:] If someone says that in this case it fits to refute the entailing factor [i.e., the pervaded object] in terms of the category of an entailing agent as being universal. Isn't it fitting to refute one unique entailing agent that has so many entailing objects?

[Answer:] In this respect, there are two alternatives: appearances and sounds, or the one and the many together with its parts, as the entailing factor and the agent of implication, respectively. The correct [view] or the truth is that when it comes to unity, multiplicity entails the negation of unity and unity entails the refutation of multiplicity. Therefore if the unity of appearances and sounds is false, then the correctness of the many is not false. If again, the correctness of unity is false, the whole of the many and its parts cannot be but false. However, if the unity of appearances and sounds cannot correctly refute multiplicity, then the multiplicity of appearances and sounds correctly refutes unity. These two separately, through the notion of the lack of inherent existence, will work at the conventional level, and one will be free from [the notions of] unity and multiplicity.

Dispelling objections

[Argument:] Third, is refuting objections done through uniting the path by either excluding unity or multiplicity?

[Answer:] In the first case, negating unity does not refute the many. The many contradicts unity. Similarly, stopping appearances does not refute darkness, just like an opposing point refutes the establishment of its antithesis.

In the second case, when multiplicity is proven, it comes [in the end] to not negating unity.

[Argument:] Someone said that if these exist conjointly or are jointly established, this proves that there are objects that are joined together. Some say: "Unity exists in contradiction to multiplicity and the two cannot exist united."

[Answer:] If that were so, multiplicity once accomplished would negate the existence of unity while its existence is not negated, and its proof would be a necessity. If appearances are proven as a unity and as a multiplicity, then their separation cannot be produced. Therefore, the unity of the whole and its parts exist in contradiction. If there were parts in a unique [thing], that would be a contradiction. [30] If there were no parts in multiplicity and it were one [thing], that would contradict multiplicity.

Again, if the appearance of the joining of the one and the many were destroyed, the power of contradiction or the power of union would both cease. In the first case [i.e., joining the one and what is disparate], one would have no ability to stop this. For one thing, if the various parts were cut off, then everything [i.e., this unitary thing] would be annihilated. Similarly, if physical heat were completely annihilated, then all various notions of physical coldness would cease. If there were no more appearances, the separation of unity and multiplicity would also completely cease. The cessation of the variety of unity and multiplicity would be extreme. The second alternative is also impossible.

[Argument:] If someone said: What if there were no annihilation?

[Answer:] Then the limits of manifestations, duality, would not be possible and unity would not exist. The strength of contradiction annihilates true and real appearances. Even one sole object with a unified appearance would be conveniently negated. When the one and the many are united in appearances and these appearances as such are proven, then they would not exist in reality.

[Argument:] Second, someone asked if reality truly exists in the entailing factor or if it just exists by itself?

[Answer:] Unity and multiplicity rest in the entailing factor. In this, the entailing factor's refutation negates implicitly the real and the true object of the entailing factor. If wood is refuted, then similarly the tree is refuted. Therefore, if the non-existence of an inherent self is false, it entails that unity and multiplicity are not false.

The reason behind establishing this convention

[Argument:] Third, someone has established that reasoning by concepts is conducted so that there is a set convention.

[Answer:] If the points on unity and multiplicity are established separately, then the meaning of inherent emptiness is proven. If proving this point were not necessary, then saying that there is a proven convention would not be correct. In the above case, separating unity from multiplicity would not come to be proven points. If this were accepted, then it would ascertain the convention of the uncertainty of the position. If so, with the negation of being able to grasp at reality, there would be no realization of intrinsic emptiness.

It is proven that a sound that is produced is impermanent. Similarly, there exist established conventions. Therefore the separate meanings of unity and multiplicity have been proven through the establishment of intrinsic emptiness. That itself is the established convention. With the complete usage of the three modes of syllogism, the conception of the absence of self-nature is proven.

Third, causality has been proven as lacking an inherent nature. It is a proven concept of the great pivotal point of everlastingness. From these two, there come the fixed concepts of mere appearances [i.e., object] and subject. These have no inherent natures. When they are naturally produced and so forth, then, using the four alternate propositions[100] of syllogism, one is free from mere appearances and subject, and they become mirage-like.

Second, there are three signs that prove the point: the subject and the two objects that need to be proven, as above.

Third, there are three signs that prove the point: (1) First, there is the analysis of a specific characteristic that is conducted using simple negation to prove the contrary. Furthermore, it is asserted that ordinary mind relies on a momentary abiding in an illusory cause from which arises interdependence. [31] (2–3) Second, the specific characteristic is twofold: recognizing production in a thesis [i.e., the property of the subject] and the modes of separation.

Production factor

First, there is the desire for substantial existence with its causes and effects coming from a self that is produced. Thus, there is a result from a cause that desires to be clearly born in order to have a true existing self-essence. This birth from another is the production proceeding from other substantial entities. To postulate that existence is coming from these two—a unitary being and something different—is to postulate that something arises in the mind without causes.

Manner of separation

Second, when the modes of separation[101] are about reversal, these consist in stopping the argument using an analysis that nullifies it. There are four possible theses here:

1. If it is produced by itself but that self is not established, it contradicts the agent of production, just like the horns of a rabbit that are blue like the sky. If these effects appear, they contradict the activity and the agent. If these effects do not appear, then this production is self-contradicting.

2. If it is produced by something other than itself, then it would be like a barren woman giving birth to a son from a father. If others were produced from others, then it would be like a pen being generated by fire. Again, if a permanent "other" were generated, that resulting product would be impermanent. If non-birth is experienced as birth and if there is the birth of something impermanent, then non-birth is transcendence. Acting and the completion of the action are negated. The future does not yet produce, and the essence of a self is not established. As for the present, if it is not simultaneous, then it contradicts the present. If it is simultaneous, then the action toward the designated benefit and the agent that is designating are not tenable [i.e., one cannot exist at the same time, since one is the result of the other], just like the right and the left horns of a rabbit.

3. Because of the inability of producing the previous two [i.e., self-generation and generation from another], then as soon as one is refuted, the

full complement of the thesis is also refuted. When one alone is refuted, the rest is also refuted.

4. A production that has no cause is then refuted, just like above.

Second, if a pervasive factor is produced, then it entails the use of the four possible alternate propositions [i.e., existence, non-existence, both, and neither]. These refute the production of karma, just like refuting a column of smoke as a sign for a fire.

Reasoning on a defined object

On the third topic, when reasoning on a defined object, if it is proven that this concept is an empty manifestation, then the main point is proven. If it is established that the concept is a convention on non-origination, then it is merely a convention.

Third, when the result is proving that there is no inherent nature, it establishes a refutation to birth and non-existence. This has two points:

Appearance-only and the subject

For appearance-only and the subject: If they are correct, then they have no inherent self because they are free from birth and are non-existent. They are similar to a magician's illusion.

Analysis on subject and objects

With the three established modes of existence above, we have explained the subject and proven objects. Analysis on this third point is threefold:

1. Basis for characteristic of a characterized object: Among existing entities are those existing with birth[102] and those without. Therefore, there are those that are clearly born and those that are unborn [i.e., non-produced]. [32] There is no point in negating this refutation.

2. Thesis and entailing factor: The first, the thesis, is what is recognized, and this is a mode of separation.

First, there is a cause that in the past generated a result. If there is no result coming, then it is said that its existence is generated only in the present. Some say that there was no past that produced the result.

Second, because of an established undermining factor, there is no need of a seed for the sprout that is produced. The moment the seed was produced, this produced sprout was already conceived. If non-existence produces, then it comes to be that a seed produced a "non-inherent production" as a result. There cannot be a fruit at the time of the seed. If there is no entailing factor, then a barren woman could be giving birth to a son. Furthermore, this seed would be producing horns on a rabbit. Since no one has seen this, neither cause nor result have been seen.

On the second aspect, entailment: entailing materialists negate truth and reality by refuting the object being inferred.

Third, the reasoning about characterizing marks is similar to the point made previously.[103]

Interdependence

The second thing concerns incompatible points that have been proven. This is dealt with in the concept of the great interdependence using two proofs:

If the thesis on manifest objects and subjects is correct and these have no inherent self, then in order to be interdependent, they have to be of the same nature as the reflections in a mirror.

The second reasoning is threefold: [Thesis:] The subject is similar to proven objects of the past.

First, on a conventional level, some causes give rise to the essence of some results. With this conventional and non-affirming negation on incompatible points, one effectively refutes this whole meaningless argument.

This **second** point is also twofold:

[Argument:] First, when someone's position on a thesis has been established through direct realization, the mutual interdependence of phenomena is proven. But when that someone proves using inference that there are hidden phenomena, then the sole reality becomes subjective.

[Answer:] Interdependence exists in the entailing agent because the phenomena exists intermittently in the entailing agent, like butter nourishing the fire of a butter lamp.

[Argument:] Second, interdependence in the entailing factor is established through the reflection of the inferential factor that has no inherent self. There is no permanence, since the referential factor is intermittent.

[Answer:] If that is so, interdependence will otherwise transform a non-existent inherent self into a substantial existence. This is because the reliance on others' categorizations always generates an essence. It is said to be like tongues of fire that are always disappearing, or like hot water.

The **third** point about reasoning is as before.

Dispelling objections

This third point concerns dispelling objections and is threefold: subject, what is to be proven, and dispelling objections on logical reasoning.

Subject

[Argument:] Are appearances only designating reality in the subject? [33] Are objects of consciousness proven by reasoning or not?

[Answer:] In the first case [i.e., appearances only being reality], the absolute would come to be reality.

[Argument:] On the second point [i.e., objects of consciousness are proven false], then one may ask if elaborations could not be cut off by maintaining this position as true.

[Answer:] That question is faultless. Inferences about the apparent are imperceptible to false reasoning.

[Argument:] Someone asked: Isn't reasoning using inference?

[Answer:] It is by means of inferences that reasoning cuts through uncertainties. Reasoning establishes inferences authoritatively.

[Argument:] Accordingly, the essence of these two [i.e., reasoning and inference] is not the same.

[Answer:] Not so! They are not the same when it concerns the one that isolates objects. However, when it concerns their differences, they are similar. When one understands the lack of inherent self in objects using the three modes, this is inference. When one ceases conceptual discoursing on truth and falseness, the ultimate nature of the object is reached in the rational knowledge of the subject.

What is to be proven

Second, dispelling the objections on what is to be proven is twofold: [dispelling objections on inclusive determination in the conventional, and dispelling objections on the exclusive determination in the ultimate.]

Dispelling objections on inclusive determination in the conventional

When inclusive determination consists in assessments on the thesis of illusory emptiness and appearances, then it is about the ultimate.

[Argument:] If there is no assessment, isn't there any inference?

[Answer:] Although there is assessment, this has absolutely no consequence.

[Argument:] Does inference have objects, since it is said that these are objects of conscious awareness?

[Answer:] First, there are no entailing factors. Second, these are not proven. In the case of a false reasoning, when consciousness accepts the absence of false inferences, then this is a different kind of deceptiveness. Therefore, in conscious awareness there are no appearances and no conflict. In self-awareness there are no manifested meanings of terms and no conflicts among appearances in conceptual consciousness. Being mistaken is different.

Dispelling objections on the exclusive determination in the ultimate

By this [i.e., exclusive determination], it is meant that there are no observable appearances in the ultimate.

[Argument:] If the concept of Suchness remains when there are no appearances, does that not establish that there are objects of knowledge [existing] by themselves?

[Answer:] First, if one sees it that way, then it is the conventional.

[Argument:] If so, then there will be no consciousness of the subject.

[Answer:] There are no objects of knowledge in Suchness and there is no non-existence of knowledge. The conventional array of appearances makes one consider that there is no existing awareness that is realizing. Since the absolute is devoid of proliferations, there is no existing consciousness that is realizing; there are no entailing factors.

[Argument:] If it is so, where are the object and the subject in the reasoning consciousness?

[Answer:] They are correctly not established. All proliferations and those free from proliferations do not exist. Mere realization of the sphere of intrinsic reality is a conceptualization of reasoning consciousness.

Dispelling objections on logical reasoning

The third topic is dispelling objections on logical reasoning.

[Argument:] Are these logical reasonings accepted or not by the subject? [34]

[Answer:] First, if they are, phenomena create discordances when entering reality.

[Argument:] Second, if they are not, then how are they not established?

[Answer:] Although it is true that they enter reality, it does not change the contradiction, since they exist in a similar category. Whatever appears—that which is debated here and that which is not included here—is established as common perceptions. Disputants understand that they are not truly existent, and their opponents have a clear knowledge of common perceptions. They resolved these by understanding the lack of inherent self. That very action of settling the dispute is established as being in a similar category. If, using valid cognition, they settle the question separating intellectual proliferations, and if there is no dissention among themselves, then their eyes are settled upon the matter.

[Argument:] If it is so, then what comes from this common understanding?

[Answer:] First, if the latter happens, then they become indivisible in their universal certitude.

[Argument:] Second, if it is so, then someone may ask if this perspective is suitably free from elaborations.

[Answer:] This is faultless. Though it is true that they are free, someone cited another person saying that there is separation from signs indicative of objects in that the object of logical reasoning is separate from the one conducting the reasoning.

Cyclic existence and liberation, the two truths and the four noble truths, the examination of the modes of being, and the various divisions of the teachings, these, by the methods of logical reasoning, scriptural authority, and the manner of their connections, are means to correct realization and to determine with certainty.

This was the first chapter on the foundation of the way of being of the so-called *Magical Key to the Precious Stages of the Path and the Grounds of the Greater Vehicle.* [35]

2. Concerning the Preliminary Practices That Are the Causes for the Generation of the Path

1. The Object of Practice on the Graded Path

The practice of the graded path is threefold: the causes that establish the path, the causes that give rise to the activities for the graduated path, and the activities of fundamental nature.

The causes that establish the path

First is the existence of karma and conduct. The scripture says:

> If the ten wrongdoings[104] are performed, one will be born in one of the three evil destinies. When the ten virtuous deeds[105] are performed, one will go to higher realms and obtain the station of the godly realm. If one practices meditation and concentration, one obtains the unsurpassable as result.

The *Treasury* (129.7) says:

> Through the power of action, one is born.

From this, one can surmise that virtuous or non-virtuous deeds will cause a stream of karma that will generate the direct causes of mental intentions, pure or not.

The nature of the causes that establish the path

Nature [of the causes] is threefold: special characteristics, the divisions of the base characteristics, and definition of the object being characterized.

Special characteristics

The first is further divided into three parts: refutation of others' positions, determining our own position, and eliminating the objections to the latter.

Refutation of others' positions concerning special characteristics

In order to refute the position that rejects general characteristics, one must refute its considerations and their false positions and refute their thesis and incorrect points.

[Argument:] First, the opinion of the glorious Me'u (1038–96)[106] is that causes and results exist before and after the path. Since there are five paths[107] and their objects need to be defined, a sole specific characteristic cannot be designated for all of them. Therefore, if there are none, it is a logical absurdity, as in the case of fire and smoke, where if one does not exist, the other cannot exist, when it is said that these do not exist. However, that cannot be validly proven.

[Answer:] There is no before and after the path or other objects to be defined. Roughly, they are solely conceptually the same. They are not many. And the special characteristic of the blissful ones cannot be conceived and established. Refuters cannot come to establish one single specific characteristic to a cow! It just shows their stupidity [lit., "ox face"]!

[Argument:] Again, if one says that everyone can see with meditation that there is a special characteristic, then aren't the concepts of the path of accumulation and the path of application merely metaphorical? They have no single special characteristic in common.

[Answer:] The "path" and "what comes later" is an erroneous array of dualistic thinking. It is an incorrect invention, an object to be eliminated. It is a thesis that originates suffering. The four characteristics of the path[108] are said to be missing; however, they do not truly exist. They cannot be validly proven; however, merely stating their existence, the non-existence of the path cannot be proven either. The entailing factor of all the paths cannot be established on the basis of the characteristics that are similar to those of the path of cyclic existence. The latter cannot be proven as non-existent. How can it similarly be proven as manifest?

[Argument:] What if someone asks if there is emancipation from cyclic existence?

[Answer:] There is, and it is emancipation from the continuum of existing. In reality, there is no limit to the continuum of cyclic existence. [36] There is no mistake here! There is no contamination in correct meditative equipoise. There is universal suffering from which there is no turning away. If those refuters maintain this attitude, they won't be coming out to the upper path by practicing the paths of accumulation and application. It will be impossible to obtain the fruits of this high path. When they reach these, they will experience what I am saying. After a person has attained the different realizations up to the seventh ground, these will become purely nominal. So says the great Lodrö!

[Argument:] Second, the opinion of Patön (b. 1040) is that there are no virtuous factors that can bring training to completion and liberation from efforts.

[Answer:] Although this saying was recorded as such, it is unsuitable to use it solely as a universal characteristic concerning all causes and results. If one states the above, then it does not follow that one can bring one's efforts to the conclusion that is liberation, and it does not follow that one can bring one's efforts to an end on the paths of accumulation and engagement.

[Argument:] Again, what if one says that the roots of virtue of compounded phenomena include the continuum of the passing beyond sorrow [i.e., nirvana]?

[Answer:] It does not follow concerning meditative equipoise. Vision and meditation are not the essence of passing beyond sorrow.

[Argument:] And again, the opinion of Dre[109] is that the activities of wandering beings are different from the activities of beings on the path to liberation. Are migrators and their activities one or different?

[Answer:] If one, then the answer rests in the experience of the one affirming this. If different, then the single continuity of traveling on the path of cyclic existence contradicts traveling on different paths.

[Argument:] Dopa says that the notion of liberation from cyclic existence entails that all phenomena have no inherent self and that whoever has this notion of no-self changes the method to achieve enlightenment.

[Answer:] Subsequent attainments happen to those who tread the path and are not encompassing conduct, phenomena, and parts of objects. Furthermore, the two defining characteristics[110] can also be applied to the object being defined with a definition that is unique. Thus the *Treasury* (212.7) says:

All paths do not include the path of cyclic existence. Furthermore, the path that exists in cyclic existence is the path of the
continuum of suffering.

Third, a mere philosophical position is an isolated meaning. This is to be
refuted. The *Treasury* (214.1) says:

> The Great Self who says that he wants to travel along the spiri-
> tual grounds does not exist. There is no entailment in the wish to
> arrive at a place to which there is no traveling. The path of "noth-
> ing whatsoever" is the circle that arrives at the place to which
> there is no traveling.

All those treading the path to liberation of the Greater Vehicle do not
come into existence. Furthermore, the lord sovereign of logic and scriptural
authority said that those treading the path, for one, are concepts. They do
not exist. There is no need to eliminate conceptions on this existing basis of
characteristics.

[Argument:] Someone said that whatever knowledge there is, it has [by
then] been reached.

[Answer:] Matter is created by causes, whereas this path comes to not
being a path [at all]. [37] This is like the saying: "The sun, the moon, and the
air are like universal emperors, while their sons are on a similar path."

Determining our own position on special characteristics

Second, [the position of] **our own tradition** consists in what the lord Lodrö
said: "One has reached [the end]."

Eliminating the objections to the latter

[Argument:] Third, someone asked: If one has reached [the end], then has
one gone? Now then, where has one gone? In the first case [i.e., one is gone],
then the paths of accumulation and engagement are not pervasive. In the
second case, it will change the fact that, in the end, there is no path crossing
over to transcendence.

[Answer:] Is there crossing over or is there more? One can posit that at
last, the crossing has been completed. The "crossing over to transcendence"

is metaphorical. In reality, there is no crossing over. Moreover, having stopped when the crossing has been completed, there is no more path. Having stopped all activities, non-existence is then proven. Furthermore, the cause that is imputed is designated by the name of a characterized cause. This is the notion of a particular cause that brings forth a particular result. If from this there is none, then it comes to be that the result that is the final end is truly non-existent.

Divisions of the basis of characteristics

The topic of the divisions of the basis of characteristics is twofold: common divisions and individual points.

Common divisions

The first point is fivefold. When the sole path with its base and divisions has been eliminated, in essence, the *Treasury* (214.2) says:

> A self is the path to the cause of inherent self. Cyclic existence is the path to the stream of evil destinies. Compassion is the path to higher realms and liberation. Cyclic existence is the path to "nothing whatsoever."

Cyclic existence and transcendence are subsumed together here [i.e., making the five points]. The *Hundred Thousand* says:

> The path of cyclic existence is the path to transcendence.

The **causal characteristics**, when enumerated in pairs, consist in those supported [i.e., wandering sentient beings] and the enlightened ones that correspond, respectively, to the activities of craving and no desire. The functional divisions are those of cause and essence [that correspond, respectively, to] the agent of activities and no one. The number of causes and afflictions are either generated or non-generated. Nature and form are either peaceful or not peaceful. Results are either pleasant or not pleasant.

Individual points

The second section on individual points regarding cyclic existence and transcendence has its first section divided into three points: cause, intrinsic nature, and activities.

Cause

First, cause is threefold: length, proximity, and secondary conditions.

On the first (**length**), it is until there are no more subtle or expansive poisons to be eliminated, and similarly until there are no more means of elimination. These are activities of the mind with the objects abiding in **proximity** that are the **supporting conditions**. Moreover, given this, the *Treasury* (92.5) says:

> The world is even more than a mistake; cyclic existence arose as poisonous frost.

The *Victorious Summit* (364.4) says:

> When imputed objects and conditions of sensory power are joined, the power of conceptual consciousness sees erroneously in the impermanent. [38]

2. Teachings on the incorrect generation of the mind of enlightenment

Definition of incorrect thinking

A scripture says:

> When thinking arises from an improper mental disposition, out of this improper mental disposition a few demons are generated.

Another scripture says:

> Thoughts arise from impurity.

[Argument:] Some say that the defining characteristic here is that a mind that is extremely agitated will aspire toward impure objects. That someone is postulating that the path of accumulation will become incorrect.

[Answer:] Regarding this, a scripture says:

> From desire there emerge activities of accumulation devoid of merit. These actions performed under suffering mean that one accumulates wrongdoing.

The bearer of characteristics

The basis of characteristics is an afflicted mind, along with its retinue and the corresponding contents of the mind.

The conduct of activities

Third is about the conduct of activities: the causes are non-virtuous actions under the conditions of the five poisons [i.e., anger, craving, ignorance, jealousy, and pride] that matured previously on the path of results.

A scripture says:

> Evil destinies are produced if one performs the ten wrongdoings.

Intrinsic nature

That second point on its nature is threefold: defining characteristic, divisions, and definition.

Defining characteristic

[Argument:] The defining characteristic according to the lord is: "An agitated state leads from any single phenomenon to another in succession."

[Answer:] This means that there is continual overextension on the paths of accumulation and application. That statement asserts that in cyclic existence there is an entity that errs and that desires to transcend suffering. But it is not so. If there were [such an entity], then it would mean that when there is no agitation whatsoever, all karma will be erased in this distinctive state.

[Argument:] The great Lodrö said: "One moves, staying in one place, then goes on to other places in succession."

[Answer:] Again, there is this continued overextension on the paths of accumulation and application. This saying does not prove that there is an existing entity that turns away.

This is not so. There is no generation of suffering in the absence of any grasping for a self. If it were so, a scripture answers this by saying:

> When one looks at the truth from the ground, it is on the other side. But when one does not see it, one is on the other side.

This is saying that they [i.e., existing entities and lack of inherent existence] are mutually exclusive. Substantial entities are devoid of inherent existence and become non-existent. If this is so, then the production of suffering is accomplished with the grasping at a self. In some cases in the Lower Vehicle, there is no consequence concerning cyclic existence and the path. When there is absolutely no grasping at a self, there is no production of suffering.

Divisions

Out of five divisions, a conceptual distinction is made regarding the basic standard that consists only in the path of cyclic existence. The *Treasury* (212.7) says:

> The essence is taught as the five paths on the continuum of cyclic existence.

The *Hundred Thousand* (21.181.6) says:

> There is the path to the hells and the paths to the hungry ghosts, animals, humans, and gods. Their causal characteristics are the five poisons [39] as causes, and because of them, there come the five tainted activities. Their essences are these five: absence of suppression of activities; attachment to existence, to various things, and to conditioned beings; delusions about causes and results; not understanding the qualities of others and the transitioning to different places; and the transmission of severe violations manifested through arrogance.

Their divisions, essential points, causes, results, and essences are different. Their numbers are ascertained with the five poisons and the actions derived from them as well as the all-inclusive set of their five essences.[111] In addition to these categories, some say[112] that there are the angry gods, but they are not added as a distinct path of reincarnation. They dwell in a higher realm and are very powerful gods with deeds that are imbued with arrogance. The angry gods and the gods are on the same path of reincarnation. Those angry gods are in a realm below and act with the same envy of power and are on the same path of reincarnation as the humans. The angry gods wander on this path and belong to the category of the gods but are cut off from the purer parts of that realm. The great Lodrö says that they wander on this path as part of the Nöjin[113] and are cut off from lower levels of reincarnation. Again, the lord said that the gods and the angry gods are on the same path of reincarnation. Merit corresponds to the life span of the body. Anger and great disputes transform [these beings] into angry gods.

Definition

The definition is that this place of cyclic existence is a single continuous path.

Activities

Third, about activities, a scripture says:

> Meritorious actions come out with meaningful results, such as incarnation as humans, gods, and so forth. The absence of virtue comes out in meaningless results, such as bad transmigrations and so forth. Unwavering actions are the actions that cannot come forth into random results. The power of actions determines the manner of abiding on the grounds of cyclic existence.

Next, the path to liberation is threefold: cause, inherent nature, and activities.

Cause

The first topic is threefold: to identify the support, which phenomena are supported, and the manner of engaging with phenomena.

Identification of the support

First, on the cause, the *Hundred Thousand* says:

> It is in order to purify the continuum of consciousness that sentient beings mature and exist in the circle of existence.

The *Summary of the Hundred Thousand* says:

> It is with the support of having faith . . .

This refers to the following three topics: identification of the essence of the support, its self-nature, and the mode of production of the continuum of any particular phenomena.

3. Teachings on genealogy[114]

To identify the support

The first topic is to identify the support, and it has three sections:

Arguments from the traditions of the others

[Argument:] First, some from the tradition of the others say that virtue is non-attachment and that whatever reasoning there is, it is about the view on selfhood.

[Answer:] But it is not so. The essence of the path of virtue is non-attachment. However, this contradicts it as the cause for the purification of the views on selfhood. Reasoning on an inherent self is not pervasive. [40]

[Argument:] Someone has stated that uncontaminated essence is newly produced, whereas old karmic seeds are nurtured. Untainted karmic seeds are continually deposited anew.

[Answer:] Karmic seeds together with their contaminated array are referred to as old karmic memories that have not yet come into existence. If untainted karmic seeds are deposited anew, then this can be countered with reasoning on inherent existence where actions come to exist from no relevant causes. This is not sound reasoning on the purification of the arrays of contaminated karma. The existence of uncontaminated karma refutes these as causes to the arrays of contaminated karma.

Our own system about the genealogy of things

Second, **our own system** on the nature of the dwelling places of the various kinds [of beings] is that there is a sole support for all transmigrations. Their genealogy changes extensively while they dwell on various paths. Members of the extended lineages of the enlightened ones [also] dwell on these paths. The *Minute Scriptures* (166.4) says:

> One's mind is enlightened from the very beginning.

The *Arcana* (3.1) says:

> Realization pervades non-realization.

From these statements, one can understand the above by deduction. One can reason on these, whereas one can apprehend an inherent mind that exists in sentient beings that establishes a support for the genealogy of beings. For instance, compounded phenomena are impermanent and, using one's own existing mind, one can say that there is an inherent mind that is enlightened from the beginning.

Dispelling objections

Third, the **dispelling of objections** is threefold: precepts and contradictions, reasoning and what undermines it, and logical absurdity.

Precepts and contradictions

First, on the proposition that all sentient beings become enlightened ones, the scripture says:

> Cyclic existence is empty; therefore phenomena are impossible.

What if someone objects to this? [Well then,] the scripture cannot be contradicted. This would be like saying [something that contradicts the scripture and going with the sense] that cyclic existence is limitless, as [if] this old cycle of existence has been enduring and existing as the pervasive factor. Furthermore, in the existing genealogies of things, conditions change so that one may wake up or not, enter the path or not. There are travelers on the path [of liberation] who are increasing, and there are supports for them [to be there].

[Argument:] And third, what if it is asked: Will these [travelers] increase in number, and will they come into being?

[Answer:] There is no fault there because as long as there are travelers on the paths, they will increase.

[Argument:] On this third point, if someone should ask whether those on the path will come to be liberated effortlessly?

[Answer:] Because the support is without faults, its manifestations do not come to truly exist. Therefore, this path exists in order to yield the result, the finality of cultivation.

Inherent nature

Second, inherent nature is threefold: [defining characteristic, divisions, and absurdities]

First comes its **defining characteristic**: Enlightenment is its substantial cause. It is the defining characteristic of the genealogy of beings. The substantial cause for arising and separation from the body of intrinsic reality is its inherent nature. It is the substantial cause for the production of the qualities of enlightenment. Virtue is the defining characteristic of the extensive lineages of the enlightened ones.

Divisions

The second point on the divisions is threefold: the demarcations of the ground of the genealogies, their enumeration, and the intent of actions. [41]

The demarcations of the ground of the genealogies

First, the support of intristic nature exists for all beings. Its expansiveness becomes the support of the path. Then compounded and non-compounded virtuous factors become the measure of their accomplishments above and below the path of accumulation.

Their enumeration

Second, with regard to the essence of their enumeration, there are these two points: self-nature and expansiveness.

They are, respectively, the results of separation and the results of accomplishments. From the provisional points of view of the Great, Middle, and Small Vehicles, there are these three paths, respectively. From the point of view of conditions, there are the ascertained and the unascertainable conditions. Conditions depend on incontrovertible proofs and false [lit. "stolen"] proofs. From the point of view of the supported, there are accomplished individuals who undertake the four particular paths [i.e., outer, inner, secret, and very secret] and their ramifications.

The intent of actions

The third point is threefold: agent; agents, faults, and qualities; and the particular modes of the exalted ones from the lower degrees upward.

Agent

First, when there is no spiritual pedigree [lit. "family, on account of what is below"], then there is no connection with the path. If there is no connection, then there are no results that can be obtained and no changes.

On account of what is the continuum of a person immanent? What makes the continuum of a person immanent? The answer resides in encountering the path. When these encounters happen, enlightenment is the result. The *Eye of the Needle* (11.102.5) says:

> Seeds of virtues and sins exist in the consciousness of the universal base. They arise in time with conditions and encounters.

Agents, faults, and enlightened qualities

The second point is twofold:
First, The *Eye of the Needle* (4.112.6) says:

> Beneficial agents are members of the lineage of awakening who do not fall into bad reincarnations and are agents for the maturing

of others. When suffering arises, they are agents who usher in a quick liberation, and are the sons of magical interventions where there are hells. They are the heroes of Everlasting Bön.

The second point is that there is an evil lineage. It consists in those from the lineage of the non-awakened ones who reincarnate because of the conditions of suffering. They meet with and are companions in sin. They are under the power of others and go through bad reincarnations and so forth. The *Eye of the Needle* (1.10.3) says:

> When the light of the sun rises, the house in darkness remains black. So it is for generations of sentient beings in cyclic existence. When one preaches honestly with words of certainty, they reject them as useless. For their sons, there is no cause for liberation.

The particular modes of the exalted ones from the lower degrees upward

As for the third point, when one's own goal is not accomplished in the Lower Vehicle, one purifies all defilements and is able to obtain all the enlightened qualities. One is eventually able to work the great expansive vow for the welfare of others and quickly obtain enlightenment. One then moves from the Lower Vehicle to the noble one.

Logical absurdities

The third topic has to do with definitions. If there are changes in support of the path, these affect the supported. If a lineage of enlightened ones is generated and it is increasing, it is a good lineage. When reliance on this virtuous [lineage] is established, it becomes the cause for enlightenment. And in particular, [42] [this reliance] abides timelessly, unfabricated from primordial beginning, enduring potentiality in inherent naturalness. When one practices the path, having planted the nourishment of Suchness by the use of virtue, the lineage of the enlightened ones will expand and be established. From this, the dwellings, the realms, and the spheres, down to the end of the continuum of reincarnation, a mind in itself with an array of impurities will become redundant.

4. Explanations on the support of the path to liberation

The manner of engaging with phenomena

Third, the topic of the manner of generating the path in the continuum of existence that comes from any particular circumstances is threefold: the support of the agent of desire, the cause for the object being appropriated, and co-emergent conditions.

The support of the agent of desire

The first point on the support of the agent of desire includes: the support inherited from previous reincarnations, and the support that is the place for beings' rebirths.

The support for previous reincarnations

First, there are two supports: the body and the mind.

The body

On the first one, despite not having been born in the eight "unpropitious" places of rebirth [hells, hungry ghosts, animals, etc.], great defilements will block awakening to spirituality. Lack of wisdom prevents the generation of an attitude of renunciation. The very few who do not have suffering and do not create sorrow thus have the support for becoming gods and humans. Although someone may say that incarnation as a god is unsuitable, the *Compendium on the Spreading* says:

> Many hundreds of thousands of sons of the gods have performed the dance of the gods.

This implies the following words from the *Eye of the Needle* (15.160.2):

> There are those endowed with a human body who enjoy leisure and fortune and possess the unswerving bodies of gods. At the time of obtaining leisure and fortune, their speech and mind

were endowed with power, whereas wherever the others are born, they wander in error and are not free.

[Argument:] Furthermore, someone said that beings in the three worlds are born from females. The latter will change the existing teachings of the enlightened ones and they won't have the virtues of those who go up to higher realms.

[Answer:] The *Eye of the Needle* (3.45.7) says:

To beings in the evil destinies, there is no sin.

[Argument:] Furthermore, a lama asked, what if there is no one endowed with the vows of a monk, or no one who has generated the thought of enlightenment for others [but] is born as a human?

[Answer:] That is not so. It is a contradiction, like mentioning the birth of the son of a god from a female water-spirit. Or like saying that there are no such things as a householder who is a hero of everlastingness, or that there are no renunciates among the gods and that liberation is attained in the continuum within phenomena, which is contrary to what is said in the *Eye of the Needle* (14.400.2)

Furthermore, there is such a thing as birth through one's own efforts. As for birth through other's efforts, it is easily possible with the support of the compassion of enlightened ones. The *Eye of the Needle* (5.112.6) says:

There are rites that have as their object the saving [of beings] from hell by heroes of everlastingness.

Again, it is said: [43] "Riding Gesar won over the understanding of everlastingness from demons, female water-spirits, and the five families of water-spirits."

The mind

As for the second point, the support of the mind, the *Summary of the Hundred Thousand* says:

A consciousness that is free from the nine limits[115] can engage [the path].

When one is awakened to the Greater Vehicle and realizes selflessness, the ground for realization is wherever the ordinary mind is. Then there is no more terror, no fear in the desire to obtain it.

The support that is the place for the beings generated

Second, concerning the container that is the place for beings, there are suitable places where there are migrating beings but where continuing predispositions remain steady. Magpies always cherish the white ground of different regions. However, at the moment that fish die in the water, there is poison that preserves them and protects their eggs. The magpies are then very cautious and so forth. These are predispositions.

The cause for the object being appropriated

The second point is appropriation. When sorrow is generated amid the suffering of cyclic existence, one should generate compassion toward sentient beings as well as faith in the qualities of the enlightened ones. The *Summary of the Hundred Thousand* says:

> If the self has no attachment, suffering has no attachment to the self. Whoever is attached to the self has the suffering of cyclic existence.

Second, the *Eye of the Needle* (6.141.3) says:

> One should obtain the basis that is great compassion.

The *Eye of the Needle* (15.509.6) again says:

> If uninterrupted compassion is generated, that is the great compassion. Then, love, joy, and equanimity are generated at the same time.

The *Eye of the Needle*[116] also (11.130.7) says:

> Unwavering faith is the cause of irreversible belief.

This last point consists in holding on to the master's instructions on the method to obtain liberation and generating the thought of enlightenment on the object conceived as the goal, as explained below.

The phenomenon of the support

Second, concerning the phenomenon of the support, there are three topics: what is a master guide, advice on his teachings, and using these as the object of observation in order to generate the mind of enlightenment.

First, the *Summary of the Hundred Thousand* says:

> Abandon bad friends and follow the lama Shenrab, who will unmistakably demonstrate the causes and results. A virtuous friend has the intention to become extensively learned in the causes and results. The teachings of Bön have unmistaken results, for they know the meanings of the difficult-to-know, and know the methods of the heroes of Bön.

These next three points concern the characteristics of a master guide, and these are the [related] topics and definitions. [44]

5. ABOUT THE MASTER GUIDE

Specific characteristics of a master

First, anyone who discloses needed advice to a trainee on the path must be at least a teacher and a master. Anyone who confers important advice to a person, if only on liberation, must be that person's master. Anyone who provides needed advice on the path of realization in particular must be an emanation of excellence. Those are the specific characteristics of a noble master.

Basis of characteristics

The second point on the basis of characteristics is threefold: boundaries, enumeration, and their activities.

Boundaries

First, when there is this first thought toward one's only friend [i.e., the master] who is the object connected with accumulated causes, one must not rely on any others. What is distinctive in this practice is to abide in the very Highest Bön. At that moment, when one seeks out the path for transcending the world, one must ponder on how difficult it is to know, and one must be made to know, how rare is this lineage. Thus, this emanation of excellence and the high vision of his purpose can be relied upon in one single place.

Therefore, here "one has to renounce all discordances, for he is the master in all manners." Once one has received teachings from this Highest Bön, there is a path that proceeds from it whereby one can engage anew, although some say that it is not proven that there is. The proof resides in the enlightened intention toward this master of distinction. For if that were not so, there would not be such a great person. There would be no supportive path that provides causes and conditions for others to enter anew on this path.

Concerning this, the *Summary of the Hundred Thousand* says:

> Since there is a ground for the universe, one can look for a path to transcend this world. And because it is difficult to make progress there, there are the teachings of the good friend.

Enumeration

The second topic consists in these eleven points: (1) the generation of the essence, (2) the noble ones, (3) the acquisition of excellence, (4) the fresh moment of entering [the path], (5) engaging in transcending the world, (6) the final purification from assuming bad states of rebirth, (7) instructions on imperfect knowledge, (8) instructions on common topics, and (9) instructions on all other aspects.

Their activities

Finally, there are these two: (10) elimination and (11) the activities for realization.

First, on the process of **elimination**, there are these topics to discuss: friends of defilement, incorrect conduct, and discarding a disheartened mind that prevents one from engaging with the Greater Vehicle.

Second, the **activities for realization** consist in skillful means. The *Summary of the Hundred Thousand* says:

> One must be knowledgeable in the methods of the path and the activities that support cause and result.

One must unite method and wisdom and realize the essential points on emptiness and wisdom while practicing in conjunction with the methods, [45] the generation of the mind of enlightenment, the dedication of merit, the purifications during the preliminaries, the main practices, and the concluding parts.

Precise definition

Third, the precise definition: "The path implies that one has to rely on the master. Planting the great tree of the virtuous path is the spiritual friend. The transformation of the traveler is conducted through the existing object of reliance, the master."

6. Teachings on advice

Second, on personal instruction, the *Summary of the Hundred Thousand* says:

> In order for me to teach the essential points of the tradition, the three worlds and the nine grounds have to be purified, and the five paths have to be communicated for liberation.

On these three points, it further says:

> About the base, the path, and the roots, the base must be taught in personal communication. With this teaching, one can enter the path. If there is no direct communication, then there won't be a basis for the production of liberation. This is the root.

Individuals who can hear, you must listen to my counsel!
First, the *Hundred Thousand* (1.56.3) says:

Because sentient beings are ripe, their stream of consciousness must be purified of miscellanea.

There are three points coming from this: From whom must one hear the teachings for support? When during one's lifetime must one hear these teachings? Where must one hear the teachings?

From whom

First, the *Hundred Thousand* says:

Whoever treads the great path of accumulation must be able to hear the teachings of Bön directly from an emanated teacher. For innumerable evils arise in this era, while one must increase one's devotion.

If one says that this is not so, then it must be refuted, for there is no genuine proof for it.

First, the advice is that there is nothing greater than distinctive personal instructions for the significance of those who listen.

Second, the *Hundred Thousand* (1.56.3) says:

Sentient beings are extremely afflicted when it comes to [following] instructions.

The *Summary of the Hundred Thousand* says:

You should know that the moment of personal instruction consists in the wisdom of hearing and reflecting!

And this is contradicted!

[Argument:] Must one examine these [personal instructions] using reasoning or must one listen to personal instruction when freshly entering the path? In the first place, the statement is corrupted. In the second place, one will not be able to enter the path, for one will not have heard the personal instructions.

[Answer:] How absurd! All this is similar to being on the path of seeing while relying on not having previously attained the supporting stages below.

[46] For that reason, when freshly approaching the path, the *Summary of the Hundred Thousand* says:

> The generation of the mind of enlightenment comes from personal instruction.

And:

> All sentient beings have to properly hear it all. Then, sentient beings will be completely ripe for entering the path.
> ... When newly approaching the path, hearing and reflecting are brought together so that one's stream of consciousness and its entourage will be purified.
> ... To acquire wisdom from listening and reflecting, remember the moment of direct instruction!

Listening and becoming familiar with the instructions is part of the great path of accumulation. There is wisdom arising from meditation, and this manifests what one hears on the path of seeing and above. It consists in seeing and meditating.

In the case of the above-mentioned scriptures and the refutation, its proof and refutation are as similar as before.

[Argument:] According to reasoning, the manifestation of excellence and newly entering the path are not antitheses in the strict sense of the word. For as much as personal instructions exist, they are not on this account distinctive.

[Answer:] In that case, there is no contrariety in acquiring concentration for one's mental continuum. Meditative concentration is not necessary just for listening.

[Argument:] Second, some say that the moment one obtains the tantric concentration formulas (*mantra*), one acquires the great path of accumulation—that is, if one concretely progresses, as mentioned above.

[Answer:] It is not so. If personal instructions are interrupted when one newly approaches the path, the transmission is also broken off. If there is concrete progress, then this has to do with the acquisition of the path of seeing. Consequently, when meeting one's tutor in order to freshly enter the path, direct experience will increase gradually.

Third, someone counters this [by saying that it] is similar to the previous assertion about emanations of excellence. Consequently, up to the path of accumulation, one is a spiritual friend to sentient beings. From the path of application onward, one becomes a noble one and an emanation of excellence.

Second, the **nature of personal instruction** is threefold: defining characteristics, the basis of characteristics, and definition.

Defining characteristics

First, the object that is the purpose of skillful methods of the heroes of everlastingness is to come forth with conviction in the words of the teacher. These are the sole instructions.

There are particular personal instructions that are distinct: having dwelled with this conviction that comes forth, the words of the teacher point one to the unadulterated methods to acquire the enlightened qualities of the heroes of everlastingness.

The follow-up instructions consist in teachings on methods for the acquisition of the qualities of the heroes when they are not yet obtained through personal instructions that arise through dwelling in conviction. The *Compendium on the Spreading* says:

> The heroes of everlastingness demonstrate the activities of this lineage that reaches to the unsurpassable great heroic mind of Shenrab.

[47] On the heart of intrinsic reality, the *Compendium on the Spreading* says:

> Teaching intrinsic reality is done by personal instruction. The significance of this is that, having taught intrinsic reality, one abides in it.

The basis of characteristics

Second, the topic on the basis of characteristics is threefold: demarcating the ground, divisions, and their nature.

Demarcating the ground

First, personal instructions are about approaching the path in a fresh manner. They are distinct from the great path of accumulation. Subsequent
teachings have little to do with the path of accumulation.

Divisions

The second point is threefold: personal instructions for the wrongdoers of
the three worlds, personal instructions on the meaning of liberation and the
five paths, and personal instructions given on final omniscience.

Personal instructions for the wrongdoers of the three worlds

On the first topic, the *Compendium on the Spreading* says:

> There are instructions on the three worlds and the nine grounds.

And the *Hundred Thousand* says:

> Sentient beings are maturing completely.
> ... The paths of the three realms of desire, form, and formless-
> ness are suitable support for the living. Wrongdoers, themselves
> living in suffering, inhabit pure and defiled places. These sentient
> beings are afflicted with separation from their own 100,000
> desires. The teachings say that they live without seeing. In the
> case where one dwells among the three evil cycles of reincarna-
> tion, one obtains liberation by only hearing the mere sound of
> these teachings.

If it is asked whether the hearers[117] had the good fortune of hearing these
teachings without previous exposure to them in the past, [the answer is:]
there is no impediment to [the argument that there was a previous exposure
to the teachings]. Tsangpa Tshukphu [i.e., Brahma, the crested one][118] said
in the *Summary of the Hundred Thousand*:

> The discipline of compassion does not change much.

Personal instructions on liberation and the five paths

On the second topic, it is said: "There are instructions on liberation and the five paths."

The essential point of personal instructions on the five paths is that these paths are all phenomena. When they were generated, they were unprecedented and were taught in order to increase their reach from before. Therefore, there are four [main points] with regard to their structure for future accomplishment:

1. If relative truth alone has not been proven, one will not be able to perceive the truth or falseness of the absolute.

2. If one has power over the object that is to perceive these two [i.e., truth or falseness], one will be able to perceive apprehending the four truths correctly.

3. Third, if one can perceive these in the support [i.e., the containing world], one will not be able to perceive the three or the four objects of refuge.

4. The perspective of the fourth special point is: having realized the above and come to them, one abandons indolence and transforms this indolence into efforts.

Therefore, the realization of the path of accumulation above is demonstrated in the *Eight Realms*, the nature of the path of accumulation in the world.

The *Summary of the Hundred Thousand* says:

> The realm of jewels is the nature of the path of engagement. Each appearance is an object of consciousness on the path, empty and unmixed, where knowing awareness is the appropriate path of approach. [48] Equal, unwavering, these are perfected potentialities.

Thus the realms of jewels are taught to be the five paths. They are taught as worldly and non-worldly all the way to the non-existent, and the like. From these teachings, the path of the various worldly realms and the arising of the paths are taught. From the precious realm onward, there are many obstacles on the grounds where urgent desires arise. Therefore, there are still many obstacles that arise even in the fields where the qualities of liberation spring forth, such as on the path of application and onward. These continuing realms are taught as part of the path of application. Appearances are taught on the path of vision as manifestations whose inherent nature transcends the world, free from the fearfulness of the world. Emptiness is consciousness devoid of inherent self, manifesting through the absolute, suppressing characteristics through brilliance. It is mirage-like, a consciousness familiar with emptiness, the attainment of meditative equipoise. It is part of the seventh ground. For each object, consciousness of the conventional remains unmixed and non-deceptive as to cause and effect. This is the clear stage of subsequent attainment. Awareness is when there is nothing arising from others while what arises from the self shines forth. In the scriptures it is called "the path of familiarization" and is part of the nine grounds. The sphere of space is where one enters into the heart of intrinsic space, completely pure of aspects, the womb of the immovable. Deeds of the body, speech, and mind arise without measure, equally moving through the ten grounds. It is said that the eleventh ground, finality, is the perfection of potentiality through perfected dynamism. It is non-existing intrinsic equanimity devoid of all that is not equal.

Thus, pith instructions say regarding the five paths: "The attainment of the final result of the *Eight Realms* is contained in the *Eight Realms*."

The three dynamisms

The third one is called "the perfection of the three dynamisms."[119] When purifying, dynamism is perfected and attains finality when one is established in non-perception. It is said that one has then reached finality, the result of the *Eight Realms*.

The nature of the basis of characteristics

The third point is about their nature. The *Summary of the Hundred Thousand* says:

> Realms and paths are altogether non-existent in the end. They are beyond finality.

It further says:

> Existence, non-existence, manifestation, and the finality of emptiness cannot be seen anywhere. It is taught as inherent reality

free from all inherent self. Being and non-being are beyond limits. As for the limits of appearances and emptiness, they are beyond permanence and annihilation. One has to pass beyond the limits of production and cessation and get clear of the twelve false misconceptions.

Personal instructions given on final omniscience

[Argument:] Concerning these personal instructions, how is one to be personally instructed in proper hearing, reflecting, and meditation? First, it is as if there is nothing to see and meditate upon. Second, it is as if there are no instructions that can come up on the path of accumulation. [49] Third, if there were instructions and one was to ask to have them, it would change existence and reality.

[Answer:] There is no fault in this. First, there are instructions on the path of accumulation. Second, there are instructions on and up to the path of application. There are instructions on purity up to the path of vision on changing reality.

Definition of personal instructions

Third, the precise definition is that there are precepts from the holy ones that are true personal instructions.

Their necessities

The third topic is on their necessities. If there were no instructions on the practice of non-apprehension, the path and its result would not arise. But there are, since there is the path of the generation of the enlightened mind and its results. Therefore, on this third point that is the generation of the enlightened mind, the *Summary of the Hundred Thousand* says:

> Thus, having obtained personal instructions, there will be faith and one will generate the mind of enlightenment that will be conducive to liberation.

On these three points, transmigrating beings are the reason for the necessity of the path of the generation of the mind of enlightenment. That was the cause of the fundamental nature of the generation of the enlightened mind. That fundamental nature is really the mode of training.

So, first, if one does not generate compassion for the suffering of sentient beings, then the mind of enlightenment cannot be generated. If it is not generated, then the streaming of the path is not generated. If this in turn is not generated, then its result, enlightenment, cannot be obtained. The mind of enlightenment is a necessity, for the *Summary of the Hundred Thousand* says:

> The result of the first ground has not been obtained because the main point of its reason has not been generated.

And again, the *Scripture of the Generation of the Mind of Enlightenment says*:

> The generation of the mind of enlightenment is connected to going for refuge. It is not the ground of phenomena.

The *Eye of the Needle* (17.521.7) says:

> When produced, the generation of the mind of enlightenment is that of a king.

Furthermore, the *Transmission of the Mind* (5.2) says:

> If I take the four lamps of the generated mind of enlightenment to a fertile field with confidence, then the sprouts of the ten perfections will indubitably grow in abundance.

And (5.1):

> When one does not previously generate the mind of enlightenment, it is like a farmer forgetting his seeds. Shenrab, the one endowed with the aim of the generation of the mind of enlightenment, is like sea foam falling from the sky.

If this is said, then the generation of the mind of enlightenment is a necessity at the outset. It is the root of all paths.

7. Teachings on the generation of the mind of enlightenment

The second point on the generation of the mind of enlightenment is about its nature and is threefold: the cause for the generation of the mind of enlightenment, the nature of the generation of the mind of enlightenment, and its activities.

The cause for the generation of the mind of enlightenment

The first point is threefold: the support for attachment, what causes its appropriation, and conditions for action.

The support for attachment

First, the reliance on the body has been dealt with above. The topic of reliance on the mind has three parts and is related to going for refuge.

[Argument:] First, on what defines it, Dopa states that one asks for refuge to be free from fear. [50]

[Answer:] Not so. An explicit refuge is made with its particular objective and function. If the refuge is real, it clears away impediments and one can go for refuge. Then, one asks to go for refuge. It is said that this particular object is to be seized so that fear is removed.

What causes its appropriation

The second point is threefold: boundaries of the ground of the mind of enlightenment, enumeration of the objects of refuge, and results.

Boundaries

[Argument:] Simply going for refuge helps with the accumulation of merit, but there is also the special path that one can enter.

[Answer:] This is accepted. While this going for refuge appears to be the deed of a novice, its ultimate end is obtained through the activity of transcending the world.

Enumeration

On the second part, the enumeration of the objects constituting refuge, there are four objects discussed in three parts: two are the greater and the smaller vehicles; two are worldly boundaries and their transcendence; and for as long there is life, one will intervene until the heart of the matter is reached.

Result

Third, the result of taking refuge consists in not being harmed by obstacles from demons and so forth. One relies suitably on the path and is protected from evil rebirth and so forth.

Definition

Third, a precise definition of refuge by the *Transmission of the Mind* (4.3) is:

> To pacify obstacles from getting into the refuge from below. If one goes for refuge in the four places of everlastingness, then one will come to be under supremely appropriate protection.

What causes its appropriation

Second, taking hold of refuge consists in having faith and compassion. Among these two, the first is what defines faith. The *Eye of the Needle* (11.130.7) says:

> One has to have real trust in the distinctive objects of refuge. Determined faith is the cause for not going back.

The basis for this characteristic consists in purity of faith, devotion, and conviction. Its precise definition is to have faith in the proximity of the distinctive object of refuge.

Second, the **defining characteristic** of compassion according to the *Eye of the Needle* (15.509.6) is:

> One is to have a kind mind toward the suffering of sentient beings. It comes from generating a limitless compassion that is

immeasurable and pure. Love, joy, and equanimity will then arise as one.

The base for its characteristic is that it is generated from seeing the suffering of sentient beings, and it is collected into the four immeasurables [i.e., compassion, love, joy, and equanimity]. Its precise definition is that compassion is generated by kind-heartedness.

Conditions for action

Third, the conditions for action are to envision this distinctive objective so that major and minor causal conditions are present and all the elements, signs, and activities arise.

Second, the topic of their nature is threefold: defining characteristics, activities, and precise definition.

Defining characteristics

The first topic is threefold: those of the other traditions, those from our own traditions, and [51] refuting others' objections.

Defining characteristics of the other traditions

[Argument:] First, what if someone said that there is no such thing as desiring to achieve enlightenment for the sake of others?

[Answer:] Not so! This is according to the followers of the Lower Vehicle, those who are not established in the mind of enlightenment, or those whose generation of the mind of enlightenment is erroneous.

[Argument:] What if someone is asking about those who want to develop the generation of the mind of enlightenment of the Greater Vehicle according to that [above], and say that it is not proven that the one who is on the path of application will really want [to attain] the path of vision for the sake of others?

[Answer:] The great Lodrö says that it is not so.

[Argument:] Again, what if another says that whatever goal one wants to obtain, it can be [obtained] with the described mental attitude.

[Answer:] Not so. Here, there is no elimination of the aspects of the ordinary mind. It is a false notion and it does not exist. Mental objects proceed only as conventions and do not entail engaging factors.

[Argument:] Furthermore, Dopa, supposed that there is a second person endowed with the semblance of the heroes' unsurpassed aspiration for the sake of others. He has what resembles the heroes' faith and aspiration for the unsurpassable result for the sake of others. He strives to produce the unsurpassed result for the sake of others, but merely possesses all that resembles the heroes' faith and aspiration in the unsurpassed cause. However, he has only generated the mind of enlightenment. He claims that he has all the respective qualifications, the aspiration, and application.

[Answer:] Yet he does not have these. The aspiration alone, the heroes' aspiration and belief, will change to isolate the mind's ideas coming from the generated mind of enlightenment and will transform it into an isolated concept of faith.

[Argument:] Yet someone said that the wish for enlightenment for the sake of others is received through a formal ceremony.

[Answer:] But it is not so. The attainment of intrinsic reality does not change the generation of the mind of enlightenment in the supremely pure absolute. These two do not entail impurity or the lower form of the generation of the mind of enlightenment.

General and particular generation of the mind of enlightenment

Second, about the general and the particular, the great Lodrö said: "First is which aspiration and in respect to what?" The one possessing the stainless vision says: "Everyone thinks and acts on their desire to realize the object of their vision. Second, the purified ones aspire to help others, and act and think with the particularity of wanting to attain enlightenment for the sake of others."

Dispelling objections

Third, dispelling objections is twofold:

[Argument:] First, an aspiration is not pervasive if it does not consist in doing the particular deeds of one's prayers. Then it does not include entering the path.

[Answer:] The meaning of entering is entering through aspiration. If it were not so, then at the time of really engaging and entering, if there is no aspiration with this objective in mind, then there will be no capacity to do it. [52] If there is aspiration with that objective in mind, then it will be done by itself.

Second, on abandoning overreaching conclusions, ideas, and statements:

[Argument:] It is said that the mind of the master encompasses all that arises in the mind as well as in cyclic existence.

[Answer:] This is not so. The answer to this is threefold:

Tradition of the others

[Argument:] First, a tradition of the others asserts that the friend to whom prayer is addressed implies a friend endowed with the generation of the mind of enlightenment.

[Further argument:] Is that so? Compassion is the cause that is addressed in the aspiration and it implies, as a result, the generation of the mind of enlightenment.

[Answer:] But it is not so! If it were so, it would not become reality. The cause of the result does not serve what is below, and it is in contradiction with the system presented here.

Our own tradition

Second, our own tradition says that the generation of the mind of enlightenment is not attributed only to the mind but considers both the mind and its mental objects.

[Argument:] Third, someone says that the one defining characteristic [i.e., the mind] changes into the mark of the second defined object [i.e., the mental object].

[Answer:] This does not exist. One alone cannot be proven; therefore, this subject matter does not exist.

Basis of characteristics

The second topic on the basis of characteristics is threefold: the boundaries of the grounds, enumeration, and the mode of the support of this continuum.

The boundaries of the grounds

The topic of the boundaries of the grounds is threefold: demarcating the grounds, seizing the essence of their characteristics, and the mode of arising in the stream of existence.

Demarcating the grounds

First, it is said that the generation of the mind of enlightenment is bent on liberation from the three worlds and the nine grounds. The generation of the mind is bent on liberation in the six paths of reincarnation. The mind of enlightenment is bent on freedom from the twelve limits. When one freshly enters the path, this is called the smaller path of accumulation that goes as far as the limit of one's continuum of existence. It is like this from the first ground up until the acquisition of the ultimate reality. It arises from accepting the path of the world. As such, conventional truth has its path for the accumulation of merit.

The absolute truth has the generation of the mind, and from treading the path of accumulation, one forms a generic mental image. Following this, the path of application becomes endowed with appearances of clarity. Then, the path of vision and above complete the experience.

[Argument:] What if someone objects to what was just mentioned and asserts that the three realms and the nine grounds do not truly exist?

[Answer:] There is no fault here. If one perceives the three worlds as endowed with faults, then from this comes the generation of the mind bent on liberation. If there is no such thing, it contradicts the very purpose of the generation of the mind of enlightenment; therefore, there cannot be an entrance to the path.

[Argument:] Someone mentioned that in the case where there is no generation of the mind of enlightenment, then the generation of the mind in the six paths of reincarnation is contradicted. If there are still the six realms despite the lack of the generation of the mind, then this changes the concept of generating the mind.

[Answer:] This is faultless! The *Eye of the Needle* (16.522.1) says:

> It may be that the lama will provide answers on the absolute and the conventional; however, it does not contradict that there are results generated by this non-existing generation of the mind

bent on liberation. The power of planting the wish of taming the world brings the teacher to lead [beings] to this place at that moment.[53]

[Argument:] Second, what if someone asks where is the support of the basis of characteristics of the generation of the mind of enlightenment? This answer is threefold:

Arguments from the tradition of the others on the mind of enlightenment

[Argument:] The countering arguments of **the tradition of the others** are two: First, they assert that the defining characteristic is an object in the mind. Then, someone posits that when praying, there is aspiration and the mind.

[Answer:] But there is no reasoning here. Mental objects alone happen to be produced here, and the supporting mental continuum transforms. The realization of the basis comes from the realization of its distinctiveness.

[Argument:] Second, they assert that it is the doing of the mind alone. When someone asks, "Why is it that one cannot see the existing universal ground of the teachings and scriptures?" It is because the mind is always afflicted with non-virtues and so forth. If the five doors of the senses are reliable, while at other times they are not reliable and do not support the generation of the mind, then it is the mental consciousness that designates. Some say that the ability to perceive this rests in pure phenomena [lit. "white bön"].

[Answer:] But it is not so. There are no changes to the essence of the vow in this generation of the mind of enlightenment. The vow exists but is taken on as a mental object and so forth. In this way, mental objects alone are generated.

Furthermore, the point of the others on defining characteristics is that for those who wish to become enlightened, mental factors and the basis of characteristics are emphasized as mind alone. The characteristic of the base then becomes dualistic and non-unitary.

[Argument:] Again, some posited that a second substantial entity arises as a mental isolate.

[Answer:] When a mental isolate exists on a non-established basis, it does not prove that an isolated object truly exists.

Our own tradition on the generation of the mind of enlightenment

Second, **our own tradition** on this topic is twofold: ·

In order to benefit others, one has to hold a distinctive mental vision. Lama Drimé Chanden[120] said: "For that reason, the eight modes of consciousness [i.e., five senses, mind, self-consciousness, and the universal basis consciousness], the five omnipresent mental factors [i.e., feeling, discrimination, intention, attention, and mental engagement], the four ambivalent mental events, and the ten virtues [i.e., three good actions of the body, four good actions of speech, and the three virtuous actions of the mind] are the basis of the characteristics of purity. The eight and the fourteen modes of consciousness, the six roots of suffering, and the twenty approaches are the bases of the characteristics of impurity."

Eliminating objections on the mind of enlightenment

Third is the elimination of objections.

[Argument:] When one wishes to generate the mind of enlightenment, it is not contradictory to generate these two [i.e., aspiration and mind]. One can assert the existence of the subject matter of the two when it concerns the generation of the mind of enlightenment. "Again, the two definable objects in the two basic characteristics come to have two intrinsic characteristics."

[Answer:] But it is not so! The many intrinsic characteristics are to be suitably defined by one defining mark.

On the mode of generating the stream of existence, the *Summary of the Hundred Thousand* says:

> Production of the mind of enlightenment consists in these three: belief, concentration, and mindful recollection. [54] Furthermore, belief is similar to the base ground. The quality of the universal ground is its base; it is like concentrated gold. Its character does not change despite the variable aspects of ordinary mind. Mindful recollection is similar to the waxing moon. [Mindful recollection] causes one to further develop [one's understanding of the path], which makes everything clear and familiar.

Enumeration

Second, the enumeration refers to these two: essence and temporary states.

Essence

First, there are these two, aspiration and application, that have to be dealt with in three parts: defining characteristic, referential aspects, and attributes.

Defining characteristic

First, the outlook is the wish to achieve enlightenment for the sake of others. The wish to achieve enlightenment for the sake of others is established through perceiving each defining characteristic with each aspiration and its application.

Referential aspects

Second, the intended objects of aspiration and their referential aspects are sentient beings. The real perception is pure realization. Its aspects are the wish to act for the benefit of others and the wish to achieve it. What is perceived as the intended object of application is pure realization for the sake of others. The objects of reality that are perceived are for the performance of heroism. Their aspects are actions for the sake of the welfare of sentient beings and the enactment of the wish to achieve its goal.

Attributes

Third, when asked what are their particularities, there are three:

Attributes from the traditions of the others

First, **the tradition of the others** is discussed in three parts: the wish to achieve pure realization or not, the outlook on not entering into pure realization and not acquiring it, and their consideration.

The wish to achieve pure realization or not

The aspiration consists in seeking the benefit of others from now until reaching the supreme absolute.

[Argument:] Having entered and acquired these, one is to engage in seizing [their realization]. This application-engagement is referred to as the path of vision, and so on.

[Answer:] Not so. For if this were so, then the aspiration and the application of the vows of the spiritual heroes of everlastingness would have to be completely adopted and, as a result, each and every living being would cease to exist. The *Eye of the Needle* (16.521.6) says:

> The teacher brings here the field of the accumulation of powerful merit that endows one with the power of faith to generate the mind of enlightenment.

Second, is a companion of the Vehicle of the Perfections[121] considered in union with this or not?

[Argument:] Some say that only friends of the Vehicle of the Perfections have the view on pure realization for the sake of others as well as its aspiration. They are said to have entered the path.

[Answer:] Not so. There are no friends of the Vehicle of the Perfections, and it is not claimed that aspiration alone makes the link to the Vehicle of the Perfections and makes one enter this path.

The third point is about the assertion that the accumulation of merit lacks defining characteristics.

[Argument:] Concerning objects perceived during the fruition of pure realization, someone said that the cause to action is initiated with aspiration and pure commitment.

[Answer:] Not so. When one engages in pure realization, there are no perceptible objects that arise. Aspiration as a cause never comes to be united with the practice of the perfections.

[Argument:] Again, someone asked whether this aspiration has to be declared during ritual performance.

[Answer:] Not so. [55] Reality itself does not change the generation of the mind of enlightenment. The absolute truth is this generation of the mind of enlightenment. There is no declaration during ritual practices.

[Argument:] What if the ritual begins with the declaration of intention? Is this engaging the path or not?

[Answer:] There is a cleansing ritual for such a declaration that was defiled, but if there were no application here, it would be in contradiction to engaging the path and contrary to the scriptural tradition described below.

[Argument:] What if someone posits that the declaration to obtain pure enlightenment for the benefit of others must be twofold: thinking of benefiting sentient beings and bringing real benefit?

[Answer:] Not so. If at the time of engaging the path there is no thought of bringing benefit, then it will not arise. If one wishes to bring benefit and it is not possible to bring benefit, then it is because the continuum of the mind of enlightenment has been severed. Pure enlightenment involves engaging with the generation of the mind of enlightenment. When all the elaborations of the ordinary mind are pacified, then all is cleared away.

Attributes according to our own tradition

Second, **in our tradition**, the great Lodrö has said that it is the intention of those completely purified to help others. This point is in the aspiration and the application for its accomplishment. The *Scripture of the Generation of the Mind of Enlightenment* says:

> The distinctiveness of that aspiration and its accomplishment is that the object of knowledge is twofold: by means of the aspiration, the aspiration is acted upon for the benefit of migrators, and the engagement is to act with effort for their benefit.

Dispelling objections

Third is the dispelling of objections.

[Argument:] There is no engagement at the moment when one is on the paths of accumulation and application.

[Answer:] If one says that there is no ability for real accomplishment, it means that concerning the acquisition of intrinsic reality and the generation of the mind of the absolute, there can be no generation of the mind of enlightenment, and so it is left for the ritual declaration only. When there is no real ability, then it is the measure of one's ability. There is no fault in this argument.

Again, when the heroes of everlastingness come to engage the reversal of slothfulness, it ceases to arise. It is no longer as it was before.

Temporary states

Second, if one divides the different points of view on temporal conditions, there are five:

First, if there are divisions concerning the object, there are two concerning the generation of the mind on the perceived object: the conventional and the absolute.

Second, from the point of view of the subtle and the coarse, one receives the generation of the mind through symbols and the intrinsic reality through the two attainments [i.e., power over birth and power over application].

Third, from the point of view of the receptacle, there are the two, the smaller and greater vehicles: the worldly and the supramundane.

Fourth, from the point of view of the demarcations of the grounds, there is the practice of belief, having a pure superior attitude, and the ripening that consists in three groupings divided with respect to the actions of the will, the action of the leading will, and the transformation into a definitely and completely purified one.

Fifth, concerning the spiritual friend, there are prayers to be done continuously [56] and there are the intermittent activities of the perfection and others.

Distinctions between the spiritual friend and the one befriending

Someone asked: What about the distinctions between the spiritual friend and the one befriending him? There are three distinctions to be made here:

[Argument:] First, in the **tradition of the others**, some say that one attains enlightenment for the sake of oneself, and the process is described as a gradual one. There is the generation of the mind of enlightenment of the higher and lower vehicles. The perception is that there are the extensive and the smaller generations of the mind of enlightenment for the sake of others and for enlightenment. Prayers are said to be the extensive perception of all the white [i.e., pure] phenomena.

[Answer:] But there are no white phenomena that cannot be included in enlightenment for the sake of others.

Second, **our tradition** sets the position that if the essence is examined, then there is the first enlightened mind that generates content in the enlightened mind. And if one examines the aspects of ordinary mind, then there is the manifestation of enlightenment.

Third is the **dispelling of objections.**

[Argument:] Is there a designated union between the spiritual friend and the one befriending him?

[Answer:] In the first case [i.e., there is a designated union], these two [i.e., the friend and the one befriending] are distinct substantial entities that refute a single entity.

In the second case, it refutes that they are arising simultaneously. If there is none of the above, then it logically follows the proverbial examples of the pillar and the vase.

[Argument:] Regarding that reply, someone has refuted the existence of the mind and its content with the example of the form and flavor of molasses. They both are a single composite. If that is so, then the main point is similar to the sun and its rays that are united at their origin.

[Answer:] The lord said: "The point here is merely that not seizing the discrete qualities of cyclic existence is not holding onto differences. Causes are from the heaven of the universal basis. Conditions are products of the four natural expressions."[122]

When it is postulated that there is no simultaneous production, then there is a gradual production that is extremely rapid.

The mode of arising in the stream of existence

Third, the topic of the modes of the support of the continuum of existence is threefold: the mode of appropriating past attainments, the mode of appropriating corrupted attainments, and faults and qualities of corrupted attainments.

The mode of appropriating past attainments

The first point consists in the teachings on the arrangement of the preliminary practices, the recitation of the rite during the main part of the practice, and the activities of subsequent practices.

The mode of corrupted attainments

There are the modes of corrupted attainments and the methods of their fabrication. The first one is threefold: characteristics that are lacking, tainted advice, and impossible offerings.

Characteristics that are lacking

The first is to have the wrong kind of faith in the enlightened ones and to have no compassion for sentient beings.

[Argument:] What about a case when whatever seems suitable for offerings, whether the items are defiled or not, one asks if that is sufficient?

[Answer:] It is not. It is called "falling into generalization." It is wrong!

Tainted advice

The second point is fourfold: First, the heretical view is when there is disbelief. Second, wrong support is when there is a loss of refuge. Third, the four wrong-thinkings are when a master worthy of respect is deceived, [57] when there is no respect toward others and regrets about virtue finally begin to arise, when evil-minded slander is committed regarding the heroes of everlastingness, and when one is acting in a deceitful manner toward others. For example, when it is said that the body of Shenrab is fake, and so forth. Fourth, a transgression regarding the period of practice is when there is no practice for a period lasting more than a third of the day.

Impossible offerings

Third is when one's offerings lose their motive. Next is when one regrets having engaged in false methods but does not confess those past deeds with regret and shame three times, or up to seven times. The *Precious Garland Tantra* says:

> Anyone who corrupts the root vows and then cuts them again three times, if it goes beyond that, will fall into the Most Tortuous Hell.

Faults and qualities of corrupted attainments

Third, the teachings on the faults and qualities of corrupted attainments are twofold:

Advantages of accomplishment

First, the advantages of accomplishment are threefold:

First is the wonderful result of having obtained birth. Immediately after having achieved this, what is said and done are transferred into a special basis. The saints praise those endowed with the highest modes of the exalted stations.

Second, the results from temporary conditions multiply, and all who are endowed with the enlightened mind to benefit others become spiritual friends. They delight those who have gone to bliss with deeds for the benefit of others. Those endowed with the power of virtue have uprooted their sins. Outer and inner obstructions and so forth become pacified. One becomes familiar with the momentary cognition of renunciation. The *Minute Scriptures* (208.6) says:

> All sentient beings filling the three realms cannot approach the production of happiness if removed from life.

The *Eye of the Needle* (13.237.1) says:

> On each and every ground is generated the mind of excellent enlightenment. If one strives to rise in virtue, demons will be crushed.

Third, a precise definition of the ultimate result is that of the *Scripture of the Generation of the Mind of Enlightenment* when it says:

> The enlightened ones are the forerunners who widely accomplish the benefit of transmigrators. The mind of enlightenment is the factor distinguishing between great and small causes and results.

Mode of appropriating corrupted attainments

The second point on the mode of arising in the stream of existence is the mode of appropriating corrupted attainments; it arises from all the reversal of the good qualities. The *Eye of the Needle* (5.86.6) says:

> There are claims put forward before evidence. When there is commitment, there are no claims. If there were contradictions concerning commitments, these would be evident [lit. "joined"] in the results. The five hundred offspring that are in bad cycles of reincarnation will go through the continuum of deceit wherever they are born.

Precise definition

Third, the precise definition: memory is lost completely through the cycle of becoming.

Function of the mind of enlightenment

Third, its function [58] is to produce the continuum of the path.

The mode of correct training

The third point, on the mode of correct training, is threefold: the objects to be abandoned, the objects of accomplishment, and training in the methods of the objects to be eliminated.

The objects to be abandoned

The first topic is threefold. The scripture says:

> One must abandon inferior friends of the Lower Vehicle, the sinful and the heretics. One should abandon those afflicted by inferior thoughts, those seeking benefit for themselves and acting in that mindset, and so forth. One must abandon those of sinful conduct, inferior deeds, and so forth. Those that support sinful friends must be shunned completely.

8. THE FOUR ACTIVITIES FOR ACCOMPLISHMENTS

The objects of accomplishment

The second topic on the activities for accomplishment is threefold: one engages in the purifying practices of the six periods of the day and the night; thereafter, the life force will come down on the body that will no longer be subject to corruption; and one should cherish enjoyments and the body at all moments and places.

Training in the methods

Third, concerning the methods of the activities causing increase, one should ponder on the countless number of sentient beings, the qualities of the enlightened ones, and the qualities of the mind of enlightenment. The third point is about how to become involved in the mode of application. The *Summary of the Hundred Thousand* says:

> First in this way, the teachings are given through the emergence of the qualities of engaging in the deeds of those who have generated the mind of enlightenment. The mindstream of consciousness, the objects to engage, and the like should be thoroughly explained by a scholar.

And again:

> Results will be achieved by means of these profound practices.

The point is to engage while accomplishing. With activities for accomplishments, one engages with the following three: cause, nature, and function.

Cause

First, reasoning on the extensiveness of the support gives rise to experiential practice demonstrating the pith instructions on the generation of the mind.

Nature

The second point is threefold and deals with defining characteristics, basis of characteristics, and precise definition.

Defining characteristics

The first is that despite not perceiving all phenomena, one is to practice with zeal and effort in order to acquire enlightenment for the sake of others.

Basis of characteristics

The second point is threefold: the stages, enumerations, and the main points on individual division.

The stages

The first topic is threefold:

The tradition of the others

[Argument:] First, someone from the tradition of the others says: "One must first prepare in order to engage the path of the application of the armor, the path of vision, the path of accumulation and meditation, and the distinctive path of definite emergence."

[Answer:] It is not so. For if it were, there would not be any application of the armor on the path of accumulation. To make this claim is to generalize, for if it were so [that is, if one would first have to prepare], the practice of the perfections would no longer be the beginning of engaging the path. This reasoning [above] is a generalization. [59] The *Eye of the Needle* (15.510.3) says:

> The method originates on the path of the ten transcendent perfections.

To that, the *Summary of the Hundred Thousand* adds:

> Having entered the Greater Vehicle, put on the armor.

[Argument:] Again, someone said: "Starting with the path of accumulation, there is engagement and armor. In order to obtain the body of the absolute, one must ponder with the motivation to apply the practices extensively, and these are the practices of the Greater Vehicle. There is the practice of the accumulation of merit coming from the teachings of Highest Bön on the ten grounds. With the practices of this Highest Bön, there is the genuine generation of enlightenment from the first ground and above. As for the grounds and the collection of the antidotes, the first ground implies that there are the ten other grounds, and the fact that there is an end to the ten grounds produces the great momentary activities that are uncontrived." He further said: "Definite emergence into transcendence exists solely at the end of the ten grounds. And it is only after having eliminated all objects to be abandoned in the three realms that the inherent knowledge of all aspects truly arises."

[Answer:] But it is not so! If that were so, then the accumulation of merit on the path of accumulation would not exist and the mere cause for the gathering of the accumulation of merit would not exist. If this is accepted, then the *White Hundred Thousand Water-Spirits* (7.380.5) says:

> It is explained that the perfection of the accumulation of merit consists in the path of accumulation.

The *Summary of the Hundred Thousand* says:

> The cause of the production of the principal deity and its retinue is the path of accumulation.

Even the realization that comes from studying and reflecting would not exist. The grounds and the collection of antidotes exist if there is a first ground. Even the suppression of the principal coarse defilements would not exist in highest reality. Even the ability to produce enlightenment from the path of accumulation would not exist. Even if the mere ability to produce enlightenment from the path of accumulation existed, there would be no real large-scale generation of merit. And if they are not established extensively, these accumulations will go against the ten grounds coming from Highest Bön.

Without real and vast production of these accumulations, there is no transcendence of the lower continuum of existence.

If there is definite emergence that transcends the continuum of being, if it exists, and if there is the continuum of the path of accumulation, then the arising of the knowledge of all aspects is not possible. The *Compendium on the Spreading* says:

> The generation of the mind of highest enlightenment arises by itself through the knowledge of all aspects.

Our own tradition

Second, our own tradition explains that there are four aspects to the path of accumulation of merit: One raises the universal and extensive mind of wishing to obtain the body of the absolute. Entering the Greater Vehicle, one takes up its practices. Relying on the two accumulations, one generates the great mind of enlightenment. Abandoning the grounds of cyclic existence, true omniscience arises. The *Compendium on the Spreading* says:

> Entering the Greater Vehicle will bring about definite emergence from the three realms. [60] True emergence comes from the knowledge of all aspects itself.

Dispelling objections

Third, the dispelling of objections is fourfold:

First, if one is endowed with the particular armor of practice and is on the path of accumulation, then there is no contradiction that they should be present there. The one who is not endowed with that will only be able to achieve this with that.

Second, if one is engaged on the path, then there is no contradiction to the existence of objects that are not obviously perceived. One is engaging the path of accumulation when there is the common realization of the essential points derived from studying and reflecting.

Third, if there are accumulations of merit, then these are not in contradiction to the real experience of achieving enlightenment. There is no real attainment when it is accomplished through the continuum of existence.

Fourth, if there is definite emergence into enlightenment, then there is no coming into existence of the true arising of omniscience. There is no arising of the experience of the ultimate reality when the continuum of existence is arising as well.

Enumeration

Second, enumeration is fivefold:

First, the benchmark that is only concerned with the achievement of the heroes of everlastingness is, in essence, made of these four: the armor, engaging the path, the accumulation of merit, and definite emergence. The *Summary of the Hundred Thousand* mentions:

> . . . putting on of the great armor . . . the path of application . . . the collection of the two accumulations . . . the result is the arising of the knowledge of all aspects.

Pondering on causal characteristics is the practice of the armor. Engaging with the practice is the application. The two accumulations are the accumulations from the generation of the result of momentary conditions. True emergence comes from generating the result of finality. These four are certain.

With respect to the mode of achieving the essence and the manner of producing the result, they are separate.

As for establishing the meaning of these divisions, these may be different from the mode of completion. Their essence is numerically divided along these two: concept and application. The results are certainly twofold: the production of the temporary and that of the ultimate.

The main points on individual division

Third, there are four main points about each and every division:

First, on the achievement of the armor, the *Compendium on the Spreading* says:

> The great heroes of everlastingness put on the armor by entering the Greater Vehicle with utter purity and abide in utter purity in the Greater Vehicle.

The *Summary of the Hundred Thousand* says:

> What is the donning of the armor in this age? It is pacifying

suffering while not being afflicted by the results of affliction that [ultimately] do not exist.

In this there are the basis of characteristics, defining characteristic, and precise definition.

First, the purpose of the body of the absolute is the practice of the non-perception of the perfections.

[Argument:] When someone asks about the defining characteristic of the perfections in detail, [61] saying that when inherent nature is realized as non-existent, it is similar to both turning away from release and entering at the same time.

[Answer:] If that were so, then the realization of the lack of inherent nature would consist in engaging the path as well as the accumulation of merit. Therefore, the realization of the lack of inherent nature would be like making friends with those who employ evil means and considering them as the heroes of this worldly continuum.

Second, from the point of view of the root, the **basis of characteristics** are the ten unsurpassables [i.e., the ten perfections]. When the different branches of practice are divided, each of the ten unsurpassables comes to have six divisions, such as giving and so forth. Scholars examine them under the heading "the Six Limbs." This is explained in the *Summary of the Hundred Thousand*. When summarized, the division into six [perfections] are gathered under these two classifications: cause and result.

Cause has five headings: giving, morality, patience, diligence, and concentration. Result has the following five: strength, compassion, aspiration, method, and wisdom. The *Compendium on the Spreading* (3.181.4) says:

If one wants to obtain the quintessential heavenly body, one must act in accord with the causes that are five among the ten unsurpassable advances. One must also engage in activities in accord with the results, which are five.

Training is subsumed under three headings: morality, concentration, and wisdom. When combined, they make four. These three [i.e., morality, concentration, and wisdom] are suitably included here in the seven. The seven are the objects to be abandoned that counteract elimination, each and every one in the wrong mental abiding in the different phenomena perceived, and the false non-perceptions of the three worlds gathered together with the three mentioned. Concerning this, then, from the *Hundred Thousand* there is love and so forth that are explained as five, and one may wonder if it is a contradiction of the path, but it is not. The five and the ten have been conveniently combined. And if, as such, they do not exist, then the no self of the path also does not exist. Then the mode of abiding will change into a trifling emptiness.

Precise definition

Third, the precise definition is this: If there is the cycle of existence, there is the action of transcending it. Diligently practicing the ten perfections, one will enter hostile cyclic existence with the armor of fearlessness.

Second, on achieving engagement with the path: The *Compendium on the Spreading* says:

> If one abides purely in the Greater Vehicle, one will be able to reason engaging with the vehicle. If so, then one enters the unsurpassed advance of giving.

The *Summary of the Hundred Thousand* says:

> One engages the object.

Furthermore:

> I, too, have engaged and also exhort others toward others.

The **defining characteristic** of these three statements is that one engages in the Greater Vehicle while practicing diligently with the mode of nonperception for the benefit of obtaining the body of the absolute.

Basis of characteristics

Second, concerning the basis of characteristics, the *Summary of the Hundred Thousand* says:

> A lifetime of practice on the true meaning of the unsurpassable
> is to experience the activities of conceptual characteristics among

affairs that are said to be devoid of meaning and coming from a deluded mind.

[62] And so forth. What is said to have form and what are said to be non-existent activities are not connected objects of activities but are not different either. They are said to be effortlessly non-dual and so forth. Similarly, the *Summary of the Hundred Thousand* says:

> There are no difficult deeds, manifested or non-manifested, eternal or not, arising or ceasing, to be abandoned or appropriated, self or no self, alone or not alone, to aspire to or not, beginning or without beginning.

And so forth. If there is a deed, then this deed has a characteristic. Therefore, when one is engaging the path without the perception of a self, and when there is an action relating to a phenomenon, this is engaging properly.

Moreover, there are nine categories [ten enumerated here]: the state of formless concentration, the practices of giving and so forth, the paths from the path of vision onward, the immeasurables, the marks of conditioned phenomena, the three worlds, intent toward the knowledge of all aspects, the six supra-knowledges, perceiving omniscience itself as being without inherent self, and engaging with non-perception so that one will achieve realization. The *Compendium on the Spreading* says:

> Abide and induce the four absorptions of the concentrated mind, the four immeasurables, the four formless concentrations, the six supra-normal powers, and non-perception.

The ten unsurpassed—love, and so forth—demonstrate that if engaging does not exist truly, it does not exist. To understand the above is to put on the armor. This is engaging the path.

The achievement of the path of accumulation

Third, on the achievement of the path of accumulation, the *Compendium on the Spreading* says:

The cause for the collections of accumulation in the three worlds and the nine grounds is the accumulation of merit.

And again:

The great heroes of everlastingness will teach you the objects of the activity of abiding in the unsurpassed advance of Shenrab. The unsurpassed advance of Shenrab is abiding in the Suchness of emptiness.

The *Summary of the Hundred Thousand* mentions "The two collections of accumulation." There are three points on this:

First, the **defining characteristic**: In order to obtain the body of the absolute, one transforms the cause of the production of momentary results through the practice of non-perception.

Second, on the **basis of characteristics**, the *Summary of the Hundred Thousand* says:

The causes are the two collections of accumulation.

The accumulation of merit is the cause and the accumulation of wisdom is the result. Like that, the training in the experience of the perfections, and so forth, are the causes for the manifestation of merit. The collection of merit is done through the accumulation of mirage-like meritorious deeds, the truly empty ones. Again, they are recognized in these two: pure truth and falsity. When practicing non-apprehension, this consists in the accumulation of insight.

Furthermore, it is similar to the *Compendium on the Spreading* on the oral teachings of the armor [63] and the oral teachings of the Greater Vehicle.

First, compassion and conduct, calm abiding and insight are grouped together into three and five. Conduct consists in the ten perfections. Thus the *Compendium on the Spreading* says:

The great hero of everlastingness, reflecting on this, said: "I declare that the immeasurable numbers of sentient beings are coming out of evil destinies."

The oral teachings of the Greater Vehicle

Second, the oral teachings of the Greater Vehicle are said to be six: expert knowledge of the methods, the practice of the perfections, the accumulation of wisdom, the experience of the eighteen emptinesses, the experiential practice of the accumulations of the paths, and the path of everlastingness.

There is the accumulation of the mystic formulas and other practices such as those of the Eight Realms of the Mother. There are the practices of the various grounds, from the phenomena of the first ground onward. Then there are the practices of abandoning objects together with the contemplative and post-meditative awareness and the application of the various antidotes. Similarly, there is the conduct during the unsurpassed journey itself in order to not remain among all phenomena. It is said: "The Greater Vehicle is the unsurpassed journey of not remaining among all phenomena." Moreover, the two above are combined.

Precise definition

Third, the precise definition: One's own continuum of existence is a gathering of accumulations. It is the result of accumulations assembled through real production.

The attainment of definite emergence

Fourthly, concerning the attainment of definite emergence, the *Compendium on the Spreading* says:

> The great hero of everlastingness trained in this and attained definite emergence into the state of intrinsic omniscience.

And also:

> How did he abide in intrinsic omniscience? Through the unexcelled entrance into non-perception.

The *Summary of the Hundred Thousand* says:

> The unsurpassed journey with the practice of ethical conduct,

and so forth, is the cause of transcending the evil destinies of the ten grounds, and because of this, definite emergence was taught.

First, its **defining characteristic**: The cause of producing the result of liberation comes from the diligent practice of non-perception.

Second, the **basis of characteristics** is twofold:

First, on "benefits," the *Summary of the Hundred Thousand* says something like this:

> The benefits of the eleven qualities of the enlightened ones are taught perfectly in the paths above as the practice of the union of method and wisdom. How so? It consists in the view of the realization of reality itself and its activities and so forth, and of guarding the vows of the mother protectress.

The *Compendium on the Spreading* says something similar:

> The eight kinds of realization are deliverance from purposeful action, arising in meditative equipoise itself, liberation for the sake of sentient beings, effortlessness, transcendence of limits, attainment of the grounds, [64] omniscience, and deliverance from the objects of the paths. These are pure and are the acquisition of liberation. Their purpose is the accomplishment of non-perception.

The above are the eleven realizations. Moreover, accomplishment is done through the abandonment of discordances. Definite emergence consists in abiding in omniscience. That is the enjoyment of bliss.

Dispelling objections on the application

Second, there is the dispelling of objections concerning the accomplishments:

[Argument:] Someone said that there is no relevance in practicing the main points of application and that there is no purpose in the teaching of any of them.

[Answer:] Not so. Application delineates the object of practice, while the accomplishments demonstrate the objects of the practice on diligence. If that were not so, teaching the unsurpassed teachings of most excellent wisdom itself would be sufficient. The four paths, the fifth, and so forth, would have no meaning and there would be no cause for practice.

Third precise definition

A third precise definition: The practice of non-perception is a result that gives rise to intrinsic omniscience. This third precise definition is the realization of Suchness.

Function

Third, the function of non-perception is to arise within the continuum of the paths. The result is the ripening of omniscience. It is said: "The support of spiritual friends is to transmit the teachings and, with these teachings, to achieve the generation of the mind of enlightenment, engaging the armor and the definite emergence of the accumulations. These constitute the limbs of the preliminaries."

This ends the second chapter on the preliminaries on the causes of the generation of the path from the *Magical Key to the Precious Stages of the Path and the Grounds of the Greater Vehicle*. [65]

3. Determining the Nature of the Common Path

I. TEACHINGS ON THE PATH TO LIBERATION

Second, concerning the nature of the path to liberation and its generation from cause, this has three parts: defining characteristic, the base for its characteristics, and precise definition.

Defining characteristic

The first topic is threefold:

The tradition of the others

[Argument:] First, a certain well-known scholar from the tradition of the others said that the root of virtue of setting time apart for gathering merit is not included within the practice of meditative equipoise. Another said that there are deeds to perform in order to transcend evil destinies.

[Answer:] But it is not so. Isn't that path itself the practice of reversal for transcending evil destinies? It is the cause of crossing over. In the first case [i.e., setting time apart, etc.], it would change the path into a session of practice to accumulate merit. And that would be contrary to going onto the path. That would also be transforming the generation of the mind of enlightenment. In the second case [i.e., deeds need to be performed, etc.], the path itself would change and would not be one of transcending evil destinies. The path on the establishment of mindfulness and so forth has been explained as part of the path, but this saying would change it into [one that] lacks a separate basis for characteristics.

[Argument:] Yet, one master has said that the action of going somewhere as a rational doctrine does not generate the base, the path, and the result.

[Answer:] This would go against the realization of insight, against subsequent attainment, and there would be no path at all!

Our own tradition

Second, our own tradition is to reach transcendence through the realization of the lack of inherent self.

Dispelling objections

Third is to dispel objections concerning the transformation on the path of the perfections. To isolate a self is a pervasive factor that reverses the path to emptiness. The *Eye of the Needle* (15.510.3) says:

> Where is the substantial entity that one wishes to encounter on the path? This is the method arising from the path of the ten crossings over that are the perfections.

Furthermore, the general meditation on vision is not pervasive. Again, there is nothing else that is pervasive to the paths of accumulation and preparation on inherent nature. Only the realization of the lack of self is necessary.

The base for its characteristics

The second topic is threefold: the person that supports the practice of meditation, the nature of application as the object to meditation, and the divisions of the path and the object of meditation.

The person that supports the practice of meditation

Discussion on the support has been dealt with earlier. Its synthesis through any of the grounds and three realms will be commented on below.

The nature of application as the object to meditation

Second, on making use of this, the *Hundred Thousand* says:

> One acquires the result of the thoroughly perfected unsurpass-

able, having performed the profound deeds of the heroes of everlastingness.

The *Summary of the Hundred Thousand* adds:

Scholars have thoroughly trained like that.

And:

What is difficult to cognize is insight, [66] and the object of insight is the method of the heroes of everlastingness.

The *Compendium on the Spreading* (3.175.2, 5, 7; 5.663.5) says:

In order to have a clear realization in all aspects ...
In order to have a clear realization of the loftiest vehicle ...
In order to acquire the path of the journey beyond limits ...
In order to completely reverse sentient beings and acquire enlightenment clearly and instantaneously ...

And so forth, with similar gradualist sayings. For that reason, if there is no one to make use of it [i.e., to apply it], the path will fail to elucidate the object of practice. This discussion is threefold: the cause, the base, and divisions.

Cause

First, I must establish the reasoning on the extensiveness of the support, give instruction on the cause, give the reasons for the generation of the mind, and give the confluence of time and place.

Nature

The second point is threefold: defining characteristic, divisions, and precise definition.

Defining characteristic of intrinsic nature

The first is threefold:

The positions of the tradition of the others on intrinsic nature

[Argument:] Someone has said that there are no general characteristics to intrinsic nature.

[Answer:] There are four marks that characterize[123] and are said to be produced at different moments. These four particular marks that characterize, once joined together, are no longer four. Their timings may be different and have many particular differences, but their common characteristic is that they are produced as a set. Thus, if they are not present, then it is not tenable that there may be only one defining characteristic concerning an object of consciousness. The objects in the realm of the mind must be set appropriately.

Our own tradition on intrinsic nature

The second point is that in our own tradition, one desires to acquire omniscience for the sake of others. Through insight during meditation, one can truly realize the lack of inherent self in all phenomena.

Dispelling objections on intrinsic nature

The third topic is to dispel objections.

[Argument:] There is one defining characteristic point [i.e., application] to the four marks that characterize.

[Answer:] Mere application is the wrong defining characteristic. "Accomplishment" is also too broad a term, and therefore is not it. There is no self-isolate; therefore essence it is! If this were not so, then the objects of meditation that are brought down through application would come to be truly existent.

The base

The second topic on the inherent base is threefold: boundaries, enumeration, and individual points.

Boundaries

The first topic on boundaries is threefold:

First, **countering the arguments of the tradition of the others** is in four parts:

[Argument:] First, someone is saying that if there is no knowledge of all aspects [i.e., omniscience] at the end of the tenth ground, then there is no known acquisition of the stage of the Peak.

[Answer:] Not so. If there is a ground for the enlightened ones, but there is no single Peak [i.e., nothing higher], then the final limit of the continuum of existence and the knowledge of all aspects do not exist. One must analyze this overreaching claim with valid cognition. If this were accepted, there would be no attainment of realization of either the transformative power in primordial wisdom or a realized body, because there would be no attainment of the Peak. If this is accepted, then the *Compendium on the Spreading* (1.49.1) responds, saying:

> It is clear that there are sixty-one aspects to the primordial wisdom of the omniscient ones.

[Argument:] Second, someone said that if there are no accumulations, there is no Peak of realization and [67] no emergence of meditation.

[Answer:] Not so. If it were so, then there would be no advent of the great path of accumulation and the two paths of accumulation mentioned above. There would be no meditative cultivation on the meaning of the desire to obtain the great knowledge of all aspects of the first accumulation.

[Argument:] Third, someone said that the graded levels, from the stage of "Heat" up to the ten grounds, are truly existing.

[Answer:] Not so. If there were accumulations, then there would be no meditation on the gradual application of the heroes of everlastingness. If this is accepted and if there is no meditation, then the path would be unfeasible. If there were no meditation, these stages would change meditation all at once.

[Argument:] Fourth, concerning the suddenness of realization: Someone said that both sudden and gradual realizations are produced and are simultaneous. Therefore, the gradual aspect exists, and it is said to be from the seventh ground onward.

[Answer:] There is no such thing. If it were so, and if there were stages emerging, then there would be no more distinct boundaries between the different grounds. The accomplishment of the concentration on proximity would be like lightning, everlasting, and so forth, as explained. The *Compendium on the Spreading* (1.59.4) says:

> The fully perfected enlightenment arises in one instant.

Second, **our own tradition** is fourfold:

[Argument:] First, concerning omniscience, one amasses accumulations until the limit of the continuum to the ground of the enlightened ones.

[Answer:] Not so. There would consequently be no meditation at all on the non-existence of the self for the purpose of acquiring the body of the ultimate, the Peak. The *Compendium on the Spreading* (3.130.1) says:

> If one accepts that there is unsurpassed enlightenment, then one realizes intrinsic enlightened mind in all its various forms.

The demarcation of the ground of the blissful ones consists in the existence and the non-existence of the extraordinary with regard to what is down below and up above.

Second, the Peak is the last stage between the path of accumulation and above. If there is the ground of enlightenment, it is the Peak. The scripture says:

> Given that one obtains realization of the transformative power of realization, one treads the grounds to the highest Peak, the vehicle from the pure primordial world of form.

Thus it goes from the former non-existent endowed with particularities to the later existing particular.

Third, the gradual path of accumulation has up to ten grounds on account of the meditative levels. Among these, if one is at the end of the stream of existence and it ceases, then there are no more meditative states. Therefore the scriptures say:

> The activity up to its limit is the path of accumulation, and the training from these limits is the path of application. Gradual progress is for the paths of meditation and vision.
> One goes past the finality of form and transcends finality.

And so forth. [68] Its particularities are the same as before.

Fourth, there is suddenness only at the end of the ten grounds. The *Eye of the Needle* (9.368.4) says:

> Immediacy is like the emission of light from a rainbow in the sky.
> That is enlightenment.

Dispelling objections

The third topic is dispelling objections:

[Argument:] If there is an end to the continuum of existence it must be because there is the knowledge of all aspects, and this will change the meditation process of the Peak. If one accepts that the state of the Peak will end, then one could ask, is there really an application of the meditation of the Peak?

[Answer:] There is no application at the stage of the Peak, for once achieved, there is only the knowledge of all aspects.

[Argument:] If there are accumulations at the level of the Peak, then one might ask if one will be able to acquire the realization of the transformative power in the path of accumulation.

[Answer:] In the affirmative, one can consider that there will be the acquisition of the realization of the transformative power that will be realized naturally by itself.

[Argument:] Then one might ask if meditative realization will arise.

[Answer:] There is only a state of meditation and nothing else in particular as such.

[Argument:] Then, someone may say that if there is no gradual end to the limit of the continuum of existence, then there are no stages to meditation and no meditative state coming from a gradual path. Therefore, there will be no sudden imminence of the body of the ultimate.

[Answer:] If one accepts this, then as far as the ten grounds are concerned, meditative states are gradual until the end of the continuum of existence when there is the sudden acquisition of realization.

[Argument:] What if the above is accepted as such?

[Answer:] Suchness is achieved in one moment and the body of the ultimate is instantly obtained. Immediately, the bright path of the trainee and all other phenomena are surmised suddenly in meditative insight. Then, either a spiritual transmission (*rigs*) is achieved or there is a substantial entity. In the case of the first one, it becomes the path of vision and realization in the lineage of the intrinsic absolute of the four noble truths. In the case of the second, the ten grounds do not come to an end.

[Argument:] Someone might say that there is no exception to the reality of enlightenment because there is no real acquisition when an ordinary mind is having a sudden realization.

[Answer:] The white of the path of the trainee and reality, without exception, are attained instantaneously by the ordinary mind.

Second, the **enumeration** is fivefold:

1. The basis of division is conducted through the defining characteristic that is applied only to the entailing factor.

2. The essence has its four aspects.

3. The causal characteristic comes down to the phenomenon lacking inherent self.

4. The Peak, whose purpose is the object of attainment, the body of the absolute, is the knowledge of all aspects gained through meditation on the lack of inherent self.

5. Suchness is meditation on the realization of the transformative power for the purpose of the object of attainment, the resulting body of reality. This is the Peak.

As for the object that lacks inherent self, when the gradual process on the lack of inherent self comes to an end and causes the sudden body of reality to emerge, if one suddenly meditates on the dominant condition lacking inherent self, then one can start the path of application instantly.

The purpose of these divisions is to show that the continuum of existence indeed ends in one moment, but meditative realization turns the path around and divides it in stages.

This comprehensive enumeration is similar to the causal reason, for the mode of production is determined by false views or by the all-knowing state [69] that has obtained the transformative power through production of the stage of the Peak. Perception in the profound meditative state is the resulting cause for overcoming false views by force.

Concerning the acquisition of the instantaneous body of the absolute, suddenly one will acquire finality in an instant after going through gradual meditative states. The bright subsequent attainment state and perception in the sphere of reality are said to be the supportive cause and the result. In the case when cause and result are one and the same, it is permissible to teach them as two distinct topics, since it would be meaningless to think about them otherwise. Or else there will be no Peak at all, or gradual cause, or result. For that reason, and if that were so, where would be the cause for practice? There would not even be any of the four modes of interpretation [i.e., literal, general, secret, and ultimate].

2. THE FOUR APPLICATIONS

Individual points on the inherent base

The third topic on individual points is fourfold: the supporting conditions for the meditator, the method (*bon*) of the preliminary practices, the phenomena of the objects of meditation, and the actual practice and meditation.

The supporting conditions for the meditator

First, there is the support of the spiritual lineage. It has an evolving potential. It has applications such as the sole meditation on its lineage, the generation of the aspiration that is conducive to liberation and above, and the first generation of the mind of enlightenment and above. Only the extraordinary meditation practices are aids to the four types of things that are truly differentiated [i.e., synonymous with the four levels of the path of application], and that is because of the irreversible signs that one obtains, mentioned above.

The method of the preliminary practices

Second, the way of the preliminary practices is necessary since one receives personal instruction on the disadvantages of not meditating, on knowing the good qualities of meditation, on abandoning disrespect and engaging in the objects of practice, and on the generation of the mind of enlightenment and aspiration, all this while performing these preliminary practices.

The objects of meditation

The third topic consists in the objects of perception and their aspects during meditation practice: perception of the two truths and views on the four truths. This we have explained above.

The second topic on the aspects of the objects of perception is threefold: defining characteristic, divisions, and precise definition.

Defining characteristic on the aspects of the objects of perception

The first discussion is on the defining characteristic.

[Argument:] It has been said that the defining characteristic is that there are many phenomena but there exist no distinctive aspects.

[Answer:] There must be some distinctions that depend on the factor isolated from the phenomena.

The basis of characteristics

Next is that which bears characteristics: the essential point and the aspects to consciousness. First, there are differences among the four truths. There are results coming from endless individual causes and individual causes with endless results. These manifest in extremely numerous ways.

Second, these are not produced in meditative states. After meditating, the meditation on what is illusionary is a form of subsequent attainment. It is based on reversing the mode of meditation on causality.

[70] Third, the different facets of their nature must be well ascertained so that after examination, one can meditate on them.

Fourth, the main practice of the path of application consists in the following categories:

First, the topic of the knowledge of all aspects is threefold: defining characteristic, divisions, and precise definition.

Defining characteristic of the knowledge of all aspects

First, concerning the activities for the sake of others to acquire the body of the absolute during the stage of the Peak, the practice is to meditate on the non-existence of inherent self. This is the common practice. Then there is the special practice of meditating on illusion-endowed phenomena and intrinsic reality lacking inherent self. This consists in defining the characteristic of each, contemplation, and post-meditation practice.

Divisions

The second topic is threefold: the divisions of [the path of] application, the modes of meditation, and enlightened qualities.

The divisions of the path of application

First, there are two divisions to the topic of application: application only and its particularities.

Application only

The first one, application only, is threefold and consists in engaging inherent nature, the moment of application, and the application through the boundaries of the grounds.

Engaging inherent nature

For the first subtopic, there are the two basic applications and three applications for realization.

First, there are two negations to be applied by the meditator at the moment of practice. These are the meditations on the objects perceived in the mind as phenomena and Suchness.

Second, there is the application of the profound concerning perception and non-perception of the base. Non-perception of objects on the path is difficult to plunge into when one applies oneself to the numerous objects of all kinds where there is no true perception [of the lack of inherent existence].

Fifth, on the basis of characteristics following the main practice of the path of application, there is the discussion on the different isolates that appear in the one essence.

The moment of application

[Argument:] Next, the moment of application, which is the fifth, is Suchness. This changes through timely opportunities. Thus, there is the realization that comes after a long period of large accumulations of merit after having been on the path of accumulation for a long time. Having heard the teachings of this vehicle, one generates a great fear that brings one to the practice of elimination and so forth. This has been said.

[Answer:] But it is not so. That is the door to enter the Smaller Vehicle where there is no path of accumulation of the Greater Vehicle. If it was not so, studying and pondering would not be combined, which is the point to the Greater Vehicle. Having studied and pondered on the path of accumulation, daily thinking and inference will not bring down the two truths. Therefore, there is the conjoined application that brings down the two truths. The path of accumulation is long and one must abide on the path of accumulation for a long time. The stage of Heat[124] on the path of application is taught in the scriptures and the level of the Peak is that of the non-returner. Then, the Forbearance level truly arises. Following this there are no more obstructions to the stage of Highest Bön.

The path of vision is located on the second up to the seventh ground where one quickly approaches enlightenment. The eighth ground and above is where one applies oneself to benefiting others by performing deeds for the benefit of the many beings. Within Suchness, fault and qualities, increase and decrease are not perceived as objects and there are no increase and decrease. [71] In Suchness, virtues and non-virtues are not perceived in meditation, and one does not see them. In Suchness, subjects are not perceived, and inherent reality is incommensurable to the mind. The mind cannot encompass it. Suchness is devoid of characteristics and characterizers and so forth, and in non-conceptuality the practitioner does not conceptualize.

Each and every ninth grounder[125] who sets out toward enlightenment with correct pristine awareness and endowed with a spiritual lineage, will go forth to that result that is extremely precious. Having trained on the paths of the ten grounds, one will come to the joint application of the very pure aspects of finality. The *Compendium on the Spreading* says:

> As such, there is no inherent nature whatsoever to the absolute. Where is the non-existing inherent nature? There is no inherently existing self.
> The inherent nature of all phenomena is completely pure.
> Once one has attained and dwelt in the unsurpassable wisdom, all phenomena will be apprehended like an echo.

And so forth.

The application through the boundaries

Third, the application through the boundaries is either conducted with exertion or effortlessly. The first is to go ahead along a previous pledge and meditate on the non-existence of inherent self, to practice without procrastination on the path of accumulation to the seventh ground and above. The practice of the seventh grounder is to abandon fabrication and characteristics. "To diligently cleanse inherent nature of marks and delusions." The second type of application is used on the eighth ground and above. The *Summary of the Hundred Thousand* says:

> The eighth grounder and above does not perceive these two: conceptual thinking or the antidotes that eliminate.

Particularities

The second topic is twofold: the moment when one is abiding in meditation, and real application.

The moment when one is abiding in meditation

On the first one, when one is at the level of Heat and above, one becomes endowed with the concept of non-returner.

Real application

The second topic has three subcategories: the application of equanimity pacifying existence, the application of the pure land, and the application of skillful means.

The application of equanimity pacifying existence

First, the timely application of cause implies meditation on equanimity. Its result is the acquisition of the equanimity of the Absolute Body. The demarcating boundaries start first with the arising of belief until the eighth extraordinary ground, where one is endowed with that particularity [i.e., the Absolute Body].

The application of the pure land

Second, the ground of the body of perfection is where one obtains the desired particularities and so forth and is established on the path leading to what one aspires to attain. The demarcation of the boundaries is as before.

The application of skillful means

Third, one joins love and compassion to the meditative state on the path of accumulation. The results are the establishment of charismatic activities and abundance in excellence. The *Eye of the Needle* (16.522.1) says:

> The power of aspiration lies in not being separated from discipline. It induces, here and now, the arising of visions.

The mode of meditation

Third, the mode of meditation is threefold: establishing concepts, accomplishing the mode, and dispelling objections. [72]

Establishing concepts

First, aspects of the path and the base are not produced by the mental properties of meditation. If meditation remains inseparable from the limbs of being consummate in the extraordinary mode of meditation, then the finality of perfectly clear appearance will definitely arise. The mental continuum of the skilled practitioner will become firm in any situation and any particular place in which one will be because it is independent of striving to hold on to familiar experiences or familiarity with objects of desire. It is the same with the frightening objects with which one is familiar.

Accomplishing the mode

Second, the mode: The subject's experience from previous meditative experiences should have been of proven benefit for one's knowledge of the base, the path, and the result. The objects that are to be proven are the host of phenomena involving subject and object. The subject proves the objects in the continuum of existence. This negates the implication that realization is a pointless accomplishment.

Dispelling objections

[Argument:] A logical reason is twofold: partial or pervasive. The first one [i.e., a partially proven concept] in the stable continuum of an ordinary mind is a former cognition that is subsequently proven. It is the awareness that recognizes day and night and that becomes a habit through the agency of the experience of meditation. When meditation is practiced with diligence and one becomes completely realized, independent realization is proven.

Second, when explicit concomitance of subject and object is ascertained, it determines that there is an isolate factor that is implied. The fact that there is awareness at the end of the cyclic continuum, that awareness proves that there is also future rebirth.

[Answer:] Third, if it is so, then the meditative state encompassing all aspects [i.e., omniscience] would be distinctly different. However, this would be meaningless because one single inherent nature refutes the many different aspects, places, and all objects that are not perceived.

[Argument:] Someone says that there is no fault in that statement.

[Answer:] Even though the essence of joint application is Suchness, because of the fact of momentary realization, whether clear or not clear, there will be a differentiation. Objection to this will be brought up below when dealing with the mode of meditation.

Completion of enlightened qualities

Third, there is the completion of the qualities of enlightenment for one's own benefit and the completion for others' benefit.

Completion of the qualities of enlightenment for one's own benefit

First, with causal joint application one gets rid of adversity and obstacles to the Three Excellences [i.e., abundance, grace, and glory]. If joint application of concordant conditions is not reversed, this will lead to distinction. Pristine awareness of the enlightened ones will bring about the distinctive knowledge of enlightened qualities.

Second, at the moment of liberation when enlightened qualities of finality are accomplished, one nears perfected enlightenment and obtains the great goal. Having been provided with an able body through all of one's lifetimes, one has the vision of the enlightened ones and performs the greatly enlightened activities. One will then come to encounter the Mother herself and obtain the inexhaustible qualities. One will acquire the inexhaustible qualities of transcending sorrow.

Completion for others' benefit

Second, one acquires pleasant speech for the benefit of others. One will meet and be instructed by the Mother herself during any rebirth. In order to fulfill the result of the generation of the mind to enlightenment, [73] one acquires realization of the qualities of many sentient beings. For the sake of sentient beings, one will be able to establish the qualities of true realization and the authentic Greater Vehicle as a reality for all sentient beings.

Precise definition

Third, precise definition: This is the achievement of complete perfection that has finalized all aspects.

The stage of the Peak

Second, the topic on the stage of the Peak is threefold:

Defining characteristic of the Peak

First, its defining characteristic: the dominant condition of all aspects does not have an inherent nature. One acquires this realization that is a transformative power when one is meditating. In particular, an illusory subject can be transformed through the acquisition of the realization of this power with meditation on intrinsic reality. This is the specific characteristic of each and every meditative and post-meditative state.

What bears the characteristic

Second, the basis of the characteristic resides in the activity of the joint application process, mode of meditation, and rejection of mistaken conceptions.

The activity of the joint application process

First, although seven are mentioned, there are in fact eight peaks: the Peak of Accumulation, the Peak of Heat, the Peak of the Peak, the Peak of Forbearance, the Peak of the Supreme Reality [i.e., Highest Bön], the Peak of the Path of Vision, the Peak of the Path of Familiarity, and the Peak of Non-Impediment.

The Peak of Accumulation

First, analyzing the lack of inherent existence on the path of accumulation, one arrives at a meditative realization and acquires the realization of the transformative power of the path of accumulation. This is the Peak of Accumulation.

[Question:] In the case of accumulation, if there is a Peak, one may ask if it is going to arise during meditation.

[Answer:] It is accepted that it arises only during meditation. However, there are traits that it is said that one should not adopt. While one abides in that state, it is accepted that this is the realization of the power to transform because there is the realization of the ability to transform [everything] into Suchness, as mentioned above.

The Peak of Heat

Second, concerning the stage of Heat, it is said that one acquires the concept of no return through the realization of the lack of inherent existence of affliction everywhere because of this power of transformation. When there are dreams, Suchness remains at the center of the dominant condition. The teachers of Bön argue that those at that stage are non-returners, and so forth.

The Peak of the Peak

Third, it is said that one should adhere to the reliance on antidotes transforming into the realization of the lack of inherent existence, and obtain the realization of the increase of all aspects. One abides on the ground of faith with particular emphasis on practice until the end of this time cycle, and so forth. These become particularly important at this stage.

The Peak of Forbearance

Fourth, concerning dedication, it has been said that one can obtain the realization of the transformative power in the realization of the lack of inherent existence of concrete individuals. Through the non-perception of the three worlds, one dedicates virtuous actions for the sake of others and generates immeasurable compassion. [74] The pure consciousness of the heroes of everlastingness dedicates this unsurpassed and completely pure and perfected enlightenment.

The Peak of Supreme Reality

Fifth, it is said that when one acquires the transformative power of the realization of the lack of inherent existence of individuals clinging to a self, one will know the virtue of merit and will abide in the enlightened mind over the finality of worldly phenomena. One will thoroughly grasp the transitioning to the unsurpassable insight and become an expert in skillful means, inseparable from the lineage of Bön.

The Peak of the Path of Vision

Sixth, it is said that when one acquires transformative power, one will have the vision of direct perception of matters seen in the past. Furthermore, having turned away from the 112 objects to eliminate through the path of vision, one obtains the great enlightenment without obstructions, the pristine awareness of release. The great heroes of everlastingness are from the lineage of those who abide in the unchanging enlightened mind.

The Peak of the Path of Familiarity

Seventh, it is said that one will have the realization of the transformative power through familiarization with grasping at what is seen. Furthermore, the concentration of the leap-over (*thod rgal*) practices will produce and generate the elimination of discarding meditation. One will abide in emptiness and will become intimate with emptiness.

The Peak of Non-Impediment

Eighth, it is said that if one realizes the lack of inherent existence in all of the above through the acquisition of the realization of transformative power, others also continuously become enlightened ones. If they belong to the Greater Vehicle, then they are in truth and reality great heroes of everlastingness.

The mode of meditation

Second, the mode of meditation is when the formulas of concentration from the past become a reality, similar to what was previously said.

Dispelling objections

Third is dispelling objections:

Even if there are knowable things present at the time of the realization of the Peak, no resulting effects will come from these productions. This will change consciousness and one's continuum of existence.

[Argument:] Some say that if there are no knowable things present, then there is no production after realization.

[Answer:] Though Suchness has no agent of production, there is the one essence that later generates different isolates.

Precise definition

Third, precise definition: That realization of the Peak arises from the power of transformation and Suchness that transforms sharply.

Sequence

Third, the sequence is threefold:

First, defining characteristic: In order to obtain the instantaneous body of reality for the benefit of others, one meditates gradually on the lack of inherent existence. In particular, one meditates gradually on the lack of inherent existence of the subject and intrinsic reality. This is the defining characteristic of each and every meditation as well as of subsequent meditation practices. [75]

The bearer of characteristics

Second, the topic of **the bearer of characteristics** is threefold: divisions of application, mode of meditation, and dispelling objections.

The divisions of application

The divisions of application is fourfold and consists in the successive transformation of the essence of the path, the cessation of obsessive clinging to the vessel of the path, the cessation of obsessive clinging to the path, and the cessation of obsessive clinging to all phenomena.

First, these practices are subsumed under the heading of the ten unsurpassed conducts[126] and special individual practices. These are gradual practices on the lack of inherent existence of perceived objects.

Second, this gradual practice on the lack of inherent existence is taken after the Bön priest the enlightened Shenrab, the object of refuge.

Third, this gradual practice on the lack of inherent existence in perceived objects is taken as the method of the god of wisdom.

Fourth, the gradual practice on the lack of inherent existence is taken through all phenomena of cyclic existence and transcendence. The *Compendium on the Spreading* says:

> If heroes of everlastingness train in complete extinction, then all scholars train themselves like this.

And:

> If the unsurpassable journey of Shenrab is accomplished, then everyone as well as scholars must themselves train like him.
>
> If one must perform in order to reach the unsurpassable wisdom, then one must perform in the vastness of the heart of intrinsic reality.

The mode of meditation

Next is the mode of meditation: First comes training, followed by gradual meditation practice on the subject, as before. Having meditated in a gradual manner on the lack of inherent existence for the benefit of acquiring the instantaneous body of the absolute, one will definitely obtain cessation, the instantaneous body of the absolute, and similarly for the mental continuum of meditators and so forth.

Third, **dispelling objections**:

[Question:] In the stage of the Peak, does one meditate in a gradual manner on knowables? For instance, if one meditates, will one gradually attain it? If one does not meditate, there will be no particular instantaneous realization.

[Answer:] There is no meditation, since one has acquired the power to transform all knowables. When one meditates gradually during the stage of the Peak, there will be a gradual realization, and so within these two, one will settle into a meditative state. Through this, one will be taught the practice of subsequent attainment.

Third, the **precise definition** is that through meditation in a gradual manner, finality will arise.

On the momentary

Fourth, the topic on that which is momentary is threefold:

First, the **defining characteristic** of the practice is to meditate using the ability of the ordinary mind, step by step from the dominant conditions up until finality, to realize in a sudden manner that all phenomena have no inherent existence. The defining characteristic for each and every meditation and post-meditation practice is the same as above.

Second, the topic of the **bearer of characteristics** is threefold: the divisions of application, the mode of meditation, and dispelling objections.

The divisions of application

The first topic is fourfold:

1. The sudden ripening of non-existent karma happens in a state of meditation when in one instant one comes to the realization that there is a unique essence to ordinary mind and to all white phenomena, such as giving, and so forth. [76]

2. The sudden ripening of aspects comes in a state of meditation with the sudden realization of the one essence of all phenomena of ripened aspects of the path of training.

3. The moment of the absence of specific characteristics comes when one meditates and has the sudden realization that there is one essence to the ordinary mind and to intrinsic reality in the inexhaustibility of all phenomena.

4. The moment of non-duality comes when one meditates and has the sudden realization that there is one essence to the ordinary mind and

intrinsic reality that is the emptiness of the duality of subject and object. Furthermore, the *Compendium on the Spreading* (3.155.1) says:

> One comes to realization in one moment. In that single moment, one becomes an enlightened one.

The mode of meditation

Next, the mode of meditation is gradual meditation as before, and that gradually gives rise to nothingness. "It is engaging in the meditation of the intrinsic absolute truth itself. It is engaging with the overwhelming ground of the universal light."

Dispelling objections

[Argument:] When there is a momentary end to the continuum of existence, others postulate that there is no possible application here. But this is contradictory! If so, then one could say that a single moment of meditation could not ever possibly exist.

[Answer:] Where there is gradual production, there is no Suchness. In the existing duality of the others, it comes to be that there is no instant of meditation. The Peak in all of its aspects and sudden realization of the single essence are different entities.

Third, the **precise definition**: Is there this single moment of realization in meditation or not? To put it this way, others will not settle this argument until they experience the sudden moment of enlightenment. On this third point, there is one certainty: there is the practice of meditation when one takes on the path of the heroes of everlastingness together with the application of the essential point of intrinsic reality.

This third topic has a **function**. It is to train through the continuum of the path. It is to practice in order to bring one to obtain enlightenment, the end result.

Activities on the path of meditation

Third, the topic of **activities on the path of meditation** is threefold: boundaries of the grounds, categories, and individual points.

Boundaries of the grounds

The first topic is threefold:

[Argument:] First, someone from **the tradition of the others** has imputed that the paths of accumulation and application have all the characteristics of the paths of vision and meditation. The last two are superior levels and cannot be directly realized as a path. The path, awareness, contemplative accomplishments, and deliverance—these four, according to the others—would then cease to be.

[Answer:] Not so. If it were the case, spiritual attainment would not even exist! And since one would be able to attain the paths of vision and meditation through the paths of accumulation and application, then as long as it would not be a subjective metaphor, the approach would be in vain. If there would be no direct realization, there would be no final realization, no enlightened ones, and a path would be preposterous!

Second, **our own tradition** is that these are dialectical answers because these are false attainments. [77] Moreover, between the stages of practicing the perfection of giving to the state of knowing of all aspects [i.e., omniscience], first there is the generation of the mind of enlightenment up to the not-yet-attained fruition. The *Summary of the Hundred Thousand* says:

> From the first ground up until the unattained result . . .

[Argument:] Third is **dispelling objections**: The point that was raised about the four characteristics of the path is that there is really no-self present on the paths of accumulation and application.

[Answer:] There is no fault here. These are not established as existing as intrinsic characteristics of the common path, the mundane in particular, or the distinctive path of transcendence.

Categories

The second topic on categories has five points [i.e., the five paths]. Whenever there is a general assertion, it includes a basis for division into categories. Essence, accumulation, application, vision, and meditation: these five represent such categories. The *Summary of the Hundred Thousand* mentions these as "the six paths."

[Argument:] Causative factors either have nothing to do with direct realization of emptiness or have something to do with direct realization.

[Answer:] In the first case where there is no understanding of the common meaning, then the path to liberation will not come to be. If there is direct realization, then with learning and reflecting one realizes that there is the path of accumulation. With the arising of meditative states, one comes to the realization that posits the path of application. Among these two, if there is only direct realization, then this will also include abiding on the path of vision, and the action of meditating on one's realization will put one on the path of meditation. These will bring one to the completion of finality.

These are the divisions based on the differences of before and after, cause and fruition.

[Argument:] Concerning their number, are there four causal characteristics? The continuum is either not ripe or ripe, or ranges from mature to liberation, and from liberation to the reaching of finality.

[Answer:] With respect to the three stages, ascertaining these is as follows: First are the paths of accumulation and application. Next, one relies on these and comes to the paths of vision and meditation. Third, relying on these, one comes to the path of reaching finality.

There are four aspects to the inherent nature that supports application on the path. They are said to be, respectively: the aspects of the Peak that are gradual or sudden, the delineation of the good mode of the path, the paraphrased commentaries on the manner of the general points of the path, and its explanation.

This ends the third chapter on the nature of the common path from the *Magical Key to the Precious Stages of the Path and the Grounds of the Greater Vehicle.* [78]

4. Teachings on the Worldly Path of Accumulation

Divisions along individual points

The third topic that is concerned with the divisions along individual points is fourfold.

First, the teachings on the path of accumulation are in three parts: cause, nature, and function.

The cause of the path of accumulation

First, the cause is a "person" that is the support. The reasoning on this has been extensively explained previously. The second point concerns the path of accumulation. Whether it takes three incalculable eons or one, and so forth, to complete depends on the power of merit. The *Eye of the Needle* (16.521.5) says:

> It is through the power of merit that the one endowed with merit, the strong one, comes to the realm of accumulation of powerful merit as a teacher.

Third, about the grounds, the *Eye of the Needle* (14.399.6) says:

> Among the three realms, it is the grounds that support the nine grounds of the three realms that are suitable to support rebirth.

Nature of the path of accumulation

Second, the topic of the nature of the path of accumulation is threefold: defining characteristic, its divisions, and definition.

Defining characteristic

The first topic has three parts:

[Arguments:] First, the teacher of the Pa clan[127] who was from the tradition of the others said that enlightenment is the cause of obtaining it. Zhang[128] said that the generation of the continuum of the path comes from the virtues of the preliminary practices.

[Answer:] However, this is an overemphasis on spiritual heroism.

[Arguments:] Dopa said that sound symbols are taken as devoid of inherent self when taken as skillful means.

[Answer:] Reasoning consciousness can correct an overextension on the path of application.

[Arguments:] Again, another said that wisdom arises from studying and pondering worldly knowledge with the generation of the mind for the sake of others. This will enable one to reach the path of application as well as transcendence of suffering of the not-yet-produced stage of Heat.

[Answer:] But it is not so. Studying and pondering generate the path of application. The path of accumulation is the essence of studying and pondering. The point reached prior to the stage of Heat demarcates these two. If one can attain these in cyclic existence or in transcendence, then there won't be any path of transcendence to Suchness. Even the great Lodrö said that to first reach the clear vision of worldly insight is an overreach concerning the path of application.

Our own tradition

Second, in our own tradition, master Drimé Chökyi Chanden (fl. twelfth–thirteenth centuries) said that one would get there through the wisdom of studying and pondering the world.

Dispelling objections

Third is the dispelling of objections:

[Arguments:] Is the path of accumulation generated by meditation or not? Someone countered this, saying: "In the first case, the path of application will not have any particularities. In the second case, what is being said about the activities of meditating on the path?"

[Answer:] However much development there is in meditation, it is but

a small understanding of the meditation process. If one is mainly studying and pondering, there won't be any changes on the path of application,
and one will not become endowed with clear visions. In the opposite case,
[79] the miraculous supporting powers will not arise despite very pure
relinquishment.

Divisions

The second topic on its divisions is threefold: ground boundaries, enumeration, and individual points.

Ground boundaries

The first division in the grounds starts with the first ground where there is
the generation of the mind of enlightenment up to the stage where the stage
of Heat is not yet reached.

Enumeration

The second point, the enumeration of the stages is twofold: the essence of
the activity of meditating and the number of its different aspects.

The essence of the activity of meditating

First, on the path of accumulation, meditation has these five paths that are
synonymous with the paths leading to liberation. The *Summary of the Hundred Thousand* says:

> The generation of the mind of enlightenment is conducive and
> partial to liberation.

On this, there are three main points:

The first is about its **defining characteristic**.

[Argument:] If someone says: "Generating the mind of enlightenment is
the virtue that is the primary cause of ripening."

[Answer:] This is an overreaching statement, since the root of virtue is a
compounded phenomenon. Therefore, the root of virtue that is the primary

cause for the transcendence of suffering cannot be the essence of this transformative power.

Second, as for the **bearer of this characteristic**, it is solely the path of accumulation that demarcates this ground and up to abiding with transformative power at the stage of Heat. In a different division scheme, having persevered with faith consists in the wisdom of mindful concentration. As such, one will rise above from below.

Faith has the aspiration to enlightenment and so forth as its object. It practices the perfections and so forth. It seizes the understanding of the method of diligence. It remembers to be mindful and not to fail the Greater Vehicle. It uses formulas of concentration in the practice of non-conceptual meditation, and it meditates on the non-perception of objects with wisdom.

Third, a **precise definition**: There are three general conducive aspects to merit, liberation, and ascertainment. First is the moment when one has not yet entered the path. Next is the path of accumulation. Third is the path of application. It is said that the realization of their aspects is analogous to the transcendence of suffering.

The number of its different aspects

The second point is fivefold: The base is the defining characteristic that is always pervasive. The essence is small, intermediate, or large. There are four objects of mindful recollection.

Causal characteristics

The causal characteristics consist in the object to be eliminated as well as being mindful of the close application of the antidote. With these, one engages the elimination process and differentiates the three attainments—the limbs of elimination—in order to separate the differentiation of entities. One can ascertain the objects to be eliminated, which are finite in number, through the mode of suppression of the above.

1. THE APPLICATIONS OF MINDFUL RECOLLECTION

This third topic on individual points is threefold: the application of the smaller manner of mindful recollection to the path of accumulation, of the middling manner that is correct elimination, and of the great manner that is "the [four] bases of miraculous power" [lit. "the four miraculous feet"].

The application of mindful recollection in a smaller manner

The first is threefold:

Cause: When a first thought is produced, one stops the object that is its source.

Second, its **defining characteristic** resides in the inherent nature of mindfulness, the manner of meditating on the variety of phenomena that are perceived, and their notable differences. [80]

First, one meditates with mindful recollection on a general imputed designation. Second, one applies the four recollections to the body, feelings, mind, and phenomena. One then engages in the contemplation of the four truths, the suffering engendered by the misfortune of abiding in this body, the arising of feelings on the basis of comfort and discomfort, and the separation of all thoughts from the notion of a self. Then eliminate all discordances of self and phenomena.

The third part deals with **perceived objects**, their aspects, and the mode of meditation.

First [i.e., on **perceived objects**], there are the five aggregates of form, feelings, consciousness, discrimination, and compositional factors. Furthermore, the five aggregates are not contradictory to the establishment of mindful recollection. The last two [i.e., discrimination and compositional factors] are part of the practice of mindful recollection on phenomena.

Second, **their four aspects** are: the body is impure, feelings are suffering, mind is impermanent, and phenomena are devoid of an inherently existent self. One must meditate that they are illusory and their inherent nature is like the sky, all-encompassing, universally outspread as one engages in each and every item above, providing the antidote to craving and so forth, [while] meditating.

Third, there are **four modes of meditation:**

First, **the application of mindful recollection to the body** is threefold:

Its **defining characteristic** is introspection on forms that are thoroughly imputed. Its **differentiation** consists in the form of its inherent nature. Then there are the following three on this topic: cause, result, and active reasoning that demonstrate non-existence. The modes of meditation of the Lower

Vehicle consist in mindful recollection of the thirty-three impure entities perceived in the body. The *Compendium on the Spreading* says:

> Who is it that goes to the cemetery? If it is the skull that is seen, then the skull of the self appears to be impermanent.

A scripture says:

> The greater ones perceive the bodies of sentient beings. The antidote to the emanation of the universal all is that one abides in meditative equipoise in non-production and one puts into practice the application of the negation of aspects. During the post-meditation period, one meditates on the mirage-like method. Form has no inherent existence. Wherever it is, it has no inherent existence. The awareness of the very pure and the learned ones rises in inherent reality.[129]

One must meditate on the pristine awareness of the antidotes to delusion that are the five antidotes, the main suppressors of any aspect [of delusion]. The *Eye of the Needle* (15.430.7) says:

> Delusion is pacified in the abyss of pristine awareness.

Second, **the application of mindful recollection to craving** is threefold:

Its **defining characteristic** consists in the introspection of the wholly designated aggregate of feelings.

Its **differentiation** consists in the transformation of the pleasure and suffering of the craving for inherent existence using equanimity toward the three [81] [kinds of feeling].[130]

The **mode of meditation** is the meditation on suffering coming from objects perceived and one's subsequent sensations until they are completely rooted out in a similar fashion as above. One meditates on the application of the antidote to craving for each of the main five poisons.[131] The *Eye of the Needle* (15.30.5) says:

> Cravings are pacified in the abyss of the application of the antidotes.

Third, **the application of mindfulness to the mind** is threefold:

Its **defining characteristic** is introspection on consciousness that designates everything.

Its **differentiation** consists in transforming using the three kinds of reversal and engaging all of the eight kinds of nature. The mode of meditation is on impermanence coming from the objects of perception in the mind and what follows, as before.

One **meditates** on love, the antidote to anger, among each of the five main poisons. The *Eye of the Needle* (15.29.6) says:

Anger will be pacified in the depths of love.

Fourth, **the application of mindfulness to phenomena** is threefold:

Its **defining characteristic** is to have introspection in regard to all that is cognized of the aggregates of discrimination and compositional factors.

Its **differentiation** consists in the two processes of discriminating their nature and compositional factors. First, there are these three: how large they are, how small they are, and the incalculability of their sizes and other factors. Next, is to investigate the fifty-one mental factors.[132]

The **mode of meditation** consists in meditating on the absence of self in phenomena and following that as before. The pacifying is done with the antidote to pride for each of the main poisons, and one meditates extensively on jealousy. The *Eye of the Needle* (15.431.5) says:

Pride will be pacified in the abyss of pacification.

The *Eye of the Needle* (15.531.5) says:

Jealousy will be pacified in the abyss of vastness.

Function

Third, their **function** is to produce elimination in one's continuum.

2. THE CORRECT PROCESSES OF ELIMINATION

The topic of the four correct processes of elimination is threefold: cause, inherent nature, and function.

Cause

First, one must have appropriated some accomplishment in the practice of the meditative application of mindful recollection.

Inherent nature

The second topic on inherent nature is threefold: defining characteristic, insight of the mind regarding elimination, and congruence with mental events.

Next, the *Realm of Emptiness* mentions that it [i.e., the **defining characteristic**] consists in the four divisions of the general class of non-virtues and the three divisions of the three doors [i.e., body, speech, and mind].

Insight of the mind regarding elimination

The *Treasury* and the *Realms of Awareness* mention the following four: traces of existence and non-existence cannot be seen, and it is correct to eliminate these false memories; one should not make use of the views of either eternalism or nihilism; one should not rationalize the mistaken views that one is following; and one should not ponder on the causes of the antidotes. [82]

The above are said to be part of the subsequent attainments, and [what comes] later are the meditative states. Furthermore, the *Compendium on the Spreading* says:

> There are these four: commitment and efforts, diligence, mental effort, and holding on to the [right] attitude.

Then, suffering is not generated. There is no production. Phenomena produced are automatically eliminated. Antidotes generate non-production as opposed to when created phenomena are increasing.

Congruence with mental events

Third, **the mode of meditation** is threefold:

First, on the perception of objects, what are those non-virtuous ones? They are the four things to abandon: the views on existence and non-existence, holding on to the views of eternalism or nihilism, lethargy or agitation in meditation, and the duality of subject and object.

Second, every aspect of the above is to be suppressed as well as rooted out completely.

Third, on the mode of meditation, the *Treasury* (18.71.5) says:

> Meditating through the practice of the meditative states and subsequent attainments is conducted in a similar manner. There is no inherent nature to the four thorough elimination processes.

For that reason, one should generate the aspiration to abandon ideas of holding on to extreme views, and keep one's ambition to make efforts. One should meditate continually with forbearance. One should train with mental effort in the use of the antidotes to lethargy or agitation. Controlling one's mind well, one should meditate continually on non-perception, joining the separate practices of calm abiding and special insight.

Third, its **function** consists in the activities of realizing the bases of miraculous power.

3. THE BASES OF MIRACULOUS POWER[133]

The third topic on the bases of miraculous power is threefold: cause, nature, and function.

First, the **causes** [of the bases of miraculous power] are the correct [manners of] eliminating, and the elimination of the five stains of wrongdoing.

Second, the topic on their **defining characteristics** is threefold:

First, there are branches to the activities of the many transformations of the many aspects, such as for one's own five aggregates, all the way to the use of formulas of concentration [i.e., *dhāraṇī*].

Second, there are three main divisions concerning the roots, intermediate period, and increase.

The roots

First, although it is said that there are four roots—concentration on devotion, aspiration, clear realization, and concentration on the state of equanimity—according to the *Compendium on the Spreading*, these [four roots] are aspiration, the heroes of everlastingness, forbearance, and deeds. These are the causal agents of production.

Second, there are the causal agents endowed with the eight compositional factors to be eliminated. These are said to be the bases for miraculous power. These eight are faith, aspiration, diligence, extreme purity, mindful recollection, introspection, heroism, and equanimity.

Third, each of the four roots can be further divided into eight, which all together make thirty-two. [83]

The modes of meditation

The third topic on the **modes of meditation** on observation is threefold:

First, one should observe these five: laziness, distracted mind, faults and qualities, dullness, and agitation. These objects once perceived should be eliminated.

Second, there are eight aspects mentioned above that are the objects to be eliminated and renounced. Furthermore, when meditation practice is not yet stable and laziness arises, it should be discarded by means of the four antidotes of faith, motivation, diligence, and pliancy. In this manner, motivation will incite the casual mode and perseverance will incite manners of results. The cause of these two is faith, while pliancy is the resulting activity.

Furthermore, at the time of the first approach, if forgetfulness arises, its antidote is to remain mindful. At the moment of engaging the main practice, when faults and qualities arise, the antidote is to guard introspection. At the moment of ending the main practice, if dullness is present, the antidote to non-action is spiritual heroism (*sems dpa'*). The antidote to agitation and non-action is to activate equanimity. These are the eight.

The great Lodrö said: "When engaging in practice, one can reject the partiality of laziness with faith, aspiration, diligence, and pliancy. When one is approaching, if one forgets the four recollections, introspection, heroism, and equanimity, one can analyze faults and qualities, and then dullness and agitation will be eliminated."

Third, the **modes of meditation** consist in these two: to recognize reality with knowledge and awareness. The first point is identical to the one mentioned above. The *Treasury* (18.21.5) says:

> The miraculous bases have no inherent existence. They are indeed
> the cognizance that there is no inherent existence anywhere.

Intermediate period

This second point is threefold:

First is the **refutation** of the tradition of the others.

[Argument:] Someone said that there is insight from learning and pondering, and that will give rise to meditative states because there must be a cause for meditation.

[Answer:] But it is not so. If it were, there would have to be a cause in order to have [final] fruition. There would have to be a sprout inside the shape of this continuum. When meditation arises, then there would have to be an existing one endowed with vivid clarity.

[Argument:] Furthermore, someone said that there is no arising of meditation from learning and pondering.

[Answer:] It is not so; otherwise, having applied mindful recollection to meditation, there would be no giving rise to the process of correct elimination.

[Argument:] Furthermore, the great Lodrö himself said: "An inherent self could be inferred and assumed on behalf of a substantial entity when there is a cognizer that makes the decision on behalf of reasoning. An individual can be assumed by inference on behalf of following after faith and knowledge (*rig pa*)."

[Answer:] Not so. The faith that follows [84] from the scriptures and the words of the masters implies valid scriptures and concepts that are correctly implicit with experience, and so forth.

[Argument:] One can counter that these two are not reliable.

[Answer:] If these do not matter, then it would seem that listening and pondering do not matter either.

Second, our own tradition [states] that indeed there is the arising of meditation and also that listening and pondering is most important. The *Hundred Thousand* says:

> Being mindful of the illusory and eliminating endowed compositional factors are the miraculous bases. Those who listen to Bön and ponder with insight are devoid of inherent self.

For that reason, if you attend to substantial entities as a subsequent knower with reasoning, valid scripture, and inferences, it will change all these three so that a person following reasoning will truly be able to infer reliable concepts. Following faith is an authentic teaching of valid cognition and the scriptures. As for reasoning, one engages holding on to realization through subsequent cognition and the concepts of existence.

Third, dispelling objections

[Argument:] It logically follows that the generation of clear and manifest perceptible objects is true.
[Answer:] But it is not so. There is meditation, but there is no production of clear appearances that are pervasive.

Function

Third, function: One eliminates the five faulty stains while one is bound to action with the generation of the mind of enlightenment on the continuum of the path of application.

Third, the **precise definition**: The accumulation of indispensable prerequisites applicable to the vessel.

Third, its **function** rests in the application of rejecting the objects to be eliminated while the fortunate one is actively producing the continuum of the path of application.

Thus it is said: "The prerequisites of merit arise when insight in meditation based on studying and pondering on the world brings realization on the path of the four and the thirty-two. Through practice, one comes to realize the concordant aspects of liberation."

This was the fourth chapter on the worldly path of accumulation from the *Magical Key to the Precious Stages of the Path and the Grounds of the Greater Vehicle.* [85]

5. Teachings on the Worldly Path of Application

1. TEACHINGS ON THE PATH OF APPLICATION

Next, there is the path of application. As such, having relied on studying and pondering, one can generate a general understanding of it. From that, one can have a clear vision of the path of application. This section has three parts: cause, inherent nature, and function.

Cause

The first topic is threefold: the support, accumulations, and the grounds.

The support

First, the support of the body has been dealt with above. The support of the mind is the collection of aspects on liberation that has been established on the path of accumulation.

Accumulations

Second, accumulations of merit rely on the work of the sense faculties and present mostly on the ground of the path of accumulation.

The grounds

Third, merit arises from the support of the six realms of rebirth and causes the path of vision to emerge.

Inherent nature

Second, the topic of the nature of the path of application is threefold: defining characteristic, subdivisions, and definition.

Defining characteristic

The first topic is threefold:.

[Argument:] Someone from **the tradition of the others** said that the vision of the arising of pristine cognition that is great compassion emerges from the practice of meditation on the worldly path of vision.

[Answer:] This is a logical absurdity.

[Argument:] Again, someone said that intrinsic reality consists in the realization of the general aspects [of the path] and that it emerges on the path of accumulation.

[Answer:] This is an overreaching statement.

[Argument:] Furthermore, Dopa said that insight arising from meditation on the world is the substantial cause for the path of vision.

[Answer:] This is only relevant for the path of application when it is conjoined with the method on insight arising from meditation on the world. The path of application of the Greater Vehicle is the substantial cause for the path of vision. That substantial cause entails the perfection of patience and the other perfections below, coming from the teachings of Highest Bön. Nonetheless, when there is a substantial cause on the stream of the continuum of existence, it entails teachings from Highest Bön. However, if one is on the path of the accumulation of merit, then this will only arise through meditation.

[Argument:] Someone stipulated that having perfected the greater path of accumulation, the path of vision would only be generated when one reaches transcendence from sorrow. And when the practice of meditation on the world begins to arise on the greater path of accumulation, then insight will suitably provide a substantial cause for the path of vision to be reached.

. The Lord said: "There are demarcations of the grounds and they do not entail that one has to have reached final completion for the processes to connect. Furthermore, the insight arising from meditation on the world produces a clear vision regarding the realization of the intrinsic reality for one, and thereby the path of vision can be reached."

Furthermore, the great Lodrö said: "When one has passed the demarcations of the grounds and the continuum of the path, it does not entail that one will reach them during meditation. But the one who has a clear vision has reached the insight arising from meditation on the world."

[Answer:] It is an overextension to state that the path of vision arises from the practice of meditation on the world. [86]

Second, **our own tradition** [holds] that the general meaning of the arising of insight can be reached through the acquisition of clear vision through meditation on the world.

Third is the **dispelling objection:**

[Question:] Extraordinary clarity of vision is the path of vision. Does it consist only in the realization of the common meaning, and does it exist on the path of accumulation [of merit]?

[Answer:] There is no fault in this! This is not the path of vision, but is only a clear vision that has been acquired.

Basis of characteristic

Second, the topic on the bearer of characteristic is threefold: boundaries of the ground, enumeration, and individual points.

Boundaries of the ground

First, the continuum of the path of vision will not be generated until one has experienced the realizations of the great path of accumulation.

Enumeration

Next, the topic on enumeration is threefold: actual divisions, their nature, and advantages.

Actual divisions

First, the basic division is the path of application only. The essential of its subdivisions are Heat, Peak, Forbearance, and Highest Bön. The *Hundred Thousand* says:

> Having obtained the manifestation of the stage of Heat, the stage of Peak then unfolds its manifestations. Forbearance then

enters the main point of Suchness itself, the unobstructed path of Highest Bön of the world.

One has realizations through relying on the four aspects of cause, characteristic, subject, and object. With respect to the four realizations of the lack of inherent existence of thorough affliction, one can then differentiate the reliance on antidotes, the holding on to the substance[134] of individuality, and the fixation on the permanence of beings. The main point of these divisions is [to identify] the modes of production of the continuum of existence that is limited to one person, the self. One has to ascertain these four objects that need to be negated.

Their nature

The second topic is threefold: the inherent nature of the objects of meditation, the mode of realization, and the mental awareness during the practice of meditation.

The inherent nature of the objects of meditation

The first topic is threefold: objects of observation, their aspects, and the mode of meditation.

Objects of observation

First, in general, grasping on an essential idea is the common basis for conceiving others' attributes, such as a vase. This, in particular, concerns the two or the four truths with perception in the mode of inherent emptiness and illusion. Using this [mode of perception], there are four kinds of objects to be eliminated, which are the four concepts, as below.

Their aspects

The second topic [i.e., their aspects] is threefold: the means to realize pristine awareness; the object of realization, the subject, and the object; and the refutation of the mode of realization as aspects of completion.

The means to realize pristine awareness

First, insight arising in meditation on the world is one that brings a clear vision to the aspects of the general meaning of inherent reality. Furthermore, these will be explained below as four.

The object of realization, the subject, and the object

Second, the topic on the object of realization is threefold: common recognition of an entity, special recognition, and the mode of conceptual consciousness of just-as-it-is (*ji ltar*).

The common recognition of an entity

The first one, the common recognition of an entity, consists in the assertion of the sensory sphere in the outer and the inner [context]. That is what belongs to the self and what is different from the self. It is considered that object and subject are in consciousness. [87] If one reverses [this process], then it is similar. The self is not proven and what belongs to the self is therefore unborn.

[Argument:] Some say that the substantial cause of object and subject exists by themselves.

[Answer:] If it is so, then as for the object possessor that is momentarily seized when it is related to the subject, the stream of consciousness has to hold both subject and object. If they are not related, then the assertion is faulty. For that reason, the *Summary of the Hundred Thousand* says:

> An object is a conception of a phenomenon, and the subject is a conception of the one endowed with the phenomenon. All isolated phenomena are what are seized, while all that are isolated and endowed with an object are the seizers.

Thereupon, the *Summary of the Hundred Thousand* says:

> The concept of the phenomenon, and the concept of the one endowed with the phenomenon [i.e., the subject] are both objects. The concept of the phenomenon and the concept endowed with the phenomenon are both concepts that are grasped.

Special recognition

The second topic is fourfold:

First, the concepts of thorough affliction, the realms of the aggregates, the sensory sphere, the twelve interdependent links, and so forth are combined in the continuum of the arising of all suffering and are related to the objects to be abandoned.

Second, the concepts of relying on antidotes, the ten unsurpassable [i.e., the ten perfections], the eighteen emptinesses, the thirty-seven paths[135] [i.e., the practices of the heroes of everlastingness], and so forth are collected in the paths and cessation and are related to the antidotes.

Third, individuality, substantial entity, and a permanent self, alone and independent, are related to the experience of phenomena.

Fourth, a being is not a concept to hold on to and to apprehend as a designation as such. Only the continuum of the five aggregates is attached and joins the action of the objects with the designated terms "sentient beings" or "heroes of everlastingness." The *Summary of the Hundred Thousand* says:

> The existence of affliction is a concept. The existence of antidotes
> is a concept.

The *Summary of the Hundred Thousand* further says:

> One pays attention and looks at other people, but one really
> looks at a body and a mental concept.

The mode of conceptual consciousness of just-as-it-is

Third, the mode of realization is twofold:

First, in **the four possibilities of real concepts**, there is what is believed to be a single object, such as the conceptual object of a vase. What is believed to be a single object is likened to a concept in a moment of consciousness. These two are like "a concept in the stream of consciousness." These two "do not truly exist, just like meditative visions in meditation."

Second, **the dispelling of objection** is fourfold:

First, the *Treasury* (62.3) says:

A color is clearly a sense object, yet color is in the expanse of the mind.

And the *Hundred Thousand* says:

Forms are the nature of the mind. Clarity brings about the result of pristine cognition.

[Argument:] Someone asked if these [i.e., forms and mind] are mutually contradictory?

[Answer:] There is no fault here. The realization is that the phenomenon itself is an object, and that indeed reflects the longing in the mind for the holder of the vase. [88] Hence, the beholder of the thought phenomenon, itself in the mind, does not exist.

[Argument:] Second, what if someone says that momentary realizations that exist do not exist as objects?

[Answer:] There is no real phenomenon at any moment in time and space. The moment has passed and one can accept the realization of that which is gone to annihilation.

[Argument:] However, if the concept of a concrete individual remains, it is because there comes to be a substantial entity.

[Answer:] There is no fault here. This is a realization that posits an explicit idea. As such, if it were not so, it would contradict the existence of the concept of object and subject itself.

[Argument:] Third, what if someone asserts that fixating concepts is akin to these two—consciousness and continuity—and change according to these two?

[Answer:] There is no fault in this. The flow of continuity here relies on isolated factors. These isolated factors do not depend on the continuum, past or future.

[Argument:] Fourth, when there is meditative equipoise during meditation practice on the path of vision, there is no mind and nothing that arises in the mind.

[Answer:] This is not a faulty consequence. When the mind is appeased— is without proliferating concepts—there is no reversion to the conceptual.

2. THE CONCEPTS OF SUBJECT AND OBJECT

Third, the topics of negating and affirming have three parts: the defining characteristic of concepts, the bearer of characteristics, and precise definition.

The defining characteristic of concepts

First, in general, despite the fact that concepts are suitably seized upon and mixed, here in this present context they are associated with clinging.

The bearer of characteristics

Second, the topic of what bears characteristics that are attributed is three-fold: the demarcation of the grounds, their numeration, and individual points.

The demarcation of the grounds

[Argument:] First, someone said: "If meditative equipoise has the stages of Heat and so forth, then in these stages there are no concepts whatsoever. When one is in the state of subsequent attainment, concepts are established."

[Answer:] Insight in meditative equipoise brings about the direct realization of intrinsic reality, free from conceptuality.

[Argument:] Again, someone said: "If there are these in meditative equipoise, then there are no distinctions between concepts that manifest, sound, and meaning."

[Answer:] Furthermore, in the state of meditative equipoise there would be no attainment of vivid clarity without elaborations. For that reason, if there is direct subsequent attainment, both are present. If there is meditative equipoise, concepts are negated. The concepts "subject" and "object" are refuted because in meditative equipoise there is vivid clarity.

[Argument:] Again, Dopa posits the idea that object and subject are used for the realization of the ultimate reality of emptiness in a non-visionary manner. Visions are discarded when not separated from karmic seeds. Ignorance suppresses direct cognition of the intrinsic reality of emptiness.

[Answer:] Not so. If that were so, then it would negate the elimination of the path of vision, and if this were to happen, then it would affirm that there is elimination on the path of vision. In the first case, it changes the path of vision. In the second case, it would reverse the concept of attainment.

[Argument:] Therefore, if direct perception of the innate reality of the negation of subject and object is the object to be eliminated, [89] then not seeing is supporting the negated concepts. The conception that antidotes exist posits the concept of attainment through concepts from the four sense-objects [i.e., sound, smell, taste, and form].

[Answer:] For that reason, if there is meditative equipoise on the path of vision and above, these two [subject and object] are not there. If there is subsequent attainment, then there is the distinct aspect of negation.

[Argument:] There is the case of some traditions that explains the idea that awareness is efficient in this.

[Answer:] There is no fault here. For that reason, it is said that ordinary mind that conceptualizes everything does not obtain the knowledge of all aspects [i.e., omniscience].

Enumeration

Second, enumeration is twofold: entities and dispelling objections.

Entities

First, grasping at subjects and objects of phenomena is to conceptualize about elimination using the antidotes as positive concepts. This conceptualizing is contradictory.

[Argument:] Second, in this case, are these positive concepts illusory objects grasping at conventional reality? First, if they are not illusory, then the misconception of the lack of inherent existence will not be severed. Second, if they are illusory, then there will be no need to abandon concepts, or so they have said.

[Answer:] The answer to this is threefold:

[Argument:] First, someone says that concepts are exclusively mistaken. The object apprehended, in truth, is a concept fixed through conceiving an accepted referent. The holder of the object, in truth, is adhering to something that he is holding, which is a concept held. For that reason, the truth on suffering that is apprehended, the object, is to have the conception hold on to the apprehended object to be purified. The object to be purified is the concept.

[Answer:] But it is not so. In that case, elimination would not be dependent on the meditative state of the four true distinctions.[136] The objects apprehended in the stage of subsequent attainment would be eliminated by the apprehending consciousness itself.

Second, **our own tradition** is that these arise in-between as subjects and objects through delusion. As such, adherence to their very own nature as apprehended and apprehender is deceptive. Therefore, misconceptions are then not severed. When the referent object is not experienced, it is because the four antidotes have eliminated it.

Third, **dispelling the objections:**

[Argument:] Someone said that when consciousness acts on an object, it changes into an upheld concept.

[Answer:] But is it referring here to the consciousness of the object or the action of realizing Suchness? First, this is included in the assertion on the two truths [presented] earlier.

Individual points

Third, individual points concern the four subjects and objects and the four antidotes. [See below.]

Precise definition

Third, the definition: The ordinary mind that grasps referents is taking in the different aspects of the processes of stopping and establishing.

The modes of meditation

Third, the modes of meditation are treated in two sections: meditations on the sensory fields in the first two paths and the two subsequent meditations on strength and maintaining concentration.

Meditations on the sensory fields in the first two paths

The first point is threefold:

The **defining characteristic** is said to be the acquisition of mastery over the general aspects of the absence of self. [90]

Second, there are these five points: faith, diligence, mindfulness, concentration, and wisdom. Above and below are the transformative powers.

Third, the **mode of meditation** is the meditation on the mode of contemplation and subsequent realization. The *Hundred Thousand* (18.71.6) says:

> There is no inherent nature in the sensory fields.

The two subsequent meditations on strength and maintaining concentration

The second point is twofold: strength and concentration.

Strength

The first is threefold:

The **defining characteristic** is the acquisition of reliance on the general aspect concerning the lack of self.

Its **divisions** are the five sensory fields and the transformation of exhaustion into great strength. What are otherwise referred to as the thirteen strengths are meditations.

The **modes of meditation** are meditations through the main practice of meditation and post-meditation attainments. The *Hundred Thousand* (18.69.4) says:

> Strength is the lack of inherent existence.

Concentration

The second point is threefold:

The **defining characteristic** consists in one-pointed mind focused on the general aspects of selflessness.

Divisions consist in the non-existent, Suchness, universal illumination, causal concentration, and completely perfected concentration.

On the **modes of meditation,** The *Hundred Thousand* (18.71.6) says:

> Suchness is the time of application. The meditation on the lack
> of inherent nature is conducted at the time of the main practice.
> There is no inherent nature in concentration.

Second, the **mode of realization** is twofold: reality and distinctive analysis.

Reality

On the first one, the *Eye of the Needle*, (14.435.3) says:

> The four causes in the eastern portal are like a hoisted lamp dispelling the darkness, illuminating all the teachings on the aggregate of form. The cause in the northern quarter is like the fruit of the Amla tree placed in the palm of the hand; it describes all the teachings on the four renowned aggregates.

This saying has three main points:

[Argument:] First, **on the tradition of the others**, Me'u Pal[137] said: "Even a slight realization of the lack of inherent existence of the apprehended [i.e., the object] belongs to the stages of intermediate Heat, Great Peak, and Forbearance." The *Eye of the Needle* (14.436.2) says:

> The realization of the apprehender is Highest Bön. It is in the south where the path of vision is generated.

[Answer:] But it is not so. The significance of this evidence is not great. There is the realization of the apprehender in the stage of Heat. Even a small amount of realization of the apprehended equals the intermediary stage of the Peak, the stage of the great Forbearance, and the Highest Bön.

Second, **in our own tradition**, the realization of the apprehended is conducted through the stages of Heat and the Peak. The realization of the apprehender is conducted through the Highest Bön of Forbearance. The *Summary of the Hundred Thousand* says:

> The two lower parts of the path of application consist in eliminating the object that is apprehended outside. The two higher ones consist in eliminating the mind of the apprehender inside.

Thus, one abandons the four aspects of conception.

Dispelling objections

Third, the dispelling of objections:

One may wonder that there are no explanations of the antidotes to affliction. They are explained implicitly. They are said to be what is apprehended during the purification process.

Distinctiveness

Second, distinctiveness is threefold:

First, [91] what is distinct, and second, what is not distinct from **the tradition of the others.**

[Argument:] First, when someone says: "The four conceptions of the apprehended and apprehender are not the same as the four alternative misconceptions and are refuted as the mass of particles, sentient beings, humans, and gods. The apprehended does not exist, the same as the four alternative imputations."

[Answer:] There is no necessity for valid cognition here about the refutation of these imputations.

[Argument:] Second, someone said that while in meditative equipoise on the four kinds of direct introspection there are no distinctions between them, but there are distinctions in the aspects of the perceived objects and the qualities of their traces.

[Answer:] Again, clear appearances do not pass the four alternatives, for otherwise there would be no elimination of the four types of conceptions. One would obtain visions in the stage of Heat. Peak would be the increase in visions. The entrance in the main point of Suchness would be Forbearance. This is said to be the path with no obstruction to the supreme reality and the conditioned world. But it is contradictory.

Second, our own tradition on the four divisions of conceptions is that there are distinctions of production in regard to the four alternate propositions, the visions, and clarity of the lack of inherent self. The works previously mentioned on consciousness know this. Thus, the aspects of the objects perceived in the Lower Vehicle have the objects of awareness of the small Heat. In this, they are the aspects of the cessation of obsessions; thereafter, the lower [aspects], which are the aspects of the perceived objects of the Lower Vehicle and the higher [vehicles], are the perceived objects of the Greater Vehicle.

Third is the dispelling of objections

[Argument:] What if someone says that at the moment of cutting off fabricated imputations that are generated by meditation, the basis of the object is cut and the object becomes established in awareness. If there are no appearances then there is no cutting away of the imputations that support the object.

The answer to this is threefold:

[Argument:] First, someone from **the tradition of the others** said that non-conceptual pristine awareness presents itself when reasoning consciousness cuts fabrication in the non-manifested. This changes into accomplished awareness.

[Argument:] Another lama has said that in the state of non-conceptual pristine awareness, there is no manifestation of an essence in the appearance of intrinsic emptiness once the object is eliminated. The inference is that essence and aspects manifest as one, therefore there is no appearance to be eliminated.

[Answer:] But this is not so. The reversal of non-conceptual pristine awareness is brought about through the constructs of the ordinary mind's conceptions where awareness becomes established. The realization that inferences are intrinsically empty brings about the elimination [of what] does not [truly] exist.

[Argument:] Again, another lama said that comprehension that arises in meditation cuts off fabricated imputations, the essence of phenomena. When reversal is not comprehended, awareness is not established, and it is the non-conceptual pristine awareness that comprehends intrinsic emptiness of phenomena. Imputations are said to evaluate the elimination of phenomena.

[Answer:] But it is not so. If one assesses an essence, it establishes awareness. The reverse is non-assessment that brings about the non-eradication of fabricated imputations that supports a reversal of emptiness. Again, the assessment of intrinsic emptiness of phenomena establishes awareness. [92]

Concerning the reversal of phenomena, there is no meditative experience rising through inference and comprehension. If there were these three [the reversal of phenomena together with inference and comprehension], these would come from study and reflection. Reasoning consciousness and inferences would come with the support of study and reflection. Therefore, at this moment, it does not occur.

Second, in our own tradition, valid cognition does not manifest the basis of severing fabricated imputations. This is the common main point. The basis of the generation of the manifestation of vivid clarity appears from what is arising in the experience of meditation. Reasoning consciousness is not established on the path of application. Reasoning consciousness exists on the path of accumulation through studying and pondering. Furthermore, in meditative equipoise the person is negated, whereas in post-meditation the person is established.

Third is the dispelling of objections. Complex elaborations do not come up in meditative equipoise. This is because apprehended and apprehenders are let go in their refutation, and vivid clarity is not eliminated. These support elimination, and elimination is the accomplishment of subsequent attainment.

Mental awareness during the practice of meditation

Third is the case of the awareness of ordinary mind.

If it is asked where does this awareness of ordinary mind on the path of application come from? There are three points on this:

First, **the tradition of the others** posits that, using valid cognition, there is no ordinary mind during the practice of meditation. It refutes it with the assertion that there is no valid cognition applicable here.

[Argument:] First, someone has posited, using valid cognition, that there is direct perception.

[Answer:] It then logically follows that real objects are not conceptions.

[Argument:] Again, someone has said that there is direct yogic perception because there is the severing of the four dissimilar misconceptions in the four concrete conceptions.

[Answer:] But again there is no such thing. If it were like that, then vivid clarity would not be able to sever the misconceptions that are being generated in the general meaning of the four dissimilarities. If direct perception of the intrinsic reality of phenomena were to be established, then there would be no distinct path of vision. If it is not established, then it is a deficient claim.

[Argument:] Again, what if someone asserts that, using valid cognition, there are inferences?

[Answer:] There are no such things! Inferences on the path of accumulation engage one in grasping for realizations.

The second section has three more points:

[Argument:] First, someone has said that one can make assumptions.

[Answer:] Not so. Assumptions do not support logic and experiences. The meaning of realization is that there are real concordant factors, and from this, these [concordant factors] are clarified through [hearing] teachings, studying, and pondering on the path of accumulation.

[Argument:] Second, a lama has posited that consciousness is an array of concepts. Thus, concerning the linkage from faith, there is subsequent cognizance generated after intellectual analysis. It relies on subsequent awareness. The inferential cognizer is a subsequent cognizer in action.

[Answer:] But then again, this is not right. If it were so, then when there was a new realization in the mind, it would have come from valid cognition. If there was no [new realization], then the four objects [93] would not be the four distinctive productions of vivid clarity.

[Argument:] Someone has said that newly arisen realizations happen in substantial entities as well as in the continuum of cyclic existence.

[Answer:] Then there would be no production of the four dissimilarities of vivid clarity in the four conceptions, and if misconceptions are not severed through new realizations on substantial entities, it would contradict these new realizations. If misconceptions are cut off, then is has to come from valid cognition.

[Argument:] On that, someone said concerning the continuum of existence that it consists in the cognition of what has already been determined. However, regarding substantial entities, they are valid cognitions.

[Answer:] But it is not so. If it were so, then would direct perception of validly cognized substantial entities be inferred? In the first case [i.e., direct perception], the claim would be wrong. In the second case [i.e., valid cognition], inference would not come to be a definitive solution.

[Argument:] Third, someone said that direct yogic perception is approximate. And also, if it happens to be mistaken, then are the phenomena of the ordinary mind even real? Or are they beyond sight? Or are they thoroughly hidden? Is there no real vivid clarity?

[Answer:] In the first case, this would be a direct perception. In the second case, correct assumptions would be inferences. In the third, it would be the ordinary mind's valid cognition based on the scriptures. In the fourth, then the claim that there is vivid clarity of nothingness would be faulty.

Second, **our own tradition** [holds] that the eight types of intellectual knowledge[138] could be nothing at all. Thus, the refutations of the others would be proven. Wrong perceptions would become doubts without ascertained meaning, and the ordinary mind would then be pure. Uncertain visions would then become non-existent. Furthermore, severing the common meaning on vivid clarity would not be cut off.

[Argument:] In that case, if someone asked, "Why is there conceptuality when there are no visions?" and "When there is clarity, are there visions?" Insights arise from meditation on the world.

[Answer:] The *Arcana* (192.7) says:

> The inherent reality of the absence of manifested being is the inherent mind of the absence of differentiation.

Third, **the dispelling of objections** is about the position that the seven kinds of knowledge and awareness[139] are not a subsumed category. The scriptures explain the eight ordinary minds and the ninth when they are grouped together.

Signs, benefits, and merit

Third, the topic on signs, benefit, and merit is threefold: permanent and real entity, the mode of application by signs, and dispelling objections.

Permanent and real entity

The first topic is fourfold [i.e., the four signs of the path of application]:

The signs of the acquisition of Heat

First, the signs of the acquisition of Heat are three: the signs that one is acquiring an auspicious support,[140] the signs that one is acquiring an auspicious conduct, and the signs that one is engaging in good causes.

The signs that one is acquiring an auspicious support

The first series of signs consists of:

The support of a body

One abides in uneasiness, a being in a bad transmigration; or one has the long life of the gods, is a demi-god, or is a being in the outlying districts of the world and the three continents; or one harbors the wrong views of heretics and does not have all of one's senses. Those are the infallible signs. [94]

[Argument:] In the case of one who acquired the virtue of forbearance, what if someone objects by saying spontaneously that to exist as a human is to be in an evil reincarnation?

[Answer:] One would most likely consider saying that those of middling faculties as well as those acute faculties are not [in an evil reincarnation]. One with a mind of the unsurpassed forbearance would also think similarly.

The support of the mind

The topic of the support of ordinary mind is twofold:

First, in reality the object of insight is to reverse clinging to characteristics, be free of doubts, and become endowed with the distinctive object of faith.

Second, one is to act on that with realization and the process of elimination. First, one is to have no doubts about the relevance of profound insight, the realization of the absence of self, and one is to engage in the activities motivated by methodical love, and so forth. One acts with the mind to benefit others.

Second, one is to abandon everything completely as well as latent tendencies. Of these two, the first[141] [i.e., to abandon everything completely] consists in not meeting with the five coarse defilements: desire for sensuous pleasures, harmful intent, doubts, slothfulness, and lethargy. Ordinary mind can be completely timid, wild, or regretful, and cannot get away from these five kinds of distractions.

[Argument:] In the case where one would ask about what happens to a mind overcome with sleepiness and dullness or one set to being wild or regretful.

[Answer:] The antidote is to be applied in accord with the cause. It is just like partaking of a medicinal elixir. When weariness and so forth arise, one engages in dissolving involuntary thoughts and uses insight meditation to interrupt and eliminate these [defilements] by means of illuminating discrimination. The lower forms of kindness, agitation, and so forth are to be contemplated with intent. Then, mental distractions are interrupted with calm abiding meditation. With the contemplation of the mind in calm abiding, they are discarded. Second, all these latencies are to be abandoned.

The signs that one is acquiring an auspicious conduct

Next, there are two points on the signs of successful practice:

First are the practices subsumed under the following two: practices for the greater majority and those for oneself. One abides in virtue while establishing others in it.

Second, what is subsumed under the benefit of the others, the greater majority, are the ten perfections and the virtues of freedom dedicated to the benefit of sentient beings.

The signs that one is engaging with good causes

Third, the topic on the signs of engaging causality is twofold:

First, the transformation into one endowed with the particular qualities is accomplished through mindful introspection on impermanence.

Second, the causal transformation of devotion toward the purity of others is, as the saying goes: "Clean the body and no more lice or their eggs will arise!"

Signs of the acquisition of the Peak

Second, the topic on the signs of the acquisition of the Peak is threefold: signs about the body, signs in the activities, and signs in the mind.

Signs about the body

First, the signs about the body, is that the five hundred kinds of worms won't arise.

Signs in the activities

Second, the signs in the activities are subsumed under what is done for one's own benefit and is further subsumed in the signs of the two natures.

First, one is to seize purity in the qualities of purification. [95] Second, one is to abide in virtue while establishing virtue in others as well as being free from the disadvantageous aspects of the ten perfections.

Signs in the mind

Third, the signs in the mind are to not act on lower imaginary impulses and have sentient beings burned by the agents of hell.

Signs of the acquisition of Forbearance

Third, the signs of Forbearance are two:

First, others have no ability to lead and control their mind concerning the deceptions of the Lesser Vehicle. One must have conviction in one's own path. Second, sinful demons do come near the heroes of everlastingness. Recognize the demons' various displays of heretical teachings!

Signs of the acquisition of the Supreme Reality [i.e., Highest Bön]

Fourth, the sign of the acquisition of the supreme reality is that whatever action is performed, there is no perceptible actor in the three worlds. These actions please the enlightened ones.

The mode of application by signs

Second, the topic of the modes of application by signs is threefold:

1. Whatever action is performed, it is done without premeditation. Wherever the action is performed, it is that of the hero of everlastingness abiding in the four kinds of true insight. When it is done in this manner, the set signs are: with respect to the continuum of these beings, they are established in the signs endowed with the distinctive activities of the speech and the body of subsequent attainment, and they are established in the continuum of those endowed with the realization of meditative equipoise. What is below this stage is then completed.

For example, it is similar to the state of mind once copulation is completed. The scriptures have proven this point. In this example, where the others' streams of being are not proper, it comes to severing faults in the continuums of others.

2. Second, an individual is proven when the sign of a subject is seen. What is to be proven is a collection of the subject and the object itself. This is the proof for the continuum of others. The signs are these two: the collection of aggregates and the entailment factor.

First, the awareness of the welfare of others is established. Next, it is established in one's continuum. Those endowed with these [realizations] are the non-returners. They are endowed with and established in the realization of equanimity on the path of application. These signs have been proven through previous signs.

3. The third consists in dispelling objections:

[Argument:] Someone said that it is not possible to analyze the mind [based] on body and speech.

[Answer:] There is no fault here, because it is impossible. However, it is possible to do so through their particularities. Again, several scriptures have explained the signs of meditative equipoise. Meditative equipoise, for instance, is demonstrated in the signs of post-meditative attainment, if not explained above as the signs of the non-returners. All these three modes have been demonstrated above. [96]

3. THE FOUR CLASSES OF THE PATH OF APPLICATION

The third topic on individual meaning is fourfold:

The stage of Heat

First, the stage of Heat is threefold:

Its **defining characteristic** consists in the acquisition of vivid clarity from what arises in meditation, which is the realization that there is no self, and to stop suffering for everyone—this is the wisdom of the world.

Second, there are the three **divisions** of highest, intermediate, and elementary capacity. Therefore, in accord with the *Summary of the Hundred Thousand*, one first reaches finality and then transforms duality.

Third, the **mode of meditation** is to meditate in the modes of meditative equipoise and post-meditation. That is said to be the consciousness of no self and so forth, in all situations.

The stage of the Peak

Second, the stage of the Peak is threefold:

Its **defining characteristic** is the acquisition of vivid clarity from what arises in meditation, which is the realization that there is no self, which supports the antidote of the excellent wisdom of the world.

The three **divisions** and the two **modes of meditation** are as before.

The stage of Forbearance

Third, the stage of Forbearance:

Its **defining characteristic** is the acquisition of vivid clarity from what arises in meditation, which is the realization that there is no self or clinging to a substantial person—this is the excellent wisdom of the world.

The three **divisions** and the two **modes of meditation** [are as above].

The stage of Highest Bön

Fourth, the stage of Highest Bön [i.e., Ultimate Reality] is threefold:

Its **defining characteristic** is the acquisition of vivid clarity from what arises in meditation, which is the realization that there is neither a self nor clinging to imputed beings. It is the excellent wisdom of the world.

The three divisions and the two modes of meditation are as before.

Precise definition of the path of application

Third, its precise definition is that if transcendence of the world is achieved through the path of application, then it is confirmed by the path of transcending the world. In particular, as occurred in the previous stage of the Heat of fire, it is the arising of the heat of realization in the application of the previous antidotes. While the previous virtues proliferate, one becomes cleverer. Unbearable harm toward others will not be produced and one will become excellent in all aspects of the phenomenal world.

Divisions

Third, the divisions are said to consist in the process of eliminating the coarse object that needs to be eliminated and the suppression of the main factors while one works at generating the antidotes in the continuum of the path of vision. Thus, true insight is a branch of realization. Negation and affirmation are the modes of the array of concepts, and with the branches of concentration and power over the senses, one will obtain the annihilation of all obstacles and the mode of ascertainment.

This was the fifth chapter of the teachings on the worldly path of application from the *Magical Key to the Precious Stages of the Path and the Grounds of the Greater Vehicle.* [97]

6. Teachings on the Path of Vision

1. TEACHINGS ON THE PATH OF VISION

The third path of vision has, as its main point, transcendence of the world arising from the emergence of perceptions. This topic is threefold: cause, inherent nature, and function.

Cause

First are the cause of reality and the cause of appropriation [of the path of vision].

The cause of reality

First is the production of the four aspects of conditions and causes:

1. The causal condition [of the path of vision] consists in planting and nourishing, through former deeds, the path of generating the mind of supreme enlightenment.

2. The predominant condition is to practice the perfections on the lower paths.

3. The referential condition related to the object consists in [cultivating the direct perception of] the intrinsic reality of emptiness through the duality of the apprehended and apprehender.

4. The condition of antecedent factors is produced immediately preceding the condition of pristine awareness of supreme reality.

The cause of appropriation

Second, the cause of appropriation, is threefold: support, accumulation, and the grounds.

Support

First, the support is the same as before where it is the activity of the continuum of Highest Bön.

Accumulation

This second topic is the same as before, and it consists in the sole practice of true insight on the activities of the coarse operation of the senses.

The grounds

Third, humans are born in the realm of desire and their minds are wandering. Individuals that are born in the formless realm have coarse and unclear minds. Consequently, beings are born in the six grounds of reincarnation according to the focus that is conveniently supportive. The first concentration state is the preparatory stage to the ground of non-agitation with its main practice, followed by the main practices that are distinct in a second and in a third moment. The fourth moment concerns beings relying on the following three points: cause, inherent nature, and function.

Cause

First, in order to attain the first concentration in the realm of desire, one has to engage with the seven mental applications. The seven mental applications are the awareness of defining characteristic and the arising of the activities of faith, isolation, joy, withdrawal, practice, and mental applications up to the limits of the path of application. The result of the limits of the path of application requires no preparation to the approach to concentration but is the main practice here.

The awareness of defining characteristic

First, the realm of desire is obstinate, rough, and miserable, and one should be conscious of its basis, which is extremely unclean suffering with sensitive results. The first concentration state is the exalted realization of a solitary peace through elimination. This meditation engages the connection between studying and pondering. It is equivalent to the path of accumulation.

The arising of the activities of faith

Second, one single-pointedly abides in the aspects of coarseness and in the peace of the pointlessness of studying, pondering on the innate reality of perceived objects and their aspects. The meditation on the mode of the general meaning of the first concentration state is equivalent to the path of application.

Isolation

Third, through meditating like this, one comes to transform the three great afflictive emotions of the realm of desire by using antidotes. This is in accord with the path of vision.

Joy

Fourth, one abandons the three middling afflictions and enhances this elimination with ease of mind and body. This is in accord with the path of meditation. [98]

Withdrawal

Fifth, one abandons the greater of the smaller afflictions and the middle ones by generating thoughts on the complete non-existence of affliction. This is equivalent to the three pure grounds.

Practice and mental applications

Sixth, one then experiences and reflects on whether afflictions truly exist or do not exist. This is the same as the path of distinctiveness. Second, seeing existence, one meditates as if there were no past. Then one can transform the smaller afflictions of desire using antidotes. This is in accord with the unobstructed path. Its acquired result becomes the main part of the practice.

These modes then transform into the first then the second part of the main practice, and so forth. What is called "elimination" is at first mere suppression.

[Argument:] In that case, what if someone inquires whether the heroes of everlastingness engage with equanimity?

[Answer:] Although it is correct to say that there is engagement here, the seven mental applications concerning what is produced within the continuum of the concentration of the heroes must be engaged. Following these is similar to non-action. Moreover, the *Compendium on the Spreading* says:

> Engagement with equanimity in the concentration of the heroes of everlastingness, and their abiding in concentration, means that these are truly non-existent. This is engaging in equanimity in meditative concentration.

Inherent nature

Second, the topic on inherent nature is threefold: defining characteristic, subdivisions, and precise definition.

Defining characteristic

First, the aspects of peacefulness and harshness consist in one's mental focus.

Subdivisions

Second, subdivisions are threefold: wrong conceptions, the extinction of contamination, and the concentration that transcends the world.

Wrong conceptions

First, the teachings on concentration states have been fully developed into sixty-two views. These are the views on the concentration states of consciousness, such as being consumed by desire, pride, doubt, and extensive delusion that are all [forms of] consciousness. Using calm abiding, the anger of envy and fresh hatred no longer arise when they manifest.

[Argument:] What if someone asked how heroes apply this?

[Answer:] Some said that mentioning "applying" here is unreasonable, since heroes of everlastingness do not have any object to eliminate. Therefore there is no engagement, though there is an object to be eliminated in the concentration state. When one says that heroes do not engage even in the mode of eliminating the object to be eliminated, it means that heroes come to eliminate these when entering into a concentration state that is non-contaminated.

The extinction of contamination

Second: What is the meditation on the four immeasurables [i.e., love, joy, compassion, and equanimity] relying on?

[Answer:] The formula of meditative concentration on the totality of the grounds is applied to all manifest grounds, and so forth. According to the *Compendium on the Spreading*, meditation is the process of suppression using the power of the five antidotes, such as shining love and so forth. Then, true knowledge arises and proliferates and the heroes of everlastingness engage in equanimity.

The concentration that transcends the world

Third: How is the activity of realizing the truth completed through meditative equipoise?

[Answer:] [99] With respect to that, there are the four and the two truths, ranging from the perception of objects, taking the aspects of meditation on the non-existence of the self without exception, to the analysis of concepts on perceived objects along these truths, and the limbs of the antidotes. When renouncing with detachment, there are the two beneficial limbs of happiness and joy.

The first concentrative state rests in the Peak, a single-pointed mindedness endowed with the five aspects of inherent essence. Second, one eliminates the analysis of concepts so that there is mindful recollection, introspection, and equanimity. These are the four internal branches of the correct antidotes, generating joy from concentration, and the two branches that are benefits and happiness.

The second, the Peak of single-pointedness, is endowed with the four limbs of inherent essence.

The third is the antidote that eliminates joy and rests in these three antidotes: mindfulness, introspection, and equanimity. There is an advantage to the absence of joy, and it consists in the limbs of happiness. This third consists in being endowed with single-minded concentration on the five limbs of inherent nature.

Fourth, using the antidote of abandoning happiness, these two, mindfulness and equanimity, become extremely pure. Equanimity makes one insensitive to benefits and is the fourth immeasurable, and one becomes endowed with the four limbs of the intrinsic essence of single-minded concentration.

These are the applications of the heroes of everlastingness. The third benefit is that this concentration state will be immutable.

Function

Third, its function is that distractions are then completely abandoned.

From the second point [i.e., the extinction of contamination], one arises onto the path of vision that is threefold: its distinctive characteristic, divisions, and precise definition.

Distinctive characteristic

The first topic is threefold:

[Argument:] First, **on the tradition of the others**, the great Me'u[142] (b. 1052) said: "Intrinsic Suchness or the sphere of intrinsic reality is really perceived by those with sharp vision."

[Answer:] There is no substantial entity to an isolated appearance itself; hence it is not an entailing factor on the path of vision of pristine awareness.

[Argument:] Again, someone said: "The union of calm abiding and insight meditation on created phenomena is subsequent to the supreme reality."

[Answer:] When a second-grounder [i.e., someone treading the second of the ten spiritual grounds] sets out an overreaching definition as an example, it makes no difference between the ground and the characteristic. Accordingly, for one of lesser capacities there is no entailing factor on the path of vision.

[Argument:] Again, the lord of scripture and reason said that the meaning of higher realizations in the mode of abiding in pristine awareness on intrinsic reality can be realized directly by anyone.

[Answer:] Yet again, this is not so. Issues on intrinsic reality and pristine awareness are not to be made all-inclusive as suited. If it is proven to be valid for one single instance, it does not encompass each and every other instance.

[Argument:] Again, lama Drimé Chökyi Chanden said that the defining character of pristine awareness of intrinsic reality is realized by intelligent ones who are able to attain this realization.

[Answer:] Again, this is almost like negating the point previously stated.

[Argument:] Again, what if some [100] made scholarly assertions, such as "the direct perception of the lack of self brings a new realization," or "the lack of self-nature of both truth and falsehood is a new type of realization," or "the direct realization of the lack of self-nature of mirage-like phenomena brings a new type of realization."

[Answer:] Here, there is no consideration of distinctive characteristics between meditative and post-meditative states in the greater and common vehicles.

[Argument:] So was there previously the realization of a no-self, or was there no previous realization?

[Answer:] In the first case [i.e., no self], it contradicts that there is a new realization. In the second, it is only coincidental.

[Argument:] Someone said that one can reach transcendence of suffering once the path of meditation of the perfected supreme reality of each and every phenomenon is no longer produced. And the attainment on the path of meditation is reached in an uncontaminated moment of practice after the perfection of the realization of supreme reality.

[Answer:] Not so. The above make demarcating limits to the grounds. There is no real transcendence and there is no suffering on the path of vision. If, as above, there is this unique uncontaminated meditative moment, then it brings one onto the path of meditation. If there is no meditative moment, then it contradicts [the assertion] that there are many different moments of meditative experience. The *Summary of the Hundred Thousand* says:

> The point of the great liberation is that the existing vision that is
> the agent of meditation does not exist.

Thus, it contradicts previous assertions.

Second, **our own tradition** is that "the very characteristic of absolute Suchness is arrived at through the realization of past misunderstanding," as per the great Lodrö's own words. Similarly, the scripture says:

> Not seeing, the door of the path of seeing opens.

The *Summary of the Hundred Thousand* says something similar to this, as previously mentioned.

Third, **dispelling objections:**

[Argument:] What if someone says that the direct experience of vision alone is good for the tenth ground?

[Answer:] It is faultless. The general reasoning is that there is vision. Again, it does not follow that there is the vision of pristine awareness. There is no such a thing. Intrinsically absolute pristine awareness is [full] realization.

Basis of characteristic

Second, the topic of what bears characteristics is threefold: demarcation of the grounds, enumeration, and the mode of rejecting the object to be eliminated.

Demarcation of the grounds

First, once the realization of the greatly excellent reality is perfected, even the realization of a very small part of the path of meditation intervenes to stop the generation of the continuum of existence.

Enumeration

The second point is threefold: the common divisions, their nature, and miscellaneous points.

The common divisions

Five points:

1. A basic distinction is that a defining characteristic goes against an all-encompassing vision.

2. The essence [of the common divisions of the grounds] rests in the sixteen moments of acceptances and cognitions of perception of the four truths.

3. This one essence consists in the enumeration of isolatable factors.

4. The causal characteristics rest in the correct or incorrect [perception] of the intrinsic reality of the subject in relation to the four truths and its objects.

5. Ascertaining these depends on the pristine awareness of realization.

The *Summary of the Hundred Thousand* says:

The objects of the pristine awareness that transcends the world
are two: Suchness and pure pristine awareness.

[Argument:] Someone asked about the point of these divisions here, saying: Are they one or different, and where is this coming from?

The answer is in three parts according to the traditions of the others, our
own tradition [101], and dispelling objections.

The traditions of the others

The first topic is in two points:
[Question:] Are these distinctions different?
[Answer:] This counters the tradition of affirming a unique essence. This
first point here in particular is used as the common refutation. This first then
has three parts: the refutation of this position in two points, refutation in
four points, and refutation in sixteen points.

Refutation in the two points of cognition and acceptance

The first topic is threefold: the position on the two moments of cognition
and acceptance, the position that there is no real subsequent cognition, and
the position that meditation and post-meditation states are different.

Position on the two moments of cognition and acceptance

[Argument:] First, someone is rationalizing that the path of vision of the
heroes has two essences. These are posited as the two factors of cognition
and endurance, as well as the sixteen facets of the four truths.[143] Furthermore, in terms of the aspects of incorrect realization of the reality of the four
truths of the realm of desire, there is cognizance of phenomena and acceptance. Therefore, each of the four truths has four facets.[144]

In terms of the aspects of incorrect realization of the intrinsic reality of the
four truths in the two realms of Suchness above, subsequent cognizance and
acceptance are transformed through the four truths. Following this, in terms
of the correct realization of the reality of the four truths of the desire realm,
having depended on the four truths at the moment of cognizing reality, then
there are these four facets that manifest. Through these themselves (*de nyid
kyis*), there will be the correct realization of the intrinsic reality of the four

truths of the two realms above. Relying on the four truths at the moment of subsequent cognizance, the four facets will manifest. Thus it is said: "Above is the path devoid of obstacles, while below is the path of release."

[Answer:] However, it is not so. Generally characterized phenomena are no support, and this changes learning.

First, when intrinsic reality and pristine awareness that have not been perceived previously are perceived, is this a general perception or is this the perception of all the particulars?[145]

In the first case [i.e., general vision], when one perceives that the one and only intrinsic reality is without impediments, then there will no longer be any point in becoming free. So it is claimed.

As for the second case [i.e., everything is perceived in all its details], again there is no support to commonly characterized phenomena; therefore, there will be no end to the path of seeing.

[Argument:] In this second case, since there are no impediments, is there any activity left to eliminate objects that need to be eliminated or not?

[Answer:] In the first case [i.e., where there is activity], it changes the path of learning. It is said: "Merely seeing truly the essential point of the great pristine awareness, one becomes familiar with the fact that existence does not exist."

In the second case [i.e., no more activity], it would negate the non-existence of impediments. Furthermore, the four moments of the path of vision based on the four truths would disappear, and this would negate the existence of the supreme reality that is without impediment.

The position that there is no real subsequent cognition

[Argument:] In the second case where there is no activity of elimination, someone said that on the path of vision and for a few moments, cognition of phenomena and acceptance are engendered. Additionally, suffering is eliminated with its perception and the continuum of existence is severed. There are no more impediments, and this is realized through cognizing and accepting the aspects of the four truths.

[Answer:] This is not presented correctly. That path of release is distant from the process of elimination. At the moment of cognition of phenomena, one instantly realizes the correct position that generates the two (cognizance and acceptance). Thus, it changes the correct reality of cognizing phenomena and acceptance into an incorrect one. These two subsequent cognitions can be subsumed conveniently in the first two cases. [102]

Furthermore, if these are gathered in the acceptance of phenomena, then the moment of comprehending Suchness becomes incorrect.

[Argument:] One can designate two kinds of realization, the realization of the superficial view that is the knowledge of the others, and the inner view where self-nature is known. When cognizance of phenomena is collected, then the moment of comprehending Suchness is correct. When Suchness of pristine awareness is apprehending factors [i.e., objects], from this fact there is the realization of an apprehender [i.e., the subject]. Then pristine awareness is said to be established.

[Answer:] However, it is not so. For if it would be like that, then the pristine cognition of the insight on self-nature, the realization of the truth, would comprehend the apprehender [i.e., the subject]. It would realize this apprehender through the six apprehended objects of the six senses, the first three truths through the six, the six apprehended objects. The four pristine cognitions of the truth of the path would be measured through the truth of the path. Concerning the realization on apprehending [objects] of pristine cognition on the ten grounds, realization is geared toward apprehending objects on the sixth ground. After that, there are no more inventories of apprehended objects.

The position that meditation and post-meditation states are different

[Argument:] Third, someone said that to postulate on two stages, meditation and post-meditation, comes to be a dualistic position. First comes the vision of intrinsic reality. Then in a second moment comes the vision of the countenance of hundreds of enlightened ones, and so forth. This is duality.

[Answer:] Again, this is not so. The mere absence of self-nature, if realized, will bring Suchness in an instant. If this is not realized, then the distinctiveness of the lack of self-nature will not emerge. When one instant becomes many, the numbers of aspects of subsequent attainment multiply. Second, the production of the four truths is also a duality. The vision of intrinsic reality produces the four truths and the second vision eliminates the production of these four.

The refutation of this position in four points

[Argument:] First, someone has said that the four moments of the path of vision [i.e., cognizance, acceptance, subsequent cognizance, and subsequent acceptance] are reproduced in sixteen moments. Furthermore, when the reality of the desire realm is realized as incorrect, the antidote of elimination is actualized as the vision that eliminates. This produces the acceptance of the cognition of phenomena, a path without impediments. Concerning the four truths, there are four moments, and after them there is the path of release where the intrinsic reality of the realm of desire is realized as pure. This produces the instant of cognition of phenomena. Concerning the four truths again, at [the onset of] the four moments and what follows, there are no impediments to realizing the reality of the two superior worlds [i.e., the form and formless realms] as incorrect. This produces the acceptance of subsequent cognition. Concerning the four truths, release is the realization of the correct intrinsic reality of the two superior worlds. When there is no production of the instant of subsequent cognition, the four truths are transformed into the four moments, as was said.

[Answer:] But again, that is not so. For if it were so, then the realization of general characteristics would be similar, as before. Furthermore, if the second vision of pristine cognition is reproduced in what followed from the previous vision, it would change the path of meditation. If it did not reproduce, or if it were produced only for a moment, there would be the experience of the four moments. If it were not produced even for a single moment, there would be no arising of the experience following reality.

[Argument:] On the second point, again someone said that all phenomena, all the way to supreme reality, are empty and devoid of a self.

[Answer:] [103] Meditation consists in realizing through the cognizance of incorrect reality the intrinsic reality of the four truths. In the case of the four truths, the four moments are similar to one sentient being having seen the four steps of a stupa. The moment subsequent cognizance of phenomena is assessed, correct intrinsic reality is realized. Release is similar to the four moments of the view on the four truths combined. The subsequent acceptance of cognition is perceived in the first two cases. The cause of the production of the enlightened ones and the heroes of everlastingness is the distinctive realization of this reasoning. Regarding the four truths as before, they transform through the four aspects.

[Argument:] It is said that at the moment of subsequent cognition, these objects, perceived as inherently existent, are assessed. And this is called "realization."

[Answer:] Not so. Such objects, when cognized at the time of realization, are implicitly apprehended; therefore there is no spiritual realization.

[Argument:] Again, someone said that cognizance of phenomena and its subsequent acceptance are similar to [how they were] before subsequent acceptance on the four truths. The instant there is subsequent cognizance, these become objects of conventional truth. Regarding these two, they are said to have been assessed previously.

[Answer:] But this is not so. For if it were like this, then that later pristine cognition, when assessed previously, would have already stopped. This would change transcendence into an accepted concept.

The refutation of this position in sixteen points

[Argument:] Third, on the position of the sixteen points, someone said that the path of vision is produced gradually in sixteen moments. If it were like that, it would be an incorrect realization of the reality of the desire realm through cognizance of phenomena of suffering at the first moment, and its acceptance in a second moment. Therefore, the instant the cognizance of phenomena is realized correctly, subsequent acceptance realizes the two superior realms as pure or impure. In the same manner, origination ceases and changes the three paths and in an instant goes through the sixteen moments. Thus, there is ignorance, omniscience, and the fifteen moments, and when these are added together with the moment of the endowment of the all-knowledge, this makes sixteen, as has been explained.

[Answer:] But again, this saying is incorrect.

The proofs

Are these doctrines of the Superior Vehicle? There is no great value in this. If it were so, then the mere absence of self-nature would be a unique production where it is seen as new without a past. If it were not seen like that, then one would see no particularities in it. It is similar to not recognizing a deer because one does not see its antlers. Again, if there exists no continuum from a past life accepted for this later life, then it would change the path of meditation and its understanding. The continuums of consciousness of past and present lives would be two separate phenomena. If that were so, then there would be no point to the path of vision. This is not what has been taught.

Common refutation

[Argument:] Second, the common refutation is that what are produced anew by acute sense faculties have different essences.

[Answer:] If this is accepted, then it makes no difference to the senses. [104] Scriptures as well as the *Arcana* (179.2) contradict this, saying:

> The doctrine of this Greater Vehicle is that all defilements are purified simultaneously at the same time.

The refutation of the position on production in a single moment

Second, the refutation of the position on production in a single moment is twofold: the position on the coarse working of the senses and the position on collective perception.

The position on the coarse working of the senses

[Argument:] First, the great being, master Lodrö, said: "Concerning the path of vision, the working of the senses is coarse, but those with sharp faculties can produce the sixteen moments in an instant. Those with dull faculties produce these gradually through transmigratory existence."

[Answer:] But it is not so. For if it were so, would there be any differences in the [sixteen] moments between the sharp and the dull ones on the path of vision? In the first proposition [i.e., there are differences], the dull ones won't have the elimination of visions that those with sharp vision have, which is the main point about pristine cognition and intrinsic reality. This analysis is accepted. Its specifics are proven through valid cognition. However, if this is accepted, there will not be any elimination of visions. The *Eye of the Needle* (14.36.2) says:

> Because one sees no visions, the door to the path of vision opens.

In the second case [i.e., there are no differences], it is claimed that although there is a gradual production for those of dull faculties, if they become familiar with past lives it will turn into the path of meditation. If it does not, since there is no cause for past life, then the continuum of production from the past is severed.

The sixteen moments are produced from a single essence

[Argument:] Second, Dopa and someone else have said that the sixteen moments are produced from a single essence. Moreover, one can truly realize that there is no production in the intrinsic reality of the four truths. Fearlessness is then generated, which brings the acceptance of the cognizance of phenomena. Does Suchness have four different modes of realization for the four sense objects? These are the four moments:

There are four moments in the category of concentration on Suchness, the acceptance of the cognition of phenomena in the four truths of the past based on the production of similar types [i.e., homologous production], and the acceptance of subsequent cognizance.

There are the four moments in the category of the instant of cognition of phenomena. These are based on true production through the non-conceptual pristine cognition of an object possessor [i.e., subject] of the intrinsic reality of the absence of production in the four truths on Suchness.

There are the four moments, as before in the category of the moment of subsequent cognizing based on homogenous production at the moment of cognition in the four truths of the past, the mind of Suchness.

In the same way, the conqueror's sons are the same as the others.[146]

[Answer:] However, it is not as this saying goes. It is refuted in the absence of proof.

First, this doctrine is concordant with that of the heroes, superior and inferior. But there is no doctrine about production at the moment of the path of vision. There is nothing greater on this than this injunction.

[Argument:] Next, the correctness or incorrectness of intrinsic reality will change if [the latter is sourced in only] one essence. Then, intrinsic reality and pristine cognition will not change from the state of meditative equipoise to a post-meditative state. [105] Are the two, acceptance and subsequent cognizance, going to be homogenous productions if these are produced from one essence to the ordinary mind? Or are they produced subsequently in a concordant manner?

[Answer:] In the first case, in which they are the same, this reasoning is faulty. In the second case, in which they are produced in one instantaneous moment, this reasoning is also faulty.

Our own tradition

Second, our own tradition on this consists in three points: the identification of the subject being characterized, the mode of instantaneous production, and the proofs.

Identification of the subject being characterized

This first section is threefold: essence, analysis, and the mode of its realization.

Essence

First, there are states of meditative concentration and subsequent attainment [i.e., following meditative realization]. Among these, there is the actuality of the fundamental level of reality, a state that is without production. From the moment of direct realization of emptiness to the realization of the limits of the self, one realizes being affected by the illusory nature of the various qualities of the knowledge of subsequent attainments. There are distinctive differences between Suchness and the essence of the timing when the different modes of realization of aspects arise.

Analysis

Second, intrinsic reality and pristine cognition are realized through the mode of vision. Thus, on the path without impediments, the realization of intrinsic reality on the path of cessation comes from the elimination of the objects to be abandoned. The specific characteristic of pristine cognition is to see directly what was not seen in the past.

The mode of its realization

Furthermore, eliminating and meditating by vision consists in seeing purity or impurity. That is the nature of the elimination process. Pristine awareness comprehends and realizes while evaluating from the viewpoint of purity and impurity. Moreover, objects in the four truths are seen as part of the sixteen moments of cognizance and acceptance of the subject. One sees with the two cognizances of phenomena in the mode of intrinsic reality. One comprehends with the two subsequent cognizances in the mode of pristine cognition. Thus, those endowed with the seven limbs of everlastingness recognize cyclic existence while engaging the path. On this, the *Summary of the Hundred Thousand* says:

> When the meaning of the great liberation is merely seen, the familiar "I" is not.

The mode of instantaneous production

The second point has two parts: the mode of the single instant of production and the identification of valid cognition.

The mode of the single instant of production

First, the sixteen moments are produced from one essence in a single instant. Furthermore, the objects that are to be eliminated are eliminated and the two productions of the continuum of the path of vision are produced uninterruptedly in an instant, or as the others [say,] without hindrance. The *Arcana* (179.2) says:

> Simultaneously, in a single instant, the meaning of what has been previously seen is truly seen. And then, due to the system of this Greater Vehicle, all defilements are purified at once.

The *Eye of the Needle* (14.4.2) says:

> Because not seeing is seeing, the door of the path of vision opens.

Second, if one asks, what is this instant? The answer is threefold:

[Argument:] **First, in the tradition of the others**, a high scholar who is [considered to be] correct said that there is no single instant of a perfected action.

[Answer:] But it is not so. For instance, is the perfect action produced in a single instant or is it produced in stages? [106] In the first case, the experience of a perfect action includes the various stages of the perfected action. In the second case, the experience of the production of the perfect action is instantaneous.

Second, our own tradition on this says: "There is no finality of time; it is merely a vision of the meaning of the great liberation."

Dispelling objections

Third is the dispelling of objections:

[Argument:] On the perfection of the realization of the meditation and post-meditation states, it is asserted that there is one essence to the ordinary mind, and when objects to be abandoned are eliminated, then for a long time there are no more obstacles.

[Answer:] Not so. The path is without impediments. It is not in contradiction with the word "post-attainment." Meditation and post-meditation are linked.

The proofs

Third, there are four proofs: cause, aspects of perception, defining characteristic, and accomplishments concerning elimination.

Cause

First, the heroes of everlastingness endowed with the Bön of the path of vision become realized in one single instant because that great Highest Bön of cause produces it immediately. The accomplishment is said to be like awareness at midday. The above breakdown entails that a wide-ranging cause proceeds unobstructed to its conclusion and that action and its results proceed simultaneously.

Aspects of perception

Second, the genuine union of meditation and post-meditation states in the four truths is said to be similar to apprehending the color blue and the realization of its blueness. This is proven. It confirms that related concepts arise interdependently. This all-reaching proposition counters the distinctions that the ordinary mind has with its perception that differentiates what is assumed to be of a single essence.

Defining characteristic

Third, because one truly sees with a sharp view, it is said to be like the rising of the sun in the sky. The sign is the fulfillment of the lineage of the one experiencing this realization. If it were not so, then the acceptance of cognizance on the path of vision would be absurd. Comprehensiveness consists in seeing with sharp vision. It is all-encompassing in a single moment. If it were not so, then such a vision would go against past and subsequent gradual realizations.

Accomplishments concerning elimination

Fourth, because the vision eliminates what is to be eliminated in one instant, it is said to be like the lamp eliminating the darkness. The sign is demonstrated by this saying from the *Summary of the Hundred Thousand*:

> Actions and suffering are not produced, and as such, liberation without impediments [becomes manifest].

Comprehensiveness is the extensiveness of this sudden realization that comes simultaneously with elimination. The *Summary of the Hundred Thousand* says:

> The first point is applying vision, and then there is no more cyclic existence produced. Thus, there is nothing that prevents the transcendence of suffering.

Dispelling objections

Third, the dispelling of objections is threefold: scripture and refutation, disproving through reasoning, and [107] abandoning logical absurdity.

Scripture and refutation

First, the *Eye of the Needle* (8.277.7) says:

> The body of emanation on the nine grounds and the three worlds is like the phases of the moon and gradually purifies the obstructions of affliction.

And if someone contradicts this, the *Arcana* (178.2) counters, saying:

> The obstructions of affliction will be gradually purified.

This is faultless.

[Argument:] The path of the world consists in the intention to first suppress the objects to be eliminated. If it is followed with the acquisition of the path of vision, do illusions still exist or not?

[Answer:] In the first case [i.e., illusions still exist], if one remains free from conceptuality, there won't be any illusions. In the second case [i.e., one affirms that illusions no longer exist], one wants to counter this assertion. The *Eye of the Needle* (16.538.1) says:

> It is similar to the eye faculty that, under the power of illusion, sees bread where there is none.

And so forth.

[Argument:] Concerning this, some say that one is free from this fault through the continuing absence of existence in a substantial entity.

[Answer:] But that is not so. For if it were so, it would change illusory phenomena and its display in the strict sense of the word, and it would be the same as dualistic appearances, consciousness, and self-awareness. If it were so, then the non-produced meditative state and subsequent attainment would be illusory. Because it would be illusory, there would be no realization. Furthermore, there would be no valid explanations on the elimination of illusion. Therefore, there is a seed to illusion but it is not coarse. That doctrine, which [states] that there is illusion on the path of the world, is the explanation for awakening to transcendence.

Disproving through reasoning

The second topic, disproving through reasoning, is threefold: mode of production, the result of engaging, and eliminating inadmissible activities.

Mode of production

[Argument:] First, is instantaneous production a meditative state or a subsequent attainment?

[Answer:] In the first case, the visions of subsequent attainment would not be part of the path of vision. In the second case, meditative states would not be part of the path of vision.

[Argument:] If one says that it is neither of these two, then it would be impossible.

[Answer:] There is no fault in this. Besides, they are connected and inseparable and are produced automatically.

The result of engaging

[Argument:] Next, someone says, what if one is engaging with the one essence of the ordinary mind but there is no result yet? If a result has been completed, then there cannot be any engaging.

[Answer:] There is no fault in this. When engaging is not impeded, results will be released.

Eliminating inadmissible activities

[Argument:] Third, when someone says that if one severs the continuum of this one essence of ordinary mind, then there are no activities of any duration. If there are no activities of any duration, then there is no agent cutting away the continuum.

[Answer:] No fault in that! When there are no interruptions in the action of severing the continuum, there are no releases of activities of any duration. If it were like that, then one might wonder whether there is duality in the path of vision. There is none. There is the excellent reality without impediments.

[Argument:] Third, what if someone asks whether production in a single moment has three phases or not?

[Answer:] In the first case [it has three phases], then production in a single moment would be wrong. In the second case, then this would become a world of sudden events without any phases.

[Argument:] If someone says that there may be no phases in the ordinary mind, then without phases there would be no changes. But there are still phenomena. [108]

[Answer:] If it were so, then the main concepts of object and subject would be different. The earlier point would be faulty and not separate.

[Argument:] Then, maybe there are not three phases among coarse objects but there is something of the three phases that is extremely subtle.

[Answer:] When someone asks about the existence of these subtleties, if one were to examine and analyze conventional reality, there is a "real" thing that has parts. And if we break this thing apart, then ultimately only separated parts will be left. This essence, limited in number as one, is produced in one moment. The sixteen moments are objects that exist through the four kinds of acceptance of cognizance in the four truths.

2. THE FOUR PATHS OF SHENRAB

Next, the topic on inherent nature is threefold: the phenomenon that is the object of vision, knowledge and awareness of the seen, and signs and benefits of vision.

The phenomenon that is the object of vision

The first topic is twofold: the nature of the principal path and the divisions of the sections of the cycle.

The nature of the principal path

First, the topic of the four paths of Shenrab has three main points: defining characteristic, divisions, and precise explanation.

Defining characteristic

First, Shenrab realized directly that there is no inherent nature in the objects of practice. And in particular, that the predispositions of sentient beings are continually imagined, and this is correct. He engaged in the cause that enabled him to assist sentient beings directly. For this reason, he worked on eliminating the line of thoroughly imputed objects to be eliminated and he became a non-returner. He reached the higher realization about the world and combined its common characteristics with the four truths.

Divisions

Second, the divisions are those based on reality and the demarcations of the grounds.

Reality

On the first, the *Rising of the Nine Suns in a Hundred Thousand Verses* (17.15.1) has these four verses:

> The white has no hindrances. One engages in the stream of compassion for a long time. There is no fairness in cyclic existence. One journeys through the middle [way].

The demarcation of the grounds

The second topic, the demarcations of the grounds, is threefold:

[Argument:] First, **the tradition of the others** assigns the first ground to the white that has no hindrances, while designating the second ground as the stage of entering the stream until the fourth ground, subsequent attainment. Meditation on the lack of beneficial conditions in cyclic existence that reaches the middle way makes the third pure ground. This sets it within the path of vision because of the realization of the ground that is then perfected. Or so said Me'u Pal.

[Answer:] But this is unreasonable. The two—entering the stream and absence in cyclic existence—are identical to the characteristic cause [pertaining] to the third pure ground, the path of vision. It contradicts each and every thing that is suitable when it concerns the journeying along the middle path.

[Argument:] Furthermore, the path of accumulation is white and has the function of separating [oneself] from negative predispositions and generating the mind of enlightenment. Entering the stream is the path of application, and one engages in the cause to assist sentient beings. There is no more cyclic existence in the meditations and the post-meditation period on the lower truth, and the continuum to all afflictive obstructions is then cut off. [109] The third ground is journeying along the middle way and is said by the great Lodrö to be the limit of the path of learning.

[Answer:] Again, it is not. These two sources, scriptures and reasoning, first make the affirmation that this is the Bön of the path of vision. But that is purely nominal. The result of the paths of accumulation and application is the cause for the path of meditation. If that is wrong, then the saying about the fourth ground being the instantaneous path of vision is also wrong. In that case, it changes the state of knowledge of all aspects into the path of vision. The paths of accumulation and application are the results of having planted seeds that exist in a former place of defect. It will not transform into the fourth instantaneous path of vision. It will transform into the four conceptual isolates of the one essence. Since that is wrong, the sixteen moments of the path of vision will transform because the sixteen phenomena exist.

[Argument:] The second of the four points is that, first, one is not to eliminate whatever obstacle presents itself on the path of accumulation. And if someone asks: "If whatever defiles mental consciousness is not eliminated, how should one eliminate bad predispositions that prevent one from generating the mind of enlightenment?"

[Answer:] One can counter this [assumption] by saying: "It is absurd to accumulate merit for a higher rebirth. Moreover, meditation on nonperception everywhere is the meditation of the path of Shenrab where there are no hindrances."

[Argument:] What if someone contradicts this?

[Answer:] Second, if there were the capacity to really assist sentient beings, then there would be nothing that one could do.

[Argument:] And when someone says that there is in reality nothing that exists to engage in the cause?

[Answer:] This would change the path of accumulation into the stage of entering the stream.

[Argument:] Third, someone could say that there is not even a stop to the stage of Heat in evil destiny, no stop to finality, nothing to do in omniscience. There is no reversal from afflictive emotions.

[Answer:] In this, only afflictive emotions are to be changed, because cyclic existence that cannot be stopped is a false conception and must be discarded. Only on the three levels of complete purity is there no cyclic existence. This is because there are afflictive emotions in the seven lower levels.

[Argument:] Fourth, the assertion at the end of the path of learning is that one acts without knowing anything of transcendence on the path of vision, journeying in the world and traveling.[147]

[Answer:] If there is no more learning on the three pure grounds, there will be no more path of meditation.

[Argument:] Also, the great lord said: "There won't be any more hindrance on the path of application. The coarse will be repressed from above. Entering the stream through the path of accumulation is engaging in the cause of the transmitted teachings. It is engaging in the cause of compassion. Unhindered and good conditions come on the path of vision. Because cyclic existence cannot be reversed, the path of release is the journeying on the middle way. It is far from the activities of elimination."

[Answer:] Not so. The assertions of the teachings of the scriptures above and the like are based only on the attainment of the common meaning gathered from studying and pondering. These must be adapted to reality.

Second, the first point on reasoning is similar to the path of accumulation. [110] And again, the door to truly taking refuge is not sufficient to function as real assistance.

Second, **in our own tradition**, it was really Lama Drimé Chökyi Chanden who mentioned Bön as consisting only of the path of vision. The argument goes like this: When one eliminates the false conceptions of the defiled mental consciousness, there are no more propensities. Then one can see one's abilities for compassion together with a real ability to be of assistance. Because of the action of eliminating the false conceptions of all objects to be eliminated, impediments do not come back. One obtains the path of vision, having reached the finality of the path of the world.

Third, the section on **dispelling of objections** treats the common and the distinctive.

[Argument:] First, there is the assertion that there are contradictions in the four moments of the path of vision.

[Answer:] But there are none. It is simply asserted that the four moments are different from the one essence.

Second, there are these four objections:

[Argument:] The first objection is that there is no knowledge of all aspects that is entirely free from predispositions.

[Answer:] If this were so, it would support a free continuity of predisposition.

[Argument:] The second objection is that this is merely engaging with the cause to liberation, which is the path of application.

[Answer:] This does not really change anything.

[Argument:] The third objection is that there is no more reverting back to evil destinies once on the path of application.

[Answer:] It is accepted that abandoning false conceptions are the objects to be eliminated.

[Argument:] The fourth objection is that it is not true that there is no knowledge of all aspects in finality.

[Answer:] This is the finality of the path of the world.

Precise definition

Third, the precise definition is that Shenrab is the path of the object that is seen, and [seeing] is similar to recognizing the details.

3. THE SEVEN LIMBS OF EVERLASTINGNESS

Second, the limbs are the seven limbs of everlastingness.

[Argument:] Someone may say that meditation on the path of vision has these seven limbs.

[Answer:] Not so. Such a statement does not reverse the essential point concerning the path of vision, and it contradicts the scriptures quoted above. Therefore, this is about realization in the mode of the limbs at the moment of direct vision. Thus, wisdom, mindful recollection, joy, diligence, pliancy, concentration, and equanimity are the seven limbs.

The first, wisdom, is the limb on the intrinsic nature of the path of vision. It is the direct vision of the lack of intrinsic nature.

The second, mindful recollection, is the limb related to events that consists in realizing the non-forgetting of Suchness.

The third, joy, is the limb related to advantage that is the focus on being of benefit to sentient beings.

The fourth, diligence, is the limb on definite emergence that will do the accompanying along the non-localized grounds. [111]

The fifth, pliancy, the sixth, concentration, and the seventh, equanimity, are the limbs of no-more-suffering.

In the higher realms, one grows away from the cause of suffering in evil places. It is the elimination of evil places. In the intermediate realms, it is to acquire the state of abiding in the pristine cognition of the absence of suffering. And in the lower realms, all the thoroughly imputed factors are entirely disjointed and non-existent. These are the only visions of the ultimate.

Knowledge and awareness

Second, knowledge and awareness consist in ascertaining and dispelling objections.

Ascertaining with valid cognition

The first one is about direct valid cognition. Furthermore, from the point of view of the object, it is the direct perception of the ultimate.

[Argument:] It is said that the face of the mind itself is the valid cognition of direct yogic perception.

[Answer:] Some particular objects of knowledge are manifest, but their embodiment cannot be ascertained. Subsequent cognition is not certain. One does not engage in pursuing conceptions.

Dispelling objections

Next is dispelling objections:

[Argument:] Concerning the inherent reality of the four truths on the future, someone said that it will change valid cognition of direct perception.

[Answer:] There is no fault in this. To see that the future depends on what has not yet been produced is valid cognition. It is to realize that the present is linked. That realization is a valid cognition of the ordinary mind.

Signs and benefits

Third, the topic on signs and benefits is threefold: the enlightened qualities of realization of the object of realization, the enlightened qualities of eliminating the object to be eliminated, and the supporting signs of the stage of Heat.

The enlightened qualities of realization of the object of realization

First, the *Eye of the Needle* says:

> If one has faith only in the object perceived on the top level of heaven, then the environment and its beings are the outward phenomena of the object apprehended while cognition and thoughts are the internal agents grasping. The power of illusion is similar to the faculty of sight that sees bread where there is none.

The *Eye of the Needle* (16.537.7) continues, saying:

> The power of merit is similar to a polished mirror reflecting virtues and sins. Ashamed and trembling with fear on the edge of a precipice, one does not truly see the objects of perception without bias.

Realizations of the meditative and post-meditative states

If someone asked what are the realizations of the meditative and post-meditative states? There are three:

[Argument:] First, Me'u Pal of **the tradition of the others** said that these realizations are not seen. He said that in the realizations of the meditative states, there are the realizations of all other subsequent attainments. Although these first subsequent attainments are realizations on the path of meditation, this is a position on the path of vision that has been deduced through the path of vision.

[Answer:] This is unreasonable. It is undesirable and resembles the position of the others, which is absurd. The first one, the realizations of the meditative states, is said to be the path of meditation and the meditative state of the first ground. If the sphere of ultimate reality is directly seen by those endowed with a sharp faculty of vision, isn't it contradicting the path of vision? This is saying that the mirage-like vision of those endowed with a sharp faculty of vision is the same as contradicting the path of meditation. [112]

Second, the meditative state of the second ground on the path of meditation is expressed as the path of vision. But even if it contradicts the visions on the path of vision, it also contradicts the path of meditation where there are no visions, as mentioned. In what manner are these similar?

Second, our own tradition is that realization of meditative states can be recognized and the proof is in that. The realization of subsequent attainment can be recognized and the proof is also there.

First, what is called "the non-perception of the meaning" is said to be merely the generation of perceived objects. Meditation on the emptiness of all phenomena is the path of accumulation. The production of vivid clarity is the path of application, while the path of vision is direct realization.

Second, what are called "objects" are what are apprehended externally as extant. Realization in a state of meditative equipoise is a realization of the illusion in an instant.

Third, on these, scriptures and the *Treasury* (215.1) say:

> First, there is the ground called Extreme Joy.

The *Summary of the Hundred Thousand* says:

> One sees the essential point of liberation.

Now, using reasoning: If the result of the path of vision is the path of meditation, then the second, the path of meditation, exists. And if the path of application is the result, then again when one becomes familiar with the second, there will be the acquisition of vivid clarity.

Dispelling objections

Third, the dispelling of objections is twofold:

First, on the elimination process in the scriptures, the *Arcana* (192.7) says:

> In intrinsic reality there are no manifestations; the mind itself is inseparable. The vision of color in a sky without perceivable objects arises as brilliant light rays.

There is no conflict here, since this is the purpose of meditative states.

[Argument:] Second, is reasoning identical to or different from meditative and post-meditation states? In the first case [i.e., identical to], then "meditative state" is a fabrication and a concept that changes when engaged in. In the second case [i.e., different from], someone can counter this by saying that reasoning is a method of elucidation and a momentary production.

[Answer:] There is no fault here. In a single essence, a conceptual moment produces a difference. The direct realization of the absence of production of all phenomena is implicitly illusory because it is a state of realization that is a subsequent attainment. Meditative and post-meditation states are dualistic. They are produced momentarily in duality while at the same time are indistinguishable and unchanged. A conceptual moment [i.e., an isolate] produces difference.

The enlightened qualities of eliminating the object to be eliminated

Second, on the elimination of objects to be eliminated, the *Eye of the Needle* (14.441.4) says:

> The Peak, which is free from the five fears,[148] is the real attainment.

On eliminating the vision of the five poisons and so forth, and being free of the five coarse things,[149] the *Treasury* (184.4) says:

> As for hatred and the hostile troupes of the parasol, who can change fear but through the great strength of great love?

This is saying that one is to acquire the thirteen strengths of fearlessness.[150] [113]

The supporting signs of the stage of Heat

The third point is about the sign of the attainment of the stage of Heat. The *Summary of the Hundred Thousand* says:

> With the acquisition of the grounds, one is free from the five fears.

One is free from the fears of fire and water, poisons, epidemics, famine, and afflictions.

Miscellaneous points

The third topic on miscellaneous points is threefold: seeing non-duality on the path of vision, seeing intrinsic reality on the path of vision, and seeing pristine cognition on the path of vision.

Seeing non-duality on the path of vision

First, having seen in one moment the inseparability of cognition and the expanse of reality, the factor of emptiness is the path of vision of intrinsic reality. The factor of clarity is the path of vision of pristine cognition.

Its **defining characteristic** is to realize, with an acute realization, the ultimate meaning of the inseparability of clarity and emptiness.

Non-dual realization

Second, there are three points on non-dual realization: its defining characteristic, the recognition of the ultimate meaning of purity and impurity, and distinctive teachings.

The defining characteristic of non-dual realization

First, this realization is the sharp realization of the expanse of reality of non-production.

The recognition of the ultimate meaning of purity and impurity

Second, [this realization] is where there is the sudden cognition of phenomena. There is perception of objects through the four truths.

Distinctive teachings

[Argument:] Third, someone said that the vision of eliminating the object to be eliminated is similar to the non-differentiation of purity. What is this view that engages in the duality of the purity and the impurity of the moment?

The answers to these are threefold: according to the tradition of the others, according to our own tradition, and dispelling objections.

According to the tradition of the others

This first topic is in three parts: the position on near and long duration, the position on purity due to being within the stains of grasping at an evil place, and countering the tradition of the position on isolation in which one makes production come to a halt.

The position on near and long duration

[Argument:] First, someone said that the stain of what is eliminated on the path of vision of the reality that is below the level of supreme reality is impure, and what is near at the moment of accepting cognizance of phenomena is impure.

[Answer:] That realization establishes the realization of what is impure. But again, when there is cognizance of phenomena and the moment between the acceptances of phenomena, impurities near and far are right then purified. The cognition of phenomena and the understanding that posits it as pure are wrong. This saying is deficient and [I am providing] the answer to refute it:

First, if there is a ground for enlightenment, then the above rationale changes it from pure to impure. It is similar to a causal characteristic. If this is accepted, then past primordial awareness is veiled. There is no realization from the past but there is realization in the future. If one wishes to analyze the timing of these two, then the case is similar to the above analysis relating to the path of vision. It is wrongly claimed that acceptance and cognizance of phenomena are inseparable.

The position on purity due to being within the stains of grasping at an evil place

[Argument:] Second, someone has postulated that although it is true that the seed of the vision that eliminates has no distinctive purity, the vision that eliminates has a distinctive purity that enables the generation of the continuum of the Superior Vehicle, despite the purity or impurities from grasping at an evil place. And because of this, [114] the path without impediments is the cutting off of hindrances. Liberation is the activity of the subject that is not produced. Because of that, when one accepts phenomena and [as a result] there is grasping at an evil destiny, this is then impure. When it comes to the cognizance of phenomena, it is said that if one is free from these, it is pure.

[Answer:] Not so. If it were so and there was the ability of generating a concordant type later within the stain of grasping at an evil destiny, then the cognizance of phenomena would become an impure concept. In the negative case, evil destinies would be produced from the second ground and above without any cause. There would be no more objects to eliminate from the second ground and above.

[Argument:] Someone said that the power, great or small, of antidotes is coarse and that in the continuum of the Higher Vehicle there is no capacity for production. And there are antidotes of greater and lesser potency.

[Answer:] Like that, all objects to be eliminated are eliminated entirely by those of the Greater Vehicle who are on the path of vision. The antidotes and concordant types of objects to be eliminated, great or small, will not be generated later. Therefore, when it concerns the objects to be eliminated, antidotes will transform accordingly in order to greatly empower their reach.

Countering the tradition of the position on isolation in which one brings production to a halt

[Argument:] Third, someone said that when one is accepting phenomena, it is similar to the action of stopping the generation of the vision of elimination and the path of vision. In this intrinsic reality that is impure, accepting the cognizance of phenomena is done through the realization in which one realizes that there is impurity. From the action of stopping production at the moment of cognizance of phenomena, there is purity through isolation. Realization of the cognition of phenomena establishes the realization of purity.

[Answer:] Not so. The production of the path of vision from a single essence contradicts the assertion of a single substantial entity in isolation, such as in the action of stopping production. Furthermore, if at the moment of accepting phenomena production is stopped, there will be no impediment to liberation. In the first case [i.e., production is stopped], it will change liberation into the path of learning. In the second case [i.e., no impediment to liberation], it could be claimed that there will be no more of this path of vision.

Our own tradition

Second, in our own tradition, the nature of this transmission is that the process of elimination through meditation is not correct. The process of elimination through the path of vision reverses that and is correct and consists in accepting [the cognizance] of phenomena. Dualistic cognizance of phenomena is established merely by having visions of both impurity and purity.

[Argument:] Again, a certain lama has said that sentient beings are impure. That the heroes of everlastingness purify these [beings] through the process of meditation on elimination, and this purifies the vision that eliminates the objects to be eliminated. And the enlightened ones are known as being extremely pure.

[Answer:] If it were so, there would be no way to ascertain the path of vision, even for a moment.

Dispelling objections

Third is the dispelling of objections.

[Argument:] Some say on the practice of accepting perceived phenomena that there is the realization of purity that changes into the realization of impurity when phenomena are cognized. The vision that eliminates is congruent with purity, and meditation that eliminates is congruent with impurity. [115]

[Answer:] Are these then called "substantial entity" or "conceptual isolate"? When the first one is posited, the second one cannot be established completely. A conceptual isolate is completely different. For example, a product is a single impermanent substantial entity and is different from a conceptual isolate. The classification "conceptual isolate" contradicts the existence of any substantial entity.

Pristine cognition

A third topic is pristine cognition (*ye shes*), whose defining characteristic consists in recognizing its essence in the mode of vision.

First, the meaning of "pristine" (*ye*, "primordial") is likened to the moment when one has a sudden and clear (*sngar*) understanding. The second syllable refers to the experience of cognizing (*shes*) a substantial entity, the instantaneous cognition of a substantial entity.

[Argument:] Someone said that the dualistic process of experiencing the cognition of substantial entities is similar to the gradual production of duality during the cognition of phenomena.

[Answer:] The pristine cognition of intrinsic reality counters the moment of production of the four truths. Because of this, our tradition on duality regards the experience of the phenomena of the four truths as an act of patient forbearance generating subsequent knowledge through comprehension in the mode of one's own awareness. It establishes an implicit understanding of a "you" and an "I" with the implicit qualities of subsequent attainment coming from what arises.

The mode of vision

The mode of vision includes the mode of self-awareness through subsequent acceptance and the experience of cognizing phenomena in relation to the four truths. The cognizance of phenomena in relation to the four truths is conducted through subsequent cognizance and with the mode of self-awareness.

[Argument:] The great lama Lodrö has explained that as a gradual process.

[Answer:] However, if it were like that, then it would imply that one would [inadvertently] turn into someone with sharp faculties and would comprehend everything in a single moment. But this outcome is contradicted. Therefore, the mode of differentiating a conceptual isolate from a single essence is understood in a single moment.

Dispelling objections

The third topic is the dispelling of objections:

The two syllables "pristine" and "cognition" (*ye shes*) refer to the two moments of assessing a phenomenon. If there is a contradiction between the agent and the object, then this [reaction] changes into an array of concepts.

[Argument:] Someone said that if there is no contradiction from the agent to the object, it makes the realization of intrinsic reality a second moment.

Another lama said that the negation of a substantial entity does not stop the lineage of production. Furthermore, this contradicts the proposition of the single sudden moment.

[Answer:] As for that, production is not stopped by the action on an object or in a single moment. Ordinary beings suffer for a long time. Because of this, the realization of the noble ones is incommensurable.

The mode of elimination of the objects to be eliminated

Third, the topic of the mode of elimination of the objects to be eliminated is threefold: the nature of the vision on elimination of the objects to be eliminated, the mode of elimination as such, and dispelling objections on the mode of elimination.

The nature of the vision on elimination of the objects to be eliminated

The first one has three parts: cause, the nature of the cause, and the activities of the agent.

Cause

First, the cause is ignorance. The *Minute Scriptures* (166.5) says:

> Through ignorance and the power of the conditions of the five poisons arises the result that is abiding in cyclic existence in the three worlds.

The nature of the cause

Second, the nature of that cause is threefold: its defining characteristic, its divisions, and the precise explanation. [116]

The defining characteristic

The first topic is threefold:

[Argument:] Someone from **the tradition of the others** said that the agents that counteract the production of the antidotes and the agents that stop the production of intrinsic reality and pristine cognition are the defilements, and this is the defining characteristic of the [practice of] eliminating by means of vision.

[Answer:] It is not. If it were so, sound would be apprehended as permanent and a conch would be apprehended as golden. However, defilement is impermanent. This proposition would change the apprehended whiteness of the conch shell as well as pristine cognition.

[Argument:] Thus, following below, if there is [any form of] production at all from intrinsic reality and pristine cognition, one would have to abandon meditation.

[Answer:] This is an overreaching conclusion, for all perfected enlightened ones wouldn't exist. And it is not so. Therefore, the mere activity of stopping production [with antidotes] would link elimination to some coarse defilement. This overreaching does not exist in the elimination through vision.

[Argument:] Again, Dopa said that the path of vision changes this refutation.

[Answer:] However, the defining mark of a particular object is fabricated.

[Argument:] The lama, lord of reasoning and scriptures, said: "The object refuted arises entirely from a cause. The condition of its refutation simply comes by means of the mere vision of abiding in pristine cognition and in intrinsic reality. This is the activity that reverses the continuum."

[Answer:] If a mark is qualified as being a part of the path of vision, then there will be no more defilements. This sole vision would reverse the continuum of defilements.

If someone said: "Who is momentarily seeing oneself as a being? For one is annihilated through the direct realization of the specifically characterized phenomena of pristine cognition and intrinsic reality. Other than eliminating through insight, who went through the activity of seeing?"

Second, what is the defining characteristic of elimination through insight in our **own tradition**? It is this momentary view of the self as a being that impedes the realization of this specifically characterized phenomenon that is inherent Suchness. That is it.

4. On eliminating through insight

Dispelling objections

Third, dispelling objections:

[Argument:] Someone stated that co-emergence is not eliminated through the path of vision, but that elimination using insight generates co-emergence.

[Answer:] There is no fault in this. There is no co-emergence in the process of elimination with insight; everything is imputed.

There are three divisions to the second point: grounds delineation, enumeration, and individual properties.

Grounds delineation

First, in the continuum of the path of vision, there are intermediaries that are truly non-produced.

The second point on divisions is threefold: the actual divisions, their nature, and dispelling objections.

The actual divisions

The basic division of the grounds is done through their defining characteristics, such as the general delimiting of elimination through insight.

Their essence is based on the defilement of suffering and the defilement of cognition.

Their causal characteristic is to interfere for liberation only. The distinctiveness of their domain creates the divisions of the two kinds of obstacles. The main divisions are based on the differences in regard to the type of defiling object. [117]

Their differences consist in their unique contexts and extents.

Their number is relative to the objects.

The nature of the grounds

Second, their nature consists in what is really seized as objects to be eliminated. Their particularities are taught here.

First, if someone asks, what are the objects to be eliminated? There are three parts to this:

[Argument:] Someone, from **the tradition of the others**, said that suffering and cognition create the defilement of suffering. Thus these two are said to be completely imputed and co-emergent.

[Answer:] However, it is not so. On the path of vision above, not even the predispositions of afflictive emotions are changed. If one accepts this, the scripture contradicts it. The *Eye of the Needle* (14.115.7) says:

On the top of the seven heavens on the walls of the indestructible
citadel, the sea monsters dry up.

These thoroughly imputed defilements of cognition are not to be eliminated
on the path of vision. If this is accepted, the *Eye of the Needle* (16.536.6)
counters by saying:

The objects of cognition—miserly pride—are lost in the pure
realized presence of the universal ground.

Second, **in our own tradition**, our spiritual forefathers have explained
this in concordance with the two afflictive defilements. Furthermore, among
these two, the imputed and the co-emergent, the thoroughly imputed have a
lineage. The above deductions are known from the scriptures.

Third, in order to **dispel objections**, the *Eye of the Needle* (96.436.5) says:

The real single cause of purifying the defilement of affliction
is forbearance in the face of the obstructions from objects of
cognition.

This is uncontested.

[Argument:] As for that, reasoning has this notion that there are co-
emergent obscurations to cognition. Having eliminated co-emergent
afflictive obscurations on the seventh ground, one intends to have no more
co-emergent obstacles to cognition.

[Answer:] This reasoning does not change the fact that the elimination
of these two, afflictions and tainted cognition, won't eliminate any object
on the path of meditation. One has to eliminate the line of co-emergent
obscurations.

Second, concerning the distinctiveness of the thoroughly imputed and
the co-emergent, the moment they are produced, the ground and its concomitant will change accordingly. As for afflictive cognition, it is the same as
what has been taught above. The *Arcana* (178.1) says:

The diminution of the obstructions of affliction is not granted at
the stations of humans and gods.

And the *Eye of the Needle* (16.536.5) says:

Great and subtle objects of cognition together with pride diminish in the pure mind of enlightenment of the universal basis.

Dispelling objections

Third is the dispelling of objections:

[Argument:] If someone asks why are co-emergent factors and the hindrances to cognition not one?

[Answer:] That proposition makes co-emergent factors concomitant
with the base. Hindrances to cognition are the agents of hindrances to subjects with distinctive traits.

Individual properties

Third, as for individual properties, the part on cognitive afflictions is twofold: first is the refutation of the tradition of the others in three parts; and
the distinctive characteristic is also in three parts.

First, the **refutation of the tradition of the others.** [118]

[Argument:] According to their scriptures and reasoning, an inherent
self—that is, the selfhood of transmigrating beings that is the view maintained as one's selfhood—gives rise to thorough imputations while preventing liberation.

[Answer:] If that were so, then the characterized marks of thoroughly
imputed objects would be distinct, and when the view on the selfhood of
beings arose, the view on the selfhood of beings would not change.

[Argument:] Again, if someone says that whoever uses reasoning on
affliction, this reasoning becomes injurious when used on the path of vision?

[Answer:] Defining marks act as distinction markers. This is an overreaching conclusion regarding co-emergent factors.

Second, the great Lodrö of **our own tradition** has said that because the
view on selfhood is maintained by beings, it is suddenly produced. It then
becomes an impediment to liberation.

[Argument:] Third, what if someone asks only about the above counter-
proposition: Are there impediments hindering cognition?

[Answer:] This question cannot be answered, since impediments are distinctive features of objects.

Divisions

Second, divisions are extremely numerous, so all these subdivisions and parts are gathered together here to dispel objections. First, there is the recognition of the essence and the aspects that are thoroughly differentiated.

The first part is twofold:

First, engaging in false reality. The *Treasury* said accordingly that there are views involving all kinds of fears, such as (1) views that grasp excessively on imputations, (2) false deceptive views, (3) grasping to a supreme view, and (4) the view on energetic activity of ethical conduct.

Second, there are the views stipulating that (5) compounded phenomena are wrong engagement, (6) one craves the objects that come to the mind, (7) one hates what does not come to be, (8) one is deluded by the different manifestations of the intermediate state [between rebirths], (9) one is proud of the qualities of the self, (10) one is jealous of the qualities of others, and (11) one is ignorant of the delusions of everything. Thus, there are eleven of these views.

Realms, grounds, et cetera

Third, there are the three categories of the realms, the grounds, and all kinds of field-objects.

First, there are thirty-three levels to the three realms.[151] Second, the *Summary of the Hundred Thousand* says:

One eliminates the ninety-one subtle proliferations with insight.

Each of the nine grounds of the three realms have tens of ten divisions, ten divisions in every one, and these come to ninety. The root of the ninety is this one root, ignorance.

Third, the one hundred and twelve transforms into thirteen roots. Thus, in this world of desire, the objects of the four truths that are perceived become forty. If one looks into the two superior worlds and also counts anger, not including the remainder and all the other nine [of the ten non-virtuous actions], it comes to thirty-six thousand, two hundred and twelve (36,212) afflictive emotions. Their root is ignorance together with these thirteen roots of ignorance.

Second, afflictive emotions can be subsumed in these three: engaging in a false reality, incorrectly entering and engaging in a false reality, and force-fully engaging with the false.

Engaging in a false reality

[Argument:] First, one will perceive oneself in the five senses as well as what is one's own with many fears and will hold on to the extreme views of either nihilism or eternalism. Because of these mistaken delusions, one will try to superimpose happiness while [119] repudiating suffering. These delusions function in one's continuum and one is unable to recognize what is correct. This is the fourth [poison], delusion. Nyö[152] (fl. eighth–ninth centuries) also discoursed on envy. That is not a concordant discussion and is said to be suspect.

[Answer:] First, it is unacceptable that the unconditioned is produced. It is unreasonable. Second, these past views are held as the most excellent, and with these, one can get hold of liberation. However, these views can be seen as impactful activities during practice. Desire and attachment, with arrogance and pride, make four. It is proper to not engage whichever of these previous four manifest. Third, whenever anger and jealousy are not produced at all, they cannot be engaged. Thus, one can engage in practice when perceiving these four. Furthermore, if suffering is produced in an object, it is eliminated through meditation. The view here is to eliminate production through insight. The lord of scripture and reasoning has said so.

Dispelling objections

Third, the dispelling of objections is threefold:

1. If there is nobody, then there is no view to have on the excellent impactful activities of morality. This objection is to be dispelled.

2. It is impossible to perceive objects on the path to cessation in the three realms. This objection is to be dispelled.

3. There is no anger in the two upper realms. This objection is to be dispelled.

[Argument:] First, if there is nobody, then are there any impactful activities of morality or not? In the first case [i.e., there are impactful activities], it changes the existence of perceivable objects in the body and in speech. In the second case [i.e., there are no impactful activities], from the point of view of the world, it is a defiled experience of the three hundred and sixty or of the one hundred and twelve.

[Answer:] There is no fault here. There are no perceptible objects of the body and speech, but the view is that there is perception of objects.

[Argument:] Second, if there is the capacity of perceiving objects on the path to cessation in the three realms, then there is no uncontaminated duality on that path. If there is none, then one could make the false assertion that the objects viewed are those in the categories of the forty, the forty-four, and the one hundred and twelve.

[Answer:] If among these there are specifically characterized phenomena, there may be no perceptions of objects, but there are perceptions of indications. Cessation consists in turning away. It is freedom and the elimination of the adventitious through insight. The path consists in insight on the untainted. When there is duality, it is stopped by the insight of elimination. Then it is no more.

[Argument:] Third, if someone says that some have claimed that there is anger in the two upper realms. This will not bring about the ripening of the practice of calm abiding in one's continuum. If someone says that it is not so, then from the point of view of the realms, this is a false experience of the thirty-three realms.

[Answer:] The reply to this statement is that this is not correct. When these realms are considered together as non-existent, this is said to be the sixteenth [aspect of emptiness]. However, this means that there will be no more proportionate predispositions. The *Eye of the Needle* (16.434.3) says:

There is nothing to seize as proportionate predispositions to eliminate in the three realms.

[Argument:] Again, the teacher of Rong[153] posits that Suchness has no self-isolate [120], while others maintain that there are existing predispositions. The latter would make the processes of the elimination of anger through vision inexistent.

[Answer:] Not so. The *Eye of the Needle* (16.451.6) says:

The form aggregate is the changing body of Garsé Tsenpo [i.e., the god who suppresses cravings].

If there is no form aggregate, it would negate a cause of cessation. But this is concomitant with the quote. If it were so [i.e., if there were no form aggregate] and if there were to be existing predispositions that would have abilities, as asserted by the others, then the practice of calm abiding would not help ripen one's continuum. If there are no abilities, then there will be no objects that can be eliminated. Therefore, the great Lodrö said: "There are predispositions without real manifestations." This is so.

[Argument:] Therefore, in this case it is contradictory to posit that predispositions will be eliminated through vision, while the others change this and say that there is no elimination of existing predispositions through meditation.

[Answer:] There is no fault here. The process of elimination is either hard or easy. The seed of hatred and its array are coarse, while the process of elimination through vision is easy elimination. It is so due to the cause of predispositions. They are produced through the very nature of the world. This changes the fact that the practice of calm abiding does not ripen the continuum. If there are predispositions, as the others assert, then there would be no separation from the past in the world. For that reason, it is the same as above. Nothing changes and there is no need for elimination. The seeds and their array are there.

Precise definition

Third, the precise explanation of this is that the continuum of the mind is the agent of suffering and its mere cessation is liberation.

Obstruction to knowables

Second, the topic of obstruction to knowables[154] is threefold:

[Argument:] First, someone from **the tradition of the others** says: "Apprehended object and the apprehending subject are only appearances."

[Answer:] Pristine cognition on the path of application pervades far into afflictive obstruction.

[Argument:] [Next], a lama said that what is thoroughly imputed arises out of the view of a self in phenomena, and that the great liberation is obtained from the cessation of that view. Furthermore, the mark [i.e., the imputed existent] creates distinctiveness.

Again, Dopa said: "Whatever conceptualization there is on the path of vision, these become harmful." They are afflictive obstructions.

[Answer:] These are overreaching conclusions. It is said that the views on the selfhood of phenomena that are suddenly produced are stopped by the inherent nature of pristine cognition and intrinsic reality.

Third is the **dispelling of objections**. It does not change anything that there are no particularities in the processes of elimination through meditation. Its nine stages[155] have no adventitious production breeding. But there is breeding of what is concomitant and at the base.

Basis of characteristics

Second, the topic on the basis of characteristic is twofold: recognition of the essence and extreme division of aspects.

Recognition of the essence

[Argument:] First, as above, someone said: "When one sees the objects perceived, past afflictive obstructions change into cognitive obstructions."

[Answer:] Not so. If the perception of anger and the like reverse into cognitive afflictions, these would be concomitant with the objects when perceived. The intrinsic nature of affliction is that it changes into the inability to perceive objects clearly, or so this imputation claims. If a pervasive valid cognition is postulated, then afflictions, apprehender, and the apprehended together with their arrays will transform in a continuum. [121] Thus anger and jealousy—excluding the ninth—actualize pride, and whatever is produced is said by the great Lodrö to be cognitive obstruction. But if it were like that, anger would be produced following the perception of cravings. And if it turned into a cognitive obstruction, as asserted, or if reversed, then these would be concomitant, as the lama said. Therefore, in the past, the common goal of pristine cognition and intrinsic reality on the paths of accumulation and application was to obtain vivid clarity. This is the generation of the mind of enlightenment that is purified of conceit. The *Arcana* (180.4) says:

> The clear conviction of the mind of purity and realization is experienced in the flesh. It diminishes conceptual fancies in the mind.

That is what the lama meant.

Next, the *Summary of the Hundred Thousand* says:

The four conceptualizations that manifest have to be abandoned.

And:

> The one that is the support to engagement is conceptual con-
> sciousness. Conceptual consciousness of this support is the
> isolated factor. A person is a conceptualization holding on to
> existing as a substantial entity. A being is the conceptual con-
> sciousness of a seized imputation.

First, the heroism that is to be cultivated is a concept to be adopted. Second, that which is to be cast out is the concept to be discarded. Third, a person is really only a concept. Fourth, a mere imputation is a concept. Each of
these are further divided into nine great, medium, and smaller categories all
the way to thirty-six. The three realms are further divided into one hundred
and eight categories.

Definition and function of objects of cognition

Third, the **precise definition** is that some objects of cognition create obstacles. Another **precise definition** of this third topic is that it is not concomitant with the path of vision. In other words, the path of vision will not be
produced. Third, the **function** of objects of cognition is to impede the continuum of the path of vision so that it is not seen.

Antidotes

Second, antidotes have two modes for the elimination of any object: recognition of the proper antidote, and the mode of annihilating the object to be
eliminated.

[Question:] First, is the process of elimination through vision accomplished by the path of vision itself, or is it at the level of the Highest Bön that
elimination proceeds?

[Answer:] In the first case [i.e., being on the path of vision], where the
process will change together with the student, the *Summary of the Hundred
Thousand* counters this, saying:

When one sees the essential point of the Great Liberation and becomes familiar with it, then it is no longer extant.

In the second case [i.e., at the Highest Bön level], one can counter this by quoting the *Summary of the Hundred Thousand*:

From the moment there is no longer an existing self, having eliminated it through vision, this vision eliminates the ninety-one objects to be eliminated through insight.

The treatment of this position is threefold, from which two topics have to do with the doctrine of the others. Assertions on the Highest Bön and assertion on the path of vision are two distinct points.

[Argument:] First, someone said that the Highest Bön level is the antidote that eliminates on the path of vision.

[Answer:] If not, this would change the learning process on the path of vision where only the production of the path of vision would be sufficient, for there would be nothing to obstruct the process of elimination through insight. Because of this, [122] there would be a very small role for the Highest Bön to play when it is first collected by the elimination of vision.

Second, this Highest Bön would have no ability in the meantime. Third, when pristine cognition of this Highest Bön were produced, the process of elimination through vision would still be produced within the confines of evil destinies and their associated conditions. Fourth, when these evil destinies and their associated conditions stopped, then at that moment the path of vision would be produced, or so they said.

[Answer:] But it is not so. If one uses valid cognition for the realization of impermanence as an antidote to grasping at sound as something permanent, this would change Highest Bön as the main antidote. And this would change the vision of Suchness at the moment of the acquisition of the Highest Bön. The process of elimination together with the antidote would therefore not be found anywhere, even minimally. The path of vision would not be produced and there would be no generation of vision through the effect of counteracting the objects to be eliminated through insight. Darkness would be like total annihilation.

[Argument:] Second, someone has asked if the path of vision is real. If it were not, then all the above would be false.

[Answer:] But it is not so. The path of vision transforms learning and its

252 The Tradition of Everlasting Bön

associated conditions. The object of the process of elimination is to perform the activities of elimination.

[Argument:] If this is accepted with the above explanations, if one eliminates harm or stops the elimination through insight at the moment of the production of the path of vision, there will be no existing antidote at all, as claimed.

[Answer:] If production is not stopped, then there is no point to all that.

[Argument:] Again, the lord of scripture and reasoning said that if the point of an antidote is the production of the non-ability of the object to be eliminated, and if this is accomplished, then that is the supreme quality and there will be no impediments. If there is the activity of eliminating the root of the seed, then there is emancipation.

[Answer:] Then, there is no more distinction between the path of learning and the path of vision.

Second, in **our own tradition:** Consequently, Highest Bön is situated above the process that causes cessation and the change to the generation of the continuum. There are no impediments above the path of vision. After birth is stopped, there is only emancipation.

Third, the section on **dispelling objections** according to scriptures and reasoning is twofold:

[Argument:] First, there are ninety-one eliminations through insight that are said to be the vision insights that eliminate.

[Answer:] There is no argument here. The purpose of the process of elimination is that there will be no more impediment. The purpose is to have no more production on the path of vision, no more elimination of objects to be eliminated through insight.

Second, the stage of Highest Bön will not change the objects to be eliminated through insight that no longer exist. The process of not having any production on the path of vision is to eliminate generated objects through insight. If this is wrong, then it changes the process of learning. Concurrently, there is no changing the contradictory nature of non-abiding.

The idea of elimination through insight is not established because of the merit accumulated in this one world and its materiality, but this merit enables one to tread the stages of Heat, and so forth, great or small. The accumulation of merit does not eliminate the subtle aspects in this world, but it has its strength, great and small. Again, the training on the path of vision will not change this. When there is new production, because of merit it will not be necessary to eliminate what needs to be eliminated. [123]

The mode of the elimination of the objects

Second, the mode of the elimination of the objects that need to be eliminated is twofold: to effect cessation and to change what was generated.

To effect cessation

First, this is the cause of the appropriation of the path of vision. Thus, the elimination of the objects to be eliminated through insight and the accumulation of merit act as one at the same time to bring about the stage of Highest Bön.

To change what was generated

Second, its function is to disable the objects that need to be eliminated and that have previously been, or are in the process of being generated.

Third, it is to stop all these at the same time.

The *Arcana* (178.2) says:

> The defilements of suffering are the causes of their gradual elimination.

The *Eye of the Needle* (8.277.6) says:

> The defilements of suffering in the three worlds, and the nine grounds, are similar to the waning moon that disappears gradually.

Therefore the great, the middle, and the smaller Highest Bön are the greatest. When things produced have no more abilities, one should suddenly stop the countering process and watch for this sign.

Second, when appropriating the path of vision, one performs the activity of eliminating the objects that need to be eliminated. Its appropriation rests in two moments: the accumulation for the production of the path of vision and the collection for the cessation of the objects to be eliminated. In a third moment, the antidote produces the path of vision when these two, elimination and cessation, become equal. This explains how it will come to be.

When these simultaneous activities are present, the one mind will counter the duality of agent and object. It is also claimed that it can be done in a gradual manner. But the *Eye of the Needle* (15.118.2) says:

> When the objects to be eliminated cease, all other traces will suddenly stop being produced. All hindrances from the object of cognition in the ten layers of heaven will be purified in an instant, just like the shining sunrise.

The *Arcana* (161.2) says:

> The system of this Greater Vehicle generates the purification of all defilements in an instant.

Dispelling objections

The third topic consists in the dispelling of objections following scriptures and reasoning.

[Argument:] First, what if someone counters the statements on gradual purification presented above?

[Answer:] There is no fault here. In this worldly path, stopping the emergence of karmic influences can be envisaged as an explanation following a gradual process of purification.

The second point is threefold: dispelling objections by analyzing the emergence of new influences and stopping these new influences, dispelling the objection on antidotes concerning the objects to be eliminated, and dispelling objections to the mode of elimination.

Dispelling objections by analyzing the emergence of new influences and stopping these new influences

[Argument:] If someone says that it is like that mentioned above, then there is no elimination through insight and it is the Highest Bön that eliminates.

[Answer:] There is no fault in this. The emergence of new influences is stopped. The path of vision eliminates. There is no change in the training, but there is still the emergence of new influences.

Dispelling the objection on antidotes concerning the objects to be eliminated

The second topic is threefold: essence, objects, and dispelling objections about the action of antidotes as being effective in one single moment or through different aspects.

Essence

[Argument:] First, someone may counter with the argument against objects to be eliminated, asking if one uses one or different antidotes?

[Answer:] If the answer suggests the first case [i.e., one antidote], then the duality of object and agent becomes a contradiction. If the answer is the second [i.e., different antidotes], then valid cognition of the continuum of others enables one to remove the speculative imputation of a continuum to the others. This second point is threefold:

First, the refutation of the **system of the others** [124] is twofold:

[Argument:] First, when asserting that there is one [essence], it is said by a lama that there are different essences gathered into one person's continuum.

[Answer:] But this is unreasonable, since if the object to eliminate is an external entity to eliminate, then the antidote is one within the continuum of the individual.

[Argument:] This assertion that the second one is different from the first one is the saying of Patön.

[Answer:] If one has to choose between these two points using reasoning, then there is no completion to the antidotes' elimination process, since they do not connect or affect each other.

[Argument:] It is said that manifestation and emptiness cannot be compared; like the temperature of fire and water, they are different.

[Answer:] But it is not so. The faults of the above [position] remain as before. When an antidote with a small potential is applied for a long time to a powerful object to eliminate, the efficacy of the antidote will be negated in the process of elimination and there will be no more antidote that eliminates the former.

Second, **our own tradition** on the antidote that eliminates is that it is valid reasoning that there is an agent harming an injured object. The point of an external object involves an essential difference in the antidote in order to process elimination. The antidote that eliminates what is in the inner consciousness has a cause that is different in essence and is free of shortcomings.

The third topic consists in **dispelling objections** about the action of the antidote as being effective in one single moment or through different moments.

[Argument:] When someone says that although the continuum of the mind that performs ritual offerings and the offerings to the gods are one, the bodies are different.

[Answer:] There is no fault in this. But it is not desirable to include in one continuum what valid cognition treats as different. The antidote to the object to be eliminated is in one continuum of consciousness. This continuum is all-encompassing and cannot be changed into an antidote that eliminates. This is because their essences are different. If it were not so, then one could produce a pencil using fire, because they would be concomitant. But they are substantially different.

[Argument:] What if someone counters this by saying that the light of the gods, the hero of everlastingness, teaches that one is to lead one's practice with the purification of defilements—the objects of consciousness—while laboring at the same time in purifying the defilements of the continuums of others.

[Answer:] There is no fault here. However, it is imputed here that only the agent of defilement can produce the antidote in one's continuum.

Objects

Second, the discussion on objects to be eliminated is twofold:

[Argument:] The first point concerns the refutation when someone says that if there is an object, one cannot locate it. If there is no object, then it will change the relationship of the antidote to the elimination process, such as a flower to the forest and a sword to the battle.

Second, the answer to this is threefold:

[Argument:] First, the saying of Patön on **the system of the others** stipulates that it is acceptable to have an antidote that eliminates within a substantial entity with aggregates and objects despite the fact that the system of perception and the mode of conception are different isolate factors. The elements (*yul*) making the objects to be eliminated are permanence, joy, and so forth. The elements making the antidotes are impermanence and so forth.

[Answer:] Not so. For if it were so, what is permanent would change into an impermanent substantial entity. And if this were asserted, it would change the antidote into an isolate, right at the moment of reversal when the object is being eliminated. An existing substantial entity is not partly an isolate and a non-isolate, such as the existing universal entity of the heretics [i.e., God].

Second, **our own tradition** finds it reasonable that, to a certain degree, an antidote could eliminate perceived aggregates and objects. [125] Aspects of the mode of perception and the mode of conception are different and do not change into a single substantial entity.

Dispelling objections

Third, the dispelling of objections is twofold:

[Argument:] First, the problem here is to have a past congruence that was eliminated as an object to be eliminated among faults that were eliminated. However, nothing has been changed in elimination and so forth by the antidote.

[Answer:] A substantial entity that has been asserted but not eliminated is the claim for an object that has been perceived. If it were not so, then valid cognition and the object of a speculative imputation would be like proclaiming that an impermanent sound could be claimed to be perceived on a permanent basis.

[Argument:] Second, one must abandon logical absurdity, such as considering identical something that is devoid of a self and grasping for a self in something [existing] among aggregates and their [sensory] fields.

[Answer:] This is similar to saying that a white conch that is validly perceived can also be falsely perceived as a golden object and made an [independent] substantial entity.

[Argument:] But what if someone asks whether this will change the reality of the lack of self on account of the reality of the aggregates?

[Answer:] What is pervasive is that in reality the aggregates are empty, but one cannot cut off the speculative imputation of the uncertainty of the lack of self.

[Argument:] On the entailing argument again, someone said that what is empty is the conch that appears and not its appearance as white.

[Answer:] The pervasiveness [of the argument] is proven here.

[Argument:] On pervasiveness here, what if someone says that this is partly real and partly not real if not contradictory?

[Answer:] There is no conflict here. The real must be separated from speculative imputation. Appearances need not be separated from speculative imputation. If it is not like that, then appearances are not real, and then it cuts off the continuum and one is not able to positively make an assertion. In reality, it is parallel to stating that yesterday's continuum ceased.

Timing

Third, the response about the debate on timing is twofold:

[Argument:] First, someone may ask about the timing of the antidote's elimination: Is this done in one moment or in different moments? In the first case, is there no change to this non-localized simultaneity? In the second case, will the different moments and the antidote of transcendence clear the object to be eliminated in the future?

[Answer:] Next is the answer in three parts:

[Argument:] Concerning **the system of the others**, the great Lodrö said that in general, the others consider the object to be eliminated and the action of the antidote, past and future, as continuous. In particular, with these two—past and future—elimination through insight and the path of vision are said to be occurring for a long and uninterrupted time period.

[Answer:] But it is not so. It is also asserted that the change of the interruption is extremely swift. If it were so, it would contradict the process of elimination through insight, since it would not be able to produce the continuum of the path of vision. The simultaneity that the others assert is thus negated.

Second, **our own tradition** from the lord of scripture and reasoning stipulates the following regarding that: The path of vision and the timing are different. The cause of the path of vision is the accumulation of merit. It first concurs with the lower level of Highest Bön, as the middle level of Highest Bön has no potentiality yet. The greater level of Highest Bön appears at the time when there are no more impediments. Antidotes have no more impediments to eliminate [126] when the objects to be eliminated and the elimination through insight both stop at the same time. Immediately following this, the others say that liberation in the continuum will be continuously generated. That is it.

Dispelling objections

Third, to dispel objections about this, we call it the "non-abiding simultaneity." There is no error here.

When the ability of an object to be eliminated is small, and it comes together with a powerful antidote to negate the impediments, then it is similar to being weak in regard to cold and powerful with regard to heat. There is no elimination through insight, and the answer, as explained above, does not change.

[Another] third point consists in **dispelling objections** on the mode of elimination, and is threefold: the time the merit is accumulated, the absence of ability, and dispelling objections on the time of reversal.

The time of accumulated [merit]

[Argument:] First, someone asks about the moment the accumulations of merit mature—does the antidote stop all objects comprehensively or not? If it does that first, then the times of causation and of fruition are equal, and the moments of elimination and of the antidote working also become equal. If [the antidote] did not stop [all objects] comprehensively, then merit could not be collected and would have no beneficial particularities.

[Answer:] Though it is true that there is not one activity that stops the process of differentiation, or the accumulation of merit, or the lack of beneficial particularities. All remain the same. When there is activity of an antidote without the ability to eliminate, it is because in the first instance karma that has accumulated arises and prevents that.

The absence of ability

[Argument:] Second, someone asks: "When the object to be eliminated has no ability, the antidote and the timing of the antidote do not connect. It is similar to subsequent production and is concomitant with reasoning. But if there is connection at that time and it is concomitant with reasoning, is there subsequent production or no production?"

[Answer:] In the first case, where there is production, the antidote is not necessary since, being too weak, it has no ability in itself.

[Argument:] And if someone said that in the second case there is production, will it change the substantial entity from being a generated product to being an agent of production?

[Answer:] A substantial entity that is generated with no ability is not produced as an isolate. Rather, it is a capable antidote that is fabricated.

Dispelling objections on the time of reversal

The third topic on the timing of the reversal is discussed in three parts: the moment of reversal, the continuity of the object to be eliminated, and the timing of the reversal of the antidote.

The segments of the moment of reversal

First, the response on this is twofold:

[Argument:] First, someone asked about the object to be eliminated: When the antidote and the moment combine, are they eliminated in an instant? Or are they three different segments in a series of three different moments?

[Answer:] The first case—where these three are eliminated in one instant—is false, and the moment of their conjunction itself is the first moment when it becomes a reversal. If someone supports the second point, then the real continuum has no segments and this reversal is impossible.

The second part to this counterargument is threefold:

[Argument:] First, there is the counterargument from **the tradition of the others**. When someone says that time is indescribable and cannot be analyzed, this is not correct. These [proponents] say that it can be described and analyzed with sensible reasoning.

[Answer:] Not so. The identification of three different moments is false.

[Argument:] Again, another lama said that at the first instant when an antidote and its object to be eliminated conjoin, there is an interval during which this process cannot be stopped. But can it be said that there are no further different segments once the process has stopped?

[Answer:] Again, this is not so. If it were so, the existence of the three moments would reverse time itself, and this would be a false reckoning of the three components of time. If this is stopped and there are no segments left afterward, this will cut off the continuum of the coarse and it will change the existence of reality with the absence of segments to that reality. [127]

Second, **our own tradition** regarding that is that it is true regarding segments; they do not exist. There are no parts. Also, we cannot support the identification of three segments in an instant because of the error contained in an action that has no capacity.

Third, the **dispelling of objections**: If someone says that there is no conflict regarding the tripartite division of the above, then there is no conflict.

Because this is easy for the mind to understand, there is this teaching on the three moments. But there is no claim to the reality of these exact three moments.

The continuity of the object to be eliminated

Second, the response regarding the continuity of the object to be eliminated is twofold: first, Highest Bön eliminates afflictive obstructions, while the path of meditation eliminates cognitive obstructions. There are no objects to be eliminated on the path of vision.

[Argument:] If this is asserted, then someone may counter this saying that afterward there will be no more hindrances. Second, someone could counter this saying that this will not change [the fact] that there are no more objects to be eliminated. It is called "the elimination of the seeds of afflictive obstruction."

[Answer:] These arguments have been negated above.

[Argument:] Here, one is asserting that there are no more objects to be eliminated and therefore no further necessity for object and agent. It is not an overreaching argument, since there are no more objects of elimination that are hindrances.

[Answer:] It is similar to clouds covering the rays of the sun. Therefore, there is no need to eliminate all existing hindrances. The world exists because of all its non-desirables.

The timing of the reversal of the antidote

Third, the topic of the timing of reversal is fourfold: reality, continuum, the many seeds, the continuum of a substantial entity accompanying the stream of being, and a fifth topic that consists in dispelling objections concerning the modes that are harmful.

Reality

First, the response to this statement is twofold:

[Argument:] First, is the antidote the real agent that harms the object to be eliminated, or is the harm coming from the continuum of existence?

[Answer:] In the first case, only in a second moment would the object to be eliminated be transformed by the antidote. But this is an immature realization of the lack of self and it does not have an antidote. So there would be no real elimination of defilements. In the second case [i.e., harm coming from the continuum], the antidote would be like firewood turning into earth and water turning into ice. The antidote would transform. Water and earth extinguish the fire engendered by kindling, as one would say.

The second response is that common reasoning on antidotes versus common reasoning on the objects to be eliminated concerns the proper suitability given to the conditions [lit. "continuum"] of reality. There is no fault in the principle of elimination. Concerning the path of vision in particular and the elimination through insight, the cause of the path of vision consists in the process of elimination [of defilements] from the continuum of reality with elimination through insight.

Continuum

The second point is twofold:

[Argument:] First is the counterargument: Does the antidote eliminate the essence of the object, or its seed? In the first case, where the essence could be eliminated, it would be similar to a vase that is speculatively imputed, apprehended as permanent, and fixed in the mind as a woolen cloth. Its removal would be the antidote that eliminates this error.

In the second case, where the seed is eliminated, only the pristine cognition of the path of vision would be the transforming antidote, and this would change it into the path of learning, and that would be the end, a logical absurdity.

Next is the answer: These two [i.e., essence and seed] have an agent that performs the elimination. In particular, the middle Highest Bön eliminates without impediments the seeds in the process of elimination. If it were not so, the elimination through the path of vision would just be a form of training.

The many seeds

Third, the topic of the many seeds is twofold.

[Argument:] First is the counterargument: In what does the process of cutting off the continuum of the objects to be eliminated consist? Does it consist in cutting the flow of substantial entities, or in cutting the flow of the continuity of their existence? [128] In the first case, it is cutting off the flow of a substantial entity. If, at the moment of the elimination of the eliminating through insight, there is the thought of a substantial entity, this will change the process of elimination of all thoughts that arise. In the second case, the cutting off of the flow of the continuity of existence, here someone can say that it makes no sense to have an existing entity doing the elimination.

Second, the answer to that is that it is said that the ability of the antidote to eliminate the chain of continuity is necessary. But this makes the process of elimination through vision into a substantial entity. Therefore, the common idea is that it might be true that there is a process of elimination in the continuity of something. There is the elimination of a substantial entity in the elimination through insight, but it does not change [the fact] that there is also continuity. The force of continuity of the ground and substantial entity are doing the eliminating. But this proposition is similar to the butcher cutting flesh and then trying to put back together what was cut off.

[Answer:] When someone says that one changes continuity by severing the flow, this is [valid only] for the elimination of a substantial entity. There is no fault in this. A scripture says:

> The substantial entity of the object to be eliminated is eliminated, but there is no elimination of the substantial entity of consciousness. Consciousness is one's nature. The object to be eliminated is temporary. Intrinsic mind exists correctly through one's nature. Suffering is adventitious.

The continuum of a substantial entity with the stream of being

[Argument:] Fourth, after the points on the path of vision above, is the practice of meditative equipoise effective or not in severing thoughts? Is it one's continuum that gives rise to thoughts?

In the first case, there is no wisdom in the process of familiarizing oneself with the practice of meditative equipoise. [Familiarization] changes the process whereby there come to be no more cause for subsequent attainment and everything becomes only delusion. In the second case, thoughts arising out of the continuum make the practice of meditative equipoise into a fabricated artifice.

[Answer:] The response to these is threefold:

First, the point dealing with **the tradition of the others**, is twofold:

[Argument:] There are two positions: the continuum is cut off, or not.

In the first case, someone said that if the practice of meditative equipoise is severing thoughts or the flow of the continuum of thoughts, both of which are non-existent, then it does not change the continuum into a fabricated artifice.

[Answer:] But this prior understanding is at fault. If it is said that the world of the conventional truth is severed and the world of the absolute is not severed, then it changes one part of the pacification process. However, this is claimed instead for the sphere of reality as a counter-response.

[Argument:] For those supporting the second case [i.e., the continuum is not stopped], the general view is that when casting one's glance inside, the continuum of thoughts is stopped; however, one becomes free from the conditions of the ceaseless flow of the continuum of existence. Another position is that stopping the others is not stopping the seeds.

[Answer:] But it is not so. Meditative equipoise and mental elaborations are contradictory. These assertions that there are thoughts and that thoughts arise in the reality of the absolute are contradictory. If there is an impediment, then these cases remain similar.

Second, **our own tradition** is that there are no changes in the fabrication of the continuum through the severing of the flow of the arising of thoughts and the tainted mind. Despite the uninterrupted flow of untainted mental arising, one becomes familiar with meditative equipoise.

Dispelling of objections concerning the modes that are harmful

Fifth [third in the text], the **dispelling of objections** is twofold:
First, in this analysis, the inadmissible will be eliminated.

[Argument:] Someone said that the unceasing flow of arising thoughts [129] makes meditative equipoise into a mental exercise [lit. "elaboration"].

[Answer:] When there is no interruption of the untainted flow, there won't be any elaborations. Elaboration is when there is no meditative equipoise and there are phenomena and the self of persons.

[Argument:] In that case, one will say that established objects and those endowed with objects [i.e., the subject] would become compounded phenomena. Pristine cognition is active in phenomena, and compounded phenomena exist during subsequent attainment. Intrinsic reality is active in objects, while there are compounded phenomena in meditative equipoise.

[Answer:] Those are unproven conclusions.

[Argument:] Second, someone said that when there are untainted thoughts but objects still arise in the mind in the state of meditative equipoise, the two truths then differentiate.

[Answer:] When emptiness has refuted the true existence of a vase, it logically follows that these two are considered very different.

[Argument:] Someone said that emptiness would not negate the substantiality of the vase, and negating the isolate [i.e., the vase] would not change the absence of difference.

[Answer:] There are no tainted thoughts arising in the mind in meditative equipoise. When there are untainted thoughts arising in the mind, there is no more differentiating of the two truths. In the cognition of the expansive sphere, one perceives no differences.

Precise definition

Third, a precise definition: The essential point of Suchness is that one can directly perceive it with a sharp vision and reach it on the path.

Third, its **function** is to go far away and become industrious in actively generating the continuum of the path of meditation. The power of purification emancipates by eliminating the objects to be eliminated with the vision that eliminates. That realization is the making of the limbs of the four paths to Suchness. Its meaning is known as "manifested vision."

This was chapter 6 on the path of vision from the *Magical Key to the Precious Stages of the Path and the Grounds of the Greater Vehicle.* [130]

7. Teachings on the Path of Meditation

1. TEACHINGS ON THE PATH OF MEDITATION

Fourth, the path of meditation is where there is the chain of continuity of thoroughly imputed objects that are eliminated and where the activity of familiarization arises, free from the former. This topic is threefold: cause, nature, and function.

Cause

The first topic is threefold: its support, the accumulation of merit, and the generation of any particular ground.

The support of the cause for the path of meditation

First, although there is an active agent of action in the three realms, its support is the production of the stream of the path of vision.

The accumulation of merit as cause

The second aspect depends on the coarse sensory inputs and the specific acquisition of the path of vision.

The generation of the ground

Third, the ground of concentration is the sixth. It is produced in the three lower realms, below that of the formless world. There, the mind meanders in the world of desire. When the mind is unclear, it wanders in the formless realm above. The four causes and conditions for acquiring concentration are similar to those in the path of vision.

The nature of the path of meditation

The second point is threefold: defining characteristic, basis of characteristic, and precise meaning.

The defining characteristic of the path of meditation

Its first topic is threefold:

First comes the refutation of **the tradition of the others**:

[Argument:] Me'u Pal said that the point of intrinsic reality is to perceive it directly. One builds up familiarity with pristine cognition on the path of vision and one becomes endowed with the three distinctions. These are said to be:

1. The distinction of the essence that is the union of calm abiding and insight.

2. The distinction of the cause that arises from the accumulation of virtue of what is below.

3. The distinction of the agent that is the agent that clears away the stains of the faults of meditation.

[Answer:] But it is not so. There is the pristine cognition of the enlightened one; however, if it were exactly like what you are saying of the other traditions, this would change meditation, wouldn't it?

Again, what is called "intrinsic reality," the subsequent attainment of familiarity in the stream of the illusory subject, is not the path of meditation.

[Argument:] Again, Patön said that Suchness is associated with the concentration of pristine cognition of direct vision.

[Answer:] Subsequent attainment is not included here, and equating it with the pristine cognition of the enlightened one is an overreach.

[Argument:] Furthermore, Zhutön[156] said that the perfection of subsequent attainment of the path of vision is associated with the production of the wisdom of calm abiding and insight, and these are combined together on the stream of training.

[Answer:] But there are no constructed aspects associated with insight. The basic characteristics of what are called "calm abiding" and "insight meditation" is that they are not different at the base.

[Argument:] Again, someone has said that what follows the completion of the path of vision is intrinsic reality. This, together with the insight coming from consummate familiarity of the subject, is said to be the complete realization of elimination.

[Answer:] However, that thorough familiarity qualifies as a defining characteristic, and that defining characteristic proceeds with the demarcation of the grounds.

[Argument:] Furthermore, Dopa said that thorough familiarity consists in directly seeing the lack of inherent nature, and that thorough familiarity also consists in directly seeing the absence of manifestation that is intrinsic reality. [131]

This familiarization process of directly seeing the absence of self in manifestations is said to be the defining characteristic of each and every aspect of the common post-meditative practice.

[Answer:] However, if familiarity is qualified as the defining characteristic, there won't be any more meditative practice on the lack of an inherent self in manifestations.

[Argument:] Once again, the lama, lord of scriptures and reasoning, said that the insight that comes with familiarization with the stream of direct vision is the entire doctrinal point of truth and pristine cognition.

[Answer:] Familiarization is qualified as the defining characteristic. Second, our own Lodrö from our tradition said that the intrinsic nature of Suchness is attained through familiarization. And thus it is.

Dispelling objections

Third is the dispelling of objections:

Meditative and post-meditative states have grounds and paths. Their distinctive characteristics are unique. These defining characteristics are dual and unchanging in their definitions. Among the many distinctions of these two, there remains this common distinctive characteristic: only the path of meditation is not a product.

Basis of characteristics

Second, the basis of characteristics is threefold: the demarcation of the grounds, enumeration, and the mode of elimination of the objects to be eliminated.

The demarcation of the grounds

First, concerning the stream of the path of vision, productions are gathered through the stream of training until the time of non-production is reached.

[Argument:] Someone said that the path of attainment is situated at the limit of the stream.

[Answer:] There is no antidote to the stains of taking on an evil rebirth but the activity of elimination.

Enumeration

The second topic is threefold: there are the common divisions, their nature, and individual particular points.

The common divisions

The first topic is fivefold:

First, the **basis of division** is merely the defining characteristic that endows meditation. In essence, there are these two: the path of meditative equipoise and the path of the post-meditation period.

[Argument:] Someone mentioned the case when there is only cognition on the causal characteristic, saying: "When freedom from hatred has been attained and won over, and when there is this cognition, the seeds of the minor marks of attainment, the flowers marking the body, will be all-illuminating and omnipresent."

[Answer:] This was said concerning the realization of the result of elimination. But it is not really as has been said. There is no doctrine of the Greater Vehicle that does not realize the elimination. Thus—concerning the object, the result and the ordinary mind—first, objects do not go beyond the two truths. In the absolute, object and agent are one in meditative equipoise. In the relative, the acting agent and the object are divided in a post-meditative state.

Second, the **results** that manifest will transform into non-manifestation depending on the kind of production.

Third, these two, **stained and unstained**, will change according to the path and the grounds of meditation and of post-meditation states. When someone asks about their differences, there are three points:

First, there are the refutations of **the tradition of the others** in three parts:

the refutations of the assertion that there are no existing concepts manifesting the meaning of terms, the refutations of the assertion that there are no existing particularities between these and suffering, and the refutations of the assertion that there are no existing impure views and ignorance. [132]

The refutations of the assertion that there are no existing concepts manifesting the meaning of terms

First, someone said that at the time of the path of meditation, there are the three meditations on devotion, dedication, and rejoicing. Thus, if there are internal contaminants, devotion must be the priority. This is the object of the exalted scripture that says:

> The point of the two natures is abundance in the three excellences.

This is the meditation on devotion. Furthermore, when one is not free from constant pride, then from that moment on, the practice of the Highest Bön will help decrease devotion to one's own benefit. Subsequently, from the first ground until the seventh, there will be a middle level of devotion and the objects will be perceived in the equanimity of the two natures. Only on the eighth ground and above will there be great devotion where perception will be aimed only at the benefit of others. After that, because there are the divisions of rejoicing and dedication, when the time comes, as long as there is no freedom from concepts manifested by the meaning of terms, there is contamination. When there are signs of compounded phenomena, there is no freedom from concepts manifested by the meaning of terms.

[Argument:] It is said that there are no contaminants from the ninth grounds onward.

[Answer:] This is not so. It is illogical to have the causal characteristics depend on various philosophical positions, and it is illogical to have the demarcation of the ground dependent on designation. First, the *Summary of the Hundred Thousand* says:

> On the two grounds below, because of conceptualizing consciousness, one should persevere with the antidote of non-conceptuality in order to eliminate these. If the eighth ground and below have these, neither can be perceived.

That intrinsic reality resides in the three higher very pure grounds. That is where there are no manifested concepts of words and meanings. The changing expressions regarding their nature exist in order to convey a word that has no characteristics. The *Eye of the Needle* (16.539.3) says:

> The mind of enlightenment is on top of the eighth level of heaven.
> It is the universal basis that is the door of non-arising sensation,
> perfected qualities without fault, free from the obstruction of
> verbal expression.

The refutations of the assertion that there are no existing particularities between these and suffering

Second, if there is a first ground and below, then it transforms existing pride. The *Eye of the Needle* (16.536.6) says:

> The object of cognition is pride, great and small, and it diminishes in the mind of enlightenment that is the universal ground.

If this is asserted so, then it must be accepted. One can diminish these a hundred thousand times while diligently undertaking difficult ascetic practices. If I can see that myself, then I should be able to do so.

Again, with respect to others, there is the exhortation of Shenrab, the hero of everlastingness, the one called "the great hero" and so forth. After the practices of devotion and dedication, there is rejoicing and so forth. The explanations on many points about this Highest Bön and below clear away doubts about the path of meditation.

[Argument:] Second, a certain Me'u Pal has explained that stains do not exist in affliction.

[Answer:] If it is stated that way, then below the manifestation of the Highest Bön there are contaminations with affliction. However, on the path of vision and above, it is said that, because of their absence, there are no stains.

[Argument:] Furthermore, Dopa said that below the seventh ground there is contamination and affliction, and the three grounds above are not stained and there are no afflictions. [133]

[Answer:] If the above is like that, then it will change what is above the first ground into stages without affliction. But this is countered by the *Eye of the Needle* (16.539.2) when it says:

> On the top of the seventh level of heaven, after the objects of suffering have been eliminated, the four sea-demons are dried up!

[Argument:] Whether it is in fact free or not free from activities, the moment the path of application is stopped, it is claimed that the path becomes non-contaminated.

[Answer:] This is the reasoning; however, there is no transformation of insight on the path from the first ground and above.

[Argument:] It is said that the path of causation is not contaminated.

[Answer:] Concerning what is below as well as subsequent attainments on the three pure grounds, contamination is non-existent.

[Argument:] It is asserted that there is no suffering and the sole identifying activities are non-existent.

[Answer:] If this is accepted, then activities performed for the sake of others come to have no causes.

The refutations of the assertion that there is no existing impure view and no ignorance

[Argument:] Third, someone said that contamination is a view, and so is ignorance; however, there is contamination on the seventh ground and below. If it is on the seventh ground and below, then there is no existence without contamination.

[Answer:] But it is not so. The eighth ground and above is attained through the elimination of the seeds of ignorance. Therefore there is contamination up until the end of the continuum.

Next, **our own tradition** on whether or not there is contamination is about conditioned and non-conditioned phenomena, the making of contaminant or not, sign and purpose, whether there is affliction or not, and whether there is the activity of antidote or not that eliminates the seeds of the view on an existing self.

Is there freedom from engaging with concepts, or not? Only when engaging in the state of meditative equipoise is there no contamination. Only then is there no arising of concepts and affliction. The *Summary of the Hundred Thousand* says:

Familiarity of pristine cognition with the non-conceptual is the antidote to the conceptual. One should not become subject to the concepts of materialism and ideology.

When there is production of manifestation during subsequent attainment, it is contaminated. If it is at that moment, then conceptions and afflictions will truly arise, and because they exist, it is logical that they arise. The *Summary of the Hundred Thousand* says:

> Contaminants are afflictions and defilements. Their resulting effects are the ripening of the three worlds and the activities of contaminants.

Dispelling objections

Third, the dispelling of objections is threefold: countering with scriptures, reasoning on harm, and elimination of logical absurdity.

[Argument:] First is the assertion about contaminated or non-contaminated meditative and post-meditative states. If someone wants to support this, the *Summary of the Hundred Thousand* counters, saying:

> As for contaminants, there are no contaminations free from affliction and its blemishes.

[Answer:] There is no fault here. Freedom from affliction consists in the activity of returning toward the meditative equipoise on Suchness. When there is no freedom from this, [134] it becomes the reversing activity of subsequent attainment.

Second, the three grounds of purity come from the supporting activities of speech and mind on devotion, dedication, and rejoicing. If the distinctive activity of awareness is present, it will transform conceptions. The *Summary of the Hundred Thousand* says:

> Concepts and the antidotes to conceptuality: these two are not perceived.

[Argument:] Someone may say that if these do not exist, then the existence of the phenomena of meditation and the superior teachings are contradicted.

[Answer:] There is no fault in this. If there is the state of meditative equipoise, then these [i.e., concepts and antidotes] do not exist. However, in the state of subsequent attainment, they are present.

[Argument:] Third, someone explained contamination as part of affliction, that its absence designates meditative equipoise, and asked: When affliction has no more seeds, does it really change anything?

[Answer:] In the first case [i.e., there are no karmic seeds left], the nine grounds and non-contaminated meditative equipoise would not exist, since seeds are only one portion of the rest of associated elements. If there were no part of the latter, it would change into the subsequent attainment stage. In the second case [i.e., there is no real change], there would be no subsequent attainments of the nine grounds free of contaminants. Therefore, that would settle subsequent attainment into contaminants and affliction, and seeds would become real.

[Argument:] What if someone asks what are the associated elements? First, meditative equipoise would be just that. Second, subsequent attainment would become free of contaminants from the self-isolate.

[Answer:] There is no fault in this. Furthermore, on the first part, when meditative equipoise operates the reversal process, afflictions and seeds really change and the two cease to exist. There would be no changes to the non-existence of non-contaminants of meditative equipoise on the nine grounds. Meditative equipoise is the reversal that frees from affliction. When meditative equipoise and its array cease, there is subsequent attainment. Second, again it may be true that there are these two (meditative equipoise and subsequent attainment) and their arrays, but there are no contradictory consequences in the absence of contaminants and self-isolate, because a self-isolate free from defilement does not exist. Therefore concepts, afflictions, and their arrays cease. However, when subsequent attainment ceases, contaminants reemerge.

[Argument:] On their **function**, someone said that one essence is different from an isolate and there is realization through the strength of reality.

[Answer:] Not so. For if it were so, one essence would encompass real realization and implicit realization. That would be like making white color and the perception of white of one and the same essence. There is neither the real realization of white nor the implicit realization of the perception of white. Furthermore, it entails that even those of the Lower Vehicle with dull faculties will not differ in their abilities on the stages of the path from the intelligent ones. For that reason, the great Lodrö said that there is a difference between the one essence and different isolates. The *Hundred Thousand* says:

> When there is realization, it is different from when there is no realization.

[Argument:] What if someone says that it contradicts the unity of contaminants and non-contaminated?

[Answer:] It is asserted that there are different reversals and it is similar to what has been taught previously.

Enumeration

The enumeration of elements on the path of meditation consists in these: objects, the two truths, the two resulting bodies, contaminated and uncontaminated ordinary mind, the manifested and non-manifested, and things as they are and all that exists. [135]

[Argument:] Now then, the scripture mentions "space." Someone said that there is no indication of this regarding the path, but it does not conflict with the two teachings on meditative and post-meditative states.

[Answer:] There is no conflict here. The sound of space really teaches meditative equipoise and of its own accord teaches the production of subsequent attainment. The *Eye of the Needle* (14.444.3) says:

> The insight of non-perception produces the elimination of defilements and impediments.

The *Eye of the Needle* (16.538.2) further says:

> All accumulated virtues and sins are cleared like dust on the surface of a mirror.

The *Treasury* gives sound as an illustration. Sound teaches the terminology of subsequent attainment. As for space, it also does so on account of its similarity. One abides in space instead of [giving] rise to desires and hopes.

[Argument:] Furthermore, someone said that direct realization of meditative equipoise and the implicit realization of subsequent attainment emerge from one single essential mind.

[Answer:] That is not an overreaching argument. One single essential mind procures the support.

[Argument:] Furthermore, the direct realization and implicit realization of meditative equipoise and subsequent attainment have this support.

[Answer:] This is not an overreaching conclusion. If it were not so, the heroes of everlastingness would again become included with the dull-witted and there would be no one with sharp or dull faculties.

2. TEACHINGS ON THE EIGHT PATHS TO EMANCIPATION

The nature of the grounds

Second, the topic of their nature is threefold: the phenomenon of the object of meditation, the ordinary mind (*blo*) as the agent of meditation, and signs and benefits.

The phenomenon of the object of meditation

First, there are eight paths to liberation and this topic is threefold: defining characteristic, function, and precise definition.

Defining characteristic

First, the branch that is the process of familiarization with the lack of self consists in becoming free from non-concordant points.

Function

Second, its function is to recognize each and every essence, to collect every part, and to practice the manner of meditating on the aspects of perception.

First, the highest discourse from the world of awareness, the *Hundred Thousand*, (4.502.6) says:

> There is the primordial path to liberation away from cyclic exis-
> tence and evil destinies. There is the primordial path to liberation
> away from the company of suffering. There is the primordial path

278 The Tradition of Everlasting Bön

to liberation away from defilements and impediments. There is the primordial path to liberation away from origination and grasping at concepts. There is the primordial path to liberation away from abiding in the eight states of bondage. There is the primordial path to liberation away from ignorance and darkness. There is the primordial path to liberation away from ordinary mental concepts and cessation of the senses.

Although eight are mentioned, these are the great insights into the path of meditation of the world. Therefore, these are in the discourse of the [136] *Eight Realms* on emptiness that similarly explains these eight points, saying:

> These [comprise] the correct view on the path to liberation, correct realization, correct speech, circumspection in action, correct livelihood, correct effort, mindfulness, and the correct concentration of the path of liberation.

Second, there are the collection of the limbs and collection of training.

The collection of the limbs

The first one comprises the transformation of the antidote and having faith in others, and these two are the principal transformative limbs.

First, there are these three: view, effort, and mindfulness.

View

Moreover, the correct view is to eliminate dullness and agitation. Correct effort is to strive to eliminate the objects to be eliminated. Correct mindful recollection is to eliminate forgetfulness and laziness while actively minding advice.

Effort

Second, there are the activities, livelihood, and four realizations. Furthermore, correct speech and realization concern the view that summarizes, the realization that eliminates the eight perverse actions, realizations from previous meditative states, and confidence regarding the correct view of suitable teachings.

Mindfulness[157]

Having obtained the previous, one should casually demonstrate the previous without errors and have confidence in others. Action and diligence should combine in conduct. The limb of activity ripens one's continuum while diligence ripens the continuum of others—that is, having confidence in [being able to ripen the continuum of] others.

The third consists in **concentration** that, according to the teachings, brings good fortune and many qualities.

The collection of trainings

Second, collecting trainings consists in the following three: view, realization, and diligence. With these, one collects training in insight. Looking within, one examines appearances in subsequent attainment, and this is the manner to eliminate the objects to be eliminated. The three—speech, action, and livelihood—are collected in one's training on ethical conduct. Thus the first two, respectively, ripen one's and others' continuum.

Third, material things are to be offered to the Bön teachings. Mindful recollection and concentration are collected in the mind-training that consists in their application and the main practice.

The mode of meditation on the aspects of perceived objects

Third, the mode of meditation on the aspects of perceived objects is threefold: perception, aspect, and the mode of meditation.

Perception

First, the intrinsic reality of the four truths and the subject is the correct perception.

Aspects

The second point is threefold: aspects of the antidote that performs the elimination, aspects of the impure objects to be eliminated, and aspects of the agent in the mode of elimination.

Aspects of the antidote that performs the elimination

The first, above, is correct speech. The second consists in incorporating this into each and every section and part.

First are the conceptual mind, fixation on concept, the power of others, wrongful action, wrong effort, non-accomplishment, non-clarity, and illusion. Together, these make eight.

Aspects of the impure objects to be eliminated

Second, the aspects that are not concordant with the three trainings are these three: fixations on concepts, conceptuality, and non-achievement. None of these are concordant with insight. The three: powers from others, wrong effort, and wrong action are the aspects that are not concordant with ethical conduct. Non-clarity and illusion are non-concordant with the mind. [137]

Aspects of the agent in the mode of elimination

Third, the modes of elimination consist in correct view, realization, correct speech and action, right livelihood, diligence, mindfulness, and concentration where impure objects such as fixation on concepts, conceptuality, the power of others, wrong action, wrong livelihood, non-achievement, non-clarity, and all illusory aspects are eliminated in stages. This was mentioned and explained by the Great Lodrö.

The mode of meditation

Third is the mode of meditation: there is intrinsic emptiness in meditative equipoise and the meditation on the mirage-like subsequent attainment. These consist in the lack of inherent self on the eight paths to liberation. Wherever there is the cognition of the absence of inherent self, it is said that it will give rise to the awareness of an authentic scholar in intrinsic reality.

Precise definition

Third, a precise definition is that the main principle of the path of meditation is to travel the path through the stages.

The ordinary mind as the agent of meditation

Second, ordinary mind and awareness turn into these three: valid cognition of substantial entity, subsequent cognition through reasoning, and unascertained appearances. From the second ground to the tenth, one uses valid cognition with intrinsic reality that is connected to each and every subject. Only reasoning on intrinsic reality is understood as being part of the practice of subsequent cognition. Any instance of a knowable object becomes an unascertained appearance when it concerns its connection to intrinsic reality.

Signs and benefits

Third, the signs and benefits consist in the following: the mind is completely pacified, numerous beings are assembled, afflictions are conquered in all their aspects, the causing of harm is appeased, unsurpassable enlightenment has been suitably obtained, and these have been transformed into appropriate bases for offerings. These are taught as six.

3. THE PATH OF MEDITATIVE EQUIPOISE

Main points of individual division

Third, the main points of individual division are twofold: the path of meditative equipoise and the path of meditation on the ground of subsequent attainment.

The path of meditative equipoise

The first topic is threefold and the subsection on the defining characteristic is also threefold:

Defining characteristic

The first point concerns **the traditions of the others**:

[Argument:] They say that in their own teaching, insight derived from the performance of meditation on Suchness is concurrent with concentration. Subsequent attainment consists in becoming familiar with it.

[Argument:] This is an overreaching conclusion.

Our own tradition is expressed by the great Lodrö, who said: "The defining characteristic of intrinsic emptiness is reached through familiarization."

Basis of characteristics

Second, the base characteristic has three parts: ground demarcation, enumeration, and the essential points of individual division.

Ground demarcation

First, perfect realization of the first ground is demarcated when the knowledge of aspects has not yet been obtained.

On the next two points, the actual first is fivefold:

1. Whatever is included in the defining characteristic is the basis of division.

2. The essence is threefold: small, middling, [138] and large. Each is further divided into three, and that makes nine divisions altogether.

3. Causal characteristics are the objects of realization, the nine expanses, and the agents for the realization of the nine concentrations that bring realization on the nine conceptions on objects to be eliminated. The *Summary of the Hundred Thousand* says:

> The smallest of the smaller pristine cognition eliminates the greatest of the greater affliction.

4. The different purpose of the divisions is to produce past and future times.

5. The enumeration is used to ascertain realization and the object to be eliminated.

Nature

Second, nature is threefold: the mode of the elimination of the object to be eliminated, the mode of realization of the object to be realized, and dispelling objections.

The mode of the elimination of the object to be eliminated

The elimination of each object to be eliminated on each ground brings the acquisition of each and every realization, the separation from the stains of the adventitious.

The mode of realization of the object to be realized

The second consists in the direct realization that the mere sphere of phenomena pervades all subjects from the first ground. From the second ground upward, the realization that each and every subject is connected to each phenomenal realm consists in the realization of the nine spheres of everlastingness. Furthermore, the *Ornament of Clear Realization* (22.2) itemizes these as:

> without end, limitless, vast without end, inside and out, immeasurable, without fear, the greatly incisive apex, without extinction, without change.

Dispelling objections

Third, the disputation is twofold:

[Argument:] First, are the realizations of the nine grounds distinctive, or not?

[Answer:] In the first case [i.e., distinctive], only false realizations begin to exist as distinct from the first ground upward, and there can be no more realization of unity [while dwelling] in the sphere of phenomena. In the second case [i.e., not distinct], these are eliminated in subsequent attainment.

[Argument:] If someone says that there appear to be no distinctions.

[Answer:] The answer to this is threefold:

First, the part for **the tradition of the others** is in three segments: the assertion that there are distinctions, the assertion that there are none, and countering both assertions.

The assertion that there are distinctions

[Argument:] First, regarding the above, someone asked whether there is vivid clarity or distinctively no clarity. This point is said to be similar to a golden vase covered with nine layers of gauze, where each removal brings it to light.

[Answer:] But it is not so. The causes of occultation come from these three: the path of the object, sensory inputs, and cognition.

In the first case, the path of the object is the occulting agent. Then, whether the phenomenon of the object in space is clearly seen or not depends on the removal of the distance.

In the second case, sensory inputs do not perceive it. If it is as above, there is no production from the senses [i.e., it cannot generate the perception], then there will be no help coming from the practice of familiarization with the lack of self.

In the third case where cognition is occulted, it is on account of the essence of the mind not free from conception. Regarding this position on conceptions and whether they are clear or not, liberation is when there is freedom from concepts and the above.

[Argument:] Again, Me'u Pal said that there are different meditative states on the nine grounds. The *Eye of the Needle* (14.448.3) says:

> There is no real entity of a sky in the sky. The way of production that generates pristine cognition is a gradation of distinctive views.

[Answer:] But it is not so. [139]

[Argument:] This traditional saying that cannot be validly proven by reasoning explains that there is a distinct realization that the space of phenomena is free of each and every phenomenon in the ten grounds.

[Answer:] However, this existing space cannot be proven, although there is a refutation to this [assertion]. In this case, if space is only realized as a phenomenon, then it would exist distinctly. Therefore, on this first point, there cannot be any further realizations.

[Argument:] Moreover, it asserts that there are distinctions in order to resolve misconception. On the path of vision, people clear whatever misconceptions on objects they have, and this severing of duality and so forth is suitable in any case.

[Answer:] First, reasoning on the intrinsic reality of emptiness as the proper end to the notion of self is not a realization.

[Argument:] Second, what if someone says that in the realization of meditative equipoise there are no distinctions?

[Answer:] It would be similar to apprehending friends and foes as gifts from the gods. There are differences in aspects.

The assertion that there are none

[Argument:] Someone said that in realization there are no distinctions, but in familiarization there are distinctions.

[Answer:] This is unreasonable. Here, pristine cognition of the realization of space would change into an illusory concept. The ordinary mind apprehends distinctions in its mode of apprehension. If there were existing distinctions in the process of familiarization, when realization of the sphere of reality on the first ground were held, it would change the existing differences and the mere mode of engagement.

Countering both assertions

[Argument:] Third, someone said that there are no distinctions in the realization of meditative equipoise. The perceptions of objects in the intrinsic reality of the four truths, the body of the absolute, familiarization, and the objects of cognition of subsequent attainment, great and small, all have differences in the process of elimination. Also, there are changes among the distinct realizations.

[Answer:] Not so. If there were no distinctions in the sphere of [ultimate] reality, then would familiarization with the meditative states of the ten grounds, downward or upward, change or not change accordingly? If changes occur, these would be claimed. If no changes occur, how could there be familiarization, since there would be no production in the continuum of the knowledge of all aspects? Then there would be only the body of the absolute existing on the first ground and there would be no production in the continuum of mere mirage-like states. This would merely be an existing distinction in isolation.

Second, in **our own tradition**, the topic of reality and its valid proof is twofold:

First, while an isolate has no distinctiveness, it does have distinctiveness in its details in the following way: The sphere of reality has no distinctive realization, while each and every subject is distinct when connected to the sphere of reality. There is the action of familiarization, and similarly only the body of the absolute and subsequent attainment have no distinctiveness in the elimination of the process of eliminating through insight. Details and objects of cognition, large and small, exist as distinct in the elimination process of eliminating through insight.

The second point is fourfold:

First, meditative states of the ten grounds consist only in the realization of emptiness in the sphere of reality through the four truths on subjects that exist without being distinct. The cause resides in engaging in the apprehension of the first insight, like seeing the light of a lamp. This is proven by the scripture that says:

> The sign is the opening of the door of the path of vision in order
> to see without perceiving.

[140] The difference in this is that in the continuum of the path of meditation, there is the application without distinction in the realization of mere isolates. Engaging successfully in the continuum of vision is likened to the translucence of a lamp. In particular, subjects that are perceived as distinct are connected to all other subjects. There are distinctions in the realization of the sphere of reality that are connected to all subjects. Because realization on each ground generates no existing common particularities, it is like a lump of crystals covered with gauze.

The *Eye of the Needle* (14.448.3) says:

> Signs are systemic productions of pristine cognition that is generated and the gradual distinctions of the view.

This statement proves it. The strength of its comprehensive reasoning is proven.

Second, realizations on the ten grounds are subject-based. Only the realization of the body of the absolute has no distinctiveness because of its application with the apprehension of insight imbued with the two purities. As for the pervasive sign, it is similar to what was mentioned. As before, on subjects with particularities, these are the particularities of the four truths that are connected to existing particularities in the body of the absolute, because they are stainless and circumstantial realizations of individual realizations. These realizations are established through the elimination of every object to be eliminated that arises, as mentioned above.

Third, the subjects of subsequent attainments on the ten grounds have no distinctiveness in mere illusory realization because of the application with apprehending direct realization becoming convinced, based on one's deceptive perception, that there is a platform in the sky above. This has been said before, and so forth. The existence of familiarity here is established as pervasive, in particular with subjects already mentioned where there are great and small objects of cognition. Because of whatever clarity there is in realization, this is similar to beholding the face of the full moon [i.e., realization becomes obvious].

Fourth, subjects are eliminated on the ten grounds. There are no more distinctions among eliminations in the process of eliminating through insight. Because one applies elimination through insight on the first ground with the elimination of the seeds, this is similar to the sun dispersing the darkness. The sign that indicates a mistake [being made] is when there is no elimination in the process of eliminating through insight because it is not suitable. This is similar to the non-production of impermanence that does not stop the grasping for permanence.

It has been said conclusively that the elimination through insight is a pervasive vision into the ninety-nine objects to be eliminated.

In particular, with subjects like the above, there are no particularities to elimination in the process to eliminate through insight, whereas there are particularities to the elimination in the process to eliminate through meditation. This is because of the elimination of the nine great, middling, and small in the process of elimination through meditation. It is similar to the remedy that purifies what is already stainless. The *Hundred Thousand* says:

The sign is the elimination of the nine ordinary deluded minds.

The process of elimination is said in the scripture to be pervasive and is known as being proven itself.

Dispelling objections

Third, the dispelling of objections is fourfold:

Dispelling objections on the sphere of the absolute

First, there are two dispellings of objections on the sphere of the absolute.

[Argument:] First, when someone says: "If there is no distinctiveness in the realization of a mere isolate, this will change the future realization of intrinsic reality of the four truths and of the first ground itself." [141]

[Answer:] There is no fault here.

[Argument:] Concerning this realization, what if the realization of the details is pervasive?

[Answer:] The juniper tree is connected only to wood. It would be like changing this realization for the realization that it is an aloe plant. Therefore, only the present is connected to realization and is designated as realization.

[Argument:] Furthermore, regarding the realization that was explained, is it only about the sphere of reality and its specificity, or is it more general?

[Answer:] If it is specific as in the first case, since the sphere of reality of the four truths in the future has not yet been produced, its absence contradicts any future realization.

[Argument:] If it is a general realization as in the second case, someone said that it changes realization into a concept.

[Answer:] It may be true that there is no specific characteristic, but the present is connected to a not-yet-existent future stream.

[Argument:] Second, the refutation regarding every subject is that one can establish the connection of every phenomenon to realization only at the time of realization.

[Answer:] If there are no distinctions in the realization of the sphere of reality, this claim is faulty.

[Argument:] If someone asks if there are distinctions, then generally these distinctions would be countered whether there would be realization or no realization of a substantial entity.

[Answer:] It might be true that there is distinctiveness, but it does not change the counterargument about realization or no realization. The moment of the recognition of a vase does not entail specific characteristics or a general realization.

[Argument:] Again, someone said that in the cognizance of a subject, there is an entailing factor. An object will become distinctive as a self-isolate in the sphere of reality.

[Answer:] This argument is not pervasive here. A self-isolate in the sphere of reality has no distinctiveness, while a manifest subject has distinctiveness. Despite the realization of its emptiness, there is still distinctiveness. The mind itself has no distinctiveness in the purity of its own nature even though it is engaged in distinguishing during the realization of the elimination process on the stainless adventitious. What is endowed with the two purities still engages in distinguishing.

Dispelling objections concerning the body of the absolute

Second, the dispelling of objections concerning the body of the absolute is twofold:

[Argument:] First, someone said that if there is no distinctiveness only in the realization of the body of the absolute, then there will be no need to progress along the second ground and so forth.

[Answer:] Only during the realization of the sphere of the absolute is there no distinctiveness, while there is distinctiveness in particular realizations where flaws are connected. There is a different realization that is stainless.

[Argument:] Second, regarding distinctions in particular, if someone says that these are undifferentiated in the realization of the sphere of the absolute, and yet this is a false claim that changes the very existence of distinctions.

[Answer:] There is no fault here. In such realization as the sphere of the absolute, existence is not established, and yet it is accepted that the sphere of the absolute is connected to each and every subject.

Dispelling objections on subsequent attainment

Third, dispelling objections on subsequent attainment is twofold:

[Argument:] **First**, if only the realization of a mirage-like state has no distinctiveness, then there is no change to the absence of distinctions of the object of cognition, great and small.

[Answer:] It cannot be claimed in particular that there is no distinctiveness in a mere isolate.

[Argument:] **Second**, someone said that if there is no distinctiveness in the particular, there will be no realization of specific characteristics of mirage-like perceived objects on the first ground.

[Answer:] There is no fault in that. While one is engaged in the mere acquisition of realization, there are also other existing realizations, great and small, and so forth.

[Argument:] But these will change into false subsequent attainments of the ten grounds. [142] In the universal ground, there are seeds of false ignorance and they arise in illusory manifestations of duality in subsequent attainment states. Someone said that if this position is accepted, then there are no false illusions in non-conceptuality.

[Answer:] Not in the strict sense of the word. There exist seeds of illusion, but the brilliance of the antidote suppresses them and they are incapable of generating illusion. Then the subtle objects to eliminate are gone and the conditions to generate illusion cannot be completed.

Dispelling objections on elimination

Fourth, dispelling objections on elimination is twofold:

[Argument:] First, someone mentioned that if there is no distinctiveness in the elimination process alone, it would change the elimination process of the objects to be eliminated on the ten grounds at the time of the first ground.

[Answer:] No fault here! As for the sole object of elimination, there is no distinctiveness in the elimination of the process of eliminating through insight. However, it does not change the elimination of the objects to be eliminated on the ten grounds, in particular when there is distinctiveness.

[Argument:] Second, if there is distinctiveness in the particular, there are seeds to eliminate through insight, and this changes the elimination process.

[Answer:] It has been said: "It may be answered that when there is one single defilement, it is not pervasive, and thus it will not change the elimination process through insight of the seeds."

[Argument:] Someone wants to accept elimination through meditation.

[Answer:] The contradiction between time and event does not really change elimination through meditation. Therefore, this is accepted.

[Argument:] But there is an impediment to seeing.

[Answer:] In that case, there is an elimination through meditation but it does not change the process of elimination itself. The essences of these two (vision and meditation) are different.

Discussion on individual topics

Third, the discussion on individual topics is threefold: defining characteristic, divisions, and the recognition of realization.

Defining characteristic

First, the defining characteristic of emptiness is that one should understand that the pristine cognition that is gaining experience is becoming smaller and smaller, and so forth.

Divisions

Second, there are greater, middle, and smaller paths of meditation and each is divided in three along the categories of greater, middle, and smaller. There are nine altogether.

The recognition of realization

Third, having realized the nine spheres of everlastingness, if there is further coining of terms to concentration, such as "smaller and smaller," they refer to the so-called concentration of the perfect insight of non-perception. The *Eye of the Needle* (24.444.3) says:

> The top of the second level of heaven comes to be similar to eliminating the obscuration and defilements of the wisdom of non-perception.

The middling of the small is the concentration of one endowed with the forceful conduct of non-attachment. The *Eye of the Needle* (14.444.6) says:

> The top of the third level of heaven comes to be similar to eliminating objects during the cycle of practice of the forceful conduct of non-attachment.

The greater of the small is the concentration of the one endowed with the wonderful strength of matchlessness. The *Eye of the Needle* (14.445.1) says:

The top of the fourth heaven comes to be similar to being endowed with the uncommon mind through the wonderful strength of matchlessness.

The smaller of the middling is the concentration of one endowed with the pristine cognition of non-conceptuality. The *Eye of the Needle* (14.445.2) says:

The top of the fifth heaven comes to be similar to acquiring the condition of matchlessness through the pristine cognition of non-conceptuality. [143]

The middling of the middle is the concentration of one endowed with the conquering characteristic of never waning. The *Eye of the Needle* (14.445.5) says:

The top of the sixth heaven comes to be similar to gaining mastery over great supernatural abilities through the conquering characteristic of never wanting.

The greater of the middle is the concentration of one endowed with indestructibility. The *Eye of the Needle* (14.445.7) says:

The top of the seventh heaven comes to be similar to drying up the four water-demons through the building of the indestructible citadel.

The smaller of the great is the concentration of the never-failing memory. The *Eye of the Needle* (14.446.2) says:

The top of the eighth heaven comes to be similar to apprehending the distinctive characteristics of the inner and outer phenomena through the acquisition of the never-failing memory.

The middling of the great is the concentration of the attainment of the non-mistaken life principle. The *Eye of the Needle* (14.446.5) says:

The top of the ninth heaven comes to be similar to engaging in the irreversible ground of the attainment of the non-mistaken life principle.

The greater of the great is the concentration of the one endowed with the quintessential advice of non-distraction. The *Eye of the Needle* (14.446.7) says:

> The top of the tenth heaven comes to be similar to the bliss in the space of inherent mind coming from being endowed with the quintessential advice of non-distraction.

Precise definition on meditative equipoise

Third, the precise definition is that meditative equipoise is free from elaborations, and the stream of vision reaches the great transcendence through familiarization.

4. THE PATH OF MEDITATION: SUBSEQUENT TO ATTAINMENT

Second, the nature of subsequent attainment is threefold: defining characteristic, divisions, and further explanations on its definition.

Defining characteristic

The first topic is threefold:

[Argument:] First, Me'u Pal of the **tradition of the others** said that transcendence of the world is concurrent with the concentration of the realization of the lack of self in phenomena. Patön said that insights from the realization of the lack of self are collected through the continuum of training.

[Answer:] However, these two are overreaches when it comes to meditative equipoise and the path of meditation. Furthermore, the lord of scripture and reasoning explained that the main point of directly seeing the mirage-like aspect of everything that lacks a self rests in insights from the activity of familiarization. All this means is that this position is overreaching concerning the knowledge of all aspects and does not include the nine grounds above.

[Argument:] Furthermore, Dopa said: "(1) Awareness that is the base of the support is merely the ground. (2) Incorrect awareness changes the ground of support, cyclic existence, and the grounds. (3) The direct realization of the heroes that is the direct realization of the lack of inherent self of objects cumulates all vehicles. (4) Through the aim of correct realization, [all sentient beings] will be placed in the state of happiness of the knowledge-holders." [144]

Someone responded to this by saying that in the first case (1), the reversal of the stream of the five aggregates is overextended. In the second case (2), the reversal of the five paths of the continuum of cyclic existence will be overextended, and so on, for the five aggregates. In the third case (3), reversal on the path will not only be overextended but there will be a reversal of the path as well as absence of differences between substantial entities.[158]

[Answer:] Properties of isolates do not change their differences and the defining characteristic of self-isolates is that they are dependent. If this is accepted, then it is wrongly claimed that they exist independently.

[Argument:] Again, someone said that the agent that supports the enlightened qualities is the ground. The agent that supports the common basis of the qualities of those with keen faculties are the defining characteristics of the Greater Vehicle.

[Answer:] Yet this is not so. First, if it were, there would be no changes on the grounds of suffering of cyclic existence. However, the three realms of desire are precisely called "the grounds of suffering of cyclic existence." There is no fault here. It is also accepted when it concerns the ground of transcendence. Owing to cyclic existence, the levels of meditative concentration depend on what will be the ground of the enlightened qualities. On this assertion, the *Compendium on the Spreading* says:

> The heroes of everlastingness engage in the fatigue of concentration.

5. Teachings on the General Nature of the Grounds

Second, **our own tradition** maintains, suitably, that there are only grounds. The ground that is the support of suffering is the ground of cyclic existence. The ground that supports the enlightened qualities is the ground of transcendence. The ground that supports the final enlightened qualities has as its defining characteristic the ground of the knowledge of all aspects. This defining characteristic is connected to subsequent attainments on the basis of familiarization with the essential point of the realization of mirage-like states. The reversal of a mirage-like state is reached through the activity of familiarization. Subsequent attainment is the defining characteristic of reversal.

Dispelling objections

Third is the dispelling of objections:

[Argument:] Someone said that even a suitable ground has only a single path.

[Answer:] Even though there is a connection with a substantive entity, there is no true existence in isolation. Again, the *Hundred Thousand* says:

> There are no perceptibles anywhere because of the concentration
> of familiarity.

There is no conflict here. That is how meditative equipoise is understood.

Divisions

The second topic on divisions is threefold:

First, the boundary demarcation is as before. Second, their enumeration is twofold and is based on their reality and nature.

Reality

First of five parts: subsequent attainment is endowed with a defining characteristic, essence is nine or ten, and causal characteristic is the object of practice, training, and differences regarding the object of purification. [145]

Defining characteristic of subsequent attainment

The first consists in the practice of each of the ten unsurpassed conducts.

Essence

Second, the three trainings [i.e., morality, concentration, and wisdom] are separated into cause, essence, and result.

Causal characteristic of the three trainings

The first cause is produced on the first ground. Its second point (essence) is threefold and is the practice of ethical conduct that opens the second ground. The *Summary of the Hundred Thousand* says:

> On the second ground, there is the practice of ethical conduct and so forth. It manifests with a partial concordance with liberation, intrinsic nothingness.

This means that as a result, the Bön of everlastingness is produced without interruption in a continuum of nine intertwined contrived activities.

Training

The training of the mind is divided into three grounds. The three grounds generate the continuum of the seven correctly discerning knowledges[159] and are divided by the training of insight. There are the thirty-seven collections of Everlasting Bön, the four truths, the twelve interdependent links, as well as the fourth, fifth, and sixth levels of correct insight.

The third section on the essence of the result consists in the seventh ground that involves signlessness. Signless and completely spontaneous accomplishments constitute the eighth ground. The ninth ground is that of the completely correct insight of every aspect. The tenth ground is that of the power of great direct cognition.

Given that the seventh ground has the character of deliberateness, the *Summary of the Hundred Thousand* says:

> The nature of a conceptual mark and reality is to purify diligently.

The third, in relation to the ten non-virtuous actions, avarice, recklessness, and so forth are definitely what need to be purified. Actions and their goals are different according to the past or future, and their enumeration is certainly in accordance with causal characteristics.

The nature of the grounds

Second, their nature consists in the manner of the objects of meditation and enlightened qualities, and this topic is twofold:

First, among the ten perfections, the first ground corresponds to giving, the second to ethical conduct, and so forth. The *Summary of the Hundred Thousand* says:

> On each ground, there is a corresponding perfection.

It has been explained completely in the expanded version of the *Hundred Thousand*.

Second, there are activities for the benefit of oneself and for the benefit of others.

The first one, giving, constitutes the first ground and will provide a vision of the Loving Mother Goddess while one realizes its import. The *Minute Scriptures* (287.3) says:

> First is the ground of the Very Joyful. The ground of the Very Joyful completely purifies the obscuration of avarice. A great host of gifts perfects it completely. By giving, one will see the face of the Loving Mother.

The second ground of ethical conduct is an insight that is similar to gradually seeing the Loving Mother and so forth. This second point is threefold: the enlightened qualities that acquire distinctive marks, the enlightened qualities of the realization of subjects endowed with distinctiveness, and the enlightened qualities of emanations endowed with distinctive bodies.

The enlightened qualities that acquire the distinctive marks

First, *Leaping the Grounds of Everlastingness* says:

> The trichiliocosm of worlds can be seen filled with myriads of precious treasuries. Yet these precious treasuries equal in number

to the trichiliocosm can be seen inside the palm of one's hand. [146] I see myself putting on the kingly armor and defeating all quarreling enemies to the end. The energy gathers all different kinds of flowers from the four quarters of the great circle of divinities, and adorns the consort. I see my head adorned with garlands of Campaka flowers. I see four staircases and a precious pond filled with golden sand. Its unsullied water is endowed with the eight enlightened qualities. I see enjoyment fields of kindness with eight Utpala flowers. To my right and left, having seen sentient beings in the abyss of hells, I perceive the return of the uncorrupted and the strong. To the left and right of my shoulders stands the king of carnivorous beasts, crowned with the mane of a lion, terrorizing all minor carnivorous beasts. Looking at this circle in front, many myriads of beings circle me as the universal monarch. I see many different precious ones under decorated white parasols looking back at me. Myriads of precious enlightened ones are appearing in all hues, circling while looking in front to the teacher of Bön.

This tenth ground is taught as the sign of the acquisition of the ten grounds. Each of these is perceived and acquired with each of their formulas of concentration.

The enlightened qualities of the realization of subjects endowed with distinctiveness

Second, *Leaping the Grounds of Everlastingness* says:

> In the teachings of Bön and so forth, there are hundreds of ordinary bodies, past and future, where one has and will abide in periods of long-enduring and fluctuating times. With the acquisition of the first ground, the heroes of everlastingness will perceive the faces of hundreds of blissful ones. They will receive blessings from hundreds of these blissful ones. They will sway toward the lands of hundreds of these blissful ones. They will go to the lands of hundreds of these blissful ones. They will dwell in hundreds of time periods. They will know hundreds of hundreds of places in the past and future. They will have the ability to manifest in

hundreds of bodies. They will have the ability to congregate in hundreds of hundreds of circles of heroes at any time. They will have the abilities of hundreds of gatekeepers of Bön. They will have the ability to bring to maturity hundreds of sentient beings, and in like manner, on the second ground this ability will multiply to the thousands. On the third it will be to the tens of thousands. On the fourth it will be to hundreds of thousands. On the fifth it will be to tens of millions. On the sixth it will be to eleven millions. On the seventh it will be to hundreds of millions. On the eighth it will be to one billion. On the ninth it will be to billions. The tenth produces enlightened qualities in innumerable numbers [of beings], greater than billions.

The enlightened qualities of the emanations endowed with distinctive bodies

Third, the cause of taking birth is twofold: the acquisition of a body, and its essence.

The acquisition of a body

First, the answer to the disputation on this topic is twofold:

[Argument:] First, do heroes of everlastingness take birth in cyclic existence, or not? In the first case [i.e., they take birth], what is the cause? If there is no cause, then the non-cause is changed [i.e., negated] into rebirth. In the second case [i.e., they don't take birth], [147] then someone may say that they cannot be agents fulfilling the welfare of sentient beings.

The answer to the second point is threefold:

First is the refutation of **the tradition of the others**.

[Argument:] Me'u Pal and others have said that the causes of the heroes of everlastingness taking rebirth are the following two: affliction and cognition. The obscurations to cognition are eliminated when there is a co-emergent production of the obscuration of affliction. They have the ability to eliminate [afflictions], yet there must be a cause of taking rebirth. If there is no application of elimination, it is like yeast and lees when making beer. When a continuum ends, elimination of the other happens at the same time.

[Argument two:] Again, someone said: "When suffering is produced, primordial cognition is impeded, cyclic existence is produced, and the existence of the four defilements [i.e., conflicting emotions, world-forming activities, the obscuration of knowable phenomena, and karmic propensities] subsequently produces concordant continuation. The first, suffering, consists in eliminating duality while not eliminating duality for later in order to precipitate a later rebirth. The cause of taking a rebirth is intention, and the ability to kill the poisons later is included in this intention."

Countering these statements is twofold:

First, these propositions cannot be accepted as such. An antidote has the potency and ability to eliminate objects of the same measure that need to be eliminated. It is similar to touch, which has the ability to sense heat and cold. Antidotes are not at the same place at the same time. Yet it is also accepted that there are objects that, once eliminated, become nothing. If only the strong antidote is perceived at a given time, it is because the object eliminated can no longer be perceived.

Second, how absurd these statements are!

[Argument:] Well then, someone else has said that the resulting acquisition of the state of Foe Destroyer of the Lower Vehicle is supported by the absence of afflictions. However, those belonging to that state are born without the cause of engaging in activities for the welfare of others, which is the entrance to the path of the Greater Vehicle. They are taught about the supports of ignorance, impediments, and so forth. If the proposition were exact, what would be supportive to both the heroes of everlastingness and the Foe Destroyers?

[Answer:] For this reason, they are independent, not the same.

6. TEACHINGS ON THE CAUSE OF SPIRITUAL HEROES TAKING REBIRTH IN CYCLIC EXISTENCE

Second, **our own tradition** is concordant with the two above. Concerning the cause of birth from the seventh ground downward, afflictive hindrances that are co-emergently produced are the causes of compassion. On the three pure grounds above, the condition for the impediment of ignorance offers the conditions for uncontaminated but conditioned factors. Former aspirations generate them. If there is an end to the continuum [of existence], it is through uncontaminated actions, concentration, and aspiration-prayers. These are the three that generate the support. It is said that this is the correct [understanding of] interdependent arising.

Moreover, the great Lodrö said: "The condition for the impediment of ignorance offers the condition for uncontaminated compositional factors. The condition for aspiration prayer among the three is supporting the taking of rebirth for the heroes of the ten grounds." The *Treasury* (129.5) says:

> The strength of actions such as these is the generator. [148]

The *Eye of the Needle* (16.521.7) says:

> After the moment when the self has completely ended and the aspiration for leading other sentient beings has been cast, the power of the aspiration that was planted to tame with fortitude to this place will now display this leadership.

The *Eye of the Needle* (1.7.4) further says:

> The migrators are led to liberation through the compassion of the four immeasurables. The welfare of sentient beings has been completed.

The third point consists in **dispelling objections**:

[Argument:] There is no need to have conditions for the cause of afflictions.

[Answer:] This is accepted and it supports uncontaminated compassion.

[Argument:] Someone said that from the division of the twelve links of interdependent origination, there are no changes in beings.

[Answer:] The *Treasury* (97.6) says the following concerning this:

> Impurity does not matter. It matters when it concerns the interdependent arising of purity only, for it teaches the correct form and names.

The *Treasury* (4.3) says again:

> Interdependence and connection are the doings of duality.

Second, based on that, the body that is obtained is the agent for the welfare of sentient beings and produces the maturation of one's principle. This is twofold:

First, it demonstrates that migrators can be tamed, just like rabbits, irritating demons, and so forth, or great whales during times of famine, or a youthful doctor and so forth during an epidemic. One can work for the welfare of sentient beings through emanations.

Second, the heroes who dwell on the first ground take on the body of a universal monarch of the world. Similarly, those on the second ground take on the body of a universal emperor of the four continents. Those on the third ground take on bodies of the thirty-three realms. Those on the fourth ground take on bodies of the realm that is free from extremes. Those on the fifth ground take on bodies of the Joyful realm. Those on the sixth ground take on bodies of the enjoying-emanations realm. Those on the seventh ground take on bodies of the realm of miraculous and powerful deeds. Those on the eighth ground take on bodies of the one-thousand-and-one highest worlds. Those on the ninth ground take on bodies of the one-thousand-and-three realms of finality. Those on the tenth ground that fulfill the essential purpose of the Greater Vehicle take on the body of a universal monarch, the dominant function.

Miscellanea

Third, discussion of the main points on different topics is threefold: ·

[Argument:] The **defining characteristic** of the second ground consists in familiarity with the mirage-like characteristic that produces the smallest of the small activity of familiarization. The defining characteristic of the second division consists in the familiarization of subsequent attainment with intrinsic reality. It is also said that the two subsequent attainments of familiarity are subject and pristine cognition.

[Answer:] Not so. There is no production in intrinsic reality, and this negates subsequent attainments. Furthermore, it changes the great, the middling, and the small sections of the path of meditation.

Third is the **precise explanation**:

First, when the qualities of the nine great, middle, and small paths of meditation arise, and in particular on the first ground of complete joy, fearlessness toward cyclic existence, the production generated in the continuum of experience from a previous birth, the body and mind, become enhanced with joy. Next, like a stainless [149] crystal, ethical conduct is freed from the stains of random activities, and the objects imputed to be eliminated are purified. Third, like light rays emanating, one emanates rays of light for the benefit of others, and one emanates light rays that pacify the distress of others. Fourth, the transformation of the seal eliminates the impediments of suffering while it seals non-arising for later. Fifth, the accumulation of clouds in intrinsic reality is the realization that collects many formulas of concentration. Sixth, the realization endowed with bliss cuts the rope of the impediments of taking a rebirth conditioned with suffering and overpowers non-concordant conditions. Seventh, the spiritual level of the Universal Tamer that fulfills all wishes eliminates the seeds of affliction from the root and establishes the wish-fulfilling compassion for the sake of others. Eighth, correct non-craving consists in having no cravings; it comes after the purification of the defilements of affliction and is made pure through the finality of one's aspiration. Ninth, the circle of letters is taking to heart the meaning of non-production of the letter A, from which knowledge of the essence of everything arises. It is established in the magical circle of the method. Tenth, the ground of everlastingness is the unchanging activity of transformation in supreme acuity, the wisdom of the unchanging activity endowed with the power of the antidote that eliminates the objects to be eliminated.

A third **precise explanation** is that all the qualities that arise—if they have a common basis—are subsequent attainments.

Another third topic is the **mode of elimination** of the objects to be eliminated, and is threefold: the meditation eliminating the objects to be eliminated, the mode of gradual elimination, and the mode of sudden elimination.

The meditation eliminating the objects to be eliminated

First is threefold: cause, nature, and function.

Cause

First, the cause is that there is no more need for the elimination of grasping in greater or smaller degree, in oneself or others. There is no more incorrect attention that arises in dualistic appearances and conditions, nor is there origination of the three impediments of inappropriate activity. The *Arcana* (180.6) says:

> The cause of the defilements of the objects of cognition arises from grasping at the self and others.

304   *The Tradition of Everlasting Bön*

Nature

The second topic is threefold: defining characteristic, divisions, and definition.

Defining characteristic

[Argument:] First, the master, the great lord, said: "There is the object of reversal of the continuum through the realization of meeting the path of familiarization that sees what arises as not being the complete cause of grasping onto a self. It operates through co-emergence." Familiarization is qualified by the object defined; however, is it the existing object that reverses the continuum when meeting with familiarization? Does familiarization meet with a real object, or is it the familiarizing agent that is not met?

[Answer:] In the first case, where familiarization meets with the object that reverses the continuum, this would change familiarization into an isolated factor, an object to be eliminated from the smallest part of the path of meditation.

In the second case, where familiarization meets with a real object, it would change the result of the elimination process [150] and the meeting with familiarization would become a false one.

In the third case, where familiarization does not meet with an agent, reversal itself would change starting on the path of vision, as is falsely claimed.

[Argument:] Furthermore, Dopa said that the path of meditation can become harmful when afflictive defilements are present. Whatever conceptualizations there are, they become harmful on the path of meditation as defilements of cognition.

[Answer:] However, the knowledge of all aspects has no harmful object, and what this refers to here is the path of vision. The object that is defined is thus qualified. Below, there are more afflictive defilements.

[Argument:] Furthermore, someone said that every aspect is impeded, and this affects the chain of co-emergence.

[Answer:] There is a chain of some hindrances but this is really about the process of elimination through insight.

7. CONCERNING ELIMINATION THROUGH MEDITATION

Second, from **our own tradition**, the great Lodrö said: "Any view on the self that is suddenly generated is reversed through the path interlacing with insight."

Third, the **dispelling of objections** on the object being defined, has the following two topics: affliction and cognition, and there is no fault in the unsuitability of using only one defining characteristic.

[Argument:] What is called "elimination through meditation" does not have a definition. Is it a gradual reversal or is it sudden? In the first case, there is no path that ends the continuum on the path. In the second case, it can be asked whether, from the second to the tenth ground and above, it is incorrectly called "the path of meditation."

[Answer:] No fault here! Of these two cases, it is the second. The tenth ground interrupts the stages below at once. It is the end of the continuum in isolation.

Divisions

The second topic on divisions is threefold: ground boundaries, enumeration, and individual points.

Ground boundaries

The first topic consists in all the agents obstructing the above, the acquisition of insight.

Enumeration

The second, enumeration, is twofold: factual boundaries and their nature.

Factual boundaries

The first topic on what are the factual boundaries is fivefold:

1. The base is the elimination through meditation of what is endowed with a defining characteristic.

2. The essence is the duality of affliction and cognition.

3. The causal characteristics concern these two: impediments and the activity of engaging.

4. Designation is done through cognition and the affliction of the thoroughly imputed.

5. The principle of these divisions consists in whether the agent of obstruction is one, or whether obstruction and principle are different.

[Argument:] The great Lodrö said that if there is no difference, then there is an isolate in the one essence.

[Answer:] If it is like that, then it changes the three pure grounds above into those that have afflictive obstructions. A single essence does not have two parts.

Enumeration concerns the activity of engaging and its reality.

Their nature

The nature of enumeration is threefold: reasoning on objects to be eliminated, the particularities of the reasoning, and dispelling objections with regard to them.

Reasoning on objects to be eliminated

First is what later comes from the thoroughly imputed and the co-emergent. [151] These are, respectively, affliction and cognition. Someone quoted the *Eye of the Needle* (16.536.5), saying:

> From the purification of the obscuration of affliction comes the
> real cause for the obscuration of the objects of cognition [i.e.,
> knowables].

It is accepted from the teachings that there are no obstructions to afflictions. If that were so, this saying from the *Eye of the Needle* (14.445.7) counters it:

> Above the seventh heaven was erected the indestructible citadel
> on the dried-out bodies of the four water-demons.

The particularities of reasoning

This second topic has already been explained above.

Dispelling objections

Third, there are two defects to eliminate through scripture and reasoning; on the first one, the *Eye of the Needle* (14.448.2) says:

> On the tenth level of heaven, obscurations to the objects of cognition are purified in one moment, as when the sun rises in the sky.

This is used to counter arguments. But it does not counter them. The important main point of the teachings here is the intention of ending the continuum. The *Summary of the Hundred Thousand* says:

> The seventh ground consists in the effortful elimination of characteristics.

[Argument:] Second, someone said: "If the seventh ground has obstructions to afflictions, it changes the process, as there will be no more elimination through insight."

[Answer:] The existence of the thoroughly imputed does not establish the existence of co-emergent factors.

Individual points

The third topic on individual points is twofold:
First, the point on obstructions to affliction is threefold:

Obstructions

The **defining characteristic** of obstructions is that the view of selfhood creates hindrances to acquiring the particular path that is concurrent with the base.

The second point [on affliction] deals with its **divisions**:
[Argument:] The lord said: "There are five poisons, such as ignorance and so forth, and they are divided into greater and lesser ones among the realms and the grounds."

[Answer:] Although he may have said so, in this case, it logically follows that the elimination through insight would be no different from [elimination through] imputations.

[Argument:] However, one may say that this was just a line of co-emergent factors.

[Answer:] For example, it is these two, anger and wrath, that take possession of oneself. Their elimination would be easily done, given the above. Therefore, the objects that come to mind and are supported by the mind are dependent, and one's qualities, too, are similarly related. What is endowed with aspects and is in-between is dependent. Therefore, along these aspects, the roots of the four kinds of impediment—ignorance, the realms, the grounds, and the objects—are so divided.

Precise definition

Third, the definition: The continuum of one's mind activates affliction, while the defilements on the path with special distinctiveness and what is concomitant with the basis still remain as they are.

Defilement

Second, the discussion on obstructions to knowables is threefold:

First is the **defining characteristic**: The view supporting an existing self of phenomena concomitant with the basis impedes the knowledge of all aspects.

Second, from the point of view of objects, there are **divisions**, and from the point of view of the essence, there are divisions, and from the point of view of gradation [lit., "great and middle"], there are also divisions.

The point of view of objects

First, the divisions consist in the teachings on the intrinsic reality of the four truths as objects, subject, the person grasping at a substantial entity, beings grasping imputations, [152] engaging with what is supported, concepts sustaining isolates, and division concerning the realms.

The point of view on the essence

Second, each of the ten grounds has its own essence that is not realized; the delusion of not recognizing the above brings one through the three [lower realms], and one falls into an evil destiny.

The point of view of gradation

Third, in accord with the nine stages, the greater of the great elimination through meditation is said to have the obscurations of impediments, the objects to be eliminated. The *Eye of the Needle* (15.555.3) says:

> Above the second level of heaven, the wisdom of non-perception purifies the obstruction of the impediments.

Similarly, the *Eye of the Needle* (15.555.36) has this to say on the greater of the middle, the impediments of things and of cyclic existence:

> Through the courageous conduct of non-attachment, the impediments of things and of cyclic existence are purified.

On the greater of the small that concerns the impediments of the nine grounds and the three realms, the *Eye of the Needle* (16.538.5) further adds:

> On top of the fourth level of heaven, the impediments of the nine grounds and of the three realms are smoothed out and cut out.

The middle of the great is the impediment of grasping objects of cognition. The *Eye of the Needle* (16.538.6) says:

> On top of the fifth level of heaven, past the objects of cyclic existence that are all suffering from illusion, rises the non-conceptual pristine cognition from the basis of the impossible imagination.

The middle of the middle is the impediment of taking birth in suffering. The *Eye of the Needle* (16.538.7) says:

> On the top of the sixth level of heaven, within the mud of cyclic existence where one has taken birth in suffering, the pure mind of enlightenment has an unlimited ability to fathom.

The middle of the small is the impediment of the four water-monsters. The *Eye of the Needle* (16.539.2) says:

> On the top of the seventh level of heaven, after the objects of suffering have been eliminated, the four sea-demons are dried up!

The smaller of the great is the impediment of forgetfulness. The *Eye of the Needle* (14.446.2) says:

> On the top of the eighth level of heaven is the acquisition of retention that does not forget.

The smaller of the middle is the impediment of the character of deception. The *Eye of the Needle* (14.446.5) says:

> On the top of the ninth level of heaven, attaining the mind of non-deception, one is established on the ground of irreversibility.

The smaller of the small is the impediment of the distraction of the aspects of the objects of cognition. The scripture says:

> On the top of the tenth level of heaven is the nail of the principle of unwavering concentration.

Precise definition

Third, a precise definition is that some objects of cognition impede knowledge of all aspects, but those that are concurrent with the base still remain. Another third definition is that with the thorough familiarization of the path of meditation there comes elimination.

Function

Third, the function is that the path of meditation above impedes the knowledge of all aspects.

The mode of gradual elimination

Second, the topic of the mode of gradual elimination is threefold: the mode of elimination as per the strong arguments of the others, the mode of elimination as per the strength of our arguments, and dispelling objections on the latter.

The mode of elimination as per the strong arguments of the others

First, the scripture says:

> On the thirteenth level of heaven, the blessings of the compassion of the perfect body of enjoyment purify the defilements of the objects of cognition. [153]

The *Eye of the Needle* (8.273.3) says:

> The bright lights of the gods of the intermediate states are the defilements from the objects of cognition of the heroes of everlastingness, so that the latter have their compassionate teachings flow out to people.

Transmission is about purification.

[Argument:] Someone said that the tantras differ regarding the objects of purification and contradict the process of elimination through absence of an agent on the objects for the antidote.

[Answer:] There is no capacity for really eliminating the objects to be eliminated. Yet, because of that, it is accepted that there is the process of elimination that the scriptures transmit. Second, what is mentioned as "the activity of eliminating, the greater of the great, the elimination through meditation" is from the *Summary of the Hundred Thousand*.

The second ground, the greater of the great object to be eliminated, consists in the obstruction of the impediments that are present in the continuum. The antidote that is the generation of emancipation, the smaller of the small, is generated in the continuum as the concentration of the perfect insight of non-perception. At first, they are assembled. In a second moment, the aptitude of the antidote incapacitates the object to be eliminated. In a third moment, the stream of the object to be eliminated is reversed [i.e., stopped], and the antidote generates the continuum that expands in realizations continually produced by others during the following moments. Furthermore, it is said that this ending of the very object to be eliminated that produced the defunct impediment is the antidote that is causing new influences to come into being. Similarly, the levels below the tenth ground are produced in like manner.

Third, overcoming the faults of scripture and reasoning is twofold:

First, the *Eye of the Needle* (8.277.7) says:

Purification is concluded in one single moment.

Furthermore, the *Arcana* (179.2) says:

The system of this Greater Vehicle purifies all defilements in one single instant.

If someone objects to this, then starting with the first quotation above, if it is the terminus of a continuum, then it is the small antidote at the moment of the elimination of the greater of the great, the object to be eliminated. When the great realm of desire is eliminated, the three great objects to be eliminated from the formless and the form realms are consequently eliminated. Similarly, the three middle and the three small ones are also eliminated.

The quotation that followed is from the scripture on the teachings of the Greater Vehicle without antidote that eliminates. In this second quotation, there is no elimination of great objects to be eliminated by a small antidote. The great antidote is not needed for eliminating small objects needing to be eliminated.

[Argument:] Someone may ask if there are greater and smaller strengths of antidote.

[Answer:] This is correct. The greater the object to be eliminated, the coarser the antidote. The smaller it is, the more difficult it becomes to easily eliminate the subtle. The *Summary of the Hundred Thousand* says:

Value the purification of the great obscuration and the stains! Clear away the smaller manifestations! Similarly, one must diligently use this great principle to purify the minute parts. When great pristine cognition is present, from here on, great affliction ceases to be. When great affliction is present, from here on, great pristine cognition ceases to be.

Simultaneous elimination

Third, simultaneous elimination is the final elimination at the end of a continuum. This topic is threefold: the nature of the antidote that eliminates, [154] the nature of the stain that is the object to be eliminated, and the mode of elimination.

The nature of the antidote that eliminates

First, the answer to the following question is twofold:

[Argument:] First, when the stream of the ten grounds ends together with the stain of taking on an evil destiny—the object to be eliminated—is this the action of an antidote that eliminates, or not? In the first case where there is an antidote, it changes the knowledge of all aspects into the path of training. In the second case where there is none, one could say that there is no acting impediment to the production of the knowledge of all aspects.

[Answer:] The response to these two is threefold:

First, the refutation of **the tradition of the others**:

[Argument:] Someone said that only the knowledge of all aspects is asserted as the antidote.

[Answer:] This changes the knowledge of all aspects into a path of training, so then it is not a result.

[Argument:] Furthermore, some said that on the path without impediments, the concentration similar to everlastingness is elimination.

[Answer:] But it is not so, for in the production of the knowledge of all aspects, obstacles are not made but are cleared away.

8. Teachings on the primordial cognition of the end of the continuum

Second, **our own tradition** on primordial cognition at the end of the continuum is threefold: cause, nature, and function.

Cause

First, there are the causes that produce these four conditions:

1. Causal condition is produced through the mind of supreme enlightenment.

2. The leading cause is the practice of the path during innumerable time periods.

3. The objective of the cause is the intrinsic reality of emptiness through the duality of apprehended and apprehender [i.e., subject and object].

4. The immediate condition stems from the past insights derived from the familiarization with the lack of self.

Nature

Second, its nature is the process that stops prior conditions and is the antidote to the process of production. First, it is the concentration that is like the indivisible equanimity of everlastingness. Furthermore, the realization of cyclic existence and emancipation as equal and non-dual is the apprehension of the concentration of the indivisible equanimity. If it is unchanging and firm, then it is the apprehension of the concentration that resembles everlastingness.

[Argument:] What is the pure pristine cognition of the enlightened one? If it is unceasing, it is said to be the path without hindrances.

[Answer:] The essence of the self is the non-conceptual pristine cognition that resembles the sky. It is the concentration that destroys all the subtle aspects of sensations.

[Argument:] Second, the pristine cognition of the enlightened ones is said to be the severing of the continuum, the antidote to prolonged distant activity.

[Answer:] Yet again, it must be.

Function

Third, its function is to eliminate taking an evil destiny while engaging in the activities to fulfill the good fortune of the two welfares [i.e., of oneself and others].

Dispelling of objections on cessation and new influences

The third topic consists in dispelling objections on the process of cessation of new conditions and the process of the creation of new influences.

The dispelling of objections is twofold:

[Argument:] First, someone may ask about the antidote of the elimination through insight that is used on the path of vision. If it is the antidote against grasping at the permanence of words, doesn't it change the realization brought about by valid cognition on impermanence?

[Answer:] Affirming the process of cessation of prior influences does not prove the assertion that it changes the process of creation in the strict sense of the word.

[Argument:] What if someone says that, like the second proposition where it nullifies valid cognition and the realization that it brings, doesn't it change the learning process on the pristine cognition of the knowledge of all aspects?

[Answer:] Upholding the process of creation does not prove the assertion that the process of cessation is unreal. [155] The existence of the process of creation does not entail the necessity of the activity of eliminating the objects to be eliminated.

The objects to be eliminated

Second, on the objects to be eliminated, the *Eye of the Needle* (14.540.1) says:

> An antidote that is non-concordant is the hindrance of a wild ass. Not realizing this, the mind pursues sensations. This mind is similar to a wild horse; it is difficult to subdue. If tamed using the doctrine of infallible compassion, the result will be lasting. The tendencies that predispose toward sensations exist only in the mind.

What is said to be the predispositions of a wild ass here are the objects to be eliminated. The predispositions of an evil mind are subtle and are said to be the stains making one take an evil destiny. The subtle aspect is the one existing at a subtle level. It is the predisposition that is set in a very subtle way in the elimination process through meditation.

9. Teachings on the Objects to be Eliminated at the End of the Continuum

Mode of elimination

Third, the mode of elimination of the objects to be eliminated is threefold: elimination through the process of cessation, elimination of the process of creation, and thoughts on their significance.

Elimination through the process of cessation

First, the cause is the pristine cognition of the enlightened ones and the other cause is the concentration that resembles everlastingness. These two go against the stains of taking an evil destiny. In the first moment, they are gathered together. In a second one, the objects to be eliminated are incapacitated and the antidote becomes extensive. In a third moment, the objects to be eliminated are stopped and become equally counteracted at the moment of the antidote.

Second, the great Lodrö said: "The same moment these two are stopped, pristine cognition of the enlightened ones is produced. It is done at the exact moment of the cessation of production. The two cognitions are held, and cause and result change at the same moment."

Again, the lord said: "Changing the process of creation eliminates the seeds by their roots."

However, this changes into training and its related limbs.

The *Summary of the Hundred Thousand* says:

> When the elimination that stops the seeds changes—the moment it ceases—other seeds begin to be constantly produced in the continuum. It is in the perfecting of the skill of elimination that one is brought to completion.

Third, when the object to be eliminated and the antidote cease at the same time, the generation of traces is stopped.

Precise definition

Third, the precise definition: The path of familiarization makes one reach the ground of the enlightened ones.

Function

Third, its function is to eliminate through the eliminating activity of meditation while activating the generation of the continuum of the knowledge of all aspects.

Precise definition of the path to liberation

Third, the precise definition: When the torments of cyclic existence are completely transcended and the knowledge of all aspects is being acquired, this is the path to liberation.

Function of the path to liberation

Third, its function is to activate the production of the continuum that is nearing the knowledge of all aspects.

Another third precise definition is whatever place one has reached, this is the path. [156]

Its functioning

Third, its functioning: The results of bliss and suffering have the function of ripening everything. The path of actualization is the activity of familiarization. Concerning the nine great, middle, and small activities, it consists in complete elimination while one progresses along the path to everlastingness, and then subsequent attainment is realized extensively. It is said: "Actualizing familiarization brings the acquisition of the knowledge of all aspects."

This was chapter 7 on the path of meditation from the *Magical Key to the Precious Stages of the Path and the Grounds of the Greater Vehicle.* [157]

8. Settling on the Results of the Teachings

1. TEACHINGS ON THE RESULT OF PRACTICE

Just as in the third point above, the topic concerning the arising of the results of practice is threefold: the cause of the accomplishments of the enlightened ones, nature, and function.

The cause of the accomplishments of the enlightened ones

First, the causal condition is first produced in the mind and afterward on the path. It is planted and then nourished, respectively. The governing condition is the practice of selflessness. The objective condition refers to the object perceived in the reality of emptiness through the modality of the apprehended and the apprehender. The immediate condition is the production through the pristine cognition of the end of the continuum.

Intrinsic nature

Second, the nature [of practice] is to come to a definitive conclusion through counterattacks and through ascertaining inherent nature.

2. REFUTATIONS OF THE POSITIONS ON THE ABSENCE OF ENLIGHTENED QUALITIES OF REALIZATION THROUGH ELIMINATION

The first topic concerns the ground of the enlightened ones:

[Argument:] Someone said that if one's own continuum is a collection of aggregates and if pristine cognition is also a collection, then both are compounded [phenomena]. If these are not compounded, then there are no enlightened qualities that realize elimination.

The answer to this is threefold:

First, the refutation of **the tradition of the others** is twofold: the assertion that the pristine cognition of the enlightened ones is not a collection, and the assertion that it is.

First, the discussion that it is not a collection is twofold: the assertion that there is no realization of elimination and the assertion of the cutting off of the continuum of cognition.

The assertion that there is no realization of elimination

First, if one includes the system of the heretics in this discussion, there are no benefits in the process of elimination for any of them. The nature of their mind is stained, so they do not succeed in the elimination process. They have no knowledge of a method to activate elimination in order to affect reversal. Elimination is not yet taught among them. There is no accumulation of benefits for realization. This lack of accumulated benefits eradicates the activity of meditation, in the same way as does striving to capture familiarization. It is said that this is because they have no teachings on realization. Since there is no activity for accomplishment, their position is harmful. This first is similar to the gradual system; it has not been proven that the nature of the mind is stained. Created opportunistically, their system is exhausted because of its proliferations.

Second, it is not proven, since the wisdom of the realization of selflessness is the result of its elimination. Insight through meditation has been proven in the above discussions of elimination.

Third, it is not proven because there is no reversal to the elimination of the seeds. A scripture says:

Because the ground is irreversible, it is inexhaustible and exalted.

Fourth, again, it is not proven. The *Eye of the Needle* (14.403.4) says:

Having subsequently produced an awareness drawn only from presence, the awareness of midday is established. The lives of all three times, past, future, and present, are causing changes that can be differentiated by cause and result.

Fifth, again, it is unproven [158] because the complete mastery of familiarization and its realization are free and independent of striving or not striving.

Sixth, again, it is unproven because of the complete mastery of realization. It is steadfast and unchanging. The *Summary of the Hundred Thousand* says:

> It is an unchanging, perfected skill . . . Unwavering, perfectly equal.

The refutation

Second comes the refutation:

If there were no past and present life, there would not be any future one. If there were no enlightened ones, then you wouldn't even know about it. If one can directly ascertain this, then it can be inferred with certainty.

Again, if the continuum of awareness were cut off, the activity of awareness of the present as well as its concordant type in the future would also not be produced.

The assertion of the cutting off of the continuum of cognition

[Argument:] On the second point and the position that the continuum of pristine cognition can be severed, Me'u Pal and and others, have said: "The main practice of the ten grounds and below is that there are defiled objects to be eliminated, and their existence means that there are antidotes. When the continuum ends, the objects to be eliminated are exhausted and pristine cognition is exhausted. It is similar to a fire dying when kindling is exhausted. Once the cause is exhausted, the conditions are exhausted. Then the transmigrators have their continuum of awareness cut off."

[Answer:] But this is not so. The scripture *Determining the Root of the Realms* (1.8.6) says:

> The all-knowing sixty-one pristine cognitions have indeed mastered clarity!

The *Eye of the Needle* (18.628.2) also says:

> From the phenomenal body is produced the body of perfection.

Reasoning does not change the essential point of continued exertion on the path. When the result arrives, the stream of cognition stops. However, having changed the result of generating the mind of enlightenment for the welfare of others, this cannot be completed. The *Eye of the Needle* (16.522.1) says:

> Through the power of planting the aspiration with fearless discipline here and now, I will demonstrate leadership.

Heretics are not different from the others. For example, the awareness of an old man about to die will later produce a concordant type, a human that resembles him. Roughly speaking, if we take the example of fire, a fire of sandalwood is distinct from the fire of the sun. The sun is unable to be similar to the fire of sandalwood. If a general refutation in particular changes into a non-refutation, for that reason it changes everything. If there is no pervasive factor, then this is also a non-existent position.

Discussing allegations on existence

Second, the position on existence is twofold: the position on manifest appearances and the position on autonomy.

[Argument:] First, someone who is an advocate of the doctrine of the Great Upholder of the Tradition posited the following in a concise manner: "One can assert that whatever has manifest appearance is a collection. Past aspirational prayers and distinctive merit manifest as the head figure of the mandala. The *Treasury* (215.1) says:

> The entourage consists in realizations of essential points around the leader. This is just like pristine cognition that shows [reality] in a fleeting manner.

This is coming from the tantric tradition, which expresses it this way. This can also be said for cognition. In the high tradition of the Dru tradition, the *Triflings of the Mind* (352.1) says:

> In a general sense, the powers of prayer and purification are concentrated drops possessing purposeful actions, as in space, where the sun, the moon, the planets, and the stars abide without ever

being mixed together. [159] Their essences dissolve into the state of pristine cognition. Their essences dissolve into the light that is pristine cognition.

However, this is not how this should be understood. For if it were like that, then this assertion on the marks of reality would change impermanence into a conceptual fabrication and a compounded phenomenon. An outer tantra, the *Very Pure Tantra* (21.172.2), says:

> Unborn, uninterrupted, it is endowed with the nature of space.

The *Roots of the Hundred Thousand* (39.76.6) says:

> Unborn, it becomes manifest enlightenment in the expanse of everlastingness.

Autonomy[160]

[Argument:] Second, someone has posited the assertion that autonomy is a composite. It is said: "What about a mind that is contaminated and the changes in what arises in the mind from a place that is uncontaminated? The universal basis and its circle of array is the mirror-like pristine cognition. The afflicted mind and its circle of array is the pristine cognition of equanimity. Mental cognition and its circle of array is the realization of its distinct parts. The five portals and their retinue are transformed abiding in earnest." This was said as a proof from scriptures and reasoning.

[Argument:] Furthermore, Dopa and so forth have said that the aggregates are transformed into Garsé Tsenpo. A contaminated place is transformed into an uncontaminated place. The result of such a practice is the ultimate finality.

[Answer:] Besides, both scriptures and commentaries have proven this. *Determining the Root of the Realms* (1.8.6) says:

> The sixty-one all-knowing pristine cognitions are clear.

The *Minute Scriptures* (289.3) proves this when it says:

On the ground of universal light, the three bodies of clarity, experience, and immovability are perfected.

[Argument:] It is said: "An inherited type is merely awareness that later generates concordant awareness, and this is particularly so when it concerns awareness at the end of a continuum of the ten grounds that will produce a later rebirth. This refutes the no reincarnation position. It is similar to being awake in the middle of the day."

[Answer:] This statement is quoted as a proof, but it is unreasonable. It is not proven and it is harmful. First, among scriptures and commentaries, the first one—scriptures—are inspirations that have come to others. The second ones—commentaries—consist in knowledge later produced. Are these ultimate or conventional truths?

In the first case, proven knowledge of awareness changes what has been established as objects. Apprehended and apprehender and their companions would change into false collection of benefits on the realization from the elimination process. The *Summary of the Hundred Thousand* explains this, saying:

The object is what is grasped and the subject is grasping the object.

It implies no conflict on the conception of the apprehended and the apprehender.

"Conceptions are incommensurable to the mind," and so forth. This statement implies the proof that compels nothing greater than saying that the ordinary mind of a person exists.

[Argument:] If conventional truth exists, can the reasoning of a subsequent rebirth be produced with firm examination or is it to be considered a shaky proposition and not examined? In the first case [i.e., subsequent rebirth is produced], is there a cause or not of the awareness produced? In the second case [i.e., no cause], having no cause contradicts rebirth. In the first case, is the cause produced from something other or is the production autonomous?

[Answer:] In the first case, from a singular self, there would be two parts: the object being produced and the agent of production. This is a contradiction. [160] It is as if a vase were suddenly produced from something else, but that is impossible.

The second proposition is as if a pencil could arise from fire. When this transformation is investigated before and after, it is proven to be impossible. In this second case, that would mean the horse of a magician would be ultimately proven to be an elephant!

The second point is about the harm that arose from the scriptures and commentaries in the first discussion above.

Realization through elimination

Second, realization through elimination is twofold:

[Argument:] First, is pristine cognition of manifest objects deliberately deceitful or not?

In the first case [i.e., if it is deceitful], then it changes all cognition to mirage-like states. In the second case, the stream of compassion would be cut off, which is a contradiction.

[Answer:] The *Eye of the Needle* (16.523.7) says:

I am like the sun that ceaselessly streams forth to all equally, like water.

This contradicts what is stated just prior to the quote.

[Argument:] Someone said that in the case of an object that is deceitfully manifest, there is no change in the illusion.

[Answer:] In that case, if there were no concepts, then this illusion would no longer be an illusion. This is not concordant.

[Argument:] Again, Dopa said: "An object is illusory; however, when its cause ceases to exist and this 'other' is eliminated, pristine cognition becomes free and pure; it is the end of the stain on Suchness."

[Answer:] But it is not so. The scripture the *Hundred Thousand* says:

The inherent self of body and mind come to be acquired as the result of the clarity of pristine cognition.

This says that if it is only an illusory manifestation, then it is not established and the argument is countered. If reasoning as well as pristine cognition on deceitful manifestation make the object in itself manifest in an illusory way, then the apprehender dwells in it because of the condition that made the concept illusory. If there is nothing manifest that places the object in the sphere of phenomena, then this is falsely claimed. It is asserted that one eliminates illusion, yet there is no elimination, because this is a deceitful grasping to an illusion. The object and the one endowed with the object are realized importantly as one.

[Argument:] Second, the moment one billion emanations are sent out, is there a pristine cognition for each and every one or not? In the first case, is cognition there from the beginning or does it come to be aware at the onset?

[Answer:] If there is nothing from the first causal moment, then the many arise at the moment of fruition. In the second case [i.e., where there is no individual cognition], it appears that there will be no benefit to pristine awareness. So, this claim is false.

[Argument:] On this, Dopa said: "The person emanating, the one awareness of Shenrab himself, manifests in many ways for those needing training. From his one body, he manifested many bodies; from his one voice, he manifested many voices; and from his one mind, he manifested many knowledgeable wisdom beings."

[Answer:] But it is not so. For if it were so, would this one awareness emanate many, or would these be many different aspects within this one awareness?

In the first case [i.e., one awareness emanates many of its aspects], this would be the experience of one. In the second case, [where there are many aspects that make one awareness], there are many beings to tame, and yet this would make their many [individual] aspects unclear. Therefore, it is a false claim. Furthermore, freedom from the one and the many negates this.

[Argument:] Third, if one supports both propositions, the lord of scripture and reasoning said [161]: "There are no manifestations of a self in the absolute, but there are in the relative."

[Answer:] But it is not so. For it would change the ultimate truth into a fabricated state. The absence of fabrication and its array, and pristine awareness in the ultimate truth, come through the cutting off of the continuum that yet transforms into no cause to emanate others.

Second, in **our own tradition**, the great lord Lodrö quotes something similar to the *Roots of the Hundred Thousand* (39.76.6), which says:

> The ultimate is free from all elaborations. All the elaborations
> that arise in the mind and the mind itself are not produced in
> the expanse of phenomena, because the vicinity of the expanse
> is pacified and is emancipated from objects with characteristics.

Without phenomena that are produced, there are enlightened ones in the expanse of everlastingness.

The outer tantra, the *Very Pure Transmission* (21.172.2) says:

The blissful ones of the three times with the retinue of their circles are, without exception, unborn, unhindered, endowed with the nature of space. Their intrinsic heart is unwavering, whatever characteristic is not originated.

The *Arcana* (207.2) says:

Without inherent self, they transcend the end of existence. Without duality, they transcend the end of everything. From the very beginning, the reality of transcendence is inexpressible.

The *Scripture of the Joyful Kunzang* says:

In the transformation of the great transcendence, how could characteristics be expressed?

And so forth.

The *Compendium on the Spreading* (1.49.1) says:

The skillful body of the unhindered trainee in conventional truth and the activities of pristine cognition, and so forth, arise in a multitude. The sixty-one all-knowing pristine cognitions dominate with clarity.

The *Eye of the Needle* (18.628.2) says:

The body of reality produces the body of perfection. The body of perfection produces the emanation body.

The *Arcana* (3.1) says:

The king of the knowledge of everything does not possess concepts, but rather clarity.

A scripture says:

> The five demons uprooted have become the five gods.
> Reasoning has nearly pacified all elaborations for the sake of enlightenment. The finality of the realization of elimination is the reason for the absence of separation of the ground and the path. It is like space. Yet others are manifest; they arise without interruption. It is the steady flow of awareness.

Aspiration is ripening the result of the mind of enlightenment. It arises as an unhindered potential, like the sun, the moon, the planets, and the stars.

Dispelling objections on ultimate and conventional truths

Third, the dispelling of objections, is about dispelling objections on the ultimate and the conventional truths, and is twofold:

[Argument:] First, it is said: "The defect of scriptures is their existence in elimination."

[Answer:] There is no conflict in this. That is the idea of the appearance of otherness.

Second, there are four defects to eliminate in reasoning. After examination, one should abandon the faults of absurdity. As a consequence, one should abandon overexertion in senseless offerings. [162] One should consequently abandon cutting off the flow of compassion. One should properly abandon extensions into heretic beliefs.

[Argument:] First, pristine awareness is not posited in terms of ultimate truth. It is asserted that when awareness is interrupted, it is the end of the continuum. However, in this position, are there antidotes or not?

[Answer:] The second case where there is no antidote—this is absurd! Only awareness cannot be eliminated. In the first case, the powers of antidotes are great, small, or of equal strength. In the first case, the antidote of great power itself severs the process of pristine cognition. In the second case where the antidote is weak, the elimination process has no capacity.

[Argument:] Some say that in the third case where the antidote is of equal power with the object to be eliminated, the past has stopped, the future has not yet come to be, and in the present, result and fruition come in an equal manner.

[Answer:] In this, where there is no antidote, there is no consequence if the cause of illusion is not eliminated. At the end of the continuum, all illusions are spent. They all originate from contaminants in the mind and the mind itself. It is said:

> Like a frozen lake melting, inherent nature is completely pure.
> The generation of the mind of enlightenment in the expanse of intrinsic reality is the vastness of the body.
>   At that moment, the manifestations of the two bodies arise equal in measure to the welfare of others.

[Argument:] To put it another way, the severance of the continuum cannot be asserted. The ultimate is free from elaborations, and when there is manifestation of otherness that is not obstructed, it arises. Furthermore, if the three bodies are absent, then there is no going into an evil destiny, and it is the same as no more rebirths.

[Answer:] But again, it is not so. It cannot be asserted that there is no "he" and "we."

[Argument:] Again, someone asked whether happiness and benefit are generated or not in a trainee [engaged] in the enlightened activities of enlightened ones? In the first case, it changes the nature of the reality of enlightened activities concerning the absolute truth. In the second case, it negates the point of any of these activities whatsoever.

[Answer:] Although these are generated, the actor is separated from activities in the absolute truth, and it does not contradict the point even though there is an impermanent phenomenon that appears as something different.

[Argument:] Moreover, do these enlightened activities have a real function or not? In the first case [i.e., they have a real function], this will change in relation to the absolute truth. In the second case [i.e., no real function], this will disable their function.

What if someone asks about the function of unreal phenomena and emptiness? Although absolute truth is free from activities, in conventional truth there is the reality of the appearance of something distinctive. That is the function. It is conventional truth. In the second point [i.e., they are unreal] someone may say that the path then becomes a useless effort.

[Answer:] Although the absolute truth is separate from activities, in relative truth, appearances of something different are not stopped. If it were not so, then any happiness, satisfaction, and so forth there might be would all go down.

[Argument:] Again, what if someone asks whether the three bodies, causes, and conditions matter or not? In the first case, where they do matter, it will change the absolute truth into conditioned phenomena, because how can anything that did not have an essence in the past come anew again? In the second case where none of the above matters, the path becomes a meaningless effort.

[Answer:] There is no fault here. The *Minute Scriptures* (166.4) says:

> There is no reliable agent of accomplishment with an inherent essence. From the very beginning, inherent mind is itself enlightened. [163] The enlightened ones of the three times are on display. That direct recognition is manifest enlightenment.

The *Eye of the Needle* (16.521.6) also says:

> The condition of special realization relies on an imputed cause that consists in the accumulations on the path through innumerable eons.

[Argument:] Third, someone said that if there is no enlightened pristine awareness, it breaks the flow of compassion, and he quoted the *Eye of the Needle* (16.523.7), which says:

> I am like the sun that ceaselessly streams forth to all equally, like water.

[Answer:] A quote from a scripture says:

> When the end of the stream of contaminated mind arises in the mind, it is appeased and compassion remains immutable. When what arises appears as different, it is not countered. It then arises like the rays of the sun. It is explained as blessing us with great compassion.

[Argument:] Fourth, when there is no pristine awareness and the flow of awareness is interrupted, as soon as the latter happens, these become alike.

[Answer:] Not so. When activities are pacified in the absolute truth, the interruption of the flow does not give rise to the stopping of the appearances of different phenomena, not completely. It is similar to the contours of the clouds in the sky.

[Argument:] Again, someone said that in general, this is similar to such a case: as soon as a fire shines forth, one sprinkles a particular kind of sandalwood on it. Then the fire's light is no longer able to emerge.

[Answer:] This posits that there is no stopping the appearances of phenomena perceived as others once the activities in the absolute truth are pacified at the end of the stream. What you posit is this. You can claim it! There is no mistake here.

Dispelling objections concerning the appearances of phenomena

Second, dispelling objections concerning the appearances of phenomena as distinct in relative truth is twofold:

First, there is nothing said in the scriptures that is without conflict. However, it is not said that there is nothing, and it is not said that there is something truly existing. Therefore, there are things that are not said. It is said: "The absolute truth is free from elaborations."

Second, the elimination of refutation based on reasoning is threefold: dispelling the contradiction that there are no benefits to elimination; realization; and finally, the elimination of contradictions on the non-existence of the knowledge of all aspects.

Dispelling the contradiction that there are no benefits to elimination

[Argument:] First, are the illusions of appearing objects in pristine awareness to be eliminated or not?

In the first case [i.e., objects have to be eliminated], it will change into cutting off the flow of compassion. The *Treasury* (181.7) says:

> The unitary principle holding all life, the intrinsic principle of
> life's power, takes hold of the distinctive characteristic of contin-
> uous compassion.

Thus, the above would be contradicting that. In the second case [i.e., there is no elimination needed], one may say that there will be no benefit to elimination.

[Answer:] It may be that limits are transcended in the absolute truth that eliminates appearances in the truth of illusion. But since an appearance is merely an appearance, manifest objects conventionally appear as distinct. There is no truth in appearances, and these mirage-like appearances arise as appearing distinctly without being eliminated.

Realizations

[Argument:] Second, does individual pristine cognition have one billion emanated bodies or not?

In the first case where there are billions of bodies, this would change everything from the very beginning of their existences, the source of awareness and pristine cognition. A single causal event would consequently bring about many results. [164] In the case of the second [i.e., there are none], someone has claimed as such.

[Answer:] Though indeed it exists, there is no fault here because it is the rise of uninterrupted dynamism. If it were not so, the light from one old sun would not appear and be interrupted. Why? Because, these are not the same.

Elimination of contradictions on the non-existence of the knowledge of all aspects

[Argument:] Third, does pristine cognition of the knowledge of all aspects know the three times or not?

In the first case [i.e., it does know], transcendence would not come and universal knowledge would become conceptual. In the second case [i.e., it does not know the three times], one could say that it makes the knowledge of all aspects nonexistent.

The response to this is threefold:

First, **the tradition of the others** has these two: the knowledge of cessation and the cessation of assumed ignorance.

The tradition of the others on the knowledge of cessation

[Argument:] First, those holding to the incomparable tradition of the champions say that the knowledge of aspects consists in not knowing specifically characterized phenomena.[161]

[Answer:] Not knowing specifically characterized phenomena will change [the knowledge of all aspects] into non-existing knowledge of everything. If it then becomes a general knowledge of the meaning of aspects, it becomes conceptual. If a specifically characterized phenomenon is known, it becomes false consciousness. And then the specifically characterized phenomenon is devoid of realization.

[Argument:] Me'u and others have said that nowadays knowledge implies direct knowledge of the past, and later of the present moment and the future.

[Answer:] A mere troubled consciousness that does not know the evidence for the existence of rebirth does not become a knower of all aspects.

[Argument:] Second, Zhuchen (b. 1092), who was a scholarly man, could not prove the point that the concept of the three times exists, but only that the existence of sentient beings could be imputed.

The *Arcana* (34.1) says:

> The state of the mind during the three times that are without beginning is equal.

[Answer:] Despite this having been said, it is not so. That scripture is not about the conceptual realization of the equality of the three times in the mind. The *Eye of the Needle* (16.526.5) mentions:

> . . . the realized ones of the three times.

On this account, is it logically possible for the three times to go away? If it is not possible, then it makes time a real permanent entity, which contradicts the claim of the scriptures on exalted knowledge of the world. If there is no exalted knowledge, the knowledge of aspects is inexistent. Now, the *Eye of the Needle* (15.497.1) says:

> There is exalted knowledge of all aspects.

Second, according to **our own tradition**, the *Arcana* (34.1) says:

> The ultimate truth is free from all these mental constructs, and

there is unity in the state of the mind of the three times that are without beginning or end.

The *Very Pure Transmission* (29.172.4) says:

The words that describe or are imagined are inadequate for the inexpressible.

The *Arcana* (207.2) says:

The Bön of transcendence is inexpressible from the very beginning.

The *Eye of the Needle* (15.497.1) says:

The mode of arising in the conventional consists in the knowledge of appearances as distinct. All aspects are but continual knowledge.

Determining the Root of the Realms (1.8.6) says:

It consists in the sixty-one all-knowing pristine cognitions.

Dispelling objections on the insight of the absolute truth

The third dispelling of objections: [165]

From the scriptures and reasoning above, the scriptures contain insights into the absolute truth. This second point is twofold:

[Argument:] First, if the absolute is free from mental constructs, then there is no change in the lack of exalted knowledge of everything.

[Answer:] Suchness is free, and there is no contradiction on appearances being distinct.

[Argument:] Second, on the exalted knowledge of the conventional, someone asked if it is a general meaning and if there are specifically characterized phenomena in the concepts and their arrays. Furthermore, does the answer change along past and future derivatives?

[Answer:] Though it is true that there is exalted knowledge of specifically characterized phenomena, this does not change their derivatives.

[Argument:] A certain Bönpo lama in Lhasa said: "The spontaneous nature of the just-as-it-is is the clear realization of the mirage-like quality of everything, because this realization cannot be encompassed by the mind. This one pristine cognition of exalted knowledge is the clear exalted knowledge of the spontaneous nature of the object of consciousness."

[Answer:] If it were not so, then wouldn't the gaze of the enlightened ones—that is, their all-knowing expressions—turn into mistaken consciousness or wrong consciousness? If there are knowledgeable men but there is no knowledge of all-aspects, why are there migrators? This is very unlikely.

The nature of clear realization

Second, on the nature of clear realization, there are these three points: defining characteristics, divisions, and precise definition.

Defining characteristics

The first topic consists in elimination, the ultimate realization, and the three exalted benefits [i.e., abundance, prosperity, and plenty].

Divisions

Next is the demarcation of the boundaries. Each and every one is threefold:

First, the only realization of the body of reality exists on the path of the world through the acquisition of the clear vision of the essential point. Its direct realization comes from treading the path of vision. With the direct realization of the lack of self comes the finality of the actualized field that is enlightenment. Once the stream is completely ended, then it is the finality of the realization of elimination.

The second point, the demarcation of the boundaries, has the following five points:

1. There are the agent, the basis, and the defining characteristic that measure in a comprehensive manner.

2. The essences are the body that supports, the pristine cognition that is supported, and performance and activities.

3. Causal characteristics consist in the base support, the mode of arising of the supported, and three types of different activities according to body, speech, and mind.

4. The main point of the divisions is to distinguish superficial aspect in the essence.

5. Enumeration ascertains the support, the supported, and the activities.

In each of these three aspects, there is nothing that is not included in all the categories of distinctive appearances.

3. TEACHINGS ON THE THREE BODIES

Individual points

Third, the meaning of each and every point is threefold: the three enlightened bodies, pristine cognition, and activities.

The enlightened bodies

The first topic is threefold: cause and condition, their natures, and function.

Cause and condition

First, the cause of the essence does not exist in the past, and it is the same for the causes of secondary conditions that consist in the generation of the enlightened mind, meditation in meditative equipoise, and meditation on pure lands [166] and spreading subsequent attainment. These three are the causes of the three bodies.

The nature of the bodies

Second, their nature is threefold: defining characteristic, divisions, and definition.

Defining characteristic

[Argument:] First, one lama said that the base, the path, the result, and the two accumulations are collected and piled up in the Bön tradition.

[Answer:] This would transform the meaning of the untainted into aggregate-isolates. This is again an overextension of pristine cognition on the ten grounds.

[Argument:] When commenting on appearances, the great Lodrö included impure objects and so forth.

[Answer:] This is also an overextension. For that reason, it does not change the point about ripening to reach finality.

The divisions of the bodies

Second, as for the divisions, scriptures have spoken of the three bodies. The *Arcana* mentioned six that are based on the locations of the senses [i.e., five senses plus the mind]. Although the tantras mentioned five bodies, two— the subject and intrinsic reality—have been absorbed [in the other three], hence making three bodies. These are reflected upon with respect to common divisions, individual aim, and the subject.

The five points on the demarcations of the boundaries revisited

1. The first point of five: the only ones endowed with the agent, the basis, and the defining characteristic are the essence of intrinsic reality and the subject.

2. The essence: each of these can be further divided into three: intrinsic essence, real enlightenment, and immutability. These correspond to the body of reality (*bon sku*), the perfected body (*rdzogs sku*), and the emanation body (*sprul sku*). Together, they make six.

3. The characteristic of the cause is twofold: manifest appearances and the absence of appearances. The absence of appearances is naturally pure, where there is the immaculate adventitious and immutability. Therefore, the three [i.e., bodies] are separated in three manifest appearances: the three pure grounds, the heroes of the ten grounds, and ordinary beings.

These three are further divided into three.

4. Function of divisions is as below.

[Argument:] Someone said that when there is only one section, it can be divided down into six.

[Answer:] If one starts to make differences, these will then proliferate. The one essence can be differentiated into isolatable factors. One is the mode of being that is then differentiated into the manner of appearance.

5. Enumeration consists in the reality concerning self-nature and ordinary mind.

The body of reality

The second point is twofold:

First, the discussion on the body of reality has three parts:

First, the **defining characteristic** is the very pure of the pure, free from the stains of the adventitious in the pure intrinsic nature of the sphere.

Second, on the **mode of abiding** in genuine spontaneity:

It may be true that there are divisions that are conventional. These are the body of intrinsic essence, the body of real enlightenment, and the body of immutability. Therefore, these are abiding in intrinsic purity, free from the stains of the adventitious. Freedom from stains is immutability. These three further become three.

Third, the **essential meaning** of the body of reality is that it is the finality of intrinsic reality, free from elaborations.

The body of the one knowing reality

Second, the body of the one knowing reality[162] is threefold:

First, its **defining characteristic** is that it is the fruit of the two accumulations (of merit and insight) and appears pure to the trainee.

Second, its **divisions** are threefold: the body of reality, the body of perfection, and the body of emanation. [167]

The first of three points is their **defining characteristics.** Despite the following saying: "Through the inherent nature of the sphere, pure consciousness that is free of adventitious stains has been greatly mixed with the intrinsic reality of non-manifested subject," consciousness of the expanse is not divisible.

Second, about the **basis of characteristics:** The essence is known as non-appearing in the manifest and is the uninterrupted body of reality, the dynamism of pristine cognition of the undifferentiated union. Elimination consists in the uninterrupted display free from elaboration. The realms to be tamed consist in the existence of all sentient beings in numbers impossible to encompass, as vast as the sky. The *Very Pure Transmission* (21.172.2) says:

> Unborn and unobstructed, it is endowed with the nature of the sky.

Another scripture says:

> It is free from complex elaborations.

The *Eye of the Needle* (14.407.7) says:

> It is similar to the sky, all-encompassing compassion.

Third, its **essential point**: Bön, the unwavering body, is unchanging.

The perfected body

Second, the topic of the perfected body is threefold:

First, its **defining characteristic** is manifested in the mind of the heroes as the five certainties that are the teacher, the retinue, the teachings, the place, and the time.

Second, the **divisions** are said to be the two peaceful and wrathful essences and the enlightened ones of the five different lineages.

Elimination is being free from stains, free from the impurities of conceptuality and the impurities of meaning, as well as free from the five uncertainties [i.e., body, entourage, time, place, and difficulties].

The realms to be tamed consist in the activities of clearing away the defilements of the heroes of the ten grounds, as is said in the *Tantra of the Secret Empowerment of Everlastingness* (28.3):

> like water or the moon appearing in a crystal or on a mirror.
> ... free from the ten signs of incorrect meaning.

The *Eye of the Needle* (18.628.3) says:

> The ground of training is to purify the defilements of the objects
> of cognition.

Third, the meaning [of the perfected body] is that it is the highest reach of enjoyment through the perfection that is unchanging.

The emanation bodies

The third topic, on the emanation bodies, is threefold:

First, their **defining characteristic** is that they appear according to the trainee's five uncertainties.[163]

Second, its **divisions** in essence are the billion emanation bodies and the disciplines of the six saints.[164] Elimination is freedom from the two obscurations [to knowledge and conflicting emotions] as well as freedom from corrupted meanings. A scripture says:

> The object of training is to tame this obdurate world and to teach wherever there are wandering beings.
> ... The hardship of discipline is to subdue the obdurate.

Third, its **essential point** is to emanate everywhere.

Dispelling objections

[Argument:] Third, whatever appears in the ordinary mind or whatever does not appear in the ordinary mind, the body of intrinsic reality exists in non-appearance. On this, someone said that when there are no manifestations, it is because they have not yet been ascertained for oneself.

[Answer:] When there are no manifestations in one's ordinary mind, this does not change that they are not yet ascertained. It is certain by itself that there are no manifestations. The body of reality is the heart of the enlightened ones, the transformation of the objects of awareness and the appearance in the mind of the three grounds of purities. The perfected body is the manifestation in the mind of the heroes of the ten grounds. The emanation bodies are appearances of purified activities to the trainee of the superior and lower Bön. [168] Therefore the heroes are not manifested. They do not exist. The one essence manifests different bodies only in different minds.

Precise definition

Third, the precise definition: Wherever there is a mind, there are appearances. However, there are [ultimately] no changes. The *Eye of the Needle* (12.218.3) says:

Attainment changes into the perfected body.

4. Teachings on pristine cognition

Function of emanation bodies

Third, their functions consist in the activities of pristine cognition that are causing the destined ones to come forth.

Support of pristine cognition

Second, the topic on the support of pristine cognition is threefold: causes, nature, and function.

Causes

First, the causes are the five aggregates and the arising of liberation in a contaminated place.

Nature

The second point is threefold: defining characteristic, divisions, and meaning.

Defining characteristic

First, although it has been said that "the actual mode of abiding of objects is exactly as seen," one has to understand this meaning with total clarity. The *Treasury* (208.4) says:

> The defining characteristic of intrinsic pristine cognition is the
> knowledge of all aspects that seizes the defining characteristic,
> realizing its meaning with total clarity."

Divisions

The second point is threefold: actual divisions, the mode of relating to objects, and recognizing knowledge and awareness.

Actual divisions

The first point is fivefold:

1. The **defining characteristic** of the basic division is to limit with circumspection.

2. If the **essence** were to be divided into primary viewpoints, it would be fivefold:[165] emptiness, equanimity, mirror-like, discriminating knowledge, and wisdom of persistent action. If one divides this based on what comes first and later, there are the all-knowing sixty-one pristine cognitions of exalted knowledge. These are arranged twelve by twelve until there are sixty [i.e., four times twelve divisions], plus the root—self-arisen pristine cognition—that is added to make sixty-one in total.

If these divisions' perspectives are expanded, they are said to be ten million, and furthermore, eighty-four thousand. If all these are combined, they become the following two: exalted knowledge of the absolute just-as-it-is and exalted knowledge of categories of the conventional.

3. The **causal characteristic** of pristine cognition is the distinction concerning taming the five poisons, the five kinds of support, and the five demonic functions. Therefore, when made to correspond to the two truths, these are known as the two primordial wisdoms.[166]

4. As for the **essential point to its divisions**, there are different isolates in the one essence.

5. The **enumeration** is there to ascertain the two truths and the cause.

The manner of relating to objects

Second, on objects, the *Key Points of Shari* (42.4) says:

> Objects in the absolute truth are empty, and one engages just-as-it-is, while in conventional truth one cognizes in earnest endeavor and engages with objects as they appear. The wisdom that is mirror-like is to engage in subsuming these two truths. Emptiness and equanimity are the insights of the absolute truth. The discriminating awareness of earnest deeds is the insight of conventional truth. The pristine awareness that is mirror-like subsumes the two truths. [169]

And again, the *Arcana* (192.7) says:

In the intrinsic reality of the absence of appearances, the undivided intrinsic mind looks without perception at the colors in the boundless sky. They rise as brilliant lights.

Recognizing knowledge and awareness

Third, someone has asked: What will the ordinary mind change into?

The answer is threefold:

[Argument:] First, on the negation of those of **the tradition of the others**, someone said that there is no direct valid cognition of the ordinary mind.

[Answer:] It is not so. Having awakened a little, the consciousness that ripens uses valid cognition. One would necessarily grasp at prior realizations. If this were accepted, then the end of the continuum would turn into the acquisition of the knowledge of aspects.

Second, **our own tradition** holds that in the absolute truth that is free from elaborations, distinct appearances arise without obstruction. In conventional truth, no sooner does the pristine cognition awaken than there is direct yogic valid cognition, through which, as soon as it expands a little, it ripens. There is cognition that is severed from [conception] and without concepts. When awakening, cognition is non-realized because there is no awareness of anything coming from the ordinary mind.

Dispelling objections on exalted knowledge

Third is the **dispelling of objections**:

[Argument:] The king of all exalted knowledge is said to have been unquestionably clear. What if someone asks whether, in the state of exalted knowledge, there is something left of the ordinary mind?

[Answer:] There is none. Pristine cognition that is without concepts perceives, in the clarity of the expanse of reality, the objects of consciousness just-as-they-are.

Precise definition

Third, the precise definition of pristine cognition is just as the *Eye of the Needle* (17.543.5) says:

344 The Tradition of Everlasting Bön

The primordial is beyond expressible object. Consciousness is perfected in the dynamism of awareness.

A commentary on the *Arcana* says: "The main point of primordial Suchness is the realization of clarity."

Function

Third, the function of pristine cognition is clarity on the spontaneity of objects, while the activities of doing are lost.

5. TEACHINGS ON ENLIGHTENED ACTIVITIES

Third, the enlightened activities section is threefold: cause, nature, and function.

The cause of enlightened activities

First, the cause is the result of the aspiration of the generation of the mind of enlightenment that arises as distinct manifestations.

The nature of enlightened activities

Second, their nature is threefold: defining characteristic, divisions, and meaning.

Defining characteristic

First, the great lord said: "The benefit of others is spontaneously fulfilled without effort." Put another way, the great Lodrö said: "The two meanings are perfected."

Divisions

The second point is threefold: real divisions, detailed classification of the mode of enlightened activities [170], and dispelling objections.

Real divisions

1. The first point of five: the agent, the basis, and the defining characteristic are the all-inclusive measures.

2. The essence consists in the four activities and the three: body, speech, and mind.

3. There are three causal characteristics: the discipline that is easy, the difficult discipline, and the very difficult discipline. These are divided among the following four: mending pride, obliteration, deeds for ripening, and continued engagement. These four are separated into four depending on how one distinguishes them.

4. There are functional divisions as well as recognizable differences.

5. Enumeration: it is certain that there are modes of training according to the number of trainees.

More on the four activities

Second, again the four enlightened activities are conducted in many ways, such as the twelve great deeds of the teacher Shenrab and so forth. Through these accomplishments, regardless of the striving, one abides continually without interruption in spontaneous compassion. Enlightened activity consists in this, that there is nothing at all to use or subtract.

Dispelling objections

Third is the dispelling of objections on permanence and the extensiveness of enlightened action.

[Argument:] First, what if someone asks if enlightened activity implies that the continuum of each instant of activity is mutating impermanence?

[Answer:] There is no proven reason for an impermanent continuum, since there is no momentary impermanence that can be pervasive.

[Argument:] Second, someone asked about the existence of a ubiquitous enlightened action that is performed by an enlightened one. Will this change the results of the activity into non-existence?

[Answer:] The ubiquity of the action has a non-established indivisible essence. Light, for example, has no ubiquitous function.

[Argument:] Third, someone said that if there is a ubiquitous factor in everything and it is permanent, this will change the function of everything.

[Answer:] If this is accepted, then everything will be liberated without effort. This is the postulate of the fortunate one. The *Eye of the Needle* (11.102.5) says:

> The desire of the fortunate one brings about the moment for meeting the right conditions.

The *Eye of the Needle* (11.103.5) says:

> There is no pervasive factor in non-possession. The compassionate teacher is the leader of sentient beings.

Again, the *Eye of the Needle* (1.10.3) says:

> The rising light of the sun is opposed by the darkness in the house. It is the same for the kinds of sentient beings that reject the demonstration of the truth's explanations as useless.

Precise definition

Third, a precise definition [on permanence and the extensiveness of enlightened action]: Does it change into the activity of praying? Pristine cognition changes into compassionate activity.

Function

Third is about function. While the object to be tamed is ripening, the goal of the welfare of others—to bring them to emancipation—is being fulfilled.

Another precise meaning

Third, the precise meaning is purification through the three benefits and the process of elimination. Realization increases the three benefits.

Function again

Third, another function is that the path that is established serves as the support for the path of trainee. The displays of the results of the path create happiness and benefits.

Thus, the path of elimination and realization is the finality. The result of the knowledge of all aspects is the object of the good teachings together with the mode of acquiring the defining properties of omniscience, the clearing away of the superimpositions of the ordinary mind, wrong views, and doubts.

This was chapter 8 of the descent of the teachings on results from the *Magical Key to the Precious Stages of the Path and the Grounds of the Greater Vehicle*. [173]

9. Conclusion: The Teachings on Entering What Follows Finality

6. THE TEACHINGS ON ENTERING WHAT FOLLOWS FINALITY

Thus, what is the goal of entering the path of the Greater Vehicle? The *Magical Key* clearly explains it well. It explains to beings the perceived phenomena that appear to their ordinary minds. Beings that are impure and bewildered must unravel the cognition of a self. Through that power, using scriptures and reasoning, they can discover the awareness of realization. They can adopt the intention of the words of the thoroughly purified, the blissful ones, and the collected meaning of the words of the noble masters. With these instructions, the knowing mind can resolve issues. The mind under delusion cannot realize the meaning of cyclic existence and transcendence. Doubts and delusion can be wiped out. In order to do this, straight and beneficial explanations have been provided herein. One can be victorious and free from cyclic existence, from doubts and extreme views. Beings that have no wisdom cannot realize the basic meaning [of victory over cyclic existence]. Ignorant and obscured minds will certainly be mistaken. Because of that, there is this lamp that explains clearly and will dispel ignorance and the obscurity of delusive meaning. Self-clinging apes will not come to comprehend this meaning. However, an established system of tenets will bring about liberation. It is for this reason that the excellent path has been well explained herein and the perverted views of foxes will be outshined. The mind collects the keys of conflicting emotions very well and will certainly experience suffering on the path of cyclic existence. For this reason, the excellent path is clearly explained herein so that one will be free from the abyss of falling onto the wrong path. Dwelling on suffering, fixations, and cravings will certainly imprison one in the cyclic existence of the three worlds. For this reason, the purified grounds have been clearly explained herein, and one will be able to be free from the abodes of deceptive fallen circles. Through exertion, one will be able to stay away from non-virtuous and impure activities and will certainly come to be purified from evil destinies and suffering. For this reason, wholesome actions have been clearly explained herein, and if there is suffering, one will be able to uproot it. When the intention of the meaning and signs do not sound right with scripture and reasoning, there will certainly be commentaries and objections on these transmitted words. For this reason, the apex of the teachings has been clearly explained in a straightforward manner herein so that one can gain the correct meaning as opposed to the second guessing of fools. Similar to possessing completely different qualities just by listening to the clear explanations in this miraculous key, these beings will come to understand, realize, and obtain the knowledge of all aspects of the stainless path. I pray for tolerance to the pure objects of refuge against contradictory false meanings and unsound intentions. This composition is varied and entirely virtuous. It is dedicated to the benefit of all beings so that they may obtain the unsurpassable. May the sentient beings pervading space come to find the excellent path and may they come to abide on the ground of the unborn essence. May I lead wandering beings to the unattained unborn essence by means of the supreme Greater Vehicle.

Thus, this so-called *Magical Key to the Precious Stages of the Path and the Grounds of the Greater Vehicle* has been completely written by Azha Lodrö Gyaltsen at the request of Lhatön Drakpa Tsultrim (fl. mid-thirteenth century). *Mutsu maro!* (May all be auspicious!) *E ma ho!* [Exclamation of joy] [176]

PART 2

*The Lore of the Root Tantra,
the Precious Universal Gathering*

Attributed to the teacher Kuntu Zangpo

To the teacher Kuntu Zangpo
who destroys the net of conceptuality,
the lord of the profound and greatly extensive body,
to this knower of everything, I bow!

Introductory discourse

From the circle of his heart, the teacher
has explained with blessings
this root tantra of the precious universal gathering.

In the citadel of Highest Sphere,[167]
in a past life, he took it upon himself to spread [the teachings] among his entourage,
where he discoursed directly from his own self-nature.

Being perceptive with great faith,
deprived of cravings and miserliness,
endowed with a mind of great power,
he taught the precepts of the root commentary of this tantra.

Being perceptive with great faith,
to those with a steady mind,
this is taught as the condensed roots of the scriptures
that meaningfully do away with conventional words.

One must have a mind steady and unmoving.
These instructions progressively integrate the teachings of the main points.

Threefold divisions

In general, the system of the secret mantra consists of the following three-fold divisions: the base, the path, and the result; tantra, transmission, and instruction; analogy, essential points, and analysis; outer, inner and secret; generation, completion, and Great Perfection; and the approach, accomplishment, and application. These are delineated as such.

These three, the base, the path, and the result, are likened to the object, the place, and the journey, and tantric transmission, scripture, and instruction, and are not dissimilar to the lord, his ministers, and his subjects.

Example, meaning and analysis are like the reflections in a mirror. The outer, inner, and secret are like a treasury, a storehouse, and a solitary place.

The generation stage, the perfection stage, and the Great Perfection are like the gradual growth of hair.

The approach, the performance, and the activities are like the hero, his armor, and his weapon. This, therefore, is what is ascertained as supreme.

Base, path, and result

The first topic, the base, is sixfold: vows, empowerments, mantras, activities, view, and conduct.

Vows

The basis of all the secret mantras consists in taking the correct pledges. Their essential attributes are divided according to their definition and the method to protect them with regard to objects and the person. They are taught using examples among the categories of faults and advantages.

Empowerments

Empowerments make one progress through stages and are divided according to the definition of their essential attributes: outer, inner, and secret.

These in turn correspond to the following threefold groups: wisdom, pristine cognition, and ultimate finality; place, time, and master; the disciple, the continents, and the divine assembly; the entrance, paying respect, and their numbered categories; the consecrated precinct, paying respect, and purifying defilements; treading the grounds, [174] concepts, and symbols and their connections; and ritual objects, necessity, and the measure of their efficacy.

These are good examples, and their results demonstrate the supreme instructions on empowerment.

Mantra

In the practice of mantra, there are the divisions of the practices, the total count of which, from the beginning, has to be observed with discrimination. These consist in the Shen of the phenomenal universe, the Shen of magical power, the method of lay practitioners, monasticism, the method of the White A, the primordial Shen, and Great Spontaneity. The total count is seven.

In total there are also these five objects: object, master, categories, intent, and purpose.

Five objects to observe

The five objects to observe are the base, non-distraction, mantras, the hand poses (*mudra, phyag rgya*), and the seed-syllables.

Activities

The main point of all these is that they are collected into the activity section.

Essence, definition, and divisions are taught by means of the following five points according to their necessary results: the activities to guard against suffering, the activities that are suitable to one's lower self, unskillful spontaneous activities, the activities of the method of the White A, and the fierce activities of pacification, expansion, overpowering, and destroying. Whatever one does, one must chiefly adopt unadulterated conduct. For example, all this is like a golden thread that strings together a necklace of jewels. It gathers around itself the activities conducted for the welfare of all.

The views

Concerning the views that sever ordinary service, they are taught by means of these five topics: essence, definition, divisions, purpose, and result.

Therefore, these views consist in the view on listening, meditating, and abiding; the view on the inexpressible transcendence of thought; the view separating concerted effort and cause; the view on separating awareness of subjects and objects; and the view on equanimity and spontaneity. One realizes these while remaining impressed, like seeing a peacock spreading its tail. It consists in oneself seeing into oneself.

Conduct

The conduct that discards various activities, its nature, definition, and divisions, these are expounded according to the enactment of blessing, the enactment of nurturing and purifying, and the enactment of establishing oneself in discipline and so forth.

These fearless activities are like an elephant sitting in water who is left unaffected no matter what.

The intermediate path

The intermediate path is taught in five parts. If one is to proceed to the ground of spontaneity and symbolic hand gestures, one must, most importantly, first receive the empowerments and pledges.

The path of empowerment

First, there is the path of empowerment. If at the onset one is not able to receive the empowerments, one will be burdened with a lack of specificity from the beginning.

It will be like the broken axle of a wheel. For that reason, the supreme path of empowerment is crucial. As for the universal basis that is the mind of enlightenment itself, virtuous tendencies must be accumulated for one to become familiar with the unsurpassed ground.

The path of accumulation

Second, the excellent path of accumulation is crucial. The bond with the blissful ones must be fulfilled in order to purify previously accumulated karmic debts.

The path of sacrificial cake offerings

Third, the excellent path of sacrificial cake offerings is crucial. The symbolic gestures of body, speech, and mind must be performed in order to proceed on the undifferentiated ground.

The path of hand seals

Fourth, the excellent path of hand-seals is crucial. Using the hand-seals of the pristine cognition of the nature of mind, the enemies of wrong views must be cleared away for one to practice in profound intrinsic reality.

The path of mantra

Fifth, [175] the excellent path of mantra is crucial. The final result accomplished is the spontaneous result of the five bodies. These [five bodies] come as the result of the very pure spontaneous perfection, which is the result of the accomplished knowledge-holders. Its lineage [of teachings] consists in the transmission from the oral source through the many complete links with all the main oral instruction compilations. Because of its sublime perfection, it is called "tantra." This tantra is the king of all tantras.

The outer tantra is illustrated in the same way as the observation of a net. The inner tantra is explained in the same way as a necklace of jewels. The secret tantra is illustrated as being similar to the abyss of the ocean.

Tantric lineage, transmission, and instruction

Oral transmissions are communicated in person because they were first conveyed orally and directly. They are the oral transmissions that convey the definitive meaning over interpretations. This oral transmission is the master's oral transmission. It is explained as the king of the oral lineage transmission.

Pith instructions are advice from the heart. The source of hearing is the lineage and the places where these were obtained. They were transmitted with small words, easy to understand but with immeasurable importance. Because of that, pith instructions are the quintessence. All aspects of knowledge are explained just like that. These three: tantra, oral transmission, and pith instructions, support one another in an uninterrupted manner.

358 *The Tradition of Everlasting Bön*

Example, meaning, and analysis

As for examples, they demonstrate in a manner using consistent illustrations that are common in the world. As for meaning, these examples express the sphere of intrinsic reality. Meaningful [categories] tightly organize what has the same predicament. As for analysis, it gathers one's thoughts. These thoughts are liberated in the unborn and changeless sphere.

The three outer, inner, and secret categories

The outer consists in unceasing manifestations. The inner consists in establishing the constituent elements [i.e., aggregates] into deities. The secret is the purity of the mind of enlightenment.

The three stages of generation, completion, and Great Perfection

The stages of the generation process

The sequence of the generation process is taught as outer, inner, and secret. The outer generation process, the generation of the mind of enlightenment, is threefold: the generation of the accumulation of merit of the faithful, the generation of the mind of highest enlightenment, and the generation of faith in the disciple toward the preceptor and his spiritual sons.

The inner generation process is also threefold: the outer generation that is concerned with the receptacle of the world that is generated as the inexhaustible mansion; the inner, where all the essential beings of the world are generated as the gods and goddesses; and self-nature that consists in the commitment of the heroes of everlastingness that is the mandala generated by itself.

The secret generation process consists in the five aggregates, the eighteen constituents, and the twelve sense spheres that are generated into the gods and goddesses; the essential drops in the castles of the knotted channels that are generated as great bliss; and the refined quintessence that is generated as pristine cognition.

The stages of the perfection process

The stages of the perfection process consist in these three: outer perfection, inner perfection, and secret perfection.

Thus, the outer perfection is threefold: the host of gods emanating messengers, perfection in the state of the syzygies (*yab yum*) of the portals, and the perfection of the host of protectors of the portals.

The protectors are perfected in their wrath at the regional boundaries. The leaders are perfected in the centers of their respective regional boundaries. The tutelary leader is perfected in the state of non-perception.

At the moment of practicing these, the two outer and inner signs arise. The outer sign is that one cognizes the illusory-like nature of wrong conceptuality. The inner sign is that one recognizes the freedom of pristine awareness.

The inner process of perfection is threefold: the characteristics of the enlightened bodies of the gods are perfected in light, the light is perfected in the state of the essential drops, [176] and the essential drops are perfected in the enlightened mind.

The secret perfection stage is fivefold:

The pith instructions on recognizing pristine awareness are perfected in the mode of a skillful physician.

The pith instructions on self-liberation from the five poisons are perfected like the all-curing ambrosia of the body of the gods.

The pith instructions on self-awareness and natural luminosity are perfected like the rising sun.

The pith instructions on the innate clarity of self-awareness are perfected like the blossoming lotus flower.

The pith instructions on experiential awareness are perfected like an inexpressible dream.

The Great Perfection

The system of perfecting the Great Perfection is threefold:

Obvious and common appearances are perfected in the state of the sky, free from elaboration. Conceptualizations perceived are perfected in the state of the pure universal ground. The dynamic manifestations that are the pristine cognition of awareness constitute the knowledge of all aspects that is the perfection of pristine awareness. Each droplet of pristine cognition is, without exception, perfected. The simile droplets are uncompounded pristine awareness. The principal droplets are marks for transcendence. The conceptual droplets abide in the unchanging sphere. The pith instruction on the empty droplets is that these are limitless. Intrinsic mind, droplets, and pristine cognition are uncompounded. In these states, everything is perfected.

The three parts of approach, achievement, and activities

The activities of accomplishing the ritual recitation consist in counting, timing oneself during the performance of the ritual recitation, and reciting the signs and characteristics. These are the sequences to the preliminaries.

Practice is conducted with the ordinary body, speech, and mind, and concludes with the establishment of the realized body, speech, and mind. The four kinds of activities of recitation are to be accomplished in concordance.

In brief, the outer, inner, and secret tantras of Bön consist in the primordial wisdom of self-awareness. This root text extracts the meaning of the scriptures. This root tantra, the precious gathering of all, is the scripture that counsels for the future. It is the great tantra of the gathering of all precious root tantras, spoken through the bestowal of blessings.

It is perfect! It is extensive in its subject matter, connecting a host of material but also concise. It is most cherished among all the secret mantras. All the main points are completely contained within. And because of that, it gathers all roots. This is the root tantra of the precious view, the one whose powerful action liberates. It is explained and praised by the glorious wise ones. Their followers have complete trust in it.

U yo ag tham! [All ills have been dispersed]

PART 3

Net of Sunrays:
A Commentary on the Root Tantra
the Precious Universal Gathering

[Attributed to] the great soul
Drenpa Namkha (fl. eighth century),
the great commander, the blaze of glory, the wall of Kailash,
the blazing fire of the citadel of the Bönpos of Tibet

I PAY HOMAGE TO the teacher Kuntu Zangpo!

1. INITIAL DEMONSTRATION OF PRAISE[168]

I first bow to the summit, the teachings from the *Net of Sunrays, the Commentary on the Teachings of the Universal Gathering*, the root tantra that is the intrinsic nature of all the secret mantras.

The teacher

When "the teacher"[169] is mentioned, it means four things:

Space is used to exemplify the teacher. Its meaning is teaching intrinsic reality. Signs are used for teaching the nature of the mind. Enlightened qualities demonstrate the source.

Using the example of space, the teacher is showing that all worldly fields of manifestations are in the state of Suchness.

The teacher is demonstrating that all manifestations of subjects with characteristics are in a state of complete purity; this is the meaning of intrinsic reality.

The teacher is demonstrating that all senses and the fields of the aggregates are in a state without production pointing at intrinsic mind.

The meaning of these three is that they are all collected within Kuntu Zangpo.

As for the teacher as the source of enlightened qualities, it is in Kuntu Zangpo himself. For that reason, Kuntu Zangpo is then mentioned.

For example, in the Golden Isle [i.e., Sumatra, according to Buddhists in Tibet] there are no stones and dirt to be named. Intrinsic mind is in the state of Kuntu Zangpo where there is not even a particle of the illusory cycle of transmigration or activity.

Therefore, if one is to make some divisions here, there are two:[170]

(1) A symbol imputes the existence of Kuntu Zangpo. It imputes that there are the higher forty-five vehicles. On top is the land of the gods, White Earth (*sa dkar*). The castle of nothingness beyond the Highest Realm is located there. In the court of the perfected circle of the seed-syllables there are the marks of the enlightened body of perfect enjoyment with all the characteristic signs.

(2) As for the Kuntu Zangpo who is without conception, Kuntu Zangpo is the body of the absolute, like the sky, free from all characterizing marks. There is Kuntu Zangpo as inherent mind, like the sky, free from all characterizing marks.

When "conceptuality" is mentioned, it refers to the suffering that should be cleared away, both good concepts and bad concepts.

When "the net" is mentioned, it refers to a conceptual example. It is like difficulties developing from the darkness of a covering net.

"Who destroys" refers to the clearing function of compassion. It is the clearing away of everything that arises into non-conceptuality through pristine awareness, which destroys the concept of "sentient beings."

When it is said "the lord of the profound and greatly extensive body," this is meant to describe the qualities of the body. It is the possession of a body difficult to realize, much like trying to measure the depth of the ocean. [178] It is as extensive as the limits of the sky, so that it encompasses the entirety of living beings.

When it says "the knower of everything," this refers to the illumination of all objects of cognition, like the sun rising in the sky that is Kuntu Zangpo.

"To" (*la*) means to establish the object of worship, the teacher.

When it is said "I bow," this refers to six items: essence, definition, divisions, example, qualities, and time period.

Therefore the **essence**[171] of worship consists in the enlightened body, speech, and mind.

The **definition** is to prostrate because of the bundles of all the defilements.

The **divisions** are threefold: the prostration of the body is to bow with the five limbs, the prostration of speech is to take refuge with a melodious voice [lit. "voice of the cuckoo"], and the prostration of the mind is to aspire with devotion.

The **example** for the prostration of the body is a tree being blown away by the wind. The example for the prostration of speech is a melodious tune. The example for the prostration of the mind is the mother of a single son.

Its **qualities**: when the body prostrates it purifies the three sins of the body—the defilements of killing, thievery, and fornication.

As for [the prostration of] speech, it purifies the four defilements of lies, slander, harsh speech, and nonsensical chatter.

As for [the prostration of] the mind, it purifies the three defilements of curses, harmful thoughts, and wrong views.

As for the **time period** [on performing these], one seeks [to practice these until one acquires] the unobtainable enlightenment of omniscience.

2. THE ACCUMULATION OF THE THREE BENEFITS

Now, as for the first of the six topics, the accumulation of the three benefits,[172] the teacher demonstrates the accumulation of the three benefits when [the tantra] says: "From the circle of his heart, the teacher."

The teacher is the accumulation of the three benefits. The teacher possesses the compounded qualities with the marks and the distinctions of the thirty-two good marks of the accumulation of the three benefits of the body, the eighty-two distinctions, the series of the forty definite marks, and so forth.

The one endowed with the four accumulations of the **three benefits of compassion** has compassion, like the limitless sky. The compassionate one is like the sun and the moon shining equally on all, like the inexhaustible earth, and like an endless stream of water.

As for the accumulation of the **three benefits of insight**, it consists in the wisdom[173] of intrinsic emptiness.

The two parts of the wisdom of intrinsic equanimity are the all-knowing wisdom and the wisdom of just-as-it-is [i.e., Suchness] without manifestation. The three wisdoms: wisdom-like-the-mirror, the wisdom of persistent activities, and the wisdom of realization of each and every thing, together with the manifestation of the wisdom of the knowledge discriminating all the details of phenomena [and the wisdom of intrinsic equanimity above] make the five great wisdoms. [179]

There are also the sixty-one wisdoms of omniscience and the 10,000 times 100,000 wisdoms of the qualities of discipline, and so forth.

As for the accumulation of the **three benefits of enlightened activities**, they are the effortless activities of the wish-fulfilling gem and the playful unhindered activities arising for the benefit of others and the suppression of the self.

The point of this is to demonstrate the circle of the exalted mind that is the accumulation of the **three benefits of the teacher**.

"Has explained with blessings" refers to the accumulation of the three benefits coming from his words.

"The blessings of compassion" is explained as the tradition's comments on the body of enjoyment. The tradition's explanations on the body of perfection was derived from comments on the letters and the words of the traditional lore on the body of emanation.

When explanations are divided up, they are threefold: the speech that bestows blessings, the speech of the spoken words directly from the presence of the holy one, and the speeches subsequently granted.

With respect to the **speech that bestows blessings**, Kuntu Zangpo's voice did not resonate with the sound of words. He does so through the private phenomena of the mantra where blessings are bestowed. Later the explanations come to the mindstream of one's awareness. These [mantras and explanations] are phenomena with definitive meaning in the Greater Vehicle of the mantras and the Great Perfection.

As for the **spoken words uttered directly in the presence of the holy one**, those are letters and words of the enlightened emanation body. Regarding **the subsequent utterances delivered**, the enlightened ones have expressed themselves through the scriptures and the teachings. Thus, these three forms of "words" are the accumulation of the three benefits from the words of the bestowal of blessings.

The expression "Root Tantra of the Precious Universal Gathering" is the accumulation of the three benefits from the teachings. The "gathering of all" is the phrase used to describe the qualities of the enlightened ones. For example, the one who possesses the kingly power gathers members of his lower circle around himself. The phrase "gathering of all" is encompassed within all the meanings of the secret mantras. "Precious" is a term used as an example. For example, the precious jewel fulfilling all wishes produces various desires and needs. This tantra itself will generate all the meanings of the secret mantras. "Root tantra" is the term for its essential point. For example, the trunk gathers all the roots of the branches. It gathers the essence of the mind and the main points of all the secret mantras. As such, it is the authentic meaning of the accumulation of the three benefits of the teachings.

"In the citadel of the Highest Sphere" has to do with the accumulation of the three benefits of the sacred place. The sacred place of the realm Highest

Sphere (*'og min*) is the abiding place of all the enlightened ones. For that reason, it is free from all the suffering of cyclic existence and is the accumulation of the three benefits of happiness. Because there exist many conditioned phenomena, [180] there is the accumulation of the three benefits of the ultimate. The abiding place of intrinsic mind is without center or limits and exists through the accumulation of the three benefits of the qualities.

"In a past life, he took it upon himself to spread the teachings among his entourage." This refers to the accumulation of the three benefits of the divine entourage. This entourage is twofold: the entourage of the host of gods of the fortress (*pho brang*) and the entourage that purifies, emanates, and appropriates.

The entourage of the host of gods of the fortress is composed of the eight kinds of deities:

1. The entourage of the five conquering families of deities liberating the intrinsic essence of the five poisons.
2. The entourage of the exalted speech of the four ranges[174] that are the complete purity of the aggregates.
3. The entourage of the eight pristine cognitions that liberate the eight collections of consciousness on their own grounds.
4. The entourage of the eight primordial consorts that liberate the eight objects of consciousness through the qualities of desire.
5. The entourage of the six taming hand-gestures that transform the six abodes (i.e., six worlds of reincarnation).
6. The entourage of the nine crowns of the nine heads that transforms the power of the senses.
7. The entourage of the four portals that conquers the demonic actions of the four: birth, old age, sickness, and death.
8. The entourage of the protectors that guards the activities under oath.

As for **the entourage that purifies, radiates, and seizes** through emanations, they are the heroes of everlastingness of the pure realms: Teacher Tsemé Öden [i.e., endowed with infinite light], Trulshen Nangden [i.e., endowed with the manifestations of a sage's conjurings], Yeshen Tsukpu [i.e., most primordial sage], Zangza Tsendruk [i.e., good woman with the six marks], Zangwa Düpa [i.e., the collector of secrets], Mönpa Kunsel [i.e., remover of all darkness], and Özer Pakmé [i.e., immeasurable light rays].

"Where he discoursed directly from his own self-nature" concerns the method of accumulation of the three benefits in the tradition of the teacher. With respect to this, the tradition of the commentaries is three-fold: intrinsic essence explaining inherent nature, the bestowal of bless-ings explaining compassion, and poetic composition involving sounds and words.

Concerning the **intrinsic essence of inherent nature**, the teacher has explained the intrinsic essence. That is understood as the circle of inherent nature.

The **bestowal of the blessings of compassion** explains the entourage, and it is understood through the entourage.

As for **poetic composition involving sounds and words**, composing verses with sounds and words brings about the three understandings of the teachings. This is done with explanations on intrinsic essence, through bestowing teachings, and blessings (*rlabs*, lit. "ripple").

Now as for the subsequent followers of these teachings, they comment with verses, sounds, and words.

3. Teachings on the Significance of the Secret Mantras

Nowadays the teachings are taught to students in this environment. There are three categories of Bön—the extensive lineage, the middle transmission, and the condensed pith instructions—and these are the three environments for individuals. They correspond to the threefold division of understanding in the minds of students: excellent, middling, and lower.

As for the [students with] excellent minds, they are said to be "perceptive in great faith." They are the students endowed with the five intrinsic char-acteristics: great faith, intelligence, little miserliness, no attachments, and endowed with a mind of great power. [181]

Therefore, the student who practices the secret mantras must be endowed with great faith as well as the four other articles of faith: faith and devotion like that of a mother toward an only son; faith that is perfectly bright, sim-ilar to the pure part of the clarity of a refined jewel; the faith of conviction, such as that of a visitor returning to his own native land; and faith in com-pletion, similar to the final gathering of the harvest. It is best if those who are endowed with these four, whoever they are, have [great] faith.

There are three kinds of "perceptive minds": one is not distracted despite whatever appears to the senses, but rather is heedful and attentive, as when straightening the shaft of an arrow; one is attentive and mindful, as when holding a metal tool to fix a tooth; and one is attentive to practice with an aim, like one suffering from thirst.

As for those "deprived of . . . miserliness": the superior ones among them have the ability to give away both their own and others' belongings, the middling ones have the ability to give their own belongings, and the lowest have the ability to give away others' belongings.

Those who are "not attached" are the master, the three entourages of the blissful ones from all quarters, and auspicious friends who do not hold on to body and life. They are not attached to food and wealth, to eating, drinking, or having clothes to wear. These auspicious friends do not care even for necessities such as food and wealth.

As for "ordinary mind," it has eight forms of knowledge and awareness: the knowledge that is expansive, like a whirling spear in the sky; the knowledge that is clear of obstacles, like casting a sword into water; the knowledge that is quick, like a fire spreading in a forest; the knowledge that is illuminating, like the raising of a lamp; the knowledge that is very powerful, like an elephant; the knowledge that is like untarnished genuine gold; the knowledge that is firm and unwavering, like the action of piercing a turquoise in a ball of yarn; and the knowledge that is unobstructed, like tumbling down a steep mountain.

The best is "endowed with a mind with great power" and must be "like an elephant." The example: like an elephant that carries a good measure of some load, the mind of the disciple has to have the power to carry whatever comes. Whatever comes, the disciple's consciousness must be fearless; in times of low spirits he or she should remain unaffected. To that sort of mind is "what is taught in the instruction to the root commentary of the tantra."

The disciple who is "perceptive with great faith" is endowed with the three intrinsic characteristics of a middling mind. He or she is endowed with great faith, intelligence, and a mind that is not changing. Therefore, this faith is the same as the former, akin to gold that does not change. This is the middling mind. For example, whatever comes, gold never changes its nature. A disciple like this will not change from virtuous to sinful.[182]

It is said that this is the "condensed root of the scriptures." Therefore, this is the Bön scriptural teaching.

"They meaningfully do away with conventional words." The disciple who is endowed with a lower mind casts aside conventional words. It is meaningful that he be endowed with knowledge of the unchanging teaching. Therefore, casting away conventional words is to use simple words and not line them up, so as not to lose hope for clear comprehension. One must meditate on the mode of pondering the meaning in between the four sessions of practice so as not to have it wither away.

"One must have a mind steady and unmoving," as when piercing turquoise in a ball of yarn. This example, piercing turquoise in a ball of yarn, must be done in such a way that the mind remains stable and is not moved by anything else. That disciple must have a steady and unmoving mind when meditating in the natural state.

"These instructions integrate the teachings of the main points progressively." To teach Bön pith instructions is to engage with the main points and discard the words. Now, to clarify the meaning of the main body of the work, there are brief explanations in separate sections.

"In general, the system of the secret mantras . . ." provides a comprehensive meaning to all the vehicles of the secret mantras. Therefore "in general" means the outer mantras.

The word "secret" is fourfold: What in essence is secret? From which objects are they secret? What is the secret mode? What is the reason for secrecy?

In essence, the oral transmissions of the secret mantras are secret.

The ten objects from which they are kept secret: (1–3) they are kept secret from the three non-abidings of the teachings, (4–6) they are kept secret from the three wrongful views on the meaning of the teachings, (7–9) they are kept secret from the three obstacles to the teachings, and (10) they are kept secret from the non-realization of the mistaken mind.

From these, the **three non-abidings of the teachings** are:

(1) Harboring wrong views that sever the root of the path to liberation. The latter [i.e., the path] is then kept concealed.

(2) The protectresses[175] keep concealed the essential point of the secret mantra, preventing the generation process so that the enlightened bodies are denied [from arising clearly].

(3) The defilements of ordinary fools cut them off and conceal the teachings.

As to **those with the three wrongful views** from whom the secrets are kept, they are: those who violate the pledges; those who have the wrong pledges; and those who slip away from upholding the pledges.

The **three obstacles** from which secrets are kept are the obstacles coming from demons, *shinpo,*[176] and enemy sprites.

As for the ignorant **mistaken mind**, it is thought to be similar to that of the mistaken heretics.

What is the secret mode?

What is there to say about the mantra formulas, the activities of the symbolic hand gestures [i.e., mudra], and the consecrated ritual instruments? It is like hearing and seeing, not to mention the least about the modes of their performance. They are not taught but are kept secret from non-initiates.

What is the reason for secrecy?

The [reason for secrecy lies in] very pure meanings of the words of the enlightened ones who are not partial in their compassion. For all of those who are ignorant, the secret itself is the means that cuts away delusion. It is a secret to those who are bewildered. An example: like the opening of a cave that faces north, into which the rising sun never shines. [183]

What is called "mantra" is threefold: the essence of mantra, definition, and divisions.

The essence of a mantra consists in its recitation to obtain one's aim.

Its **definition** is that the main point of the mantra consists in its aim. The object that is recited is a mantra. The objective of pronouncing the mantra is to transform the five poisons into wisdom. The objective of pronouncing the mantra is for the mantra to transform a deluded mind of ignorance into an enlightened mind.

The divisions are twofold: division in terms of categories and division in terms of action.

Division in term of categories is fourfold: mantras for families of deities, mantras for recollection (*gzungs, dhāraṇī*), mantras for forceful actions, and secret mantras.

Mantras for families of deities are mantras involving the lineages of peaceful deities, mantras for the lineages of wrathful deities, mantras for deities that overpower, and mantras for deities that [bring about] increase.

The mantras for recollection are mantras that are entirely for protection alone.

Forceful mantras consist in the following three kinds of mantras: mantras for fierce accomplishments, mantras for the casting of fierce spells, and mantras for fierce magical stabbing.

There are three kinds of such mantras: (1) mantras against heretics, mantras of the priestly class (*bram ze*), and mantras of the sages (*drang srong*); (2) mantras from Zhangzhung; and (3) mantras that are spells against deadly poisons.[177]

The secret mantras are those of the universal ground of the most perfect meaning. Those endowed with the mind of enlightenment will use these to transform the five poisons into the five wisdoms.

Now this kind of tantra of the secret mantras here teaches the transformation of the five poisons into wisdom in conjunction with completely demonstrating their qualities to all the other lineages of mantras.

The division in terms of action is fourfold: the mantra that is the unmistaken root, the mantras of the root for the minor causes of production, the mantras for the activity of recitation, and the mantras of the root to the extraordinary.

The mantra that is the unmistaken root consists in the seed-syllables that are the root cause for the generation of the deities.

The mantras that are the minor cause of the production of the deities are those generated in the heart.

The mantras for the activity of recitation consist essentially in those whose number of recitations should be counted.

The [roots] to the extraordinary consist of the mantras of the different families.

"The system" means that there are different traditional systems of the secret mantras. Those subsumed under the families are the five different kinds of enlightened families displaying the activities of secret miraculous displays. These five kinds correspond to the body, speech, mind, qualities, and enlightened activities.

(1) The emanation section has the peaceful and wrathful families for the attainment of the immutable body.

(2) The deity and the prognostic sections are for the attainment of unobstructed speech.

(3) The sections "The Essence of the Transmission of the A" and "The Heart of the Goddess" are for the attainment of the unborn mind.

(4) The sections "Abiding in the Six A" and "The Droplets of the Peaceful Deities" are for the attainment of abiding in the enlightened qualities.

(5) The enlightened activities of the Hero Spreading the Words, the activities for magical rites, for precepts, for protection, for the reversal of spells

with casting stones, and for the Sharp Black Peg (*phur nag*) rites are for the attainment of the enlightened activities of countering and liberating.

The five classes of special attainments are the five classes of the Perfection Vehicle: the completely perfected pacification, [184] the everlasting wrathful perfection, the perfection of the power of the summit of the gods, the perfection of medicinal ambrosia, and the deep perfection of secret illusions.

The three classes of critical pith instruction are Black Mountain (*ri nag*), Black Peg (*phur nag*), and Black Waters (*chab nag*). These and so forth are the systems of all the Illusion-Using Secret Mantras that are similarly related to this tantra.

4. Brief teachings on the base, the path, and the result

"These three: the base, the path, and result." This means that this [tantra] teaches about the base, the path, and the result of the Vehicle of the Secret Mantras. The object of the base, if different, is therefore non-existent.

The universal ground is the mind of enlightenment and the basis for all cyclic existence and its transcendence.

"The path" is the method of realization of the base with objects of the view and conduct.

"The result" is in making the base manifest. This has two meanings:

(1) The mode of abiding[178] that is the object of the activity under the influence of reality is taught as the base, the path, and the result.

(2) The greater activity is chiefly the method of achievement [i.e., the process] that is taught as the base, the path, and the result. Therefore the mode of abiding, which is the Greater Vehicle, is the system of the secret mantras. The base is without production or cessation. The path is without method and wisdom. The result exists without space and consciousness.

The base

First, the base is fivefold: the essence of the base, the system encompassing enlightened qualities, examples, divisions, and the elimination of the flaws of illusion.

As for **the essence of the base**, it has no production or cessation. A scripture[179] says:

> There is no production and cessation. Primordial wisdom has no
> differentiation. Everything is undifferentiated. Self-origination is
> the expanse of the universal basis.

The nature of the mind appears unceasingly in its variety. The emptiness of
intrinsic essence does not produce any measure of arising. These two that are
inseparable do not have the duality of generation and cessation. The universal base is the inherent mind of enlightenment.

The system encompassing enlightened qualities

The traditional system of the qualities encompasses the base that is at its
highest the court of the conqueror, and whose lowest point includes the
frightened hosts of the hells. It includes all of the above.

An **example** for the base is where it is likened to the sesame oil pervading
the sesame seeds. A scripture says:

> How wonderful! Sentient beings in cyclic existence are from the
> beginning in the heart of the enlightened ones. These [sentient
> beings] are the natural aspects to delusory conceptions.

Another example likens the base to arable land where seeds are a simile for
three outcomes: any seed that is produced is planted and then ripens. Any
[seed] that is harvested but not eaten performs a function [i.e., is reserved
for future planting].

As for **divisions**, the base is originally pure and unborn. Yet the base displays a mode of arising, spontaneous and unceasing, from an indivisible
essence. Someone asks: "If illusion is eliminated, does the base still have
illusions?" If yes, then it follows that enlightened ones are illusions as well,
and that would include the god conqueror above. If no, then it follows that
moving away from cyclic existence entails breaking it up, which would also
include the hells.

The intrinsic essence of the enlightened ones that is all encompassing
[185] is no illusion. What arises in the conditioned mind includes present
illusions.

The path

The topic of the non-duality of method and wisdom on the path is three-fold: the essence of the path, an example, and divisions.

With respect to **the essence**, there are these two topics: the path of wisdom, meditation, and the view, and the path of method and conduct. A scripture says:

> When there is no duality of method and wisdom, result will come in the end.

As for **wisdom**, it is the concentration formula (i.e., mantra) of the view.

As for **conduct**, it consists in the recitation of the mantras, the performance of the mudras, the four activities, and the required ritual paraphernalia.

An example is a stretched rope made of golden hair. This example is threefold: the main point of the gold is that it does not change, the hair has growth, and growth is clearly perceivable [i.e., the performance is indicative of progress along the path].

The topic on **the divisions of the path** is threefold: the outer path, the inner path, and the secret path.

Concerning **the outer path**, it has the three paths of accumulation with nine stages.

The inner path is the path of engagement with the four wisdom families.

The secret path is the path of vision leading to the ultimate.

The outer path

From these, the path of accumulation is first in the following three points: The path of accumulation is first and is all about the objects to be eliminated. There are three objects of the middle accomplishment. There are the three objects of the great concentration.

First, then, there are **the three objects to be eliminated**. A scripture says:

> Life is cut short, stolen, and has lust, passion, and excess. It is said that these are the three objects of the body to eliminate. False-hood, innuendos, harsh words, and pointless talk are said to be the four objects of speech to be subdued. Vindictiveness, cruelty,

and wrong views are said to be the three objects of the mind from which to take refuge.

As for the three objects of middling accomplishment, the scripture says:

> With regard to the body, it is to adopt the positions and accomplish the hand gestures. With regard to speech, it is the activities of recitation. With regard to the mind, the nature of illusion is impermanence. Abide in the accumulation of merit with continued efforts.

As for **the three objects of the great concentration**, they are the concentration on the non-existence of whatever is [imputed as] their basis, the concentration of kindness toward the objects of knowledge, and the concentration for the emanations of compassion.

Thus elimination, practice, and meditation, these three in the outer, are the common path of vision and the vehicles of monastic vows and lay vows.

The inner path

The inner path of application of the four enlightened families regarding Heat, Peak, Forbearance, and Highest Bön are the pristine cognition of Heat, the pristine cognition of the Peak, the pristine cognition of Forbearance, and the primordial wisdom of the Highest Bön.

Once these four primordial wisdoms have been attained, there is the achievement of the state of No-More-Return. The defilements of suffering are then cleansed and the accumulations of the auspicious causes are perfected.

Thus, the view of these four primordial wisdoms ranges from the stage of the Great Realm to the Finality of all worldly views. It is the greatly efficacious practice that completes the accumulation process. This is the inner path. [186]

Moreover, these two, accumulation and application, are mundane paths. The mundane and supramundane paths are different. A scripture says:

> When duality manifests, one apprehends duality and focuses on the practice of worldly concerns that is suffering. When duality

manifests but is not apprehended dualistically, then the truth is perceived and one transcends the world.

The secret path

The secret path is threefold: the path of vision, the path of meditation, and the path to transcendence.

The first one, **the path of vision**, is fivefold: its essence, defining meaning, divisions, the culmination of vision, and the elimination of any defilement that is present.

Its essence is the pristine cognition that is self-arising.

Its definition is that when one is able to see the past, that is the seeing on the path of vision.

The divisions consist in these two: the primordial wisdom of deliverance and the primordial wisdom that is not realized.

The culmination of vision is being able to see over the whole world like the rising sun in the sky. It is to clearly see intrinsic emptiness and to transcend beyond suffering.

As for **defilements**, one eliminates the defilement of afflictive emotions. Once the path of vision has been attained, there is no return to cyclic existence.

The path of meditation is fivefold: essence, definition, divisions, the culmination of vision, and the elimination of any defilement.

From this, its **essence** is to abide in equanimity in the natural state.

Its **definition** is that if one meditates along the main point of vision, as earlier, this is what is called "the path of meditation."

Divisions are twofold: meditative equipoise and subsequent cognition.

The culmination of vision is the vision of non-duality of primordial wisdom and of the expanse.

The elimination of defilements consists in the elimination of the defilements from the object of cognition. From the second up to the ninth ground, there are dense portions of defilements. Those indeed are eliminated through familiarization with one's own realization and the compassion of Kuntu Zangpo.

The suppression activity from the eighth ground onward is where the oral teaching of the enlightened one are applicable, since its characteristic is the activity of suppression on the ground of no-more-return. Its result is the perfection of the collection of primordial wisdom.

The tenth ground is the path of the finality. A scripture says:

> The spontaneous path is reached at long last.

That is said to be the finality of all paths and the path to the ultimate. As for all the very subtle defilements of the objects of consciousness, they are exhausted and eliminated there. This third path is the path to transcend the world.

The result that is the non-duality of the expanse and pristine cognition is the emptiness of the expanse and the clarity of pristine cognition. [187] This non-duality of the expanse and pristine cognition is the body of the absolute. A scripture says:

> There is no duality between the expanse and pristine cognition.
> It is liberation in the body of the everlasting absolute.

On this topic, the three bodies of the absolute great bliss correspond to these: the eleventh is the ground of the universal light, the twelfth is the ground of the lotus of passion, and the thirteenth is the ground of the perfected circle of letters.

The thirteenth ground is the ground of the body of the absolute. Its teachings on the essential points of the body of the absolute have six aspects: its essence, its divisions, an example, the circle of words, pure lands, and the nature of the body of reality.

Its essence is the non-duality of the expanse and pristine awareness.

Its divisions consist in the solitary droplets that are great in number and are not established in the body of the absolute.

A good example is to see it as the sky.

The circle of words consists in inexpressible description and imaginings.

The pure fields of training are limitless like the sky.

Its inherent nature is endowed with the five non-established natures: the non-established object with graspable characteristics; the non-established measure to seize a real body; the non-established circles of listening to manifested form; the scriptures, tantras, and commentaries that are non-established Bön; and the non-established fields of training where there is grasping for a self.

The twelfth ground is the ground of the body of perfect enjoyment. The body of enjoyment has six main points:

Its essence is endowed with characteristics and signs.

Its divisions go according to the five families of peaceful and wrathful deities.

A good example for it is the sun and moon.

Its circle of words is the Greater Vehicle.

Its pure fields of training are the ten grounds of everlastingness.

Its nature is what is endowed with the five accumulations of the three benefits: (1) the three benefits of the body are to be endowed with signs and characteristics, (2) the three benefits of life are the life of changeless ever-lastingness, (3) the three benefits of the circle of listening are those of the heroes of everlastingness on the ten grounds, (4) the three benefits of the Bön of explanations are those of the promise of definitive meaning, and (5) the three benefits of the fields of training are the ten grounds.

The eleventh ground of the universal lights refers to the ground where emanated enlightened bodies are everywhere. The emanation body also has six points:

Its essence is proper emanations everywhere.

Its divisions are the billions of emanations.

A good example is the metaphor of the rainbow.

The circles of words consist in the four portals with the Treasury that make five, the hierarchy of the nine vehicles, and the 84,000 portals of Bön.

The pure fields of training are the unceasing worlds of the trichiliocosm, the one billion universes.

As for the five undefined **natures**, they are the undefined appearances of the body, the undefined measure of life, the undefined circles of the listeners, the undefined doctrines explained, and the undefined pure fields of training.

Those indeed are great major achievements that are taught as the base, the path, and the result. The basic intention of this root tantra is sixfold [188] and is taught as the five paths and the three results, demonstrated below. But contrary to that, the intent of the secret mantras is the universal ground.

Someone said that the mind of enlightenment that is asserted, the six basic positions, and the intention of this tantra are not concordant. Each of them has its own intent. The basis of the teachings that has something comprised of the base, the path, and result is for the common secret mantra. The basis of the practice of achievement of this tantra is taught as mainly performance.

"There are these three: tantra, transmission, instruction" that are the three categories collected in this tantra on intrinsic reality, its transmission, and its pith instruction. There is the class of the expansive tantras, the middle class of transmission, and the class of collected instructions.

"There are these three: analogy, essential points, and analysis." Analogy is the method using illustrations. The essential points are used to define reality. Analysis is to impute using the connection between the example and the meaning.

"There are these three: outer, inner, and secret." The outer is the object. The inner is the subject. The secret is its intrinsic mind.

"The three stages of generation, perfection, and Great Perfection" make for the gradual generation of a superior body over the ordinary manifested one. When one is not abiding in gradual perfection, this is the stage of gradual generation. When one is not abiding in the practice of the Great Perfection, this is the gradual perfection process.

"There are these three: approach, accomplishment, and application." The approach consists in the practice of the preliminaries. It is said that all these have been established from that point of view. Whenever the lore of these activities is conducted, the intention here is that it must be done according to their particular defined performances.[180]

Presently, a good example that is composed [in this tantra] as a brief explanation of these [practices] is when it says: "These three: the base, the path, and the result, are likened to the object, the place, and the journey."

The base that is likened to a phenomenal object is threefold: the teachings are all in the object, the ripening is all in the object, and whatever is done is as if one cannot go beyond the object.

The teachings are all in the base. The ripening is all in the base. Whatever is done is as if one cannot go beyond the base.

The path is similar to a journey. Everything is a journey as such on the path, and as such has limitations on its going.

Result is similar to abiding. Abiding is finality; it does not change into something else.

The tantra is like a **lord**, endowed with rulership. He is exalted with eulogies of greatness and as a total refuge, and his sayings are strictly ordered.

The transmission is similar to a **minister**. This minister is endowed with methods that cannot be incorrect and whose decree is accordingly settled. [189]

Pith instruction is similar to a **foundation**. This foundation is painstakingly done for its own sake so that wherever a door is skillfully placed, the edifice will not fall under the sway.

Analogy is similar to a **mirror**; it has the ability to illustrate. It is similar to a design that sets forth the goal.

To **analyze** is similar to a **reflected form**; it is like recognizing a face.

The **outer** tantra class is like a **treasury** from which all needs and desires are fulfilled.

The **inner** is like the treasury in a storehouse; it is secure.

The **secret** is like a very solitary place that is difficult to get to.

The **generation practice** is similar to hair; it radiates.

The **perfection** stage is similar to the rung of a ladder; it is one of many, and one does not dwell on it. One does not dwell on the stages of the perfection practices, for they are inherently empty.

The propitiation rite is similar to a **hero**. The body of the hero has great strength. Speech is a forceful hero. The mind is similar to a hero who remains undiminished. Ritual practice is like putting on armor. It provides a hard protection that will not yield under the attacks of the others. The application of activities is like a sword. It is able to strike decisively. It fulfills the purpose.

"This is therefore, what is ascertained as supreme." All the secret mantras together with these examples and meanings must be known.

5. On the four kinds of activities and the six families of the Vehicle of the Secret Mantras

From now on, the traditional lore will be taught extensively. "First," at the beginning the base will be taught. "The base is sixfold," the enumeration of the divisions is a synopsis. "Vows, empowerment, and mantras, activities, view, and conduct" is a clear summation of the six divisions. Whatever is mentioned here is taught individually.

Then there are the four causal characteristics: the definite amount of causal characteristics, the definite order of causal characteristics, the definite causal characteristics of each and every defining characteristic, and definite synonyms of the causal characteristics.

With respect to the **amount of the causal characteristics**, the number regarding the basis for the secret mantras was articulated to be six and it was not necessary to increase it to seven. Previously there was no consensus; it was ascertained as six in number.

The definite order is the following order of layered elements:

The pledges are like the basic ground and must first be taught.

The empowerment is similar to building (or masonry) and is taught as second.

The formulas of concentration are like presences and are taught as third.

The activities are like painting and are taught as fourth.

The view is like the eyes and is taught as fifth.

Performance is like a supervisor and is taught as sixth.

For each and every defining characteristic:

The pledges are the defining characteristics of the object to be protected and are expressed verbally.

Empowerments are the defining characteristics of the objects to be brought to maturity and are done orally.

The formulas of concentration are the defining characteristics of meditation and are recited.

Activities are the defining characteristics of ritual accomplishment and are explained.

The view is the defining characteristic of the teaching of the mode of abiding and is pointed out.

Performance is the defining characteristic of the action of the inherent nature of the view and is demonstrated.

Meaning is certitude. All these are for the one accomplishment of the unsurpassable enlightenment. [190]

"The basis of all the secret mantras" as well as the extensive traditional lore "consist in taking pure pledges." These teachings are concise root words that are extensive in meaning. From these, and from the six main points above, the explanations of the pledges are taught. Their main points, which are extensive, are that "their essential attributes are divided according to their definition" and so forth.

These have been taught as the nine essential points of the pledges: (1) the essence of the pledges, (2) definition, (3) divisions, (4) whosoever needs protection, (5) whatever object needs to be protected, (6) the method of protection, (7) the disadvantages of not being protected, (8) the qualities of protection, and (9) providing good examples.

6. ON PLEDGES

On **the essence of pledges**, the *Tantra of Secret Everlastingness, the Secret Life Bearer* (5.425.5) says:

> One's own mind is pure. There is neither cunning nor deceit, for pledges are called pledges! There may be losses or not, but one's own mind has pledged. One's own nature is just pure.

As for **the definition of pledges**, if their meanings are protected, then they are pure. When the words are not protected there are faults because of conceited qualities. The first is what is called a "pure pledge." For when the words are protected, there is the example of the blissful ones who have abided by the purity of their words; they promised.

As for the words, as an outward action, they can turn into enemies and hindrances. As inner concepts, they can turn into predispositions. As secret, words under the influence of ignorance can turn into suffering. If they are not guarded, they are just words. A promise, if acted upon, is a bond in cyclic existence toward alleviating suffering. It is pure. Words, then, are expressions of the continuum of one's body, speech, and mind.

The divisions consist in root pledges and secondary pledges.

There are two kinds of root pledges: the pledges of the exoteric teachings of Bön and tantric inner pledges.

The exoteric secret pledges are those guarded by monastics and the laity. They are these four actions to guard against: the taking of life, taking what is not given, not observing ethical purity, and lying. These four root defilements are further developed into the ten non-virtues[181] that one must guard against. Those indeed are the pledges of the exoteric teachings of Bön. But the inner tantric practitioner guards these pledges as exoteric.

As for the inner tantric pledges, they are twofold: the root pledges on the object to be eliminated and the pledges on the observance of the root vows.

The root pledges on the object to be eliminated are threefold according to the class of the pledges of the body, speech, and mind.

The pledges regarding the body concern the master, the parents, and the siblings [i.e., kinfolk or spiritual]. This is the first set of pledges. In regard to this one teaching, one must rely on it at face value. [191] As for spiritual consorts, when menses or blood comes out, one must not beat, throw dirt, or kill the consorts. These behaviors must be abandoned. A scripture says:

> The root to the generation of the mind of enlightenment is the master. The roots to the generation of the body are parents and siblings. This is one teaching on pledges. As for consort and so forth and other wandering beings, one should eliminate drawing blood, beating, and killing.[182]

As for **the pledges of speech**, a scripture says:

> The words of the blissful ones have not passed away. Their words of truth have not been broken, while people have turned their backs on the words of the enlightened ones. The truthful words of the master have been cut off. That is equal to killing sentient beings of the three realms.

The object of the pledges of the mind is to refrain from the erroneous. A scripture says:

> Erroneous views of the mind, such as negativities that are mischievous, are to be burned in order to have the result of liberation.

The pledges of the objects to be eliminated, when damaged, have three options:

If corrupted, there is no method of repair but a birth in the Hell of Endless Torment.[183]

If the root pledges are not maintained, it will be similar to seeds being burned. There will be no results.

If the root pledges are lost, it will be similar to cutting the tip of a palm tree. The tree will be severely weakened and will be destroyed. It will be like the body of a dead flower, separated from the radiant luster of life. The compassion from the blissful ones of the three times will become the same as the sun seen from the northern opening of a cave. There is no way for compassion to shine in, even for an instant.

The *Tantra of Amrta Kundali, the Golden Tree of Paradise* (18.4) says:

> The pledge of abiding by the words is such that to violate the

pledges will simply cut short the descendants of one's family. The ruin will be for an entire eon. Sentient beings that commit an infraction to their vows will end up in the Never-Ending Hell.[184] There will be unending suffering without release.

The pledges on observance of the root pledges are threefold.

The pledges of the body are to observe the seals of the body: the master, the parents, and the everlasting siblings. This is the first set of pledges. Concerning spiritual friends and consorts, the pledge is to forever generate love and not abandon them. It is to praise their body, speech, and mind with devotion. This is the superior pledge of the mind of all the blissful ones. It is the vitality of the accomplished Shen priests of future generations. One abides on the ground of the pledges while holding on to these purifying and powerful vows. Do not abandon the seals of the body, and practice continually during the three times.

The *Tantra of Amrta Kundali, the Golden Tree of Paradise* (17.2) says:

> Toward the master, parents, and everlasting siblings, as well as toward consort friends, I make this one pledge in a state of great love, that I will not abandon and will always produce ardent love. I fervently praise your body, speech, and mind. This is the pledge of the body. If I defile it, then for the intervals of two eons, I will wander in the circle of black darkness.

As for **the pledges of speech** [192], the *Tantra of Amrta Kundali, the Golden Tree of Paradise* (17.6) says:

> I will strive not to sever the connection with the compassionate pledge in regard to the mantras, the heart-seal, and the formulas of concentration. I will abide by the seal of speech and ceaselessly strive toward the tutelary deity. I will never sever the generation and perfection stage, the seeds, the seals, the connection with the mantras, the heart empowerment, the hand-seals and the formulas. This is the pledge of speech, and if I have betrayed it, I will enter the prison of the cycle of hunger and thirst for the interval of two great eons. I will wander unceasingly in this cycle.

As for **the pledges of the enlightened mind,** the secret instructions that are the essential points of the mind will not prosper in an unworthy recipient. If they prosper, one will be born in the Hells of Endless Suffering for a period of three great eons. In the words of the *Tantra of Amrta Kundali, the Golden Tree of Paradise* (18.2), the pledge is:

> I will abide in the seal of the mind undisrupted without change in the circle of the mind. The secret instruction has as its goal the inherent mind. I will not teach it to an evil recipient, to an unworthy recipient, or to an unsuitable recipient, even if they practice in the proper way. This is the pledge of the mind. If I betray this, then for an interval of three great eons I will fall into the Most Tortuous Hell of Ceaseless Torture[185] where it will not be possible to be released from suffering.

Thus, those three root pledges have to be protected from being impaired at the root. If this is not done during one's lifetime and the pledges are in the process of being corrupted, one can properly repair them three times. If the reparation goes over that limit, the results will be ashes. As for the person who regrets having broken the pledges and has not turned away from the outer tutelary deity, the *Tantra of Amrta Kundali, the Golden Tree of Paradise* (21.6) says:

> He has the means to nurture and repair [the root pledges], like mending a damaged golden or silver vessel. If one has not separated from the underlay of the teachings, then there is a method to rebalance and mend them. If the root pledges have been corrupted, they can be repaired up to three times. Past that, one will fall into Tortuous Hell. The secondary pledges can be continually repaired.

Now the six secondary pledges are taught as the common outer pledge, the particular accomplishment pledge, the pledge of continual practice, the pledge of the view on inherent self, the pledge of exceeding importance, and the pledge of the distinctive **samaya**.

Among these, **the common outer pledge** is to guard the pledge through the mode of non-aversion. It is, in brief, to protect equanimity.[186]

That lion of supreme skills, the white snow mountain [i.e., the teacher], must not die!

That tiger's skin, the predator of the forest, is now spread out on the lower seat. Refrain from this! [i.e., Do not use the wife of the teacher!]

Do not make the conqueror's precious jewel fall from the top! [i.e., Do not belittle the body of the teacher!]

Do not destroy any bit of the great cliff that is the face of everlastingness! [i.e., Do not be devoid of moral boundaries!]

Do not throw that beautiful lump of stainless crystal into the swamp! [i.e., Do not tear to pieces one endowed with insight!] [193]

Refrain from using a sickle made of meteorite on that precious willow twig! [i.e., Do not kill monks, friends, brothers, and sisters!]

Do not kill that splendid white bull of the gods with the tip of your spear or the tip of your arrow! [i.e., Do not abandon your tutelary deity!]

Do not activate or send hail to that garden of lotus flowers! [i.e., Do not disparage sisters and brothers!]

Do not throw a guest arriving from afar after a long journey down a precipice! [i.e., Do not teach the wrong transmission!]

The glorious meteorite, Phurpa, kills the sacrificial effigy using troubled waters! [i.e., Don't get drunk on alcohol!]

Do not collect the rotten remains of the pleasures of Tagzig! [Do not make portions of the offerings fall on the ground!]

Do not fight inside the meteorite of Urmo! [Do not support feuds between tantric practitioners!]

Refrain from sitting on a fierce tiger's skin.

Do not put poison in your casket used for ritual items.

Refrain from using a torn mat with the design of a demoness as a seat.

Do not slaughter a black goat to the lower worlds.

Do not drink rainwater given by a mute.

Do not open the gate to the nine levels on the ritual Destruction Pit.[187]

Do not separate the anther and pistil of a lotus flower.

Do not pour ambrosia into a bad vessel.

In the evening, do not milk a calf that has been milked in the morning.

Do not separate the wings of the feathered garuda.

Beware of the wind against the lamp that dispels the darkness.

Do not tear down the protective wall of the swastika.

Do not divert the water of the empowerment from your mouth.

Do not break the seal of the decree.

Do not destroy a stronghold of Everlasting Bön.

The carcass of an eagle, a vulture, and human are three different things!

The above pledges are to be kept pure.

The *Tantra of Amrta Kundali, the Golden Tree of Paradise* (20.5) says:

If one sees and realizes these practices, then they are great ambrosia. They are lamps of wisdom. They are great pledges. Whoever is not endowed with these [realizations], death will be like drinking poison, and one will wander through the nine continents of darkness. As time passes, the words of the pledges have changed.

There are twenty-five **particular accomplishment pledges**:

(1–5) the five pledges on the activities of ethical behavior
(6–10) the five pledges not to be relinquished
(11–15) the five pledges to follow in earnest
(16–20) the five pledges that must be known
(21–25) the five pledges to be attained

On the five **pledges on the activities of ethical behavior**, the *Tantra of Amrta Kundali, the Golden Tree of Paradise* (19.3) says:

To abide spontaneously in the proper conduct without any indolence and laziness; to practice union as well as liberation; to not steal, speak harsh words, or lie. Those are the five pledges on the activities of ethical behavior.

As for the **pledges not to be relinquished**, the five aspects of causal spontaneity that are to be eliminated are jealousy, hatred, greed, delusion, and pride.

On the categories of **causal spontaneity that are not to be eliminated**, the *Tantra of Amrta Kundali, the Golden Tree of Paradise* (19.4) says:

> The spontaneously accomplished body of the five families—this foremost constant necessity is never to be eliminated.

As for the **five pledges to follow** in earnest, the *Tantra of Amrta Kundali, the Golden Tree of Paradise* (19.6) says:

> Everything is ambrosia for one's inherent nature. Meat, excrement, urine, and blood from the lotus [i.e., menses], the spirit of enlightenment [i.e., semen], are conferring blessings from the heads of the five blissful ones through which Suchness of the five wisdoms and the five bodies [194] are manifesting in the seal body of the syzygies (*yab yum*). Always do this in earnest.

On the **five pledges that must be known**, the *Tantra of Amrta Kundali, the Golden Tree of Paradise* (20.2) says:

> The five aggregates are known as the five fathers. The five elements are known as the mothers. The seals that are the bodies of all the gods represent the five aggregates and the five elements, the five senses and the colors, the bodies and the couples of wisdom beings—these must be known as one, undifferentiated.

As for **the five pledges to be attained**, the pledges on behavior according to the traditional lore, the *Tantra of Amrta Kundali, the Golden Tree of Paradise* (20.3) says:

> The five head figures that must be achieved through the five seals are the sacred (*gsas*) dance of Kuntu Zangpo, the sacred eagle, the sacred sky, and the five sacred lords. If these are wrongfully changed, many types of illness and suffering will arise in this life, besides wandering in evil destinies and experiencing various types of suffering [in future lives].

The pledge on the flow of practice is threefold. *Transforming the Root of the Five Poisons* (191) says:

... to abide in the body, speech, and mind while you apply yourself against your enemies; to abide in purity and stop intoxication; to abide in the importance of practice and eliminate the
enemy of laziness.

The pledge on the view of inherent nature is fourfold. *Transforming the
Root of the Five Poisons* (191) says:

... the view of the complete liberation of the three worlds of
cyclic existence; the view of the purity of the grounds of the three
realms; the view of transforming the five poisons into elixir; and
the view to transform cyclic existence.

The pledge of definite importance is threefold: the mode without shame,
the importance of non-defilement, and the realization of the ultimate.

The four modes without shame are no shame about the view on recitation
and achievement practice, no shame in honoring the master, no shame in
feeling affection for the consort, and no shame about the deceptions of one's
mind.

The importance of non-defilement is fourfold: non-defilement of the
moon, non-defilement of incidentals, non-defilement of inherent self-
nature, and non-defilement [when in an apparent state of] powerlessness.

On the examination of reaching the ultimate and the common accomplishments, the one endowed with pledges must develop great power and
skill in the fields of those who are to be tamed. He must give great blessings
while being aware of being detached. He must accomplish his desired goal
in the fields of becoming, and then he will attract fame and the respect of
many.

The fifty distinctive samaya

The pledges for the distinctive samaya vows are the fifty necessary pledges.
They consist in the pledges on the five key points, the pledges on the five
poisons, the pledges on the five essences, the pledges on the five views, the
pledges on the five causes, the pledges on the five abidings, the pledges on
the five environments, the five pledges of activities, the five pledges of harmony, and the five pledges of training.

Key points

The five key points are about heavy meat, alcohol intoxication, being over-taken by torpor, laziness, and neglect. If there is great faith in meat and blood, then there will be no time to save the resulting meat from the semen and blood of the parents [i.e., one's own body]. If there is great faith in drunkenness, [195] the mind will be overpowered by demons. If great torpor is clouding the mind, then the tutelary deity, the gods, each and every one will go away. If laziness is great, one will not be able to realize the meaning of the pith instructions. If one is lost in indifference, results, however plentiful they might be, will not come.

Poisons

The five poisons are the poison of a prideful mouth, the poison of a lustful eye, the poison of a hating mind, the poison of the torpor of sleep, and the poison of the body of jealousy. From that, when pride is produced, one is born as a carnivorous animal. When hatred is produced, one is born as a Shin (*srin*) demon. When jealousy is produced, one is born as a dog. When lust is produced, one is born as a bird. When torpor is produced, one is born as a beast of burden.

Essences

The five essences are: the master is the essence of the pledge of learning, har-monious friends are the essence of the pledge for a harmonious mind, good causes and conditions are the essence of the pledge for gathering goods, the gods are the essence of the pledge of a good eon, and vision is the essence of the pledge for treading the grounds.

Elixir

A learned master is the great elixir for teaching pith instructions, harmoni-ous friends and siblings are the great elixir for curing an illness, and the cause and condition to gather goods are the great elixir for gathering harmonious conditions. As for the good eon of the gods, the great elixir is a cheerful mind. As for becoming familiar with the ground of vision, the great elixir is to generate a radiating faith.

Views

The five views are: for the tutelary deity god, the view on real accomplishments; the view on the heart inside the chest of the master; the view of the eyes of the heads of siblings and friends; for the celestial citadel (*gsas mkhar*) where the sages (*gshen*) are gathered, the view on the qualities of the body; and for the commingling of the signs of the sages, the view of them in the minor parts of the body.

If one does not have these views and is forgetful of the tutelary god, then a place will be generated in the form of the head of a bull burning with the fire of the god of death. When one cannot hold the view of the heart in the chest of the master, then the lord of death, Kamala, will remember to cut up the body with his razor-sharp sword, severing life; if one does not have the view into the eyes of the head of the friend of the one master, one will fall into a bottomless saltwater lake. If one does not have the view into the qualities of the siblings of the sages of that one celestial palace, one will fall into dark cycles of existence. If one does not have the view, through signs, of the minor parts of the body as mixed with sages, one will experience innumerable eons of repulsive sufferings.

Causal pledges

The five causal pledges are the causal pledge that is like the causal lamp; the causal pledge that is like the water, the sphere of causality; the causal pledge that is like the basic ground, the power of the Greater Vehicle; the causal pledge that is like wind, the power of the mind; the causal pledge is clear, like the vast expanse of the sky. Furthermore, the meaning of the metaphor of the causal lamp is that it is the great cause of the path of vision; the metaphor of the water of the causal sphere is that it is the great cause of not abandoning the pledges; the metaphor of the basic ground of the power of the Greater Vehicle is that it is the great cause of voluntarily assuming happiness; the metaphor of the wind—the power of the mind—is that it is the great cause of not becoming discouraged; the metaphor of the vast expanse of the sky is that it is the great cause of universal harmony.

Abiding

The five abidings are abiding in the pledge of being endowed with love, abiding in the pledge of being endowed with the mind of enlightenment, [196] abiding in the pledge of fright through the ripening, and the abiding in the pledge of understanding the suffering of cyclic existence.

Environments

A good temperament is an environment for pledges; one who is in harmony with the explanations of the master is an environment for the pledges; one who behaves according to the word of Shenrab is an environment for the pledges; a distinctively truthful one who does not kill is an environment for the pledges; one who is reverent toward the spiritual lineage is an environment for the pledges; and one who follows with action an environment [that help maintains one's] pledges. These are the five environments.

Activities

Chanting (*gyer*) induces one forward. Ritual proclamations (*smrang*) clarify the traditional lore. Magic rituals (*gto*) bring conclusions. Pith instructions are to be remembered so that there is no foolish chatter with the master. Secret Bön, when pledged wrongly, will not prosper. An old Bönpo priest will not be sending praises to a group of friends. One must act in harmony with the pledges. Those are the five activities.

Harmony

One must act in harmony with the tutelary god. One must act in harmony with the teacher's words. Inner and external worlds, gods and demons, all must act in harmony. The minds of friends must act in harmony. And retinues and servants, all must act in harmony.

Training

The five pledges of training are: offer and confess continually 83,000 times, tame the ten ground of negativities with the teachings, do not confer on others what you have not been empowered to confer, and do not teach others what you don't know. If you make up points that you don't know and convey them to others, you yourself will fall into the three evil destinies.

The eighteen pledges of conduct

The eighteen pledges of conduct are the three things on which one does not sit, the three actions to refrain from, the three things not to eat, the three things one should not cut, the three things one should not abandon, and the three things not to drink.

Three things to not sit on

The three things on which one does not sit are tiger skin, horse skin, camel skin, or a skin concealed. If there is a tiger skin, the course of the path to the gods will disappear. If there is a horse skin, the four horses of the wind will be defiled. If there is a camel skin, one's power will be robbed by the Shinpo (*srin*) demons.

Three actions to refrain from

The three actions to refrain from: invoking (*mi'i bon*) for the mundane needs of humans on the full moon; shooting arrows at the sky where there is nothing firm; and being overindulgent with friends and enemies you may not know well. If you perform rites for humans at the full moon, you will be exchanging your life for the lives of other people. If you shoot arrows at the sky without any focal point, gods and demons will strike your body as they please. If you are overindulgent with friends and enemies you don't know well, their careless mouths may greatly affect you.

Three things not to eat

Do not eat the flesh of these three—goats, horses, and birds. If you eat goat meat and then have to take powdered medicine, it will not work on your body. If you eat horse meat, worldly gods will become resentful and will poison you. If you eat the flesh of the *chiawang*,[188] you will be menaced with contamination.

Three things not to cut

The three things that one should not sever: do not cut a lock from the mane of a lion, do not cut the tree beneficial to the Lü water spirits, and do not drain a soul-lake of the Nyen spirits, so that Dukje Nagpo [i.e., the black lord of poisons] won't be able to seize you. As for the mane of the lion, it means do not unwrap the coverings of scriptures and reliquaries. If you unwrap these needlessly, you will be reborn among the hungry ghosts (*yid dwags*). Destroying a tree that is beneficial to the Lü spirits is like cutting off the script from scriptures, and you will fall down into the Naraka hells for 10,000 kalpas. Draining the lake of a Nyen [197] is to kill one's wife. One will be reborn in the Hell Clouded with Darkness. If Dukje Nagpo takes hold of you, you will be born in the Endless Torture Hell (Avīci).

Three things not to abandon

The three that should not be abandoned are the god, the master, and the parents. If one abandons one's tutelary deity, the path to liberation cannot be aimed for. If the master is abandoned, one will wander in cyclic existence away from accomplishments. If one abandons one's parents, one will be born as a discarnate spirit.

Three things not to drink

The three that one should not drink: Drinking the blood of a goat will corrupt one's brilliance. Drinking fish blood will confuse one's moral power. If one drinks the sap of the poplar, one's power over proper conduct will be corrupted. Whoever teaches when people are merry must be careful. When people gather in small groups and debase their vows, their fall will be frightening.

The object of the pledges

When "object" is mentioned, what is the object to protect? The objects of the pledges of the root qualities. What is called the "method of protection" becomes the object of observance. The pledges of the body—there is no need to mention refraining from beating and striking, let alone playing sport—yet again one indulges in these instead of protecting the body. Similarly, for sexual misconduct and stealing, these should not be done even for a moment.

The pledges for speech relate to false speech and divisive speech, not to mention harsh speech and meaningless talk. Teasing and joking should also not be done.

As for the pledges of the mind, from the point of view of the ordinary mind, a vindictive attitude, harmful thoughts—not to mention wrong views, jokes, mind games, and snapping one's fingers—these should not be done even for a moment.

Flaws

When "flaws" are mentioned, there are four flaws of non-observance: the five corruptions, the result of the ripening of aspects, the method to correct deteriorations, and the standard for making amends.

The five corruptions

On the five corruptions, a scripture says:

> There are many interruptions suffered due to having fantasies. These are about the past, or that one's wife and children do not die, or ugly things that arise in the mind. What if there are no indications that the pledges are corrupted? Because happiness is exhausted, there will be roaming in evil destinies and the endless experience of suffering.

The result of the ripening of aspects

Ripening: In general, all corruptions of pledges bring about birth in the three evil destinies, and in particular, corruption of the root pledges brings about birth in the Endless Torture Hell.

The method to repair

For the method to repair deteriorated vows, if the pledges of the body have been defiled, one should invite one's own root master, and if there is no such master, invite one important master. One should gather friends, spiritual siblings, lamas, and a master with whom one has affinities. Do not throw away your body, your life, and your wealth. Make offerings to the teachings with words of sadness and with suffering. Be very regretful and sorrowful and offer confession. If you give gifts, the pledges are repaired. [198] The disciple must offer regretful confession. If the lama is deaf to the regretful plea, then both you and the lama will roam in the cycles of evil destinies.

If the pledges of speech are impaired, sit in a solitary place and exert yourself to practice meditation, then give praises and recite mantras. If signs appear, make entreaties for reparation.

If the pledges of the mind are impaired, then in front of the lama, the precious body of the master, construct a thousand mandalas and so forth. Make extensive offerings, praises, and proclamations, and make heartfelt confession. Pleasant sounds and light visions will accompany your expiation rite.

If the ancillary pledges become impaired, the *Tantra of Amrta Kundali, the Golden Tree of Paradise* (22.3) says:

> Do circumambulation for merit. Make molded clay figurines (*tsha tsha*) and recite the prayers for overcoming evil. Repair treacherous mountain trails with wood, save some animal life, and give alms. Generate the mind of enlightenment with feeling and offer a confession.

"Qualities" means the qualities that should be protected. In this life, one should think about the end of the life of the body and make friends with accomplished ones and vow-holders while seeking assistance from those gone beyond. This pleases the lama, spiritual friends, and siblings.

The later results of the path are those of the knowledge-holders. The results of [reaching ultimate] finality consist in the acquisition of the body, and of wisdom. Thus, if the pledges are repaired, the great pledge of wisdom, the results obtained will be the enlightened bodies and wisdom.

The realization of the meaning of the patriarch (*dpon gsas*), the accomplished sage, is the pledge regarding activities that protect the body, speech, and mind. The *Tantra of Amrta Kundali, the Golden Tree of Paradise* (23.3) says:

> All of one's own observances are the excellent droplets of the mind of the enlightened universal perfection, the unsurpassable sphere, so that deeds that violate the vows will not arise.

What is called a "concordant example" is the example of the qualities of attainment. It is similar to the consequence of the eyes seeing. It is like the protection given by a fort along the borders. It is like the bowstring of the champion. It is like the immutability [lit. "frozen"] of a hermitage.

Examples of the fault of non-attainment: When the root pledges are broken, it is like seeds burned by fire. When the ancillary pledges are broken, it is like wind blowing out the fire of butter lamps. When the pledges are broken accidentally, it is like turning one's back. When they are broken through turning a blind eye, it is like golden and silver vases destroyed. When they are broken through one's spouse, it is like being powerless in the face of flooding. When all are broken, it is like cutting the head of a tree.

7. On empowerment

"Empowerment progresses in stages." This teaching of the scripture is a series of empowerments following stages in the pledges. The extensive form of empowerment is fourfold: the essence of empowerment, the definition, the divisions, and [199] the method of conferring empowerments.

The essence

The essence is that there be no mistake in conferring the objects of knowledge. These are free from defilements, and one must have mastery over the common and extraordinary attainments.

Definition

For what reason is there an empowerment? The activities of the blissful ones empower by means of empowering one to practice. Because the empowerments have a perfect and unmistaken aim, they confer power. Because they confer mastery over one's mind, the ultimate object, they confer power.

Divisions

The divisions are fivefold: outer empowerment, inner empowerment, secret empowerment, the empowerment of pristine awareness of wisdom, and the empowerment of the unsurpassable finality.

The method

Each of these five empowerments, in turn, has twenty-one teachings. Thus, the topic of the place where the rites are performed is the first teaching. The timing is the second. The master is the third. The student is the fourth. The fifth is the four continents.[189] The circle of deities is the sixth. The stages of the entrance is the seventh. The eighth is the stages of conferring empowerment. The numbers of aspects is the ninth. The place of the empowerment is the tenth. The method of transmission is the eleventh. The measure for the purification of defilements is the twelfth. The grounds that are trodden is the thirteenth. The fourteenth consists in the signs. The fifteenth consists in the symbols. The sixteenth is the instructions on union. The seventeenth is the ritual paraphernalia. The eighteenth consists in practical purposes. The nineteenth is the measure of abilities. A consistent example is the twentieth. The twenty-first is the results of the empowerment rites.

1. The place

The first teaching on the location of the rite is fivefold: the external place should be auspicious, attractive to the mind, pleasant, and with heavenly qualities; the internal place is a consort endowed with favorable signs, pure with the aspects of the celestial space. The secret place is the expanse of the complete purity of the universal ground. The place of the pristine awareness of wisdom is awareness free from elaboration. And the place of the unsurpassable finality is the complete purity of the space of reality.

2. Timing

The topic on timing is fivefold: The outer time is when faith is generated in the disciple. The inner time is when precious advice comes directly from the countenance of the master. The secret time is when the lama master bestows the main points. The time for pristine awareness of wisdom is when the rite of the empowerment has been bestowed. The time for the empowerment of the unsurpassable finality is when the empowerment has been obtained through one's own awareness.

3. The master

The topic on the master is fivefold: the outer master is the master who confers the empowerment but also everything else that has not been said here. On treading the ground of patience, the great *Stainless Splendor* says:

Through the agency of the father, the lineage of the clan is not severed, thus the sounds of drums and bells are not stopped. [200] The acquisition of the greatness of the clan and its fame for learning is everything that is sought. One endowed with the majestic empowerment dwells in the highest honor and, as such, with the exception of his activities, he is not mentioned as an object of activities to others.

This is what is said about the master.

The inner master is to gain mastery over the crucial points of the three aspects of the generation and perfection practices. The secret master is to gain mastery over the crucial points of the three results of the base and the path. The master of pristine awareness of wisdom is mastery over the crucial points of the inseparability of method and wisdom. The mastery of the unsurpassable finality is mastery over the crucial points of the following three: the meaning of the unborn intrinsic reality, the sphere, and the great inherent self of one's own nature.

4. The student

The topic on the student is fivefold. The outer student is the object for which the empowerment is conducted, but the final word has not been spoken on this. It is said: "He should have great faith and little miserliness, little laziness and great diligence. One should not reject his offerings, made with devotion, as the master looks around with his all-seeing eye (lit. "the eye of the forehead"). He believes in the words, the tantras, and the scriptural transmissions of the blissful ones. He strives to measure up to the sages. He has tremendous devotion to the secret mantras of Bön. To that sort of disciple, the perfected outer and inner empowerments are conferred."

The disciple is endowed with the eight non-declining qualities as well as with extremely diligent enthusiasm. These eight non-declining qualities consist in non-declining tireless faith in the lama, non-declining clarity on the mantras of the tutelary deity, non-declining exertion toward the accomplishment with the consort, non-declining earnest discipline toward the sacred items, non-declining pure pledges toward accomplishments, non-declining great love toward spiritual siblings, non-declining great compassion toward sentient beings, and non-declining good behavior toward everything. These make eight.

The secret disciple is one endowed with forcefulness. The disciple of the pristine awareness of wisdom is endowed with awareness. The intelligence of the disciple of unsurpassable finality goes straight to the fundamentals of practice.

5. The continents

The topic of the continents is fivefold. The outer continents are the teacher of the past, Shenrab Miwo, who at that time was born in Olmo Lungring, in the country of Tazig; the king of the water deities (*klu'i rgyal po*), Gawo Jokpo,[190] who is in the water in the vase used during the empowerment-ceremony purification rite; and the goddess of the earth, also called Serdoma [lit: "golden mother"], the Tenma (*brtan ma*) goddess of the earth who comes to rest on top of the empowerment vase and to whom one prays for blessings. These are the outer continents.

The inner continents consist in the teacher Shenrab, who settled on the summit of the mountain of the god of light; the goddess of trees, Öchagma [lit., "mother of light rays"), [201] to whom all trees and the Bilva fruit are auspicious; and the eight auspicious ritual items for the empowerment ceremony. These constitute the inner continents.

The secret continents are the teacher Shenrab, in the lower fortress of the gloomy turquoise tent; syzygies conferring the rite of empowerment; and the definitive points on body, speech, and mind. These are the secret continents.

On the continents of pristine awareness of wisdom, in the cave of the sinking black mountain of the demons, the teacher Shenrab gathered under his power all the outer and inner demons. The goddess of compassion, Chamma, gave him the transmission and teachings. At that time, after receiving the power to subdue demons, a demoness revealed a sign to the teacher. Once more, the teacher Shenrab obtained the empowerment of wisdom, which is the continent of the pristine cognition of wisdom.

The continent of the ultimate is the teacher Shenrab's empowerment rite on self-clarity of awareness in the cave of the crystal valley of turquoise. This is the continent of the ultimate.

6. The mandala

The topic of the mandala is fivefold: the outer mandalas of colored powders, the inner mandalas of the aggregates, the secret mandalas of the mind of enlightenment, the mandalas of the pristine awareness of wisdom, and the mandalas of the lack of inherent self in the intrinsic reality of the ultimate, making five.

7. The entrance

What is called the "entrance" consists in the five stages of entering. The outer aspect of entering has thirteen parts: first, it consists in voicing a request, then offering a request prayer, generating determination, the descent of blessings, analyzing the signs, the opening of the portals, opening the eyes, removing the face cover, the lustration rite, discarding the twigs and the seeds of the necklace, sitting toward the seat of power in the west, completing the empowerment rite for the empowerment of the ritual items, and casting the seal of power.

The inner entrance is to engage with the consort who possesses the signs.

The secret entrance is to enter the great bliss of the mind of enlightenment.

The pristine awareness of wisdom is to enter in the experience of bliss without proliferation.

As for the ultimate reality free from proliferation, it is to enter in the correct meaning.

8. Conferring empowerments

What is called "conferring the mandala" (*bskur*) refers to the stages of the empowerment ritual. The outer aspects are fivefold and consist in the drum, the bell, the rosary, the vase, and the name. The name is the sage white god, Shenlha Karpo. Its secret characteristic is designated by the letter A. The drum is Garsé Tsenpo [lit. "the Tsan spirit lord of the holy dance"]. The bell is Gösé Sangwa [lit. "secret of the holy eagle"]. The rosary is Sejé Mangpo [lit. "the holy lord childless"]. [202] The vase is Namsé Yingrumlha [lit. "the god of the womb of space, the celestial citadel"]. The gods and the ritual items are methodological aspects. They are the outer aspects.

The inner aspects of the method are the ritual items connected to wisdom. The secret aspects are the ritual items connected to pristine awareness and space, the formula of concentration of the experience of pristine awareness of wisdom, and the items of performance connected to great bliss. The ultimate aspect is the established conclusion in intrinsic reality, absolute, the great clarity of self-awareness.

9. The numbers of aspects

As for what is mentioned as "the enumeration of aspects," these five numbered root aspects have twenty-one elaborations.

10. The places

"Place" refers to the places of the empowerment rites: the outer mandala of the body, the inner mandala of speech, the secret mandala of mind, the mandala of awareness for the empowerment of primordial consciousness, and the mandala of the unsurpassable finality for the empowerment in the mind of enlightenment. These make five.

11. The transmission

Again, the "bestowal" of the mandala refers to the methods of the empowerments that are five: the outer transmissions are the mantras, the seals, the formula of concentration, the ritual items, and the pronouncements, which make five from the point of view of the conferral of the rituals.

From the point of view of the inner transmissions, they are the white and red minds of enlightenment. From the point of view of the secret transmission, it is the experience of great bliss. From the point of view of the transmission of the pristine awareness of wisdom, it is the bliss that is free from conceptual constructions. From the point of view of the ultimate bestowal, it is the unobstructed production of intrinsic reality.

12. The purifications

What is referred to as "the purification of defilements" is fivefold: the purification of the defilements of the body is done through the perfection of the outer empowerment; the purification of the defilements of speech is conducted through the perfection of the inner empowerment; the purification of the defilements of the mind is done through the perfection of the secret empowerment; the purification of the defilements of the afflictive emotions is conducted through the perfection of the pristine awareness of wisdom empowerment; and the purification of the defilements of the objects of consciousness is accomplished through the perfection of the unsurpassable finality empowerment.

13. Treading the grounds

"Treading the grounds" is the fivefold treading on the various grounds: the treading on the first ground through the acquisition of the outer empowerment; the treading on the fifth ground through the acquisition of the inner empowerment; the treading on the eighth ground through the acquisition of the secret empowerment; the treading on the tenth grounds and below through the acquisition of the empowerment of the awareness of the mind of wisdom; and the treading on the ground of the great perfected circle of letters, the thirteenth ground, through the empowerment of the unsurpassable finality. Together these make five.

14. Signs

What are called "the signs" (*rtags*) consist in these: the outer sign is that snow (or rain) falls during the empowerment ceremony; the inner sign is that a good omen manifests; the secret sign is that the haughty (*bsnyens pa*) great bliss of accomplishment arises; for the empowerment of the pristine awareness of wisdom, the sign is that the heat of realization arises; and the sign of finality is the mastery of non-apprehension. These are the five signs.

15. The symbols

The "demonstration of symbols" is fivefold. It is mentioned that the symbols are of body, speech, and mind. They are taught like that because they are secret conversations.

Symbols have flawless meanings, words of brilliance, and symbolic seals. These are their three aspects.

The Vase Empowerment demonstrates a symbol. [203] Symbolic hand-seals are taught as a collection of ten. As for the words, they come straight from the sounds of Zhangzhung words. The symbol that is demonstrated for the inner empowerment is taught as the hand-sign of the wheel of mastery. The symbol that is demonstrated for the secret empowerment is taught as the hand-sign of the vase of ambrosia. The symbol that is demonstrated for the empowerment of the pristine awareness of wisdom is taught as the hand-sign of the frown of magic. The symbol that is demonstrated for the empowerment of the unsurpassable finality is taught as the hand-sign of intrinsic equality. All of the accompanying sentences that are pronounced come straight from the Zhangzhung language.

16. Union

What is mentioned as "uniting with that" are the five pith instructions: during the completion of the outer empowerment of the vase, counsels (*gdams ngag*) are given on the three vows; during the completion of the inner empowerment, counsels are given on the two truths; during the completion of the secret empowerment, counsels are given on the two, the generation and perfection stage practices; once one has acquired the empowerment of the pristine awareness of wisdom, counsels are given on great wisdom and method; during the empowerment of the unsurpassable finality, counsels are given on the experience of intention These are the five.

17. Ritual paraphernalia

The meaning of "purpose" lies in the fivefold necessity: The outer items are the arrow and the sword, the arrow with silk bands, the mirror, and the vase, which make the five precious items and so forth. The inner item is the endowed consort. The secret items are the first pouring and the ambrosia of blood. The item of the pristine awareness of wisdom is awareness free from elaboration. The item of the finality is the pervasive stainless ground.

18. Practical purposes

The "purpose" rests the meaning of necessity that is fivefold: The outer purpose is auspiciousness, force, and magnificence in this world. The inner purpose is the necessity of passion that is similar to a powerful force and a high official position. The secret purpose is the exclusion of interferences. The purpose of pristine awareness of wisdom is the necessity of being enabled for the sake of others. The purpose of finality is the accomplishment of the unsurpassable yet extremely pure result.

19. The measure of abilities

What is called the "measure of one's ability" is the grade of potency that is a fivefold topic: It is to meet a lama master and at that time request empowerment and instruction. It is at first not to have one's body and life interrupted. To offer one's body, speech, and mind, a son and small ones and uninterrupted resources, a horse and an elephant with a symphony of music, the precious world with gold and turquoise, the most precious of all—these are offered without attachments. If one is not endowed with the cause of the best resources, then one makes soup with plantain, collects some pure beautiful flowers, and together offers one's body, speech, and mind.

20. Consistent examples

What is mentioned as "consistent examples" is included within these fivefold examples, three of which are: like the rung of a ladder, like the levels of a glacier, and like the decorations of the costumes of heroes.

21. Results of the empowerment rite

What is called "fruition" is the result of achievements [204] and has five parts. It is overpowering the four demons.[191] Thus, like the above, when one offers one's body, speech, and mind and one's own aggregates with devotion, then gods and goddesses through their wisdom destroy the demons that are the sons of the gods. The gods of the aggregates and the gods and goddesses, through their wisdom, do not have the pain of afflictions. They have vanquished the demons of affliction. Since they do not have the pain of afflictions, they do not take future rebirths. They have vanquished the demons grasping at the aggregates of the body. Not taking future rebirths, they have no birth and no death, because the demon of death has been vanquished.

8. FORMULAS FOR CONCENTRATION

The teachings on practice through the experience of the formulas for concentration are, as stated, "the practice through the experience of the formulas of concentration." To demonstrate this succinctly, after receiving empowerment, one proceeds to the practice of meditation.

In this tantra, it is said: "It is separated into the topics on the general body, explanation of the parts, and visualization." This clearly demonstrates it in brief.

To explain it more expansively, it is threefold: it teaches how to make the divine bodies linked to the formula, it teaches the explanation of the parts making the formula, and it teaches the visualizations accompanying each section of the formula. These make three.

Thus, first come the sevenfold teachings that constitute the body of the formula: the words of the proclamation (*tshig smrang*) that are meditated upon is the way of the vehicle of the Shen of the visual world; the ferocious heart that subdues enemies and hindrances is the meditation of the vehicle of the Shen of illusion; the lay practitioner [lit. "the one approaching virtue"] consists in the meditation of the vehicle of the virtuous adherers; the undisrupted meditation on the main point of awareness is the way of the great ascetics; the mind of enlightenment being in equipoise over illusionary thoughts is the meditation of the way of the White A; the point of focus of awareness, where conceptual objects can be changed into anything according to one's wish, is the meditation of the way of the primeval Shen; and whatever arises without conceptualization is the meditation of great distinction, the spontaneous accomplishment from the very beginning.

Shen of the visual world

Among these, the Shen of the visual world consists of activities along divisions corresponding to the gods and demons of the manifest world. The practitioner of the Shen of the visual world meditates on the aim of the words in the ritual narratives (*smrang*), and these are not distinct from the ritual chanting, the ritual dances, the songs, fables, and riddles where there is no meditation. In each of these sessions (*leu*), the Bön priest mentions the sponsor without fail. Nowadays, he meditates as if the sponsor is actually present. The Bön priest never fails to mention this, and the present-day Bönpo meditates on the presence. As such, it is impossible that beneficial results do not come, for this meditation practice brings the acquisition of the sought benefits to the present-day sponsor. The formulas of concentration [i.e., spells, mythical narratives, mantras, etc.] are the settings for this.

Shen of illusion

What is called "Shen of illusion" is to act using illusory manifestations to subdue enemies and hindrances. The Shen of illusion uses aggressive emotions to subdue enemies and hindrances. The demonstration of the elimination of impediments is done from the sphere of the tutelary deity. [205] Thus, there are ten fields of activities of elimination. These are the eliminations of contempt for the teachings, breaking of oaths, vanity with regard to these tantric cycles, breaking the power of blamelessness, the baleful influence (*phywa*) on the body of the teachings, inimical demons, the Shin demons, pledges that eliminate violations, hateful enemies, and harmful hindrances.

The virtuous adherers

What is called "the one approaching virtue" [i.e., the lay practitioner] is the object that abides in compounded phenomena. The lay practitioner meditates on being close to the virtuous mind. One practices the ten authoritative virtues by inclining the mind toward good works despite the contradictory conditions. One meditates eliminating the ten defilements.

The great ascetics

The monastic has the objective of guiding the continuum of others through self-correction. The monastic [lit. "guiding to the straight"] meditates without distraction on self-clarity in the focal point (*don*) of awareness.

The White A

The White A is the action of achieving the approach. The White A is the generation of the mind of supreme enlightenment through maintaining the mind in equipoise while meditating.

The primeval Shen

The vehicle of the primeval Shen has primordial Suchness as the object of meditation. The primeval Shen consists in the cultivation similar to a wheel of light reverberating awareness everywhere.

Spontaneous accomplishment

"Spontaneity" is the object that is free from concerted efforts from the very beginning. It is the distinctive feature of the Greater Vehicle, the meditation on the all-pervading spontaneity of the mind of enlightenment.

Thus, among the nine vehicles, the meditation practices of the Shen of prediction (*phywa gshen*) and the Shen of the visual world (*srid gshen*) are not taught. Why is that? With respect to the meaning of the words of these two, meditation practice is above their ritual narratives. Because the meanings of the words are concordant with the Shen of the visual world (*snang gshen*), they are not taught.

Now, calculations (*rtsis*) relating to the formulas of concentration are first. Their teachings come under five sections: In which direction is the activity performed? Which master will be conducting the activity? To which category does it belong? For what reason/purpose is the activity performed? And what are the teachings' imperatives?

What is mentioned as "calculations are first" means that former explanations on the roots lead to later explanations.

The "object" is where the object of enlightened activity is. It is performed in the cave of crystal of the turquoise valley.

What is "the master"? The master is Sangwa Düpa [lit. "the secret assembly"] that performs the enlightened activity.

What is the "category to which it belongs"? The category of the mantra of the White A to which it belongs.

The "reason/purpose" is the reasons of the deeds of the sages (*gshen*) of past generations.

The "necessity" is the necessity of the object to be attained during one's lifetime concerning the accomplishment.

The "five" are the five principal aims that are first concerned with the calculations of the aim of the formula of concentration.

The activities associated with the various visualizations of the formulas are taught in five parts: the meditation on the basis of the gods for setting up their attributes, the undisrupted meditation on the aim of the formulas, the meditation on the mantras that generate the bodies of the gods, the meditation on the identification of the gods through hand gestures, and the meditation as the cause of the gods through seed-syllables. These are the five.

Again, "visualization" is [206] taught laying aside the root texts of the past.

The "basis" is the meditation on the basis of the gods through stabilizing their various attributes. On these, their two parts consist in stabilizing the vestments of the enlightened body and stabilizing the ornaments. Furthermore, on the appearance of the enlightened body, there are the five seals of the appearance of one's nature. There are five ornaments to be stabilized: the head ornament, the upper body ornaments, the skirt, arm ornaments, and pure silk garments. As for the five wrathful ornaments, they are the stance, the haughty pose of the enlightened body with eyes crossed in anger, bare fangs, and threatening hands. The wrathful deities have five more ornaments [one is missing in the text]: a tiger's hide, a human skin, a necklace of human skulls, and a black serpent belt. As such, if all ornaments are combined with those of the peaceful deities, all together there are thirteen. As for the wrathful deities, there are the eight cemetery ornaments. These are all the ornaments of the ritual for realization for the practitioner.

The undistracted aspects of tantric meditation

"Undistracted" refers to the five undistracted aspects of meditation: the essence of the formulas of concentration, definition, divisions, methods of practice, and the results of meditation.

The essence

The essence is the quick transcendence of all accomplishments, the pristine awareness through the knowledge of the aspects of Suchness.

Definition

The definition follows along the words of the formula of concentration [*ting nge dzin*, i.e., mantra]. *Ting* [the sound of a metal bell, also meaning concentration] is the undistracted. *Nge* means to stay. *Dzin* [to grasp, to hold] is to stabilize relentlessly.

Divisions

Divisions are twofold: the general divisions and the detailed divisions.

The **general divisions** are threefold: the formula of concentration on inherent Suchness, the formula of universal manifestation, and the causal formula. The detailed divisions are explained in eighty-one elements or otherwise as traditional textual lore.

The formula of concentration of inherent Suchness

Therefore, on this, the first of the three general divisions of the formulas of concentration, the formula of concentration of inherent Suchness is without errors. Its countenance is non-fabricated. Intrinsically, it goes to the fundamental. Its "concentration" [*ting*, as above] is unwavering. Its grasp means that it cannot be cast away. On this, there are seven further points: the causal characteristic of the necessity of meditation, the cause to engage, the method of meditation, the measure of vision, the system of abiding, a relevant example, and the result of meditation.

Causal necessity: Moreover, the three poisons of afflictive emotions come from the five poisons. They increase the power of the impediments of afflictive emotions and karma. They are durable when they are very heavy, but arrogance can soften them.

The cause to engage: The cause of engaging is the antidote to deluded appearances of the coarse conceptual consciousness.

The method of meditation consists in the non-conceptual consciousness that enables one to enter the realm of the great freedom from proliferation, inherent reality. The method of meditation is to have ordinary mind drawn to the sphere of the great all-pervasiveness of the non-self, the field of emptiness. [207] Whichever peaceful or wrathful aspect it is focused on, one mediates on the clarity of the space.

The measure of vision consists in the awareness that any phenomenon there is, is witnessed as a non-perceivable [i.e., it is not perceived as a dualistic isolate].

The system of abiding is to have no conceptualization whatsoever, where there is no abiding in anything whatsoever, no craving for anything whatsoever, no hope for anything whatsoever. It is where there is no cutting off after what has passed. There is no meeting of the past in the future. There is nothing to plant in the consciousness of the moment. The mind continues to continuously self-liberate.

A relevant example is the simile of the sky.

The result of meditation consists in the acquisition, without hindrances, of the generated body of reality without perceivable objects.

Then, there is the formula of universal manifestation. Universal means without exception. Manifestation is the clear and unobscured object of compassion.

Ting nge [i.e., clearly] is measureless, continual, and instantaneous compassion. Grasping refers to non-dual grasping of all the minds. These, too, have seven points.

The causal characteristic of meditation is to meditate on the journey from the depths of the ocean of suffering in order that I and the limitless number of sentient beings that cannot be encompassed by the mind be liberated from suffering.

The cause to engage consists in engaging with the point of view of the great all-encompassing compassion. Ignorant and deluded minds do not realize the meaning of very pure compassion or the import of intrinsic reality. It is determined compassion toward those whose main focus is grasping at a self, which is nothing but self-delusion.

The method of meditating consists in the meditation on the compassion of the four immeasurables, the six families, and the four categories [of activities], gathered in the five tantric cycles. It is to bind activities and afflictive emotions with determined compassion toward the crux of the matter: false illusory conceptions. For among these there is immeasurable compassion. One meditates on the metaphor of the mother with an only son. Then there is immeasurable love. One meditates on the similitude of the lama as the pure refuge and protector. As for immeasurable joy, one meditates as if one discovered a splendid and wonderfully potent treasure. For immeasurable equanimity, one meditates on the allegory of the sun's rising, which is all-encompassing in its splendor. Then there are the meditations on the peaceful or wrathful tutelary deities where there are [required] visualizations.

The measure of vision is to envision everything as objects to be apprehended with compassion.

The system of abiding is to have compassion abide in the sphere without partiality for self.

The relevant example is the eyes of the crow. The crow's vision is like a straight wooden stick falling from above. The unchanging shape of its vision comes straight and head on. In a similar fashion, the eyes must be looking straight ahead, as if looking from above, and in one moment one will be able to see everything that dwells below.

The formula is to manifest everything that is, at the moment, in the imagination. Whatever there is, it is empty of inherent nature and one sees no-self. [208] Just as below, one can see the suffering of non-realized sentient beings. In short, one knows and realizes this from the mandala of the supreme king to the lower host frightened in hell and above.

The result of meditation consists in the acquisition of the perfect enjoyment body of great bliss.

As for the **causal formula**, the cause of sentient beings not being born again is the production of this end result from the causal seed-syllables and the lights miraculously displayed at birth.

The causal characteristic of meditation: The causal characteristic that is necessary for the meditation on causal formulas is to meditate for the sake of turning away from the causal fields of cyclic existence. Birth comes from karma and the causes and conditions of afflictive emotions while existence amplifies the fields of cyclical existence. That is the activity of reversal.

The cause of engaging the vehicle of formulas is to engage in the lights, the letters, the colors, and the hand-seals.

The method of meditation consists in envisioning the three types of mandalas: the mandala of inherent nature, the mandala of the formulas, and the mandala of colored symbols.

The measure of vision: There are three stages to the generation of the mandalas: the generation outside oneself, the generation of the seats, and the generation of the gods.

System of abiding: From that, whatever it is, peaceful or wrathful, with meditation comes the visualization process. The system of abiding also consists in the mode of manifesting the residence that is to establish the mandala of the gods.

Relevant examples

A relevant example is that it is similar to a precious jewel that fulfills all wishes. For example, there is this island in the ocean outside where there are the mighty and resplendent lights of these great jewels, and one can appropriate the precious jewel that fulfills all wishes.

The victory banner that does not wane marks the apex. One circumambulates it and makes offerings to it. If one recites prayers, then whatever is wished for will come true, for that precious jewel has inexhaustible qualities. Thus, to follow up on these examples, the meaning is that one's own awareness is inclined to transmigrate. Whatever may be taught to trainees, the peaceful, the wrathful, or the mandala of Phurpa, the formulas to the mandala of awareness are inexhaustible. They are without deficiencies. There is nothing that arises from emptiness while activities for the welfare of transmigrators are wide-ranging.

The result of meditation is to acquire the extensive emanation body and to send it everywhere.

The methods of practice

The methods of practice are threefold: Concerning the formula of Suchness, it is to practice with limitless selflessness and emptiness. One practices the activities done for the sake of transmigrators. These are great compassion that manifests universally and the four immeasurables.

The causal formula consists in the visualizations of the three seals of the body of the gods that are practiced through activities for the sake of the transmigrators. From that, the causal formula is practiced in three sections:

One practices the mode of the gradual generation of one's commitment beings; then it is certainly suitable to have among one's sons the blissful ones. [209]

Then one practices the mode of gradual perfection of the heroes of everlastingness; the wisdom beings, the commitment beings, the sons of the blissful ones are suitable for the self.

One practices the mode of the Great Perfection of the heroes acting in non-duality so that all activities are conducted without obstacles [and these are performed] for the transmigrator's sake.

Each of these methods belongs to the category of the outer practices, the inner practices, the secret practices, or the ultimate practices. All these practices have two aspects to them: the practices related to the purification of coarse phenomena and the practice concerning the formulas of the subtle that is non-perceivable.

The purification of the coarse phenomena

The purification of the coarse phenomena is that all the realms of the world without exception are burned and washed using the seed-syllables *Ram, Yam, Kham*. Then one meditates on the clarity of the main import of intrinsic emptiness.

The practice of the formulas of the subtle non-perceivable

The practice of the subtleties is to abide in the unwavering sphere. It is the meditation on clarity and the essential point of the pristine cognition of inherent emptiness. The result of practice is the spontaneous accomplishment of enlightened body, speech, and mind.

The main points on the meditation on the generation of the mantra body of the deities are fivefold: the essence of the mantra, definition, divisions, the system of recitation, and the result of recitation.

The essence of the mantra

The essence of the mantra is the inexpressible, the unmistaken object of the sound.

Definition

The definition is: because the practitioner of mantra (*ngags pa*) works toward a purpose, it is called "mantra" (*ngag*).

Divisions

The divisions are threefold: the unmistaken cause, the root of the mantra; the mantra and the defect of generation; and the recitation as the activity of the mantra.

The unmistaken cause

The unmistaken cause, the root of the mantra, is threefold: the essence of abiding, the essence of changelessness, and the secret essence.

The essence of abiding is twofold: the essence of abiding in the cause and the heart of the inherent essence.

The essence of abiding in the cause is the universal ground, the mind of enlightenment.

The heart of the inherent essence is the white letter A.

The essence of changelessness is twofold: the changelessness of inherent nature and the changelessness of abiding.

The changelessness of inherent nature is the pristine awareness of self-knowledge.

The changelessness of abiding is the essence of one's own continuum, and has six parts: abiding in the *A*, abiding in the *Ni* (*rni*) syllable, abiding in the *Su* (*su*), abiding in the *Tri* (*tri*), abiding in the *Thri* (*pri*), and abiding in the *Du* (*du*).

Furthermore, the essence of the one aspect is threefold: the essence of unchanging life, the essence of the abiding life, and the essence of real life.

Among these, the essence of unchanging life is the existence of the six essences of changelessness of the six enlightened families.

The essence of the abiding life is the body of the deity.

The essence of real life is the name of the deity.

The secret essence is twofold: the secret cause and the secret result. [210]

The secret cause is refined essence. The secret result is the enlightened one.

The mantra for the condition of generation

The mantra for the condition of generation has to do with whether it relates to the mantras for the mandala of the peaceful deities or to the mandala of the wrathful deities. The action of reciting consists in the repetition of the mantra of the ferocious wrathful ones or the repetition of that of the peaceful gods, these two. The systems of recitation, as well as the unmistaken cause with regard to the root mantra, consist in the internal recitation of the precious heart of *citta* [i.e., the mind].

The mantra and the defect of generation

The mantra and the defect of generation is the recitation about defects to the inexpressible wind horse. The action of reciting the mantra is similar to the gait of the tortoise separating each movement. This is the manner of recitation.

Following this there are the mantra, the essence, and the repetition. The provisional particularity to that unique designation is labeling it with these three names.

The result of recitation is the acquisition of the speech of the lack of inherent self.

The Great Seal

The topic of the Great Seal, the meditation on the representation of the body of the gods, is fivefold: essence; definition; divisions; fabrication, transformation, and release; and the result of the seal.

Essence

The essence of the Great Seal is the unmistaken action of the body.

Definition

The definition consists in the five afflictions that are impressed with the seals of the five wisdoms. These are the seals.

Divisions

The divisions are fivefold: the seal of the wheel of power that transforms existence, the seal of the wrathful grimace of magical illusion, the seal of the subjugation that brings [any being] under one's power, the seal of the display of the generated body, and the seal of the splendid suppression.

Fabrication

Fabrication, transformation, and release consist in the mind-essence of the abode of construction, the mind-essence of the abode of transformation, and the mind-essence of the abode of release.

The result

The result of the making of the seals is the acquisition of the changeless body.

The syllable body of the deities

The topic of the body of the seed-syllables of the deities during meditation is threefold: essence, definition, and divisions.

Essence of the body of the deities

The essence is the unmistaken object of knowledge.

Definition

The definition is that the *Yi* [of *yige*, i.e., syllable or phoneme] is wisdom and the *Ge* is rising compassion.

Divisions

The divisions have two aspects: the syllables and their authentic meanings and the syllable of exemplary display.

Syllables and meaning

The syllables of exemplary display are divided into the thirty letters of the alphabet and the lower glyphs, making thirty-six. If they are not thus particularly divided but instead are taken together, they make the display in thirty letters. The diacritical vowels and punctuation signs [i.e., the vowel sound indications in superscript, subscript, and so forth] are the *I*, the *U*, the *È*, the *O*, the vertical punctuation mark (*shad*), and the dot between syllables of the script (*tsheg*) that are directly apparent, such as for the pure letter *Ka* and the pronounced letters.

The syllables and their authentic meanings are: *Ka* is for one's breath, *Kha* is for the power of one's tongue, *Ga* is for speech, *Nga* is for the consciousness of the mind, *Ca* is for the consciousness of the tongue, *Cha* is the moisture that is sprinkled, *Ja* is the consciousness of the body, *Nya* is the mind, *Ta* is the visual sense, *Tha* is the eye consciousness, *Da* is the means of expression, *Na* is the consciousness of the ears, *Pa* is the brain, and *Pha* is the top of the cranium, the aperture of Tshangpa. It is similar to when a female dog is sleeping (making a circle with its body) and a blade of grass is sticking out in the middle; *Ba* is said to be for the six great roots of the senses that is the navel. [211] *Ma* is said to be the base of origination of everything that is the universal basis, the mind of enlightenment. *Tsa* is the nose, *Tsha* is the consciousness of the ears, *Dza* is the warmth of fire (i.e., the heat of the body), *Wa* is the root of one's life force, *Zha* is the blood, *Za* is the sense of smell, '*A* ('*a chung*) is the consciousness of smell (*sna*), *Ya* is the mind with conflicted emotions, *Ra* is the wisdom of awareness, *La* is compositional factors, *Sha* is the very essence of semen, *Sa* is one's own flesh, *Ha* is the breath, *A* is primordial purity, the *I* vowel is the apprehending consciousness, the *U* vowel is the secret root, the *È* vowel[192] is the root of the celestial pull from the crown of the head, the *O* vowel is the compositional factor of one's own consciousness, the vertical punctuation mark (|) is the activities of the feet, and the dots (˙) between syllables of the script are, in worldly activities, where the source of the letters of non-deluded actions come from. It is the heart of the teachings. As for the letters arising from this heart of the teaching, the topic is threefold: the colors of the letters, the phoneme of the letters, and the meaning of the letters.

What is mentioned as five, in this regard, is practice from the point of view of the five senses' activities, such as vision and so forth. Among these five senses, the basis remains undistracted. Those are the teachings on the minor factors of the concentration.

9. ACTIVITIES

Now, the activities conducted for the welfare of all are taught together. "The activities conducted for the welfare are all combined." The brief explanation is that it is necessary to perform the activities when one is familiar with the practice of concentration.

"The essence, definition, divisions, necessities, and the teachings on the results together make five points." The extended explanations are fivefold: the essence of activity, definition, divisions, necessity, and the teachings on result.

Essence of activity

The essence of activity is that mind and very pure pristine awareness are not mixed, are not dissolute, and are not disordered.

Definition of activities

The definition is that oneself and the heroes are bound by their words to the mind of enlightenment, and together with the divine actions of the heroes and wisdom beings, act in order to bring all karma to finality. Those are the activities. Moreover, the arrangements, with none left to waste, are that activities are to be conducted entirely for the sake of others.

Divisions of activities

The divisions are fourfold: to act as a total refuge from suffering, to conduct the activities of the lower vehicles oneself, to conduct the activities of the recitation and accomplishment of the rites of the peaceful and wrathful deities and the White A, and to perform the self-arising of the droplets without unskilled motives.

To act as a total refuge from suffering refers to "The activities of refuge from suffering . . ."

They are composed of these two: the objects from which one becomes a refuge and the one performing the activities of protection.

The objects from which one is a refuge are the torments of sickness, of hunger, of extreme temperatures, of transition and changes, as well as of the vagaries of unhappiness and suffering. [212]

As for the one who protects, [the protector] acts against the above for the sake of others and generates compassion. These others are seeking refuge in vital antidotes. The antidote against the torments of hunger is to give alms. The one against the torments of extreme temperatures is to give medicine. In short, whatever is of benefit involves providing what is necessary. "Whatever is of benefit, do the necessary accordingly."

Activities of the lower vehicles

The lower vehicles are the Shen of existence, the way of virtuous conduct, and the way of the great ascetics. These are mundane works and views, the deeds of the priests. One has to pull oneself out from these mundane vehicles. Whenever their practices come, they incite the pride of superiority. Generating activities that are more concordant with oneself makes one enter into virtue.

Other activities

"Without skill, the activities are spontaneous." The meaning of the unborn intrinsic reality, free from elaboration, is the completion of accomplishing the welfare of transmigrators.

"The activities conducted through the way of the White A . . ." The teacher divides the activities of the recitation and the accomplishment rituals of the peaceful and wrathful deities in five sections: "pacification, increasing, overpowering, wrathful, and violent activities." These are the activities for pacification, to provoke increase, to overpower, for wrathful subjugation, and for violent action.

The twenty-four lores

Each of these traditional activities can be stretched out to twenty-four points of traditional lore:

1. Consecrating the food and the place
2. Erecting the mandala of the citadel
3. Accumulating merit and preliminaries
4. Setting out valuables and goods
5. Setting up the outer, inner, and secret boundaries
6. Confession
7. The main liturgical procedures of the three formulas of concentration[193]
8. Prayers for the erection of the mandala
9. Invitation
10. Obeisance
11. Request to sit
12. Taking the pledge
13. The main traditional practice of the hand-seals for the wrathful assembly
14. Presenting the five kinds of offerings
15. Offerings of ambrosia and medicinal substances
16. Offerings of meat, blood, and bones
17. Offering of the dance of the seal
18. Offerings of mantra repetitions and heart mantras
19. Offerings of the host of enjoyments
20. Reciting entreaties to fulfill commitments
21. Adopting the dancing position of trampling transgressions
22. Installing the host of ritual cakes
23. Arousing the gods of the measureless mansion to activity
24. Collecting long-life prayers for auspiciousness and the four roots

Consecration

The first topic, which consists in consecrating the first part of food offerings and the place, is fivefold: setting up while consolidating the place, blessing the place, blessing the food, blessing the congregation [lit. "brothers and sisters"], and blessing the ritual items and goods.

Setting up the items and their consolidation consists in following the general procedures to get rid of apparitional manifestations.

The blessing of the place is threefold: It consists in purifying the ritual area of coarse appearances through the self-purification of the three eons. [213] Once purified, the five illusory elements are then generated in the consecrated space. This is followed with the blessing of the immeasurable palace of the deities.

Concerning purification, one first meditates on oneself as the lord of compassion, the primordial sage Tsugphu [i.e., Yeshen Tsukphu]. From his heart are emanated the seed-syllables *Raṃ*, *Yaṃ*, *Maṃ*, from which arise fire, wind, and water as extensive as those appearing at the end of an eon. With these, the place is purified and one thinks of it as empty.

The elements for the transformation of the consecrated space are then generated. One recites the seed-syllables *A*, *Yaṃ*, *Raṃ*, *Maṃ*, *Khaṃ*, *Bruṃ*. From *A* arises the circle of the [unconditioned] space. From *Yaṃ* is the mandala of wind. From *Raṃ* comes the mandala of fire. From *Maṃ* comes the mandala of water. From *Khaṃ* comes the mandala of earth. From *Bruṃ* the immeasurable mansion of the deities is produced.

Blessing the food

The blessing of the first part of the food offerings is sixfold: the essence consists in the first parts of the offerings, the defining characteristics, divisions, the purification process, the multiplication, and the blessing.

Essence

The essence of what is called "the first part" is that it is yet undefiled [i.e., it is the food that has not yet been touched].

Defining characteristic

Its defining characteristic is that it is ascertained as dignified.

Divisions

Its division is threefold: the first part with the meaning of very pure, the first part coming from the elements, and the first part that consists in the realization of its compositional factors.

The very pure

The very pure first part is the first part of the body of phenomena arising from the three enlightened bodies [i.e., body, speech, and mind] and the enlightened bodies of the five families. This consists in the first of the five wisdoms, intrinsic emptiness. It is the first clan of Kuntu Zangpo, among the five enlightened] clans.

The elements

The first part among the elements consists of things that have been produced, such as the palace of the gods, the citadel, the drawn decorations, the elongated fabrics, the metal castings, the words, the silk paper, and the book cover boards. These are considered the dignified first part. The first sublime part of cyclic existence consists in the lamas and the universal king of the people; they are the very first part of dignity.

Compositional factors

The first part of compositional factors is the realization that they are arising from swarms of forces of curd-like interdependent factors that are the causes. These are called "the first part of items and characteristics from exalted apprehending and their perception through realization."

Purification and multiplication

The purification and the increase are concordant with the dwelling.

Blessing

As for the blessing, all three places of the body are anointed with the tip of the finger of one's right hand with every droplet of nectar gathered at

424 The Tradition of Everlasting Bön

the place. From the seed-syllable *A* produced amid the wheel of the moon, Kuntu Zangpo is generated. On the tip of the forefinger one then generates a light illuminating a sun wheel. Then one recites the mantra:

> So om ba wa de na hum ra sa ya na g.yu drang dü tsi om hum so tha![194] [*So! Om! Bawadena hum! Ambrosia! Drink of nectar! Om hum so! All!*]

Then, one should visualize that from the heart of the gods, mother-father, light rays emanate that strike the crown of one's head with a stainless pearl of white nectar. [214] There on the crown is generated the enlightened body. One makes the hand-seal of the wheel of transformative power that confirms the seal.

Blessing of the congregation

Following that, the blessing of the congregation consists in anointing everyone with the droplet of nectar on the congregants' three places while one recites:

> Om ha hum.

One should meditate that they all transform into gods and goddesses.

Blessing of the ritual items

Then, the blessing of the ritual items and goods consists in blessing the ritual items, alcohol, and water torma [*gtor ma*, ritual cake]. One should visualize these [becoming] pure and clean. One should fumigate with incense and bless the items with the five desirable qualities pleasing to the five senses.[195]

The erection of the mandala-citadel

The erection of the mandala-citadel is fivefold: the earth ritual, the walls of the fortress, sprinkling, drawing the architectural lines, and erecting the mandala.

Earth ritual

First, the earth ritual is fivefold: searching for the ground, assuming the ground, ground divination, removing the corpses from the ground, and placing a treasure in the ground.

Searching for the proper ground

Searching for the ritual ground is to seek a wholesome area, comely to the mind, where there is no inconvenience to the god of the land.

Assuming ownership of the ground

The rite of assuming the ground consists in assuming ritual ownership and displaying one's power. When the Tenma goddesses existed before, there were no displays of power. Assuming is like circling around. Nowadays, followers put roasted barley flour on the large boulder of the lord of the soil, and with a handful on the top, they assume mastery over the land. That is the assuming part. Some polish the crown of the boulder with items such as alcohol, the first portion of gold powder, or bless it with medicinal powder poured in milk. This is the blessing by nectar. When are the activities relating to the earth ritual to be assumed? Once the prognostication of the location is done.

Divination

After digging a hole in a high plateau, one pours in liquids. If it overflows, it is good. If it dissolves in the hole, it is a bad omen.

Removing the corpses

The five corpses of the ground are removed from the mandala. These are:
The two corpses of the wind that are the clear and the murky slime that should be carried away.
Fire corpses are charcoals, baked clay, fungus, and ashes.
Water corpses are remains of claws and potholders resembling fish.
Corpses of the earth are cutoffs and rotten grounds.

Corpses of the element of space are the acrid smells of cremation grounds and the clusters displaying illusions of rotting animals.

When the five corpses of the five elements are present, or if fewer than five, they must be removed. If they are too numerous, one must change the location. If there are no other grounds to move to, one must fix the place with the five potent essences. The five potent essences: the potent essence of wind is metal, the essence of fire is copper, the essence of water is silver, the essence of earth is gold, and the essence of space is turquoise.

Placing a treasure

One must then place an earth-treasure, the earthenware of a precious vase, and put in medicine, grains, silk brocade, and cast items. This earth rite is put together according to whether the place is new or old. If new, it can be done. If old, this is not required.

The walls of the citadel

What follows is the construction of the palace. The mandala is a fathom square. It must be one cubit in height and have four opposite sides toward the cardinal directions. One must build it with the four corners. The outside of the mandala is four fathoms square. Its inside is the size of four fathoms square of one's body. If it exceeds this by a cubit, then it becomes [215] a place for the sky-soarers, the holders of the lineage. If it is less, then it will violate the rules of [mandala] construction.

Sprinkling

Therefore, when sprinkling the place, there is sprinkling of a bad place and sprinkling of a good one. Sprinkling a bad place is done with perfumed water, pure liquid substances, and precious water that is fumigated. Sprinkling a good place is done by fumigating with the five ambrosia and pure items.

Drawing the lines

Following that, there are the nine guiding lines: the main causal lines, the symmetrical lines, the "mirror" lines for survey, the technical lines, the lines demarcating the boundaries, the lines for rite, the divisions, the lines for efficacy, and the actual straight lines that are cast. These make nine kinds of lines. There are two kinds of base for the lines: the basic lines are made with a thread and the vermillion lines are drawn on the base of a drawing. The thread line is made of wool. If you don't have wool, a yarn made of cotton will do.

There are the vermillion and the white lines following the natural method. The red ones are of the nature of wisdom. The measurement for their size is four fathoms. The measurements for the mandala are four square fathoms. Thinness and thickness at the corners are combined into one to symbolize the endowments of body, speech, and mind.

The analysis for prognostic is that if the teacher falls into extremist views, it is bad. If the disciple falls into extremist views, it is bad. If the center of the mandala is broken, this is bad for the patron.

There are three methods: the projection method, the method of reception, and the method of meditation.

The method of projection is that the master projects from his heart to the crown of the disciple's head. He then receives it. This is the method of reception of the mandala.

The meditation method is to meditate on the five kinds of light that emanate from the five wisdoms and overcome the five poisons.

Concerning the four boundaries, there are the object to be cut off, the agent that cuts off, the method of cutting off, and the results of the cutting off.

Therefore, the objects to be cut off are the obstacles and the agents of perversion.

The agents of the cutting off are the masters and those knowledgeable about ritual activities.

The methods of cutting off are five: mantras, formulas of concentration, hand-seals, ritual instruments, and activities.

The necessary results of the activities of setting up the boundaries consist in, to put it concisely, the absence of hindrances.

As for the rite of drawing the lines of the mandala, they are drawn according to the focus of the activities of the rite. The divisions of the lines are lines for the symbolic items and those for the mantra formulas.

The function is to be able to realize the mandala of self-nature through the casting of these measuring lines. The casting of the demarcating lines enables the placement of the colors of the mandala. The actual markings of the lines are done according to the traditional lore of the activities performed and set together accordingly.

Erecting the mandala

The erection of the mandala is twofold: the consecration of the colors, and drawing the mandala.

Consecration

The system of consecration is fourfold: blessing the space of the mandala with the five wisdoms; blessing the mandala with the mantra formula of the five: enlightened body, speech, mind, qualities, and activities; blessing the mandala with the five elements of the material world; and blessing the mandala with the colored symbols in the five colors. [216]

As for the grounded colors that are spread in all directions, one writes the *A* in white, the *Yaṃ* in green, the *Raṃ* in red, the *Maṃ* in blue, and the *Khaṃ* in gold. One thinks that from the heart of the meditating Tshugphü, the primordial Shen, the five seed-syllables emanate rays of light and transform everything into the five wisdoms.

Mandala of space

The mandala of space is blessed with wisdom in the manner of fire and wind with the white color. The blue color blesses with the wisdom of equanimity. The red color and so forth bless with the wisdom of realization. The green color blesses with the all-accomplishing wisdom. The golden color blesses with the wisdom of intrinsic emptiness.

Mandala of mantra

The mandala of the formulas of the mantras blesses the body with the white color. The green color blesses speech. The golden color blesses the mind. The red color blesses the qualities. The metal-gray color blesses the activities.

Mandala of the material world

As for the mandala of the material world, white [*dkar* i.e., transparent actually] is for space, green is for the wind element, red is for fire, blue is for water, and gold is for the earth that is used to confer the blessings.

Mandala of colored symbols

As for the mandala of the colored symbols, white blesses the seeds for the colors. Gold blesses the ground. Green blesses the ornaments. Red blesses its luster. The metal-gray color blesses the vessels. One thinks of summoning the five seed-syllables that then transform into the five elements. By pronouncing *A Yaṃ Raṃ Maṃ Khaṃ Bruṃ*, the colors gradually fill the pegged palace [*phur khang*, i.e., the mandala] and the five bodies are hereby gathered together with the five wisdoms, the five elements, the five colors, and the five qualities.

Drawing the mandalas

There are two aspects on drawn mandalas: the colors that are used and the material used in making the mandala.

The colors that are used are those chosen according to the mandalas associated with the peaceful deities, the wrathful deities, or the Phurpa deities. They are concerned with the activities of abiding [i.e., pacifying], corpses [i.e., overpowering], scorching, and so forth, respectively. They are drawn according to associated traditions from tantric practice and as methods for illusory achievements.

As for the mandala, the palace of the gods, it should be drawn exceedingly beautifully and equivalent to what does not exist or is judged as surreal.

In general, mandalas of colored powders have three kinds of visible flaws: the pure realms can be incomplete, full, and replete with the visible; the visible flaws can be due to a decision in the drawing of the picture and can be either as small as a dog's tooth or as narrow as the neck of a gorge; the visible flaws can be due to the composition of the elements, either unconnected or forced. In order to optimally execute the composition of the palace, one must draw well, applying the colors at the moment when the they are most beautiful.

Teachings on the composition of the mandalas

As for the teachings on the composition of the mandalas, there are two:

the teachings on the systems of practice according to the four categories of activity, and the teachings on the composition according to local traditional methods. [217]

The methods of practice according to the four categories

"The meditation on the sacred palace causes the mandala to arise. It is the object that causes the categories of contemplation. It is the cause of reversal from cyclic existence and the place of uplifting. The seats and woolen draperies are naturally set and the walls and the portals separate the inner from the outer. The pillars support the beams adorned with rainbows. Beams support the dark blue tent. These are the objects of the practice of the mantra formulas."

The palace is where the arrays of the seats of the gods are set. The arrangements of the four portals, the elements, and the walls separate the outer from the inner. In the veranda the attributes of the desire realm are set. They go from the rim of jeweled bricks down to the inside swastika (*yungdrung*) designs. The ornamented portals together with the pediments set the gates above the courtyard. Copper mountains are set and the Iron Mountains are established. The pillars lift up the rafters, the beams, and the dark-blue tent.

Composition according to local traditions

The teachings on composition according to local traditions are fourfold: the oral explanation on the composition of the support, the divine mansion; the deities of the teachings; the trainees in the pure realms; and the explanations on the application of the trainer with compassion.

Composition of the support

For the compositional merging of the support, the divine mansion, the peaceful, the wrathful, and all the Phurpa deities, the seats consist of lotuses, wheels, and seal-knots. The divine palace has at its center the assembly hall, the intermediate courtyards, and the Iron Mountains circling its periphery. These are the three main areas.

The deities

The peaceful deities are placed on lotuses that are their support. The wrathful deities and the Phurpa are placed on wheels and seal-knots, respectively. The protectors are placed on triangles and on the Iron Mountains.

The trainees

In general, if there are pure realms and their disciples [i.e., the trainees], the disciples of the enlightened ones fill the limitless sky. However, there must be these three: emptiness, pure realms, and the disciples of the teacher. The arrays of the four portals, the elements, and the walls comprise the first one-thousandth part that is the uppermost layer of the world. The attributes and the arrays of the pediments constitute the second one-thousandth part that makes the middle layer of the world. The arrays of the iron and copper mountains are the third one-thousandth, the limits of the world.

The trainers

If the compassionate trainers [i.e., masters] are added to the representation, then the four knowledge-holders of the quarters and the three bodies become the essence of the gods of the mandala.

Collected topics on the mandalas

Thus, if all these are brought together, mandalas have four main points: the essence of the mandala, definition, divisions, and necessity.

Essence

"The mandala is the place where all the objects of cognition of cyclic existence and transcendence are represented."

Definition

Its definition is that the center of the circle is where the chief is, and he is surrounded by a retinue. These make the mandala.

Divisions

The divisions are: "The mandala of transcendence, the non-transcendent mandala, the mandala of inherent nature, the mandala of mantra formulas, the mandala of colored powders, and the mandala of the body, speech, and mind."

The four categories are those of the four divine palaces of perfection of the enlightened body, speech, and mind. [218]

Necessity

Their necessity is the need for a place of realization that contains equivalences to all the objects of cognition of cyclic existence and of the transcendent realm.

Accumulating merit and preliminaries

Now, these two—preliminaries and amassing merit—are conducted in a manner similar to receiving guests from outside, bending over backward for them, and accumulating merit. These outside guests are the gods and demons of the phenomenal world coming from the four quarters. They are subdued with golden libations (*gser skyems*), by casting ransom [to the obstructing spirits] while keeping one's consciousness in a state of equanimity, casting sacrificial cakes in a three-part ritual, and the thread-cross exorcism ceremonies.

Amassing accumulations consists in making molded figurines (*tsha tsha*), reciting the scriptures, sending pure water offerings (*chab gtor*), and offering sacrificial cakes.

Setting out valuables and goods

There are the four valuables and goods to set up for offering: the goods to enjoy one's livelihood, the goods offered during the approach and accomplishment of the ritual of the peaceful and wrathful deities, the goods consisting of weapons to overcome enemies, and the objects of medicinal value to overcome sickness. Furthermore, the preliminaries and the collection of accumulation, the arrangements of the valuables and goods for offerings, these two in the end come up during the ritual construction of the citadel-mandala.

The main liturgical procedures

The main liturgical procedures of the three formulas of concentration and so forth consist in first setting up the outer, inner, and secret boundaries. One then engages the rituals associated with propitiation, arranging the ornaments, confession, the liturgical procedure for the mantric formulas, and so forth, in accordance with one's tradition and the activities related to the host of the mandala and their function.

"One focuses mainly on what needs to be done unadulterated."

Whatever is mainly taken up as one of the activities of the five families is conducted exclusively. As an example, it is said: "Like a string of gold threading a necklace of jewels." The illustration here is that if a string of gold is used to thread a necklace of jewels, each of their individual qualities shines accordingly. The results of each activity will be individually obtained.

The Collected Discourse says:

General welfare is collected in the activities themselves.

The discourse on all actions is subsumed under activities. It is necessary that there be no disturbances and no confusion. The results are the three bodies.

10. THE VIEW

The view teaches what is to be determined. This saying, "The view decides what is to be determined," merits a brief explanation. The view indicates that at the end of these activities there must be some sort of realization.

"There are five teachings on the view: essence, definition, divisions, necessity, and result."

In the extensive explanation, the general idea is that there are five definitive views: the essence of the view, its definition, its divisions, their necessity, and the end result.

Essence

Therefore, as for the essence of the view, it is unfabricated and unadulterated.

Definition

The definition is that the view regarding all the phenomena of cyclic existence and transcendence is in the mind. [219] The view is ultimately in one's mind.

Divisions

Divisions are fivefold: the view of the primordial mind that abides in meditation, the unfabricated view on transcendence of the mind, the view that is free from cause and potential object, the view that is free from objects of perception, and the view of spontaneous accomplishment in equanimity.

View of the primordial mind

The view of the primordial mind that abides in meditation consists in the primordial mind of enlightenment that is free from potential objects. Where there is nothing in the mind, meditation becomes free from concerted effort.

The unfabricated view

The unfabricated view of the transcendent mind is free from all elaboration.

The view that is free from cause

The view that is free from cause in potential objects rejects striving and is free from all good and evil.

The view free from objects of perception

The view that is free from objects of perception is that when there is nothing in characteristics that can be seized, then it is free from all objects of perception.

Spontaneous accomplishment in equanimity

The view of spontaneous accomplishment in equanimity is that all inner and outer phenomena, enlightened ones and sentient beings, cyclic existence and transcendence, are spontaneously accomplished in the sphere of the great bliss of the mind of enlightenment.

"One realizes while internalizing." The meaning of this view is that realization occurs within the continuum of existence. This is taught in the following example on the view: "It is similar to a peacock seeing its own radiance. One will see oneself." The example here is similar to the moment the peacock sees its own radiance; it realizes its own inherent radiance without being distracted. That view comes by itself without any wavering.

Necessity

The necessity here is to see in a state of realization and to meditate abiding continually in this state. It is the practice of not passing beyond, the spontaneous accomplishment of the result.

11. PRACTICE

"Now, practice demonstrates renunciation, but practice also rejects renunciation." A brief explanation is that this is similar to the view that conduct is a necessity.

"By means of essence, definition, divisions . . ." An expanded explanation is that performance is threefold: the essence of conduct, its definition, and its divisions.

Essence of practice

With respect to its essence, practice consists in the uncontrived pristine awareness of the very pure mind (*thugs*).

Definitions

Its definitions: Practice is for the sake of experiencing the point of utter purity. It is for the sake of experiencing the words of the blissful ones. It is for the sake of experiencing the union of faithful beings.

Divisions

The divisions are threefold: the practice of blessings, the practices of restoring vows and purifications, and the practice of engaging with discipline.

Practice of blessings

The practice of blessings is threefold: blessings from reality (*bon*), conferring blessings on oneself, and the blessing of non-duality.

Blessings from reality

The practice of receiving blessings from reality: there is no distinction of good or evil when it concerns each and every particular phenomenon all the way from the distinct unsurpassable uppermost extreme above, down to the last level of the Vehicle of Prediction (*phywa gshen*) [220]. All accumulations and purifications that have been demonstrated as non-dual make no true distinction between good and evil in ultimate reality. Teachings on the welfare of any sentient being are limitless and impartial in ultimate reality. The essential point of the scriptures is that there is no individual self in reality, all the way to the unity of inherent emptiness.

Conferring blessings on oneself

The practice of conferring blessings on oneself is done when one does not yet have realization and there is still duality between self and Shenrab. It is when the distinction between enlightened ones and sentient beings is maintained. There is true realization when oneself realizes that one is Shenrab and Shenrab is oneself.

The blessing of non-duality

The blessing of non-duality has been taught by Shenrab himself. It happens when there is no distinction between Shenrab and reality (*bon*). Similarly, the practice of this blessing is that there is no duality between oneself and ultimate reality.

The practices of restoring vows and purifications

The practices of restoring vows and purifications are twofold: the practice of restoring and the practice of purifying.

The practice of restoring is twofold: restoring one's vows and restoring for others.

Restoring one's vows

On restoring one's vows for oneself, a scripture raises this point:

> The circle of protection of the cyclical world is surrounded with layers. One protects oneself as others protect life and fortune. Because the world is being protected, it protects against escapes.

If one is to illustrate this, one could say the foundation of time is like a butter lamp. The basis of life is like leather and reeds. The body and the mind are like bees and a flower. Therefore the ground of time is like a butter lamp that is extinguished by the wind. The basis of life is like reeds or a leather bag broken apart by water. The body and the mind are like bees and a flower. The bees circle while contending with each other. This illustrates the separation between body and mind.

"One will protect oneself so that there will be glory for the lives of the others." And thus, it has been said.

When the consciousness of a being abides on the seed-syllable *Raṃ*, there it exists. When it dwells on the light issuing forth from the seed-syllable, there it is. Therefore, from one's heart, one emanates light from the seed-syllable. When the consciousness of a being grasps at something, then the letters *A* and *Ni* (*nri*) dissolve in my heart.

For example, this practice is like sustaining a butter lamp.

"The basis to life is like reeds and leather bags."

As in the case of a renegade monk or an evading idea, a monk running away is like noon and midnight; an evading thought is like the light of the sun or light at night. One must protect the object at work in a timely manner. One must meditate during the dark of night and at sunset and recite mantras and so forth, as well as enjoy the performance of good deeds. It is said that Shenrab practiced equanimity at noon and at midnight.

The mind focuses on the letter *A*. [221] One examines the movement of breath going through the root of one's nose while concentrating on the letter *A* between the eyebrows. In coordination with the breath, as it goes in and out it pulls in light. The A letter is made to circle three times and then light and the letter A are pulled in together. The aim of this practice is to have both, the letter *A* and light, brought together in the expanse of the mind of non-perception of the self and dissolve there. At noon, one should have the intention of doing just that. Then there is the practice of restoring one's vows.

Restoring vows for others

When one wants to restore the vows of someone else, one makes a protection circle in order to perform the restoration of the vows. In the circle, one draws five *Dza* seed-syllables and four lines that are divided into nine subsections. In the center of the circle is the letter *A* with the name of the person for whom one is accomplishing the rites. Around it, one writes the root-essence mantra of the tutelary deity one is practicing. Along the edge of the circle, write wrathful mantras. Having set the center of the circle, one performs the generation stages, and once completed, one makes the invitation, renders homage, and invites the deities to sit. One does the accumulation of merit, offerings, and empowerments while all this is summarily conducted within the circle of protection. The ground is affixed with the six sorts of offerings,[196] with the highest at the core, and the four holies[197] are visualized in this circle. That is the practice of restoring the world.

Purification

The practice of purification is twofold: the purification of one's continuum and the purification of the body of misconceptions.

One's continuum

The purification of one's continuum is twofold: purification by display and purification by fire.

Purification by display

The purification by display consists in effecting purification with ritual tools and precious items and purifying with the presence of the host of deities of the mandala.

The purification by fire

The purification by fire is twofold: purification with a fire-offering ritual and the purification conducted with the burning of a corpse.

Fire-offering ritual

There are five kinds of fire-offering rituals: burning offerings for pacification and for increasing, overpowering, and wrathful action, and burning offerings for violent activities.

The pacification fire-offering rite is conducted facing an eastern direction; for overpowering, one faces south; wrathful action is west-facing; activities for increasing are done facing north; and for violent activities one faces the center. As a rule, the realm of the fire god is situated in the southeast. As for the traditions on burnt offerings, the outer method is to burn enemies and hindrances, the inner method is to burn coarse conceptuality, and the secret method is to burn wrong conceptions of the five poisons and connect the traditional lore of each and every one of the five families and their activities.

There are five modes to be known for burning a corpse: knowledge of how to deal with the material aspect of the body, knowledge of the departed, knowledge of the disciple, knowledge on offering articles, and knowledge of the deities. Furthermore, there are minute details to be known for the cremation following the ritual of the five Shen[198] priests. The purification of the body of the conceptions of the self consists externally in prostrations and internally in confessions. The purification of the body of the conceptions of others consists in the use of the material thread-cross and the various ransom rites. These are the practices for restoration of vows and purification.

The practice of engaging with ascetic discipline

The practice of engaging with ascetic discipline is threefold: the conduct of the reckless intrepid, [222] the conduct of the unobstructed push of an elephant, and the conduct of an inconsiderate child.

Conduct of the reckless intrepid

The deportment of the crazy intrepid is said to be "to act fearlessly." It is to change into a great scholar, correct in words and meanings, and behave like a foolish herdsman who is without fear.

The unobstructed push

The unobstructed push is said to be similar to that of an elephant sitting in water. The great strength of a standing elephant is such that others cannot move it from its position.

The inconsiderate child

The conduct of an inconsiderate child is said to be that there is no change in one's conduct despite the changing conditions. That child has no preconceptions toward friend and foe, love and hate.

In general, practice is threefold: the practices of the scholars as means for [achieving] the welfare of beings, the uncontrived and spontaneous performance in one's continuum, and the practice in the mode of conduct of taming wrong actions. Thus, there are six teachings on the six grounds of reincarnation.

12. ON THE PATH AND THE KNOWLEDGE-HOLDERS

"It is taught that there are five paths, and among these five, there is the path in the intermediate state." This scriptural teaching says that it is necessary to continue practice above the four paths.

"The intermediate state" is taught as being the intermediate state between the first ground and the two final results [i.e., direct and indirect].

"The path," even apart from when there is progress, is not that. It is a means to the realization of the grounds.

"There are five" represents the divisions enumerated from the scriptural teachings.

"Spontaneous hand-seals on the journey along the grounds consist chiefly in empowerments and vows." This demonstrates the cause and the results of the paths. This topic is twofold: the teachings on the journey that is the result of the path and the traveler as the cause of the path.

The nine topics

The knowledge-holders include nine topics: the essence of the knowledge-holders, definition, divisions, the supported body and speech, the power of abilities, the measure of realization, the hindrances that there are, the antidote to be used for elimination, and the end result that is obtained.

The essence of the knowledge-holders

Because of the true non-existence of sentient beings and enlightened beings, there are really only heroes of everlastingness on the ten grounds. Because of this, there are no enlightened beings. There are only defilements of the objects of knowledge. Because there are no existing sentient beings, the defilements of suffering are purified and mantras are the common speech of the heroes of everlastingness. The inner speeches are those of the knowledge-holders.

Definition

There are enlightened knowledge-holders because they have gone beyond evil destinies. These are called "knowledge-holders."

Divisions

Divisions have six aspects: [223] The "Great Seal" is the knowledge-holder of the Great Seal abiding on the first ground. The "spontaneous" is the knowledge-holder abiding in spontaneity on the ten grounds. There is the knowledge-holder of the eternal gods. There is the powerful knowledge-holder of life. There is the knowledge-holder who transforms powerful illusions. There is the fully matured knowledge-holder.

Great Seal

"The knowledge-holder of the Great Seal" refers to the namesake of all the defilements of cyclic existence that are in reality the marks of non-conceptual wisdom. Because he is the holder of the knowledge of how to transcend the world, from the first ground up to the superior one he is called "the knowledge-holder of the Great Seal."

Spontaneously accomplished

The knowledge-holder of spontaneous accomplishment brings all the paths of the world and the transcendence of the world to the ultimate end. It is the spontaneous accomplishment in the formula of concentration of everlastingness.

Eternal gods

The knowledge-holder of the eternal gods has acquired the changeless body, the speech beyond words, and the mind of spontaneous accomplishment in the profundity of intrinsic reality.

Holder of life

The powerful knowledge-holder of life can hold the body of any being by using his great and independent production abilities. If this great and independent isolate cannot assist the welfare of a migrating being through a past incarnation, he has the ability to emanate other bodies and to abide in many lives at the same time while going from and returning to his existing body.

Transformer of illusions

The knowledge-holder transformer of powerful illusions is endowed with all the various magical powers of illusions, such as changing anything into water, controlling the timing of winter, the ability to stand still in the sky, and the ability to enter into the ground.

The mature knowledge-holder

The knowledge-holder that is fully matured has the ripened body, speech, and mind of the gods. The particularities of the nature of this knowledge-holder cannot be conceived by the mind.

The support of body and speech

The body and speech are supported according to mode of being of the body obtained in its present reincarnation and the body that is emanated for the sake of others. The body that is obtained, in accordance with the mode of existence, is taken as the body of a deity of the realm of form, the realm of desire, or of humans, according to the practices of the tantric path. The body that is emanated for the sake of others is a body taken in any form that is of benefit to sentient beings.

The strength of the disciple's ability

The strength of this ability is to be able to emanate many different bodies, to teach many doctrines, to encompass many worlds, and to project many emanation bodies.

The measure of realization

It is the endowment of the wisdom on the self-arising of inherent emptiness.

The hindrances

Hindrances consist in hindrances abiding in the objects of knowledge.

The antidote to be used for elimination

The antidote to be used for the elimination process is the compassion of Kuntu Zangpo and the meditation of self-realization.

The end result

The final result consists in the fruition of the spontaneous accomplishment of the five bodies that is enlightenment. Therefore, it is the end result of the journey on the path.

"Now, the teachings on the cause of the path to be traveled consist mainly of empowerments and pledges."

The particularities of the results of the path

The causes of attaining the position of knowledge-holder and enlightenment consist in empowerments and pledges. [224] Furthermore, empowerments come from the scriptures, where empowerments are the bodies endowed with splendor and the fulfilment of the welfare of transmigrators.

The result is the completion of unsurpassable enlightenment.

The methods consist in causes, conditions, and result.

Causes

The causes are faithfulness, diligence, devotion, and aspiration. Entering the mind of enlightenment engages one into the unobstructed purpose.

Conditions

Conditions are taught to be of four kinds: the conditions of encountering the empowerment implements and the master; the conditions that cause the bestowal of the gradual series of empowerments; the condition of the master that cause one to obtain empowerments from him; and the condition that causes purity, similar to what follows—that is, where there is a sudden cognition, the enjoyment of signs of progress, or the arising of an expanding delight.

Result

The result is the finality of inherent enlightenment.

Ways to confer empowerments

The manner of conferring empowerments is threefold, according to the categories of outer, inner, and secret. Furthermore, there is the fourth category that is finality.

For those fortunate ones endowed with excellent faith, the outer empowerments are bestowed on them. For the diligent ones endowed with understanding, the inner empowerments are bestowed. For those worthy vessels endowed with fierce discipline, the secret empowerments are conferred. As for the conferral of the empowerment of final perfection, it is meaningful here to abandon words.

Outer empowerments

The outer empowerments are conducted with colored mandalas filled with vases, ritual items, and so forth. The master who is familiar with the scriptures bestows great power through the successive stages of the generation processes, with power from the mantras, the formulas of concentration, and the hand-seals, to the worthy and respectful disciple when he has arrived or has nearly reached the end of the path of accumulation. He purifies his body from arising impurities with lustration. Along with the bestowal of profound instructions, these will be completed by activities such as the conferral of a secret name and the declaration of royalty by means of the coronation.

Inner empowerment

The inner empowerment uses pure ritual items, the white and the red of the purified mind in the space of the lotus. It consists in the master, endowed with the profound instructions, who confers the empowerment of the great application of bliss to the knowledgeable and diligent disciple. He instructs in the methods and insights of the experiential knowledge. This is for those nearing the end of the path of application. Connected to that, treading the grounds also teaches profound insight.

Secret empowerments

The secret empowerments are about the pure items of consciousness in the mandala of the universal ground. They involve a master, who is settled, conferring the perfection of empowerment of dynamic awareness to the disciple endowed with a fierce sense of discipline. He teaches the experiential instructions on non-transitoriness and changelessness. This is for the training of those who have reached the end of the path of vision and the path of meditation.

Fourth empowerment of finality

The teachings of the profound instructions on self-awareness and self-clarity represent the ultimate finality, the circle of the space of intrinsic reality where in the heart of the awareness of self the master transforms into space and bestows the self-empowerment of awareness. This becomes effortless to the disciple abiding in the meaning beyond words. These profound instructions on the severing of the view are then taught. The *Tantra of the Wonderful Demonstration of the Universal Gathering of Great Power* (2.2.2) says:

> There is the path of complete finality that is called "spontaneous accomplishment."

The pledges will protect these very teachings from the ground up. [225] Empowerments and pledges will enable one to acquire the station of knowledge-holders and enlightenment.

The path of empowerment

First, there is the path of empowerment. The path of empowerment is for the practitioner of mantra to tread. On this, there is the empowerment of the preliminaries to all the Bön teachings on the outer secret mantras.

Nine common points to empowerment

There are nine common points to empowerment: divisions, essence, cause, conditions, definition, faults and qualities, defilement and purity, sequential activities, and results obtained.

Divisions

There are two main divisions: the concise divisions and the expansive divisions.

Concise divisions

The concise divisions consist in benefits, secret abilities, the empowerment of great bliss of self-empowered pristine cognition, and five brief teachings on objects of consciousness.

Expansive divisions

There are eighteen expansive divisions: the empowerment vase, head ornaments, necklaces, parasol, victory banner, silk hangings, drum, bell, food offerings, and armor. These represent the ten beneficial powers. Furthermore, there are the empowerment of the listener, the empowerment of elocution, the empowerment of the four activities and meditation, and the empowerment of the billions of empowerments of everlastingness. Those are the objects to know in order to be able to perform the five empowerments. Together with the three secret empowerments and so forth, they make up the eighteen practices of empowerment.

Essence

The essence of these empowerments, the essential point of all of them, consists in unmistaken realization.

Cause and conditions

There are two aspects to cause and conditions: those that are concomitant and those whose conditions are co-emergent.

Concomitant conditions

Those that have concomitant conditions have not been produced from the very beginning. The four aspects of conditions are causal conditions, the main condition, the objective condition, and the condition of what immediately precedes it.

"First, purifying the ground of all impediments is defined as the **causal condition**."

The mandala, the ritual items, and so forth, are posited as constituting the **main conditions**. The **objective condition** is the master who is perceived as dominant—that is what is perceived by the senses by the excellent and middle-level practitioners. The **immediately preceding conditions** consist in what comes from the scriptures. The correct modes are the gradual divisions leading to the result. They make the conditions that come before and after.

Definition

The definition is that the empowerment of perfection, from the very beginning, is a power that cannot be forfeited by others. From primordial time, empowerment has existed by itself from the very beginning. Empowerment conferral is an expression of these primordial qualities.

Faults and qualities

Empowerments are containers for amassing the two accumulations. If they are properly conducted, there should be no impediments. However, if the traditional lore is not properly conducted, this will give rise to obstacles to life and so forth. There are outer, inner, and secret mantras that overpower evil spirits [the nyen, or *gnyan*]. The benefits of the ten empowerments can be obtained by gods and humans. There are no obstacles concerning working for the welfare of oneself and others. The secret mantras can be applied to all of them, and will bring about endowment in this age.

The pure potency of the five empowerments of abilities is contained in thirty-five ancillary formulas of concentration. The enlightened qualities obtained from the secret empowerment are known as the unmistaken conduct of the secret mantras. The attribute of abiding in the inherent pristine cognition [226] is effected while breathing in and out. Once great bliss has been obtained, objects of the mind appear as mere conceptions and Suchness shines in intrinsic pristine cognition.

When there is no conferral, there is the condition for not obtaining empowerment—this is contrary to traditional lore. The *Very Hidden Heart, the Tantra of the Mother Tukje Nyima* (522.1) says:

> The master is not pleased if empowerment rituals are not conducted. Similarly, students will obtain no results and will become lost.

Defilement and purity

It is explained that any defilement there is, is to be purified successively through the outer, inner, and secret categories. One purifies the defilements of the body, speech, and mind. Fourth, the defilements of the objects of consciousness are then cleansed.

Sequential activities

These deeds are effected through seven gradual points, and these empowerments are granted with respect to the person, the mandala that is conferred, the master who confers, the ritual items used, the place of conferral, the manner in which they are awarded, and the time of the bestowal.

With respect to the person

There are three kinds of persons: the faithful, the diligent, and the well-disciplined.

The diligent

There are three kinds of diligent persons: the one who is diligent for his own sake is the vessel to receive the empowerments, hearing, thinking, and meditating; the one who is diligent for the sake of others is the vessel for the four activities and explanations; and the persons who are endowed with these two are then given the excellent empowerment of the billions of everlastingness.

The disciplined and the well-disciplined

As for the persons endowed with discipline of the secret, strong in the discipline of equanimity and the traditions of the lineage, they are given the secret empowerments and so forth.

With respect to the mandala that is conferred and the master who confers

If someone asked what kind of mandalas can be ritually bestowed? There are the symbolic mandalas of colored powders, the mandalas of the formulas of concentration, and the mandalas of the pure mind of enlightenment and perfected with the five powers of the master.

The ritual items used

As for the ritual items, they are the two attributes of compassion.

The places

The places of empowerment are the crown of the head and so forth, just like the tongue and the heart.

The manner in which they are awarded

The manner and methods are those of the king to his children, similar to the bees and flowers that are transformed into gold.

Timing

As for the time, it is according to the person himself when doctrine has been joined in the mind.

The results that are obtained

There are results for body, speech, and mind that are inexhaustible, similar to garlands of ornaments. They are commonly called "empowerments."

First of all, as far as transmigration is concerned, the traditional lore says:

> If excellent empowerment is not supported in oneself, then there is no acquisition of its bestowal. One's ability is tainted and one is entangled in the phenomena of cyclic existence. A polished agate is without any great unevenness. When excellent empowerment is supported in oneself together with pith instructions on ritual items and so forth, one is firmly established with clarity in the essential points.
>
> When one has not obtained empowerment through persistent actions, then it is like a pack animal afraid of weight or a broken axle.

The meaning of these sayings is that without receiving empowerment for the benefit of oneself and others, [227] one is like a pack animal afraid of weight or a broken axle. If empowerment is not received, it is like not letting the earthen jar be filled with water. When empowerment is received, it is like letting the earthen jar be filled with water. As said, if empowerment is not received, it is like not letting the earthen jar be filled with water.

A scripture further says:

> If the master is not pleased, there will be no gradual progress through empowerments. Then all efforts in the accomplishment of the practice of mantra recitation will bear no fruit, and one will fall into evil destinies. If there is no progress through the empowerments, mentally deciding not to care whoever teaches the gradual pith instruction, then both aggregates and agent of action will become hell beings. One will become a spirit transgressor of promises. One's mouth and tongue will plough fields. One will roam in the abode of the Hells of Unending Torture. What if it is asked if it can be talked about with a person who did not progress through the empowerments and these can be gradually communicated but not stated overtly? That evil question should not even be mentioned! If someone has perfected the gradual path and has become a worthy vessel, and then talk is instigated about him and people ask about him, this will not become a good demonstration of the meaning of truth. That will spoil empowerments. Therefore, the sublime path is cherished.

When the teaching is without method, there is no empowerment. One will move away from the path of empowerment.

The path of accumulation

The path of accumulation is fourfold: The ground of amassing the collection of merit, the modes of accumulation, the qualities of collecting, and the teachings on the meaning of the path of accumulation.

The ground

Regarding the ground of amassing the collection of merit, it is said:

> The universal ground is the inherent enlightened mind. All virtuous and sinful deeds are collected on the universal ground. The universal ground is collected in intrinsic mind.

The modes

How does one proceed with the accumulations? It is said:

> Predispositions and the host of virtuous deeds are accumulated.
>   The mode of these predispositions is to accumulate on the universal ground.

The qualities

On amassing the enlightened qualities, it is said:

> These are amassed on account of familiarization with the unsurpassable ground.

Familiarization is obtained on the ground of enlightenment.

The teachings

Regarding the teachings on the meaning of the path of accumulation, it is said:

> Second, the path of accumulation is declared as sublime.

Six points on accumulation

In [the teachings], there are six main points concerning accumulation: the essence of accumulation, definition, divisions, blessings, action, and meaning.

Essence

The essence is the unstained object of cognition.

Definition

The definition is that it is called "accumulation," since it accumulates the sublime and common merit.

Divisions

The divisions are twofold: the accumulation of rebirths and the accumulation of experiences [*rol pa*, lit. "play"].

Accumulation of rebirths

The accumulation of rebirths is threefold: the accumulation of rebirths among the gods of the phenomenal world, the accumulation of rebirths among the gods along one's own continuum, and the accumulation of rebirths among the arrogant ones of the phenomenal world of enjoyment.

Accumulation of experiences

The accumulation of experiences consists in the realization of the equanimity of impermanent phenomena.

Blessings

Blessings are twofold: worldly blessings [228] and the blessing of the elixir.

Worldly blessings

The first one consists in meditating on the primordial sage Tsukphu as oneself. One utters the syllables *Raṃ*, *Yaṃ*, *Maṃ* that emanate from one's heart and strike the container of accumulation [i.e., the person]. One meditates on the fire element that burns up, the wind element that scatters, and the water element that purifies filth and defiled accumulations. Then one pronounces the syllable *A*. One then meditates on the worlds of the trichiliocosm, the excellent mountain at the center of the universe with all the surrounding areas conjoined, and extensive fields and vast vessels filled with the five precious substances [i.e., gold, silver, turquoise, coral, and pearls].

The blessing of the elixir

Next is the blessing of the elixir. The blessing starts with the hand-seals called "the hand-seal of the mouth poised in enjoyment." It is done in a manner reminiscent of a reliquary [i.e., this is the name of a specific hand-seal], blessing this with the mantra of the five seed-syllables of the heroes. One then pronounces: *Oṃ, A, Huṃ, Raṃ Dza*! One meditates that, coming from the concentration on these syllables, all the realms of the universe are endowed with the five desirable qualities [i.e., of form, sound, smell, taste, and tactile impressions] and all the enjoyment of the collection of food offerings. The light rays of wisdom emanate and pervade the circles of the inexhaustible eight, the dense masses of the central mountain of the universe, the lofty elevation of the sky, the multitude of the constellations, the extensiveness of the four corners of the earth, and fulfill all the needs and wishes to their greater degrees with all the collected treasures.

Teachings on action

Teachings on action consist in offerings first, then confessions, and conclude with the remaining servings.

First, in order to accumulate merit for oneself, one makes offerings to the expanse of the peaceful and wrathful deities. In order to purify resentment and discord, one makes confession. Finally, serving the remainder is threefold: cause, method, and necessity.

Cause is action and the ten grounds of liberation from suffering.

Method consists in the recitation of the formulas of concentration, the hand-seals, and mantras.

The necessity is that these are performed in order to pacify conceptualization.

Two main points

Their main points are twofold: the cause is the accumulation of merit and the result consists in the accumulation of insight.

Cause

The cause that is the accumulation of merit is threefold: the accumulation of the gods of fortune, the accumulation of human wealth, and the accumulation of non-dualistic action.

The accumulation of the gods

The accumulation of the gods of fortune is threefold: the accumulation of the sphere of primordial wisdom, the accumulation of the means of insight, and the accumulation of the power of the wrathful deities.

The accumulation of the sphere of primordial wisdom

The first one, the sphere of primordial wisdom, is threefold: From the unceasing sphere of intrinsic reality, awareness originates as measureless varieties of accumulation of primordial wisdom.

The accumulation of the means of wisdom

The accumulation of the means of wisdom refers to the unborn state that manifests circles of peaceful and wrathful deities for the sake of sentient beings. [229]

The accumulation of the power of the wrathful deities

The accumulation of the power of the wrathful deities refers to the cause that the five poisons of suffering and the three poisons are the play of the primordial wisdom of compassion without attachment.

The accumulation of human wealth

The accumulation of human wealth is twofold: closeness is the cause of the accumulation of merit and distance is the cause of the accumulation of merit.

Closeness

Thus, closeness to human wealth as a cause for the accumulation of merit comes from the prior aspiration for the mind of enlightenment of the universal ground. In that, there are also two points: the amassing of accumulation of wealth and enhancing the accumulation.

Amassing accumulation

Amassing the accumulation of wealth consists in having one's continuum amass a collection of virtuous predispositions in the measurelessness of the haughty universal ground.

Enhancing accumulation

The enhancing of accumulation is to increase the number of virtues of compounded phenomena in the cycle of accumulation.

Distance

The distance as the cause of the accumulation of merit is also twofold: the accumulation of cause for oneself and others and the accumulation of the support of perceived objects.

Accumulation of cause

The accumulation of cause for oneself and others is that, from the elements of fire, water, earth, space, and so forth, there are an immeasurable billions of phenomenal universes.

Accumulation of the support

The accumulation of the support of perceived objects is twofold: the collection of the support and the accumulation of perceived objects.

Support

The collection of the support consists in collecting without exception the roots of virtuous compounded phenomena, clay imprints of holy items (*tsha tsha*), water offerings, the taking of vows, and taking refuge from fright (*nye'u 'don*).

Perceived objects

The accumulation of perceived objects consists in materials, displayed goods, things seen and heard, smells and tastes, tangible objects, and so forth. It consists in the collection of enjoyments of the attributes of the desire realm such as the nine goods, the nine beloveds, the nine beautiful ones, the nine melodious ones, the nine dances, and the nine delights. It is the display of feast offering articles, enjoyments, noble offerings, and food.

Accumulation of non-dualistic action

The accumulation of non-dualistic action is said to be "the five passionate actions that are the ornaments of Everlasting Bön."

These are the five kinds of offerings as well as meat, blood, and bones, and the five kinds of sensual pleasures. These, together with the pure mantric formulas belonging to the Bön of powerful transformation that are numerically inconceivable to the mind, arise out of dualism on the pure mind of enlightenment of the universal ground.

Divisions

Divisions are said to be "the accumulation of non-dualistic deeds in non-separation."

Resulting accumulations

The resulting accumulation of primordial wisdom is threefold: the accumulation of resulting insights on the ripening of aspects, the accumulation of resulting insights on unlimited expansiveness, and the accumulation of resulting all-pervading insights. Or in another way, the sudden accumulation of resulting wisdom is threefold: the accumulation of resulting insights of awareness, the accumulation of resulting insights on purity, and the accumulation of resulting insights on liberation.

The accumulation of resulting insights of awareness

In the state of the pure enlightened mind of the universal base, the accumulation of the qualities of great primordial insight of awareness arises for the trainee as an antidote.

The accumulation of resulting insights on purity

The accumulation of resulting insights on purity is taught to be similar to awareness being an antidote for the trainee. [230] Reality itself is pure and in a state of great bliss.

The accumulation of resulting insights on liberation

As for the accumulation of resulting insights on liberation, one vividly recognizes the great bliss of self-arisen primordial insight through the intrinsic mind of pure enlightenment of the universal basis.

As for the moment of remaining in the ultimate state, it is when one is self-liberated from all ordinary mental contents, predispositions, and conceptualizations. It is liberation on the path of accumulation.

Sacrificial cakes

The topic of the path of sacrificial cake offerings is twofold: the necessity for the path of sacrificial cake offerings and the teachings on the meaning of this necessity.

Necessity of sacrificial cake offerings

On the necessity of the path of sacrificial cake offerings: "In order to atone for previously accumulated karmic debts and repair broken pledges, the heroes of everlastingness . . ."

One invites guests of reverence—all the enlightened ones of the three times—in order to repair broken commitments. One invites guests of quality—the seventy glorious lords and guests who are karmic debtors from the eight classes of gods and demons as well as guests of compassion, sentient beings of the six realms of reincarnation—in order to relieve the load of karmic debt and retribution from the beginningless series of rebirths.

The meaning of this necessity

The teachings on the meaning of this necessity are said to have six main points: "Third, it is called 'the sublime path of sacrificial cake offering.'"

These consist in the essence of sacrificial cake offerings, definition, divisions, analysis, manners of doing, and demonstration of the view.

Essence

The essence of sacrificial cake offering is that the outer and inner essences appear as they are. These are all real things.

Definition

"Non-apprehension spreads all over [*gtor* in *gtor ma*]. . . . equally to all mothers [*ma* in *gtor ma*]."

Divisions

Divisions are twofold: the sacrificial cakes as causes of enjoyment and the sacrificial cakes for intentional formulas of concentration.

Sacrificial cakes as causes of enjoyment

The sacrificial cakes that are causes of enjoyment have five aspects: the sacrificial cakes are causes for oneself, support for visualizations, support for targets, support for the activities of oath-bound protectors, and support for the auspiciousness of yogic practices.

Sacrificial cakes for one's own causes

The sacrificial cakes offered for one's own causes are those that transform causality for all the world's transmigrators as well as the outside world.

Support for visualizations

The sacrificial cakes as support for visualizations use the twenty-one grains, the three offerings of meat, blood, and bones, and various white and sweet food offerings.

Support for targets

The sacrificial cakes used as support for targets are those used to "capture" a result and are kept as long as the activity is not concluded. These cakes function with oath-bound spirits like flies attracted to rotting flesh.

Support for activities of oath-bound protectors

The sacrificial cakes for the activities of oath-bound protectors are used for casting away to obtain swift results from the activities of helping spirits. This is like giving away alcoholic beverages to military troops before sending them to war.

Support for the auspiciousness of yogic practices

The sacrificial cakes for the auspiciousness of yogic practices are to be dedicated to local earth goddesses, the Tenma, and the guardians of the precepts in order to reverse interfering conditions and powerful evils.

Sacrificial cakes for intentional formulas of concentration

The sacrificial cakes for intentional formulas of concentration are of six kinds: sacrificial cakes for the expanse of reality, sacrificial cakes for the enjoyment of primordial wisdom, [231] sacrificial cakes thrown for general soaring in the sky, sacrificial cakes for waves in the river of great bliss, sacrificial cakes for the emanation of compassionate blessings, and sacrificial cakes for non-dualistic concentration. There are also particular ones for certain formulas of concentration.

Analysis

When sacrificial cakes are not cast away, one comes to the conclusion that one does not attain the path of enlightenment. Analysis on the elements of extraordinary and common attainments brings up the need for diligence in offering sacrificial cakes.

Manner of operation

The manner of operation is sevenfold: first is the manner of making them, then the manner of casting them, purifying them, understanding their uses, inciting, concealing, and exhortation.

Manner of making

First, the manner of making sacrificial cakes. The three summer months are for making flower sacrificial cakes. The three months of winter are for making meat and blood sacrificial cakes. The three months of spring are for making medicinal sacrificial cakes. The three months of fall are for making fruit sacrificial cakes. The sacrificial cakes for the expanse of reality are made of heaps of sacrificial cakes. The sacrificial cakes for the enjoyment of primordial wisdom are made of pieces of sacrificial cakes. The sacrificial cakes for the emanation of compassionate blessings are made of small pieces of kneaded dough in the shape of horns. The sacrificial cakes of the four types of activities are prepared with the ingredients for pacifying, increasing, overpowering, and forceful activities.

Manner of casting

One casts sacrificial cakes in a manner that will stir the oath-bound spirits to action in the locale of the sacrificial cakes. One throws the sacrificial cakes to make these spirits obedient to the command. The sacrificial cakes for the auspiciousness of yogic practices, for instance, are offered in that manner.

Externally, these cakes are offered to the twelve Tenma earth goddesses who are external guardians and to the external residences of the twelve classes of gods. Internally, these cakes are offered to the internal mothers and child protectors of the inner spaces and to the internal residences of the nine internal gods. Secretly, these cakes are offered to the host of wrathful gods, the four kings, and to the above-mentioned mandalas.

Manner of purifying

Purification is done with formulas of concentration and with purifying ritual items.

Understanding

Understanding is threefold: sacrificial cakes are offered to the host of gods as objects of consciousness for the enjoyment of the attributes of the desire realm; sacrificial cakes are offered to disciples as objects of consciousness for the activities of the gods and others; and sacrificial cakes are flung as weaponized objects of consciousness, like swords and poisons.

Manner of inciting

Inciting is fivefold: inciting with formulas of concentration, inciting with hand-seals, inciting with mantras, inciting with entreaties and exhortations, and inciting with ritual items.

Concealment

Concealing is fourfold: one is to conceal a sacrificial cake of the space of intrinsic reality with a sacrificial cake dedicated to the mind of enlightenment; one is to conceal a sacrificial cake for the emanation of compassionate blessings with a sacrificial cake dedicated to the space of intrinsic reality; one is to conceal a sacrificial cake of playful primordial wisdom with a sacrificial cake dedicated to the aggregates of one's continuum; and one is to conceal a sacrificial cake for the causal accumulation of inherent nature with a sacrificial cake dedicated to the four elements.

Exhortation

Exhortation is threefold: exhortation through the continuum of commitments, exhortation through following promises, and exhortation through throwing a sacrificial cake at vital points.

View on sacrificial cakes

The view is like this: to view all sacrificial cakes as appearances without change, as if the sacrificial cakes were curded milk.

This counsel is for the tantric practitioners treading the path of sacrificial cake offerings. [232]

The way of the hand-seals

The path of hand-seals is threefold: cause of hand-seals, their necessity, and the point of hand-seals on the sublime path.

Cause

About the cause, it is said: "With the hand-seals of body, speech, and mind…"

There are hand-seals of the body, speech, and mind. The body hand-seals are fluid dance movements and turning hands. The activities of speech are mantra recitations. The hand-seals of the mind are emissions and reabsorptions of the formulas of concentration.

Necessity

On the necessity of hand-seals, it is said: "Because of the journey on the grounds of indivisibility…" This is a necessity for the journey to the eleventh ground of the universal light.

Meaning of hand-seals on the sublime path

On the meaning of hand-seals on the sublime path, it is said: "Fourth, it is called 'the sublime path of the hand-seals.'" This has five main points: the essence of hand-seals, definition, divisions, the path, and the result.

Essence of hand-seals

The essence is the exalted primordial wisdom of the mind.

Definition

The definition is that hand-seals are a manner of labeling the essential of a revolving epithet. Hand-seals indicate the representation of the body of the gods.

Divisions

The divisions are twofold: the hand-seals of intrinsic reality and the hand-seals of accomplished Shen.

Hand-seals of intrinsic reality

The hand-seals of intrinsic reality are of six kinds: the hand-seals of the original state, the hand-seals of ornamental enjoyments, the hand-seals for emanations, the hand-seals of powerful transformation, the hand-seals of adornments, and the hand-seals of the syzygies.

Hand-seals of the original state

There are four kinds of hand-seals of the original state: the hand-seals of uncontrived phenomena, the hand-seals of the intrinsic equanimity of the mind, the hand-seals of the lack of inherent self of the secret voice, and the hand-seals of the unchanging body.

Hand-seals of ornamental enjoyments

There are five kinds of hand-seals of ornamental enjoyments: the hand-seals of perfected enjoyment of the body, the hand-seals of perfected enjoyment of speech, the hand-seals of perfected enjoyment of the mind, the hand-seals of perfected enjoyment of the qualities, and the hand-seals of perfected enjoyment of activities.

Hand-seals for emanations

There are nine kinds of hand-seals for emanations: the hand-seals for emanations of awareness, the hand-seals for emanations of virtues, the hand-seals for emanations of the melodious voice, the hand-seals for emanations of accoutrements, the hand-seals for emanations of action and agent, the hand-seals for emanations of sounds and speech, the hand-seals for emanations of magical power, the hand-seals for emanations of production, and the hand-seals for emanations of master-guides.

Hand-seals of powerful transformation

There are four kinds of hand-seals of powerful transformation: the hand-seals of powerful transformation for faithful request, the hand-seals of powerful transformation for increase, the hand-seals of powerful transformation for ripening, and the hand-seals of the all-encompassing powerful transformation.

Hand-seals of the adornments

There are five kinds of hand-seals for the adornments: the hand-seals of the adornments of the sky, the hand-seals of the adornments of the elements, the hand-seals of the adornments of the cosmic central mountain, the hand-seals of the adornments of the ocean, and the hand-seals of the adornments of sentient beings. [233]

Hand-seals of the syzygies

There are two kinds of hand-seals of the syzygies: the hand-seal of the union of father-mother in intrinsic space, and the hand-seal of the union of father-mother for all beings [lit. "the nine beings"].

Hand-seals of the accomplished Shen

As for the hand-seals of the accomplished Shen, there are three kinds: the hand-seals of the body of Shenrab, the hand-seals of the speech of Shenrab, and the hand-seals of the mind of Shenrab.

Hand-seals of the body of Shenrab

There are two hand-seals of the body: the hand-seal of the manifestation of inherent existence, and the hand-seals of the hand of transformation.

Hand-seals of the hand of transformation

There are five kinds of hand-seals of the hand of transformation: the hand-seal of the wheel of powerful transformation, the hand-seal of the teacher's incarnation body, the hand-seal of the deceitful wrathful mien, the hand-seal of the powerful subjugation, and the hand-seal of the visualizations of the leading imperative summon.

Hand-seals of the five conquering gods

Again, there are the hand-seals of the five conquering gods where there are five kinds of transformation of the hands in succession: the hand-seals of equal pacification and increase, the hand-seals of the protector from violent activities, the hand-seals that dissolve enchantments and wrathful actions, the hand-seals of the transformations of expansion and splitting, and the hand-seals of the deception of the celestial wrath.

Hand-seals of the speech of Shenrab

There are five kinds of hand-seals of the speech of Shenrab: the hand-seal of the absent continuum of the elixir emanating from the seed-syllable *A*, the hand-seal of the absent continuum of the elixir emanating from the seed-syllable *Oṃ*, the hand-seal of the absent continuum of the elixir of pacification, the hand-seal of the absent continuum of the elixir of wrath, and the hand-seal of the absent continuum of the elixir that gathers the very essence.

Hand-seals of the mind of Shenrab

There are four kinds of hand-seals of the mind of Shenrab: the hand-seal of the primordial wisdom of the mind without conception, the hand-seal of the primordial wisdom of the mind of Suchness, the hand-seal of the primordial wisdom of the all-illuminating mind, and the hand-seal of the primordial wisdom of the mind of the highest of causes.

The activity of the hand-seals is such that one binds while releasing its results in the accomplishment of the five wisdoms of the five bodies. This is liberation on the path of the hand-seals for the mantra practitioner.

The path of the formulas of concentration

The path of the formulas of concentration also has four categories: the causal formula of concentration, performance, necessity, and the meaning of the formula of concentration on the highest path.

Causal formula of concentration

On the causal formula of concentration, it has been said: "The inherent mind is expressed through the hand-seal of primordial wisdom. The hand-seal of the mind is the deity emanating as aspects of primordial wisdom. The hands are illusory aspects of Suchness. They are cast extensively in the space of natural abiding.

Performance

On performance, it has been said: "It is to clear the impediments of wrong views." With performance of the formulas of concentration, all the mistakes creating obstructions on the path are cleared.

Necessity

On their necessity, it has been said: "They are necessary because one trains in profound intrinsic reality."

Meaning

On the meaning of the formulas of concentration on the highest path, it has been said: "Fifth, it is called 'the highest path of concentration.'"

To become familiar with the path, one must meditate with concentration. Therefore, there are five points about concentration. These are similar to the teachings about the basis. Thus, from the teachings on the five paths the mantra practitioner obtains release on the path of the formulas of concentration. [234]

13. TEACHINGS ON THE RESULT

Now, about the teachings on the result, it has been said: "The result is the final accomplishment." The brief explanation is that the wholesome end result has been taught in these three: the base, the path, and the result.

Extensive explanation

The extensive explanation is threefold: the result of the spontaneous accomplishment of the five bodies of final great transcendence, the result that is the intrinsic reality of absolute spontaneous perfection, and knowledge-holders as the result of the path of transcendence of suffering.

The great liberation from suffering is said to be "the result is the spontaneous accomplishment of the five bodies." The five are: the body of the absolute that is non-perceivable, the body of perfect enjoyment, the body of emanations in all directions, the body of manifested pure realization, and the body of inherent essence. This is the concise explanation, but it is a deceptive generalization.

"The result is absolute spontaneous perfection." Intrinsic reality is empty and selfless.

The result of the path of liberation from suffering is said to be "the result is the accomplishment of the knowledge-holders."

Knowledge-holding has been demonstrated by the nine points coming from the four types of activities on the path of empowerment. Thus, the base, the path, and the result have been taught.

14. Tantra, oral scriptural transmission, and instructions

Now for the teachings on the tantras, oral transmissions, and instructions, this section on the tantras is eightfold: the essence of the tantras, the measure of their numbers, extensiveness, divisions, traditional explanation, activities, concordant examples, and demonstration of their necessity.

Essence of the tantras

Concerning their essence, it is said: "Tantras are transmissions from the revelatory source." Because they are transmitted from the source of revelation of those who have gone before, they are called "tantras" [i.e., continua].

The measure of their bundles

On the measure of their bundles: "Because these are manifold, extensive, and interconnected, they flourish and encompass all meanings; the host of the three excellences, these are called tantras."

These so-called tantras are like the multitude of dust particles. They are like Tshangpa the size of the universe. They are like the connected patterns of a leopard's fur. They are like all the objects of knowledge, above and below, showy and flourishing while the orb of the sun is showing clearly. This means that they are like the precious treasury of Tshangpa. They are called tantras because they demonstrate the three supreme benefits of traditional lore. As for oral transmissions and instructions, their measure is noble.

Extensiveness

On the extensiveness of this tantra, it is said: "This tantra is the king of the tantras." Other tantras are the same as vassal states. This one is like the king of transformation of the trichiliocosm.

Divisions

The divisions of the tantras are threefold: the outer tantra, the inner tantra, and the secret tantra. The traditional explanation of this tantra is that, in general, it is explained as the three supreme benefits of all the tantras. [235]

Outer tantras

The particularities of the outer tantras are explained as the connecting cross knots [lit. "the eyes"] of a net.

Inner tantras

The inner tantras are explained as precious garlands that are inexhaustible.

Secret tantras

The secret tantras are explained as exceedingly deep, like the ocean.

Activities

Their activities demonstrate an extensive range of purposes.

Concordant examples

Concordant examples: The tantras are inexhaustible, like garlands of gold. Similar to the treasure chest of the king, they manifest everywhere.

Demonstration of their necessity

Their necessity is that there is the imperative to liberate the excellent mind.

Oral transmissions

Oral transmissions of the tantras have seven points: the essence of the oral transmissions, the divisions, the greatness of their scriptures, the manner of transmission, activities, concordant examples, and necessity.

Essence

On the essence of the oral transmissions, it is said: "Because it is an oral pronouncement, it is an oral transmission." It is an oral transmission because the mouth of the enlightened ones spoke it.

Divisions

On the divisions, it is said: "The oral transmission of the tantra has interpretable meanings and definitive meanings." There is the transmitted explanation of the interpretable meanings and the transmission of the definitive meanings. The interpretable meanings are mentioned as the conventional method of interpretation. The definitive meanings are made of ultimate sayings.

Greatness

On their greatness, it is said: "These scriptural transmissions are the lama's oral transmissions." In other words, oral transmissions are like humans going away. Inside of a tantra are contained oral transmissions of the teachings. The lama is like the lord of refuge.

Manner of transmissions

On the manner of transmissions: "Tantras are the king of oral transmissions." Oral transmissions are commentaries on the source of the tantra.

Activities

Concerning activities, having cleared doubts away, one can be guided toward definitive knowledge.

Example

A common example is that of selected stakes where the dance goes straight for practicability.

Necessity

Tantras are necessary, for it is imperative to liberate middle-level minds.

Direct instruction

There are eight points on direct instruction: the essence of instruction, the divisions of the systems of practice, the qualities, the greatness of these instructions, the ways of explaining, activities, concordant examples, and necessity.

Essence

The essence of instruction is said to be: "Advice on essential counsels." These are teachings on the essence of the mind.

Systems of practice

About the systems of practice, it is said: "The transmission is from the source of revelation in order to acquire the grounds." They consist in instructions on the transmission from the source of revelation, instructions on the revealed words on the acquisition of the grounds, instructions on the revealed words for obtaining the empowerments in the five abodes of awareness, and words from the face of the deity seen in visions.

Qualities

Its qualities are said to "consist in easy-to-understand small words, and in meanings without limits." "Easy to understand" means clearly understanding the different aspects of their meanings. "Small words" means collecting meanings concisely. "Meanings without limits" means that they demonstrate methods of abiding.

Greatness

About the greatness of direct instruction, it is said: "Because of that, instructions are the very essence." Instruction to others is like the cream of the essence of the best part of the grass. These instructions on the teachings of the inner tantras are like refined butter.

The manner of explanation

About the manner of explanation, it is said: "How is it that the knowledge of all aspects has spoken?" This is the explanation of the canon of revelatory teachings.

Activities

Activities consist in the performance of the infallible meaning.

Example

A concordant example is that of a learned woman teaching her child. [236]

Necessity

Their necessity consists in the dire necessity for the final liberation of the mind: "These three, tantras, oral scriptural transmission, and instructions, are there to support one another."

The understanding mind of the trainer of sentient beings has exhaustively taught the differences between tantra, oral transmission, and instruction. These three together are one in meaning.

15. ANALOGY, MEANING, AND ANALYSIS

Now, these three, analogy, meaning, and analysis, will be explained.

Analogy

First, the teachings on analogy are demonstrated like this: "Searching for a good example of the world." This topic is threefold: analogy on the formulas of concentration, analogies on generation and perfection stages, and analogy on impermanence.

Analogy for the formulas of concentration

The topic of the analogy for the formulas of concentration is threefold: an analogy for formulas of concentration of intrinsic similarity is "the same as the sky," an analogy for formulas of concentration that are thoroughly illuminating is "compassion for the sick and the destitute," and an analogy for causal formulas of concentration is "that they are the same as the meaning of 'outer' and 'inner' concerning the container and its content [i.e., the world and its denizens]."

"The same as the sky" is about the sky that is uncompounded. It means that it is broad without limits. It will not fall from its position. It is, in essence, non-established and free from fabricated characteristics.

"Thoroughly illuminating" is the same as "compassion for the sick and the destitute" and means that it is similar to the spontaneous compassion generated for a stranger [lit. "not a friend"], a destitute person, and a sick person. "Thoroughly illuminating" means that one is to generate a spontaneous compassion that manifests to all suffering sentient beings of the six realms of reincarnation.

"The causal formulas of concentration are the same as the meaning of 'outer' and 'inner' concerning the container and it content." This analogy is that the inestimable mansion that is built in stages from the elements is a container-like world. The other analogy is that gods and goddesses are the essences that sentient beings' streams of consciousness gather.

Analogies to generation and perfection stages

The analogies for the generation and perfection stages have to do with the generation stage, the perfection stage, and the Great Perfection practices. The analogy is that the generation stage is like making a sketch on the ground. The analogy on the perfection stage is that it is the same as generating a full picture. The analogy for the Great Perfection is: there is no abode there.

The analogy on impermanence

The analogy on impermanence is that impermanence is like clouds.

Meaning

About meaning, it is said: "These are the teachings on the expanse of intrinsic reality." All these analogies have meanings that do not waver from the inherent emptiness of the expanse of intrinsic reality. It is said: "They are tight in their common predicament." This common predicament does not go beyond the state of inherent emptiness.

Analysis

It is said: "Analysis is the gathering of one's thoughts." Analysis is analogous to this very world that is manifested. [237] Various recollections appear in thoughts. The main point is that intrinsic reality is not identifiable through analysis. Thus, emptiness is not a product and in emptiness there is nothing produced. Substantially, there are no changes in emptiness; therefore, ultimately there are no changes. Space is free and inherent emptiness is itself empty.

Now these three levels of arcana that consist in outer, inner, and secret categories, the two truths, the distinctive teachings on the outer, inner, and secret, as well as the explanations on the particularities of the outer, inner, and secret, are as follows:

The particularities of the categories of outer, inner, and secret are twofold: the particularities of the outer, inner, and secret mantras and the particularities of the outer, inner, and secret objects of knowledge.

Particularities of the outer, inner, and secret mantras

The particularities of outer, inner, and secret mantras consist in the following:

Since one has not yet relied on sacred ritual items and the five ambrosias, one first uses the outer vehicle of the mantras for the accomplishments on the path to enlightenment.

Having relied on the use of ritual items and the five ambrosia, one can then use the inner vehicle of the mantras for the accomplishments on the path to enlightenment.

Having used the inner vehicle with the view of the *Scripture of the Great Realms*[199] along with the great ripple effects of its conduct, one will realize the accomplishments of liberation. This is the vehicle of the secret mantras.

Particularities of the outer, inner, and secret objects of knowledge

As for the particularities of the outer, inner, and secret objects of knowledge: In the outer tantras, the deities, mandala, and so forth—the objects of knowledge—are manifestations that appear external to oneself [lit. "external to one's own aggregates"]. In the inner tantras, what was manifested as external objects of knowledge are now in oneself [lit. "one's own aggregates"]. In the secret tantras, objects of knowledge [lit. "the others"] consist in inherent mind abiding in Suchness.

The outer tantras

Now, on these explanations of the particularities of outer, inner, and secret, it is said: "The outer is unimpeded manifestation." This has five aspects: the cause of manifestation, essence, definition, divisions, and the necessity of ascertaining manifestation.

Cause of manifestation

The cause of manifestation is illusion.

Essence

The essence of illusion is the six destinies.

Definition

Its definition: "In the sphere of the activities of the senses, appearances manifest as external."

Divisions

The divisions of manifestations are threefold: illusory manifestations appear as sentient beings in the three realms, manifestations of the realization appear as heroes of everlastingness, and what spontaneously manifests becomes the natural state.

Necessity of ascertaining manifestations

According to the tradition of the others, sensory perceptions are artificial and are manifested by the mind as inferences. It is necessary to decode perceptual manifestations. This continuity of visible manifestations is the reason for the necessity of the realization in the natural state where there are no manifestations.

The inner tantras

"In the inner tantras, the aggregates are established as deities." This has six aspects: the causes of the aggregates, the conditions of the aggregates, their essence, definition, divisions, and the necessity to ascertain the aggregates.

Causes

The causes of the aggregates are the five poisons.

Conditions

The conditions are the positive, the negative, and the undetermined karma.

Essence

The essence of the aggregates consists in the collection of the five causes.

Definition

The definition is that all aggregates destroy one another.

Division

The divisions are twofold: the aggregates as secondary conditions to the three worlds and the aggregates that exist through the qualities of the enlightened ones of the three times.

Conditioned aggregates

The aggregates that are secondary conditions to the three worlds are those coming from the four causes to the aggregate of form [238] and those of the four names coming from the aggregate of the mind.

The **four causes** of the aggregate of form are the four great elements. Thus, it is the compositional aggregate of the collection of the four elements. Again, the four causal forms and the ten resulting forms are forms that do not truly exist but appear as aspects to the intellect [i.e., not objective phenomena].

The **four names** of the four parts of the aggregates of the mind are the aggregate of feelings, the aggregate of distinctive perception, the aggregate of formation, and the aggregate of consciousness.

The aggregate of feeling is threefold: the feeling of happiness, of suffering, and of indifference.

The aggregate of distinctive perception is threefold: the perception of extensiveness, the perception of smallness, and the perception of indeterminateness concerning size.

The aggregate of formation has fifty-one categories: the six roots to suffering, the twenty secondary afflictions, the four changeable mental factors, the five omnipresent mental factors, the five distinct objects, and the eleven virtues.

The eight consciousnesses are combined to form the single category of the aggregate of consciousnesses.

These aggregates are present when there is no realization, in the intermediary state between reincarnation in cyclic existence as well as in the production of illusions. At the moment of accomplishment and realization, the aggregates spontaneously become gods and goddesses.

Aggregates of the qualities of the enlightened ones

The aggregates of the qualities of the enlightened ones of the three times consist in the quality of non-conceptuality of the Absolute Body, free from elaborations; the qualities that make the major and minor marks of the perfected body of enjoyment; and the qualities of the billions of emanations of the body of manifestation.

Necessity

The necessity resides in ascertaining the aggregates and pertains to the necessity to release the composition of the enlightened qualities from faulty aggregates. In the inner tantras, the aggregates begin to be established as deities.

The secret tantras

"The secret consists in the purity of the purified and realized mind." This has four points: the essence of the mind, definition, divisions, and the necessity to ascertain inherent mind.

Essence

The essence of mind is that what does not truly exist is manifested in every way, incessantly, without increase, and is all pervading.

Definition

The essential point of this definition is: "Virtues and sins exist on account of the mind that thinks they do."

Divisions

The divisions are chiefly: "The purified and realized mind that is nothing in and of itself, and its manifestations appearing in multifarious ways in the eight groups of consciousness."

Necessity

The necessity resides in ascertaining the mind and pertains to the necessity to release all illusory experiences into non-existence.

16. ON THE STAGES OF GENERATION, PERFECTION, AND THE GREAT PERFECTION

Now, there are the teachings on the stages of generation, perfection, and the Great Perfection. "First the stages of generation are taught." [239]

The concise explanation is clearly mentioned: "The generation of appearances is produced from a state in which there are no appearances. This consists in producing the seed-syllables in stages and gradually from light. Deities are then gradually generated from these seed-syllables. One then gradually produces the attributes and ornaments of the deities in stages."

The categories are duplicated in the following quote that concisely and clearly explains their names. "These three are outer, inner, and secret . . . ," and "Concerning the outer, there are three generation processes." This is the concise explanation on the outer generation process.

1. The generation of the accumulations

"The faithful produce [the two] accumulations." Among the supports [i.e., beings] that are generated, it is the faithful who generate these [accumulations]. The meaning of what is being generated is that it is the accumulations that are being generated. There are eight topics on the generation of the accumulations: the cause of the gathering of accumulation, the conditions, the essence, the divisions, the objects gathered in these accumulations, the collections from any beings [i.e., support], the collection in any manner, and the result of these collections.

Cause

The cause of the gathering of accumulation is fourfold: generation of accumulation from the point of view of the body, generation from the point of

view of speech, generation from the point of view of intention, and generation from the point of view of goods and fortune.

Condition

The condition is the unceasing exertion of everyday activities.

Essence

Its essence consists in producing many pure thoughts.

Divisions

Its divisions: The causes are the activities of the many accumulations of merit
of the body, speech, and mind. The results are non-conceptual from the [rec-
itations of] various formulas of concentration that accumulated primordial
wisdom.

Objects

The objects gathered in these accumulations are the accumulations of peaceful, wrathful, and Phurpa deities; the accumulation of masters and lamas for
myself; and to accumulate the sons of compassion from the six realms and
friends.

Supports

The supports are the collections on the universal ground.

Mode

The mode is to gather the manners of predisposition.

Result

The result of these accumulations is the acquisition of the result of enlightenment from the purification of the two kinds of defilement.

2. Generation of the mind of enlightenment

"One is to generate the mind of highest enlightenment." The generation of the mind of enlightenment has six points: the cause of its birth, the conditions for ripening, the essence, the divisions, the qualities, and the result.

Cause

The cause of the generation of the mind of enlightenment is the existence of virtue, the seed for the sake of others, on the universal ground.

Condition

The condition is the suffering of sentient beings.

Essence

In essence, it is love and compassion.

Divisions

Its divisions are aspiration toward the Bön teachings on accumulation and applying the Bön teachings on miscellaneous activities.

Qualities

The enlightened qualities consist in the welfare of others, the accumulation of the three supreme benefits, and the avoidance of a rebirth in the hells.

Result

The result is acquisition of the two bodies.

On teachers

"Abbot-preceptors, the master-teacher, and sons produce the students."
    The abbot-preceptor is the one who has bestowed his lineage. He is the

root master, the one in whom one generates conviction to take permanent refuge.

The master-teacher [240] is the leading master who generates conviction into a place of ease.

The sons are the brothers and sisters that have generated their conviction into a common vow.

The disciple is the pupil possessing favorable signs who has generated the conviction to establish the teachings widely.

3. The inner generation process

"Concerning the inner generation process, it also has three points."

The outer process of inner generation

These are the concise explanations on the generation process regarding the inner generation aspect. "The outer generation process consists in generating this universe as an immeasurable mansion."

This is threefold and consists in generating all the universes into immeasurable mansions, like filling the entire sky; generating the trichiliocosm universe as an immeasurable mansion; and generating the world issue from Tshangpa [i.e, the creator] as the immeasurable mansion.

The inner process of inner generation

"The inner is to generate the contained sentient beings as gods and goddesses." This is also threefold and consists in generating the contained as wide as the sky, the contained in the trichiliocosm, and gods and goddesses in the world that issues from Tshangpa the creator.

"I pledge to generate myself into the mandala as a hero of everlastingness." The outer and inner pledges generate the mandala of the heroes, and one's own aggregates are pledged to be generated as the mandala of the heroes.

The secret process of inner generation

"The secret is to produce in the same way." This is the concise explanation on the secret generation process. "Constituting elements and the sensory sphere are generated as gods and goddesses."

Causes

The five aggregates, the eighteen sensory-bases, and the twelve sensory spheres are the causes of the generation process.

Results

The results of this generation process are gods and goddesses.

Thus, the five aggregates are the aggregate of form, the aggregate of feeling, the aggregate of perception, the aggregate of formation, and the aggregate of consciousness.

The eighteen sensory bases are the six bases of the sense-possessing objects, the six bases of the outer objects, and the six bases of consciousness.

The twelve sensory spheres are the collections of the six senses and their six kinds of objects.

Therefore the aggregates, the sensory bases, and the sense spheres that are generated as gods and goddesses have three aspects: they are generated as peaceful deities, as wrathful deities, or as Phurpa deities.

Peaceful deities

Concerning the peaceful deities, the five poisons of affliction are the five gods of the conquering expanses. The five aggregates are the five palaces of the five families. The eight collections of consciousness are the eight primordial Shen. The eight objects are the eight primordial consorts. The six places are the six disciplines. The three doors are the trichiliocosm of the three times. The vertebrae are the nine crowning summits. The four limbs are the four portals. Hair and body hair are generated into the collections of aspirations. One meditates that one has scattered the perceived aggregates as deities.

Wrathful deities

Concerning the generation of wrathful deities, the five poisons are generated as the syzygies, the couples of wrathful deities in the four directions and the center. The five aggregates become the wrathful deities of the boundaries and above. [241] The four limbs become the four portals and the six abodes (*gnas drug*) become the six protector deities.

Phurpa deities

Concerning the generation process of the Phurpa deities, the five poisons are generated as the syzygies of wrathful deities of the four directions and the center. The five aggregates become the syzygies of wrathful deities in the intermediate directions and above. The four limbs become the four portals and the head becomes the fierce host of guardians. The waist is generated as the host of gatekeepers, the guardians of the passageways, and the feet become the host of Mamo [i.e., fierce mother goddesses], the root protectors.

Channels and knots

"Channels and knots, the citadel, and the droplets are all generated as great bliss." The meditation practice on the channels and breath-energy is two-fold: the meditation of the blissful heat of the body and the meditation of the concentration on bliss.

Blissful heat

As for the meditation on the blissful heat of the body, the channel of the "physician" is right and the channel of "non-apprehension" is left. At the center is the channel "universal strength." One meditates that at the top of one's head there is a single letter *A* in the aperture of Tshangpa [i.e., the fon-tanel]. One meditates on a single red letter *Raṃ* in the center of the navel. Then one either sits cross-legged or crouches and expels the poisons of the breath with three long breaths through the nostrils. Then one sucks in the air, and with the air in, presses down from above.[200] The lower air is left wait-ing and the middle air is made to stir. The upper air must be strongly main-tained. One must maintain the air to the limit of one's capacity and then expel the air through the nose in a long and soft manner, leaving a little bit of air. One then sucks in the air again and holds it. Like that, again and again, one meditates.

The red seed-syllable *Raṃ* at the navel transforms into fire. Maintain it inside, without holding, for a count of three, and then imagine that the fire blazes upward. Tongues of flame make the *A* syllable at the top of the head drip. It flows down into the channel and strikes the fire of the *Raṃ* syllable. The fire melts it and it sinks down and fills up the channel. This transforms it into a great mass of fire, and one meditates that the whole body transforms into the very nature of fire. All of that should be made very clear. One will be certain to attain this also using the view on emptiness.

Furthermore, one meditates in four sessions daily until Heat is gained. The benefits are that impediments will not be established and it will spontaneously generate formulas of concentration. Cold illnesses will not be able to develop; stomach and swelling sicknesses will be cleared away. These sicknesses will not be experienced by the body and one will attain a state of equanimity.

Concentration on Bliss

The meditation on the concentration on bliss is as follows: Having emitted fire from the syllable *Raṃ* at the navel, and having gathered light in the syllable *A* at the crown of the head, one then makes the three white droplets move along the three channels. One first nurtures them and lets them fall three times. In the secret path, the three white droplets gather together. The white droplets are not made to enter abruptly into the secret path but are gulped down, and one imagines making a *lulu* sound. Again, these are made to go up and down in the bellows of the consort, whether it is for bliss or to gain experience, and one meditates day and night in six or four sessions daily. At that time, all experiences of bliss are made to join with emptiness. [242] Quality in this is generated essentially by concentrating on bliss while one remains aware to capture the essential point.

Subtle essence

"The subtle essence generates primordial wisdom." The subtle essence is the subtle essence of awareness. It is the essence of the primordial wisdom of the Suchness of the mind of enlightenment. The word "primordial" is used analogously rather to illustrate the inherent emptiness of transcendence. Wisdom [i.e., insight] is the mode of awareness, the factor of clarity that is unimpeded. The primordial wisdom of the non-duality of clarity and emptiness is like a butter lamp; it remains in a state free from conceptuality and is generated by the primordial wisdom of the subtle essence.

The perfection processes

Now for the demonstration of the stages of the perfection process: "There are three stages to the process of perfection." The concise explanation of the divisions: "This consists in the outer perfection, the inner perfection, and the secret perfection." "Clarity" is the applicable word for this concise explanation. The third stage of perfection is demonstrated as separated from perception.

Extensive explanation of the perfection process

On these three parts on the extensive explanation, first is the outer process of perfection.

The process of outer perfection

"There are three processes of outer perfection." This is the concise explanation of outer perfection. To expand, this is threefold: the stage of perfection of the messenger at the portals, the stage of the perfection of the wrathful protectors, and the stage of perfection of the non-perceivable chief. From that, there are three further categories of the three stages of perfection of the peaceful, wrathful, and Phurpa deities.

The stage of the wrathful protectors

"The stage of perfection of the messengers at the portals consists in the host of deities emanating as messengers." This concerns the peaceful deities and the messengers. There are 360 of them, scattered. At the top, there are 120 messengers accomplishing the activities of Gekhö.[201] In the center, there are 120 messengers for the activities of Thanglha.[202] And below, there are 120 messengers for the activities of Pomra,[203] thus making 360 all together.

> Previously, the Teacher Shenrab himself made a point to subdue the haughty spirits who were harming all living beings. He scattered secondary emanations from the depths of his mind to the Slate Mountains and the Snow Mountains. And in order to set them up to protect the teachings, he distributed these deities.[204]

The continuum of the world is not very small. These secondary emanations are subtle emanations of the nine classes of worldly deities from the Sé citadel and numbered into the twenty-five thousand.

"The host of deities . . ." is the host of these exceedingly numerous ones that are scattered, and the subtle ones are from the Sé fortress.

"Perfected in the state of the syzygies of the portals . . . ," these are all messengers, perfect emanations of the various portals [of the mandala] and are perfected in the state of the very portal into which they dissolve.

"Perfect as the guardians of the portals . . . ," these are the seven guardians, the collection of medicine of the seven who are perfected in their state of protecting.

On the wrathful guardians in the stage of perfection: "The guardians in the boundaries of the quarters are the perfection of wrath." The guardians, embodiments of the primordial wisdom at the boundaries of the quarters, are the primordial medicine, the five conquering gods, and are perfected in the portals of the four sides of the mandala.

"Perfected is the chief in the middle of the boundaries of the quarters." [243] The deities of the boundaries of the quarters who, in that case, are the deities standing at the corners are emanations of Kuntu Zangpo. In the case of the peaceful deities, they are conjured in the corners [of the mandala] and are perfected in the state of the great space of Mapang.[205]

As for "perfected is the chief in the middle of the boundaries of the quarters," that chief's mode of existence is perfected in the state of non-perception.

Non-perceptible

There are four non-perceptibles: the ground that, from the very beginning, cannot be apprehended as a place, a visible distance that cannot be apprehended as having an end, the force whose source cannot be apprehended, and intentional action that cannot be apprehended. The non-perceptible here is the ground that, from the very beginning, cannot be apprehended as a place.

Mode of abiding

The mode of abiding of all objects of knowledge is perfected in the state of Suchness in the non-perception of an end seen in a distance. This non-perception is free from any grasping.

Perfection and wrathful deities

Now as for perfection regarding the wrathful deities, there are the twenty messengers and familiar spirits that are perfected in the state of the syzygies of the portals. They are perfected in the state of the six guardians of the portals. They are perfected in the wrath of guarding the boundaries of the quarters. They are perfected in the state of the supremely great chiefs at the center of the boundaries of the quarters. The supremely great ones are themselves perfected in the state of the emptiness of non-perception.

Mamos and protectress

The perfect host of Mamo in the portals are perfected as protectresses of the portals. The leader at the center of the boundaries of the quarters is the perfected, Druksé Chempa.[206] Druksé Chempa himself is perfect in the state of inherent emptiness of non-perception.

"During the time of practice, the dualistic imputation of outer and inner arises. The demonstration of the qualities of the realization of the stages of perfection is that the imputation of an 'outer' is a wrong conception from a deceived consciousness." For example, a magician recites a magical incantation on a pebble and on a piece of wood and these appear to men and women as a horse and an elephant. The intrinsic natures of both of these mere appearances are similarly empty. The point about the host of peaceful, wrathful, and Phurpa deities is that the false conceptions of the practitioner manifest as mere illusions and their real essence is emptiness. What is manifested is devoid of inherent self, like reflections in a mirror. Deeds have no attachments, like the moon disk on the water. Equanimity has no partiality, like the design of a rainbow.

From the expanse of reality, which is empty and has no [inherent] self, the host of peaceful, wrathful, and Phurpa deities manifest as real for the sake of the trainees. These mere manifestations themselves have no inherent self. When the meaning of this is not realized by the deluded mind, it grasps for permanence, forever dependent. The result is to stray among the great collectors of the realms of the Shin demons, the demon Rudra and so forth who eat their meat and drink their blood. [244]

Inner perfection process

"The inner sign is that primordial wisdom is free from any grasping." This is the realization of not grasping at all in the primordial wisdom of inner awareness.

"Concerning the inner process of perfection, it is threefold." The inner is the process of perfection. This is the concise explanation.

The extensive explanation: "First, at the moment of the generation process, droplets of clarity are generated from the empty inherent mind. Light is produced from these droplets. And from these lights, the deities are generated. At the time of the perfection process, one becomes perfect in the mode of gathering these droplets and deities. The marks of the bodies of the deities are perfected in the lights. Deities transform into light, and this light is perfected in the form of droplets. Light proceeds as droplets with the non-duality of clarity and emptiness. The droplets are perfected in the mind of enlightenment." Clarity and emptiness remain unmoving in intrinsic mind.

The secret process of perfection

"There are five perfections concerning the secret process." This is the concise explanation for the secret perfection process. The extensive explanation is: "Through the instructions on grasping at primordial wisdom, it is perfected in the mode of the skilled physician." This, in accord with the final state of the mind and the final mantras, is the perfection in the activity of abandoning the objects to be abandoned. The example is the skilled physician who alleviates sickness by prescribing medicine that acts to take away the sickness.

The one who eliminates is the accomplished Shen who uses antidotes as agents of elimination of the five poisons at the time of annihilating the objects to be eliminated. Delusion is transformed into pristine awareness. Anger is transformed into love. Pride is transformed into peacefulness. Desire is transformed into giving. And envy is transformed into generosity. "The instruction on liberation from the five poisons consists in the perfection entailing the nectar of the body of the gods."

Concerning those of middle mental capacities and [their practice of] the inner mantras, they are perfected by the object of release and the activity of releasing. Furthermore, among the three classes of deities, there are the three bodies of the supramundane gods and the three classes of deities of the three realms, the gods of cyclic existence. These two do not include the three lineages of the heroes of everlastingness or the deities of the ten grounds. For that reason, the supramundane deity is Kuntu Zangpo, the great primordial wisdom whose body is like nectar, where the five poisons are completely non-existent. Because he is the liberator, he is the accomplished Shen, and through the action of releasing he releases the five wisdoms for the objects to be released from the five poisons. He releases from delusion with the pristine cognition of inherent emptiness. He releases from anger with the primordial wisdom (*ye shes*)[207] of the mirror. He releases from pride with the primordial wisdom of equanimity. He releases from cravings with the primordial wisdom of discriminating knowledge. He releases from envy with the primordial wisdom of persevering action.

"The instructions on self-awareness and self-clarity perfect [the whole process of perfection], like the rising sun." This consists in the perfection of the excellent mind, the Greater Vehicle. For example, there is no darkness in the disk of the sun. When the sun rises, the sun drives away the darkness. Darkness does not run away, but all the mountains and valleys become illuminated naturally. [245] At the moment of realization, the mode of abiding becomes innately aware and self-luminous. One's own nature is liberated spontaneously from all defilements and awareness is perfected, free from obscurity.

"The instructions on the sprout of wisdom are perfect, like blossoming lotuses." The thoroughly enlightened qualities are analogies for extensive perfection. For example, the elegance and colors of blossoming lotuses are such that [their luster] shines distinctly for each flower. Intrinsic mind, the sprout of primordial wisdom, makes all the various enlightened qualities rise.

"The instructions on the awareness of experience are perfected, like stammering in dreams." The perfection of one's experiences is likened to stammering in dreams, not knowing how to convey one's experiences to others in words. The main point on the perfection process is that the instructions on these particular experiences release one from knowing how to convey them in words.

Great Perfection

"The modes of perfection of the Great Perfection are threefold." This is the concise explanation on the mode of abiding in the Great Perfection. From the very beginning, this perfection is accomplished effortlessly. Cyclic existence and transcendence are perfected, for there is no good or evil. All the non-existent is perfected; there is nothing to adopt or reject.

The extensive explanation: "Manifested external evidences are free from conceptual inferences; they are perfected in the sphere of space." The example is about the perfected mode of space, which does not experience fluctuations and is free from the conditions of limits, colors, and shapes. Like the senses that perceive external evidences as appearances, fire, water, earth, and air, all existing worlds and their contents are perfected in the sphere of unconditioned space.

Mode of perfection

"The experiences of the arising of conceptualization are perfected in the sphere of the pure universal ground." Meaning: the mode of perfection is mind itself. All that arises from happiness and suffering, the concept of good, and the concept of evil are perfected in the sphere of the pure universal ground. The universal ground itself does not experience the fluctuations of arising concepts.

"The dynamic of awareness and primordial wisdom is all-knowing. Primordial wisdom is perfection." The mode of the perfection of primordial wisdom is knowledge. The potentiality of awareness is everything that manifests. This [awareness] never fluctuates in the primordial wisdom of the omniscient enlightened ones.

"Each single droplet of primordial wisdom—without exception—is perfected." From the very beginning, the consciousness of thusness is primordial wisdom. Its droplets shine unimpeded, expanding in inherent emptiness. "Each single" means without count. "Perfected" means inexpressible by words or imagination.

Enlightened qualities

Now, from the point of view of the enlightened qualities, the divisions of the mode of arising of the droplets are taught as fivefold: example, meaning, and signs, then instructions and the mode of abiding for the droplets of intrinsic mind. These make five. [246]

Example

"The example for the droplets is that they are uncompounded pristine cognition." An example is a way of representation, such as "droplets shine unimpeded, expanding," "empty from the very beginning," and "consciousness shining." "Uncompounded" means ultimate. The example "uncompounded" means this is similar to space.

Meaning

The meanings for droplets, names, suffering, and transcendence are modes of existence expressed by means of examples. "Droplets" is concordant with the previous examples. "Names" has to do with manifestations of conventional truth. "Suffering and transcendence" are, respectively, for conventional truth and the process of liberation toward the happiness of freedom from the elaborations of the first.

Signs

"The signs for droplets are to abide in unchanging expanse." Example and meaning are connected as signs abiding in the inherent emptiness of the unchanging expanse.

Instructions

"Instructions are that droplets are innumerable in emptiness." Example, meaning, and signs have to do with this saying on instructions that teach with clarity. These three, example, meaning, and signs, demonstrate emptiness unfettered.

The mode of abiding of the droplets of intrinsic mind

"Intrinsic mind, droplets, and pristine cognition are uncompounded." "There are no causes that arise in this intrinsic mind. Secondary conditions are not produced. Names are not established. Through the non-manifestation of reality, intrinsic mind is uncompounded. In this state of view, everything is perfected." The mode of abiding does not deviate from thusness.

17. Approach, accomplishment, and activities

Now here are the demonstrations on approach,[208] accomplishment, and activities. "Approach, accomplishment, work . . ." is the concise exposition. The concise explanation on approach is twofold: the explanation on the particularities of approach and accomplishment and the explanation on the words "approach" and "accomplishment."

Explanation on approach

The explanation on the particularities concerning the approach is fivefold: the essence of the approach; definition; divisions; how to practice the mode, path, and method; and the qualities of the approach or the teachings on the result.

Essence of the approach

The essence is that the perfection of the approach of the body, speech, and mind is for those excelling in faith, aspiration, and devotion. Therefore, the perfection of the approach of the body consists in acting with a body free from defects, missing parts, deafness, or blindness. One begins first with composition, the seal of the preparation of the field. Then the transformation with the seal of offerings to the field of merit follows as the middle part. Lastly, one concludes with release, the seal of dissolving the field and so forth. This is the knowledge of transformation.

The perfection of the approach of speech consists in the causal activities of speech of the root mantra that is recited without error, free from a loud or muted voice. Then the generation with the mantra for conditions and the recitation with the mantra for activity and so forth are pursued. This is the knowledge of mantra repetition. [247]

The perfection of the approach of the mind consists in the activities of the mind being free from madness and depression, and in conferring knowledge to others on the activities of the formulas of concentration and so forth. This is the knowledge of meditation.

These are the approaches of the body, speech, and mind for the mind endowed with the correct teachings, devoted to the master-preceptor and to the deities of perfection.

Definition

The definition of approach: Because one approaches the essential point that is pure and profound, it is called "approaching." Furthermore, this is the body approaching with hand-seals. This is speech approaching with the heart-mantra. This is mind approaching with concentration. This is approaching the mandala of the deities that are manifested.

Divisions

The divisions of the recitation are five. "The nature of the recitation is timing and numbers, the recitation of names and signs." These are the nature of the recitation, the timing for the recitation, the number of recitations, the names for the recitation, and the signs for the recitation.

Nature

"Recitation is natural." Natural recitation consists in staying in a solitary place and practicing the mode through whatever one is doing, such as moving or lying down.

There are innumerable hand-seals. As for the magic wheels,[209] they change according to context. There are innumerable heart-mantras, enough for endless streams of parrot-like recitations. The innumerable formulas of concentration [i.e., mantras] for meditation are like the wish-fulfilling tree.

Timing

As for the timing of the recitation, when it says "timing," it means the time of year, the time of the month, the time of day, the time for eating, the time for the number of lives, the time of the constellation and so forth, as well as the duration of activities to be performed in accordance with the teachings. "From the first moment one sits to the last moment this is happening."

The objects and deities that are not manifesting, the apparent objects, the consent given in proximity to the master-preceptor when taking on the pledges, all these are about the stakeholder himself.

Numbers

As for the numbers to be recited, when it says "numbers," is this about the time used for the recitations or is it about the numbers of mantras to be recited? Is it a hundred, a thousand, ten thousand, a hundred thousand, or more like ten million? The measurement the reciter is to employ for development sets the number for the repetitions of the mantras.

Names

As for the names of the recitations, when it says "names" it means formulas of concentration, heart-mantras, hand-seals, activities, the offerings of the ritual items for every single occasion for offering.

Signs

"As for the signs during the recitation . . . ," for the highest disciple these consist in the vision of ultimate reality. For the middle-level practitioner these consist in experiences. For the last level of practitioner, these consist in seeing the bodies of the deities, hearing words, manifestations of changing lights in the mind, a smile on the face of a wrathful deity, the shaking and twisting of a Phurpa deity, flaming ritual items, arising heat or wind, and so forth. In the course of activities, memorable [lit. "marking"] events arise. However, when there are no [notable] experiences coming up that can be seized, that is also the sign of successful recitation.

Practice

How to practice the mode, the path, and the method? First, there is the setting up of the outer, inner, and secret boundaries, [248] and finally the recitation count that one will adopt until the signs of accomplishment gradually develop, which is the object of the recitation.

Qualities

The qualities of the recitations or the teachings on the result concern the activities that caused transformations by the recitation of the heart-mantra; the concentration; the hand-seals of the body, speech, and mind; the purification of all sins and defilements of affliction; and the experience of the Great Seal of the body of the deity.

"First go by stages," because the recitation is preliminary and at the same time one approaches the inner aspects—this is the first move toward the achievements of these two outer and inner realizations.

Accomplishment

Now, for the teachings on accomplishment: "One progresses with the ordinary body, speech, and mind to achieve the enlightened body, speech, and mind."

The meaning of accomplishment is eightfold: the cause of accomplishment; the essence; definition; divisions; what is being accomplished; who accomplishes it; the mode, path, and method for what is being accomplished; and teachings on the result of the accomplishment.

Cause

On the cause of progress: "One progresses with the ordinary body, speech, and mind . . ." The practitioner, having perfected his approach with his own ordinary body, speech, and mind, works conjointly on being pure himself.

Essence

The essence consists in abiding in the essence of the view on the ordinary body, speech, and mind.

Definition

The definition is to progress in order to accomplish the extraordinary and common attainments.

Divisions

The divisions are "to achieve the enlightened body, speech, and mind." These are the accomplishment of the enlightened body, the accomplishment of the enlightened speech, and the accomplishment of the enlightened mind.

What is being accomplished?

Temporary and ultimate accomplishments are being achieved.

Who accomplishes it?

The accomplishing Shen is achieving these.

Mode, path, and method

As for the mode, path, and method, they are respectively conducted with the hand-seals of the ordinary body, the repetitions of the recitations of ordinary speech, the concentration of the ordinary mind, the ritual activities, the incantations, the offering rites, and the ritual goods and items. That is the accomplishment of enlightenment.

Results

As for the results of the accomplishments, their temporary results are the great gifts of spiritual power, long life, as well as an increase in spiritual companionship and the acquisition of the appropriate ritual items.

The results of ultimate fruition consist in a changeless enlightened body, spontaneous enlightened speech, the equanimity of an enlightened mind, and the enlightened qualities of the three supreme benefits.

Activities will consist in working for the benefit of beings. The practitioner will have his body, speech, and mind spontaneously perfected into enlightened body, speech, and mind in the great primordial purity where nothing can be added or subtracted from their inherent nature. The pit of cyclic existence will be shaken, karmic predispositions will be cut off at the root, and the body of the absolute, the great self-liberation of primordial purity, will be spontaneously accomplished.

Explanations

Now there are four aspects to the explanations commenting on the recitation (*bsnyen sgrub*): the approach, the close approach, [249] the accomplishment, and the great accomplishment.

The approach

Drawing the mandalas of the citadels of all the peaceful, wrathful, and

Phurpa deities without entering the ground of approach and setting the ornaments of the above, this is the Bön of the approach.

The close approach

Having dedicated oneself to three kinds of formulas of concentration and the above, this is the Bön of the close approach.

The accomplishment

Having accomplished the host of the generation process, the recitation of the traditional lore, the hand-seals, and all of the above, this is the accomplishment.

The great accomplishment

Exhorting the messengers to activity, this is the great accomplishment.

Teachings on activities

Now for teachings on the activities, there are four kinds of activities regarding the work: "Whatever is concordant with the accomplishments..." There are four topics on activities: the essence of activities, the definition, the divisions, and the results.

Essence

The essence is the fundamental meaning that must be applied.

Definition

The definition is to apply the activities to what is desired.

Divisions

The divisions are said to be "the four kinds of activities . . ." These are the activities of pacifying, the activities of overpowering, wrathful activities, and the activities for increase. "The activities of pacifying consist mainly of the practices for purifying and obtaining the realization of enlightenment. The activities of overpowering are practices conducted in order to ripen the continuums of the disciples. Wrathful activities consist in practices to subdue enemies. The activities for increase are practices for the welfare of the departed. These are the four kinds of activities."

Results

The results are that the welfare of beings is fulfilled, enemies are not able to strike, life and power have increased, and the essence of everlastingness has been experienced. "In short, this is the outer, inner, and secret reality (*bon*), it is the primordial wisdom of one's awareness."

18. THE CONDENSED ROOT OF THE MEANING OF THE SCRIPTURE

Now the essential points from the scriptures on perfection have been collected in this scripture: "The meaning of the scriptures has been condensed to its roots."

Having brought together all the illusory aspects of the secret mantras, all the meanings of the teachings, the grounds, the paths, the result, and so forth, having taught the six meanings, I have discoursed extensively on the meanings in these short words.

"This is the root tantra of the precious gathering of all." All meanings are collected in it, just like a precious jewel. The root of all the secret mantras was transmitted directly from the enlightened mind of Kuntu Zangpo.

"Pure counsel for the future . . ." In the future, disciples who are vessels worthy of the tantras, the scriptures, and the pith instructions will be able to uphold these teachings. These are words of advice from the accomplished Shen who held the teachings. This doctrinal advice provides counsel, like precious jewels among dirt and stones. And among these precious jewels, this tantra is entrusted like golden advice.

"The great tantra of the gathering of all roots is the precious jewel." "The object is in its perfect title, explaining through blessings."

These doctrinal explanations have expressed the body of perfect enjoyment with no need for further explanations. They have explained compassion with concentration. "They are perfect." There are no further explanations.

Net of Sun Rays: A Commentary on the Root Tantra the Gathering of All has been finalized and explained with the blazing splendor of eloquence by the great pandita, the Kailash, the translator, the Bönpo of Tibet, the blazing fire of the towering sacred citadel, the great lama Drenpa Namkha. It is complete.

The Bön of illusion has been thoroughly purified by the lineage of the Mula Ratna [lit. "the root jewel"], the great Gyerpung (Gyerpung Nangzher Löpo, fl. eighth century). This, together with the commentary on the *Precious Root Tantra, the Gathering of All,* of the northern treasure from Shangpa, have been produced from a treasure text discovered by the three ācāryas in the storehouse of Samyé Monastery after a request by these three men to a venerable Buddhist monk. It was then requested by Neljené from Sebön Gurpo (Gze bon rgur po). The female meditator Reng mo transmitted it to Mengrok Walpo, who passed it to Jé Lhari Nyenpo. Jozhön from Shangpa then requested it. Someone called Pel from Tsang requested it, and it went to the teacher from Yo, Namkha Rinchen (fl. 1390?). Then it went to the teacher from Zhang, Sherzhön, who passed it to the spiritual head of Bön, Sherab. It then went to the chief disciplinarian Mönlam Logrö.[210]

In the presence of the great and precious teacher of Yo, Namkha Rinchen, during his great transmission of the canonical scriptures, the teacher from Zhang, Sherab Zhön, requested it. Then the scholar among all the disciplinarians and Shen, Yeshé Lodrö, requested it together with an oral transmission. Then I, Mönlam Lodrö, the head of disciplinarians, requested its transmission together with a copy of the book and an empowerment. Then the teacher from Sum, Lhayi Lodrö, requested it with explanations and comments.

From the storehouse of Samyé Monastery to the three ācāryas who excavated it, the crucial moment is when Sebön Gurpo passed it down with accompanying words and it became famous through the northern treasure-text transmission. The commentary on this root tantra contains the middle exposition from the three extensive, middle, and concise explanations. [251]

PART 4

The Magic Key That Disentangles the Secret Meaning

By the monk of the Shen lineage
Sherab Gyaltsen (1356–1415)

Ségyer pung la dungu hrün![211]
I pay homage to the master, Bön priest of the gods!

To the most excellent object, the protector of wanderers,
to the masters, the tutelary deities, and the sky-goers,
I pay homage with devotion with my three doors!

Herein I will explain the profound in a gradual manner, the door to enter the
profound and the great method that fully leads the trainees, relying on the
excellent words of the scholars.

In the expanse, unwavering from the intrinsic reality of the highest realm,
at the castle of the nine elegant continents, the teacher Kuntu Zangpo, in
the middle of the circles of emanations of primordial wisdom, gave explanations from the point of view of the blessings of inherent nature. At that
moment the knowledge-holder, the excellent Shen, began to gradually transmit the teachings using methods of compassion. From above came the pure
counsel of the powerful scholars and from below, the wondrous display of
the knowledge-holders, ushering sentient beings toward liberation by generating the excellent primordial wisdom for all the worlds of cyclic existence.

In order to reverse the illusions of various errors, I will explain the Bön
teachings on the Secret Heap of Universality (*spyi spungs*). Its basis is in the
two truths, the endless modes of manifesting enjoyments, the infinite imagination of the gods and goddesses, the unimpeded primordial wisdom, and
the emanated enlightened bodies that are assembled in the heart of Suchness, free from elaborations.

1. Sources

Regarding the superior ultimate and the conventional, the *Heap of*

Universality of the Precious Heavenly Citadel[212] is first the root, and then there are the limbs. The root text is the *Secret Capable Sen-Demoness*[213] itself.

The limbs are comprised of four groups: the extensive, the middle length, the abridged, and the cycles of the Heavy Loaded and the Trap (*yang khol gal po*).

The extensive limbs

The extensive is twofold: the cycles with the aim at pacification and the cycles of the wrathful tantras. Furthermore, there are three more classes in the main corpus. These are the six main traditions (*don drug*), the Mirrors, and the Two Sharpnesses (*rno la gnyis*).

Six main traditions

These are the six main traditions, enumerated in the following manner:

1. The *Collection of the Nine Trunks*[214] on the main points of the view.
2. The *Cycle of the Nine Arcana*[215] on the main points of meditation.
3. The Three Twisted Strands of Droplets[216] (*thig le sum sgril*) on the main points of practice.
4. The Hundred Thousand Samaya Pledges [i.e., a general nomenclature for pledges].
5. The Completely Perfected Activities of Everlastingness (*zhi ba g.yung drung yongs su rdzogs pa*) [instructions on peaceful deities].
6. The Secret Key to Accomplishments (*gsang ba lde mig*) [pith instructions].

The nine mirrors

The ancillaries contained in the *Cycle of the Nine Mirrors*[217] are:

1. The Mirror of Method, a practice conjoined with the Wild Ass (*rkyang*).
2. The Mirror of the Apprehender that is the Great Suppression from the oral transmission.
3. The Mirror of Abiding that consists in very concise oral transmission.

4. The Mirror of Enlightened Speech, the *Proclamation of the Cuckoo* (*Khu byug sgrogs*).
5. The Mirror of the Enlightened Mind, which is the practice of imperturbable resting (*cog bzhag*).
6. The Mirror of Clarity, the *Ornament of Awareness* [several cycles bearing similar names].
7. The Mirror of Familiarization, the *Continuum of the Oral Transmission*.
8. The Mirror of the Eon, the *Distant Sphere*.
9. The pointing of the finger at the immaterial among manifestations.

The two sharpnesses

The Two Sharpnesses, the fabricated essence of the *nyen* spirits, consists in the white from above, ancient *rākṣasa* spirits, and the black from below, the great sword of the black *khyung* spirits.[218]

Wrathful tantras

As for the wrathful tantric cycles, there are three classes: the tantras, the ritual practices for accomplishments, and the ancillary rites. [252]

The tantras

The six secret tantras of everlastingness consist in the two cycles on The Great Khyung (*khyung chen*), the *Magical Net* [*Sgyu 'phrul*, see K137], the four tantras on the Nine Life-Sustainers (*srog 'dzin dgu*), the two on the Phar ma [lit. "leaping"] spirits, the two Action Droplets, and the Lasso of Method.

Ritual practices

The ritual practices for accomplishment consist in the great empowerments, the moments reserved for practice, and connected activities.

Ancillaries

The ancillary practices have the following two sections from the Point of the Arrow (*mdel kha*) ritual practices:

(2) The ancillary practices of the *Nine Gates of the Small Gems*[219] that consist in:

1. The Two and the Nine Droplets of the Royal Peak (*rtse rgyal thig le dgu dang gnyis*).
2. The *Secret*[220] and the *Spinning of Light Rays.*[221]
3. The four actions and the continuum as fifth from Universal Awareness, the Lasso of Sunrays (*kun rig las bzhi rgyun lnga*).
4. Appeasing by the Billion Highest Droplets from the Balmo Goddesses (*dbal mo las thig rab 'byams skong*).
5. The Nine Intrinsic Mirrors of Verbal Expression (*gsal byed me long nyid dang dgu*).

(2) The activities of the four Short Points of the Arrow (*las kha'i mdel thung kha bzhi*) that consist in:

1. The two reversals for protection, the Armor of Walsay (*go char dbal gsas srung zlog gnyis*).
2. The *Heart Pain of Concerted Action.*[222]
3. The Arrow Point that is Sufficient as Repayment to Heaven and Earth (*gnam sa'i skyin 'dang mdel thung*).

The middle cycles tackle two classes of deities: the peaceful and the wrathful. Ancillary practices are either extensive or concise.

The concise traditional lore, the ancillary practices, and the various implements are associated with the Sharpness (*rno*). The lore that is assembled in the peaceful, the wrathful, the secret categories, and so forth, are ancillary cycles such as the Nine Lamps and the ancillary on concordant conditions that comprise the Lamp of the Power of the Trap.

The Sharpness category consists in texts such as the *Cheeks of the Meteorite* (*Gnam lcags za 'gram*) and so forth.

The Trap (*gal po*) class is also twofold and consists in the cycles of the tantra, the oral transmission, and the essential cycle, and the cycle of the Key to Revelation (*snyan rgyud lde mig*).

The cycles of the tantra, the oral transmission, and the essential cycle are, respectively, the tantra, the oral transmission, and the ancillary practices.

The tantras are twofold: peaceful and wrathful.

The oral transmission consists in these two: the peaceful and wrathful cycles.

The ancillary rites consist in those linked to the Vehicle of the White A and so forth, the reversal rites against death, the subjugation for life, the rites for achieving long life and prosperity, and rites against mental illness coming from enemy demons and so forth.

2. INSTRUCTIONS

The instructions are part of the ancillary texts from the Key and from the *Cycle of the Nine Arcana*,[223] and so forth. As for those with pure intention and motivation, let them recite these.

As for the gradual practices toward the realization of intrinsic reality, they are explained from the viewpoints of the base, the path, and the result. Objects of knowledge are the basic natural disposition of the mode of abiding, but their ancestral source has its meaning in inherent essence.

The root base of all cyclic existence and transcendence is awareness that is the intrinsic mind of enlightenment. The sensory aspects of thusness are endowed with the seven aspects of inherent nature:

1. The inherent nature of the non-produced is clear light.
2. Non-duality is great bliss.
3. On the other hand, that which does not arise is unobstructed.
4. The prime ancestor is endowed with the nature of greatness and has a non-produced nature.
5. The space of unobstructed playfulness shines with variety.
6. Its essence does have the duality of differences.
7. Its innate characteristic abides in the great freedom from extremes.

As for how error arises, it is similar to the error of taking a rope for a snake. There is no truth in a mistaken truth. From such an error, name basis becomes truly established, and from that comes the cause of the three realms and the six destinies in cyclic existence.

There is no illusion existing in the base. Its nature is pure in all aspects from the very beginning. Therefore, there is no existing cycle of illusion. In the dynamism of playfulness, there is error and realization. At the moment of realization, pristine cognition shines forth. Thus, dynamic energy accomplishes both realization and error.

There was no illusory cycle [253] in the beginning. Since there is endless ignorance, it is accepted that there was no beginning to cyclic existence. There was production from the base, and because of that, there were impediments. This is why it is said that there was cyclic existence from the start.

The external environment is the immeasurable mansion of the gods. One can clearly see that there is no inherent self. In the world of the aggregates and the sphere of the senses, the playfulness of pristine cognition is unimpeded. It is the immeasurable mansion of the gods and goddesses. One can see that the gods and goddesses are the inner life, the content of the world. It is the way of seeing the playfulness of relative truth.

As for the mode of being of the basic disposition of the ultimate, purity and impurity, truth and falsehood, gods and the immeasurable mansion, and so forth, all are subjects displaying their characteristics. Purified thoughts, without exception, combine perfectly into one single droplet. Thusness is isolated from the characteristics of proliferation. The non-existent is free from the extremes of eternalism and nihilism. The non-produced is the reality of primordial purity. How can the inexpressible be described? Although inherent nature is non-compounded, it is perfected in the playfulness of pristine awareness and the enlightened body. The base shines through all realizations and errors.

The objects that are perceived have two aspects: the objects perceived as objects of compassion and the beings of the six destinies.

[Topics on realizations] to be accomplished: Kuntu Zangpo, action and agent, and the recognition of the ground of perception as Suchness.

The droplets from the mind of Kuntu Zangpo are sent forth for the welfare of sentient beings. They are the doors of Bön, the vehicles, the tantras, view, and action, followed by their subsequent aspects. The droplets abide in the six worldly destinies. Their vitality awakens through the fluctuation of predispositions within whichever sentient beings they have gathered. With faith and devotion, the person carries on activities with aspiration and then awakens through various conditions. A particular attribute is to be endowed with leisure and good fortune. The human of this world is the one endowed with attributes. The attribute of intention emerges according to previous accumulations, and good predispositions awaken in the continuum as devotion to the precepts on [taking] refuge.

Refuge

It is explained that there are four divisions to the taking of refuge. They are the outer, the inner, the secret, and the very secret. The outer refuge consists in the four abidings in everlastingness. The inner consists in the four gates to perception. The secret consists in the four continuums of wisdom. The very secret consists in the four confirming seals.

The modes of going for refuge are four:

1. In the outer, the four abidings in everlastingness are the lama, the blissful ones, the support, and the wisdom of the ten directions.

2. In the inner, the four doors to perception are the master, the crown of the head, the tutelary deity, and the sky-goers. Whatever you encounter is the tutelary lama. Quickly beg for refuge, and so forth! Perceive all beings as closely protected.

3. The secret, the four continuums of wisdom, consist in the clear mind that illuminates each and every [aspect of] knowledge, the unlimited wisdom of method, and the continuum of the wisdom of non-perception.

4. The very secret that consists in the four confirming seals: the seal confirming the sky of the manifested world; the subject of Suchness as intrinsic reality; all conceptions, without exception, as intrinsic mind; [254] and everything, without exception, as the ultimate—the great intrinsic self as the confirming seal.

When one has properly practiced the whole sequence of methods this way, one will be able to engage by confronting the heretic with distinctive superiority; demons and non-humans will not be able to intervene and cut down meditators. Having suitably relied on pledges, the two defilements will be purified. One will protect others so that there will be no more birth into evil destiny.

One must quickly actualize these so that one will never be struck by sickness. Then, one's decrees will all be melodious songs. Then, accordingly, all sentient beings that have been one's mothers but have no realization will be seen with compassion and be freed from all suffering. This is how one should meditate.

Love and pleasure will be produced from increasing levels of realization in equanimity. Then, having generated the mind of enlightenment, this becomes the path that will quickly lead to the attainment of the experience of enlightenment as a result. Vivid belief, conviction, and faith in that attainment will help generate it, as well as fear of death; those without faith search [in vain] to bring it forth. Faith activates going for refuge and pro-·· duces closeness to the mind of enlightenment and so forth. Someone who knows the grounds will lead on the speedy path.

A good master's characteristics

As for the characteristics of a good master, he has great compassion and skill-ful methods. He is knowledgeable on everything in particular and should be viewed as a perfectly enlightened one. One should rely on a preceptor for all knowledge and should not separate oneself from him. One should aspire to enlightenment for the sake of others and generate mindfulness and great confidence. Aspiration and engagement are separated into two. From the point of view of aspiration as a mental object, this is twofold: there is the generation of the mind of enlightenment in the conventional and in the absolute.

One should continuously think of one's aspiration and rarely spend time with friends who are without a master.

Qualities of the applied mind

There are four particular qualities of the applied mind: awareness, yogic dis-cipline, compassion, and the four modes of immeasurable union.

In general, one should know the object of friendship above. These friends should make causes and conditions meet so as to be able to engage in the proper modes of practice. Then the blissful ones will be pleased and one will accomplish one's aim. One will become pure while purifying sins and defile-ments. Interferences will be pacified and the roots of virtue will flourish. One will then quickly obtain perfect enlightenment.

Empowerments

The door to the path of the profound is divided by the empowerments. There are four empowerments for the unperfected yogi. To be without a lad-der is like jumping to reach up. It is like a lower jaw without a skull or having a left hand but no right hand. One will not be able to enter the door to the path of the profound, and if one enters, enlightened qualities will not arise.

Conditions for obstacles to empowerment and so forth will come up. If the empowerment for listening is not received, then when one listens, a great deafness will be produced toward the secrets. If the superior empowerment to commentaries is not received, then when one tries to explain, one will turn mute. Having no empowerment is like having a mouth full of feathers. Listening, explaining, practicing, and so forth are said to be the activities received during the empowerment. For these reasons, the one who knows values empowerments.

Empowerments are divided into four: outer, inner, secret, and very secret. [255]

The outer empowerments have to do with the leader of the celestial citadel; the enlightened body, speech, and mind; the enlightened qualities and activities; method and wisdom; meditative absorption; the nine vehicles and each of their empowerments; and the eight limbs.

The inner empowerments are threefold: the empowerment that transforms the aggregates into deities, the one that transforms conceptions into primordial wisdom, and the one that transforms secret knowledge into intrinsic reality. These are the three inner empowerments.

The secret empowerments are threefold: the empowerment of the emptiness of the unwavering essence; the one that displays inherent nature that is the manifestation of the truly non-compounded; and the consciousness of clear light that is illuminating all aspects.

The very secret empowerments are fourfold: the sky-like direct introduction that is the spontaneous achievement, non-fabricated and unwavering; the direct introduction that is like the white crystal that consists in the luminosity of emptiness, the luminosity of manifestation, and the luminosity of light rays; the one that is like the butter-lamp illuminating all aspects that is the manifestation of inherent nature in the essence of emptiness; and the signless one on the reality of inherent nature, free from all recognition of any essence.

Non-conceptual grasping of aspects is like [the empowerment of the] conferral of the mirror. Once received, the pledges must be guarded properly. Receiving an empowerment is like Mount Meru and the cosmic ocean. They by far surpass the splendor of the world and the ten grounds. The power of the empowerments suppresses the sons of the demon. Opportunities give rise to all qualities, and in the end, bad rebirths will be completely eliminated and great liberation attained.

The path of the profound

The path of the profound is divided into five stages: the direct introduction to the mode of abiding according to established instructions; after that, one rejects any training program; one then practices; one grasps the subject at the root; and one accomplishes the two benefits [i.e., for oneself and others] with the arising of finality. These are similar to the divisions of the five stages of the view, performance, meditation, pledges, and activities.

The view

The view is taught in three aspects: total ignorance, partial realization, and completely correct realization without illusory conception. These three are respectively divided as incorrect (*ma dag*), self-realization (*rang rtogs*), and completely correct (*yang dag*) views.

The view of total ignorance

The incorrect view is threefold. There are the intelligent and the wrong positions regarding cause, result, essential points, and the natural state. These two intents change according to the view. They are divided as no realization, wrong conception, and doubt.

No realization

The no realization views are explained as ten and consist in: (1–6) the karma [lit. "completed actions"] that brings about the six illusory appearances in the six destinies, and (7–10) virtuous, evil, and unspecified deeds not noted in the scriptures together with the rites, the diagnosis (*dpyad*), the manufacturing of items, and the restoring to health make the last four. Among these, strict adherence to the pledges brings about the thorough purification of forgetfulness in the continuum of cyclic existence.

Wrong conception

The views based on wrong conception have sixty-two aspects. These afflictive emotions depend on which of the following two is prevalent: the views along the sixty-two different aspects or Suchness.

Repudiating primordial wisdom generates wandering in evil destinies. It obscures the path to the union of method and wisdom.

Doubts

There are forty-two views on doubt: one consists in extensive reliance on the five powers [i.e., faith, diligence, mindfulness, concentration, and wisdom]; then there are the ten opposites to the ten perfections. If one is looking for a single definition of these: One single mistaken view can be divided into various aspects. Therefore, forty-six statements can be summarized in two statements: [256] "There are obstacles on the path to the profound. These generate abiding in anguish."

Self-realization

Eighty-four statements can be subsumed under these two: co-emergence and erroneous conception.

As for "intrinsic mind, freed from elaboration—that is intrinsic reality," grasping at a self is fluctuating ignorance. Intrinsic mind, free from elaboration, is intrinsic reality. The fluctuation of grasping at a self is ignorance. That itself [i.e., ignorance] consists in abiding in causes and conditions and in analyzing whatever is distinct from an essence. There are no characteristics to complete freedom from causes and conditions. If you know that, it is the recognition of ignorance. Stopping at that, which is similar to imputation, is knowledge.

What is pleasant or not, fame and so forth, is known through analysis to be unreal and uncertain. Objects and senses, virtues and non-virtues, as above, are analyzed and known in a similar manner. Self-knowledge is the intrinsic essence of primordial wisdom. It is unobstructed, self-luminous, and self-manifest. These five wisdoms are spontaneously perfected and are not different from the five powers. Thus, they arise variously and unceasingly. They are analyzed as separate from causes and conditions. This is it, the knowledge without characteristics. The deity with its entourage is self-liberated from ignorance. The deity and its entourage are the pristine cognition of awareness. Its essence is not differentiated from the realization of intrinsic reality.

If ignorance were pure presence, then pristine cognition of awareness would appear in oneself. The view is to transform manifestations as the playfulness of pristine cognition without exception. The world and its inhabitants, gods and goddesses, the aggregates, the realms and all sensory spheres, the enlightened body and primordial wisdom, are playful transformations. All these are manifested without a self. They shine without conceptual grasping. Awareness is self-luminous, in a state of pure enlightened mind, unwavering and uncontrived. It is spontaneously accomplished with fulfilled intent.

The essential meaning of the mode of subsistence is that the essence of cyclic existence and transcendence is purified enlightened mind. That itself is the enlightened body of reality, the Great Perfection, unborn, pure from the beginning, spontaneously accomplished, and transcending mind, concepts, and grasping. It is free from elaborations. It is illustrated as free from extremes and inexpressible. It is the realization of thusness and that which is to be believed. It is ascertained as pristine cognition, pure, the antidote that strikes the crucial point. One is liberated from grasping at manifestations through the reversal of illusory manifestations. Not going away from scriptural transmission will make virtues flourish. Overcoming afflictions will make primordial wisdom arise. Overcoming doubts will make one discover the path to the profound. The undifferentiated essence is liberated in itself.

The nine vehicles of self-realization

The nine views of the vehicle of self-realization are related to the nine distinctive aspects of the senses. They are:

1. The vehicle of the Shen of prediction (*phywa*)
2. The Shen of the visual world
3. The Shen of illusion
4. The Shen of existence

These are the causal vehicles. The vehicles of result are:

5. The virtuous adherers
6. The great ascetics
7. The White A
8. The primeval Shen
9. The Unsurpassed Moon (*zla bla med*)

Each is said to have its own view. These points can be expanded at length.

The Greater Vehicle is connected to this and consists in acquiring the very result of finality.

The completely pure views

Concerning the three pure views, these are the views regarding the continuum of the path, the mode of subsistence, and the mode subsuming the main points. They are, respectively, the divisions of the view along the general, the extensive, and complete eradications; freedom from elaborations of the nine extremes; and the three views expressed as metaphor, actuality, and indication.

The teachings on the general, the extensive, and complete eradication [257] consist in these divisions: the definitive meaning as opposed to afflictive emotions; the condition of true existence on the path, the three gradual views expressed as metaphor, actuality, and indication; and the complete eradication of the five paths to affliction.

On the path, as the realization of the great distinction arises, one becomes free from grasping and fixation. In order to become free from the nine views holding to extremes, there are the nine views that are free from extremes. One becomes free from these nine views holding to extremes as one has realizations that liberate from extremes. The manifested world is pure in the state of space. Phenomena dissolve in the realm of intrinsic reality. Thought activity is liberated in the expanse of intrinsic enlightened mind.

On the three views that are metaphor, actuality, and indication, one becomes completely released from grasping to cyclic existence and transcendence.

The mode of manifestation appears just as it is, playfulness. When it arises by itself, unimpeded, the unproduced mode of subsistence is then achieved through freedom from elaboration. It is intrepid while being free of the dynamism of action.

If there is eradication through the general, the extensive, and the complete, it is like the horned-eagle that demonstrates its ability to float in the sky. Non-dual emptiness and clarity support one's continuum so that it becomes free from extremes, giving and taking.

Outwardly, one is liberated from the subject and object of manifestations. One realizes the expanse of visible emptiness.

Inwardly, one is released from thought activity, and the pinnacle of realization arises in intrinsic pristine cognition.

Secretly, one is liberated from grasping at a self and ignorance, and co-emergent wisdom arises naturally. Then one obtains the enlightened body of reality in the undifferentiated cognition of the expanse. Non-realization, wrong conceptions, doubts, and deviant adherence to the vehicle below will be completely cut off through realizations on cyclic existence and transcendence.

Authentic view with authentic instructions will liberate one from the extreme of exaggerated views. Realizing the mode of subsistence for what it is and so forth, intrinsic mind will be explicitly realized as the enlightened body of reality. Cyclic existence will become liberated and naturally pure. Natural realization will flare up the four causal ways of Bön. As such, the vehicles of the virtuous adherers, the great ascetics, the White A, and the primeval Shen, these unsurpassed and distinct vehicles will be exalted. This is the realization of the view of the Greater Vehicle.

Four contentions

As for the views of the Lower Vehicle and so forth, the practices of elimination and transformation are not distinct. The acquisition of liberation is to be understood by itself. If things are eliminated, then the path of elimination becomes pure. If there is transformation, it is because the agent of transformation is the conception. Free from conception, primordial wisdom is gained just as it is. Non-dual fundamental nature is similar to charcoal when primordial wisdom of realization is obtained. It does not change. The first cause of dispute does not exist.

As for conception as a factual basis in itself, when pristine cognition is produced, there are no more concepts. These two contentions here do no harm. There is no recognition and so forth of pristine awareness when abiding in the inherent essence, for the one who realizes is dependent on circumstances.

The third contention is isolated on this account. Furthermore, non-recognition and pristine awareness and so forth, if there is contradiction, the undifferentiated arises just as it is. If they are connected, then how can they arise as the same entity? An agent releasing an object released from a single entity is a contradiction. To come into being implies cause and result and so forth.

The fourth contention, there are no existing others, [258] does not contradict the duality in a single entity. The distinction of realization and non-realization lies in ignorance and primordial wisdom and so forth. That contention is free from faults. Exaggerations have explained the many views, but basic unconditioned disposition (*gshis*) is one mode. That itself rests in the authentic view. Because of that, the mode of subsistence is released from exaggerations through proven instruction in its own natural state. Deliberate refutation is not needed. Non-dual self-liberation is realized. Having been freed from exaggerated elaborations, the realization of the meaning of the mode of subsistence arises. Having separated the meaningful from the non-meaningful, one enters the authentic meaning.

Conduct

The two kinds of conduct are taught as maturing from pleasurable and non-pleasurable. They are taught as divided into the two categories of virtuous and non-virtuous.

Eighteen non-virtuous actions have been mentioned, and they are subsumed under the three categories of the deeds of body, speech, and mind. There is no escape from wandering in cyclic existence. It is to be purified by the three kinds of virtuous conduct.

The gateway to the pinnacle of realization is separate. It is the particular domain of the conduct of the secret mantras. Therefore, these have different modes of conduct. They are taught under the topics of the divine citadel, the secret of illusory emanations, and the particular objects of perception.

The divine citadel

The essential points of conduct related to the divine citadel are threefold: it is perfected in the mind, it is emanated from one's intention, and it is concretely realized. These divisions of the conduct relating to the citadel have to do, respectively, with the pristine awareness aspects of wisdom deities, the awareness at the time of reciting the formulas of concentration, and the emanation of the signs.

There are 120 wisdom beings in the divine citadel. Sixty of them are expanding droplets. The mode of arising of the qualities of the droplets is in the sixty limbs free from extremes.[224] Elaborations and emptiness are said to be all-encompassing. Intrinsic mind is taught in the tantras as being free from elaborations. Marks that are used are completely empty.

There are 120 formulas of concentration of the celestial citadel. These are subsumed under the five kinds of formula of concentration: non-produced emptiness, unfabricated equanimity, the four immeasurables, the seed-syllables of light, and the enlightened body and completely perfected pristine awareness. These are nothing whatsoever but thusness.

Together, there are 120 marks of the divine citadel that are subsumed under the categories of enlightened body, speech, mind, and the root. The enlightened body is spoken of as having psychic channels for the twenty-one major and forty-eight minor marks. Enlightened speech is said to have eighteen, and those of the mind have thirty-three psychic channels.

The practice of the profound

The practice of the profound is the flawless action of reversing antagonism. It is the threefold secret practice of illusory emanations: the domain of the object of practice, the conditions for the practitioner, and the visualizations as the manner of practicing. These are further divided into abiding, the items, and the letters, also classified as abiding with a friend, the visualizations, and the letters.

As for the abiding process, there are the ultimate and the conventional, and the process consists in the performance of the union of method and wisdom.

As for the ritual items, these are the ritual tools, the hand signs, the supports for yogic accomplishments, the offering substances, and so forth. These grant blessings and fulfill all needs and wishes. [259] They are metaphors, meanings, and signs as well as ritual symbolic items, aggregates, and the three seed-syllables of the deities.

Seed-syllables are used for the bodies of the deities and so forth, particularly with the threefold practice of visualization of the body, speech, and mind.

As for the hand-seals, the essence, and the concentration, the hand-seals are of three kinds: those used in the mode of arising of the enlightened body, speech, and mind; those used during the taming of beings on the path; and those used for marking the strength of wisdom beings and the expanse of intrinsic reality during the enunciation and the making of the signs of the deities. These kinds of hand-seals are changing constructs that reveal the enlightened bodies. Intrinsic reality arises and brings intention to completion.

There are three kinds of particularities to essential mantras: the meaning of the mantra is its root, the conjuration is the particular process of emanating and reabsorbing, and the mantras establish the bodies of wisdom beings. They are, respectively, emanation and reabsorption, mantra repetitions, and meditative equipoise.

The process

Light issues forth from the enlightened bodies and becomes primordial wisdom beings.

There are three kinds of formulas of concentration: for uncontrived limitless compassion, for the production of light, and for the production of seed-syllables. These three are, respectively, Suchness, all manifesting, and causal. Free from correcting and modifying, one guides transmigrating beings. One becomes familiar with pure visions, and meditates.

There are three aspects to the reasons for practice. The practice of the method to enter the path is to purify body, speech, and mind with virtues.

The three kinds of practices

The practice of the wisdom that realizes the intent is threefold: the secret practice, the secret practice of forceful yogic discipline, and the practice of the boundless conqueror.

Insightful realization comes through perfecting the skill of pristine awareness. It is illustrated by the analogy of a pouncing lion.

The practice of the union of method and wisdom is to become free from the dualistic fixations of refuting and proving. It is to free clinging to a self and thought activity through emptiness.

As for the unskilled practice that requires forceful yogic discipline, nonsensical chatter makes one stray in evil destinies. It should be curtailed by hitting the crucial points of method and wisdom in order to achieve the three enlightened bodies.

Faults and qualities should be separated, and in particular, what should be abandoned is to be eliminated. Then, meditating on the view, the perfected result will be obtained.

Meditation of the profound

The meditation of the profound is of three kinds: conquering the mind, calm abiding, and gradually manifesting stabilization by means of the symbolic attributes that are without distinguishing marks.

There are three kinds of meditation on the main point of the natural state: the three kinds of concentration formulas on symbolic attributes; the visualizations of the marks of the generation process; and dependence on droplets, energy, and the channel practices of the perfection stage. The traditional lore on activities and the path of stabilization, together with the meditation on the methods of the droplets, respectively, make these three.

The nine cultivations

There are nine cultivations concerning the traditional lore of the activities. These nine are the preceptor, spiritual friends, the deities, the immeasurable mansion, offering substances, visualizations, meditation, stabilization, and meditative development on the path.

Clinging to the eight modes of consciousness must be destroyed because of the destruction that comes from clinging to the aggregates. The related practices are divided along the four signs, the five seed-syllables, and the two kinds of mental fixation; the three meditative cultivations on the method of the droplets; the reliance on the method applied to one's own body [260]; reliance on the wisdom of the body of others; and the practice of the union of bliss and emptiness.

One must reverse hanging on to manifestations, the aggregates, or sexual intercourse, so that pure visions, non-conceptual wisdom, bliss, and emptiness will arise.

There are three kinds of signless concentration formulas. This means that there is meditative equipoise, followed by undisrupted abiding, and then discordances and clinging to extremes are cleared away. That brings about the continuum of the unfabricated contemplative equipoise of droplets.

The narrow path of duality and the dispelling of darkness are divided into three sections: the nine cultivations of the meditative equipoise of the droplets, the unreal and effortless non-duality, and the meditation on the undifferentiated mind of pure enlightenment.

There are nine meditations on the uncontrived continuum:

1. The meditation on the inseparability of the signless meaning.
2. The nine cultivations on the dispelling of darkness on the narrow path of duality.

3. The meditation that is uninhibited non-duality, free from extremes.
4. Liberation from dualistic clinging and the distraction of signs that give rise to uninhibited and continuous non-differentiation.
5. The three cultivations of the authentic natural state that are the recognition of the self-originated wisdom, the freedom from the stains of corrupted experiences, and their transformation into undifferentiated experience and realization. This is perfected in the primordial wisdom of the unceasing freedom from perceivable objects.
6. The nine cultivations of unceasing non-perception, the meditation on the non-perception of the five wisdoms and so forth.
7. The nine meditations on the completely perfected primordial wisdom and the mind of enlightenment that is without bondage or release and that transcends analysis, investigation, and named characteristics.
8. The meditation without partiality, uninhibited and unceasing.
9. The nine cultivations of the state without distraction, which is the spontaneous realization of the three enlightened bodies, primordial wisdom.

Undefiled primordial wisdom arises truly while the clarity of the non-differentiation between bondage and release is realized. Then, the finality that is the spontaneous accomplishment of the three enlightened bodies is obtained.

There are the three divisions that are the sessions for the cultivation of the concentration formulas, the cultivation of the state of the mind of enlightenment, and the cultivation of the depth of realization.

There are meditative cultivations below that are complex elaborations. "There is nothing to be meditated on." This becomes the common view of nihilism. If it is the common view, then ask why is there hanging on to conception? "This is the sign of reality," they say. There is no meditation here, because when there is cultivation, it relies on the process of familiarization.

The fault of that objection is isolation. The pleasure of the others is to uproot fleeting movements of thought. The state of clarity and emptiness is imperturbable. It can be illustrated by the turtle raising its head up from the ocean.

The stages of the generation stage process involve concentration, while the stages of the perfection process involve meditative equipoise.

The Great Perfection is friendly. All external objects are freed from recognition. The internal thoughts are without fixated attachments. One's inner secret state is clear, without any satisfaction. The adherence to bliss, to clarity, and to non-conceptuality, and so forth, is completely severed; one is free from attachment.

The five hazardous grounds of realization are the three mazes and the two deviances. The three mazes are generalities, mental maze, and involvement. Those are the three mazes of intellectual theorizing. It has been said that one has to study and reflect in order to increase direct introduction [261] so that unmistaken practice will be improved and the result of realization, the knowledge of all aspects, can be obtained. The non-differentiation of view and meditative cultivation make one exit the gate of reality.

Pledges

There are three kinds of pledges on the profound path. Externally, there are those of the secret mantras. These are in order to really accomplish the welfare of others. Their secret meanings are to condense the essentials. The three external ones that are superior and particular are the three kinds of external pledges. They are divided according to the branches of cause, action, and condition; along the five poisons, virtues, and defilements; and food, clothing, and friendship categories.

Their fundamental principle is transformative, in order to eliminate the five poisons: anger, delusion, cravings, envy, and pride. Each of these is then subdivided into ten. One has to protect this transformation of the five poisons into wisdom. The fundamental principle is in the respective adoption and rejection of virtue and defilements.

The three pledges of the body are not to take life, not to take what has not been given, and no sexual impropriety.

The four pledges of speech are no nonsensical speech, no harsh speech, no false speech, and no divisive speech.

The three pledges of the mind are no cursing thoughts, no cruelty, and no wrong views. Each of these can also be subdivided into ten more. One abandons wrongdoing and practices the guarding of virtue.

As for livelihood, support, and friendliness, these three are about food, clothing, and friends. The fundamental principle is to partake appropriately and to not discard food.

As for the three categories of meat, alcohol, and garlic and onions, there are ten explanations each for meat and alcohol. These are enjoyed only as blessings for yogic accomplishments.

The fundamental principles about clothing and ornamental articles are explained in ten sections. These should be well protected from the viewpoints of refuting and defending.

The fundamental principle with regard to adopting and discarding friendship is to rely on the blessings of genuineness.

As for the two superior pledges, the first fundamental principle is related to the conditions of action. Foremost are the five poisons and the ten wrongdoings. The elimination and transformation of these is to protect the pledges. There are 44,300 individual explanations on their different aspects.

The three kinds of special pledges are the pinnacle of realization of self-nature, the door to the Superior Vehicle; the special method on the union of method and wisdom; and the manner of realization of the mode of existence, finality.

The vehicle of self-realization, the White A, has the three special and unsurpassed pledges. The pledges of the vehicle of self-realization are explained in nine points over eight categories. Each is concerned with traditional lore on the practice of union.

The pledges of the secret White A have three divisions on the main root principle and branches. The root principle is elucidated in the traditional lore dealing with the five aspects, the transformation of the five poisons into wisdom, and the transformation of the aggregates into the five enlightened bodies.

The ancillary branches are said to have ten divisions. The section on the five kinds of pledges is about the secret, the transformation, the practice, no transgression, and elimination. The method on the manner of the union of method and wisdom is to be guarded.

The pledges of the special unsurpassed are explained as four kinds: when there are no longer any differences between killing and reviving, or between giving and taking, or between sexual intercourse and celibacy, or between truth and lies.

As for observances, guarding, and the manner of protecting [pledges] and so forth, one is to remain unmoved from the state of a purified mind, [262] free from extremes, and to guard them without transgression.

The three kinds of observances are for individual liberation, the heroes of everlastingness, and the Greater Vehicle of the secret mantras. Individual observances are for those who want peace and happiness for themselves only. Observances for the heroes are aimed to accomplish the unsurpassable for oneself and others. It is the opportunity for everyone to gain the nature of the enlightened ones through the use of mantras and visualization. The exalted ones exist to generate in individuals the three vows, respectively, and so forth.

As for those belonging to the others [and their practices], their generation is uncertain. The marks of the rules regarding the protection of the pledges are varied. These rules are followed in order to release the essence of the non-produced intrinsic mind. It is the pledge of the great protection of the primordial.

When the mantras and the vows are generated in the continuum of a being for the necessity of individual liberation, one will get to the intermediate state of the house of the gods. When the mind of the mantra comes to interrupt the stream of the pledges, they become useless for leading the traveler on the path. If one then asks whether this relates to the practice of non-involvement, there is no absolute necessity to rely on individual liberation. Individual liberation itself breaks down. The vows of the heroes of everlastingness are necessary. When they are acquired through the gradual process described above, the essence of the vows, above and below, unify. Then the pinnacle of realization becomes one.

If this is statement is accepted, then one could say that these distinctions [i.e., individual liberation, the heroes of everlastingness, and the secret mantras] contradict this unification, for distinctions would mean that the stream of consciousness would be many.

If one responds: "Aren't ornaments laid out in variety?"

If this is accepted as the mode for the transformation of the deities, then there will be no elimination, as they will be extensively filling the abodes above, and each will be equally filled with details. The gait of the goose demonstrates this with its dangling feathers.

The general and the superior pledges have three particularities: the attitude for realization, the method that guards with unobstructed purity, and the sole uncontrived inherent mind that is the intrinsic wisdom confirming this.

The outer sign is that oneself and others will be released from desire and hate. The internal sign is that whatever one is intent upon will be spontaneously realized. The secret sign is that non-production will begin to shine purely. The defects of fixation, partiality, straying, and sidetracking will stop through the consciousness that protects the unhindered primordial. Thus, in regard to these pledges that protect the primordial, if there is rejection and acceptance of defilements and virtues, then there is no protection and there is no protection of the primordial. Is this not any different from the lower vehicles?

Someone said that where there is no protection of the pledges, it is just the same as the common vehicle, and not different. This is the mode of conventional means. There is nothing in it concerning ultimate wisdom. Therefore, these two arguments pose no damage.

It is the same for the secret pledge on the root of life. Concerning temporary conditions and finality, qualities and increase, if these are inseparable from the pledges, then view, meditation, action, and fruition would be generated as [mere] continua [in cyclical existence].

The three kinds of activities of the profound are effected for the welfare of oneself, for the welfare of others, and for the welfare of both. The meaning of the scriptural transmissions and the meaning of the traditional lore are in the end transformed into gems. The welfare of beings is divided according to the mark of the activities.

There are three types of capacities for activity according to the traditional lore and the meaning of the scriptures: the superior, the middling, and those of inferior capacities. They are further divided into the extensive, middle-sized, and abridged activities.

If the object to be pacified is not placated, then it becomes the same as a wild antelope pursuing a mirage. When it is an activity under the mark of the wrathful deities [263] and there is no success with fierce activity, then it is said to be similar to progressing toward the border of a dangerous passage. For that reason, these two, peaceful and wrathful deities, are two.

The secret collections and so forth teach that in order to thoroughly purify for the welfare of oneself and others, one must accomplish the activities of the wisdom beings and their enlightened bodies. The Nine Activities of the Agate Gem[225] that transform limits are divided among the nine vehicles. These are accomplished for taming beings according to what is appropriate to each one.

There are three types of activities to benefit beings: the sequential activities for the ritual recitation, appropriate action according to the mind of each individual, and last rites to fulfill the two welfares [i.e., of self and others].

The ritual recitations can be divided in three for the full extensive recitation, along their different sorts, or to affect extreme cases (*las kha mtha' bsgyur*).

There are two kinds of extensive ritual recitations: those divided according to the traditional lore and those divided according to the Jewel tradition.[226]

The bundle of the former [i.e., the traditional lore] is further divided into two: a group of texts on of the activities of accomplishment and another group of texts on the deities as objects of accomplishment.

There are two sections on appropriate action according to the mind of each individual: the divisions of the extensive, the middle-sized, and the abridged; and the Rolling of the Mound.[227] The abridged meaning consists in rolling these three aforementioned divisions together. They are rolled into one category and are used appropriately for the perfection of the body and so forth.

As for those that are rolled into one category, this is about the great self-liberation from the five poisons. Awareness does not apprehend the eight modes of consciousness, and when one emanates, there is no attachment to marks. The female wrathful deities, the Balmo, annihilate enemies and obstructing spirits, while the heroes, the spirit generals, and the great kings accomplish the reversal of obstacles and their minor causes by themselves.

The nine workings are the Nine Activities of the Agate. They are said to be the divisions of the nine vehicles. Everything without exception is the mind's expressive power that is unborn, is free from elaborations, and acquires what is extensive.

The four kinds of secret activities, the activities of the one perfected awareness following the direct recognition of pristine cognition and self-awareness, are the aims of the activities accomplished. Once realization has arisen, the twofold goal has been attained.

As for the activity of integrating various elements on the path, what is the use of activities that are spontaneously accomplished by themselves? One has to view the world and its contents as the immeasurable palace and the deities. The three doors, the hand-seals, the recitation of the mantras, and the concentration formulas are the plays of pristine cognition. Sights and sounds, offerings and ornaments, and enjoyments are conceptions made complete within pristine awareness.

The activities of the union of method and wisdom, which are union and liberation and so forth on the path of the practice of the profound, are the unceasing play of those endowed with marks. It is the practice from the point of view of the unstoppable method among the ornaments. These are practiced without fixation, undifferentiated, by non-observable insight. These are sealed by the non-produced intrinsic mind.

As for the activities that bring the welfare of beings to completion, there are those of the nine vehicles, the four actions, and so forth. Whatever objective is to be accomplished for the welfare of others, it is completed for the sake of beings to be life-bearing of realization, because in order to accomplish the two goals, there must be no wavering or decline. This is illustrated by the sounding of the melodious voice of the cuckoo.

Hand-seals, the generation matrix (*snying po*) [i.e., the mandalas], the concentration formulas, the ritual items, the chanting, and so forth, are accomplished without differentiation. What is to be accomplished, the accomplishing agent, and the mode of accomplishment [264] are considerations of the unborn intrinsic mind. They demonstrate the undifferentiated processes of generation and perfection, the mind of enlightenment, the continuum that transcends the ordinary mind, the Great Perfection.

The outer sign of success is that the welfare of beings is fulfilled without partiality. The inner sign is that the variety of manifestations is liberated through the bodies of the deities. The secret sign is that the welfare of beings is fulfilled without partiality. Hanging onto a reality connected with effort and struggle stops. There is no more grasping for a self and fixation on concreteness. Effortlessly, fundamental reality is settled through accomplishment. Supreme and common supernatural accomplishments are quickly attained. The two benefits are brought to completion. Not discarding fading results, the welfare of self and others is carried out until the end. The objects observed are not differentiated within the knowledge of the expanse.

If the enlightened body of the deities and so forth were to reside in the meaning of reality, then the mode of subsistence would come to be conceptual proliferation itself. There is no such abiding because there is no object of meditation. That above-mentioned meditative concentration would come to be artificial.

Someone said that in this present mode of basic disposition, the body of the deities and so forth are not established but they arise with the dynamism of the playfulness of conventional reality. The contention of these two conditions [i.e., basic disposition and conventional reality] here is not proven.

The deities and the immeasurable palace all exist because of the playfulness of the mind. But the intrinsic mind is non-arising and devoid of constructs. When considering the genuineness of mind and awareness here, they are not equivalent.

Conventionally, there is no inherent nature in the manifestation of the gods and goddesses. The mandala is the unimpeded dynamism of playfulness. Ultimately, there is intrinsic mind only because it is non-arising and unconditioned. The illusory freedom from the constructs of conventionality and the consideration of the ultimate here are not equivalent. The essential point here is that one's mind abides in the deity. This non-duality is the great intrinsic being because of the assertion that it is itself in the mandala. The wisdom beings and the pledges are not equivalent to the assertion that the self produces the others. Consciousness becomes familiar with the processes of generation and perfection.

Are there concepts or no concepts? If there are concepts, there are no concepts when primordial wisdom is acquired; it is just-as-it-is. If there are no concepts, although the body of the deity appears as really having its own presence, it is not established.[228]

If someone asks about how these changes effortlessly occur by themselves? Studying and reflecting produce thoughts corresponding to reality due to the ability to produce non-conceptual primordial wisdom. That contention here poses no harm to the argument.

Ordinary mind, according to one's capacity, may be by itself without conceptuality. This tantra teaches the two modes of production, and shows the transitory path of the profundity of power and the supreme path of liberation of the knowledge-holders.

The outer empowerment is the acquisition that counters hanging onto true existence. The inner empowerment liberates from clinging to the marks of the aggregates. The secret empowerment makes the untainted arise in the mind. The very secret empowerment brings up the realization of self-liberation.

As such, there is application through belief on the first ground. When the ten grounds are overcome with the great bliss of intrinsic reality, one is released from objects, from the ignorance of conceptualization, and from the clinging to taking on evil destinies.

The knowledge-holders' eight paths to liberation are the realizations of the perfected ground, the three enlightened bodies. [265]

The two results of the profound

There are two results of the profound: the necessary temporal and the ultimate.

One acquires the supreme and common accomplishments thanks to the teachings on the qualities of the five families. Each is explained in five points.

The five common accomplishments are: long life, the body, goods, blessings, and the power over illusion.

The supreme accomplishments are the five realizations of the view, meditation, performance, pledges, and enlightened activities. There are also these three: the enlightened body of inherent nature, primordial wisdom, and the actions of enlightened activities.

The five enlightened bodies are the body of ultimate reality, the body of perfection, any emanation body, the body of primordial wisdom, and the body of real enlightenment. These can be further expanded into forty-five.

There are the eighty-six limitless contemplations and so forth, such as having the clarity of everything and all possibilities, intrinsic emptiness, the intrinsic equanimity of the mirror, realization regarding everything, and accomplished activities. These five are further elaborated to sixty-one. They go beyond 84,000 expressions.

The activities that are careless spontaneity are of these four kinds: pacifying, increasing, overpowering, and wrathful activities. Each and every enlightened body, speech, and mind corresponds to the five emanations of the activities and qualities that come to 84,000. The actions of enlightened activities go beyond understanding.

In short, the necessity of the profound is to have the strength of the families of the enlightened body of the deities in this life, and having acquired intrinsic perfection—the eye of primordial wisdom—to extensively perform the activities of spontaneously realizing the two meanings. And this is because one will attain the supreme body for oneself and others.

* * *

The subject matter of the profound has been put together above. Thus, as for faulty explanations, I confess openly to the relatives of the objects of refuge. May virtuous merit be dedicated to all beings pervading space, so that they will obtain the supreme body of union!

Those who follow this will achieve supreme victory over demons. May they raise the banner of the teachings!

The fully ordained monk Sherab Gyaltsen, who was in retreat at Menri, composed this writing in a solitary place. May it be virtuous! May this be auspicious!

PART 5

The Practice Manual of the Revelatory Tradition of the Great Perfection from Zhangzhung

Drutön Gyalwa Yungdrung (1242–90)

Warning! This manual of meditation introduces practices on the control of breath as well as positions and movements of the body that may be hazardous to one's health if carried out improperly. As mentioned later in the main body of the text, these instructions need to be followed with care and under the guidance of someone who has previously mastered these exercises.

1. Preliminary Practices of the Great Perfection from the Revelatory Tradition from Zhangzhung: Devotional Prayers

I PAY HOMAGE TO Kuntu Zangpo, who has accomplished the two benefits for myself and others.

The preliminaries in Bön consist in nine successive meditation practices in accord with traditional lore.

Meditation on impermanence

Here is the recitation on impermanence.

Alas! Since phenomena of cyclic existence have no essence, it is pitiful for one to be grasping at a true existence. Grant the blessing of generating in our mental stream the realization of impermanence!

Its pleasures last only a moment—how pitiful that one hopes for permanence in this continuum of existence! Grant the blessing of generating in our mental stream the realization of impermanence!

One wanders forever, and even now, one still does not worry! It is pitiful for one to be deluded without reason! Grant the blessing of generating in our mental stream the realization of impermanence!

There is no pleasure in the toils of cyclic existence. Now, it is pitiful to be ignorant, one must be alarmed! Grant the blessing of generating in our mental stream the realization of impermanence!

One still does not sum it up so that one can be dissuaded from this life! It is pitiful to still hope for real permanence! Grant the blessing of generating in our mental stream the realization of impermanence!

There comes a time when there is no more life. It is pitiful that then, one still wishes for permanence amidst impermanence! Grant the blessing of generating in our mental stream the realization of impermanence!

Whatever time brings is unraveled, and more of this will definitely come! It is pitiful that people still hope for life and death! Grant the blessing of generating in our mental stream the realization of impermanence!

Everyone experiences the moment when one sees and hears death! It is pitiful that one then still hopes for a permanent self! Grant the blessing of generating in our mental stream the realization of impermanence!

Everything changes among circumstantial phenomena. It is pitiful that one still hopes for the one permanent thing! Grant the blessing of generating in our mental stream the realization of impermanence!

When one ponders, there is no moment without distraction. It is pitiful that one is lazy and procrastinates! Grant the blessing of generating in our mental stream the realization of impermanence!

The moment of death is uncertain, yet one still likes to rejoice in flavors. It is pitiful that what one likes is to rejoice in rags! Grant the blessing of generating in our mental stream the realization of impermanence!

All beings are active in their respective places, only once. It is pitiful that they wish to escape from this!

> Grant the blessing of generating in our mental stream the realization of impermanence!
> Grant the blessing of remembrance after death!
> Grant the blessing to turn away from the depths of attachment!
> Grant the blessing to generate renunciation in our mindstream!
> Grant the blessing of the realization of the cause of everything!

Confession

Here is the recitation for the confession of wrongdoings.

> [268]
> What non-virtuous actions and wrongdoings
> I and other sentient beings present have done in all of our previous lives—
> our deeds, our pretenses, our impulses, and our own intentions,
> actually conjoined with thoughts and spoken words,

deeds done for the sake of these [pretenses, impulses, etc.], per-
    formed or not,
all proper and faulty deeds, subtle or brash,
carried on as such or changed, even the slightest,
not forgetting any, and remembering,
for my ordinary mind subsumes all
the wrongdoings and defilements—
in the presence of the most excellent objects of refuge,
we confess them all profusely with a fearful mind, full of sor-
    rows and regrets.

Generation of the mind of enlightenment

Here is the recitation for the generation of the mind of enlightenment.

Just as the victorious noble ones and so forth of the three times
have manifested the power and brilliance of their virtue in order
to bring enlightenment to sentient beings, so am I likewise generating the mind of excellent enlightenment.

Going for refuge

Here is the recitation of going for refuge.

To the lama Shenrab who is the glorious source of the three
    bodies,
to the blissful ones of the three times, overall protectors of wan-
    dering beings,
to his images, relics, and scriptures that are the receptacles of his
    body,
to the most excellent Shen of the ten directions that are the
    lamps of his teachings on the path to liberation,
to these four holies I prostrate and go for refuge!

Offering of the mandala

Here is the recitation for the offering of the mandala. One recites this first
to set up the practice.

*Nama a kar sha ya ni shag sa le sang ngeye soha! Drum ri ti gar ma
la Ho! A Yaṃ Raṃ Maṃ Khaṃ Druṃ shag sa le sang ngeye soha!
Chopur sa le ha lo seng!*

Ema ho! These countless fantastic and marvelous pure realms are beautiful, washed of impurities, bright, made of heaps of perfect jewels. The excellent mountain, encircled by the seven mountain ranges, the Sea of Enjoyment, the continents and so forth, the wish-fulfilling tree, the sun and the moon, I contemplate these and enhance them with jewels, the eight auspicious articles, the seven precious jewels, butter lamps, flowers, pure water, and incense to wake up the gods, and gold, turquoise, copper, iron, crystals, pearls, white sugar, objects pleasing to the sight, harvests, grains and nectars, ornamented fabrics, silk ribbons, pleasant and attractive offering substances, beautiful shapes and pleasing sounds, fragrant aromas, delicious tasteful flavors, and objects that are soft and harmoniously interlaced.

My fortune, together with all that is seen and heard, are presented along with my mind's imaginings. Life, body, ornaments, and enjoyments, power and so forth, these articles as vast as the sky of the universe, I offer to the lama, to the enlightened ones, and their sons!

I and others pray that, for the sake of wandering beings, you partake of these, and that you care for us at all times.

I pray to be filled with experiential realization and accomplished conviction, and to have the wisdom of self-awareness arise. [269]

I pray that conquerors, their sons, and friends of the teachings reside continually and always with us.

I generate them before [me] to entreat them to accomplish the accumulation of virtue.

I rejoice in all collections of merit.

May the precious words, the miraculous teachings of the Teacher, disseminate and fill the ten directions!

May we be endowed with the manner of conduct of the spiritual heroes throughout all our lives!

May there be great masters that lead me to virtue!

May each [being] have a place of refuge from everything in the end!

May we quickly attain the great intrinsic self, the protector!

May I accomplish the welfare of beings with compassion, method, kindness, and exalted knowledge without ever complaining!

I dedicate whatever virtue may arise and accumulate toward the acquisition of the body of intrinsic Suchness!

May we quickly attain the highest result, the certainty of the incontrovertible!

Here is the concise formula.

Om A da da de de chö chö sa le ha lo seng![229]

Meditation on the processes of emanation and absorption

Here, then, is the transmitted recitation for producing the emanation and reabsorption.

I bow to the glorious one that leads all sentient beings in cyclic existence to liberation, the foremost teacher Shenrab!

Akar ame dutrisu nagpo zhizhi melmel soha![230]

Akar means that all aspects of intrinsic mind are pure.
Ame means that pristine cognition manifests clearly in light.
Dutrisu cleans evil destinies.
With *nagpo*, evil deeds and obscurations are purified.
With *zhizhi*, the sufferings of cyclic existence are pacified.
Melmel is the mind endowed with happiness.
With *soha*, wrong views and Rudra are overcome.
This is the essence of pacifying suffering.

May evil destinies in cyclic existence be shaken from their depths, and beings become enlightened in the expanse of intrinsic reality!

Offerings

Following this is the recitation for offering the collection of one's illusory body.

Kyeho! Please receive the offering of my body!
My four limbs are a support, planted to form a tripod for a piercing flame. My precious skull serves as a vast cauldron. My flesh, blood, body heat, breath, skin, fat, ligaments, and nerves, all the constituents of my senses, and my wind channels, are all

arranged inside with my limbs, together with the various sense faculties and sense organs, internal organs, the viscera, the skeleton, teeth, nails, and body hair.

They are divided in three parts: the pure, the impure, and with my own essence, and all these are made to expand greatly.

I bring as offerings this inferior body, which is contaminated.

I ask you, who have a realized view, to grant me exceptional experience and insight this very moment!

Having been cleansed without exception of karmic debts from my creditors as well as of all damages, may I acquire the excellent mind of enlightenment!

May the blessings of this boundless and extensive dedication liberate beings from the view of clinging to a self!

Supplication

Hereafter is the recitation for the supplication.

> Emaho! I pray to the pure lamas, the continuum from which
>   arise the three bodies, [270] and all the enlightened ones!
> I pray to the compassionate lamas to bestow empower-
>   ments, oral instructions, and procedures with victorious
>   compassion!
> I pray to the lama-guides to introduce me to the steps along the
>   path to liberation from this perilous circle of transmigration!
> I pray to the lamas of the lineage to engage in leading me from
>   the lower paths to that of the supreme holders of the lineage!
> I pray to the lamas who resonate with this lineage to destroy, by
>   means of the higher knowledge, the continuum of the self in
>   cyclic existence!
> I pray to the root lamas to sever the innermost illusions with
>   profound instructions!
> I pray to the enlightened ones of the ten directions to be of assis-
>   tance to beings as if they were their own children, with love
>   and knowledge!
> I pray to the host of inner and outer deities to send forth emana-
>   tions of all kinds with compassion and means!

I pray to the knowledge-holder heroes to expand our wisdom
through realizations on the path and the grounds!
I pray to the mother and sister sky-goers to bestow accomplishments, empowerments, blessings, and power!
I pray to the oath-bound protectors to entirely disperse inner
and outer obstacles!
I pray that once I have been freed from the ignorance of the
duality of subject and object in cyclic existence, pristine cognition of self-awareness may arise!

Emaho! As to the lama who manifests the three bodies,
Kuntu Zangpo is the sphere of the bliss of the body of reality.
Shenlha Ökar is the body of perfection endowed with the major
and minor marks.
The victorious Shenrab is the priest [*gshen*] endowed with the
four compassions.
Tsemé Öden is the priest that leads beings.
Trulshen Nangden is the priest of the self-arising self-awareness.
Barnang Kujung is the father of the play of consciousness.
Zangza Ringtsun is the mother of cyclic existence and
emancipation.
Chimé Tsukphu is the chief who teaches the subjugation of
demons.
Sangwa Düpa is the lord of the profound tantras.
I pray to the nine transmitters of the intent of the victorious
one!
I pray that once I have been freed from the ignorance of the
duality of subject and object in cyclic existence, pristine cog-
nition of self-awareness may arise!

The lamas who transcend[231] to greatness in the natural state are:
Yongsu Dagpa, who was without partiality, like the sky.
Lubön Banam, who was immovable, like the expanse of space.
Tridé Zambu, who remained in the state free from delusion.
Banam Kyölpo, who abided in the midst of non-conceptuality.
Trishö Gyalwa, who cut off the glimmers of the objects of
consciousness.
I pray to the five priest-subduers of beings!

I pray that once I have been freed from the ignorance of the
   duality of subject and object in cyclic existence, pristine cognition of self-awareness may arise!

[271] The lamas who focused on the essential points of the six
   topics[232] are:
Rasang Samdrup, who was pure from the very beginning, like
   the sky.
Darma Sherab, who was immovable, like space.
Darma Bhodé, who spontaneously achieved the three bodies.
Zhangzhung Triphen, who was able to apprehend without loss.
Muyé Lhagyung, who remained in the condition without
   foundation.
Mashen Lekzang, who attained the pure flawless body. I pray to
   the six unequaled heroes!
I pray that once I have been freed from the ignorance of the
   duality of subject and object in cyclic existence, pristine cog-
   nition of self-awareness arises!

The lamas who liberally taught the ninefold advice are:
Gyershen Takla, who arose with intent without production.
Rasang Yungdrung, who truly realized the mind of
   enlightenment.
Sechen Yungphen, who had control over the essence of duality.
Gewar Döndrup, who was truly an enlightened one and
   attained the supreme.
Gyerpung Gephen, who abided in the condition of
   one-pointedness.
His son Gegyal saddled himself to the ultimate.
Zhangzhung Namgyal realized self-awareness.
Mugyung Karpo destroyed the illusion of subject and object.
Horti Chenpo was a haughty priest (*gshen*), learned and
   accomplished.
I pray to the nine accomplished knowledge-holders!
I pray that once I have been freed from the ignorance of the
   duality of subject and object in cyclic existence, pristine cog-
   nition of self-awareness may arise!

The lamas that are the four crown ornaments of instructions are:
Dönkun Drubpa, who taught the view without foundation.
Rasang Phengyal, who practiced clarity and bliss.
Guru Sega sustained the practice of equanimity.[233]
Dawa Gyaltsen took hold of intrinsic reality as his natural place.
I pray to the four greatly accomplished translators and scholars!
I pray that once I have been freed from the ignorance of the
    duality of subject and object in cyclic existence, pristine cog-
    nition of self-awareness may arise!

The lamas, source of advice, counsel, and sayings are:
Tapihritsa, who is the emanation body of exalted knowledge.
Nangzher Löpo, who attained the accomplishment of the
    prophecy.
I pray to the two kind emanations!
I pray that once I have been freed from the ignorance of the
    duality of subject and object in cyclic existence, pristine cog-
    nition of self-awareness may arise!

The lamas who were endowed with the marks of accomplish-
    ment are:
Gyalzig Sechung, who was free from the care of the prison of the
    physical body.
Mushen Tsogé, who was unceasing clear light.
Gyershen Dzotang, who demonstrated magical emanations and
    the marks of accomplishment.
Shötram Chenpo, who perceived any appearances as magical
    illusion.
Mugyal Lodrö, who cut off the twilight of cyclic existence and
    emancipation.
Pöngyal Tsenpo, who tamed the noxious *rākṣasa*[234] demons.
I pray to the six excellent fortunate ones!
I pray that once I have been freed from the ignorance of the
    duality of subject and object in cyclic existence, pristine cog-
    nition of self-awareness may arise!

[272] The lama meditators endowed with dignity are:
Gugé Loden, who rose in the transmission of the great bliss.

Pureng Kunga, who was skilled in obtaining liberation.
Naljor Sechok, who sustained the fundamental of spontaneity.
Chungji Muthar, who possessed the power over vitality.
Dewa Ringmo, who attained the accomplishments instantly.
Tokmé Shikpo, whose self-awareness was a rising sun.
I pray to the six realized ones, destroyers of illusion!
I pray that once I have been freed from the ignorance of the
     duality of subject and object in cyclic existence, pristine cog-
     nition of self-awareness may arise!

The lamas who possessed the quality of non-partiality are:
Lhundrup Muthur, who resounded with the intent of the gener-
     ation and perfection stages of the tantra.
Shengyal Lhatsé, who dwelled in the condition of the Great
     Perfection.
Lhagom Karpo, who demonstrated true secret practices.
Ngödrup Gyaltsen, who was proud to have arisen in accom-
     plished realization.
Orgom Kundul, who was endowed with an unfailing memory.
I pray to the five greatly accomplished manifestations!
I pray that once I have been freed from the ignorance of the
     duality of subject and object in cyclic existence, pristine cog-
     nition of self-awareness may arise!

The authentic lamas for this revelatory transmission are:
Pangla Namshen, who is the priest leading beings.
Lungom Tokmé, who is the priest of self-arising self-awareness.
Nyelgom Trulmé, who solved illusion completely.
Nyakgom Shertsul, who cleared away the darkness of ignorance
     and covered defilements.
Uri Sögyal, who flourished in the demonstration of meritorious
     activity.
Dronya Söyé, who accomplished activities with spontaneity.
Gyagom Yerin, who demonstrated the intent of Kuntu Zangpo.
Gyatang Chenyi, who has been established in the natural state.
Lentön Sönam, who was purposefully learned and righteous.
I pray to these nine authentic lamas!
I pray that once I have been freed from the ignorance of the

duality of subject and object in cyclic existence, pristine cognition of self-awareness may arise!

The lamas who demonstrated the vehicles of the revelatory transmission, the mantras, and mind teachings are:
Kangtsa Tradar, who was a priest of self-illumination of self-knowledge.
Mönlam Lodrö, who obtained the accomplishment of realization of purification.
Khetsun Tretön, who proclaimed the sound of Bön, demonstrating without partiality.
Patön Nyipal, who showed the intrinsic self of the vehicles of mantras and Mind.
Gyagom Tensang, who was the priest for pith instructions for the Fire Mountain cycle.
I pray to these five lamas of the mantras and mind vehicles!
I pray that once I have been freed from the ignorance of the duality of subject and object in cyclic existence, pristine cognition of self-awareness may arise!

The lamas who impartially served the welfare of beings are:
Yangtön Chenpo, who was the emanation body of exalted knowledge.
Dampa Bumdzé, who was most familiar with the collection of scriptures.
Tashi Gyaltsen, who made servants of demons (*bdud sri*) and vampires.[235] [273]
Tokden Bönpo, who liberated everyone without partiality.
Gyaltsen Rinchen, who was loving toward beings as if they were his own children.
Jigchö Déshé, who liberated himself from clinging at a self.
Khetsun Gyalwa, who acted as a master holder of the teachings.
Ripa Sherlo, who was a priest teaching the canon of scriptures, tantras, and spiritual instructions.
Yeshé Rinchen, who was a scholar-priest and proud in accomplishments
I pray to the nine lamas, knowledge-holders of the canonical scriptures and the tantras.

I pray that once I have been freed from the ignorance of the
   duality of subject and object in cyclic existence, pristine cognition of self-awareness may arise!

The lamas who became liberated with the intent, like the sky,
   are:
Lama Gyaltsen, who was a priest-leader of beings.
Sonam Lodrö, who manifested true self-awareness.
Tengyal Zangpo, who knew the three times and was without
   defilements.
Tsultrim Gyaltsen, who explained and understood the natural
   state.
Ngari Sögyal, who was endowed with the nourishment of pro-
   found advice.
Tashi Gyaltsen, who realized the sameness of cyclic existence
   and transcendence.
Paljor Lhundrup, who was a priest of the profound path of Meri
   [i.e., The Fire Mountain Cycle of Gekhö].
Kunga Gyaltsen, who led beings through the four
   empowerments
I pray to these eight masters of the profound path!
I pray that once I have been freed from the ignorance of the
   duality of subject and object in cyclic existence, pristine cognition of self-awareness may arise!

The lamas endowed with loving compassion for the welfare of
   others are:
Tsenden Ripa, who was endowed with the nourishment of the
   profound.
Namgyal Kara, who selflessly spread love and knowledge.
I pray to these two lords of wandering beings.
I pray that once I have been freed from the ignorance of the
   duality of subject and object in cyclic existence, pristine cognition of self-awareness may arise!

The lama holders of pith instructions, the canonical scriptures,
and the tantras are:
Tokden Shepal, who spontaneously demonstrated freedom from
extremes.
Namkha Özer, who met others feeling deeply as if they were
sons or mothers.
Yungdrung Yeshé, who realized things as one, without
separation.
I pray to these three lamas endowed with the lineage of
transmission!
I pray that once I have been freed from the ignorance of the
duality of subject and object in cyclic existence, pristine cognition of self-awareness may arise!

The lamas who truly demonstrated the profound meaning are:
Rinchen Lodrö, whose qualities spread without partiality.
Sherab Gyaltsen, who was endowed with pledges and
empowerments.
Rinchen Gyaltsen, whose view and practices were completely
pure.
Namkha Yeshé, who was a priest and the source for the extraor-
dinary and the common [attainments].
Kunzang Gyaltsen, who spread widely the love and knowledge
of scriptures and reasoning.
Rinchen Gyaltsen, who was endowed with ethical behavior
without exhaustion.
Tsultrim Gyaltsen, who had the vision of the self, the intrinsic
mind.
Sönam Yeshé, who was a lamp of the teachings.
I pray to these eight lamas unequaled in teaching and life! [274]
I pray that once I have been freed from the ignorance of the
duality of subject and object in cyclic existence, pristine cog-
nition of self-awareness may arise!

The lama holders of the teachings on the three trainings[236] are:
Sönam Yungdrung, who conferred as offerings the three
trainings.
Shetsu Drungmu, who liberated enemies of the teachings.

Sherab Özer, who possessed the essential points of learning and
   righteousness.
Yungdrung Gyaltsen, who spread the teachings on the three
   precepts.[237]
Sherab Lodrö, who held on to the teachings on the three trainings for dear life.
Sherab Özer, who truly realized self-awareness.
Tsukphu Özer, who was pure in the aspects of the three trainings.
I pray to the seven lamas, the powerful lords of the three
   trainings!
I pray that once I have been freed from the ignorance of the
   duality of subject and object in cyclic existence, pristine cognition of self-awareness may arise!

The lama holders of the treasury and the nine vehicles are:
Yungdrung Tsultrim, who selflessly and widely spread loving-
   kindness and knowledge.
Rinchen Özer, who truly demonstrated the profound meaning.
Rinchen Lhundrup, who realized all desires spontaneously.
Sherab Tenzin, who shone with the intent of Kuntu Zangpo.
Sherab Wangyal, who cut off illusion completely.
Yungdrung Wangyal, who ascertained the tradition.
Phuntsok Namgyal, who illuminated self-awareness.
Sherab Gongyal, who knew the three times without defilements.
I pray to the eight confident and unequaled lamas!
I pray that once I have been freed from the ignorance of the
   duality of subject and object in cyclic existence, pristine cog-
   nition of self-awareness may arise!

The lamas who demonstrated acceptance of the natural state are:
Nyima Tenzin, who demonstrated the non-difference between
   consciousness and space.
Choklé Namgyal, who self-liberated from cyclic existence and
   emancipation.
Sherab Yungdrung, who gloriously illuminated the teachings to
   beings.
Sangyé Tenzin, who became liberated in one single manner into
   the natural state.

Tenzin Tsultrim, who genuinely realized non-foundation.
Phuntsok Lodrö, who turned whatever appeared into ornaments [i.e., into blessings].
Gyalwa Lodrö, who was liberated from cyclic existence and
emancipation in his mind.
I pray to the seven who were liberated from everything,
impartially!
I pray that once I have been freed from the ignorance of the
duality of subject and object in cyclic existence, pristine cognition of self-awareness may arise!

The lamas, haughty in their accomplishments of the secret and
mind teachings, are:
Tenpa Lodrö, who achieved the intent of the great space.
Nyima Wangyal, who was released from his physical body into
the realm of the gods.
Sherab Lodrö, who truly realized the awareness of the
primordial.
The root master, who is the emanation body leading transmigrating beings.
I pray to these four noble ones for their activities!
I pray that once I have been freed from the ignorance of the
duality of subject and object in cyclic existence, pristine cognition of self-awareness may arise!

[275] The certitude that arose in the mindstream of these lamas
consists in:
The universal ground that is without foundation and is completely pure from the very beginning.
Awareness that is self-luminous, free from faults, and uncovers
defilements.
Sound, light, and rays that express the dynamism of self-
manifested mental perception.

These are the devotional prayers in stages of this particular experiential lineage, the limbs of pure perception composed for later generations by the
priest of Dru, Gyalwa Yungdrung. May one be associated with these and
may virtuous goodness increase! [276]

2. Prayers to Lord Tapihritsa, Emanation from the Heart of Kuntu Zangpo

EMAHO! EMANATION FROM THE heart of Kuntu Zangpo of crystal colored light, undefiled and lustrously clear, issuing rays of light in the ten directions.

Unadorned and naked, you are the purpose of the essence of the original state!

Through the two knowledges[238] and compassion, your purpose is the welfare of beings.

The heart nectar of the blissful ones is the Great Perfection, the most excellent of all.

It is the sublime peak of the vehicles, the heart of the tantras, the oral transmission, and pith instructions.

The base is the natural state, while cyclic existence and emancipation are delusion and liberation.

As sounds, lights and rays, and faults and qualities become self-evident, having illuminated all the darkness in the mind of beings, one realizes suddenly that the path and the grounds are primordially empty and without foundation.

Experience and true realization free the mind from cyclic existence and emancipation.

The results make the three bodies settle into space.

To you, Tapihritsa, leader of beings, I pray single-pointedly with devotion!

I request you to bestow empowerments on me and other wandering beings!

Pacify outer, inner, and secret obscurations!

Once liberated from ignorance and the delusion of self-clinging, self-awareness will truly manifest, and view and practice will be brought to completion.

Primordially empty and without foundation, beyond the mind, this is the great meaning!

This very moment, please bestow these on me, Lord Tapihritsa, guide of wandering beings.

We pray that you seize, with your compassion, the six kinds of wandering beings and remove them, and myself, from the continuum of existence!

Gyerpung Nangzher Löpo ardently offers these prayers to the emanation Tapihritsa. [277]

3. The Stages of the Preliminary Practices of the Revelatory Transmission

TO KUNTU ZANGPO, WHO is the all-encompassing leader of transmigrating beings, manifest self-awareness, I pay homage!

Host of knowledge-holders, masters, sky-goers, and guardians of the precepts, you emit the light of compassion from all ten directions. I pray that you unravel the sealed decree on the essential points of the profound path!

The scripts on the revelatory transmission had no arranged organization. I pondered these with loving-kindness in order to purify them from bewildering opacity. So I have prepared these in accord with the meanings [of the tradition] and collected them together. I pray for the forgiveness of the sky-goers and the guardians of the precepts!

These scripts are the heart-essence of Kuntu Zangpo, the oral instructions from the blissful ones, the direct advice of the noble knowledge-holders, the quintessence of all advice, the innermost mind of all revelatory transmission, the finality of all intent, the pinnacle of all realizations of the view, the summit of the scriptures, the essential point of all tantras and spiritual writings, the essential extracts of all pith instructions. They are the feat accomplishments of Gyerpung Nangzher Löpo. These are the visionary experiences of the greatly accomplished ones named above. The ones that have done the above are guides on the path. They are the final advice on the profound essential points of the Great Perfection. They eradicate the reach of delusion and bring out what is concealed. They actualize naked awareness while offering appearances and mind as its mother and sons. Having cast away the falsity of cause and effect, one vigorously achieves enlightenment. Once one leans on the continuum of practice, one's faith will be refreshed through demonstration. One severs the inner glimmers, and then the outer signs of achievements will manifest.

The four topics of the text

This advice, from the revelatory transmission of the Great Perfection from Zhangzhung, discusses the following four topics: the general understanding of the view, the direct instructions to the inner pith advice, the vision of the naked secret awareness, and the innermost conclusions on the very secret natural state. The key points are extracted from all of them, and the significances are then summarized.

The task of disclosing the hidden arcana is taken up in three ways: First, one's continuum must become completely pure, and one engages in the purification practices following the stages of the preliminary practices. Next, once the continuum ripens, one is released and engages in the main practices. Finally, one continues practices to actualize the realizations in the continuum of being with the ancillary practices that follow. [278]

Preliminary practices: purification

The first topic, purifying, is threefold: disciplining one's continuum with the three preliminary practices of general importance, cleansing one's continuum with the three preliminary practices that are universal and common, and purifying activities of one's continuum with the three preliminary practices that are distinctively noble.

1. Disciplining

The first topic, disciplining, is threefold: it consists in the directives on empowerment with blessings conferred on one's continuum, directives on impermanence in order to thoroughly discipline one's continuum, and directives on the confession of defilements in order to purify one's continuum.

Receiving blessings with empowerments

First, one retires to an isolated place where one's virtues will be increased. The method is to separate oneself from mistaken understandings and diversions. Then one becomes the devoted and faithful disciple of a lama who is endowed with all the marks and has the highest view and intent. As part of the circle of his entourage, one will request instruction, empowerment, and oral transmission. One's merit will be increased by the practice of the elements of the rituals. The benefits are that outer and inner obstacles will be pacified and one's wishes will be accomplished and included in the above supreme objects of refuge. These are the instructions on receiving empowerments. *Uya maro!*[239]

Impermanence

Second, on the practice of disciplining one's continuum, one sits upright with the five postures of the body,[240] with the gaze focused between the eyebrows. One's mind concentrates on the fact that all compounded phenomena are impermanent, everything in reality changes, all produced things disintegrate, all composite things fall apart, all beings that are born will die. When one thinks about and analyzes any of these, one understands that there is no essence residing in any of them. But one has seized them as real, as true, as permanent, and as existent! You then think to yourself how pitiful this is!

Endless wanderings

One has roamed endlessly. Again and again, whatever comes, one just wanders. One has no regrets about past actions but is not satisfied with suffering. One consults the inevitably of the above, but no matter what, one will not be associated with these facts and one continues to grasp for permanence. You then think how pitiful this is!

Inevitability of loss

One imagines that one sits on a beautiful throne in a royal castle in the middle of many cities. All the threefold excellences are present there: power, amusements, food, gifts, enjoyments, and circles of attendants. Then the entire assembly turns away and rebels. All food and gifts are carried away. People close to oneself are all killed. The cities all collapse. Alone, with nothing in one's mouth and hands, destitute, one is cast away. One meditates on impermanence for one session.

Illness and decay

Again, [279] one imagines that one's upper body dries out while the lower part is rotting away, affected by a disease that is excruciatingly painful and unbearable. Then, consider that relatives and loving friends all gather and cast divination, have religious ceremonies performed, and look for medicine. Even with the aid of the nine perceptions[241] and the ten recollections,[242] one still moves toward the utmost limit [i.e., death]. One meditates on impermanence for one session.

Death

Then one imagines that one arrives at the moment of death, like the fading moon in the sky. Every month it fades into the ground. There is no spell to cast away the experience of death. Nothing may arise or anything may arise in one's awareness. One meditates on impermanence for one session.

Dying and the intermediate state

Then, imagine that the strength of the four elements slips away. One has no power over one's desires and subsistence. One's outer faculties stop and consciousness is expelled. The appearances of the intermediate state, the illusory body, arise, and the corpse that remains is discarded. Subsequently, food and gifts are set up and people cry out and wail. One meditates on impermanence for one session.

Wandering and lost

Then one imagines oneself empty-handed, stripped naked, having nothing, alone with no companions in an unfamiliar country, moving like a ghost. There is no place to stay, no place to go. One can bring anything back to mind, but one cannot find anything to do. One meditates on impermanence for one session.

The others that have died

Furthermore, one thinks of those one previously saw and heard about who have died. One thinks that they were just like oneself, could understand things, and were able to speak. One meditates on impermanence for one session.

Never-ending changes

Moreover, one imagines how worldly pleasures and disappointments, rich and poor, friends and foes, good and bad, high and low born, come to be. One meditates on impermanence for one session.

Time's inexorability

Furthermore, one imagines the number of eons, years, months, and days and how these periods of time come to be. One meditates on impermanence for one session.

Inevitability of death

Also, one imagines that the place of death, the time, conditions, and manner are uncertain. But in any case, death is certain. Therefore, the moment of death is unpredictable, but the time comes, no matter what. One meditates on impermanence for one session.

No one escapes death

Furthermore, one thinks that there is no one in the past who has not died. It is impossible that anyone in the present will not die. In the past or subsequently, not even one has ever been spared. One meditates on impermanence for one session.

Thus, one meditates and cultivates one's three doors side by side with this set of enumerated meditation sessions. At a certain point, the power of one's ordinary mind will turn away from cyclic existence and the notion of impermanence will be generated in one's continuum. The illusory nature of all appearances will arise. Fondness to attachment to true existence will be cut off. Worldly appearances will arise according to what one is familiar with. The *Six Transmissions* [142.6] says:

> As it is imputed, thus does it arise.

And again:

Since it is by generating the notion of impermanence in one's continuum that one achieves remembrance of death, all priests [*gshen*] of succeeding generations take time for it. [280]

The great soul, Drenpa Namkha, said: "Meditate following these nine ways [of thinking] about impermanence and death."

These were the instructions on the exhortations on provisional meaning. *Uya maro!*

Confession

Third, one generates the lamas and blissful ones in the sky in front of oneself, and then they merge into oneself. [One recites:]

I, and all sentient beings in successive lives until now, have been wandering in cyclic existence. We have been tortured by cleansing our measure of karma. We are bound by grasping at a self. This process of cleansing gives us no opportunity for happiness, and since we have persisted in committing these deeds, there are no limits to our wrongdoings. Thus I, and all sentient beings, have committed great sinful deeds from lifetime to lifetime, such as the five inexpiable sins,[243] the five nearly inexpiable sins,[244] the four heavies,[245] the eight perverse actions,[246] the nine deceptions,[247] the ten non-virtuous[248] actions, and so forth. I committed these wrongful and non-virtuous actions myself, or urged others to do so. Afterward, I rejoiced in these and presented them to others and so forth. All these actions committed by myself or all other sentient beings, all past actions that I was unaware of, that I did not know of, or had done because I was ignorant, all of these combined, of which the omniscient ones in their heart clearly know, I offer before their eyes this confession with a mind full of shame and remorse!

Having generated a fierce remorse toward all these non-virtuous actions performed in the past, like goose flesh where flesh and bones are separated, one offers confession. From now on, one inclines toward having an assuredly stainless mind and becomes a follower of the Greater Vehicle. One abandons entirely the host of sinful and non-virtuous actions. One must engage in the ever-subtle application of the roots of virtue. For all those beings in the realms of the world who engage with purity in compounded and non-compounded virtues are exceedingly amazing! One must rejoice exceedingly in one's mind's continuum as well as offer confession. The *Lore for the Accomplishment of the Very Pure* [17.77.5] says:

> One must confess each and every non-virtuous and wrongful action, and one must bind oneself to all virtues.

Then, having cleansed all past non-virtuous and wrongful deeds, one becomes fit for the Greater Vehicle. If this is not the case, then it will be similar to writing a letter on oiled paper. One will not be a fit vessel for the Greater Vehicle.

These were the instructions on cleansing and confession. *Uya maro!*

2. Cleansing one's continuum with the three preliminary practices that are universal and common

Second, the three preliminary practices that are universal and common for cleansing one's continuum consist in [281] establishing the foundation for unlimited compassion with the generation of the mind of enlightenment, establishing the foundation with faith and devotion by going for refuge, and establishing the foundation of pure self-manifestation by offering mandalas.

Generating the mind of enlightenment

The first, generating the mind of enlightenment, is as follows. Before one's eyes, in the sky, one generates the place of refuge with the blissful ones present and recites the following:

> Not even one among all sentient beings has not been my father, mother, son, and friend. Yet they wander in cyclic existence. I feel compassion toward those who experience suffering, and I generate an uncontrived wave of fierce compassion.
>
> But now, despite my lack of ability to create the cause of their welfare, and because of this, I will achieve the intent of the enlightened ones in this body for the welfare of all sentient beings who are as numerous as the sky is vast.

I will endure to lead them until cyclic existence is empty. Past and future exist in relation to the welfare of sentient beings, so from this very moment onward, I intend to acquire the result of enlightenment for the sake of sentient beings.

These were the instructions on the generation of the mind for the welfare of others. *Uya maro!*

Going for Refuge

Second, one imagines that before one's eyes, in the sky, sitting on thrones supported by lions, on a lotus, sun, and moon, sits the root master with the appearance Kuntu Shenlha [i.e., the divine Shen of All]. In all directions as well as further in front are the host of tutelary deities, deities of the outer and inner cycles, the enlightened ones of the ten directions, knowledge-holders, heroes, lamas of the lineage, sky-goers, and oath-bound protectors sitting on arrays of clouds and rainbows. In the rear are all the pure realms of the ten directions. The excellent supports of the enlightened body, speech, and mind are set upon mountains and rock-like faces, present and vivid.

Then one's body is multiplied by eleven million, hundreds of times. Each of these leads a great many sentient beings. Imagine that all together, with a great clamor, they take refuge with great faith and devotion, single mindedly focusing their three doors.

One then recites the relevant words.

These were the instructions on taking refuge with devotion. *Uya maro!*

Offering of the mandala of the universe

Third is the offering of the universe. The best materials for the ritual articles are gold and silver. The middle quality is metal for bells, or bronze. The lowest kinds are wood and clay. Their shapes have to be made with the right measurements and their ornaments have to be in the right numbers.

First, one thinks that one will be cleansing defilements and one's own and others' obstructions. One then recites well:

Oṃ namaḥ a kar shag sale sang ngeye svāhā![49] [282]
Oṃ! Hommage! How white is the A! Clear! Pure! Svāhā!

Then, while still holding the mandala implements in one hand, one recites the following while setting up the heap of material [i.e., jewels, pearls, stones, etc.] in the center:

> *Brum ri ti gar ma la ho!*[250]
> *Brum!* Here is the first excellent mountain! Ho!

One then recites the following, starting directly in front (representing east), going around to the right (counterclockwise), while placing the material in the eight directions:

> *A yam ram mam kham brum shag sale sa ngeye svāhā!*[251]
> Clean! Clear! Pure! *Svāhā!*

One recites the following while placing the material in the center of the four quarters:

> *Chöd phur sale ha lo seng!*[252]
> Directional Pegs! Clear! Rising as beautiful flowers!

Thus, these seventeen heaps must be arranged appropriately and beautifully while thinking of their qualities and defects, without crowding them, or dispersing them, or scattering, or decreasing their numbers.

Then in front, in the sky, one imagines the objects of refuge gathering like clouds above, or like the shining stars showing everywhere. As for the mandala, the best way is to generate it as equal to the sky, the middle, as the trichiliocosm,[253] and the lowest, as our universe [lit. "the universe of Tshangs pa"]. Below is the golden stainless ground on which are arranged the Excellent Central Mountain Meru, the seven mountains, the four continents, the minor eight continents, and the circles of the iron mountains. Inside that are the host of clouds of offerings carrying the eight auspicious items and the seven precious jewels, desirable attributes adorned with sights, sounds, smells, tastes, and tangibles. There are wish-fulfilling gems, enjoyments for gods and humans. One thinks of these as being on inconceivably vast clouds everywhere.

One's body is multiplied by eleven million, hundreds of times. Each of these lead sentient beings, waving like crops, who are then transformed into gods and goddesses. Whichever offerings arise, they are offered everywhere.

While doing this, one imagines that whatever is perceived becomes an offering. One completely offers attachments from the point of view of non-attachment, while praying to generate in one's continuum the exceptional realizations of the Greater Vehicle, the natural state. One offers the words while offering this prayerful resolve.

When one later collects the material from the base of the mandala, it is not done haphazardly. One gathers things from the left direction (clockwise) until the end. Following this, one does the dedication.

Morning and evening, one meditates as above, that one's body becomes the realms and fields of the mandala. One's sense consciousness is transformed into innumerable goddesses making offerings. One imagines doing this while giving offerings, and, as above, what is perceived is offered.

These were the instructions on mandala and clouds of offerings. *Uya maro!*

3. Directives on the confession of defilements in order to purify one's continuum.

Third are the purifying activities of one's continuum with the three preliminary practices that are distinctively noble:

1. The purification of obscurations and defilements with the recitation of mantras and the process of emanating and reabsorbing.
2. The gradual-manner offering with groups of illusory bodies to collect merit.
3. The gradual steps for casting prayers in order to receive blessings.

The purification with recitation of mantras and emanating-reabsorbing

First, in the sky in front, [283] one's root lama sits in the aspect of Kuntu Shenlha. He is surrounded by the outer and inner tutelary deities, the enlightened ones of the ten directions, knowledge-holders, heroes, lamas of the lineage, sky-goers, and oath-bound protectors. While one prays, numbers of them are generated that fill the intermediate space in the sky, which becomes full. They then merge together.

Then, while intoning *Hum* many times, innumerable lights emanate from them [the *Hum* syllables] and completely pervade the sky. The bodies of all sentient beings transform into aspects of rainbows. One imagines that these are all being summoned from all directions and are collected into one's own sense consciousness. One imagines that the entire outer universe becomes rainbow light and all of my emanations from the ten directions are summoned and absorbed.

Next, when sounding *Phat!*, one's body together with its array of consciousness grows larger and larger until what is encompassed by the heavens is within one's body. One's own sense consciousnesses similarly encompass this. One's body transforms into the innumerable realms of the universe. The magical displays of awareness generate innumerable sentient beings in the three realms. One thinks of purifying the measure of karma of each and every one. Then one meditates on this with yearning and compassion.

Then, the hearts of the blissful ones generate masses of fire, lightning, and thunder. Innumerable flashes of lightning emanate. Instantly, all the obstructions and defilements of sentient beings are suddenly burned with the roaring sound of the wind of primordial wisdom. Just like shooting stars, they vanish while all the pure realms burn. All the obstructions and defilements of sentient beings burn up in purple vapors. Again, primordial wisdom makes the sound of drizzling water, and just like shooting stars, it cleans the black slime of the obstructions and defilements of sentient beings.

Then, A letters in one's heart spread everywhere, manifesting sometimes in subtle or in coarse forms, and then go and melt on the crown of each and every being. All sentient beings transform into Kuntu Zangpo. Then, as the light spreads over them, all the pure realms transform into the great immeasurable mansion. With the bodies of the gods, they all perform the activities of the Great Seal. Their intrinsic minds receive the empowerment, the intent of the profound, free from elaboration. One imagines a melodious, self-sounding voice proclaiming the murmur of the *Dutrisu*[254] mantra. One counts these recitations to one hundred, one thousand, ten thousand, or one hundred thousand and so forth, remaining silent [i.e., repeating in a silent murmur]. Afterward, [284] one remains sitting, developing non-perception while dedicating this for the enlightenment of sentient beings. Due to these practices, if one maintains the effort at all times, one's defiling karma from reincarnations will be unable to endure. They will be like chaff dispersed by the wind or will go away like dew touched by the sun. One should continually make efforts.

These were the instructions on the recitation of mantras and the cleansing of defilements. *Uya maro!*

The gradual-manner offering with groups of illusory bodies to collect merit

Second, in the sky, in front, are generated lamas, blissful ones, tutelary deities, a host of gods, sons of the victorious ones, heroes, sky-goers, and oath-bound protectors, together with arrays of the glorious protectors of the eight classes and the beings of the six kinds in inconceivable numbers. They are everywhere. Suddenly, directly in front of one's heart, there is this great innermost cavity of primordial wisdom that spontaneously bursts open. All at once, it opens up from the inside and sends forth a droplet of light. This is one's own conscious-ness. It fades just like a spark of fire, then rushes out. Dissolving into light, it transforms into the bluish wrathful deity of primordial wisdom with one face and two arms, brandishing a sword with the right hand. Severing one's own four limbs with the sword, it arranges them to form the hearth of a fire. Trim-ming off of the top of the head, it places it on the fire, where it becomes wide and spacious. Inside the head, it puts one's own flesh and blood, skin, entrails, and all internal organs, which it cuts into many small pieces, filling it up. Then these are multiplied and expanded. This wrathful one transforms into innu-merable offering goddesses. These seminal (*dwangs ma*) goddesses offer clouds of offerings to the gods of primordial wisdom. This ocean of the ambrosia of regenerative fluids they have swirled together aptly and completely satisfies the glorious protectors. This [ocean of ambrosia] in so many ways transforms the murky worldly attributes, and the eight classes [of spirits] and the beings of the six kinds are appeased. It delights the conquerors, satisfies the oath-bound pro-tectors, and appeases the gods and demons (*srin*). The transmigrating beings of the six kinds are satisfied. One then imagines these illusory bodies departing this gathering of sacrificial offerings, and one offers the words.

With these words, understanding karmic debtors of the body and mind leave of their own accord. Defilements are all simultaneously cleansed. The two accumulations are joined together. This is the advice on receiving the simultaneous accomplishments.

These were the instructions on the sacrificial offering that accumulates the two accumulations. *Uya maro!*

The gradual steps for casting prayers in order to receive blessings

Third, on the crown of one's head one generates one's root lama who sits radiant in his perfected body on a seat of lotus, sun, and moon. On top, above, sit all the lamas of the lineage, one above the other. They are surrounded by arrays of the outer and inner deities, the enlightened ones of the ten directions, knowledge-holders, heroes, mother and sister sky-goers, and oath-bound protectors. [285] One must have great and single-minded devotion and faith, and must not be inconsistent, irregular, or tenuous. One must essentialize the practice wholeheartedly. The generated beings disperse as lights of primordial wisdom and come to dissolve into the crown of the head of all sentient beings and oneself. They transform into streams of ambrosia that really purify accumulated obstacles from past and present lives, all obstacles and defilements. These lights, white, red, and dark blue, dissolve into the three places of the body, and one obtains the attainments of the enlightened body, speech, and mind. These [lights] confer the blessings of the empowerments. One imagines that one has obtained all their enlightened qualities—the highest view, the realization of equanimity, their activities, and their knowledge. One prays with yearning and devotion so that one's awareness will become strong and steady. And therefore one receives blessings and vigorously clears away impediments. The enlightened qualities are obtained and accomplished with speed. Experience and realization become abundant and one is seized with kindness.

These were the instructions on praying with devotion. *Uya maro!*

Common general practices

Second, one practices the common forms of the nine gradual practices of Bön multiple times, every day, from morning until dusk. Assuming a good position, one meditates fiercely on impermanence, again and again. Then one confesses one's defilements, generates the mind of enlightenment, goes for refuge, offers mandalas, recites mantras, accumulates merit, and recites all these prayers three or five times. Afterward, one dedicates all these pure activities toward enlightenment for the sake of wandering beings. Thus one practices in this order without confusion.

At noon, one does prostrations with the cycle of daily liturgies and so forth, or engages in other activities according to one's circumstances. During this period, one remains within the boundaries of the practice space. One does not mix with others. One does not break from mental concentration. Furthermore, one must not bring about distaste for oneself by destructively spinning one's thoughts. The *Eye of the Needle* [15.457.6] says:

Do not waver [away] from the words of the teacher over time.
Do not forget these truthful words! Hold on to them! Hold on
to them!

Drenpa Namkha in his *Lamp Dispelling the Darkness of Provisional
Meaning* [5.6] says:

Defiling oneself by cheating oneself and being pleased is a disser-
vice to oneself.

The signs of Heat

Second, when one is practicing these ancillaries of the preliminary practices
[286] irregularly and haphazardly, only for a year, or saying so, there won't
be signs of Heat. One should involve one's three doors single-mindedly. One
practices observing that the body and mind are entangled. Then, the qualities will arise. The signs are said to be like the sun rising, or swimming, flying,
climbing upward, reaching an island with flowers, the sounds of swimming,
or seeing the face of the tutelary deity, eating delicious food, and purging
vomit, blood, or insects. Prophesizing will arise, the body will become light,
and awareness will become quintessential (*dwangs*). These will be experienced in reality, in visions, or in dreams. These signs are of superior, middling, or lower values. One holds to the essential points until beginningless
conviction arises.

Thus these pithy instructions are the essentials from the intent of the
innermost Great Perfection. They are advice on the main points of the
essentially profound revelatory transmission. These are the limbs of the
preliminary practices of the path of initiation. I dedicate the merit of these
instructions on closeness joined with striving, for the sake of all wandering
beings on the path to everlastingness. May worthy vessels obtain realization,
experience, and liberation!

These were the graded preliminary practices for cleansing and purification
from the the revelatory transmission of the Great Perfection. May there be
auspiciousness and virtue! [287]

4. The Main Practices on Dark Retreat, Advice on the Profound Points

TO KUNTU ZANGPO, who is the all-encompassing leader of transmigrating beings and manifest self-awareness, I pay homage!

Second, the intermediate section consists in the graded principal practices that ripen and liberate one's continuum. These are threefold: (1) At first, the mind that was not seized is seized. (2) Midmost, when mindfulness is not present, one makes it present. (3) Last, when self-awareness is not limpid, one makes it limpid.

1. Preliminary Instructions

Concentrating the mind

First, the *Lamp*, (221.5) says:

> The mind that is mindful must be fixed on the light.

The *Dark Blue Paper* says:

> The sphere of light is directly taught as cyclic existence.

Therefore, there are three points: the key points on the body, the key points on the gaze, and the key points on training.

The key points on the body

First, it is said that the five postures of the body control vitality. In order to restrain the lower channels and winds (*rtsa rlung*), one must sit cross-legged.

Because the vertebrae must be bound together, they must be kept straight. In order to seize the main points of exercising restraint, one places the hands in the position for meditative equipoise. Because one must break the urges to speak, the neck is slightly bent. In order to cast away and tame the dichotomy of subject and object, one's gaze must be straight ahead. Furthermore, the left hand is placed on top of the right pressing down below. The ring fingers are slightly bent. These are the essential points. At that time, one regulates oneself by striving to be aware of the position of the body, the muscles of the legs and arms, and so forth.

The key points on the gaze

Second, one stares to the front, neither near nor far. There is a nimbus surrounding in various degrees the sight where awareness is focused. One's vision must not go up and down, nor left and right. The eyes must stare intensely, piercingly ahead, like boring a hole in a path, or passing a thread through the eye of a needle, or shooting an arrow at a target. There must be no physical expressions, nor efforts to speak, nor external mental considerations on the past, but only vivid alertness. One must gaze straight, clearly, steadily, single-mindedly, naturally.

The key points on training

Third, at that time, if saliva drips from the mouth, or tears come up from the eyes, one should naturally let them drip. One is training body and mind to bring them to their natural state. As for the length of the periods of practice, in the first morning session one should recite the *Saleyö* mantra[255] two hundred times, three hundred times in the afternoon session and so forth, or raise the amount according to one's commitment.

Again, during morning and afternoon sessions, one considers the existence or lack of existence of the enlightened ones, sentient beings, good and evil, and the one that is looking and the one that is meditating, all of them remaining as such. One tries to understand their intrinsic characteristics, their color, physical appearances, essences, causes and conditions, and engages oneself in seeing what they are like, the one sitting, over and over again.

Again, one first engages in looking at their origins, their mode of abiding in the middle, and the mode of where they are going in the end.

Again, is the origin [of all these] outside or inside the body? One engages in investigating up from the crown of the head [288] and down to the tip of the feet. One works out the cases of their faults and qualities, and effectively severs their roots with the mind.

Thus, what if the practitioner has a flow of memories while in a state of calmness? The best practitioner who is devoid of thorough grasping sees them just like a tortoise who remains immobile in a bronze basin. Whatever the case may be, that one has no fear.

The middle-level practitioner remains undistracted, like water flowing through a metal tube staying continuously in the middle.

The lower one is like a bee sucking nectar, where only small changes occur.

While in a state of tranquility, signs of spiritual progress will become full. One will go into meditation where no characteristics will appear. However, if the signs are not complete, one should fixate one's awareness on the sky. While in the middle of this, one can utter suitable neutral sounds like *Huṃ* and *Hṛi*. Furthermore, if there are difficulties, for these activities are exhausting, there are instructions on recovering from exhaustion. One can also make use of visual supports such as a mirror, the tuft of hair on the deity statues, and so forth.

Moreover, for those whose fire and wind elements are greatly dominant, signs will come early but will subsequently be obstructed. For those predominantly of the earth and water elements, signs will come later but subsequently will become favorable. It is easy to explain this interconnectedness as symbols and means, but it is difficult to get rid of daily unpleasantness from distractions.

When a master possesses this ambrosia, it is impossible not to arrive somewhere. Moreover, once one has successfully captured the king of awareness, one will come headlong into the soldiers of mindfulness, the source of the mind. Conceptions are obstructions, the fall of the wild dogs of delusion. The outer tantra, the *Clearing Away of the Limit to the Primordial Throne*, in its section entitled "Moon" (246.6) says:

> Seize the king, and its base will be annihilated. It will bind down the wild dogs of suffering.

The *Six Transmissions* (141.4) says:

> Mind pays attention to characteristics. More peace, more peace

will pacify conceptions! More clarity, more clarity will make primordial wisdom clear!

These were the instructions on the grasping of the mind for characteristics.

2. Dark Retreat

The practices for part two change an unsteady mindfulness into a steady
one. The place of meditation itself must be completely dark. It can be a hole
in the ground, or a cave in a cliff side, or a straw hut. Its ceiling must be elevated and broad, the faces of its walls well made. The light openings must be
closed to the outside. The inside must be broad. There must be three doors
arranged at angles and there must be no light coming in from the windows
at all. It must be made pleasant.

The mode of practice

The method of practice is threefold: how to meditate, how to train, and the
mode of emergence in one's continuum.

How to meditate

First, the *Little Nails* (310.3) says:

> Having abandoned distracting activities with the three restraints
> (*sdam pa gsum*), the three loosening activities will bring the ordi-
> nary mind into tranquility.

This mentions three points: having restrained the activities of the body, one
becomes tranquil without activity; [289] having restrained the expressions
of speech, one becomes tranquil in non-expression; and having restrained
the attachments of the mind, one becomes tranquil, transcending thoughts.

Essential points on the body

First, all of us assume a body from a previous life to this present one. We
engage in activities, whether pure or impure. We act on senseless endeavors, taking us solely into suffering. Having circled in delusion as an object

known and used by demons, one will neither engage one's body in the three unwholesome activities[256] nor seek out business outside of what is in the scriptures; no running about angrily, no thrashing around; not indulging in food, arts and crafts, nor even engaging in virtuous activities such as performing prostrations, circumambulations, hand signs, yogic exercises, and so forth; nor engaging in rest and relaxation, nor giving up or delaying one's practices. One will not engage in these activities as such, since the various activities of the body disturb the psychic channels. They agitate the winds. Having disturbed the mind, they will then obstruct the generation of non-conceptual concentration. Relaxing as such will help control the channels. It will calm down the winds. Having fallen to the ground, one will attune one's consciousness to abiding in non-conceptuality.

Thereupon, it is said:

> The essential point on the body is that the five postures help control the vitality of the body.

One sits crossed-legged, both hands in equipoise, the spine straight, the neck slightly bent, the eyes looking straight forward.

Essential points on speech

Second, all of us, from previous lives until this day, have expressed ourselves verbally for good, for bad, or in the middle. Whatever these endeavors of meaningless expressions were, they brought only suffering. From today on, I will abandon the four non-virtuous speech actions[257] and so forth, that are impure—that are not according to scriptures, such as joking, laughing, advising, meaningless leisurely chatter—as well as what is virtuous, such as the repetition of mantras, recitations, charms, singing, and all spells. I will rest in the mode of mute inexpressibility.

Accordingly, one will become intimate with not moving one's breath to stir verbal expressions, shake the psychic channels, or stir up thoughts, and will have the insight that generates non-conceptual concentration.

Essential points on the mind

Third, all of us, from previous lives until this day, have intentions that we remember as good, bad, or in the middle. Whatever these endeavors of meaningless thoughts were, they brought only suffering exclusively. And because I have circled in delusion, from now on I will refrain from the three non-virtuous unwholesome thoughts,[258] from the five poisons and so forth that are not according to scriptures, and all analysis, considerations on the natural state, or the cause that created the present, or existing conceptions on goodness; nor will I indulge in meditations on the gods while emanating and reabsorbing seed-syllables, or concentrate on characteristics. [290]

I will be entirely without conflicting emotions such as desires, hopes, fears, doubts, and indecision. I will engage in loosening and relaxing, in transcending thoughts with mindful awareness in the depth of the universal base.

Accordingly, there will be no movement from one's impulse to ride the horse of the internal winds along the path of the channels. This would obstruct the production of non-conceptual concentration. Consequently, one's natural condition will repeatedly correct and modify itself so as to be naturally in its place, without errors, spontaneously. It will suddenly stay free from any roots and will be without a basis. One will not decide the future from the past, nor look for the past in the future. One will be in one's own condition in its own place, natural, free from roots, aware in the depth of the great pervasive universal base. There won't be any tremulous thoughts about food and making things, but only presence in accord with one's innate condition.

How to train during dark retreat

Second, practicing for the first time, if one does long sessions, there will be drowsiness, agitation, drifting attention, and so forth. If it goes too quickly, experience and realization will not be produced. After reciting rounds of the *Saleyö* mantra a hundred times, each day the session can be increased by an increment. In between the sessions, one can meditate generating strong devotion and compassion. Do not eat garlic, onions, spices, and so forth, or food that is not bland, or whose elemental nature is partial, or contaminated food, or funeral food. Food and clothing must be paid equal attention. Do not sit close to fire or in the sun. Cut out going in and out. Primordial cognition is lost during noon and midnight or when one is fatigued, and one should then take a little break. One should not be separated from a lama who is learned in the method and endowed with the essentials. If laziness and neglect arise, one should enumerate one's defilements and offenses and urge oneself to make intense efforts again and again. One must not be discouraged by loss but rejoice and be inspired by self-development.

Experiences

Third, practice consists at first in generating in the mind a state of calm abiding. Then, it is to have the natural state arise during the state of calm abiding. Finally, it is to acquire firmness and stability when the state of calm abiding finally arises. The *Twenty-One Nails* (309.5) says:

> Having dissolved impurities in space, pure essence shines as light.
> Having expelled the dust from the mantle of the mind, naked
> awareness arises. Having cleared away the host of clouds of conceptuality, pristine cognition is unveiled.

Impurities are the causes that stir conceptions. Being mindfully aware of the ordinary mind will cause all impurities to dissolve into the universal basis. Pristine cognition is the self-arisen quintessence that arises as clear light, just like pure water without impurities. Having removed the dichotomy of subject and object, which is similar to a mantle covering, the naked pristine cognition of awareness arises. It is like removing the clothes of an infant. Having purified thought processes of good and evil that are like clouds, one discovers the natural color of the universal base. It arises in one's continuum just like the clear sky.

Furthermore, one can use a pale light in the dark house. What is outer or inner then manifests with a neutral brilliance. [291] When the lower five elements are thus analyzed, little of them appears. Setting in motion nonconceptuality in consciousness generates in one's continuum a concentration that does not let go.

These were the instructions on calm abiding without characteristics. *Uya maro!*

3. Practices with open sky and sunlight

Part three consists in advice clarifying what is unclear, and is threefold: general practices, distinctive practices, and important advice for enhancement.

General advice on general practices

First, the *Lamp* (221.2) says:

> The great ocean was moved up and fixed at the edges by the dark
> iron mountains. The mindful mind is held by light. Moving
> impulse will be subdued by sound. The dynamism of awareness
> will be purified by rays.

There are three points on this: adjusting the five essential points of the body,
paying due diligence to the conditions on the path of method, and the mode
of vision dependent on one's continuum.

Adjusting the five essential points of the body

First, the place for the practice of meditation is very important. Though the
inside may be completely illuminated by a great fire, it still will not be able
to shine light on everything. But a small lamp in a great darkness will be able
to shine bright. This path and method are extremely swift. Therefore, there
must not be even the smallest hole that lets light into this great darkness.[259]
It is vitally important that it should be a hermitage in an isolated place. If
these elements are not all there, one can cover the eyes. The method is to use
a curtain or a part of the hand to bring about darkness.

It is a very important to correct the position of the body. This incarnation
has hands and feet, yet if these are not disciplined, then there will be no
clarity. If the body is twisted, then the four limbs and four channels will be
twisted.

The big toes are drawn in to bring the two legs close to one's chest and
imprison the calves by the elbows. The two ring fingers of the hands press
down on the big toes. The two elbows are kept perpendicular and the two
shoulders crouch over the legs. The tongue connects to the palate and the
mouth is managed. The nose is managed into an angry frown, and the space
between the eyebrows is brought together with the nose. The eyeballs are
turned up and the eyelids are closed. The two ears are kept erect. The spine
is vertical and kept straight, the neck and throat are collected. The left foot
and hand are kept on top [of the right foot and hand]. The stomach and its
"knots" (*gsus pa shigs pa*) are continually pulled in.

The gaze is foremost. Awareness is present in the channel pathways. If the gaze is not trained, the qualities will not really manifest. For that reason, morning and evening, one focuses the gaze one cubit in the air above the crown of the head. This is the gaze of the fierce one turning the wheel. During the heat of the evening, the gaze should come down slightly to the eyebrows and be fixed about sixteen fingers high in the air. This is the gaze of the lion. At midday, it should be focused just a little in front of the eyebrows. This is the gaze of Sangwa Düpa.[260]

Foremost is the main point of the mind. If awareness is not trained [292], the qualities will not arise for real. Besides, at that time, one should abruptly eradicate thinking about the past, pondering about the future, or engaging any circumstantial thoughts and memories that come up suddenly, and keep a sharp consciousness. One should remain clear-sighted without base and roots.

Breathing and internal wind-energy

The point about winds that is very important for luminous and clear awareness is that awareness has light in itself. One must differentiate between pure or impure winds, otherwise the sign of Heat will not arise suddenly. For that reason, engaging in the first session of practice, one must expel the poisons from the winds. After that, life-sustaining winds and awareness are wrapped up together and directed to the crown of the head or between the eyebrows. The breath is powerful and should move in and out gently through the two nostrils.

In particular, when the elemental earth wind is on the move, or when it is time for the elemental space wind to be on the move, controlling the posture of one's body and gaze is very important during meditation so that wind-energy will transform and grow. Then, a particular wind will form and start moving, and it will grow larger when moved through the left nostril.

In the evening, before adopting a sleeping position, and upon waking for the day, one will practice the yogic exercises and the key points on breathing and so forth. One will use the hand method to make the breath move through the left nostril. The reason is that the left is the root door to pristine cognition and cuts off the streams of conceptuality and suffering.

Paying due diligence to the conditions on the path of method

Second, on the length of the practice session, at first, meditation sessions are short but numerous. Every day one makes changes and prolongs the sessions so that, in the end, one will be able to remain in calm abiding. Only then will the yoga in dark retreat become of foremost importance. One must remain in the state of equal meditative contemplation when eating or on the path of practice. Pristine cognition will diminish by a small amount at noon and midnight; therefore, at these times one should relax. In general, a good outcome depends on zeal and diligence; there should be neither laziness nor indifference during practice.

The mode of vision dependent on one's continuum: special insight and visions

Third, when one has practiced like that, impurities should have been separated from the pure quintessential awareness. One continues to follow the main points on mind and awareness. The gates of the channels become open and the causes and conditions can be completed so that the fire-wind can flare up. This is the natural radiance of awareness dwelling in luminous clarity. Apart from that, there is no method for this rising. The *Six Essential Points* (215.3) says:

> The base is abiding in the middle of the heart. The [visualized energy] streams along the pathways through the channels and rises up to the gate that is the lamp of water. In the center of the conch house is the circle of the brain. The middle channel is called "Tsangri Purlang."[261] This channel then divides into two peaks. The gate of this channel is like a fully opened sesame flower; this is an equivalent expression for the gate of awareness. It is said that the five lights rise up through the downward mouth of this channel and look like the eyes on a peacock feather.

The *Lamp* (221.4) says:

> In the darkness of Radiant Darkness (*mun par zer ldan*), one can see an immeasurable mansion of shining light.

There are many modes of arising, but for the beginner, the visions manifest externally. [293] The *Instructions of the Gods of Revelation* (505.5ba5) says:

When the elemental earth wind enters the central channel, apparitions are like smoke. Similarly, when the elemental water wind enters, apparitions are like a mirage. When the elemental fire wind enters, apparitions are like fireflies. When the elemental air wind enters, apparitions are like the twilight of dawn. When the elemental space wind enters, apparitions are like the sun rising in the sky or like pure sky. These arise as vivid experiences or as reality.

When the elemental earth wind arises, internal consciousness is in a supported and relaxed mode. Similarly, when the elemental water wind is present, body and mind feel happy, pliable, and supple. With the elemental fire wind, one feels light and trifling. With the elemental air wind, one feels light, high, and wildly vigorous. With the elemental space wind, one feels spaciousness and brilliant purity, and no apparent obstruction emerges.

Furthermore, the inside and outside of the retreat room become clear without obstructions. The body, inside and out, becomes clear—flesh, blood, channels, tendons, and ligaments. Visions can arise that are explained as day visions—with these, one may feel delight and become conceited. If they do not arise, then one has to continue practicing with zeal.

These were the instructions on special insight and clear light. *Uya maro!*

Distinctive practices

Second, distinctive practices are twofold: the practice of purification by concentrating on clarity and the brightness of space, and the practice of purification by concentrating on the self-luminosity of a lamp.

The practice of purification by concentrating on clarity and the brightness of space

The first one is fourfold: the place of practice, the timing of practice, the method of practice, and the methods to arouse clear light and experience visions.

The place of practice

The place is a ground where one can see the vast open sky: the summit of a high mountain, the middle of a wide field, or a lower place, such as the roof of a house or under the eaves, and so forth.

One's body must be propped up and hidden. The spaces above and in front must be vast. The space must be particular in that light arises and is manifest. One must find a method so that the light of the sun does not shine directly on one's body or head. The *Instructions of the Gods of Revelation* (4.3) says:

> The method for gazing is to put up a half-house or a shelter, and one should stay in a healthy place or a high mountain. One meditates gazing at the vast expanse of the sky. In the evening one looks east, gazing for longer and longer sessions.

The timing of practice

Second, regarding time, once signs from the dark retreat practices above have begun to manifest to the ascetic practitioner, and one has acquired some stability in concentration, one can then meditate from early morning when the sky becomes light, until late in the day when darkness begins its cover, with a little rest at noon. The *Instructions of the Gods of Revelation* (4.2) says:

> Early morning, when there are no clouds and a fresh breeze, one can gaze at the pure sky. In the evening, looking east, one gazes for a longer session.

The *Dark Blue Paper* says:

> In the morning, one looks in the direction of the powerful water spirits. In the evening, one looks in the direction of the scent-eating spirits. [294]

The method of practice

Third, on the mode of practice, the *Lamp* (222.1) says:

> Universal clarity is the mirror of the mind. Its lights support visions in the sky.

Concerning the practice of the five main points on the body, it should be done in the same way as the points explained above on adjusting the position of the body. As for the gaze, on the point of the sensory activities, the *Instructions of the Gods of Revelation* (6) says:

> One gazes like a crouching lion or like Sangwa Düpa.

Whichever of these two methods one employs, one should engage in joining the three spaces.[262] One should focus on the space "in between" that is the emptiness in the sky of this external world. One should train the subtle channels that are empty inside, like one's sensory perception in relation to the sky. One should sharply bring forth the emptiness of intrinsic mind, which is the very secret meaning of the mark of space.

On holding the breath, the main point on breathing, the *Dark Blue Paper* says:

> One must cast aside subject and object, while the main point
> with awareness is to hold the breath.

One should engage in the practice of the threefold not-letting-in:[263] Do not let in the breath of vitality from above. Using the horse of awareness, one holds the breath while combining breath and awareness. Do not stop the breath forcefully. Breathing should be balanced and should come in and go out softly. Do not pass out while engaging with hidden breathing. Particularly during the time of the elemental air wind, one does this very gently.

Following this, on the main point of the pledge of non-separation, the *Root Commentary on the Little Nails* (4.2) says:

> You must contemplate without closing your eyes so that you can
> recognize the universal base without conceptuality.

The practices of the three immovables: If the body does not move, the channels are not moved; therefore one does not move, so that action and agent are not in contradiction. If the channels do not move, so that the eyes do not move, the mind won't be moved. Refrain from blinking, squinting, and side-glances. Afterward, one should be conscious of what arises before the eyes. This is the main point about the eyes.

Then, for the main points on the three relaxations, the *Little Nails* (310.4) says:

> With the three methods to stabilize meditation, one apprehends
> the ground of the mind.

The *Root Commentary on the Little Nails* (4 *ba* 5) says:

> Using the three methods to stabilize meditation, one applies this:
> refrain from fabrication and remain fresh.

[And]:

> One remains continually stable in the great natural state.

One must be set in the immediacy of the mode of reality of the universal base. The *Root Commentary on the Little Nails* (4 *ba* 5) says:

> One is established in reality without modifying it.

The methods to arouse clear light and experience visions

Fourth, on the mode of arising, the *Lamp* (221.3) says:

> One will see luminous visions in the darkness. These will be seen
> as mirages and nets of rays, like the filaments of a spiderweb.

In that way, when one gets into practice, these arise as the natural radiance of one's inner awareness on the path of the channels. They arise as visions in midair. These are signs of the winds of the five elemental powers, [295] and they appear like gray-colored ribbon-like signs, flickers, flashes, and lightning, or like crystal mirrors, or wings of bees, or golden eyes, smoke, or clouds, or like dyed garments, mirages, water ripples, and change their color to that of the sky.

Furthermore, coming from the natural radiance of the five wisdoms, various reflections arise, such as rainbows, or woolen-like silk brocades woven with full blossoms or with configurations of nets, latticework, checkerboard patterns, triangular motifs, reliquaries, lotus petals, and so forth.

Visual appearances will arise in inconceivable forms, such as glass-colored droplets of awareness scattering like quicksilver, droplets looking like tents made of five-colored lights, sets of five rings of light circling, bright silver chains of compassion rays stretching out, chains of metal links, or arrangements of canopies, parasols, or something like scattered hair combs in mid-air, and so forth.

One piece of advice on the main points regarding the path and method is to make primordial cognition and the blissful wind gather slightly in the central channel. The wind united with the mind will slightly open the door of the channel. By the force of practice, the quintessence will be slightly separated from impurities. While the clear light of insight begins to make visions arise externally, the primordially pure naked awareness expels [impurities] from the inside. This will be the time for experiences and realizations to shine. Internal and external qualities will be generated in one's continuum as one, and at that time it will be very important to be zealous in practice.

These were the instructions on the concentration on the sky and clear light. *Uya maro!*

Daylight practice

Second, the practice of concentration on the self-illuminating lamp has four topics: the place of practice, the time for practice, how to practice, and the mode of the arising of the qualities of practice.

The place of practice

First, having experimented with the general and distinctive essential points, the signs of Heat will come to one's continuum. Then, in an isolated place where one can see clearly, such as from the edge of a rooftop, or where one has a wide vision of the rising sun's rays, or on a cliff or a rock face, or a tree, or in a cave, and so forth, one practices in a retreat where there are no broken pieces of stone, or where there is a ravine for shelter in the shade.

The time for practice

Second, as for the times, one practices in the early morning immediately after the sunrise, and also on the verge of the sunset, or whenever the wind and clouds are not obstructing.

How to practice

Third, on how to practice, the *Lamp* (222.2) says: [295]

> Mindfulness is the spear of the mind. With it, one should stab
> through the shield of light visions.

The great soul Drenpa Namkha said: "The fortunate being with good karma
should cut off all illusions from the rays of the sun.

In these four topics on practice, there are three further points: the postures of the body, the gazes, and the main points on the mind.

(1) Postures of the body

First, the essential points on the body are the five postures that will tempo-
rarily generate clear light: the awe-inspiring pose of the lion, the reposing
elephant, the crouching ascetic, the swaying goose, and the crystal wild goat
scaling a cliff.

The awe-inspiring pose of the lion

For the first position, one should squat like a dog. The top length of the
feet are on the ground while one is kneeling. The feet carry one's weight.
Hands are perpendicular to the feet and stretched out between the knees,
supported by the palms on the ground. The waist is straight and one sits still
while the lower winds are slightly controlled. The neck is bent.

The qualities of this posture are that the winds are suppressed from moving and the mouth of the central channel is open a little to pure realization.
Externally, visions arise immediately. Internally, the intent toward the transcendence of the ordinary to the body of reality arises.

The reposing elephant

For the second posture, one lies facing down, one's weight supported by
the two elbows and the two feet. Both hands support the jawbone, and the
knees should not touch the ground.

The qualities of this posture are that it suppresses the winds that are moving while it stops longings, desires, and clinging. It uproots phenomenal

existence and has extensive power, like that of the elephant. Externally, the pure realms arise perfected, while internally, experience, realization, and so forth, are generated.

The crouching ascetic

In this third posture, the soles of the feet are planted firmly on the ground. Sitting in an upright posture, the calves are drawn in by the inner elbows, and both hands seize hold of the middle of the forearms. The lower winds are bound, and the feet support one's weight. The neck is bent only slightly.

The qualities of this posture are that it ripens and increases the heat of the inner fire while it pacifies the coarse and subtle discursive thoughts. Externally, it gives rise to the manifestations of the emanation bodies. Internally, it produces particularly clear visions in one's continuum.

The swaying goose

In the fourth posture, the right elbow is planted firmly on the ground, the right cheek supported by the palm of the hand. The right leg lies over the left leg, in the manner of pressing the buttocks together. The legs are slightly bent at the knees, the right calf on top of the left leg. One gazes ahead.

The qualities of this posture are that the winds having been well received in the central channel, now illusory disturbances in the form of small worms are produced. Visions immediately arise.

The crystal wild goat scaling a cliff

In the fifth posture, one crouches with the knees pressed to the chest. The two elbows press the knees together [297] while the thumbs pull the left and right ears. The spine is straight and the two feet support one's weight.

The qualities of this posture are that having stopped the dichotomy of subject-object with auto-generated bliss, the right channel of primordial wisdom is opened. Externally, conceptual patterns emerge in pristine cognition, while internally the intent of non-grasping clear emptiness arises.

(2) The gazes

Second, concerning the gazes, it is said that when one adopts the first posture of the body [i.e., the pose of the lion], one gazes upward toward the body of reality. One bears upward through the eyebrows with a piercing gaze.

Similarly, when taking on the second posture [i.e., the reposing elephant], one performs the gaze of the body of perfection looking at the eye level [i.e., the middle level]. One fixes an unmoving and piercing gaze directly in front.

When assuming the third posture [i.e., the crouching ascetic], one performs the gaze of the emanation body looking downward. The eyelids are down and one focuses the eyes downward.

When assuming the fourth posture [i.e., the swaying goose], one gazes to the right and the eyes are made to look toward the right corners.

When assuming the fifth pose [i.e., the crystal goat], one adopts the gaze of the excellent wisdom looking left. The eyes are made to look out toward the left corners.

(3) The main points on the mind

Third, subduing the mind is here the main point. Whenever one adopts the various gazes, one should practice the three lamps: (1) The lamp of the external world is suppression using fixation. One focuses on the sun, and so forth. (2) The internal lamp of the sensory powers is to focus on the syllable A, which is concordant with the eyes. (3) The secret lamp of awareness is to focus on a non-defined space in the middle. Free from thoughts, one generates being in a non-defined space with intensity.

Meanwhile, one should know the three points of value:

(1) One must highly value the essential points on the body. Arriving fully in dealing with the channels and the winds has the purpose of using special insight on adventitious thoughts that are produced. One must not be unstable nor inconsistent here but must apply the key points well.

(2) One must highly value the essential points on the gazes. One is actually causing the hidden to become fully manifest. But one must abstain from generating ordinary thoughts.

(3) One must highly value the essential points on the mind, for everything runs into it. Do not be lazy! On account of this, you must combine [these postures, one after another,] together. It is important!

The mode of arising

Third, on the manner of arising, internal awareness abides by itself as five lights. It flows in the channels and opens them. It meets up with what it seizes externally as the orb of the sun, which then manifests as the many lights, rays, and droplets of light. Thus, as demonstrated above, these particular outer and inner grasping encounters that previously appeared were brilliant, quintessential, beautiful, and shining vividly in multicolored fashion. These displays, vibrating slightly, [298] arise fully as visions in the space of the sky. One does not make an effort to investigate them, but practices extensively, as mentioned above, letting them self-originate, self-arise, and be self-liberating. On their qualities, the *Instructions of the Gods of Revelation* (6.2) says:

> It generates a concentration like pervading the entire sky in one's continuum.

The *Hundred Thousand* says:

> A concentration that shines and flashes quickly.

Furthermore:

> Having grasped, one obtains the great liberation.

Moreover, the *Commentary on the Sun* says:

> These two methods above of day visions and night visions are there to create progress. If one practices them according to their timings—whichever they are—and relies on them continually, then they may affect one's constitution and senses. One should know what to adopt and what to discard.

In general, in these three practices the main point of one method over the other should be carried over the other.

If these practices are unbearable to one's constitution and senses, then one can use a piece of transparent Chinese cloth similar to dark-blue paper and follow the essential instructions. One places one's head inside a piece of blue cloth, following the method described above on gazing.

These were the instructions on the sun, the lamp on self-illumination. *Uya maro!*

Advice on particular points for visions

Third, advice on three essential points to improve the practice of visions: enhancement of the points of practice on the path and method on vision and gazes; enhancement of the purification of the mind and the winds; and enhancement with counsel on visions during the night.

Enhancement of the points of practice on the path and method

First, lights, rays, and droplets will appear during visions, and their colors will be perceived as white. If many meditators come up with the shape of the crescent moon, it is because the lights, rays, and droplets are conjoined with the elemental space wind. One then mainly employs the upward-looking gaze of the body of reality.

If the lights, rays, and droplets appear as lozenge shapes and are predominantly red in color, it is because they are conjoined with the elemental fire wind. One then mainly employs the downward-looking gaze of the emanation body.

If they appear as square and predominantly yellow, it is because they are conjoined with the elemental earth wind. One then mainly employs the gaze of the skillful means.

If they appear predominantly spherical and green, it is because they are conjoined with the elemental air wind. One then mainly employs the gaze of wisdom.

If they appear predominantly triangular and dark blue, it is because they are conjoined with the elemental water wind. One then mainly employs the middle-looking gaze of the body of perfection.

When all the lights, rays, and droplets have all the shapes in equal number and they are full of the five colors with all five shapes, it is because all the main five elemental winds are under control. One then chiefly or exclusively employs one of the three gazes: the gaze of spinning the wheel, the gaze of the poised lion, or the gaze of Sangwa Düpa.

These gazes are essential points on the path and method and are concordant with the mode of arising of external visions. You should know well the condensed and the general practices for all daytime and nighttime visions!
[299]

Enhancement of the purification of the mind and the winds

Second, the purification of the winds and the mind is threefold: the mode of abiding of the channels, the winds, and the droplets; the reason for the necessity of purifying them; and how to purify them.

The mode of abiding of the channels, the winds, and the droplets

First, in the main region [i.e., the heart], the central channel is hollow. One opens it by drawing the wind into it and upward. It enters the gate of Tshangpa and is led along the path to transcend sorrow. The wind is then moved downward to open the lower part. It goes through the secret gate along the path of cyclic existence. Having made it enter through the large mouth of the white right channel at the spine, it spirals up in the channel to the left of the central channel and comes forth through the gate of the left nostril. The rigid kind of breathing caused by ignorance and suffering move along this path of error.

Alternatively, having journeyed up to the left of the central channel, from the spine up through the left red channel it then comes out through the left nostril. This is the path of the enlightened qualities where the blissful wind of the pristine cognition of awareness moves. These channels spread out into limb channels and then into 84,000 branches and smaller leaves to the minor parts of the body. Body and mind rely on them. However, they can be condensed into three. Most of the winds are gathered in the right channel, where moves the rigid wind of sorrow; the left channel, where moves the blissful wind of pristine cognition; and the central channel, where the natural wind of awareness moves.

Furthermore, one must draw inside the blissful wind of pristine cognition, and for this, the rigid wind of sorrow must be expelled. Holding the natural wind of awareness is the main point.

Most of the droplets are pure droplets of awareness. The impure ones hold the body, but both kinds of droplets are gathered in it. Moreover, having so far relied on the impure droplets, holding the pure droplets is the main point here.

The reason for the necessity of purifying them

Second, the central channel is the king of the channels. Having made the blissful wind of pristine cognition enter, if one holds the quintessential droplets of awareness to abide here, then external visions of clear light will arise from all the internal dynamism of experience and realization. The *Little Nails* (318.3) says:

> Having purified awareness in the paths of the channels, there is
> no longer any wrong place on the paths.

The *Lamp* (207.2) says:

> The universal base and awareness abide in the heart from the very
> beginning. Dwelling in the circle of heart, it rises up naturally
> along the paths and channels.

Furthermore, it (214.1) says:

> The universal base is similar to the space that is contained within
> an anointment vase. Covered by the clouds of illusion, there is no
> clarity. The path of the central channel is like the cloudless sky.
> There is the pristine cognition that abides in great transparency.

How to purify them

Third, the methods of purification are threefold: purification in gentle breathing, subduing rigid breathing, and tending the natural breath.

Purification in gentle breathing

The first method is threefold: the main points on the body, the main points on the intellect, and the main points on breathing.

The main points on the body

The time: practice depends on the time—morning, evening, night, and dawn. [300] The great soul Drenpa Namkha said: "There is no point in meditating at noon or midnight or when one is drowsy."

The place: in a dark house, awareness is supported and enhanced. As for the place, [it must be] where there is no disturbance.

The method: The *Little Nails* (309.4) says:

> The essential point on the body is restraint.

This refers to the five postures of the body as detailed above. One should remain vigilant in observing the rules and constantly control the body. One should move forward with these essential points.

The main points on the intellect

Second, inside one's body the right channel is white, the left channel is red, and the central channel is dark blue. At the secret place, the right and left channels connect and become one with the inside of the dark-blue central channel. At the crown of the head, the central channel is cut off, similar to the tip of a writing reed. Each of the right and left channels has knots, similar to a twisted rope. Each has its opening in the right and left nostrils. With respect to these, there are three wheels [i.e., cakra] generated, the *Pu She Li*,[264] that are, respectively, above, beneath, and in the middle of the central channel. Each of these wheels has four-by-four petals expanding into channels. The extremities of these channels divide further into 84,000 channels with wheels at the top, bottom, and middle parts. In the manner of the fine roots of trees, one's body generates webs of channels.

The main points on breathing

Third, on the winds, the *Little Nails* (309.4) says:

> Hold the horse of the wind.

One should hold the breath and air should not move through the nostrils. Then one makes the movements of the silk-weaving Chinese maiden as one expels the air. One does this a few times to equalize miscellaneous thinking. In that way, one inhales and exhales equally nine times.

Then, like in the *Dark-Blue Paper* method, the antidote to conceptual thoughts is to move the breath in and out. Afterward, mindfully following the instructions on the three seed-syllables, one emanates and reabsorbs the *Oṃ* in the left channel, the *A* in the right channel, and the *Huṃ* in the middle channel in coordination with breathing. Again, one should think that the *Huṃ* remains in place, the *Oṃ* enters, and the *A* is expelled while breathing normally and not holding the breath deliberately. With these, the pathways of the channels will be cleansed, their doors opened, and the channel knots released, for it is necessary to clear the conduits of the channels.

Subduing rigid breathing

The second topic has two points: how to meditate and the mode of arising of meditative experiences.

How to meditate

First, on the points on the body and the channels, as seen above, at the junction of the three channels is a green seed-syllable *Yaṃ*. Inside and four fingers above, there is a red seed-syllable *Raṃ*. Directly in front of the heart, one's own self-awareness appears naturally as the seed-syllable *A*. Seeds of the five lights twirl out, expanding. One meditates that these are the size of small sparrow eggs setting off and shining brilliantly. One blows off the air. The air in the right and left channels that was held in place is propelled. Then the vital wind of pristine cognition becomes pink as it rises and bellows the *Raṃ* [301], which lights like a copper needle on fire. It feels hot as fire. The wind meets with fire and these two potencies burst together. The door of the central channel opens uncontrollably and abruptly, and the tongues of flame go higher and higher toward the gate of Tshangpa, carrying the droplets. The seed-syllable *Huṃ* stands inverted, is struck by the tongues of flame, and drips down droplets of pristine cognition like human fat melting. One meditates that all the channels with their associated parts from the heart downward are purified, and the droplets of the mind are filling them to the brim.

Then there are two seed-syllables *Huṃ* standing combined, white [right] and red [left]. When one inhales them through the nostrils, they join together like feet at the secret place. One imagines that, through their strength [i.e., the combined *Huṃ*], all the droplets are completely gathered together and abide there, empty and brilliant. You then utter a long *Hum̐* nine times.

Then one puts one's fists on the ground firmly and forcefully shouts *Hum̐* nine times. These go to the crown of the head along the central channel. One then shakes one's head and upper body parts while roaring nine *Phat!* One then imagines that the many droplets of pristine cognition are distributed from the crown wheel of bliss down to all the channels and tributary channels. One should assume the main points of the body well and focus one's awareness with the gaze of wheel-turning or the gaze of the lion pose. During these moments, one brings the winds face-to-face, reducing, increasing, and holding the "horse,"[265] wisely discerning the main points of breathing.

The mode of arising of meditative experiences

The second point is that for each cycle of purification of the winds like these, one should alternatively meditate on the cycle of the visual perception of clear light. When one meditates like that, the visions arise externally just as above. These visions may increase, and the coarse may increase and become numerous. The sky and the space in between will be full of objects of visions, sharp and brilliant in shape and form, standing out very little in the sensory fields. They will arise vividly, pleasant or unpleasant, radiant, clear, in rays of light, in droplets, reflections, and threads. Internally, the experiences in the channels will be such that one will feel pain, as if large stones are in the channels. Pain in the bones or joints, shaking and swift jolts, may also come up.

During the experience of the winds, feelings of lightness, disturbance, and intense restlessness may arise. During the experience of the droplets, one may experience bliss and pliability. When eating or if touched, one may sense tingling. Later, all these feelings of droplets coming down, bundling up together, being pulled, and scattering, may come up. The experience of the mind may be that when the mouth of the central channel opens up slightly, the controlled winds can be brought along the main points by the mind.

The droplets may be stuck in the upper parts and have little clarity in appearance. They may arise in unidentifiable aspects, and these outer and inner manifestations have no power to deceive or defile. Awareness abides there without distraction in the condition of non-apprehension of emptiness and bliss. [302] All thoughts and conceptualizations, good or bad, are self-arisen and are cut off decisively of their own accord. The *Clear A*[266] says:

One merges with the ability to focus effortlessly and continually, while relaxed and without becoming distracted.

The *Little Nails* (318.3) says:

Because the pathways and channels have been purified, there can be no deviance on the path of awareness.

These were the instructions on the purification of the pathways and channels of awareness. *Uya maro!*

Night sleep visions

Third, the advice on night visions is threefold: combining clear light and sleep, the manner in which qualities and faults arise, and intense focus on the *A*, grasping the main point.

Combining clear light and sleep

First, the *Great Lineage of Revelation*[267] says:

The advice is that predispositions converge with the intermediary state of dreaming, like the course of a river.

Its practice is that one lies down in the posture of the sleeping lion on an elevated and comfortable pillow [i.e., mattress]. Below the right side of the body, one applies thumb, index, middle, and ring fingers to block openings.[268] The right side is where the door to the channel of sorrow is, and one blocks the gate for its wind. Then one imagines oneself on a seat supported by lions, elephants, and Khyung[269] birds, on a lotus with sun and moon. Three times, one expels the poisons from the inner winds. Awareness, inside the central channel at the center of the Aksho[270] wheel [i.e., the throat], has the appearance of a ball of luminous threads, like a peacock's egg. One should not wander off over past considerations or ideas about the future. Eyes are closed.

Then, one lies down to sleep without distraction. For the best practitioner, all illusory visions of dreams will then arise as clear light. Furthermore, when one goes into sleep, one will retain the memory of details. One will be inseparably performing virtuous work. Then, visions of clear light will be uninterrupted. If sleep is intense, then clear light will also be intense. If thin, then clear light will arise thinly. One will then become conscious within the dream. At that time, one must mindfully engage in virtuous activities. Having meditated on the practices above, the flow of all dream consciousness will then stop, ordinarily in an instant without exception. Virtuous daytime practices will increase nighttime experience. Daily activities will greatly increase nightly results. Even though the thread of mindfulness will not be cut off at that time, diligence must be increased in practice. Purification having increased greatly, one will recognize these well. At that time, one must strive as above.

The manner in which qualities and faults arise

Second, in general, the causes for not recognizing the dream state are: there is no devotion in one's continuum, one has not developed confidence in the oral instructions, one has no ability to muster appropriate effort, and the ideas in one's continuum are conflicted. [303] One should eliminate these four existing faults in one's mind.

The elements of the body may be unbalanced due to the kind of food eaten. One may be fatigued due to one's activities. One may be craving the pleasures of male and female. One's bodily powers may be degenerating. One should eliminate these four existing faults in one's body.

The first instance above is imbalance caused by [eating] the wrong food. One should slightly hold [oneself] to stay awake [when lying down to sleep]. When the urge grows stronger and one is on the verge of falling asleep, one wakes up and immediately goes into the main position of the body posture. One strives to remember the previous dream images just perceived while not wandering elsewhere into thoughts, and lies down to sleep. Morning and evening, during daytime or any other time, all daily visions that appear are dreamed visions. Even though they are dreams, they exist, but since there are no predispositions in them, one considers them not to be real but only dreams.

When one remembers in the midst of dreaming, or when one remembers but half of it, what is to be done? One goes on doing the practice mindfully and diligently and becomes skilled at it. This is vitally important. In the end, when sleep becomes intertwined with clear light, tricks and temptations from non-human beings will come up. Visions, all manner of sensations, whatever will occur—one familiarizes oneself with them as illusory self-manifestations. One must refrain from feeling conceited, cheerful, or happy here. For in the end, dreams will turn into space, one's consciousness will become independent, and the flow of memories will pass by as displays. Abiding this way, everything—high and low, good and bad—is merely thoughts passing. One goes in transforming any visions as such. They are pure self-manifestations that are, in general, properly transformed. Similarly, these transformations arise as visions. The flow of hallucinations of the intermediary state itself will be interrupted by all the manifestations. Flesh will be reversed, hair will be reversed, and there will be no more fear in the intermediate state of wandering through birth and death. At that time, moreover, all various manifestations in the state of dreaming will be carried on the path as activities refining one's training. They will be immediately loaded as empty. Loss and victory will be integrated and practice will become unbounded. At that time, when engaging in any virtuous practice, all will be transformed right away and enhanced greatly nine times over.

Intense focus [on the A], grasping the main point

Third, despite whatever one practices, if one not does remember, one will fall asleep happily, as above, and fixate on enjoying images seen. Then, one should slightly constrict the two veins on the neck. As soon as the visions in one's continuum stop and one feels dizzy, stop holding until the dizziness goes away. It is dangerous! Awareness must be strongly exercised here. If one slightly loses control over the channels, one must do this on a cold floor. If one presses the two veins for too long, there is a risk of consciousness leaving the body. Be careful! Then it will be impossible to control dreaming.

These were the instructions on integrating sleep and clear light. *Uya maro!* [304]

Colophon

Thus, the final advice on the essential profound meaning has been happily arranged in a series of practical instructions on the main practices of the nectar of the intent of the quintessential instruction from the Zhangzhung Oral Transmission. May these come to be meaningful to all fortunate vessels! This advice on clear light and the principal practices will ripen one's continuum and free it. These instructions should not be conveyed to those with wrong views and those who are not destined to receive them. [305]

5. Instructions on the View for Seeing in Its Nakedness, the Direct Introduction to the Nature of the Base

I PAY HOMAGE TO Kuntu Zangpo, the all-encompassing leader of wandering beings who is manifested self-awareness!

Third, having realized one's continuum and made it manifest, there are four branches to follow further: (1) the instructions on the view for seeing in its nakedness, the direct encounter with the nature of the base; (2) the instructions on the contemplation of clear light, the practices of the path; (3) the instructions on the practices of yogic exercise training to undertake the secondary conditions on the path; and (4) the instructions on the clear elucidation of the three bodies, holding the natural ground of the result.

The instructions on the view for seeing in its nakedness, the direct encounter with the nature of the base

This first point is threefold: direct introduction through relying on the essence and nature of the base, direct introduction by relying on particular activities, and extensive explanations on liberation and delusion.

Direct introduction through relying on the essence and nature of the base

This is fourfold: direct introduction to the essence of the mother, direct introduction to the son, direct introduction to dynamism, and direct introduction to the undifferentiated union of the mother, son, and dynamism.

Direct introduction to the essence of the mother

First, the mother is the natural state of the basic disposition, the universal base. It is the root base of all, cyclic existence and transcendence, the great ancestor of all sentient beings and the enlightened ones. If one could express it in words, it could be naturally designated in all ways. If one could essentialize its meaning, one could not point to any whatsoever.

As for its first expression in words, its essence is unobstructed, naturally luminous, empty, and rootless. It is naked and denuded. Originally, it was not covered by delusions, defilements, and afflictions. It is called "the great primordial purity."

It is not subject to any obstruction; it is colorless and unchanging. It is pure and transparent. It was not created by cause, nor fabricated by secondary causes. It is achieved without efforts. It does not fall into fabricated limitations; therefore, it is called "the great self-originated."

All objects of knowledge in cyclic existence or transcendence are already perfected in their condition. Now there is nothing that needs to endure ripening or be liberated. Without having to be realized, it is called "the great spontaneous accomplishment."

As to being recognizable [i.e., the mother], it has no identifiable body, form, color, size, or identity whatsoever. Whatever its essence is, it has not been established yet. It is called "the great freedom from extremes."

It does not side with either cyclic existence or transcendence. It cannot be divided. From the smallest of insects up to the heights of Kuntu Zangpo, it cannot be divided. It is neither great nor small, subtle nor gross, and cannot be included as being either thin or thick. It is called "the great all-encompassing."

Everything in its space arises, abides, and fades. All the various displays that arise dependent on any kind of body or by themselves neither diminish nor increase it. It is neither narrow nor wide. Everything anywhere cannot transcend it. It is called "the great intrinsic-self."

Therefore, the deeds of the enlightened ones and of cyclic existence have passed as neither good nor bad. There is no hope in the highest. [306] The ultimate does not glow. There is no nearing to the one. The one has no duration. It is called "the great universal heap."

A name cannot be imputed to it, yet it does not go beyond one meaning. One can see its one essence, yet different manifestations emerge from it. In this one basis are contained the great particularities of happiness and suffering. Great variety arises, yet what is called "this" cannot be defined, for at some point, it is hidden. It cannot be seen at all, yet everyone is connected to it. Its essence is unknown. It is all-encompassing. It is non-existent to others, for it is beyond the mind. It is called "the great inexpressible one."

The *Lamp* (186.5) says:

> The universal base, which is the intrinsic mind of enlightenment, is the clear light of unadulterated emptiness. It is the body of reality, the great primordial purity. It cannot be tainted by anything. It can be approached, yet remains untouched. It is the body of spontaneous perfection. It is the universal perfection, the supremely perfect, perfect in every way. It is an emanation body that is unverifiable, not spoken of in the scriptures. Impartial, it arises everywhere with magical displays, but each of these has no differences. It encompasses the whole of cyclic existence and transcendence. It is the space, the one brilliance, that encompasses all. It is limitlessly impartial in its luminous space. It arises everywhere as the one great expanse. In the expanse of emptiness, it is spaciously inexistent. In this one expanse, everything abides. In this expanse of equanimity, there are no upper or lower. Therefore it is called "the mind of enlightenment." It is explained with these three expedient meanings.

These three [universal base, space, light] referred to above use example, meaning, and sign. However, one can only use two of these [expressions]. This way, there may be many expressions using words, but understanding and knowledge only amount to so much.

Meaning is summarized and descends upon one's continuum. But if one relies on putting these [three] into practice, due to the fact that none of them exist, and having taken the above-mentioned practices on the three places [i.e., body, speech, and mind], putting trust in these, it is like staring fixedly at the point of clarity[271] of non-conceptual natural clarity, the universal base. Then, in this respect, one will acquire conviction and will come to a clear elucidation that the explanations above have great import.[272] At that very moment, one's own mind will cease grasping and will become self-luminous, just like the clear and cloudless sky. And the three bodies will arise by themselves. This is self-luminous self-awareness, spontaneously accomplished pristine cognition. The *Little Nails* (312.2) says:

The king of awareness is self-originated luminosity. He is formless pristine cognition, free from colors, shapes, and forms. He
is inexpressible pristine cognition, free from name, words, and
letters. He is non-conceptual pristine cognition, free from the
activities of ordinary mind.

The *Six Transmissions* (122.1) says:

> There it is! It arises there! See!

Where is it now? Although it pervades the body in general, it dwells in the
brown cornelian tent with crystal beams, which is precisely the heart. Inside
the heart that holds the channels,[273] the five lights are pitched like a tent in
its midst. It is unmixed with whatever is there. It dwells in the great primordial purity. The *Lamp* (205.6) says:

> Inside the heart, free from darkness, like the sun, self-awareness is
> continually completely self-arising. [307]
>   It dwells there like a butter lamp inside a vase. Now one can-
> not see it due to the covering of the body. It is explained that it
> will come out once awareness is freed from the corpse.

On that occasion, one will be directly introduced to the circle of the base.

Direct introduction to the son

Second, pristine cognition of awareness is twofold: the natural state of the
son and direct introduction to the son.

The natural state of the son

First, the universal base is like the sky. The awareness of the son is like the
essence of the sun, it arises like nectar. The essence of this rising is in its
uncovered nakedness that is illuminating clearly. It is intrinsic emptiness that
abides immaculate without foundation. The essential point of the aspects
of objects is perceived just as it is with vivid awareness. Pristine cognition
is naked. It is polluting to exert and move with adventitious conceptualizations and analysis. In this life, one is confused by absent-mindedness and

haunted by the unpredictable. Non-conceptuality is fresh. Alert without grasping, the pristine cognition of awareness is originated by itself. So it has been said. The *Lamp* (190.1) says:

> The activity of pristine cognition of awareness is similar to the sun in the expanse of the sky. Awareness arises from the expanse of the universal base. Its essence is naturally empty in brilliance. Cognizing aspects do not distract awareness.

Direct introduction to the son

Second, the exertions of the body postures bring about the union of winds and mind. Quintessential awareness is separated from the impure by drawing forth the valuable luminous radiance, which is cognition. At the time conviction is formed, one engages in gazing fixedly at its essence. That is direct introduction being applied. Awareness in its pristine cognition is enlightenment in its natural state. The very moment consciousness is in a state of non-conceptuality, it becomes vividly brilliant. It then appears in full transparency, undefiled. The *Little Nails* (317.7) says:

> The six glances[274] arise at the forehead.

And again:

> Direct vision is the thorough perfection of the intent.

Furthermore, on Suchness, the *Little Nails* (312.3) says:

> The hue of pristine cognition has no appearance whatsoever. It is the body of reality. The white deity of Shen (*gshen*) who is self-less is the universal base. It is famously called "the awareness of intrinsic essence."

On the pristine cognition of awareness, the *Hundred Thousand* says:

> It does not arise from outside. It does not arise from inside. It arises by itself, naturally.

And so forth. This was the extensive direct introduction.

Direct introduction to dynamism

Third, dynamism, sound, and light rays; these three have two further points: the natural state and direct introduction to dynamism.

The natural state

Thus, first, dynamism and the radiance of pristine cognition of awareness do not have an agent as a primary cause. They arise without interruption as self-manifested rays, lights, and sounds. The radiance, which has no shade, is the factor of the clarity of awareness that arises as the light that is self-illuminating awareness, like a rainbow. Its capacity, which is completely without roots, is the factor of the emptiness of awareness [308] that arises as the sound that is self-sounding awareness, like an echo. Dynamism, which is devoid of the duality of an intrinsic essence to clarity and emptiness, arises as the sound that is self-sounding awareness.

Furthermore, the natural radiance of awareness arises from the base connected to the five lights as all the manifestations of the changeless bodies of the enlightened ones. It also arises in sentient beings as the many birth emanations of the four kinds. Similarly, awareness arises from the base as connected sounds that are all the manifestations of the speech of the enlightened ones. It also arises in all sentient beings as all the emanations of speech. Awareness arises from the base as connected rays that are all manifestations of pristine awareness, the all-knowing mind of the enlightened ones. It also arises in all sentient beings as all conceptualizations of mental intent and memories.

The pristine cognition of the awareness of the son is not created by anyone. The activities of the three great manifestations arise as self-manifested. The *Lamp* (190.6) says:

> From that arise the three dynamisms of manifestation. These three are sounds, lights, and rays. They arise as lights in the bright sky. Sound is self-originated from the expanse of emptiness. These [dynamisms] emanate as rays of non-dual awareness. They are said to be the objects of visions.

The *Lamp* (192.4) further says:

Although essence is primordially unstained, it is the ground of both faults and qualities of cyclic existence and transcendence. Light and awareness are connected and transform in the base as enlightened body and ordinary body. Sound and awareness are connected and transform in the base as enlightened speech and ordinary speech. Rays and awareness are connected and transform in the base as enlightened mind and ordinary mind.

Direct introduction to dynamism

Second, once the winds and the mind are joined and awareness has separated the pure from the impure following one's training with the body postures as above—such as pressing upward the ocean and so forth, and having the gaze focused between the eyebrows without distraction—there comes a distinguishable break in clarity. One then holds on to the echoes of the continual sounds self-generated by the mind and focuses uninterruptedly on memories as the natural rays of awareness, just like the rays of the sun. Confidence will generate a firm conviction. That is direct introduction.

These three: sounds, lights, and rays, which arise in self-radiance from the pristine cognition of awareness, have from the very beginning never been made by anyone nor accomplished through exertion. It is not an exaggeration that awareness is arising, self-manifesting uninterruptedly in the sphere of pristine cognition. The *Lamp* (221.5) says:

The moving mind can be subdued by sound. The recollecting thoughts can be grasped by light. The three dynamisms of awareness can be purified by rays. Once the three dynamisms have been purified by rays, the circle of the three bodies will arise by itself.

The *Lamp* (223.7) further says:

Sounds are the natural sounds of awareness. The natural sounds of emptiness are aspects of echoes. Lights are the natural lights of awareness. The natural lights of emptiness are aspects of sunlight. [309] Rays are the natural rays of awareness. The natural rays of emptiness are aspects of sunrays. These are the primordial natural dispositions.

This was the extensive direct introduction.

Direct introduction to the undifferentiated union of the mother, son, and dynamism

Fourth, the direct introduction to the union and inseparability of the mother, the son, and dynamism is twofold: the natural state on union and direct introduction to this union.

Natural state on union

First, wherever the mother, the son, and dynamism are revealed, the continuum of one's essence is, from the very top, undifferentiated from mother and son. Their very nature is united. Their innate characteristics do not possess any differences. The mother, the universal base, is pure like the sky. The son, pristine cognition of awareness, is uncovered and self-luminous, and arises like the heart of the sun. And from their dynamism, sounds, lights, and rays arise as magical display, like the light rays of the sun. Furthermore, they exist in their integrality, without addition or subtraction. The *Lamp* (194.3) says:

> The base, heart-essence, and factors of display are the mother, the
> son, and dynamism. In the continuum of a person, their mode
> of abiding is without subtraction or addition. The universal base
> is like the shore of the sky. Awareness is like the heart of the sun.
> Dynamism is like the light rays of the sun.

Direct introduction to this union

Second, having strictly followed the rules of conduct and having disciplined one's consciousness methodically, one disciplines these three: winds, awareness, and concentration. Having practiced the three relaxations, one looks spontaneously within at the mother, the universal base that is intrinsic emptiness without roots. This immaculateness is the body of reality. The son is awareness, self-luminous, pristine in its nakedness (*rjen pa ru ye*). This intent is the body of perfection. Dynamism is self-arising and the self-originated factor of display. This free flowing is the body of emanations. From the very beginning, mother, son, and dynamism have been abiding intrinsically in the great inseparable intrinsic self of the three bodies. The *Little Nails* (319.2) says:

The empty luminous universal base is the sphere of reality, the expanse of the sky. The thumb-sized pristine cognition is the body of reality, self-originated.

The *Little Nails* (318.4) further says:

Self-awareness in the space of the heart (*tsi ta*) is the body of reality. One's nature in the pathways of the channels is the body of perfection. Natural arising in the gate of the lamp is the body of emanation.

The *Lamp* (214.4) says:

Primordial greatness is the body of reality. It is unblemished by anything. What approaches cannot touch it. It is similar to the sun rising in a cloudless sky. Mother and son arise in an inseparable manner in the pathway of the central channel.

This was the extensive direct introduction.

Direct introduction by relying on particular activities

Second, the direct introduction to the special activities of the base is fourfold: direct introduction through thoughts and memories, which are like the clouds in the sky; direct introduction by conceptual patterns, which are like a gentle breeze in the air; direct introduction through afflictive emotions, which are like waves on the sea; and direct introduction through the six collections of consciousness, which are like vast rainbows in the sky. [310]

Direct introduction through thoughts and memories

First, there are two considerations: teachings on the natural state, and its direct introduction.

Teachings on the natural state

The first topic is awareness is like the heart of the sun. Thoughts and memories are like the rays of the sun, and whatever may arise is uncontrived.

Furthermore, mind is making up its own objects. Therefore, the meaning of the object in mind will be remembered just as it is. It has been said that the intellect is the experience of the meaning from memory. The *Lamp* (193.13) says:

> Although the king of consciousness has no thoughts, it is the basis from which the various thoughts and memories arise, just like the light rays from the dynamism of the sun. The ordinary mind arises from the dynamism of awareness.

Its direct introduction

Second, after controlling awareness with the three postures, one settles into tranquility, relaxing. At that moment, one gazes with wide-open eyes into the one in control, the one who relaxes, and the thinking of the one making categories. At that moment, if there is a memory that is retained for examination, one will know. If it is not examined, these unclear memories cross the mind uninterruptedly. These two are called "the knowing awareness of thoughts and memories."

There are collections of concepts of good and bad, subtle and coarse. All theorizing and examining past [and future] thoughts are fabrications. Those [thoughts] themselves abide in the essence of pristine cognition, self-originating from the very beginning. The *Lamp* (193.4) says:

> They arise in the ordinary mind from the dynamism of awareness.
> They arise in dynamism as the six collections and the six objects.
> These are called "the thoughts of the ordinary mind." They are memories from knowing and remembering. This is called "the mind," for it is moving toward objects.

Direct introduction through thoughts

Second, on the collection of thoughts, non-conceptual awareness is like the sky. From within that state [i.e., non-conceptual], one produces thoughts of any type for their own sake. They arise long and unsteady. One first examines those that arise, their secondary conditions, and their production. These are free from basis and roots.

Then one examines what their essence is. They are devoid of reality, shape, and color. In the end, they are purified into their own natural purity in the state of intrinsic mind. They are destroyed in their own destruction. They are lost into their own loss. They are liberated into their own self-liberation. Their empty movements become like a breeze manifesting. They arise in non-conceptual, self-originated pristine cognition. The *Little Nails* (320.6) says:

> Non-conceptual pristine cognition is the base. The various memories and thoughts are dynamism. Following after them is the way of delusion. Looking at their faults is the place of error. The method is to relax into the natural ground. In the end, they are released into the expanse. This is the idea of non-duality.

The *Little Nails* (322.1) further says:

> Memories and thoughts are ended in the sphere of non-conceptuality. What makes the ordinary mind is ended in the sphere that transcends the ordinary mind. Sectarian clutching to partiality is ended in the sphere of impartiality.

The *Lamp* (220.6) says:

> After there are no more memories and thoughts, one just settles into non-acquisition.

This was the extensive direct introduction.

Direct introduction to self-liberation from afflictions

Third, direct introduction to self-liberation from afflictions consists in the following:

In the sphere of the great clear light of non-conceptuality, [311] one can intentionally generate anger and so forth. As soon as it arises, one observes its self-origination, its self-arising, and its self-liberation. Like a wave returning to the ocean, afflictions are liberated in pristine cognition. The five poisons are purified in their own condition and faults arise as qualities. It is said that there is a high value in poisons, for they arise on the path and need not be abandoned. The *Little Nails* (320.7) says:

The base is self-originated pristine cognition. Dynamism is the five poisons of afflictions. Pursuing them is the way of delusion. Looking at their faults is the place of error. The method is to relax into the natural ground. In the end, they are released into the expanse. This is the idea of non-duality.

The *Six Transmissions* (126.4) says:

If the five poisons are not something concrete, then making use of the five poisons is the superior practice.

The *Commentary on the Arcana* (21ba5) says:

When there is anger, one will reach freedom from anger in the end.

Direct introduction through the six collections

Fourth, direct introduction with the six collections is like a vast rainbow in the sky. When each of the six collections arises from the sphere of the great clear light of non-conceptuality, it engages in meeting with its object naturally. Now and then, they are brought together just as they are. They are seen vividly in the consciousness of the agent joining the six collections. They arise in the sphere unimpeded. They arise in the emptiness without roots. They are empty, like a vast rainbow rising in the sky that is liberated. This rising of liberation is the various visions of the six collections. They have been abiding in the essence of pristine cognition of self-awareness from the very beginning. The *Lamp* (216.3) says:

From pristine cognition of self-awareness, dynamism has been arising as the six objects of the six collections. These make the various activities of the body, speech, and mind. They arise as emanations and abide in their own realms of emanations. Not realizing this, they arise in the forms of the six destinies.

The *Little Nails* (326.2) says:

The clear elucidation on destinies is that they are pure from the coverings of delusion from the very beginning. When this has been plainly clarified in the ordinary mind, then the dynamism of pristine cognition arises.

The *Six Transmissions* (142.6) says:

> The base of these phenomena is without roots. Just as they are imputed, so do they appear.

Extensive explanations on liberation and delusion

Third, the extensive explanations on liberation and delusion are twofold: not realizing the mode of delusion, and realizing the mode of liberation.

Not realizing the mode of delusion

This first one is twofold: co-emergent generation and ignorance that imputes everything.

Co-emergent generation

Sentient beings have not committed even a single hair of defilement. When first in such delusion, the above-mentioned base was just like the sky from which arose the pristine cognition of awareness. In there, moving memories and thoughts wavered and one was ignorant of the natural radiance that self-manifested in the visions of sounds, lights, and rays. It is like a lion mystified by its own reflection. [312] Behaving as such, the three natural dynamisms [i.e., sound, lights, and rays] rose as enemies. There, the pristine cognition of awareness was covered, just like the sun covered by clouds or a naked person dressed in clothes. Awareness was encased in a web of light. Grasping at a self in even a minor way stirs the subtle factor of an entity, and it is then very difficult to purify one's inherent nature. Doing so [i.e., grasping at a self] covers the universal base. Before that, there is no other ignorance. The base of ignorance is identical to grasping at a self. This is called "co-emergent ignorance." The *Lamp* (198.5) says:

> The reason sentient beings are deluded just like that is that when the three manifested objects arise as real, the ordinary mind's

consciousness, memories, and awareness are obscured by these objects. They do not know that the illusion is self-manifested. They truly see these as something else. What is seen as something else conceals the essential from the awareness of ordinary mind. The intellect that does not know does not understand the meaning of the universal base. That is co-emergent ignorance.

Ignorance that imputes everything

Second, co-emergent ignorance changes the complexion of the pristine cognition of awareness, and this causes greater distraction. Because the self-manifestations of sound, lights, and rays are apprehended coarsely as real, there arise subject and object. At that moment, object and consciousness are not recognized and mental states spread. Fluctuating winds encourage the spread. The three kinds of manifested objects are then in commotion, like clouds stirred by interfering winds. The visions of lights become like an extensive tent, and the manifestations of the five lights arise. They arise in five colors: white, green, red, blue, and yellow. This is called "conceptual ignorance." The *Lamp* (199.3) says:

> The power of ignorance stirs consciousness toward objects. The manifested objects are labeled, and the objects of consciousness stir fresh fixations. These fresh fixations agitate the three kinds of manifest objects. The agitation of the three kinds of manifest objects brings up the continuum of the five elements. That is conceptual ignorance.

These lights give rise to the five great elements. And among these, the five poisons that are the roots of afflictions arise. From these, the manifest elements arise into the five realms. And these elements mature into the five heaps[275] as a result. From these, the five main organs are formed. In these, the five limbs that give rise to dynamism are established. And in these originate the five sorts of vessels. In these vessels, the five working senses are established. These senses give rise to the five apprehending sensory consciousnesses. These consciousnesses establish the five objects of enjoyment. In these objects originate the five conditioning activities. From these conditioning activities, the five doors that generate impurities spring forth. These impurities ripen into the five categories of illness. When one interacts with them, one then engages with the continuums of the five paths. These five paths, in turn, ripen into the five existing realms. Among these, the continuums of the five pure lands arise.

One should be directly introduced to the cyclic existence of the extensive dependent arising that is the mode of delusion, just like that. [313]

At first, when all these simple aspects of predispositions did not exist, delusion had no form. Then delusions slowly began to take form. When more and more fixating concepts were produced, this turned into delusion in the form realms. From that moment, forms spread greatly, just like that. Having been led astray into the realm of desire, individualized sentience became part of cyclic existence in the three realms. These then incarnated in the six causal destinies, migrating in cyclic existence from one body to another.

Step by step, the *Lamp* (201.2) says:

> When the karmic propensities of these [i.e., individualized sentience] became mightier, mental bodies of discursive thoughts were conspicuously established. Under the power of delusion, they drifted into the formless realms. From that, the capacity of the karmic propensities became mightier, and bodies of manifested light were conspicuously established. Under the power of anger, they drifted in the cyclic existence of the form realms. From that, the capacity of the karmic propensities became greater, and corporeal bodies made of flesh and blood were established. Under the power of passions, they drifted in the desire realms.

Furthermore, from subtle bits of afflictions they strayed further into coarseness.

At first one must gradually train. In the end, one is instructed in the deeper points. Accordingly, one is no longer deluded to err lower, and this is the single main point. If one practices, in the end one will become liberated from the existing initial source of cyclic existence. All of these I consider as the single main point.

The mode of liberation by realization

Second, realization and its mode of liberation is twofold: what is the manner of liberation, and extensive explanations on the system to liberation.

What is the manner of liberation?

First, since Kuntu Zangpo did not do a hair's worth of good deeds, how was he liberated? Like the sun, pristine cognition rose unceasingly as sounds, lights, and rays, its natural dynamism. Not engaging the ordinary mind to grasp these three self-manifested dynamisms, the condition for liberation arose. Having looked at the countenance of the base and awareness, one identifies with mother and son. The nature of the mind draws near to the kingdom of Kuntu Zangpo. Having grasped that, the mind is not contaminated by the senses and arises in pristine cognition. At that moment, the increasing qualities of the enlightened body, speech, and mind that transcend conditioned experience, enlightened activities, and all the emanations of method and compassion naturally arise without depending on effort and striving. The *Lamp* (196.3) says:

> What is the reason for realization? When dynamism arises as the three objects manifesting, the consciousness of the ordinary mind that knows and recollects, surpassing the illusion, sees these as self-manifestations. Because these objects were self-manifested, awareness arises bare-naked. The universal base is vividly realized as unobscured. Through this realization, awareness holds on to its natural ground and does not pursue manifested objects. At that moment it becomes really independent, and emanations transcending suffering [314] arise implicitly without having anything to undertake.

Extensive explanations on the manner of liberation

Second, pristine cognition of awareness is the natural radiance of being liberated in the essence of the base. From the dynamism of the capacity for pure vision, the five lights[276] arise naturally as visions, and from that, everything is produced. The spheres of the five elements[277] arise. From these, the five expanses[278] of the wombs arise. From these, the five wide spaces arise. From these, the five existent deities[279] arise. From these arise the five bodies[280] of the places. From these originate the five rising destinies.[281] In these arise the five bases[282] of support. From these are accomplished the five limbs[283] of the symbolic gestures. From these arise the five treasuries[284] originating everything. From these arise the five uncontaminated sensory powers.[285] From these arise the five unobstructed pristine cognitions.[286] From these arise the five completely pure objects.[287] From these arise the five completely pure pristine cognitions.[288] From these arise the five unimpaired strengths.[289] In these arise the five clear pristine cognitions. From these arise the five unsurpassable results.[290] From these arise the five perfected mandalas.[291] In these are established the five realms[292] that arise in reality.

This was the manner to understand extensively direct introduction to the cycle of dependent-arising.

The qualities, which understand and are aware regarding the meaning of the mother, the son, and dynamism, have been pure from the very beginning. Kuntu Zangpo has been enlightened without regard to proceeding along a path. The *Lamp* (198.3) says:

> There was no collecting the two accumulations, and this implies
> that realization occurred in the very beginning.

Now again, the rationale is that one is purified on the path through the power of familiarization through effort, until in the end it becomes a reality. As for this enlightenment, the path to liberation is enlightenment.

These were the instructions on the view of seeing nakedly, the direct introduction to one's own base. *Uya maro!* [315]

6. Instructions on the Meditation on Clear Light, the Practice of the Path

To Kuntu Zangpo, who is the all-encompassing leader of transmigrating beings, manifested self-awareness, I pay homage!

Second,[293] these instructions on meditation on clear light, which are part of the practices along the path, are twofold: the manner of meditating with the extended methods of the gradual path, and meditating in a manner that gives rise to clear light and its experience.

The manner of meditating with the extended methods of the gradual path

First, the depths of birth and death are terrifying, and one should pursue the aim of enlightenment. One should carry one's lama on the crown of one's head with an invincible faith. Having cast away worldly deeds, an individual with the ability to be attached only to awareness has to thoroughly acquire the clear elucidating advice above on the practices and the direct introduction. If one wants to guard these, one goes to an isolated place, a great place that increases virtue, or to an island, a forest, a cave, a glacier, a rock pass, and so forth, where there is a clean, elevated field. It should be a place where days and nights are particular as described above, a land that is workable and easy to settle. There should be no work activity and very few attendants. Distractions should be eliminated, otherwise one will not attain stability. When meditating in retreat, one should refrain from working when tired. One should not mix and chat with others. One should be content with one's food and clothing. One should completely sever traveling for entertainment. One should gather all good and amiable conditions.

Although there have been many mentions of the path and its methods, the manner of instruction, enhancements to proceed further along the path, direct introduction, and so forth, it is most important to rely on oneself, and with a single-pointed mind, to completely merge awareness with the main great unobscured clear light.

There are practices for the key advice on the winds and the mind, and for the appropriate use of characteristic visions. One must have an essential lama who knows the meditation and comprehends the profound advice. With fierce efforts, one meditates vigorously without for a moment relinquishing equanimity. One meditates capably, with fortitude, for a long time—this may take a number of years, months, and days—until the experience enters one's continuum. One meditates uninterruptedly, chasing [results] like this, without interruption at any time or occasion.

There are four ways to practice: meditate on nurturing what is favorable, meditate on how visions arise externally, meditate on all the ways of generating inner experiences, and then engage in increasing the meditational experiences so that these flourish like the waxing moon.

The *Little Nails* (309.2) says:

> In a pleasant mountain retreat in a solitary place [316], an individual, deeply terrified of birth and death, having recognized the universal base, should elucidate awareness clearly.

The *Hundred Thousand*[294] (19.303.7) says:

> With resolve to practice in every way, one completes it without tiring at all.

Removing obstructions

Second, when one takes on the practices of the main point of the Greater Vehicle, the natural state, external obstacles from humans and non-humans, obstacles from sickness collecting internally, and secret obstacles experienced during meditation may arise.

Obstacles from humans and non-humans

For the first, the strings of worldly obstacles such as the affection of friends or attachment to wealth, one should know that they are all demons. Even the company of good men should be shunned. One should engage in ceremonies to expel disturbances, in exhortations, in ritual cake offerings, and the ritual of severance of the body.

Obstacles from sickness collecting internally

Second, when sick, one may engage in yogic exercises, controlled breathing, visualization, sounds, and so forth, in order to clear out obstructions. One should let go of the smaller [chores].

Secret obstacles that are experienced during meditation

Third, many obstacles arise during meditation. To summarize them, there are three related to the practice of meditation: view, meditation, and conduct.

Obstacles to the view

One can be attached to entrenched explanations on the view. This can be an obstruction to the essential point, and one can lose one's way in senseless chatter and feel disgust.

Even though one's ordinary mind has an understanding, when specific signs do not arise, one can get lost in speculation.

At present, one does not take on the practices. One escapes into hope and planning for the future.

One does not recognize one's mode of being and gets lost in intellectual speculation .

While holding two views, one is indecisive due to conceptual limitations.

Obstacles to meditation

There are five places where one can go wrong. (1) One may be really gripped with bliss during meditation, and this may generate confidence in this instance. One will then misconstrue this momentary state of bliss for non-conceptuality. (2) If there is no presence of mind, one will continue to meditate in a daze. (3) When one is enveloped in drowsiness and torpor, luminous radiance will not emerge. (4) When one is agitated, floating about, and distracted, there will be no stability. (5) If one slips up, makes changes, and quarrels, there will be no progress and one will get lost in error.

Obstacle to conduct

As for conduct, one should not proceed into error with these five: nonsensical chatter and phoniness; acting with the aim of opportunistic gain; laziness and indifference; acting out of self-imposed, relentless asceticism; and behaving with ordinariness, holding on to wrong views.

The *Eight Realms*[295] (589.6) says:

> When one enters the path of the merchants to seek the precious wish-fulfilling gem, because there are many enemies that will do harm, one should put on armor. [317]

Meditating in a manner that gives rise to clear light and its experience

Third, the manner of making experience and clear light arise through meditation is threefold: initiating the arising of visions, increasing visions in meditation, and the gradual stages of the path in connecting these together.

The manner of initiating the arising of visions

This first point is twofold: the manner to perceive external visions, and the manner to generate internal experiences.

The manner of perceiving external visions

First, the *Lamp of Clear Expression* (222.1) says:

> The teachings on the forceful method to purify dynamism are as follows: One is to capture the fish with flickering rays in the net of light in the dark retreat house. The mirror of awareness, which is all-illuminating, reveals the clear visions in the expanse of the sky. The spear of mindfulness should be fixed on the shield of radiating lights. Then one will see the seeds of the form-bodies[296] that will rise like stars in the sky.

At first when one practices one will see the marks of the five elements, as mentioned above. Furthermore, lights and rays and woolen-like multicolored brocade will spread out [in space]. Rainbows will arise together with mandalas, as if drawn, in numbers too large to conceive. Something familiar to the practitioner will arise. It will be like seeing the grid patterns of a town through a canvas or a piece of felt, and everywhere in the space of the sky. The *Little Nails* (319.3) says:

> Visions will arise in various forms through insight, such as the five lights that will be the basis for pure lands and mandalas, immeasurable palaces of the five wisdoms, tents, and droplets.

The manner of generating internal experiences

Second, when practicing these virtuous activities, it will be similar to trying to see the sun through clouds. The vision will be blurred and one will start to have doubts and so forth. At the beginning of the meditation sessions, it will be like the first and second days of the waxing moon cycle.

The manner in which visions will increase

Second, after that, when one is familiar with the visions, the manner in which they will grow is a fivefold topic: the manner in which visions will increase, the manner in which visions will spread as visions, the manner in which they will intensify, the manner in which they will be perfected, and the manner in which visions will reach finality.

The manner in which visions will increase

First, as mentioned above, one practices single-mindedly, and after a while one will experience that visions are increasing. Internally, these rising visions become innumerable visions of clear lights. These are pea-sized droplets of awareness, the color of crystal. Then these become larger, spread, and two can be connected, or they can be combined in threes, or many joined together, connecting upward, linked across, and so forth. These heart-droplets of awareness are called "threads of compassion." The silver or white threads are like chains of white silk scarves. They look familiar, like droplets on strands of sheep yarn, or [318] not strung together but connected one by one by a thread. Droplets may appear as many but not be connected along a line, alone, and so forth.

Because all of one's elements are not yet in a state of balance, a greater number appear all white, or each is alone individually, or a small portion are fully in the five colors and arise individually. They arise in a greater measure with single or multiple colors.

Inside the circle of these droplets, a few may appear in the aspect of deities. Upon examining them, they do not appear clearly, and each one abides in a subtle manner. Furthermore, these lights, rays, and droplets remain but for a single moment and are like water falling down a mountain slope, or like rolling balls of mercury. They appear to vibrate, scatter, and come back together. The *Lamp* (222.3) says:

> As one becomes more familiar and gains experience with these, five particular aspects will manifest. At first, the vision will increase and one will see something scattering and re-combining like quicksilver.

The *Little Nails* (311.2) says:

> Rays of awareness are threads of droplets. At first, they appear like water falling from a mountain cliff.

How internal visions are produced

Second, when the experience of single-mindedness appears, consciousness will experience stillness, utterly fresh and brilliant, with a clarity that is not diffuse. This is the meeting of emptiness and awareness, of mother and son, which is tranquil and smooth. One should enter a practice session during the day when the light is most clear. This will generate a particular bliss, but once stabilized a little, it still will not be clear enough. When the generation of virtuous practice of this coarse body depends on the above conditions, the meditation session will be brought to a state of culmination, like the third and fourth days of the waxing moon.

The manner in which visions multiply

Second, the manner in which these multiply is twofold: First, they arise as internal visions of clear light in all quarters. Inside these again arise scattered droplets of crystal color. The colors of the five elements being stable, they

are calm. When they are stronger, each of the droplets of the tent is surrounded with the five lights, five lights by five wheels, radiating in multi-
color luminosity. The threads also arise, some white. When strong, they arise
like lone strands of droplets of multicolored sheep yarn surrounded with five
rings. In these circles there are subtle aspects of form-bodies, seed-syllables,
reliquary towers, and so forth, in various appropriate forms. Between these
there are further lights, rays, and different aspects, reflections, and so forth.
It is uncertain whether these will be arising. These manifestations may arise
as before, slower and tamed, more controlled, and may remain a little longer.
The *Lamp* (222.4) says: [319]

> Then the visions will proliferate and one will see them like the
> sun and the moon rising in the sky. One will see wheels of lights
> of awareness. One will see tents of light-droplets.

The *Little Nails* (311.3) says:

> Second, it is like water falling through a chasm.

When the visions multiply, all the former rays, lights of the droplets, and
threads will be a little slower and will remain. The rays, threads, and ropes
will manifest quickly, in a walking manner.

Second, the experiences of single-mindedness above are still thin. They
arise as experience of Suchness, free from elaborations. In one moment, the
loosening that is the great self-liberation of all that is inner and outer is happening. There is nothing beyond the sphere that is completely self-luminous
and unwavering. It is like the wind that is not stirring the ocean. It is vividly
rising solely free from all fabricated characteristics. For example, it is like the
waxing moon in its fifth and sixth days. These will proliferate greatly while
meditating, and will even spring up while not meditating. Then one will
have arrived at the meditation in the state of enlightenment.

The manner in which visions will intensify

Third, the manner in which they will intensify is twofold: First, because
visions due to the winds have stopped in one's own continuum, the excellent clear light will arise from inside. The sort of impure manifestations
of the elemental fire, water, earth, and air winds having stopped in one's

continuum, the seeds of pure bodies and the visions of pure lands arise. Visions in the nature of clear light arise in all quarters, in front, above, below, and behind; droplets of the five lights, some like shields, some like felt, or as if seen through felt made from yak hair; or a grid-like pattern of a city, tiny seeds, and so forth. Each of these five droplets will further split into five. Out of these, some will be embellished with vertical side strands of lights, surrounded with circles, and so forth. They will be surrounded at the periphery by lotuses of light, wheels, swastikas, jewels, and so forth. Outside these, there will be outer portals, with gate ornaments set forth or completed with their proper equivalents. The inside of these circles will be filled with various divine forms, in part or complete, or filled with just heads, brilliant seed-syllables and letters, and so forth, together with strands of light rays, large and small, in numbers inconceivable by the mind, arising as objects. These visions abide sometimes without moving and shaking, sometimes rolling up a bit. The *Little Nails* (311.3) says:

Third, they transform to resemble hawks searching for food.

The *Lamp* (222.6) says:

These visions will intensify and you will see the mandalas of the perfected bodies of the five families. [320]

The manner in which to generate internal experiences

Second, as in the above, once one has achieved deep stability, self-liberation, and freedom from elaborations, then after a while, awareness becomes baseless, primordially empty, abruptly and completely rootless. Whatever external and internal objects of consciousness occur, no matter what, everything that arises in either cyclic existence or transcendence becomes of one singular taste in the natural state.[297] This is called "the meditation where the many has a single taste." It is similar to the eighth and ninth day of the waxing moon. Here, one has only reached halfway toward the intent of enlightenment. Having reached the end (*zad sar*) [lit. "extinction"] of the practice of meditation on essential nature, one then begins with the meditation on space.

The manner in which visions will be perfected

Fourth, there are two points on the manner in which arising visions will be perfected. First is to make manifest the excellent clear light. The bodies of the enlightened ones and the pure lands emerge spontaneously by themselves. They themselves arise really without ever having been hidden. Thus, they are self-manifestations of the mandalas of activities of pacification, increase, overpowering, and of wrathful activities. These great palace-fortresses are separate, and each is radiantly illuminated. They are layered with gates, gate ornaments, cornices, horned-eagle tents, horned-bird feathers, pillar decorations, vases, parasols, and bird horns. The inside of the mandalas for the activities of pacification and increasing have suns, moons, lotuses, swastikas, wheels, jewels, and so forth, for seats that are pure and without flaws.

The mandalas for overpowering and wrathful activities have these five: haughty spirits, gods, subterranean Lu, scent eaters, and Tsen,[298] and so forth. Their seats have their characteristic cloaks, and their entourage, together with further emanations, messengers, and attendants, surround the chiefs of the five outer and inner lineages. The number of deities from the various families dedicated to pacification, increase, power, and wrathful activities is inconceivable. They are all sitting on their appropriate seat with their customary ornaments. They have the major and minor marks, the colors, symbolic hand gestures, and all the characteristics of perfection. The magnitude of their size is beyond measure. They arise in incommensurable numbers. Now and then they arise five-by-five everywhere, back and forth, above and below, as droplets of the five lights. At their centers, the five families sit, perfected. Again, the inside of each droplet is demarcated with the four pure realms in the quarters and the fifth in the center. Inside these sit the five families. Furthermore, between the droplets are set the emblems of the five families. And again, in each mandala and so forth, the deities sit on their thrones, shining. These gods, perfected bodies, their emanations, and so forth, manifest everywhere. The [various] ways in which these pure visions arise are unquantifiable. The moment these presences manifest, the immeasurable lights, droplets, rays, threads, and bodies—all these together—remain unmoving and stable. The *Lamp* (222.6) says:

> Then these visions will be perfect and one will see mandalas of spontaneous symbolic seals. [321] One will see pure lands of visionary lights. One will see unmoving wonders.

The *Little Nails* (211.3) says:

> Fourth, they become like a turtle in a basin.

Second, the virtuous practice of making the many into the single taste will bring but little conjecture to one's experience and realization. Whatever there is, all the objects of meditation and the endeavors of the ordinary intellect that is meditating, will be released in the mind. Awareness will come to abide continuously in an undisturbed state, without meditating. What emerges from that will not go beyond. From that moment on, the ordinary intellect will not need to meditate deliberately. In this state it is necessary to be only slightly mindful. This is called "meditating undisturbed without meditating."

It is similar to the thirteenth and the fourteenth day of the waxing moon. One is starting to reach the ground of enlightenment. Finality is rising for real in one's continuum with the meditation on the expanse of realization, but at this moment it has not yet arisen enough to be evident.

The manner in which visions reach finality

Fifth, the manner in which final visions arise is twofold: First, just as in the rising of the pure lands, the droplets, the lights, the rays, the body of the gods, and so forth arise pure by themselves. Conceptual elaborations are everything that has the characteristic of reality. Intrinsic emptiness is rootless. It is the universal base in the space of non-conceptuality, the resting place to dissolve. Having collected, now all at once, efforts and everything that has the mark of conceptuality is liberated by just letting go. Sounds, lights, rays, the bodies of deities—all manifestations of pristine cognition— are collected in the mind. And with clear elucidation they are abruptly cut off. The *Lamp* (222.7) says:

> Rays are the natural rays of awareness, the wonders of emptiness
> as reflections. Sounds are the natural sounds of awareness, the
> natural sound of emptiness in the manner of echoes. Bodies are
> the natural forms of awareness, the natural forms of emptiness in
> the manner of water moons.

The *Six Transmissions* (133.5) says:

One sees the blissful ones existing in grains of sand. It is like drinking honey in a dream, where [all these experiences mean] nothing to the one awakened. Nothing remains, nothing is seen, for emptiness is free from partialities. This said, it is difficult to explain, like a mute person trying to explain a dream.

The *Little Nails* (311.3) says:

Fifth, they are like the sky fading away the elements.

The manner in which these visions arise, all of these, sounds, lights, rays, and so forth, everything that arises in these self-manifestations presently fades. They fade in the expanse of the universal base, vanishing by themselves, self-releasing, eliminating themselves, rising by themselves in the finality of extinction. This is the single essential point in regard to delusion. The *Little Nails* (322.3) says:

The innermost ground of origination is released. Having reached this, this is the finality of liberation. [322]

Second, being mindful, unwavering without meditating, is accompanied by a slight binding. At some point, one must cut the rope of mindfulness. For having developed a tethering pole in meditation regarding everything that one does, one can otherwise never get beyond into the state of effortlessness. Whatever arises, it arises in pristine cognition. Whether one meditates or not, it makes no difference. Whether one sleeps or not, it makes no difference. If one is established, one stays. If one focuses, it will go away. When necessary, it arrives. It is independent and transforms by itself. An enemy becomes the same as a son. Gold is the same as dirt. There is no hoping for something higher. There is no fear of the lower. The meditation on the expanse of realization becomes manifest. It is similar to the fifteenth day of the waxing moon. It is the completion of familiarization. One has gained the natural ground of Kuntu Zangpo.

Furthermore, for example, if a liar completely cuts away his deceit, he will go away ashamed of himself. These visions of sounds, lights, and rays have been thoroughly crushed, for they have met with the source of the mind. Delusion has been completely severed. This is the one good merit, the perfect enlightenment, and the result. There is no need to hope for something else.

Present visions are understood as deities in their immeasurable mansions. Hopes and desires are reversed and evil actions are rightfully eradicated. Henceforth, wicked actions are, accordingly, no longer done. Having well and completely severed delusion in the primordial ground, from now on one is never deluded again. Awareness is primordially pure and stainless in essential actuality. At the original onset, dynamism is perfected and any remaining exertion is severed. Once this becomes evident, there is no more wavering from that state, which is the body of reality. From that state the defiled composite aggregates are released into the uncontaminated state. The trainee will then have pure visions. One's body will arise as a body of perfection adorned with the major and minor marks and with displays of ornaments, thrones, and pure realms.

The manner in which these will arise, constituents and sense spheres, channels and limbs, the six collections, the five doors, and so forth, are outwardly as the one-hundred-and-eight deities of increasing, and inwardly as the forty-five deities of pacification, and secretly as the eighty-six wrathful deities. They will arise in these perfected bodies.

All these will emanate and use various paths and methods to lead wandering beings in whatever manner is appropriate. They will undauntedly fulfill the welfare of wandering beings and will emanate forms that will originate spontaneously, so that there will be no need to sow for the three enlightened bodies in the future.

Then, at that time, there will be no need to purify karma and defilements or to generate the path and strive for many eons, because all provisional meanings, the divisions of cause and effect, will be false and cast away. This empty compulsion of an enclosure that is the physical body will be enlightened at that very moment. The *Lamp* (223.2) says:

> Manifested falsehoods become extinct in the mind. It is decisively clear that form bodies [323] are determined in the mind. Delusion is completely cut off, so that error is impossible. The three bodies now become manifest. The power of action, cause, and effect are a great fiction. This is the powerful method of the enlightened ones.

Now then, having brought to completion this advice, with however many visionary experiences, the *Little Nails* (310.7) says:

The number of pulses of the arteries should be measured. Their frequencies should be neither long nor short. Calculating a hundred as one unit, with eighteen thousand of these, one will conclusively become familiar with visions.

The median number of breaths for a person in a cycle is a hundred. This is the measure for one count on clear light. The full measure for this is then eighteen thousand. If one with medium capacity practices without interruption, given other conditions, the vision of finality, following the above, should reach completion as said.

Furthermore, there are five ways in which these visions appear directly, and these are shown in a corresponding diagram.[299]

Combining visions with the stages of the path

Third, combining visions with the stages of the path is like the tradition of the charioteers: one travels along the path like the conquerors and the saints of the past. Moreover, one first purifies sins and defilements with the nine gradual practices of Bön. In order to amass the two accumulations, one acts in accord with the path of accumulation. From that comes the advice concerning the practices related to those using symbolic attributes and those without attributes. The generation of clear visions on intrinsic essence, and the connection with the essential point on the natural state, correspond to the path of application.

Furthermore, there is the general and the particular advice on clear light. The direct teachings concerning the pristine cognition of awareness correspond to the path of vision.

Moreover, there is the advice on how to extract maximal benefits. There, the real meaning of the essence itself arises, and one becomes acquainted with this familiarity. This corresponds with the path of meditation. Once again, having been directly introduced to the true nature, there is the definitive conclusion, which is reaching finality.

Furthermore, regardless of how one toiled for many eons and rebirths abiding on the path of method, one can in this one rebirth prevail and self-liberate without treading the path for one instant and without abandoning illusion. One then spontaneously achieves the resulting three bodies. The *Six Transmissions* (144.1) says:

624   *The Tradition of Everlasting Bön*

The path: It is perfected in this short path.

The *Lamp* (223.3) says:

> The power of action, cause, and result are a great fiction. This is
> the powerful method of the enlightened ones.

If one joins realization and experience at the time of the meditation session,
one will become familiar with the mode of the essential point of the pristine
cognition of awareness. This is concordant with the path of accumulation.

When one is in the state of meditation and is endowed with clear visions
that arise, this is concordant with the path of application. When one is in
the state of meditation and visions begin to arise, one realizes afresh one's
natural characteristics. This is concordant with the path of vision. [324]
Then again, while this state is becoming familiar, one finally crosses over.
This is concordant with the path of meditation. It turns into the expanse, the
result in which one is brought to completion.

Furthermore, during the meditation session, when one acquires stability,
one will have acquired the enlightened qualities of truly knowing delusion,
the qualities of the essence of knowledge, the qualities of pure speech, and
likewise of the view, meditation, deportment, activities, clear visions, and all
these experiences. In all pure individuals, the arising of all these enlightened
qualities will occur.

Similarly, when in a state of meditation, all these arisen enlightened qualities will become more and more exalted. The true knowledge of the mira-
cles of the heroes of everlastingness, their activities, their enlightened body,
speech, and mind, their view and intent, their conduct, all these enlightened
qualities will be acquired. When in the state of meditation, one will become
extremely exalted in them all. The five enlightened qualities of the body,
speech, mind, activities, qualities, and so forth of the supremely perfected
enlightened ones will truly arise in one's continuum.

Furthermore, the manner in which the outer visions arise is that of seeing the clear light. Internally, the manner in which experiences are generated comes from proficiency with virtuous practices. Between clearly seeing
through the artifice of delusion and all the enlightened qualities and so forth,
the individual will produce these experiences gradually. All these outer and
inner interconnections will become united in the same manner as before,
and they will arise in a similar manner, gradually.

For the one who realizes instantly from the first moment, visions arise in concordance with the state of meditation. One skips stages and moves in great leaps in so many ways. Advice appropriate to one's intellect, such as direct introduction and so forth, is given directly. For the one who proceeds suddenly, advice is also given directly. It is not desirable to teach using the gradual generation process here. For those leaping over stages, it is necessary to train with a variety of methods along the path of skillful means. Thus, cultivating advice appropriate to one's intellect is very important and is a crucial point.

These were the explanations on meditation on clear light and taking on the practice of the path. *Uya maro!* May there be virtue![300] [325]

7. Instructions on Conduct to Purify Dynamism That Comes Up as Conditions on the Path

TO KUNTU ZANGPO, who is the all-encompassing leader of transmigrating beings, manifested self-awareness, I pay homage!

Third,[301] these instructions on conduct to purify dynamism that comes up as conditions on the path are threefold: forceful purification in this life, forceful purification at the time of death, and forceful purification during the intermediate state.

Forceful purification in this life

This first section is fourfold: to carry on along the path of the three doors, to carry on along the path with the six collections,[302] to carry on along the path with conceptual patterns, and to carry on along the path of diversity.

To carry along the path by means of the three doors

First, the activities of the three doors [i.e., body, speech, and mind] are all the activities of the path of conduct, pure or not. When engaged in virtuous practice [i.e., ritual or meditation practice] during meditation or post-meditation, these must be integrated, such as the virtuous activities that are attributed to the body: circumambulation, prostrations, symbolic hand-gestures, and yogic exercises. Non-virtuous conduct as such consists in striking, beating, [uttering] angry words, jumping, running, and so forth. Activities not indicated in the scriptures consist in eating, walking, sitting, dancing, cooking, and so forth, all of which concern actions done by one's body.

Concerning the highest-level practitioner, there is no conduct among the above that is prohibited. For the middle-level practitioner, during meditation one is to practice self-release without grasping. As for the last level, one should not prevent [lit. separate] oneself from using the antidote of fixed mindfulness.

In the great state of clear light of empty awareness, one's conduct should arise by itself from the pristine cognition of self-awareness. The *Root Commentary on the Little Nails* (5.3) says:

> The various actions of the body arise with the energy of non-action.

Similarly, pure activities of speech consist in the repetition of mantras, essential mantras, daily liturgy, explanation and debate, signing and ritual chanting, and so forth. Impure activities consist in harsh speech, lies and slander, crying and wailing, and so forth. Activities not indicated in the scriptures consist in singing, ancient recitations, mythical narratives, conversation, jesting, random talk, spells, discussion and solicitation, and so forth, all speech expressions.

In regard to the superior practitioner, it is the same as above. The middle-level one is the same as in meditation. The lower-level one's conduct should be the same as well, applying fixed mindfulness.

In the great state of the clear light of empty awareness, one's conduct is unobstructed when coming from the state of the clear, naked, pristine cognition of self-awareness. The *Root Commentary on the Little Nails* (5.3) says:

> The various expressions of speech arise with the energy of speechlessness.

Likewise, pure mental activities are respect and devotion, generation-stage practices, concentration, meditation, and so forth. The impure ones are the five poisons, cursing thoughts, cunning thoughts, wrong views, and so forth. Activities not indicated in the scriptures are minding one's country, wealth, profit, reminiscing about the past, considerations about the future, ideas and scrutiny, judgments [326]—in brief, all measure of mental activities.

One's conduct is unobstructed when coming from the state of the clear, naked, pristine cognition of self-awareness. The *Root Commentary on the Little Nails* (5.4) says:

> The various memories and concepts of mental intent arise with the energy of non-conceptuality.

The *Little Nails* (320.1) says:

> It [pristine cognition of self-awareness] is entirely pervasive without outside or inside. The measure of manifestation is the play of the enlightened body. The measure of fame is the play of enlightened speech. The measure of memory is the play of the enlightened mind. The measure of occurrences is the play of the enlightened qualities. The measure of action is the play of enlightened activities.

In fact, all actions of the three doors that are not perceived as deliberate deeds, performed from the state of intrinsic emptiness, which is the highest wisdom, must arise unobstructed in the nature of skillful means. The *Elucidation*[303] says:

> Whether going or sitting, eating or drinking, facing up or on one's back, lying sideways, in stable contemplation or in the post-meditation state, whether dreaming or in the intermediate state, if one does not know and is not continually connected with awareness, it is like a stream dried out by drought. One will not be able to acquire the conditions of both the view and meditation.

The practices of yogic discipline involve all activities of the three doors and are performed with complete sincerity. When first engaging in these, one must integrate them well with religious practices. In the middle it will be insufficient to slightly integrate yogic discipline with religious practices; however, one must not harm one's religious commitments. Finally, it will be insufficient to not harm them even a little [i.e., one must only keep the bare minimum of religious commitments]; however, yogic discipline and religious practices must still continue to appear as friends.

To carry on along the path with the six collections

Second, as for carrying on the path with the six collections, whichever visual object is perceived as having a beautiful form, it is likewise not beautiful. All visual objects arise in the visual sensory field as big, small, good, bad, near, far, and so forth. However, for the superior practitioner, they arise very much by themselves and self-liberate. For the middle-level one, they will be seen directly as what they are and will be directly freed. For the lower-level practitioner, they will be good or bad. Each doubt will be eliminated once it has been appropriately repudiated, and there will be no more conceptualization and examination.

In the great state of the clear light of empty awareness, forms that are seen are empty, completely rootless, and unreal; like mirages, they are to be forcefully purified. The *Hundred Thousand* says:

> Forms are like mirages. Since they do not exist whatsoever, there is nothing whatsoever to be done with them.

The *Treasury* (22.3) says:

> Regarding a brightly colored object of the senses, it is said that color is bright only in the expanse of the mind.

Similarly, a pleasant word that is perceived as an object of the auditory sense is not a pleasant word in itself. All musical sounds, the signs of living beings originating from languages, are empty sounds to be forcefully purified, just like echoes, in the same manner as noted above for superior, middle-level, and lower practitioners.

A pleasant scent is not a pleasant scent in itself. Clean scent, unclean scent, scent joined with another fragrance, all scents by themselves, and so forth, all these aspects of scent are empty feelings without traces that are to be greatly and forcefully purified by all three, the superior practitioner, the middling, and the lower. [327]

Gustatory sensations that are objects of the taste sense, delicious or not, good or bad, subtle or coarse, and so forth, all tastes are to be forcefully purified, as above, when perceived by the superior, the middle-level, and the lower practitioners who practice cutting off. These experiences are completely empty, without roots.

Those objects of the tactile senses that are soft to the touch or rough, hot or cold, light or heavy, good or bad—whatever arises, when perceived by the superior, the middle-level, and the lower practitioner, they should practice forcefully purifying these through self-liberation and non-apprehension in awareness and emptiness.

The *Lamp* (212.3) says:

From the pristine cognition of one's awareness, the six dynamisms arise as the six kinds of object through which various activities are performed. These are emanation bodies existing naturally.

The great Shen, Drenpa Namkha, said: "One should not pursue the objects of the five senses. If one follows [them], one must not distinguish between their aspects. Although one may distinguish them, one should not grasp at a self. And although one may grasp at the latter, one should not cling to its predispositions."

Even those with very little strength to practice can engage in grasping at whatever comes up and so forth, just when looking. They can identify, for the benefit of their own knowledge, the one doing the action from the one looking. When pristine cognition of one's own awareness is in the state of clear nakedness, one sees unceasingly while not engaging the dynamism of concepts and discrimination. One integrates everything [such as subject and object] into one's own continuum without losing this abiding in pure naked awareness even for a moment. But one must go beyond merely integrating so that all the visions should arise together as friends. It is not sufficient for them to arise as such; they must become of one taste in non-duality.

To carry on along the path with conceptual patterns

Third, it is said that every day the continuum of an individual is moved 84,000 times with conceptual patterns, and there is no way to carry any of them on the path. It is for that reason that memories are produced suddenly. Although whatever is produced may be great or small, subtle or coarse, numerous or not, good or bad, they are deliberately either eliminated or not, with or without effort. One does not cast away their power.

The view of the best practitioner overcomes these conceptual patterns in the manner of snow falling into a lake. As for the middle-level practitioner, during meditation she overcomes these protrusions in the manner of the sun striking frost. As for the lower-level practitioner, while upholding mindfulness he pursues them in the manner of giving appropriate counsel to one who is angry. One practices not engaging frivolously in one's afflictions, but rather looking into the essence of these conceptual patterns. One meets closely with the source and cuts its roots at the base. One regrets these afflictions and sets out to renounce them. Afterward, one puts on the armor of not generating them again. The *Little Nails* (320.7) says:

The base is self-sprung pristine cognition. Afflictions are the dynamism of the five poisons. Realizing non-duality, one concretely manifests the result. [328]

To carry on along the path of diversity

Fourth, to carry on along the path of diversity has three conducts: the secret conduct, the secret ascetic conduct, and the conduct of complete victory that is without partiality.

The secret conduct

First, the secret conduct is like the fire of a lamp that can be extinguished through bad conditions such as wind and so forth. For individuals with inferior abilities, at the beginning of their work, all activities of body and speech will be affected by their practices on the path of conduct. At that time, all non-concordant obstructing conditions should be eliminated. They should rely on friends and all harmonious conditions, and take on all manner of conduct of the heroes, such as the ten perfections[304] of skillful methods. The *Hundred Thousand* says:

One will engage intensely in the profound conduct of the heroes.

The *Directed Meaning* (20.1) says:

When hurt manifests, one should rely on a helpful friend.

The secret ascetic conduct

Second, the lamp is now bigger and it is like holding it for a friend against the wind and so forth. The middle-level practitioner is at this time able to practice on one's own a little. One can carry on along the path of forceful purification to make progress, applying the key points in one's practice of yogic exercises.

This conduct is like that of a dog or a pig to whom nothing is clean or dirty. Clean or dirty, tasty or not, good or bad, right or wrong, friend or foe, one behaves such that everything is of equal taste, accepting and rejecting nothing. Behaving like a lunatic, unconcerned, one does not take sides through one's conduct. One does not reject or accept. One does not calculate for profit and loss. One does not give in to concepts and discriminations. One is settled in behaving completely spontaneously.

This conduct is like that of a child who has nothing to stop or accomplish and who neither does good nor eliminates the bad. One behaves unbounded. One lets loose, free and relaxed. One's conduct is like an avalanche, completely free of doubt. One countenance reveals neither cheerful hope nor hesitation. One is completely cut off, giving away instantly, behaving without fluttering.

This conduct of the great yogic discipline is like a peacock. One carries on in a friendly manner in adverse circumstances. One summons poverty as wealth and takes on obstacles as accomplishments.

This conduct is an antidote, like a heroic person who carries on to the summit. One practices above sickness and anguish. If frightened, one practices above fear. If disgusted, one rises above it. If sick, one carries on above sickness. If hungry, one carries on above hunger. If cold, one practices intentionally overcoming cold and so forth. One is fighting a battle and integrates defeat and victory. The *Directed Meaning* (20.4) says:

> Visions, during the time of plenty, all arise as friends.

The *Six Transmissions* (126.4) says:

> Engaging the five poisons is the most excellent of conducts.

Furthermore (126.7):

> When one is able to perform the great yogic practices, whatever one does is neither good nor bad. That is praised as the vessel of the Great Perfection.

And (126.4):

> Such conduct is unstoppable. [329]

The conduct of complete victory that is without partiality

Third, at the time of the finality of experience and realization, the highest practitioner's conduct integrates the many into the one taste, much like the golden continent. Nothing surpasses that state. Everything in that state is of equal taste. Through realization, all these experiences are mirages. This state surpasses all objects of performance and performers. It is the conduct of the complete victory that is without partiality. The *Coming of the Three Meanings*[305] (6.3) says:

> If one realizes the self as the blissful one itself, then everything is the conduct of the blissful one. It is a measure that cannot be measured.

Forceful purification of dynamism at the time of death

Second, on forceful purification at the time of death, the *Lamp* (224.7) says:

> At the time of death, there is a boundary separating happiness and suffering. The mind has the greater power to decide between the good and the bad. I offer this unfailing advice on the union with the vessel of the senses.

The *Little Nails* (322.4) says:

> The moment when, finally, body and mind dissociate is when the boundary separates the two, happiness and suffering.

There are three points here: the practices according to the disintegration of the elements, the practices according to their assemblage, and advice on particular points.

The practices according to the disintegration of the elements

First, when the spleen, the earth element, disintegrates internally, the external tactile sensations of the body are no longer noticeable. Concomitantly, one cannot raise the left hand. As a result, the contaminants of the nine orifices naturally flow out.

At that moment, for the best practitioner, being in the state where view is uniquely perfected, objects of knowledge, even the abusive ones, arise as friends. The middle-level practitioner remains inseparable in intrinsic essence and unwavering from the state of meditation. The lower-level practitioner, who merely followed this advice, should recollect that moment of disintegration, the first of the six recollections, the remembrance of death. Understand the disintegration of the elements! These external and internal realities, whatever the case, are relentless.

One recollects the lama sitting on the crown of one's head, and one meditates with fierce devotion. Then one should remember one's tutelary deity. One imagines one's body as that of the tutelary deity, reciting its mantras and not forgetting one's secret name. Then one should recollect the intermediate state. As such, visual objects that arise are manifestations of the intermediate state. One should think, these are unreal, like mirages. Thereafter, one should recollect the words of advice and the point on rootlessness, that one should be stable in one's own naked awareness.

Similarly, when the kidneys, the water element, disintegrate, sounds are no longer heard. One cannot raise the left leg. One cannot hold urine.

When the liver, the fire element, disintegrates, the tongue cannot taste. One cannot raise the right arm and blood comes out from the nose. [330]

When the lungs, the air element, disintegrate, the nose does not perceive smells. One cannot raise the right leg and one cannot hold feces.

When the heart, the element of space, disintegrates, the eyes cannot see. One cannot raise the head and sperm is expelled.

For each of these moments, again, the best and middle-level practitioners do as above. The lowest practitioner should remember the advice of the five recollections. One meditates by oneself or is confirmed[306] by another.

The practices according to their assemblage

Second, on the manner in which the elements are reabsorbed, the *Lamp* (224.5) says:

> Earth dissolves in water, the strength of the body is lost.
>
> After this single element is finished, internally, where the earth elemental wheel is located at the navel region, there are signs indicating that its ability is dissolving into the water element. Externally, the body's strength is dissipating. The body feels like it is sinking to the ground, heavier. The yellow-color elemental earth radiance will then arise in self-awareness. All visions spring up

as pure yellow to the one traveling this path. The water element dissolves into the fire element, and the luster of the body is lost.

The ability of the wheel of water at the secret place dissolves into the fire element. Its sign is that the luster is lost, the mouth and nose become dry, and visions come up with blue light. The fire element dissolves into the air element and the body and the heat of the body is lost.

The *Lamp* (224.6) continues:

> When heat is reabsorbed, one's tongue stutters and one cannot talk. All visions arise with this red light. The air element dissolves into space and breath will collect and then be lost.
>
> One will become terrified and will try to catch the ground, but one's breath cannot be held. Visions will arise as green lights. Then the mind will dissolve into the universal base. Breath will stop and body and mind will become separated.

Then it becomes darker and darker and the eyes close, no longer perceiving, and they turn upward. Visions then arise as white lights. At that moment, the superior and middle-level practitioners' views and states of meditation are as indicated above.

As for the lower-level practitioner, the lama or spiritual friends will remind one, clearly saying: "Here are the signs of the dissolution of the earth element into the water element. Leave them for the state of the great clear light of unstained awareness. That golden light that arises in self-manifestation is the natural radiance of pure awareness. Know that this natural radiance is illusory. These visions of light are like the intermediate state of the clear light of reality. Be familiar with these self-manifestations!"[307]

One should become familiar with these visionary elements in this manner. Those who will follow later should meditate with visualizations in a straightforward manner.

Moreover, these elements are gradually reabsorbed in great measure. In the case of an adventitious illness, they can be reabsorbed abruptly. Even at that moment, the external breathing may not be cut off, but when it stops, there are two reabsorptions. At that moment, all the blood in the smaller veins, having gathered in the central channel, falls three times into the heart. The vision will be of a rain of blood, or like being squashed by demonic spirits. [331] It will be difficult to be mindful then. At that moment, the body of reality will be thrown along the central channel of awareness and will be sent out through the doorway of the lamp. It will be expelled through the right eye for men and through the left eye for women.

Advice on particular points

Third, in regard to particular points, in case the external breathing has stopped but the internal breathing has not, awareness becomes like the sun in a cloudless sky, unstained and bare in its nakedness. At that moment, all changes arise clearly and advice on particular essential points must be given.

The body is placed facing east, along the five postures, or in the squatting position, or even in the sleeping position of the elephant. Then generate the three channels as above. At the heart, one's mind is generated in the seed-syllable *A*, in a grain made of five lights that spreads and spins, the size of the little finger. Then the breath is expelled from the corpse with as much effort as possible. Filth that is inside the path of the central channel is thrown out and the space of clear awareness is cleansed of dirt and obstruction. One then thinks that the door of Tshangpa at the crown of the head is opened.

Then while pronouncing *Hrig* in coordination with the breath twenty-one times, the *A* jumps up in increments through the door of Tshangpa. As it rises through little by little from below, one imagines the door of Tshangpa closing behind.[308] Then again, twenty-one times, this grain of light is collected into the *A*, and another grain of light is displayed in space. This *A* melts into the heart of one's lama. As this lama disappears like a rainbow, one imagines that one is thus enlightened. At that moment, the purification practice consists in the *Hrig* seed-syllable that goes through the door of Tshangpa while the *A* syllable falls back into one's heart. When awareness is clear, it has been purified and the signs will arise without the slightest distraction.

When resting, the *A* syllable descends back into the heart while one performs the dedication to enlightenment. The *Little Nails* (316.5) says:

> Awareness is the little man of the mind, mindfully riding the horse of the intellect. The unobstructed wind lifts him with its wings, and he departs up the path of enlightenment, the central channel. He arrives at the secret door of bliss at the crown of the head and rises up as the naked king of awareness. Discursive

thinking, the skin of the ordinary mind, is shed so that one can see the countenance of naturally-arisen pristine cognition. One is then purified from the mystifications of dark ignorance.

The enlightened qualities of this advice consist in what the *Little Nails* (312.1) says:

> The pathways that generate impure places; the ordinary three: body, speech, and mind; the nine orifices; the five senses; the six destinies; the qualities and so forth, these close the door to the transference of consciousness and to ordinary consciousness such as "heat." They completely reverse the nine grounds and the three worlds so that the continuum of the path of the five poisons and afflictive emotions is severed. The six destinies and the ocean of cyclic existence dry up. The four kinds of births and the gate to cyclic existence become empty, and the three enlightened bodies arise naturally and multiply widely to help [others].

One has to be established gradually in this.

Furthermore, at the time of death, for the practitioner of superior capacity, the knowing awareness of the moment will spontaneously achieve the three enlightened bodies and the integrality of enlightenment. [332] Self-awareness will become realized, fully rising, and pristine cognition will manifest completely in the concrete reality of the nature of the mind that is. The secondary conditions that are [included] in the admonitions should be clearly mentioned so that with the direct introduction, one will no doubt have the vision of the self.

For the practitioner of middling capacity, the *Little Nails* (n.p.) says:

> At the moment of death, what is untrue and illusory-like will arise fully in self-manifested appearances. All of these are of the nature of intrinsic mind. This intrinsic mind is complete rootless awareness of that moment. The body of reality exists within one-self. Having been directly introduced to the primordial abiding, one's confidence becomes definite and there are no more doubts about eliminating the door to rebirth.

For the practitioner of lower capacity, the *Little Nails* (322.7) says:

One engages in activities with the highest faith and devotion.
One engages in meditation with compassion and love toward the
lower beings. One is directly introduced to non-conceptuality
and non-attachment, with all that is in between. With this
advice, one will undoubtedly come to abide in happiness.

Furthermore, sounds, lights, and rays have been significantly cleared. The
highest practitioner arises self-liberating. The middling one arises in the
pristine cognition of the body of the deity. And the lower practitioner is
directly introduced to the self-generated sounds, lights, and rays when body
and mind separate.

The *Little Nails* (322.7) says:

Refuge, the mind of enlightenment, the tutelary deity, and so
forth, these are to be remembered well, together with the power
of good intention, at the time of dying. And one will certainly be
taking on rebirth in a happy place.

One will then become just like a glossy, clean wick nurtured with butter!

The forceful purification of the intermediate state

Third, the forceful purification of the intermediate state is threefold: the
intermediate state of the abiding base, the intermediate state of the clear
light of reality, and the empty intermediate state of becoming.

The intermediate state of the abiding base

On the first intermediate state, the *Little Nails* (323.2) says:

The conceptuality of subject-object dissolves in the expanse. At
that moment, awareness abides in nakedness. Self-originated
pristine cognition is devoid of obscurations and coverings.

As soon as body and mind separate, at that one moment there is no longer
any direct encounter between pure and impure activities. For all sentient
beings, there are no more distinctions between large or small defilements.
The universal base and awareness become like the sun and the clouds

parting. At that moment there are no more obscurations, and pure penetrating self-luminosity abides in all its nakedness.

As for its mode, the universal base and the king of awareness come off from the dust [i.e., one's corpse and cyclic existence] from the right or left eye, respectively, for men and women. Then, they dwell between the eyebrows for a while. At that moment there will be a radiance remaining uncorrupted in one's face and particularly between the eyebrows. At that moment it will be very difficult to be mindful, and one will barely remember. As soon as there is recognition, mother and son will immediately meet, and the three expanses of the ordinary body, speech, and mind will be torn apart, and the three dynamisms of the enlightened body, speech, and mind will be perfected. It is by way of wrapping the two lamps into one that there is enlightenment. This is called the narrow path of the heroes.

Furthermore, one becomes liberated through the gathering of the three key points. For now, one becomes familiar with the main point of direct introduction, becoming well acquainted with it over and over again. The moment of death [333] should be repeatedly visualized so that one can become well acquainted with and can resolve karmic predispositions. One is enlightened through being ravished by the three intermediary states of the abiding base. The *Six Essential Points* (223.3) says:

> This is the coercive method to enlightenment, for activities and
> results are themselves the great lie.

At that moment, mind is connected with Heat. Due to previous activities and the power of the thoughts at the moment of dying, as mentioned above, consciousness can nevertheless come out from any of the orifices of the upper or lower sections of the body. If one follows the words of this advice, the transference of consciousness can be done through the door of Tshangpa.

As for the karmic propensities of the intellect that make it impossible to be reborn in a place of happiness, they will circle near the body with greater or smaller attachment for three, two, or some other number of days. During this time, do not perform the cremation and so forth. This measure for purification is needed because subtle visions are still occurring due to karmic predispositions as well as desperate attachment.

If one is not freed from these subtle visions, the son-awareness will dissolve into the expanse of the universal base, the mother. Mindful awareness will become dormant in that state, and the dynamism—that is, the sounds, the lights, and the rays—will be completely eliminated. Lattices of light will cover self-awareness. The universal base will be dense and one will be in a state without anything—clear appearances, memories, or thoughts. One will abide there for three days until the fourth noon, or five or seven days, and so forth.

The intermediate state of the clear light of reality

The second point is twofold: recognition and the elimination of the intermediate state.

Recognition

First, the *Little Nails* (323.3) says:

> In the case where one is not free from that, this will give rise to
> two intermediate states.

If the body and mind do not separate, and one is not freed of the abiding base at the moment of the intermediate state, then one will awaken to the experience that is called "the intermediate state of the clear light of reality." It will be like a second awakening where awareness is clearer than before. Secondary conditions will make changes easy to originate. Then one's bodily karmic propensity will appear in its own form from the space of the heart of light[309] as one-inch-sized pristine cognition. That done, awareness and thoughts will awaken, and memories will begin to flow again. The lattices of light will be torn apart and something looking like a butter lamp in a vase will appear. The clear light of consciousness will arise for real. Now then, visions of fire, water, earth, and air having been stopped, the manifestations of sounds, lights, and rays will arise without being hidden.

Moreover, above, below, and in all the intermediate directions, rainbows of the nature of the five lights will appear like drawings, radiant and luminous. Self-generated sounds of awareness, self-arisen, will resound in the manner of discontinuous, roaring thunder. They resound variously, as distant, long, short, large, small, pleasant, or not. Self-generated rays of awareness are like satin, spread woolen cloth, or sunrays and spearheads. They arise variously as weak, strong, long, short, thin, bulky, and in all sorts of ways. The *Little Nails* (323.4) says:

Lights are pure lands without center or limits. They arise like
rainbows in the sky. The sounds roar in the expanse without reality, [334] self-arisen in the manner of the sound of thunder, dis-
continuously. The rays show up as unreal displays, like a sort of
satin or woolen cloth.

The *Little Nails* (324.5) further says:

As for the duration, they arise over the course of five or seven
days. They arise in stages of luminescence for seven days.

Thus, each day corresponding lights arise in stages: white, green, red, blue,
and yellow. For the superior practitioner, these self-arisen lights self-liberate.
For the middle-level one, they become the five deities, the five bodies, and
the five pristine cognitions. The lowest practitioner will then have to meditate on the illusory nature of these self-generated visions, similar to what was
mentioned above.

The elimination of the intermediate state

Second, here, the advice for those having great strength with purification
practice is that the three manifestations—sounds, lights, rays—arise as if one
is meeting a man from one's past. Once more, the exhortation on the secondary conditions should be re-emphasized so that one can proceed with
the elimination. Here, practice brings about final liberation. For the person who is familiar and acquainted with this, divine bodies and mandalas
will arise perfected. At that moment they will arise escorted by the threefold vision with clairvoyance and recollection. It is said that these familiar
accompaniments and so forth, are self-manifested.

As for purification for the middle-level practitioner, there will be a release
of the three key points. The previous advice on clear light has produced a
little understanding of acquaintance and familiarity. The main point about
the moment of death is to have suitable mindfulness with visualization so
that the intermediate state of the clear light of reality will truly arise. With
the key points of meeting the three, it is impossible not to be liberated. The
Little Nails (324.3) says:

In order to completely reverse the cycles of the three realms, one purifies the non-duality of cyclic existence and transcendence in the base. The three enlightened bodies and mandala will then implicitly arise.

The *Little Nails* (324.5) further adds:

> At that moment, one must first remember one's lama. Then one must remember the words of advice and so forth, so that, through the reawakening of accumulated latencies of secondary conditions, there will be release. The secondary conditions will bring release from the intermediate state.

The lowest-level practitioner, having been somewhat purified with this advice, will not fall under the sway of the self-arising of the three manifestations of that moment. These three—sounds, lights, and rays—will arise as delusional, self-generated manifestations. Longing, desire, fear, and panic will not be produced, and one will understand these delusional self-manifestations as pristine cognition in the bodies of deities. One will not be deceived by these and will be released.

Furthermore, for the best practitioner, the manifestations of these three—sounds, lights, and rays—will rise as friends at that moment. The middle-level one will remember that these come up only as minor factors. And for the lowest-level practitioner, liberation is assured through knowledge and self-radiance. The *Little Nails* (323.7) says:

> Visions make one see one's own face. Self-awareness encounters one's face in oneself. One is then purified of the delusion of ignorance in one's own ground. [335]

At this instant one is directly introduced to the cycle of time, the intermediate state.

The empty intermediate state of becoming

Third, the topic on the intermediate state of becoming is fourfold: the manner of its arising, the manner of severing it, the manner of being free from it, and the manner of delusion for certain persons.

The manner of its arising

First, for those above who have not been liberated, the intermediate state of becoming arises. Having stopped the manifestations of sounds, lights, and rays, awareness pours out, carried away cleaned, like a baby chick displaced and coming out depressed. Consciousness then has no support and wanders while becoming attached to karmic predispositions. It goes to kindred terrain, but there is no recognition. One longs for food, wealth, objects, and houses, but there is no power to use them. There are no sense faculties, yet all senses are complete. One can pass at will through the ground, stone, mountains, and cliffs without obstructions. One needs only to think to go. One knows all past and present lives, places high and low, internal and external things.

As for the body, it takes a form concordant with predispositions that were self-manifested in the past life, or that arise in the third part of the future life when one will roam through the gate of rebirth to seek out a new ground to engage. One tries again to enter the previous body, for one may not have had the opportunity to cut ties. Although one has the eyes of pristine cognition, one cannot see anyone except those in the intermediate state. At that time, one is like a bee cut off from nectar and hovering in the sky. Without support, one roams haunted in the intermediate state. One is aware and remembers. But one emerges as one that cannot find anything to do.

The *Tantra Explaining the Primordial Throne*[310] (295.2) says:

> In the manifestation of the clear light of reality, the highest wisdom of realization is not produced. Previous pristine cognition lies dormant, and past karmic propensities arise as visions. One is endowed with a form made of flesh that originated in a previous existence, which is the cause for all the senses to be complete and unobstructed, the strength of the delusion of karma. One can see with pure eyes divine concordant beings. But one actively searches for an ordinary body and a place to stay.

The manner of severing it

Second, at the moment the physical body is cremated, some [mourner] may call one's name, or cry, but one cannot answer. One cannot offer a portion of food. For instance, [the deceased] is unable to sit in a separate place or have a suitable support for any action.

In the intermediate state of becoming, one knowingly wanders. Remembering advice, one becomes hopeful and cheerful and does not despair or doubt for even a moment. One then actualizes the practice by condensing all points with focused single-mindedness. Mother and son will then meet and one will take one's place in the sphere of enlightenment.

But if one is not able to do that, at that moment one should think and remember that all manner of external arisings are mirage-like, natural self-arisen manifestations that are like a dream. Practicing like this, one will not be deceived by these manifestations. One will not pursue them, and they will be released through self-annihilation. [336]

As for those of lower abilities, they should engage in the generation and the perfection processes of the tutelary deity. Having practiced with faith and devotion toward the lama, one applies the key points and cuts off the gate to impure rebirth. Having reawakened the accumulated propensities from one single life, one becomes liberated.

Therefore, faith and aspiration are golden to the one who is presently familiar with the manner of the arising of the essence. When one clearly remembers the ideas that were heard at the moment of death, having died, one can arrive at sustaining the good karmic propensities. Once defilements have been cleansed, it is very important for others to practice meritorious deeds for seven weeks for the deceased. The causes of the intermediate state should be prompted clearly in order to be recognized and remembered. Having remembered the advice by that prompting, one can energetically engage in the practice of purification. If [these purification practices] are not effective, then positive results will not be possible. The key point here is irreversibility [i.e., to practice without compromise in order to succeed]. This is an unerring path. The result will be effortless, like a pig pacing along a narrow path. The *Little Nails* (316.5) says:

The path of the droplets is not crooked.

And again (324.6):

From the continuum of a good place, one is quickly liberated.

The manner of being free

Third, the manner of release is threefold:

First, for the superior practitioner, the realization that arises in the intermediate state of the abiding base is like meeting a previously known man. It rips the lattice of the three: ordinary body, speech, and mind. Having perfected the three dynamisms of the enlightened body, speech, and mind, he is like the lion cub or the horned eagle. Immediately after the separation of the body and mind, there is the transformation into the three enlightened bodies from which one will be working continually and extensively for the welfare of wandering beings.

Second, the practitioner of middle capacity is to be well acquainted and familiar with this advice on the intermediate state of the clear light of reality. So that at that moment, wherever the hues of pristine cognition and whatever the hues of light arise in the base, one's body will manifest as an enlightened body of light without span or limits in the directions, above or below. An immeasurable number of immeasurable droplets and tents will arise in the ten directions of the heavens. In the center of these tents that arise five-by-five, the five enlightened bodies will arise by fives. They will manifest in the manner of the arrangements of mandala clusters.

At that time, the six clairvoyances and the six recollections having arisen, they will be like lamps that illuminate extensively. Furthermore, from each of these will arise lights in fives for five days. Awareness will be well acquainted with these wheels and domes of lights. They will arise in pristine cognition as divine enlightened bodies and will then be eliminated in the self-manifestation of enlightenment.

Third, the manner of liberation for the lower-level practitioner will be by remembering the existence of the intermediate state, the conditions, and the intermediate state of becoming. One remembers the words of advice on these, and with practice one will know that this lowly vagabond is the conquering child. One seizes one's natural ground of enlightenment. One grasps in one instant the status in the unborn sphere.

Once those with little purification recognize these intermediate states, they will understand their meaning. [337] They will not follow after them and will not fall under the sway of natural inclinations. They will assume their rebirth under their own power. Having brought learning, reflection, and meditation to completion, they will accomplish the great and extensive welfare of self and others. Activating past karma, there will be no intermediate state, and they will become enlightened.

The manner of delusion for certain persons

Fourth, if one's continuum does not embrace this advice, or if one is a follower of the tenet systems and does not heed the key points of this advice, these intermediate states will not be severed. Then, as mentioned above, one will be without a basis for consciousness. While roaming in the intermediate state, pure visions will arise for the virtuous one. Impure visions will arise to the sinful one. These visions will come up quarreling about confused activities.

Furthermore, afflictions, anger, cravings, and torpor will be generated in one's continuum. Lights that are yellow, red, and dark blue will be generated and apprehended on one's path. These visions will naturally occur at the crown of one's head. Snow, blizzards, and gales will pursue one, and one will have to proceed through ravines, gorges, and caves. The result is that, having gone into the three evil destinies, one will take impure bodies with similar associations.

Next, affliction, pride, and envy will be generated in one's continuum and white and green lights will be produced and apprehended on one's path. In these visions, one will be tottering on one's feet and doddering sideways. One will proceed through fog, rusty mist, mirages, and so forth. Having been housed in caves and tents, the result will be a projection to be reborn among the gods and the demigods with similar associations.

Having been peaceful and gentle, having generated the mind of enlightenment and produced devotion in one's continuum, one will not have to engage with the five lights on the path, and the visions will be of climbing upward along steps carried by rainbow clouds and sunrays. One will reach an immeasurable divine mansion. The result will be independent rebirth in pleasurable destinies, and having worked for the welfare of wandering beings, one will receive all similar benefits as those that are reborn in pure realms.

In general, one should know that the intermediate states are like dreams. In case this is difficult to remember, one must remember that it is like looking at someone swimming across water. Conditions change easily. And in case they change, one must do what is necessary, like making gold with copper. There will be great profit. Therefore, one must proceed according to the key points of this advice. If one happens to experience [positive signs following these spiritual exercises], and [continues with] practice, this will not be less than practicing virtues for many lifetimes. Just because this advice might not agree with all the scriptures and precepts, in the same way, taking on this practice does not agree with all individuals on the path.

These were the instructions on conduct with forceful purification of the conditions that arise on the path. *Uya maro!* Virtue! [338]

8. Instructions on Decisively Elucidating the Three Bodies by Seizing the Natural Ground, the Result

To Kuntu Zangpo, who is the all-encompassing leader of transmigrating beings, manifested self-awareness, I pay homage!

These, the instructions on decisively elucidating the three enlightened bodies by seizing the natural ground, the result, are threefold: direct introduction where example and meaning are connected, direct introduction to the dynamism of self-manifestation, and direct introduction on the resulting three enlightened bodies.

Direct introduction where example and meaning are connected

First are the symbol and the example. The lamp symbolizes the principle of the example. The lamp is pointing directly to the sign. The sign is pristine cognition. Both should be joined to each other. Furthermore, the *Lamp* (218.5) says:

> As for illustrating these principles with examples, the butter lamp symbolizes the natural clarity of pristine cognition. The lotus symbolizes the unstained original purity. The sun symbolizes the spontaneous clear light. The mirror symbolizes the unobscured natural clarity. The crystal ball symbolizes transparent nakedness. The sky symbolizes the all-filling pristine cognition.

At first the butter lamp should be shown. Its reflection arising in the mirror becomes the focus of one's awareness. Then one directs one's attention inside. With eyes wide open, one sees into the essence of awareness. One becomes confident and comes to be directly introduced. The essence of the butter lamp is to be free from the darkness of obscurity and coverings. It is limpid in its natural brilliance and it shines accordingly.

As for the universal base and awareness, having been totally freed from the covering of darkness at the gate of the lamp, one is clear and limpid in natural clarity. This is called "direct introduction."

Similarly, one should also perform these practices with other examples in order to well illustrate the main principle. Then, the internal conviction that arises will develop. One should continue with adequate direct introduction.

Although the lotus dwells naked in mud, it is unsullied and unstained by the mud. The universal base and awareness exist in the interior space of karmic predispositions and arise unsullied in their naked primordial purity without being stained by the impurities of karmic predispositions.

The sun rises resplendent in its great primordial luminosity without having been created by anyone.

The universal base at the door of the lamp has also not been created by anyone. Yet it is spontaneously accomplished as the great clear light from the very beginning where it originated by itself.

The reflections in the mirror arise clearly without obstruction, this clearly without having a nature of their own. The universal base at the door of the lamp arises vividly without grasping.

The crystal ball abides in immaculate transparent nakedness without obscurities. The universal base at the door of the lamp is free from being covered by obscuring overlay. [339] It arises wide-eyed in limpidity.

Just as the sky encompasses all in its general immersion, so does the universal ground at the gate of the lamp encompass in complete immersion the great pristine awareness without outer and inner.

Direct introduction to the dynamism of self-manifestation

Second, the direct introduction of self-manifested dynamism is two-fold: direct introduction to self-arising and direct introduction to self-manifestation.

Direct introduction to self-arising

On the first, the *Little Nails* (314.4) says:

> The example that illustrates the integration of object and aware-

ness is the manner in which light is in water, crystal, the sun, and the butter lamp.

Water

The first of these four examples is when sunrays strike water. Clear rays are reflected back and arise. This is the direct introduction. Awareness is like water. Sounds, lights, and rays that manifest are like the light on the water. This is the direct introduction to the self-originated arisings.

Crystal

The direct introduction to self-originated lights displayed in the sunlight on water are the same as those lights seen in crystals. Awareness is like the crystal. The three kinds of manifestations are like the lights reflected from the crystal.

Sun

Furthermore, awareness is like the sun in the manner of sunlight and the three manifestations.

Butter lamp

Again, awareness is like the butter lamp. The three manifestations are known in the manner of their lights.

Direct introduction to self-manifestation

This second point is threefold: direct introduction where the lights are of the nature of the lights of the rainbow, direct introduction where the rays are of the nature of reflected rays, and direct introduction where the sounds are of the nature of the sounds of echoes.

Direct introduction where the lights are of the nature of the lights of the rainbow

First, one can be directly introduced at the same time to lights and rays. The modes are: the outer lamp of existence that is the pressing down, the inner lamp of the senses that is the fixation of the seed-syllable *A*, and the secret lamp of awareness that is the direct introduction to turning away at the crucial point.

The outer lamp of existence

First, one takes hold of the radiance of the sky with the key points of the body, the key points of the senses, the gaze, and so forth. The lamp of existence consists in pressing down during the confines of daytime visions, according to the practices of waving the tent pole,[311] where lights, rays, droplets, and so forth arise in numbers. One should become familiar with these direct introductions to self-manifestations.

The inner lamp of the senses

Second, the inner lamp of the senses, which is the fixation on the seed-syllable *A*, consists in pressing down the door of the lamp with the two imperturbables.[312] After breathing in, the breath is held, and from this, various lights and rays will arise. These autogenerated lights and rays are directly pointed out. When one is twisting, one takes a short breath. One relaxes, and from this, lights like rainbows will arise. This practice directly points out one's natural lights. Finally, when relaxing, one need not fixate on the seed-syllable *A* but rather look into the previous state. The manifestations of lights and rays are liberated in self-liberation. This is directly pointing at the natural dynamism of awareness.

The secret lamp of awareness

Third, the lamp of awareness comes down to the main points—the key points of the body, the gazes, the practices of the winds, [340] and so forth, that command each of their individual cycles during meditation. Awareness is fixed in midair when there is no hail or clouds. Separating the pure from the dross, the luminous radiance can emerge and the many manifestations of clear light arise. One is directly introduced to these illusory self-manifestations.

The sounds are of the nature of the sounds of echoes

Third, the topic on sounds that are sounds with the nature of echoes is three-fold: direct introduction to the natural echoes of external empty sounds, direct introduction to the conditions of other methods using internal signs, and direct introduction to the natural sounds of secret self-awareness.

Natural echoes of external empty sounds

First, one shouts against a cliff, in a ravine, and so forth. That empty echo is the direct pointing out to the undifferentiated, the self-rising, and the self-originated.

Direct introduction to the conditions of other methods using internal signs

Second, when one is practicing, one plays loud music abruptly in one's ear canal and stops. Then one presses down over the ears. This is directly pointing at self-generated sounds.

Direct introduction to the natural sounds of secret self-awareness

Third, one presses down the secret gate of the two imperturbables. One fixes one's intellect on the inherent sound of awareness that resounds continually and arises naturally. This is the direct introduction. The *Lamp* (221.4) says:

> In the central core of the swirling ocean of the conch arises the
> gate of the sound of empty winds. From the secret hollow of the
> sounds, the crescent moons resound with self-originated tunes.
> This irregular whistling subdues the moving mind with sounds.

Direct introduction on the resulting three enlightened bodies

Third, the topic on the result is threefold: direct introduction to the enlightened one existing naturally within oneself; the manner of the arising of pristine cognition, the divine body; and indirect teachings on accepting and rejecting.

Direct introduction to the enlightened one existing naturally within oneself

On this first topic, the *Lamp* (216.4) says:

> The natural state is the universal base, the pure and perfect mind itself that is great, all-encompassing, and without partialities. This non-restriction is the expanse of reality itself. In that sacred place, awareness dwells as the great primordial purity. This is the enlightened body of reality. The pure realm of the body of reality exists naturally within oneself and is forever in close association, unrecognized.
>
> This sacred place is the brown cornelian tent in the heart that is endowed with crystal beams. This shining immeasurable mansion of light is the incomparable pure land Unsurpassed.[313] In that sacred place, the pristine cognition of awareness is spontaneously accomplished in the dynamism that is sounds, lights, and rays. Here, all of cyclic existence and transcendence are spontaneously perfected. This enlightened body of perfect enjoyment exists naturally within oneself as arrays of pure lands and enlightened bodies of perfection. When not understood, they are mirages.
>
> This sacred place is perfected with its three channels, six sorts of wheels, trunk, branches, and limbs, together with minor parts. It is the pure land of the perfect wheels of letters. In that sacred place, the six dynamisms, the six objects, and so forth, arise as myriads of miraculous displays in the pristine cognition of awareness. This is the enlightened body of emanation that abides naturally within oneself, accompanied by pure lands and emanation bodies. If this is not realized, the six kinds of destinies arise manifest.[314]

This is called "direct introduction." [341]

Inside the heart self-awareness rises, and this is the enlightened body of reality that exists naturally within oneself. All the miraculous displays of the mind arise at the gate of the lamp without exception. This is directly pointing at the self-arising of the body of emanation. The *Little Nails* (318.4) says:

> In the expanse of the heart abides self-awareness, the body of real-

ity. Along the pathways of the channels, intrinsic nature abides, the body of perfection. In the gate of the lamp it arises by itself as emanated bodies.

Furthermore, the existing pristine cognition of awareness, which is without roots and is pure from primordial beginning, is the enlightened body of reality. Because of the strength of the union of ordinary body and mind, the strength of the forms of the divine families give rise to all wisdom beings [i.e., embodied pristine cognitions]. These are the enlightened bodies of perfection. The conduct of the various activities of the three ordinary doors is the enlightened body of emanation.

The *Little Nails* (318.2) says:

> Self-awareness is the enlightened body that is pure from the very beginning. The union of the ordinary body and mind is the enlightened body of perfect enjoyment. Any of the various actions and agents is an enlightened emanation body.

Moreover, in the circle of the heart, awareness burns along the pathways in an enlightened state. This is primordial enlightenment. The three dynamisms are completely inseparable in the hollows of the channels. This is perfect enlightenment. The vivid experience is uncovered limpidity that arises at the gate of the lamp. This is real manifest enlightenment.

The *Little Nails* (318.4) says:

> Within, self-originated primordial enlightenment dwells. In the hollow, spontaneously accomplished perfect enlightenment resides. Seeing it is the real uncovered manifest enlightenment abiding.

Furthermore, the empty essence of intrinsic mind exists naturally within oneself as the enlightened body of reality. The clear aspects exist naturally within oneself as the enlightened body of perfection. The various miraculous displays that arise, which exist naturally within, are the enlightened emanation bodies.

Emptiness, clarity, and manifestations are directly pointing at the three enlightened bodies. Furthermore, all the modes of arising—outer and inner—remaining in the intrinsic empty essence are the enlightened body of reality. Intrinsic nature remaining in unimpeded luminosity is the enlightened body of perfection. The unreal miraculous displays arising are the enlightened emanation bodies.

Furthermore, all of one's subtle and coarse conceptualizations, being factors of emptiness, are the enlightened body of reality. Similarly, the manner in which external visions arise, and all the modes that produce experiences and understanding, are connected. This is directly pointing at enlightenment.

The arising of pristine cognition and the divine enlightened bodies

Second,[315] the topic of the manner in which pristine cognition and the divine forms arise is threefold: the manner of arising of the divine forms, the manner of exalted knowing of pristine cognition, and the manner of performing enlightened activities.

The manner of arising of the divine forms

First, about this conjunction of inert matter and awareness at the base, the three bodies that abide naturally within oneself are the three bodies of the base. The moment one practices exactly that, they will arise in one's continuum. These are the three bodies of the path.

When they reach originations, they develop as power, strength, and force. [342] Once they are completely actualized, they become concretely realized as the three enlightened bodies of fruition. There are two topics on these: the base for arising and the manner in which they arise.

The base for arising

First, having been freed from the corporeal and devious manifestation of one's body, which is characterized by contamination, one sets forth an emanation into an uncontaminated body of excellence, ornamented with the major and minor marks and established in a pure realm, sitting on a throne. This arising in perfection is the materialization of the enlightened body of perfection. One's intrinsic enlightened mind is free from ruination and is in a profound state that transcends ordinary mind. Having given away the conditioned body, one remains without separation, merged in this enlightened body of perfection. One's enlightened melodious voice that radiates, is without inherent existence, and communicates the 84,000 revealed words and so forth, which materializes as embodied enlightened emanations. The *Six Transmissions* (139.7) says:

> The moment the ordinary body, speech, and mind turn into enlightened body, speech, and mind, the dynamism of the sounds, the lights and the rays, the aggregates, the constituent and sense spheres, the channels, the limbs, the mind and its products, all, whether outer, inner, or secret, arise as the extensive host of deities. The state of fulfilling the welfare of wandering beings, regardless of efforts, originates naturally from its own strength. There are no fluctuations in the enlightened body of reality. Nevertheless, it sends forth emanations everywhere to fulfill the welfare of wandering beings.

The manner in which they arise

Second, in general, sounds, lights, and rays are released in the essence of awareness's self-manifestation. In particular, the white light that is visualized as deities, the enlightened mind of liberation, is the god of the authentic enlightened mind, Kunang Khyabpa [i.e., the one encompassing the manifestation of all]. He is in the central position, the head of the enlightened family of inherent Suchness (*de bzhin nyid*), with the wheel as its hand symbol. He abides in the state of great bliss of the enlightened body of reality with his two hands in the meditative position. Having command over the expanse of heaven, his consort is the goddess of space (Namkha'i lha mo). He suppresses anger and sits on a lion. He is endowed with the power of great love. He overcomes the suffering of the hot and cold hells while producing benefit.

Similarly, from the yellow light originates the changeless enlightened body that is Salwa Rangjung [lit. "self-originated luminosity"]. He is the clarity of the mirror-wisdom in one's continuum, his yellow body. He is in the eastern direction and is the head of the enlightened family, the gold scepter with a swastika as hand symbol. He is the symbol of the enlightened body of perfect enjoyment, his hands playing in the gesture of wonder at the heart. He has command over the expanse of the earth element. His consort is the goddess of earth (Sa'i lha mo). He suppresses dullness and sits on an elephant. He is endowed with the power of the great primordial cognition. He overcomes the senselessness of the animal realm while producing benefit.

Similarly, from the green light originates Gelha Garchuk [lit. "the wealthy dancing god of virtue"].

From the red light originates Jedrak Ngöme [lit. "the valuable that is immaterial"].

From the blue light originates Gawa Döndrup [lit. "the joy that is the accomplishment of the purpose"]. Each of these five also has its own symbol, and one should be introduced to all of their methods extensively.

Moreover, in their outer aspects they are the five Shenlha [lit. "the gods of Shen"], [with an aspect of Kunang Khyabpa in the center followed by]: Gösé [lit. "the palace of excitement"], Garsé [lit. "the citadel dance"], Sejé [lit. "the lord of the citadel"], and Namsé [lit. "the celestial citadel"]. In their inner aspects, [343] these five are mentioned as Kunang and so forth. In their secret aspects, they are the five chiefs [with an aspect of Kunang Khyabpa in the center followed by]: Trosé [lit. "the citadel of wrath"], Ngamsé [lit. "the citadel of desires"], Walsé [lit. "the citadel of the burning tip of the blade"], and Tumsé [lit. "the citadel of fierceness"]. When they appear to ordinary beings, they are in their transformed states as different aspects of one identity. One is pointed directly to this teaching.

In the same way, the eight collections[316] are the eight primordial Shen. The eight groups of objects[317] are the primordial enlightened ones. The fixed concepts of the five poisons[318] are the five stainless ones. The head, feet, eyes, and tongue[319] are the four flower-mother goddesses. From the grasping of the six types of causes[320] come the six Shen of discipline. The four times[321] are the four queens of fixed concepts, and so forth. These arise into the forty-five peaceful deities. Moreover, the one hundred and eight assemblies of the deities of prosperity [i.e., *rgyas*, lit. "increase," one of the four classes of tantric activities] are the outer aspects. The inner aspect is the assembly of the forty-five peaceful deities. The secret aspect is the assembly of the eighty-five wrathful deities.

The manner of liberation from the continuum of cyclic existence as well as the manner of arising are as mentioned above. On the rationale for these modes, the root tantra that is the *Secret Capable Sen-Demoness of the Universal Heap* (9.95.2) says:

They originate in a common base but point directly to different ways of teachings in order to directly entreat those who need to be tamed. The outer, inner, and secret are the magical emanation net.

Accordingly, the meaning of the mother-father syzygies that arise in the rising assemblies of deities is that they abide in the union of method and wisdom, clarity and emptiness, and so forth. The chief and the assembly are the particular strength of the liberation of the mind and its objects. The risings of outer, inner, and secret are the symbols that clearly reveal the doors that engage in conjunction with their environment. The arising of the activities of pacifying, increasing, overpowering, and forcefulness are the methods of the four activities to lead wandering beings.

In connection with the qualities of the enlightened body, speech, and mind, the meaning is that they have abided as the intrinsic nature of the three enlightened bodies from the very beginning, so they are adorned with the major and minor marks and the superior qualities of great thrones. Their definitive inventory of attributes arises in the pure lands that are established together with their emanations, which have eliminated all impurities and defects. These enlightened qualities of goodness are the symbols of the perfection of the purity of finality. Even more than these, the origination of eleven million different and dissimilar circles of outer, inner, and secret assemblies of deities are the symbols showing the corresponding antidotes to corresponding trainees.

The manner of exalted knowing of pristine cognition

Second, pristine cognition is the concretely actualized principle of Suchness, which is the pristine cognition of awareness that is self-originated. It arises and is established as dynamism, strength, and force. Its manners of emergence are the five wisdoms of emptiness, equanimity, earnest endeavor, discriminating realization, and the wisdom of the mirror. If these are combined, they can be gathered into these two: the knowledge of seeing as the absolute nature and the knowledge of seeing as the relative nature.

The activities of these pristine cognitions follow the fragmentary perceptions of the behavior of the objects of knowledge. There are 84,000 pristine cognitions. Furthermore, at any given moment thoughts arise, abide, and are liberated in sentient beings. There are countless hundreds of thousands of gateways to concentration that illuminate the enlightened mind. The moments of their causes arise in the liberation of the various thoughts and memories. [344]

The lights rays that emanate and are then reabsorbed, filling the entire world, are symbols, respectively, of the elimination of all the objects to be eliminated in one's continuum and the purification of all defects of the continuum of others.

The manner of performing enlightened activities

Third, the topic of enlightened activities is twofold: actualization and the mode of exalted activity.

Actualization

First is great compassion, then skillful means, and then the knowledge of everything.

Compassion

The first, compassion, manifests concretely as these four: It is immeasurable like the sky. It shines equally like the sun. It is continuous like water. It is inexhaustible like earth. The *Eye of the Needle* (16.523.7) says:

> I am like the sun that is equal toward all, and like water that streams endlessly.

Skillful means

Second, with the activities of the enlightened body, speech, and mind, one will be able to subdue anyone accordingly, anywhere, with the twelve enlightened activities of pacifying, increasing, overpowering, and violence.

On leading wandering beings with various uncertainties, the *Discourse on the Stainless Root* (8.6) says:

> The path of skillful means is to effect activities and use all there is for the welfare of those to be subdued, whose number is incommensurable to the mind.

The knowledge of everything

Third, not knowing, being unclear, and being a brute and ignorant of the natural condition of the objects of knowledge, one will not be able to do anything about anything. It is said:

> This one pristine cognition of exalted knowledge is that it reveals
> all there is on the natural condition of the objects of knowledge.

Mode of exalted activity

Second, on these activities, there are exalted activities that are all-encompassing, and where there is no single apparent purpose solely for sentient beings, or occasionally none, there are always non-partisan courses of enlightened action. They can be accomplished spontaneously, disregarding any effort. They can be manifestly accomplished by no indirect ways. If not apparently present in one's continuum, they can be accomplished by one endowed with compassion. *Ascertaining the Root of the World* (8.5) says:

> I, myself, am of the nature of impartiality, the one with the intrinsic self of peace.

Although the enlightened ones' activities for the benefit of others are effected by the exertion of the three doors at the causal moment, they are liberated from all efforts and characteristics of suffering.

Indirect teachings on accepting and rejecting

Third, the gradual method of casting commands and permissions after accepting or rejecting is twofold: permission and casting commands.

Permission

First, a fortunate person with good karma should be held as the chief prospect for the future. He must be diligent and have a great capacity for generosity. He must have faith and devotion joined with compassion. He must have gathered enthusiasm and dedication, having great forbearance for austerities. He is serviceable in attitude and conduct, and endowed with mindfulness and introspection. He appears suitable and in the prime of life. In brief, he understands pith instructions, has obtained them, and has the ability to practice and the knowledge to profess them. To such a person who concentrates on this single pursuit, [345] one should teach the whole completely without making impossibilities, without hiding anything, and without keeping secrets.

Casting commands

Second, for an individual who is the opposite and does not possess good fortune or karma, whose deeds and thoughts are not united and appropriate, who has no grasp on introspection and mindfulness, who is deviant with perverted views and conduct, whose four elements are causes for deterioration, who is affected by the stains of youth, who is contemptuous about avoiding criminal involvement and practices, who encourages deprecation and carries on with evil, who is not able to engage in austerities with fortitude, who does not let go of mental manifestations, who is skillful in dissimulation and deceit, who does not abandon pride and self-aggrandizement—in brief, for a person who does not have the key points of the teachings or the profound pith instructions, who does not notice them, and has no room for, is unable, or has no developed lineage, these teachings should be kept very secret, completely concealed, well hidden, without even saying a word.

Furthermore, these essential instructions, the rubrics, together with writings, should only be given to the few fortunate ones as well as to those who are clean in their pledges. If they are given out to obtain wealth or reputation, and to whomever appears to be good, then the blessings of this advice will disappear and the sky-goers and the oath-bound protectors will issue a command to proceed with punishment. Therefore, be careful about who you accept and reject.

These were the instructions on decisively elucidating the three bodies by seizing the natural ground, the result. *Uya maro!*

Thus, these pith instructions that collect the essential points of the advice have been drawn out from the heart. These rubrics from the innermost mood of enlightened intent are the condensed roots of the scriptures. Although this quintessential exalted intent of the profound revelatory transmission was appropriately arranged with pure intention, whatever confusion and impetuous shortcomings may have been combined, I confess without reservation my faults and ignorance! May this merit bring about the realization of the meaning of excellence, the empty clear light of awareness, to others, to all wandering beings without exception, and to myself.

Having done this, the key points together with the outer, inner, secret, and most secret elements of the revelatory transmission from Zhangzhung have been collected here, the quintessence of the profound advice. This is the ultimate advice from the oral instructions of the superior and greatly accomplished masters. The monk from Dru, Gyalwa Yungdrung, composed in due order this manual at the monastery of Yeru Bensakha with the purpose of fulfilling the repeated demands of the spiritual friend Tashi Rinchen, holder of the saffron-colored robe. *Mutsu maro! Emaho!*

These writings and figures[322] should not be shown to anyone except to the lama and the one giving this advice. May it be auspicious! Virtue! [346]

9. Notes on the Removal of Obstructions and the Perception of the Clear Light

I PAY HOMAGE TO Kuntu Zangpo, who is manifest self-awareness!

Since there were no writings on the Zhangzhung Oral Transmission, this script was set forth. I pray for forgiveness to the assembly of lamas, tutelary deities, sky-goers, and protectors of Bön!

This advice came from the mouth of the lama. Having cut off at the root the ties to cyclic existence and transcendence in this life, realization and experience arise. The counsel is to condense winds and mind in the central channel. This itself is to be brought into one's experience as one dwells in a pleasant and isolated place.

The general program

The steps to the preliminaries are to go for refuge, generate the mind of enlightenment, offer the mandala of the universe, request blessings, fix the mind, and receive pointed instructions on the ground, the path, the result, the lamps, the *Little Nails*, and the six key points of practice. It is to be directly pointed to like this and explained in that [ordered] manner.

Then one has to be directly introduced to reliance on the external lamp of the world and the internal water lamp of Bhiguta, which have been clarified separately. One must rely on the secret section that relates to the channels, winds, and droplets that is called "understanding according to the direct introduction." The essential point here is to begin the dark retreat on the practice of the lattice of light.

Sleeping practice

With regard to sleeping, on top of becoming quiet, one has to arrange one's hand in the meditative position with thumbs pressing on ring fingers.

Key points on the visualization practice

As for the key points on visualization, one visualizes the three channels like this: the right channel is white, the left channel is red, and the central channel is dark blue. The central channel has the thickness of a metal cane, the color of lapis lazuli, and is hollow inside. Inside the back are petals at the wheel in the heart with a pillar-like standing structure, above. At the upper extremity is the mouth opening, which is equivalent to the aperture of Tshangpa. The junction at the lower extremity pierces the "threshold of the great mouth."[323] It is from there that the right white and the left red channels radiate. They are only as thick as an arrow's shaft, the right and left channels supporting the central channel. One imagines that these reach up to the two ears, then come together at the curved bones below the nape of the neck where they project over the "two mountains" along the pathways to the doors of the channels.

Sitting posture

Then the manner of sitting is like this: One steadies oneself in the posture of the "great serpent spirit."[324] One joins the ocean to the excellent mountain,[325] the tongue is affixed to the palate, and the luminaries [i.e., the eyes] are reversed upward.

Purification breathing moving winds and mind

Then, one expels the breath three times while imagining one's obscurations being purified. Next, one tilts the head slightly to the right, breathing in gently and exhaling through the right nostril, then holding. That wind-energy is similar to the dust particles in sunrays, it travels back and forth, alternating, shimmering in the right white and the left red channels while moving upward in the central channel. One then thinks that it exits shimmering above through the crown of the head. Then again it moves back down, [347] spreading out in the right and left channels. One imagines it exiting through the two nostrils. Both wind and mind are fixed on expelling the air. Then again from the right channel the wind is held once more, and as before is made to move, becoming purified in the mind. One does this through the right nostril three times. Then one does it through the left nostril three times. Holding the breath is also done three times with the central channel. One visualizes as previously described. One goes on with training and purifying the channels and the pathways. One does this nine times. At the time of purifying, when the air is completely out, it is very important not to get distracted.

Key points to moving winds, mind, and droplets

Furthermore, having counted the days of practice for a suitable number along the key points of the body position and held the breath and the channels as mentioned above, the winds must be subdued as above. Moreover, when holding the breath in the right channel, wind and mind must be together and the essential aspect of the droplets of light must be white coming from the right and proceeding as white, and red coming from the left and proceeding as red. The droplets from these two must be like whirling balls. They go up and go down and away. When they are made to enter the central channel, they go up and down and then are exited through the door of Tshangpa.

Again, when the breaths are returned to circulate below through the right and left channels as before, they spread and then move out and are made to reach the two nostrils. Purification expels the breath as dust. Moreover, it is similar to before, as the wind is held through the right channel to be purified. It is the same with the right, left, and central channels: three ninefold breath-holding sets make one practice session. One flashes these [whirling balls] out in the sky through the crown of the head and sends away the dusty stale air. In that manner, having separated impurities and limpid awareness, the experience of luminous emptiness arises and one is able to make the transfer through the gate of Tshangpa by oneself. At that moment, if awareness surges, the damage to the winds rests in the old droplets. When there is no drowsiness, one should let the two channels loose to fall in their own natural places.

Purification with father-mother

Again, the key points regarding the body are similar to the above. One should clearly visualize the three channels in the crown of the head. Above the right white channel sits the father, called "the king of the light of the sky"—Kuntu Zangpo sitting approximately in the center of a moon-seat. Above the left red channel sits the mother, called "queen Nang Makö," sitting [besides him] on a sun-seat. The father looks at the mother from the corner of his right eye, and the mother looks at the father from the corner of her left eye. One meditates on the light coming from the enlightened bodies of these two. Again, one holds the breath [, letting it in] from the right channel while dispersing the winds in one's controlled body. The two enlightened bodies flow in and dissolve inside. One imagines that the droplets from the right white channel are white and the droplets from the left red channel are red. They move and are purified as before. Accordingly, for the right, left, and central channels, one does this purification in a three-times-three set, the ninefold breath. Beginning with the first session of practice, experience and understanding will gradually come.

Deities as white and red droplets

[348] Again, as for the two deities above, at the time of meditating on the central dark-blue channel, one expels stale air as before. One then holds one's breath, as above. The deities father-mother melt into light and move up and down inside the central dark-blue channel one by one like whirling balls, reaching everywhere in the three channels. The white droplets from the right white channel and the red droplets from the left red channel move up and down. Then they move higher and higher and exit the mouths of the two channels, dispersing above. The winds are stripped clean with purification.

Again, one holds the breath through the right channel. Droplets in the central dark-blue channel descend as before, cleansing. Moreover, the two right and left channels as well as the central channel are purified nine times for one complete session. At that time, experience and understanding will gradually come.

Droplets with rainbow colors

Furthermore, the method of meditating on the central channel is as before. When the three channels are fully replenished, one visualizes that the conduits to the two ears, from the vertebrae of the right white and left red channels, are piercing paths through the two mountains [i.e., the brain]. Again, one expels stale air and then holds the breath from the right white side.

One imagines changing the droplets into rainbows of five colors. Again, one imagines that they fill the three channels and ascend through the central channel. One imagines them going away, shimmering like a rainbow through the crown of the head. Again, they fall down as before, purified. Thus, the number of sessions is as before and identical.

Breathing meditation using the three seed-syllables

Then one meditates that inside the center of one's heart is the seed-syllable *Hum* with the rainbow of five colors. One expels stale air and holds one's breath. The *Hum* syllable moves up inside the central dark-blue channel and one imagines it going through the crown of the head, flying away. It then goes down into the central dark-blue channel again and reaches everywhere, filling the three channels. From the seed-syllable *Hum*, two seed-syllables *A* in the nature of rainbows issue forth. They go up the right and left channels, reaching through the pathways to the gates of the mountain. The winds have been cleansed. One imagines that rainbows are emitted from inside the *A* syllables in the sky. Then one inhales air and all the rainbows are completely scooped together, and one imagines the rainbows transforming back into *Om* syllables inside the two nostrils. They descend inside along the two right and left channels and reach everywhere, filling the three channels. Then again, the two *Om* syllables turn into rainbows and become one with the *Hum* syllable at the heart. One then imagines it going up along the inside of the central dark-blue channel and exiting by flying out through the door at the crown of the head. It then descends again as before, purified. Thus, this time one imagines the *A* syllables going out, inhaled back as *Om* syllables, and resting in the *Hum* syllable at the heart. Inhaling, filling up, and expelling nine times makes one round. [349] When concluding the session, these seed-syllables are gathered back into the seed-syllable *Hum* at the center of the heart. One then exhales stale air.

Moving the three seed-syllables along the channels

The manner of abiding of these seed-syllables is similar to before with the central dark-blue channel. With the right white channel, the course runs from inside between the eyes and circulates inside the left channel all the way to the vertebra, then by the ear, and finally pierces through the right nostril. One imagines that for the left red channel the course runs from inside between the eyes and circulates inside the right channel all the way to the vertebra, passing by the ear and finally piercing through the left nostril. Furthermore, in the meditation involving the dark-blue *Hum* syllable in the center of the heart, once the stale air is expelled, one holds one's breath. The *Hum* syllable inside the central dark-blue channel moves up and comes flying out through the door at the crown of the head. It returns again descending and reaches everywhere, filling the three channels. Then, having transformed into two white *A* syllables, the right wandering *A* syllable does the circuit as before with the right white channel all the way along the course to the left vertebra and ear, exiting through the door of the right nostril. The left wandering *A* syllable does the circuit as before with the left red channel all the way along the course to the right vertebra and ear, exiting through the door of the left nostril. With that, one meditates that suddenly the winds are dispersed and the sky is filled with white *A* seed-syllables. Inhaling again, one imagines them transforming into red *Om* syllables. The method of purification for the *Hum* is the same as above. This includes all the practices of the key points of the body as well as concentration on ninefold breath control. As before, one expels stale air and follows this with a second expelling of stale air everywhere, which is very important.

Time required for practice

On the time required for performing these practices, the *Little Nails* (310.7) says:

> Calculating the leaps along the channels, one takes the measure of their intermediate space. The full number of their spaces, which are neither long nor short, can be counted in some cases from one up to eighteen thousand. Familiarity with the visions finally reaches the full measure.

The *Six Essential Points* (177.3) says:

> For the best practitioner, one week; for the middle-level, twenty-one days; for the lowest, it takes one month and ten days to reach perfection.

In this, according to karmic connections—the measure of diligence, the abundance or scarcity of cause and necessities, violations of pledges or adherence, the measure of faith and devotion, good and bad wind channels, dwelling in solitude or not—the distinctive attributes of success will arise indeterminately.

Prerequisites

When someone requests practical instructions on the profound advice that is the revelatory transmission, first it is important that the person be a worthy vessel. Then it is important to extend excellent offerings and sacrificial cakes. Furthermore, it is important to clear away obstacles, carve scriptures, and give feast offerings to oath-bound protectors and non-human spirits. Then it is important to live in a solitary place. Then again it is important that one clears away defilements with lustrations and clears away corruption and hindrances. Having arranged for clothing and food, and depending on essential provisions, [350] it is important to fill one's belly by only two-thirds, leaving one-third in air. It is important to pray for blessings from the lama three or four times a day.

Virtue!

I pay homage to Kuntu Zangpo, who dispels outer and inner obstacles!

Six preliminary yogic exercises[326]

This Zhangzhung Oral Transmission has a series of yogic exercises to clear the obstacles from the three types of channels and limbs. Yoga purifies the channels and the pathways so that the channels and the winds illuminate from the inside. In order to expel the poisons in the winds, I will explain how to train the channels. For the preliminaries, I will teach the special series of six yogic exercises.

Expelling stale air

One sucks in the air and then expels it forcefully. One then inhales softly with long, gentle breaths right and left. Hold the breath in order to have the neutral wind[327] pervade one's entire body.

Upper body exercise

Massage all the limbs, the head and body. Arms and legs are straightened, like those of a wild antelope. This is followed by expelling stale air. In order to expel impurities, one pronounces the word *Ha* three times while exhaling.

Leg exercise

Breathing practice is conducted after massaging the whole body. The right leg is thrust forward with the thumb of the right hand, and [the leg] is shaken seven times, in the manner of a wild ass. The practice of breathing as well as the wild shaking is done in a similar manner on the left side.

Arm exercise

Practice the breathing above in order to apply the main points. The right hand rubs the inside of the arm along the crease of the elbow and the head. Shake like a wild ass seven times and then expel stale air. The yoga for the left side is done similarly.

Entire body exercise 1

Perform the breathing practice with the forearms parallel, palms facing the ground. Then the legs are stretched in front of one and the hands rub the head and chest. Then after shaking the legs seven times, one exhales the stale air. While [jumping] shaking the body, one pronounces the word *Ha* three times, exhaling.

Entire body exercise 2

The yoga for the entire body is done as mentioned above, and the body is twisted four times, shaking like a wild ass. One then expels stale air while pronouncing *Ha*.

Controlling the channels is done as a yoga to balance the four limbs. I composed this outline with keywords as a reminder of these six yogas for the preliminary yogic exercises. In conjunction with these teachings, the qualities of the preliminary yogic exercises are that they balance the channels and winds and clear the hollows of the channels. The four elements become balanced, and these capture the essential points for the aggregates. These exercises separate the quintessence of awareness from impurities, while differentiating the winds and their existing qualities. These exercises were envisioned by Pöngyel Tsenpo.[328]

Five yogic exercises

The teachings on the essential points of the yogic exercises for the channels consist in these: (1) striking the skull of the hero, (2) the window of primordial wisdom, (3) spinning the four wheels, (4) loosening the corner of the intricate knot, (5) waving the pennon upward. These are the five yogic exercises for the channels. I have added (6) the forceful leap of the tigress. [351]

Striking with the skull of the hero[329]

First is the yogic movement striking with the skull of the hero against anger. Place your hands on the nape of the neck with the five fingers interlaced. Having knelt on the ground, the front part of the legs and feet on the ground, lean backward. The weight is carried by the legs, the waist kept straight, perpendicular. Then recline the neck and chest and bend forward. The two arms are folded with elbows [forward and hands holding the back of the neck] . Do this, reclining [and then stretching backward, back and forth], seven times. Then shake [the body] and bend backward, expelling the breath while making the sound *Ha* to expel stale air.

The window of primordial wisdom[330]

The second yogic movement, the window of primordial wisdom, is used to counter delusion. Sit crossed-legged with four fingers pressing and holding the hip joint, right and left, your fingers at the front and your thumbs to the back. The right and left crooks of the arm are then placed on top of the folded legs, the right and left armpit forming a triangular opening. Then roll backward and forward, from the back of your neck to your forehead, on the ground seven times. Then shake your fingers.

Spinning the four wheels[331]

Third is the yogic movement spinning the four wheels against pride. Sit crossed-legged placing the right and left foot under the thighs, and draw the head forward. With the palms of the hands, grab the right and left big toes and roll onto your back until the nape of the neck is pressing on the ground. Then roll forward until the lower front parts of the legs press the ground. Then straighten up, unfolding your knees and and extending your legs. Do these counterclockwise rolls seven times. Then shake your fingers as above.

Loosening the corner of the intricate knot[332]

Fourth is the yogic movement loosening the corner of the intricate knot against attachment. Sit crossed-legged and raise your right and left elbows perpendicularly, squaring the shoulders.[333] The two thumbs are pressed into the right and left armpits with the four fingers set on the crest of the breasts. The left elbow touches the right knee. Then, the right elbow touches the left knee. Alternate this right and left movement across seven times. Then shake your fingers.

Waving the pennon upward[334]

The fifth is the yogic movement waving the pennon upward to counter jealousy. One kneels with the two palms pressed to the ground. The forearms and the legs below the knee are extended straight. The [opposite] hand and foot move upward three times so that one's weight is entirely on the left palm and knee. Then alternate the right and left sides, waiving the extended arm and leg seven times. Then shake out your fingers [at the end of the exercise].

The forceful leap of the tigress[335]

The yogic movement the forceful leap of the tigress counters drowsiness and agitation. One stands in a cross-legged *vajra* position and touches the ground with hands and head. The body is raised and then lowered. Do this seven times. Then shake out your hands.

These are the basic five yogic movements of the revelatory transmission envisioned by Pöngyal Tsenpo. One should also put into practice the ten gazes that were also transmitted.

The resulting qualities of these six yogic movements

The qualities of striking anger with the skull of the hero are that the channels and pathways of the space element are freed and the door of the channel carrying anger is blocked. The aggregates of consciousness [352] being freed, the pure land of the body of reality arises. When the radiance of space arises, one perceives the mandala of the body of reality. While one is then freed from the illnesses described in the four medical root texts, the outer and inner interferences are cleared away. Having liberated the objects of consciousness on their own ground, the primordial wisdom of intrinsic emptiness arises. Then consciousness, on its own power, soars like a bird in the sky.

The qualities of the yogic movement the window of primordial wisdom against delusion are that the aggregate of form is liberated onto its own ground, the radiance of the earth element arises, and one perceives the bodies of perfection and sees the mandala of the conqueror. The door of the channel carrying delusion is blocked and the primordial wisdom of the mirror arises. The forms are brought under control and mountains and rocks are no longer obstructing.

The qualities of the yogic movement spinning the four wheels against pride are that the aggregate of compositional factors is freed, the radiance of the air element arises, one will be released in the bodies of intrinsic essence, and the mandala of the three enlightened bodies will arise. The door of the channel carrying pride is blocked and the primordial wisdom of Suchness expands. The winds are brought under control and the power of speed increases.

The qualities of the yogic movement loosening the corner of the intricate knot against attachments are that the aggregate of discrimination is liberated, the radiance of the fire element arises, and perfected, separate, enlightened emanation bodies and mandalas of enlightened emanations arise. The door of the channel carrying attachment is blocked and the primordial wisdom of discrete realization expands. The fire element is brought under control and the fierce one[336] will blaze without heat.

The qualities of the yogic movement waving the pennon upward against jealousy are that the aggregate of feelings is freed, the radiance of the water element arises, and one will reach the perfection the enlightened body of priceless objects and the five kinds of mandala. The door of the channel carrying jealousy is blocked and the primordial wisdom of appropriateness will expand. The element of water is brought under control and the power of not sinking[337] increases.

The qualities of the yogic movement of the forceful leap of the tigress against drowsiness and agitation are that the power and strength of the winds will be perfected while sluggishness will be purified in its own ground. Winds and mind will enter the central channel and one will be liberated from moving conceptual patterns.

Those are the qualities of the basic yogic movements.

Clearing obstructions with the five gradual yogic movements

Second, the five gradual yogic movements to clear obstructions that are taught here are (1) the duck drinking water, (2) the female yak nudging, (3) the wild ass sleeping, (4) the hovering hawk, and (5) wrapping up the four continents.

The duck drinking water[338]

First is the method of the yogic movement of the duck drinking water. The body stands straight. The waist is seized with both hands, the thumb pads pressed to the body. The top of the head is brought down to touch the ground, then brought back up and backward. Do this seven times. Then shake your hands and expel the stale air while making the *Ha* sound. [353]

The female yak nudging[339]

Second is the method of the yogic movement of the female yak nudging. Standing up, the fingers grasp the waist. The trunk then leans toward one leg, stepping across seven times. The feet stomp the ground as if to flatten it down. Then, shake your hands and expel the stale air while making the *Ha* sound.

The wild ass sleeping[340]

The third is the method of the yogic movement of the wild ass sleeping. The body is balanced, the hands holding the waist. Moving the trunk, the inside of the right elbow touches the top of the left knee. This rotation right to left is done seven times. Then, shake your hands and expel the stale air while making the *Ha* sound.

The hovering hawk[341]

The fourth is the method of the yogic movement of the hovering hawk. Hold the waist and raise the heels so that the feet are partly on the ground. The trunk moves as before, leaning downward and allowing the right elbow to touch the left knee. Do this seven times. Then shake your hands and expel the stale air while making the *Ha* sound.

Wrapping up the four continents[342]

The fifth is the method of the yogic movement of wrapping up the four continents. While the body stands straight, the right and left hands are moved downward across each other. Do this seven times. Then shake your hands and expel the stale air while making the *Ha* sound.

Qualities of the five gradual yogic movements

The clear elucidation of their qualities was initially given orally:

The qualities of the duck drinking water are that one will be free from the illnesses as described in the four classics of medicine and will unlock the channels of the space element.

The qualities of the female yak nudging are that one will be free from fevers and will close the door to the channel of the earth element.

The qualities of the wild ass sleeping are that one will be free from the sickness of phlegm and bile and will close the door to the channel of the air element.

The qualities of the hovering hawk are that one will be free from heat illnesses and will close the door to the channel of the fire element.

The qualities of the manner of wrapping up the four continents are that one will be free from the cold sicknesses and will close the door to the channel of the water element.

The common qualities are explained as: one will acquire swiftness, strength, blazing heat, and long life.

These were the teachings on the special yogic exercises that clear obstructions.

The graded auxiliary yogic exercises

Next are the graded auxiliary yogic exercises. There are five main and five secondary practices.

The five main graded auxiliary yogic exercises

The five main yogic exercises are (1) bringing down the five elements naturally, (2) the peacock drinking water, (3) the four intertwined tree trunks, (4) the fourfold rolls above and below, and (5) striking the fourfold intricate knot.

Bringing down the five elements naturally[343]

The first consists in bringing down the five elements naturally. Sitting crossed-legged, palms flat and pressing down on the thighs, bring the torso forward and down, while shaking, then back, seven times.

The peacock drinking water[344]

Second is the peacock drinking water. [354] Right and left legs are stretched out in front, the waist upright. The forearms are crossed behind the back, the thumbs pressed on the ring fingers. Bend the body so that the forehead touches the knees, then return to the upright position, seven times. Then the head moves from left to right, seven times.

The four intertwined tree trunks[345]

Third is the four intertwined tree trunks. Hold the big toes of the right and left feet and roll until the back is pressed to the ground, then stretch out your hands and feet. Do this bending and stretching seven times. Then shake.

The above and below fourfold rolls[346]

The fourth is the fourfold rolls above and below. Hold the right and left soles of the feet together. Roll onto your back until head and feet touch the ground. Then, roll forward until the forehead touches the ground. Do this cycle from back to front seven times.

Striking the fourfold intricate knot[347]

The fifth is striking the fourfold intricate knot. Sit in the *vajra* crossed-legged position. The right and left hands are in back of the knees, grasping the ankles, then bounce in a circle. Do this seven times.

The qualities of the five main auxiliary yogic movements

The qualities of these main auxiliary yogic movements are: (1) One is freed from the sickness of the four elements and can capture the essential points of the winds and mind. (2) One is freed from the illusory appearances and one overcomes fixations on delusory appearances. (3) Bodily strength increases and one obtains control over the four elements. (4) Outer and inner obstructions are removed and one captures the essential points of the channels and winds.

The five graded limbs for clearing obstacles

Next come the five graded limbs for clearing obstacles. These five exercises for clearing obstacles are (1) flapping the wings of the horned eagle, (2) the peacock drinking water,[348] (3) clearing out the fourfold gathering, (4) the black antelope[349] hopping to the side, and (5) shaking the sides of the deer.

Flapping the wings of the horned eagle[350]

The first is flapping the wings of the horned eagle. Stand straight, hands to the sides, feet together, then kick the left leg backward, standing now only on the right foot, at the same time as one raises the left arm above the head. The left arm and left leg are drawn back simultaneously, again and again, while the right arm and leg remain stationary.

The peacock drinking water[351]

The second is the peacock drinking water. The hands are stretched out to the sides while the trunk of the body twists right, then left, toward the back, seven times, hands flapping.

Clearing out the fourfold gathering[352]

The third is clearing out the fourfold gathering. The soles of the feet are flat against each other and the hands grab the large toes. Drawing up the legs to the chest, one bounces backward and forward seven times.

The black antelope hopping to the side[353]

The fourth is the black antelope hopping to the side. The sole of the left foot is moved to connect with the right thigh[354] while the left hand holds the left foot in place. One hops forward and backward on the right leg, shaking the free hand gently [355] seven times. Do the same on the left leg.

Shaking the sides of the deer[355]

The fifth is shaking the sides of the deer. Stand straight, the sole of the right foot pressing against the inner left thigh.[356] The right and left hands are gently shaken while one hops forward and backward, just like above.

The qualities of the five graded practices of the limbs for clearing obstacles

The qualities of the five graded practices of the limbs for clearing obstacles are: (1) One is free from the obstacles of the five senses while the door of the channels of the four elements is closed. (2) When the four elements are balanced, sickness will not enter. (3) Joints, flesh and blood, and channels and winds will become balanced on their own ground. (4) It is said that those performing these exercises will be endowed with innumerable exalted qualities. These were the graded practices of clearing away hindrances from the mind of master Lhundrup Muthur (fl. ninth–tenth centuries).

The particular graded practices that clear away hindrances

Next are the particular graded practices that clear away hindrances, taught for the head, the torso, the arms, the waist, and the legs.

First is the clearing of hindrances for the head[357]

Circle the head, bending it right, then left, seven times. Then bend the head backward and [then forward, first going] sideways seven times.

The fettered Gyiling[358] steed for the torso[359]

Second is the fettered Gyiling steed yogic exercise for the torso. The arms are crossed in front, the palms of the hands holding the right and left shoulders. The lower legs touch the ground. Rotate the body to the right, then to the left, seven times.

The crow fighting[360]

Third is the yogic exercise of the crow fighting. Thrust your claws upward, shaking, stretching them right and then left seven times.

The vajra stomach for the waist[361]

Fourth is the vajra stomach exercise for the waist. Cross the right and left hands, holding the upper part of the arms. The forearms are in a row fastened to the waist. Sitting crossed-legged, turn at the waist to the right, then to the left, seven times.

The lower stance of the camel[362]

Fifth is the yogic exercise of the lower stance of the camel for the legs. The lower legs are held with the hands. Roll backward until the back of the head touches the ground. Then stretch the legs straight out, shaking them. Reverse the movement and repeat the sequence seven times.

The qualities of these particular graded practices that clear away hindrances

The qualities of these particular exercises for clearing away hindrances are taught as clearing away every disease of the bile, and of hot and cold winds. Whatever illnesses there are in the upper and lower parts, these exercises will clear them away.

After performing each of these yogic exercises against winds and illnesses, the oral transmission of this yoga says that one has to shake the hands and expel the air with the *Ha* sound. All the exercises should be performed in a similar ordered manner. These limbs are clearly elucidated as the knowledge directly transmitted orally. The coded notes are compilations by Orgom Kundul[363] of these particular exercises for clearing away hindrances. It is said that you should intend to practice them in a similar ordered manner.

These were the teachings on the particular yogic exercises for clearing away hindrances.

The common exercises for dispelling hindrances

Fourth in the series of the graded auxiliary yogic exercises are the common exercises for dispelling hindrances. These three are called (1) churning the depths of the ocean, (2) loosening the nine intricate knots, and (3) loosening and controlling the channels.[364]

Churning the depths of the ocean[365]

The first is the yogic exercise of churning the depths of the ocean. [356] Sitting crossed-legged, reach for the legs, then bounce holding your lower legs right and left. The lower arms and the waist are straightened so that the whole body bounces seven times, nine, thirteen, or as much as one can.

Loosening the nine intricate knots[366]

The second is the yogic exercise of loosening the nine intricate knots. The body sits on the ground, the two legs separated and stretched out a little. The palms of the two hands are crossed at the back of the head. From the forehead to the back of the neck, the right and left cheeks, the right and left shoulders, the outside of the right and left eyes, the right and left knees, pat each seven times. Then the right and left heels are crossed and pressed to the ground so that one jumps high and the sole of the foot strikes the ground, three times. Do this seven times for the practice session of the winds and yoga.

Loosening and controlling the channels[367]

Third is loosening and controlling the channels. The ground should be good; best if it inclines upward. Stand straight, thumbs pinching and holding the waist. The four muscle groups in the arms and legs and joints are well aligned. One clearly visualizes the three channels and the six wheels. The winds are made to join the seed-syllables *Yaṃ*, *Raṃ*, *Khaṃ*, *A*, *Oṃ*, *Huṃ*. Light rays emanate from the three seed-syllables of the enlightened body, speech, and mind. One meditates that the three white, red, and dark-blue droplets joined these.

The oral directions state that during the practice session the air, once inhaled, should not escape to the extent possible. One draws in the leg, up and down three times, while jumping in the air as before. Then one shakes the body and exhales while sounding *Ha*. The oral instructions mention that in general this should be done quickly.

Furthermore, Yangtön Chenpo had three particular and generally quick yogic exercises. These were mentioned by his son, Dampa Bumjé Ö.

The qualities of the common exercises for dispelling hindrances

The qualities are that illnesses arising from conditions of the four elements, as well as the outer and inner hindrances, are all cleared away. The upward channels, the sunken winds, winds that are disordered, highly spirited, crippled, bent, and so forth, all obstacles from the conditions of the channels and the winds are cleared away. One can apply the key points of the five elemental winds and dispel general hindrances to the channels and the winds. One can focus on the fast-running four elements while exalted qualities arise with the experience of non-grasping luminous emptiness.

Taking and augmenting the jewels[368]

One dispels the hindrances of growths in the upper part of the body with the yogic exercise of taking and augmenting the jewels. The fingers are interlaced, the index fingers pointing forward together. The right thumb is pressed by the left thumb. One stirs the hands outside and then draws them in, the back of the thumbs hitting the muscles of the center of chest three times, in a sequence. This exercise particularly focuses on the diseases of the eyes. They are done in one's spare time as practical procedures to enable the winds. Its qualities are such that one will be freed from the sicknesses of depression, of whistling lungs, of the heart, and of growths on the upper part of the body.

The Chinese maiden weaving silk[369]

The method of the yogic exercise of the silk weaver is threefold. In the first movements, the left hand goes into the hollow of the knee [357] and then comes out and grabs the toe [same side]. The right hand grabs the upper part of the right foot. The left foot and hand are brought in and out in circles, seven times. Once the leg and foot are stretched out and straightened, one expels the stale air to clean it.

Next, the method of the second yogic movements of the silk weaver. The right hand is under the head, and with the index finger and thumb of the right hand close the right nostril and press the right[370] artery, respectively. The left hand pulls in the left leg. The left index finger grabs the toe and brings the leg in and out in a circular movement seven times. Then, do the same with the other side.

Finally, the third yogic movement of the silk weaver. Sitting in the tent posture, both hands stretch out between the legs. Grasp the right toe with the right hand and the left toe with the left hand. The heel kicks at the hipbone, then stretches and pulls in the leg crossing. Do this cycle and its reverse seven times. Then stretch the four limbs of the body. Shake the body and expel stale air with the corresponding sound.

The qualities of the movements of the Chinese maiden weaving silk

The qualities of the silk weaver movements are: First, it opens the door to the left channel and makes the rigid wind enter. Second, it blocks the door of the right channel and severs the stream of afflictions. Third, it captures the two winds and one attains outer and inner mastery.

These were the teachings on the graded yogic movements of the silk weaver and its three rapid general performances. These were the instructions of Dampa Bumjé.[371]

These were the graded yogic exercises, particular and common, of the ancillary and main practices of the revelatory transmission of the Great Perfection from Zhangzhung. I received the sets of six yogic movements of the system from Tö,[372] from Pöngyal Tsenpo, and from the five great accomplished ones of the lower system, the lineage of practices in stages from Yangchen and his son the young master.

Virtue! May it be auspicious! [358]

10. The Cycle of the Seven Clear Lights from the Single Transmission of the Cycle of the Revelatory Transmission of the Great Perfection from Zhangzhung

EMAHO! I PAY HOMAGE to the enlightened body of the primordial teacher!

This advice on the key points of the practices of the channel and the winds is part of the revelatory transmission of the profound Great Perfection of the secret tantras. The blissful and accomplished lama has revealed in these writings the manner of accomplishing the practices along a gradual line, similar to a rosary of pearls, for the benefit of individuals of future generations. One must have previously completed the preliminary practices.

At present, one must meditate according to the oral directions on the practices of the channels and winds. The key point of the yogic exercises, the basic preparations to control the channels, consists in stabilizing body and mind and bringing the winds and the mind under control.

Stabilizing body and mind

Stabilizing body and mind consists in adopting the five body postures. The legs are crossed, the hands are in the meditative posture, and the spine is straight as an arrow. The neck is bent like a metal hook. The shoulders are split apart like an eagle soaring. The tongue does not touch the palate, even a little. The mouth and lips are free and slightly apart, as if to subtly sound the letter *A*.

Controlling the winds and the mind

For the generation process, the key points on the channels: the right channel is white, the left channel is red, and the central is dark blue. These should be clearly visualized.

The winds are thrust together into the channel below the tip of the spine and form the shape of the seed-syllable *Cha*[373] with its two feet. The channel splits in three at the level of the heart, and its central part has its upper tip spread open like a meadow flower above the crown of the head. The right and left channels depart from inside the central channel at the level of the vertebra; they follow inside the cup shape of the skull over the brain matter and exit at the opening of the two nostrils, piercing free. Furthermore, the main point of these channels is that they retain the size of silk threads. The central channel is to be generated to be the width of a metal cane and opens wide at its end. The two right and left channels are nearly as straight as an arrow shaft; the right is a crystal color similar to a white mountain crane. The left is vermillion, like the color of coral. The central channel is the glorious Nyelo'u,[374] like the color of the resplendent light-blue sky. This is how these three should be generated.

As for exhalation while training the winds and the mind, stale air should be replenished with fresh air multiple times. To top off one session of practice, consciousness should be stabilized for a short time. One trains the channels by purifying the right, left, and central channels nine times.

The key points for the practices of yogic exercise are that they are done within the four limits of the retreat boundaries, the body and mind are composed, the body and mind are put down for training, and the churning of the winds to control the channel and so forth are done as mentioned above.

The key point on the body is [359] to take the bodily position of the wrathful awe-inspiring posture.

The key point on the generation of the channels is to clearly visualize the three channels as mentioned above.

The key point on holding the breath is to replace stale air with fresh air.

The key point on the meditation on the droplets is to recite the seed-syllable *SO*.[375] From the sphere of the non-manifest come the dark-red *SO* syllables. These jingling miniatures of pristine cognition emanate and enter through one's crown to melt inside one's continuum. In the circle of one's heart they merge as one in non-duality with the essence of one's awareness. I become the wrathful one with a dark-red body, one face, and two arms. I am the hero with awesome splendor!

One then recites the seed-syllable *SO*. The *SO*, which dwells in one's base, emanates jingling dark-red *SO* syllables, miniatures of pristine awareness that fill the flexible dark-blue central channel everywhere. One recites the seed-syllable *SO* while slightly holding the breath from the right channel. The seed-syllable *SO* of the central channel emanates countless *SO* [syllables]. They fill the interior of the flexible white right channel. They then push out the wind from the flexible right channel upward, emanating the jingling miniatures of pristine cognition as dark-red *SO* syllables together in the darkened interior of the retreat cell, the sky, and the earth everywhere.

One recites the seed-syllable *SO* while slightly holding the breath from the left channel. The seed-syllable *SO* of the right channel emanates countless *SO* [syllables]. They fill the interior of the flexible red left channel. Then countless jingling miniatures of pristine cognition come out from the left channel, filling the trunk of one's body, front and back, the aggregates, their constituents and sensory fields, the channels and focal points, and the pores and hair of the body. These jingling miniatures of pristine cognition are issued forth using one's imagination everywhere, so that obstructers, demons of perversion, and sprites cannot strike with mischief, no matter what. One fixes one's consciousness on that and meditates within the space of seven in-breaths[376] while still suppressing the breath. Then the process is completed [i.e., one exhales].

Perfection stages

As for the perfection stages process, having melted the *SO* syllables into light outside, they are reabsorbed into the *SO* of the right white channel and those of the red left channel. Having melted these *SO* of the right and left channels into light, they are reabsorbed into the *SO* of the central dark-blue channel. Having melted the *SO* of the central dark-blue channel, they are reabsorbed into the abiding base. The *SO* syllables abiding at the base together with the wrathful deities in the sky dissipate like a rainbow into the seal of non-perception.

The instructions on the practice in the dark, in this little writing on establishing the boundaries with clear light, are completed. [360]

11. Clear Light, Yogic Exercises, and Channels and Winds of the Revelatory Transmission from Zhangzhung

EMAHO! I PAY HOMAGE to the enlightened body of the primordial teacher! I bow to the lamas of the lineage!

The visualization of the channels, the practices of the channels and winds, and the yogic exercises of this revelatory transmission are similar to the advice on the vitality[377] of the blood in the heart and consist in the visualizations for the weekly cycles of clear light. The accomplished yogis of the past gave this advice in the single, one-to-one transmission. Since that time, it has not been taught to a second person and has been under the seal of this command. For the sake of future generations, I have established this outline of the oral instructions for the visualization of clear light in a seven-week cycle.

First week

The first week, the key points on the yogic exercises and the basic arrangements to the sun-particles practices consist in establishing body and mind in stability, finalizing the control of the winds, and training the channels with the ninefold breathing and so forth, similar to the above.

Continuing with the key points of the body postures, this consists in the position of the hands and the five natural customary postures of the body, the strenuous practice of the great expanse,[378] the formula of the ocean and the excellent mountain,[379] keeping the tongue in its prison,[380] and turning the great luminaries upward.[381]

The points on generating the channels consist in clearly visualizing the three channels as mentioned above.

The point on holding the breath is to expel the stale air nine times, replacing it with fresh air.

The point on meditating on the droplets is to meditate on the two glitters that are blue and green and guide them splendidly with breath and mind to the nostrils, like reining in sunrays that are the essence of the droplets. That is to say, holding one's breath a little while fixating one's attention will transmit them to the interior of the right and left channels. At the lower end of the dark-blue central channel and the three channels, having fused the wind with a maroon-colored droplet, one proceeds to make it go up along the inside of the central dark-blue channel, exiting through the crown of the head, a finger-width out. One lets the wind fall back slowly, where it comes to rest in the center of the heart, filling it. For that, one fixes the attention, meditating on exiting the wind back and forth seven times. Once this is completed, one imagines the droplets disappearing, becoming inseparable with non-conceptual space. One expels stale air for fresh air and seals this in non-perception.

Second week

The second week's basis consists in the practice of the movement called "rays of the sun." The yogic exercise, key points of the body, and channels and winds are the same as above.

The point on the droplet consists in the white-yellowish droplet [361] in the right nostril and the red-yellowish of the left that are but the size of a lentil.

Lights of the five colors of the rainbow are then emitted from these droplets and fall downward inside the right and left channels. The droplets then rise up through the central dark-blue channel like whirling balls, ascending above the crown of the head, like sputtering flames, and exiting to just about a finger's width. Then the droplets gently fall back down and come to rest in a row in the circle of the heart. They abide face-to-face, joined in this sphere. There, fixing one's attention, they melt while one holds one's breath, interspersing the breath with seven small breaths. Once this is completed, when one feels drowsiness glooming, one has the droplets absorbed in the conch housing of the brain. When one becomes agitated, one has them absorbed in the center of the heart. When there is no drowsiness or agitation whatsoever, one imagines them resting naturally in the two nostrils, then fading. One expels stale air for fresh air and seals this in non-perception.

Third week

The third week focuses on the essential points of the basic yogic exercises for the right white channel and the left red channel. The body position and their key points are as above.

The key point on the generation of the channel is that the lower point below the end of the spine at the mouth of the great pillar where the three channels meet looks like the letter *cha* [ཆ] standing up. The upper end divides in three in the center of the heart. The three channels reach the crown of the head and cut through like wheat straw. Their hollows glow. Their color and thickness are as mentioned above.

The key point on the retention of the breath is to expel the stale air nine times and take in fresh air.

The key point on the meditation with the droplets is that one meditates on the king of heaven, Kuntu Zangpo, who is the essence of the moon, sitting above the right white channel the size of a grain of barley. The queen Nang Makö,[382] who is the essence of the sun, sits like a rainbow above the left red channel. Furthermore, the father looks at his consort from the corner of his left eye, and the consort looks at her spouse through the corner of her right eye. These two are generated in their enlightened bodies endowed with love and exalted knowledge. They emit rays of light into the expanse and invite divine couples to be present, who dissolve into them in non-duality. One fixes one's attention on that as long as one is holding the breath. The rising heat from respiration, which is a little like a rainbow, strikes the divine couple. The divine couple melt into light and become white and red droplets, merely the size of a lentil. Lights of the five colors of the rainbow are then emitted from these two droplets; they fall down inside the right and left channels and then rise up through the central dark-blue channel like balls ascending above the crown of the head, like sputtering flames, exiting to just about a finger's width. They then gently fall back down and come to rest in a row in the circle of the heart. They abide face-to-face, joined in this sphere.

There, fixating one's attention, they melt while one holds one's breath, interspersing the breath with seven incremental breaths. Once this is completed, when drowsiness glooms, one should have these dissolve at the mouth of the central dark-blue channel. [362]

When there is agitation, one should meditate on the center of the heart. When nothing whatsoever appears, one imagines them fading into their own place at the mouth of the right and left channels. One expels stale air for fresh air and seals this in non-perception.

Fourth week

The key point of the fourth week is the yogic exercise on the basic position of one's central channel.

The key points of the body and the channels and winds are as mentioned above.

The key point on the meditation on the droplets is to generate a lotus petal above the central dark-blue channel, on which the king of heaven on the right and the queen Nang Makö on the left come to sit as mentioned above. One then fixes one's attention on that and holds one's breath.

The hot air from respiration strikes the divine couple to a certain degree. The divine couple melt into light and become white and red droplets merely the size of barley seeds. Lights of the five colors of the rainbow are then emitted from these two, and they fall down inside the central dark-blue channel. From the junction of the three channels below, they ascend upward inside the right and left channels, exiting through the crown of the head to just about a finger's width. They then gently fall back down. They then ascend like whirling balls inside the central dark-blue channel, going up to the mouth of the central dark-blue channel and exiting above to just about a finger's width.

They then gently fall back down, where they come to rest lining up in the center of the heart. One meditates on them face-to-face in this sphere. There, fixing one's attention, they melt while one holds one's breath, interspersing the breath with seven incremental breaths.

Once this is completed, when drowsiness glooms, one should have these lights of the five colors of the rainbow dissolve at the mouth of the central dark-blue channel. When there is agitation, one should meditate on the center of the heart. When nothing whatsoever appears, one imagines the lights fading into their own place at the mouth of the central dark-blue channel. One expels stale air for fresh air and seals this in non-perception.

Fifth week

The key point of week five is based on the yogic exercise with the basic position of the rainbow.

The key points on the body, the channels, the winds and sunrays are as mentioned above.

The key point on the meditation on the droplets here is that inside the two nostrils [one imagines] the essences of the droplets of the winds and the mind. These are like the sun surrounded by rainbows, just about the size of a lentil. Lights of the five colors of the rainbow are then emitted from these two droplets and follow the course down inside the right and left channels. The two droplets then rise up through the central dark-blue channel like two whirling balls, ascending through the crown of the head and exiting to just about a finger's width above. They then gently fall down and come to rest lined up in the center of the heart. They rest in the sphere, face-to-face. There, fixing one's attention, they melt while one holds one's breath, interspersing this breath with seven small breaths. Once this is completed, when there is agitation one should meditate on the center of the heart.

When drowsiness glooms, one should have these droplets of light dissolve at the mouth of the central dark-blue channel. [363] When nothing whatsoever appears, one imagines them fading into their own place above the channel. One expels stale air for fresh air and seals this in non-perception.

Sixth week

During week six, the keys points are on the basic yogic exercises of making the seed-syllable *Hum* rest, emanating the seed-syllable *A*, and collecting the seed-syllable *Om*.

The key points on the position of the body are as above.

The key point on generating the channels is to clearly visualize them stable, like a mother.

The key points on holding the breath are as above.

The key points on the meditation on the droplets are as follows: One's awareness is essentialized as the completely dark-blue-colored seed-syllable *Hum* in the center of one's heart. It emits the five colors of the rainbow, and one's attention is fixed on that. One holds one's breath and makes the *Hum* syllable go up inside the central dark-blue channel, the winds chasing after it. It exits through the crown of the head to just about a finger's width. It then gently falls back down until the junction of the three channels, where there are [two] white *A* seed-syllables. One imagines that these two seed-syllables emit rays of light in the five colors of rainbow. They course through the right and left channels and reach the two nostrils. One then expels the air, cleaning it out. One then meditates that the inside of the dark room, manifesting in the sky outside together with the earth, is filled and sealed with the seed-syllable *A* in the nature of rainbows. One fixates one's attention on that while holding the breath. These *A* syllables melt into a single *A* syllable, which is then transformed into two white *A* syllables for the two nostrils. Having dissolved these *A* syllables into light, they become two orange-colored *Oṃ* seed-syllables. One meditates that these two seed-syllables emanate rays of light in the five colors of the rainbow. They then course through the inside of the right and left channels. One then meditates that at the base of the central dark-blue channel they turn into the seed-syllable *Huṃ*. The seed-syllable then ascends and exits through the crown of the head to just about a finger's width. It then gently falls down and comes to rest, clearly tranquil, in the center of the heart. One fixes one's attention on that while it melts, holding the breath and interspersing the breath with seven incremental breaths. Once this is completed, the *Huṃ* syllable in the center of the heart dissolves. One expels stale air for fresh air and seals this in non-perception.

Seventh week

The last week is concerned with the key points on the yogic exercise of the basic postures using the abiding *Huṃ* seed-syllable, the emanating *Oṃ* seed-syllable, and collecting the *A* seed-syllables.

The key points on the body and the yogic exercises are as above.

The key points on the meditation on the droplets consist in one's awareness essentialized fully as a dark-blue-colored seed-syllable *Huṃ* in the center of one's heart. It emits the five colors of the rainbow and one's attention is fixed on that.

One holds one's breath and makes the *Huṃ* syllable go up inside the central dark-blue channel, the winds chasing after it. It exits through the crown of the head to just about a finger's width. It then gently falls back down until the junction of the three channels, where it transforms into two orange *Oṃ* seed-syllables [364] that emit rays of light in the five colors of a rainbow. They course through the inside of the right and left channels and arrive at the two nostrils while one expels one's breath for fresh air. One then meditates, imagining that the inside of the dark room, the sky outside, and the earth are filled and sealed with the seed-syllable *Oṃ* in the nature of rainbows. One fixates one's attention on that while holding the breath.

These *Oṃ* syllables melt into a single red *Oṃ* syllable, which is then transformed into two white *A* syllables for the two nostrils. One meditates, [imagining] that these two emanate rays of light in the five colors of the rainbow. They then course through the inside of the right and left channels.

One then meditates, imagining that at the base of the central dark-blue channel, they turn into a dark-blue seed-syllable *Huṃ*. The seed-syllable then ascends and exits through the crown of the head to just about a finger's width. It then gently falls down and comes to rest, clearly tranquil, in the center of the heart. One fixes one's attention on this as it melts, holding the breath and interspersing it with seven incremental breaths. Once this is completed, the *Huṃ* syllable in the center of the heart dissolves. One expels stale air for fresh air and seals this in non-perception.

Conclusion

On concluding activities, there are the general, the partial, and the reverse. These are the pith instructions that should be known directly from a master.

There are five systematic postures and the three channels that have to be clearly visualized, similar to the above. Stale air needs to be expelled nine times for fresh air.

The points on the meditation on the droplet consist in the brain as a red *Hri* seed-syllable on top of an orange sun-seat. The "clouds"[383] of the brain become two white *Hri* seed-syllables on white-yellowish moon seats. They emit the five colored lights of the rainbow. The two *Hri* syllables are method and wisdom, and they dwell there vividly, stacked up. One fixates one's attention on that. Once this is completed, the two *Hri* syllables and the sun and moon-seats dissolve, disappearing naturally. One expels stale air for fresh air and seals this in non-perception.

The seven-week cycle of clear light has a general compression process. The principal practices of the seven-week cycle on clear light consist in illuminating, what is called "the projection of the object of awareness in the sky," and is similar to the purification process of the Victorious Summit.[384]

The general compression process on purification is to meditate concentrating the object of awareness in the center of the heart while compressing seven-times-seven times to dissolve the winds.

The oral instructions mention that a paired object of awareness is transmitted to each of these objects of awareness of clear light. For each paired object of awareness, the body has to be in a meditative-state posture and the three channels clearly visualized. One then expels the stale air.

As for the meditation process, one meditates imagining that the light in the center of the heart becomes a white *A* syllable endowed with the five colors. One meditates that inside the right and left channels are two green *Yaṃ* seed-syllables, and there is a wheel of light at the crown of the head. [365] One holds one's breath while [the breath itself is imagined to] course through the right and left channels. It strikes the two *Yaṃ* seed-syllables, and green lights, like strands of silk thread, stream down, pass by the junction of the three channels, and move up, ascending to the central channel. They dissolve into the *A* syllable in the center of the heart. At that, one holds the breath for one cycle then expels stale air.

One holds the breath, having made it travel in the right and left channels until it strikes the *Yaṃ* syllables. After melting the *Yaṃ* syllables into light, the green droplets shrink to the mere size of lentil. They move to the juncture of the three channels and merge into one. They move up inside the central channel and fade into the *A* syllable in the center of the heart. One fixes one's attention on that. One meditates seven times and makes compressions to dissolve winds.

The completion process consists in making the *A* seed-syllable go inside the central channel and out through the crown of the head. It then dissolves into the wheel of light. Furthermore, the wheel of light then fades into the sky. Awareness is stabilized in clarity and emptiness without grasping. This is the gradual manner of the general practice.

As for the partial manner, following the above-described ancillary body postures, one engages in the key points on breath control in four sessions and pursues this day and night.

The reverse manner is to pursue day and night the particles of sunlight moving upward with the seed-syllables *Oṃ, A, Huṃ*.

This is the traditional lore on the cycle of visualizations. *Samaya!* Sealed! Sealed! Sealed! *Atham!* Virtue! [366]

12. The Oral Advice of the Knowledge-Holder Lishu[385]

I PROSTRATE TO ALL the reverend lamas whose view and conduct are inseparable! They are free from activities and unstained, and their realization of the meaning is like the sky. Although they engage in activities as such, their enlightened conduct is well and appropriately done.

Alas! Yogis whose intention is the realization of the meaning, carry on the crown of your heads the lama who taught you the definitive meaning of these pith instructions! Doing that, you will permanently keep in your heart the pith instructions on these teachings. Yogis, the range of your view is not small, but the range of your conduct is not great. The blissful ones have realized the intent, but their enlightened conduct is not in accord. You may have realized the intent of the blissful ones, but your conduct is not in accord.

Virtuous ritual activities are an undisputable path, a conduct that is favorable with everything. Realization, although arising by itself, generates generosity and compassion. The nine vehicles are true on their own grounds and can be used for one who is about to start on the [Greater] Vehicle, but the profound view of the ultimate curtails partiality regarding reality.

Listening to one's own continuum does not skillfully satisfy the reality of liberation, and it brings false meanings and contradicts the words of the blissful ones. Therefore, put that aside! If it were true, pure in meaning and correct, then one would be able to enjoy secret activities, rape, and perverse conduct!

One may have great confidence in oneself, but question everything! One's experience may be profound, but you there, keep secret and speak little of it!

One does not examine other people's mistakes when one's own mistakes occur. Carry all the different convictions of sentient beings and do not cast them away. Offer exalted knowledge, but curb your arrogance, stubbornness, and pride.

If one accepts a great and elevated status for oneself, one must abandon insulting the lowly others. There is no point in producing afflictions, therefore renounce disputation and doubts!

If you wish to engage in the various ritual practices of Bön, you must conduct yourself according to Bön. Explanations do not tame humans! Tell this to yourself!

The yogi who meditates to ascertain knowledge for oneself must be resilient. Refrain to the utmost from wrongdoing and from accumulating faults in this life!

If you hold on to meditating single-mindedly, go live in a remote place alone! Whatever truth there is in realization, renounce that which there is to know! It conflicts with phenomena, therefore let go of activities for worldly success!

Rely little on desires and abandon your own country to practice virtue! If you know how to free yourself from cravings and hatred, then wherever you stay, you'll be alone. When there are contradictory conditions to Bön, abandon distraction and entertainments.

When you cognize any phenomena, abandon whatever it is, for it is without cause. When one's view causes something hidden to come out, that is a cause for confusing meaning. In reality the path of conduct is not fabricated, therefore reject confusion, and I urge you to peace!

If you become conceited after receiving adulation, then each of you yogis are very weak! If you debate and assert yourself as a scholar, there is no purpose there for you to create afflictions. [367]

If you cheat and so forth, you sin for selfish, concrete benefits. If you allow the cause of deceit into your mind, the gods and the sky-goers will be ashamed of you. If you pretend to realization without realization, you yogis will shame yourself! If you knowingly deceive, the assembly of scholars will shame you. If you are tormented by desire for wealth, you yogis will feel hungry for yourselves! If you hold fame and merit high, you yogis are monstrously duped! If the limelight of glory torments you, each of you yogis is weak! If your attachments to subject and object are great, O yogis, you'll remain permanently in cyclic existence.

Bring down the roots of intrinsic reality that are indeed in your own mind! Bring down the roots of discursive thoughts that are indeed the making of your conceptual self! Finalize the three enlightened bodies that are indeed the root to transcending misery! Discard the cravings of subject and object, for indeed they are the roots of cyclic existence and transcendence! There is no compounded intrinsic reality; it goes unnoticed when you rely on discursive thoughts. If there is no cause for perceiving discursive thoughts, then because of that you will see the real intrinsic reality. If you do not take readily to happiness, it is because you have not abandoned suffering. If there is no cause for eliminating suffering, then there is simply just happiness.

If you do not cut off the roots of your words, then cut off the roots of your meaning! If you cut away the roots of your words, then you will become the boundless sky. If you cut away the roots of meaning, then simply cut your words to the end!

If you do not cut away the roots of intrinsic reality, then cut away the roots of your mind! If you cut the roots of your mind, then there is the sovereignty over reality.

If you do not seek, then there will be no enlightenment and you will have to rely on the defining marks in your mind. If you know the defining marks of your mind, then with that you shall discover enlightenment.

Having asked for advice on the evident roots of enlightenment from a compassionate one endowed with exalted knowledge, then see for yourself and research what there is and what there is not. If you have doubts, then look at all these tantric texts! If you are okay with these three, then you will soon have no more doubts.

For diligent yogis, an unassailable attitude in this life will produce enthusiasm. If you will consider this, then since at this moment it is not in my power to remain, you should quickly take the practice into your own hands. When mental objects have no more energy, then set yourself aside in the state of realization. You yogis who have realization for the sake of others, practice at length and stay at your leisure!

Listen a lot and collect little. Sift the relevant from the confused mixtures. Understand the coarse, yet practice thoroughly. Understand broadly, yet protect the details. Realize greatly, yet avoid pettiness.

The world has been brought to extremes. There, you say! But it is unfinished! There are still subtleties. Do your virtuous practices! You should be ashamed!

Indolence, beer, and cravings, these three are poisons to virtuous practices. These are extremely unhappy doings.

Evil objects, evil friends, and evil teachers, these three are in contradiction with Bön. If you wish to eliminate them, skillful means will eliminate them.

Fame, glory, and merit, these three are in contradiction with Bön. [368] Really, they are not to be trusted!

Companionship, one's own country, and wealth, these three are demons to virtuous practice! Really, they are not to be trusted!

If you carry on in accord with Bön, afflictions, external foes, thieves, causes of deceit, and internal ulcers will depart. Do not be short tempered with conditions of suffering. Your state in cyclic existence will not last long.

Internally, human customs eventually become self-defeating. Units of measure do not enter into Bön. You should expel false spiritual siblings from among you, as well as afflictive emotions, conversation left and right, the unintelligent, slighting and not taking seriously the words of the blissful ones, sustaining mentally devious spiritual teachings, treating one's selfish aims as not small but as rather urgent, and taking the [use of the] Bön practices for worldly gain as not of great concern but as rather urgent.

Objects that are manifestly illusory do not endure for long, and the state of realization does not last for a short time. If you are not endowed with experience and confidence, self-liberation from the five poisons won't be coming. If reincarnations and deaths endure for long, then you will meet death throughout the three evil states of reincarnation, and engaging in virtuous practices will not be you, sir! Then faith and confidence will not be produced, while you will not fear reincarnation and death. If you cannot turn away from the phenomena of cyclic existence, then you will not be mindful at the moment of death, and these virtuous practices I mentioned are then false.

Consider gradual studious efforts as opposed to working in the field, gradual positive practices as opposed to the consequences of harvesting, gradual roots of virtue as opposed to the existing contempt toward servants. Those who are knowledgeable and can explain Bön are proverbial! Gradual virtuous practices are better than superficial religious practices. With the former, faith in Bön will be assured. Demons lure humans into deception in order to make them crave fame and glory. Be diligent in virtuous activities of the body and speech! Whatever is the fault of the cause of deceit of the body, practices for one's own reputation are afflictions and suffering. That form of Bön is not it.

In every quarter, the fortunate one will be practicing conduct concordant with the realizations of all the ways of the heroes. He will be neither exclusive nor inclusive of the outer and the inner purposes. He will have destroyed discursive conceptuality, suffering, and afflictions. This is the essence of the blissful ones in the body of sentient beings. As such, they are extremely rare among beings, for it is held in the essence of the profound view. If you know the conduct that is in harmony with it, then you are the most excellent of beings among individuals. Because of that, view and conduct coincide with the practices conducted for the mothers [i.e., sentient beings that have been our mother in one reincarnation]. For myself and those like me, Lishu Takring, I have written this small manual, which is the root of the scriptures, as a testament for my rough-mannered spiritual siblings. I pray to the exalted scholars for forgiveness! May it bring fruition to those in delusion. This is complete. Samaya! Seal! Seal! Seal! *Aya ag tham! Shu bam!*[386] Virtue!

Table of Tibetan Transliteration

Phonetic Spelling	Transliteration
Anyé Machen	A myes rma chen
Azha Lodrö Gyaltsen	A zha Blo gros rgyal mtshan
Balkhyung Monastery	Dbal khyung dgon
Banam Kyölpo	Ba nam skyol po
Barnang Kujung	Bar snang khu byung
Chala Yungdrung Gyaltsen	Phya bla G.yung drung rgyal mtshan
Chikchö Deshé	Gcig chod dad shes
Chimé Tsukphu	'Chi med gtsug phud
Choklé Namgyal	Phyogs las rnam rgyal
Chungji Muthar	Khyung byid mu thar
Dampa Bumzé	Dam pa 'bum rdze
Dampa Bumjé Ö	Dam pa 'bum rje 'od
Darma Bhodé	Dar ma bho de
Darma Sherab	Dar ma shes rab
Dawa Gyaltsen	Zla ba rgyal mtshan
Dewa Ringmo	Bde ba ring mo
Dönkun Drupa	Don kun grub pa
Dopa	Do pa
Dopa Töntsul	Do pa ston tshul
Drak Yungdrungkha	Brag g.yung drung kha
Drenpa Namkha	Dran pa nam mkha'
Drimé Chökyi Chanden	Dri med chos kyis spyan ldan
Dronya Söyé	Sgro snya bsod ye
Dru Namkha Ö	Bru nam mkha' 'od
Dru Namkha Yungdrung	Bru nam kha' g.yung drung
Druksé Chempa	'Brug gsas chem pa
Drutön Gyalwa Yungdrung	Bru rgyal ba g.yung drung

Dutsi Gyaltsen	Bdud rtsi rgyal mtshan
Garsé Tsenpo	Gar gsas btsan po
Gatön Tsultrim Gyaltsen	Sga ston Tshul khrims rgyal mtshan
Gawa Döndrup	Dga' ba don 'grub
Gawo Jokpo	Dga' bo 'jog po
Gegyal	Dge rgyal
Gekhö	Ge khod
Gelha Garchuk	Dge lha gar phyug
Gewar Döndrup	Dge 'bar don grub
Gomchen Barwa, Tokden	Rtog ldan Sgom chen 'bar ba,
Gösé Sangwa	Rgod gsas gsang ba
Gugé Loden	Gu ge blo ldan
Gurup Sega	Gu rub gsas dga'
Gyagom Tensang	Rgya sgom bstan bzang
Gyagom Yerin	Rgya sgom ye rin
Gyaltsen Rinchen	Rgyal mtshan rin chen
Gyalwa Lodrö	Rgyal ba blo gros
Gyalzik Sechung	Rgyal gzigs gsas chung
Gyatang Chenyi	Bya btang mched gnyis
Gyermi Nyiö	Gyer mi Nyi 'od
Gyerpung Gephen	Gyer spungs dge 'phen
Gyerpung Nangzher Löpo	Gyer spungs snang bzher lod po
Gyershen Takla	Gyer gshen stag la
Gyershen Dzotang	Gyer gshen dzo btang
Horti Chenpo	Hor ti chen po
Jé Lhari Nyenpo	Rje Lha ri gnyan po
Jedrak Ngömé	Bye brag dngos med
Jigchö Déshé	Gjig chod dad shes
Joyung Khyungom	Jo g.yung Khyung sgom
Jozhön	Jo gzhon
Kangtsa Tradar	Rkang tsha bkra dar
Khetsun Gyalwa	Mkhas btsun rgyal ba
Khetsun Tretön	Mkhas btsun tre ston
Khutsa Dawo	Khu tsha zla 'od
Khyungö Tsal	Khyung rgod rtsal
Kunga Gyaltsen	Kun dga' rgyal mtshan
Kunang Khyabpa	Kun snang khyab pa
Kundröl Drakpa	Kun grol grags pa

Kuntu Shenlha	Kun tu gshen lha
Kuntu Zangpo	Kun tu bzang po
Kunzang Gyaltsen	Kun bzang rgyal mtshan
Lama Gyaltsen	Bla ma rgyal mtshan
Latö Tokden Depa Sherab	La stod Rtogs ldan Dad pa shes rab
Lentön Sönam	Glen ston bsod nams
Lhagö Thokpa	Lha rgod thog pa
Lhagom Karpo	Lha sgom dkar po
Lhatön Drakpa Tsultrim	Lha ston Grags pa tshul khrims
Lhayi Lodrö	Lha yi blo gros
Lhundrup Muthur	Lhun grub mu thur
Lishu Takring, Nya	Snya Li shu stag ring
Loden Nyingpo	Blo ldan snying po
Lopön Mé	Slob dpon me
Lozang Drakpa	Blo bzang grags pa
Lubön Banam	Klu bon ba nam
Lungbön Lhanyen	Lung bon lha gnyan
Lungbön Tashi Gyaltsen	Lung bon Bkra shis rgyal mtshan
Lungom Tokmé	Lung sgom rtog med
Lungtok Tenpai Nyima	Lung rtogs bstan pa'i nyi ma
Machen Pomra	Rma chen spom/pom ra
Mapang Lhachen	Ma pang lha chen
Mapang Yutso	Ma pang g.yu mtso
Marpa Dopa Wangchuk	Mar pa Do pa dbang phyug
Mashen Lekzang	Rma gshen legs bzang
Matön Drangsong	Rma ston drang srong
Matön Sherab Sengé	Rma ston shes rab seng ge
Matön Sölzin	Rma ston Srol 'dzin
Mengrok Walpo	Rmeng rog dbal po
Menri Monastery	Sman ri dgon
Metön Drakpa Pal	Me ston Grags pa'i dpal
Metön Kunzang Gyaltsen	Me ston Kun bzang rgyal mtshan
Metön Sherab Özer	Me ston shes rab 'od zer
Me'u Gongzö	Rme'u dgongs mdzod
(alias Dampa Ritrö Tröpa)	(alias Dam pa ri khrod pa)
Me'u Lhari Nyenpo	Rme'u lha ri gnyen po
Me'u Pal	Rme'u dpal
(alias Tsultrim Palchen)	(alias Tshul khrims Dpal chen)

Me'u Rok Walmo	Me'u Rog dbal bon
Mongyal Lhasé	Smon rgyal lha sras
Mönlam Lodrö	Smon lam blo gros
Mönpa Kunsel	Mun pa kun sel
Mugyal Lodrö	Dmu rgyal blo gros
Mugyung Karpo	Mu rgyung dkar po
Mushen Tsogé	Dmu gshen tso ge
Muyé Lhagyung	Mu ye lha rgyung
Naljor Sechok	Rnal 'byor sras mchog
Namkha Özer	Nam mkha' 'od zer
Namkha Rinchen	Gnam mkha' rin chen
Namkha Tsultrim	Nam mkha' tshul khrims
Namkha Yeshé	Nam mkha' ye shes
Namgyal Kara	Rnam rgyal ka ra
Namri Löntsen	Gnam ri slon btsan
Namsé Yingrumlha	Gnam gsas dbyings rum lha
Namtso Dopa	Gnam mtsho do pa
Nang Makö	Snang ma skos
Nangzher Löpo	Snang zher lod po
Neljené (alias Neljigur)	Rnel byed ne (alias Rnel byid gur)
Ngamsé	Rngam gsas
Ngari Sögyal	Mnga' ri bsod rgyal
Ngödrup Gyaltsen	Dngos grub rgyal mtshan
Ngorchen Kunga Zangpo	Ngor chen kun dga' bzang po
Nya Lishu Takring	Snya Li shu stag ring
Nyakgom Shertsul	Nyag sgom sher tshul
Nyelgom Trulmé	Snyel sgom 'khrul med
Nyen Takpung	Gnyan Stag spungs
Nyenchen Thanglha	Gnyan chen Thang lha
Nyenthing (alias Sherab Sengé)	Gnyan 'thing (alias Shes rab seng ge)
Nyima Tenzin	Nyi ma bstan 'dzin
Nyima Wangyal	Nyi ma dbang rgyal
Nyö Arin	Gnyö A rin
Öchagma	'Od chags ma
Ökar Nezin	'Od dkar gnas 'dzin
Olmo Lungring	'Ol mo lung rings
Orgom Kundul	'Or sgom kun 'dul
Özer Pakmé	'Od zer dpag med

Paljor Lhundrup	Dpal 'byor lhun grub
Pangla Namshen	Spang la nam gshen
Patön Nyipal	Spa ston nyi dpal
Patön Ösal Gyaltsen	Spa ston 'od gsal rgyal mtshan
Patön Palchok	Spa ston dpal mchog
Patön Tengyal Zangpo	Spa ston Bstan rgyal bzang po
Phuntsok Lodrö	Phun tshogs blo gros
Phuntsok Namgyal	Phun tshogs rnam rgyal
Pöngyal Tsenpo	Dpon rgyal btsan po
Pönsé Gyalpo	Dpon gsas rgyal po
Pönsé Khyungö Tsal	Dpon gsas khyung rgod rtsal
Pureng Kunga	Pu reng kun dga'
Rasang Phengyal	Ra sangs 'phen rgyal
Rasang Samdrup	Ra sangs bsam 'grub
Rasang Yungdrung	Ra sangs g.yung drung
Rinchen Dopa	Rin chen do pa
Rinchen Gyaltsen	Rin chen rgyal mtshan
Rinchen Lhundrup	Rin chen lhun grub
Rinchen Lodrö	Rin chen blo gros
Rinchen Özer	Rin chen 'od zer
Ripa Sherlo	Ri pa sher blo
Rongtön Chöjé	Rong ston chos rje
Rongtön Sheja Kunrik	Rong ston Shes bya kun rig
Salwa Rangjung	Gsal ba rang 'byung
Sangnak Lingpa	Gsang sngags gling pa
Sangwa Düpa	Gsang ba 'dus pa
Sangyé Lingpa	Gsang rgyas gling pa
Sangyé Rinchen	Sangs rgyas rin chen
Sangyé Tenzin	Sans rgyas bstan 'dzin
Sebön Gurpo	Gze bon rgur po
Sechen Yungphen	Gsas chen g.yung 'phen
Sejé Mangpo	Gsas rje rmang po
Sengé Rikzin Nyima	Seng ge Rig 'dzin nyi ma
Sengé Tulku Rikzin Nyima	Seng ge sprul sku Rig 'dzin Nyi ma
Serdoma	Gser do ma
Shen Naljigur	Gshen Rnel byid gur
Shen Yeshé Lodrö	Gshen Ye shes blo gros

Shenchen Lüga	Gshen chen klu dga'/Gshen sgur klu dga'
Shengyal Lhatsé	Gshen rgyal lha rtse
Shenlha Karpo	Gshen lha dkar po
Shenlha Ökar	Gshen lha 'od dkar
Shenrab	Gshen rab
Shenrab Miwoché	Gshen rab mi bo che
Sherab Ganden	Shes rab dga' ldan
Sherab Gongyal	Shes rab dgongs rgyal
Sherab Gyaltsen	She rab rgyal mtshan
Sherab Lodrö	Shes rab blo gros
Sherab Özer	Shes rab 'od zer
Sherab Tenzin	Shes rab bstan 'dzin
Sherab Yungdrung	Shes rab g.yung drung
Sherab Wangyal	Shes rab dbang rgyal
Sherzhön (alias Sherab Zhön)	Sher gzhon (alias Shes rab gzhon)
Shetsu Drungmu	She tsu drung mu
Shötram Chenpo	Shod khram chen po
Sipé Bön	Srid pa'i bon
Sokdé Tenpai Nyima	Sog sde Btan pa'i nyi ma
Sönam Lodrö	Bsod nam blo gros
Sönam Yeshé	Bsod nams ye shes
Sönam Yungdrung	Bsod nams g.yung drung
Songtsen Gampo	Srong btsan sgam po
Takla Mebar	Stag la/lha me 'bar
Tapihritsa	Ta pi hri tsa
Tashi Gyaltsen	Bkra shis rgyal mtshan
Tashi Rinchen	Bkra shis rin chen
Tengyal Zangpo	Bstan rgyal bzang po
Tenpa Lodrö	Bstan pa'i blo gros
Tenzin Tsultrim	Bstan 'dzin tshul krims
Tokden Bönpo	Rtogs ldan dbon po
Tokden Gomchen Barwa	Rtog ldan Sgom chen 'Bar ba
Tokden Shepal	Rtogs ldan shes dpal
Tokmé Shikpo	Rtog med zhig po
Tönpa Salwa Rangjung	Ston pa Gsal ba rang 'byung
Tönpa Shenrab	Ston pa gshen rab
Tridé Zambu	Khrid sde zam (zab) bu

Trishö Gyalwa	Khri shod rgyal ba
Trisong Detsen	Khri srong lde btsan
Triten Norbutsé	Khri brtan nor bu rtse
Trosé	Khro gsas
Trotsang Druklha	Khro tshang 'brug lha
Trowo Tsochok Khaying	Khro bo Gtso mghog mkha' 'gying
Trulshen Nangden	'Phrul gshen snang ldan
Tsangpa Tsukphu	Tshangs pa gtsug phud
Tsangri Purlang	Tsang ri pur lang
Tsemé Öden	Tshad med 'od ldan
Tsenden Ripa	Mtshan ldan ri pa
Tsewang Rikzin	Tshe dbang rig 'dzin
Tsukphu Tumsé Özer	Gtsug phud gtum gsas 'od zer
Tsultrim Gyaltsen	Tshul khrims rgyal mtshan
Tsultrim Palchen	Tshul khrims Dpal chen
(alias Me'u Pal)	(alias Me'u dpal)
Tumsé	Gtum gsas
Uri Sögyal	U ri bsod rgyal
Utsé Karpo	Dbu ste dkar po
Utsé Marpo	Dbu tse dmar po
Walchen Gekhö	Dbal chen ge khod
Walchen Trogyal	Dbal gshen khro rgyal
Walsé	Dbal gsas
Walsé Ngampa	Dbal gsas rngam pa
Yangtön Chenpo	Yang ston chen po
Yeru Bensakha	G.yas ru dben sa kha
Yeshé Lodrö	Ye shes blo gros
Yeshé Rinchen	Ye shes rin chen
Yeshen Tsukphu	Ye gshen gtsug phud
Yölmo	Yul mo
Yotön	G.yo ston
Yongsu Dakpa	Yongs su dag pa
Yorpo Mepal	G.yor po Me dpal
(alias Metön Drakpa)	(alias Me ston Grags pa dpal)
Yungdrung Gyaltsen	G.yung drung rgyal mtshan
Yungdrung Tenpai Gyaltsen	G.yung drung Bstan pa'i rgyal mtshan
Yungdrung Tsultrim	G.yung drung tshul khrims
Yungdrung Wangyal	G.yung drung dbang rgyal

Yungdrung Yeshé	G.yung drung ye shes
Zegur	Gze sgur
Zangwa Düpa	Bzang 'dus pa
Zangza Ringtsun	Bzang za ring btsun
Zangza Tsendruk	Bzang za mtshan drug
Zhang Löngom Ringmo	Zhang Blon sgom ring po
Zhangtön Sonam Rinchen	Zhang ston Bsod nams rin chen
Zhangzhung Namgyal	Zhang zhung rnam rgyal
Zhangzhung Triphen	Zhang zhung khri 'phen
Zhotön Ngodrup	Bzhod ston dngos grub
Zhuchen Yeshé Rinchen	Zhu chen Ye shes rin chen
Zhutön	Zhu ston

Notes

1 According to Bön historical sources, Shenchen Lüga (996–1035) inaugurated a renewal of Bön in Tibet with the discovery of a cache of texts in 1017 after the persecution of Bön by the pro-Buddhist king Trisong Detsen (r. 756–c. 797). See Martin, *Unearthing Bon Treasures*; and Karmay, *Treasury*, 117–18, 126–31.

2 Gurung, "Emergence of a Myth," 9.

3 Lalou, "Rituel bon-po," 339–61.

4 These ransom rites are common in Bön and among Tibetan Buddhists who adopted them with enthusiasm. They consist in offering a substitute for the person/family/animal afflicted by inimical spirits. This substitute can take various forms, from that of a sacrificed animal to offering cakes (gtor ma) and so on. In Everlasting Bön there are no blood sacrifices, as opposed to other forms of Bön such as Sipé Bön (srid pa'i bon). This is one important point made repeatedly by its adepts.

5 See Dotson, "Complementarity," 44–45.

6 See for instance the four collections of Lü Bum (Klu 'bum), Nyen Bum (Gnyan 'bum), Sadak Bum (Sa bdag 'bum), and Tö (Gto, also Gtod 'bum), K135–42.

7 See Dotson, "Complementarity." It is also quite possible that lineage could have been the differentiating element in these attributions.

8 See Torri, *Landscape*.

9 Yeru Bensakha was destroyed by flood in 1386. This precipitated one of its abbots, Sherab Gyaltsen (1356–1415) to found Menri Monastery in 1405, which still posits itself as the headquarters of Everlasting Bön. The actual situation is more nuanced, since there are many independent Bön monastic settlements. Although Menri is acknowledged as extremely important, most of these institutions do not consider themselves bound to Menri. See Des Jardins, "Notes on the History of Bon."

10 Phun tshog, *Bod kyi bon dgon khag*, 21. Unlike contemporary historians of Tibet, Everlasting Bön proponents do not consider monasticism and its accompanying vows to be newly introduced during the Yeru Bensakha Period. On the contrary, its adherents support the view that the founder of the creed, Tönpa Shenrab, introduced this practice. In any case, taking on monastic vows was a small movement among Bönpos in the twelfth century. It is only with the development of large temples and changes in social practice over the course of several centuries that monastic Bön became prevalent in local village temples. The abundance of Bönpo geshes (*dge bshes*), or scholar-monks, is a very recent development in Bön. Sengé Rikzin Nyima (b. 1986) believes that a hundred years ago, scholar-monks were a

minority and lineages of Bönpo lamas were still passed mainly through hereditary lines (personal communication 2004). This growth could be attributed to changes in Tibetan society since the founding of the People's Republic of China as well as recent educational policies developed by monastic institutions.

11   See Ryavec, *A Historical Atlas*, map 16, as well as his article "Regional Perspectives," which highlights the locations of Bön and Buddhist monasteries during the period 900 to 1240. It is important to note here that Ryavec's survey does not include village temples where Bönpos operated who were not part of the monastic tradition. The Kadam monasteries recorded in his survey might have been simple temples with a few monks at most. However, due to the focus of later Tibetan histories on Buddhism, they do not mention already existing or new temples that were not Buddhist. For key works of the Kadam tradition, see Jinpa, *Book of Kadam*.

12   The best survey of its canonical texts up till now remains Martin, Kvaerne, and Nagano, *A Catalogue of the Bon Kanjur*.

13   Cech, "History, Teaching and Practice of Dialectics," 22n18, lists the names of the eighteen abbots of Yeru Bensakha.

14   On the development of tantric ritual cycles in Bön, see Des Jardins, "Tantric Ritual Standardization."

15   These are Tsultrim Palchen (1052–1106), Meton Sherab Özer (1058/1118–1132/1192), and Patön Ösal Gyaltsen (tenth–eleventh centuries). See Gurung, "Emergence," 4, 36n36, and 46.

16   The best historical and critical study of this scripture is Gurung, "Emergence," which analyzes its composition and the rise of Shenrab Miwo as a pseudo-historical character.

17   The *Gyacher Rölpa (Rgya cher rol pa)* is the earliest translation of the *Lalitavistara*. See Gurung, "Emergence," 5, 16, 35, and 53–56.

18   For a good rendition of the various aspects of Shenrab's life, see Gurung, "Emergence"; and Ramble, "Ston pa Gshen rab." See also Tardar, "The Twelve Deeds of Shenrab."

19   See Blondeau, "Le Lha-'dre bka'-thañ." For a more recent reappraisal of the contributions of Bön texts to the treasure-text tradition of the Nyingmapa, see Mayer, "Rethinking Treasure."

20   An eighth-century master, Tongchen Mutsa Gyermé (Stong chen Dmu tsha gyer med), is credited with the transmission of this twelve-volume text to Loden Nyingpo. O-thog bsTan-'dzin dbang-rgyal, "An Introduction to the Index."

21   See Kvaerne, *Bon Religion of Tibet*, 36–37.

22   See discussion on Shenrab's chronology in Gurung, "Emergence," 20–24. Many contemporary Bön lamas and their followers seem to take this chronology as historical fact, which is a serious pitfall. This unfortunate stance is severely hampering the critical study of Bön records. The value of mystical stories and myths rest in the ideas that they are carrying. Taking symbolic numbers and giving them historical (Gregorian) dates is as reasonable as the creationists who believe that the world was made in 168 hours (seven days) 6,000 years ago.

23   See Dagkar, "gShen."

24 On this lineage and the Master Tagla Mebar, see Des Jardins, "About the Zhang-zhung master Stag la me 'bar."

25 See for instance Lhagyal, "Bonpo family lineages."

26 These nine commentaries have been published together in volume 9 of the series *Gangs ti se bon gzhung rig mdzod* (*Mount Kailash Treasury of Bön Knowledge*) edited by Tsering Thar et al. The nine texts are the following:

    1. *Byams ma chen mo rtsa ba' 'bum bzhugs*, attributed to Shenrab but discovered as a treasure text by Trotsang Druklha. Karmay provides for him the unusual dates of 956–1077, conferring a life span of 121 years. See Treasury, 124n3. These dates, to my knowledge, have never been investigated.

    2. *Byams ma 'bum lnga'i bka' 'grel*, a commentary on the first title written by Rongtön Sheja Kunrik (1345–1429/1367–1415). See Karmay, *Treasury*, 141n3.

    3. *Sa lam 'phrul gyi lde mig* by Azha Lodrö Gyaltsen.

    4. *Gzhi lam 'bras bu'i rang 'grel gsal byed me long* by Gatön Tsultrim Gyaltsen (fourteenth century).

    5. *Sa lam 'phrul gyi sgron ma* by Sherab Gyaltsen.

    6. *Sa lam 'phrul gyi sgron ma'i rang 'grel*, an autocommentary by Sherab Gyaltsen.

    7. *Thar lam gsal sgron nyi ma'i 'od zer*, again by Sherab Gyaltsen.

    8. *Bsam gzugs brgyad kyi rnam bshad rin chen phreng ba* by Lopzur (slob zur) Namkha Tsultrim (1930–2019).

    9. *Zhugs 'bras brgyad kyi rnam bshad mu tig phreng mdzes*, also by Namkha Tsultrim.

27 Karmay, "Cult of Mountain Deities," 400.

28 Reynolds, *Cult and Practice*.

29 For a good summary of the meditative traditions in Bön, see Jurkovic, "Prayer to Ta pi hritsa."

30 On the Atri system, see Kvaerne, "Bonpo Studies"; Bru-sgom, *Stages of A Khrid Meditation*; and Geshe Sonam Gurung and Brown, *Pith Instructions for A Khrid Dzogchen*.

31 See Achard, *Enlightened Rainbows*, 263–88.

32 See Shar rdza, *Self-Arising Three-Fold Embodiment*. See also Achard, *Enlightened Rainbows*.

33 See Dalton, "A Crisis of Doxography."

34 Snellgrove, *Nine Ways*, 16–19.

35 *Eye of the Needle* (*Gzer mig*), in Snellgrove, *Nine Ways*, 16–20.

36 Yorpo Mepal, alias Metön Drakpa Pal; on this character, not mentioned in other biographies, see Karmay, *Treasury*, 110.

37 See Cech, "The History, Teaching and Practice of Dialectics according to the Bon Tradition", 22n18.

38 On Khutsa Dawo, see Mayer, "A Bon Tantric Approach to the Senses."

39 Achard, *Les instructions sur le A Primordial*.

40 Other works of Lodrö Gyaltsen's in the canon of commentaries are:

    • *Zhi ba A gsal gyi mngon rtogs chung ba gsal byed* [*Concise Explanations on the Actualization of the Peaceful Asel*], written at the monastery of Snying mo glang ra, T27.6: 45–48.

On the secret rite of Drenpa Namkha (*dran pa gsang sgrub*):

- *Nang sgrub phyag bzhes [Rubrics on the Inner Rites]*, also *Nang sgrub gsal byed sgron ma rin po che [The Precious Lamp That Clearly Explains the Inner Rites]*, written upon the request of a monk from Upper Dölpo, T48.2: 35–66.
- *Gsang ba yab yum gyi phyag bzhes gsal ba'i sgron ma rin po che'i bcud [The Elixir of the Precious Lamp Elucidating the Rubrics for the Secret Syzygies]*, written in Yeru Bensakha for upon the request of a monk from Upper Dölpo, T48.3: 35–66.
- *Gsang ba bla chen sgrub pa dran pa gsang sgrub kyi phyag bzhes gsal byed sgron ma [The Lamp That Elucidates the Rubrics for the Secret Rite of Drenpa, the Accomplishment of the Great Secret Lama]*, written in Yeru Bensakha for upon the request of a monk from Upper Dölpo, T48.4: 67–102.
- *Phyi sgrub phyag bzhes [Rubric for the Performance of the Outer Rite*, also called the *Precious Lamp for the Supplications (Section) for the Outer Rite]*, T48.7: 123–28.
- *Snyan rgyud kyi phyag bzhes [Rubrics for the Oral Transmission].* This contains directives on the empowerment rite of the Secret Accomplishment of Drenpa. It was written for Khatsun Namdak (Mkhas btsun rnam dag ming can/'od zer) at Paldenna Monastery (Dpal ldan sna'i dgon), T48.24: 443–98.
- On the *Rig 'dzin mkha' 'gro'i zhus len [Asking the Sky-goer Knowledge-holders]* that is a collection of practices of a revelatory nature attributed to the visionary Shensé Lhajé (Gshen sras lha rje, 1215–68) and linked to the Ma rgyud tantric cycle and Tsewang Rikzin (Tshe dbang Rig 'dzin):
- *Tshe dbang gsang sgrub kyi phyag bzhes gsal ba 'phrul gyi lde mig [The Magical Key to Elucidating the Practice of the Secret Rite of Tsewang]*, T61.37: 635–55.
- *Tshe dbang rgya gar ma'i skong ba [Summoning Tsewang in India]*, T61.50: 798–806.
- *Tshe dbang skong bshags tshangs pa'i gter [Treasure Text for Full Confession and Amends of Tsewang]*, T88.28: 525–47.

On the Father Tantra class and its purifying practice (*pho sbyong*):

- *Mdo sde gsar rnying lung gi dgongs pa tshig spyi dril nyams su len thabs [The Intention of the New and Old Traditions of the Scripture Category, the General Method to Practice the Recitations for (transference of) Virtue/Merit]*, T207.11: 123–206.
- *Spyi spungs zhi ba g.yung drung yongs rdzogs kyi phyag bzhes gsal byed sgron ma [The Lamp That Clarifies the Rubrics of the Very Perfected Everlasting Peaceful Deities of the Universal Heap]*, T230.1: 1–35.
- *Thar glud mdos kyi lag len gsal ba'i me long [The Mirror That Elucidates the Directives for the Liberation Rite, Ransom Offering, and Thread-Cross Ceremony]*, to be used for the Bön of the secret tantras, T232.15: 471–77.

On the rites of Phurpa:

- *Phur pa'i phyag bzhes me ri bkod legs [The Well-Arranged Mountain of Fire, Rubrics for Phurpa].* This text is attributed to Lodrö Gyaltsen; however, the colophon mentions three contributors to this text—namely, the uncle and master Dutsi Gyaltsen, Lodrö Gyaltsen, and the Lady of Dong (ldong btsun), Lady Drugyaltsen (Btsun 'Grus rgyal mtshan), T245.1: 1–95.
- *Gsang sngags lam gyi 'jug chog mu tig 'phreng ba [The Method of Entering the Path of the Secret Mantras, the Necklace of Pearl],* written at the request of Sönam Gyal (Bsod nams rgyal) from Menyak, T251.1: 1–60.

41 A current typeset edition has been published in volume 6 of Tsering Thar, *Gangs ti se bon gzhung rig mdzod.*

42 A current typeset edition has been published in volume 12 of Tsering Thar, *Gangs ti se bon gzhung rig mdzod.*

43 The very existence of this lost vernacular as a distinct language on the Tibetan plateau is currently debated by scholars, but with no clear outcome. Some dictionaries have been compiled. The study of Zhangzhung as a former kingdom in the western part of Tibet, its history, and geography have been supported by Chinese and Tibetan archeologists and Tibetologists. The data amassed up until now is highly susceptible to interpretation, which makes for heated debates in academia.

44 The first commentary on the *Innermost Treasury* is attributed to the eighth-century sage Drenpa Namkha and is a treasure-text titled the *Great Commentary on Sound* that was brought up as a treasure-text by Gyermi Nyiö (b. 1108). The second commentary, posterior to Lodrö Gyaltsen's commentary, is that of Gatön Tsultrim Gyaltsen (fl. fourteenth century), the *Kun las btus pa srid pa'i mdzod gzhung [The Tradition of the Treasury of the World, the Compendium]* and its autocommentary. The first treasure text of Gyermi Nyiö was published as part of the *Bden pa'i mdzod phugs rnam par 'byed pa'i lde mig,* 1–35. The text of Gatön Tsultrim Gyaltsen was published in *A Treatise with Autocommentary Presenting the Bonpo Abhidharma* by Sga ston Tshul khrims rgyal mtshan in 1974. This information was gleaned from Dan Martin's handout in 2016 at the Bon Manuscript Conference in Hamburg. A third commentary on the *Innermost Treasury* is attributed to Sherab Gyaltsen and is titled *Srid pa'i mdzogs phugs kyi tshig don gsal bar byed pa'i 'grel ba 'phrul gyi sgron me.* It was privately published in a typeset edition as volume 11 of the Yungdrung Bon Teaching and Practice College series for the students of the monastic school at Menri Monastery in India.

45 A current typeset edition has been published in Tsering Thar, *Gangs ti se bon gzhung rig mdzod,* 15: 105–428.

46 The three tantras in the cycle are associated with the father, the mother, and son, respectively: the *Gsang ba 'dus pa,* the *Gsang ba bsen thub,* and the *Gsang ba don grub.* This "mother" tantra involves the Secret Mother, Goddess Senthub (Yum gsang ba'i lha mo bsen thub ma), and contains early myths and narratives on the origin of evil and the assembly of twenty-seven Walmo female spirits (*dbal mo nyer bdun*). See Blezer, "The 'Bon' dBal-mo Nyer-bdun(/brgyad)."

47 A current typeset edition has been published in Tsering Thar, *Gangs ti se bon gzhung rig mdzod,* vol. 19.

48   A current typeset edition has been published in Tsering Thar, *Gangs ti se bon gzhung rig mdzod*, vol. 20.

49   Dharmakīrti (d. 660) was an important theoretician of the Yogācāra and the Sautrāntika schools. His *Commentary on Valid Cognition (Pramāṇavārttika)* was extremely influential in Tibet and one can clearly see his vocabulary and his style of reasoning, as well as its categories, reflected in Lodrö Gyaltsen's text. See Dunne, *Foundations*.

50   Dignāga (480–540) was an important Indian commentator of Buddhist Abhidharma philosophy who established through his work the fundamental tenets of Buddhist logic and epistemology. His main thesis is that only perception and inference can be relied on as instruments of knowledge. See Hayes, *Dignāga*.

51   "A large commentary and a small one were discovered together" (*rtsa rgyud la 'grel ba che chung gsum*). For the story of this discovery, see Karmay, *Treasury*, 120–21 and 284, for the untranslated portion naming the texts.

52   Gurung, "Emergence," 9.

53   In Karmay, *Treasury*, 91.

54   See Ramble, "Tsewang Rigdzin."

55   On New Bön, see for instance Achard, *A Fourfold Set of Emanations*.

56   For his biography by Tashi Gyaltsen, see Karmay, *Treasury*, 141–45.

57   Sherab Gyaltsen's *Collected Works* recently reedited in Sichuan are computer-typed and total ten volumes with 111 titles of various lengths. See Sherab Gyaltsen, *Bka' 'bum*.

58   On the contributions of Menri's pandits to the formation of the tantric tradition in Everlasting Bön, see Des Jardins, "Tantric Ritual Standardization."

59   On his life, see Achard, *Les instructions sur le A Primordial*, 61–63; Karmay, *Little Luminous Boy*, 53–55; and Shar rdza bkra shis rgyal mtshan, "Man ngag rin po che."

60   On the link between Gilgit and Bön, see Des Jardins, "About the Zhangzhung Master Stag la me 'bar."

61   Khyung rgod rtsal, alias Dbyil ston He ru ka Khyung rgod rtsal.

62   On his life and the list of his transmissions received directly from the hermit Tsewang, an emanation of Tsewang Rikzin, see Karmay, *Treasury*, 113–15.

63   On the treasure texts that were transmitted to him from the son of Matön Sölzin, see Karmay, *Treasury*, 169. These consisted of tantric texts as well as Great Perfection material.

64   On his life, see Karmay, *Treasury*, 167–68.

65   See his *Man ngag rin po che A khrid kyi bla ma brgyud pa'i gsol 'debs* in T265.6: 45–70.

66   Lishu Takring, alias Nyachen or Nyen Lishu Takring (Snya chen/snyan Li shu Stag ring)

67   The five supreme tantric deities are the Five Supreme Ones of the Celestial Citadel (gsas mkhar mchog lnga): Phurpa, Gekhö, Trowo Tsochok Khaying, Lhagö Thopa, and Walsé Ngampa. See Karmay, *Treasury*, 45n2.

68   See Karmay, *Treasury*, 56–58.

69   *Dri med gnyis tshogs*: the two accumulations of stainless merit and wisdom.

70   Here, I interpret *'phrul dum* for *'phrul du ma*, many emanations.

71 *Don gnyis*: the two aims are to attain enlightenment for oneself and others. Tado, *Dictionary*, 12.

72 Tshangs pa is generally considered as the Tibetan name for Brahma, the Indian head of the Tripura. It is questionable to assume that the Bönpo would have the same conception of Tshangpa as the Indian or Tibetan Buddhist. The "indigenous" deity (*lha*) Tshangpa is a multifaceted persona linked to ancient myths, such as the origin accounts of some Tibetan clans. The Lang Lazik (Rlangs Lha gzig) clan in the *Rlangs kyi po ti bse ru rgyas pa* (Lhasa, 1986) is a good example of this. Toni Huber, in *Source of Life*, theorizes that this deity may be the source of the Sipé lha (*srid pa'i lha*, lit.: the gods of the world) cults, a form of Tibetan ritual practice linked to the cult of celestial deities. Sources of these myths and practices can be found in the Bön canon under the generic title: The Four Compendiums ('*bum bzhi*). Each is dedicated to one of the pantheon of worldly spirits that are the Nyen (*gnyan 'bum*) deities, the To (*gtod 'bum*), the Sadak (*sa bdag 'bum*), and the Lu (*klu 'bum*). Tshangpa is therefore a complex figure, and in order to highlight this, I chose to use his Tibetan name in this volume unless the Tibetan word in the text is written in an Indic transliteration or refers to a known Indian or Buddhist reference. Despite that, Bönpos will usually assign a Zhangzhung provenance to Tshangpa instead of an Indian one.

73 *Gnas gsum* here seems to refer to the three world systems of cyclic existence following the Buddhist conception and mentioned in the next paragraph. These are the realms of desire, form, and formlessness. In Bön however, there is the frequent mention of the three abodes of the sky, the earth, and the underground or land of the Lu (*klu, nāga*). See Huber, *Source of Life*.

74 *Shing rta'i srol*, the traditions of the charioteers or the two chariots, are those of Nāgārjuna and Asaṅga. The twelfth–thirteenth centuries was a period of intense eclecticism in Tibet, when Bönpo masters went to Buddhist institutions to study philosophy, grammar, and so on. *The Eight Realms*, for example, is the Bönpo version of the *Perfection of Wisdom*.

75 *De nyid bdag tu sgros btags kyis*. This means that one holds on to the notion that one has a true self that is absolute as such. This is the classic mistake, according to Buddhist and Yungdrung Bön philosophies, where one attributes individual existence to phenomena and gets sidetracked into believing in their reality.

76 Here the Tibetan editors mention that the list of Lodrö Gyaltsen is incomplete. Other sources, such as *Treasury*, actually list nine points instead, with a further fourteen. See 368n20 of the original edition of this text.

77 See "eighteen emptinesses" in the Glossary.

78 This example of a faulty vision that perceives the moon or a conch shell as being double is often used in philosophical discussion as a metaphor to point out the faulty perception of reality. See Coseru, *Perceiving Reality*.

79 See the above heading "Divisions" under "Inherent nature." The author constantly jumps from a subsection to one of the main sections without further indication for the most part. Hence the text itself goes from first, to second, to second again, or to several third topics in a row, making it extremely challenging and confusing. To ease our understanding of the core text, I have added subheadings throughout, although these are not to be found within the original text.

80 Dru Namkha Ö is presumably another person from the Bru clan and not the Dru Namkha Ö (1268–1321) who lived shortly after the author Azha Lodrö Gyaltsen (1198–1263).

81 Lit., "similar to the pillar-and-pot equivalence." This is a classic idiom used in Buddhist philosophy for ascertaining whether there are one or separate essences for phenomena in theory. If the pillar and the pot are of the same essence, their differences refute this. If they are two distinct essences, they contradict each other. See Cabezón, *A Dose of Emptiness*, 121, 168, 180–81, for further considerations.

82 Is this Marpa Dopa Wangchuk (1042–1136), who is chiefly known as a translator of tantric scriptures from India, in particular the Cakrasamvara cycle, the same as the Dopa repeatedly mentioned in Lodrö Gyaltsen's text? It is also possible that this Dopa Wangchuk may have been both Buddhist and Bönpo, something not uncommon throughout history and even today.

83 Namtso Dopa (fl. twelfth century), a contemporary of our author, is an enigmatic character. Little is known except that he was one of the six mind disciples of Tokden Gomchen Barwa (fl. eleventh century). Both Dopa and his fellow-disciple Joyung Khyungom (fl. twelfth century) were from Central Tibet. According to the *Rtogs ldan nyams rgyud kyi rnam thar* (on this text see Achard, *Enlightened Rainbows*, 303), both disciples were conversant with the Perfection of Wisdom section from the *Eight Realms* (*Khams brgyad*) scripture as well as with the Madyamaka philosophy. I want to thank Sengé Tulku Rikzin Nyima (b. 1967), who kindly pointed me to this source. Although there seems to be no obvious connection between Dopa Wangchuk above and Namtsho Dopa, the latter's arguments are always countered by our author. This needs further examination. Namtsodo or Namtso Tsedo (*gnam mtsho lce do*) is a peninsula in Namtso Lake in the northern regions of the Jiangthang (*byang thang*) in Tibet. It was a sacred place for Bönpos until the twelfth–thirteenth centuries when Buddhists took over. The land is riddled with caves, and many ascetics practiced there. Consequently, yogis from the place were often just called Namtsodopa, "the person from Namtsodo." See Bellezza, "Notes on Three Series."

84 *Mtshan mtshon gzhi gsum* consist in the defining characteristic (*mtshan nyid*), the object that is being characterized (*mtshon bya*), and the bearer of the characteristic (*mtshan gzhi*). This is a common distinction within Buddhist hermeneutics. The classic demonstration used is: The supporting power of a pillar is its defining characteristic (*mtshan nyid*). The pillar itself is the object being characterized (*mtshon bya*). The description of the pillar's qualities is the bearer of the characteristics (*mtshan gzhi*). See Hugon, *Trésors du raisonnement*.

85 The three kinds of conventional truth are: the relative aspect of the relative truth (*kun rdzob kyi kun rdzob*), the relative aspect of the non-existent completely pure (*yang dag pa ma yin pa'i kun rdzob*), and the relative aspect of the completely pure (*yang dag pa'i kun rdzob*). Tado, *Dictionary*, 74.

86 The original text has "defining characteristic" (*mtshan nyid*), but the editors of the text stipulate that here it should be read as "basis of characteristics" (*mtshan gzhi*). See the Tibetan text 271n45.

87 An entailing factor (*khyab pa*) is what points to a fact. For example, a column of smoke in the middle of a forest entails a fire. See Duckworth, "Two Models."

88 *Rnam gcad*, or "eliminating categories," refers to the process used by consciousness and perception to decide on the nature of an object. The elimination or decision process referred to in this expression means that the knowledge of an object came from inference or the elimination of other possibilities. Hence, the burning properties of a fire can be known through inference and rationality as opposed to unilateral decision (*yongs gcod*) based on experience or direct perception. See *yongs gcod* entry in Duff, *Illuminator Dictionary*.

89 This affirmation is among the logical propositions used when studying the veracity of any statement. It is a common heuristic device used by both Buddhists and Bönpos. A proposition can specify that A exists, A does not exist, A exists while not existing at the same time, or A neither exists nor does not exist. The last two propositions are self-contradictory, and any other of these propositions excludes all the other possibilities.

90 As mentioned in note 88, *yongs gcod*, or "unilateral decision," is the alternative way to knowing, as opposed to knowing through inference (*rnam gcod*). This is the determination based on either direct perception or intuitive understanding that one applies to any given phenomenon. It is similar to knowing the heat of fire based on direct experience.

91 Shes rab dga' ldan might be a reference to the historical Buddha Śākyamuni as suggested by the context of this passage. There is no recorded character with this name living prior to the thirteenth century that I have been able to find.

92 *Dgra bcom* is the destroyer of the enemies (i.e., afflictions) and is the Tibetan translation of the Indian Buddhist term arhat. The latter is one who has managed to become free from cyclic existence and reincarnation. See *dgra bcom pa* entry in Duff, *Illuminator Dictionary*.

93 The identity of this individual, Mu stegs rgyal mtshan, is uncertain. Most likely he is an avatar of Shenrab.

94 *Ji ltar ji snyed pa'i mkhyen pa* are the two ways of knowing of enlightened beings, describing the true ultimate nature of things and omniscience. Tado, *Dictionary*, 5.

95 These are the reflections in a mirror, the moon in water, echoes, rainbows, dreams, the city of celestial beings (gandharva), mirages, and magical illusions. See *sgyu ma'i dpe brgyad* entry in Duff, *Illuminator Dictionary*.

96 *Tshad ma bzhi*, the four syllogisms, are, respectively, valid cognition through direct perception (*mngon sum tshad ma*), valid cognition through inference (*rjes dpag tshad ma*), valid cognition through scriptures (*lung gi tshad ma*), and valid cognition through evaluation of an example (*dpe nyer 'jal gyi tshad ma*). See Tado, *Dictionary*, 155.

97 *Gcig dang du ma bral ba' rigs*, a reasoning that is free from singularity and multiplicity, is a form of reasoning used in Madhyamaka philosophy to investigate a concept to see if it corresponds to only one object or to many. It is a process of elimination to prove the inherent emptiness of all concepts and things. See, for instance, Shinya Moriyama, "Ratnākaraśānti's Theory," 339–51; and Cabezón, *A Dose of Emptiness*, 147–52.

98 The threefold criterion or three modes of syllogism (*bsgrub pa tshul gsum*) are used to determine if the proof is valid or not. In order to do so, one examines the argument along three aspects: the nature of the subject (*phyogs chos*), its pervasion

(*rjes khyab*), and its counterpervasion (*ldog khyab*). In other words, is the object relevant to the topic? How widespread is it as an entailing factor? How is it not connected to entailing factors? See Doctor, *Tibetan Buddhism*, 43n56.

99   The six parts of a spatial position are best conceived by imagining that one is in a box. The four quarters plus the nadir and the zenith make the six directions of space.

100   The four alternative propositions (*mu bzhi*) consist in the four possible assertions that can be made during philosophical inquiry. Objects or propositions are existent, non-existent, both, and neither. See Cabezón, *A Dose of Emptiness*, 93, 291.

101   The modes of separation (*bral ba tshul*) are manners of using reasoning to effect a separation from the objects that need to be eliminated (*spang bya*) on the path.

102   The basis for any phenomenon to be recognized as "something" is birth or production. A product is cognized by its characteristic, the property that is noticed by consciousness. The phenomenon is the bearer of characteristic.

103   See the discussion following the earlier heading "Identifying the essential of the indication of characterized objects."

104   The ten wrongdoings are killing, stealing, sexual misconduct, lying, creating enmity, harsh language, gossip, evil thoughts, harmful ideas, and wrong views.

105   The ten virtuous deeds are not killing, generosity, mindfulness, moral discipline, truthfulness, fostering harmony, using pleasant language, reciting prayers, freedom from evil thoughts, and cultivating perfect view.

106   This identification of our protagonist with Rme'u dgongs mdzod, alias Dam pa ri khrod pa, is tentative but contextually probable.

107   The five paths are accumulation, application, seeing, meditation, and no-more-learning.

108   The four characteristics of the path are causal, immediately preceding, objective, and predominant conditions.

109   This person from the Dre ('bre) clan is unidentified.

110   In the writings of Dignāga, these two defining characteristics (*mtshan nyid gnyis*) consist of the two views of examination (*gzhal bya*): the first is one seen under one's own view and the second is observed from an external view. These are the only possible ways to valid knowledge. However, defining characteristics can be particular. That is the case for all isolated phenomena, or universals. See Hugon, *Le rTags*, 41n30.

111   This passage explains that there are five paths, adding a sixth in the realm of the angry gods, to possible reincarnations. This, again, is a standard Buddhist understanding of conditioned existence in the cycle of reincarnation. To each of these five realms corresponds one of the five poisons that is dominant in that particular realm.

112   This addition of the angry gods as a supernumerary category is noted by Tibetan editors as coming from the *Activities of the Mother of Namdak Padma* (*Rnam dag Padma yum gyi 'phrin las*, T245.131 Ba4) of Dru Gyalwa Yungdrung. See Tibetan original, 373n102.

113   *Gnod sbyin*, Skt. *yakṣa*.

114   *Rigs* here means a line, a lineage of things or beings. Having a wide range of meanings, it is a difficult word to translate. It can also signify reasoning, as in a line of

argument. It deals with the chain of cause and effect in a variety of ways and on a variety of topics. Therefore, in this section I opted for "genealogy" in the sense of lineages of causes and effects.

115 The nine limits or the nine extremes (*mtha' dgu*) are empty appearances (*snang stong*), existence and non-existence (*yod med*), negation and affirmation (*dgag sgrub*), rejection and adoption (*spang blang*), arising and ceasing (*skye 'gag*), eternalism and nihilism (*rtag chad*), wavering and firmness (*g.yo rtsol*), emerging and entering (*'byung 'jug*), and emanation and reabsorption (*'phro 'du*). Tado, *Dictionary*, 348.

116 Erroneously refers to the *Mdo phran* in the original; see 374n123.

117 Hearer (*nyan thos*; Skt. *śrāvaka*) is a common technical term in Buddhism and Bön for those entering the path by listening to the teachings of enlightened ones.

118 On Tshangs pa gtsug phud as Brahma in Tibetan Buddhist narratives, see Obermiller, *History*, 41n252.

119 The three dynamisms (*rtsal gsum*) are the powers or abilities of the body, speech, and mind. Tado, *Dictionary*, 71.

120 Possibly Drimé Chökyi Chenden, who may have been a contemporary of the author, but who is otherwise unknown. The only reference I have found is on a fifteenth-century bronze statue in a private collection shown on Himalayanart.org as item no. 57378.

121 The Vehicle of the Perfections (*phar phyin theg pa*) refers to following the path as described in the Perfection of Wisdom literature adopted by the followers of the Everlasting Bön tradition.

122 Four natural expressions (*rang bzhin brjod pa bzhi*) are: the nature of reasoning (*rigs kyi rang bzhin*), the nature of objects (*bya ba'i rang bzhin*), the nature of enlightened qualities (*yon tan rang bzhin*), and the nature of substantial entities (*rdzas kyi rang bzhin*). Tado, *Dictionary*, 154. However, the text here mentions only the four natures (*rang bzhin bzhi*), and this could refer to other secondary conditions, such as the four kinds of birth, etc. Even in context, the referents are not clear here.

123 There are four marks that characterize, i.e., define (*mtshon bya*) and indicate compounded phenomena: cause and conditions (*rgyu rkyen*), the conditions immediately preceding (*de ma thag rkyen*), conditions that are observed (*dmigs rkyen*), and empowering conditions (*bdag rkyen*).

124 Heat (*drod*) is one of the four stages of the path of application together with the Peak (*rtse mo*), Forbearance (*bzod pa*), and the Highest Bön (*bon mchog*).

125 A bodhisattva who has attained the ninth ground.

126 *Bla med spyod pa bcu*; see Glossary for the ten unsurpassed conducts.

127 Note 229 on page 379 of the original Tibetan text stipulates that no character by that name is known and that it might be a fabrication. However, could this be Patön Tengyal Zangpo (b. 1014)?

128 This Zhang is an unknown character belonging to the "lineage of the others" and therefore cannot be either Zhangzhung Triphen or Zhangzhung Namgyal, both being earlier Bönpo characters. It could possibly be the diminutive for the teacher of the Pa clan member just mentioned, Patön Tengyal Zangpo.

129   There was a Lama Zhang (1122–1193) that was influential in Buddhist circles of his times. See Yamamoto, *Vision and Violence*, in passim.

130   The three kinds of feelings are pleasure, pain, and neutrality.

131   The five poisons (*dug lnga*) are ignorance (*gti mug*), craving ('*dod chags*), anger (*zhe sdang*), pride (*nga rgyal*), and jealousy (*phrag dog*). See the lengthy entry in Tado, *Dictionary*, 193.

132   These most likely refer to the fifty-one mental factors (*sems byung lnga bcu rtsa gcig*) of the *Abhidharmasamuccaya* of Asaṅga (fl. fourth century), since this section deals mainly with Abhidharma categories. These are present in Bön and mentioned in the *Treasury*. See Martin, "Comparing Treasuries," 37–42.

133   The "miraculous feet" (*rdzu 'phrul gyi rkang*) is a common expression used mainly in Buddhism and alludes to the miraculous deeds of buddhas and enlightened beings. The simple term "miraculous deed" is used for saints and other thaumaturgists. The four legs here refer to four bases of miraculous power acquired by practitioners. These concern motivation ('*dun pa*), mental powers (*sems*), perseverance (*brtson 'grus*), and analysis (*dpyod*). The Bönpo list of these focuses on four types of concentration that are their roots, as the author explains below.

134   Holding on to the substance of individuality (*gang zag rdzas 'dzin*) presumably refers to the process of grasping that makes the notion of "individual identity" concrete.

135   The thirty-seven paths and the thirty-seven collections of Everlasting Bön mentioned later by our author in his section "Teachings on the General Nature of the Grounds" may refer to the thirty-seven collections of the heroes of everlastingness. These consist in the four recollections, the four thoroughly abandoned, the four miraculous feet, the five sense faculties, the five powers, the seven enlightened limbs of everlastingness, and the eight limbs of Shenrab. Tado, *Dictionary*, 457. See each individual entry in the Glossary.

136   The four true distinctions (*nges 'byed bzhi*) refer to the four levels of the path of application that leads to the next level, the path of seeing. Its full name is the four types of things to distinguish (*nges 'byed cha mthun bzhi*). These are the four stages of the path of application—namely, Heat, Peak, Forbearance, and Highest Bön, discussed previously. Tado, *Dictionary*, 105.

137   Tsultrim Palchen, aka Meu Pal, b. 1052.

138   The eight types of intellectual knowledge (*blo rig/rigs brgyad po*) are the eight means of knowledge of ordinary mind. These are doubt (*the tshom*), non-ascertainment of meaning (*don du ma nges pa*), wrong consciousness (*log shes*), non-ascertainment of visions (*snang la ma nges pa*), mental assumptions (*yid dpyod*), decisive cognizance (*bcad shes*), direct valid cognition (*dngos sum gyi tshad ma*), and inference by valid cognition (*rjes dpag tshad ma*). See Tado, *Dictionary*, 324.

139   Those are the same as the eight types of intellectual knowledge (*blo rig/rigs brgyad po*), where direct perception is counted here as "awareness."

140   *Phun sum tshogs*, lit. "the three benefits."

141   In this argument-answer section, nothing is said about the second point—that is, abandoning latent tendencies—except below: "Second, all these latencies are to be abandoned."

142 Rme'u dpal, alias Rme'u Tshul khrims dpal chen, b. 1052. See Karmay, *Treasury*, xxxvi.

143 The sixteen facets of the four truths (*bzhi ldog pa bcu drug*) are the same as those of Buddhism on the four noble truths. The truth of suffering: impermanence, suffering, emptiness, and lack of self. The truth of the origin of suffering: causes, origin, production, and secondary conditions. The truth of the cessation of suffering: cessation, pacification, excellence, and definite emergence. The truth on the path: the path, awareness, achievement, and deliverance. On the path of vision, one goes through each of these in sixteen moments. One first cognizes (*shes*) one of the four aspects of the four truths and then accepts it (*bzod*) as a moment of realization.

144 These four "facets" (*ldog pa bzhi*), which are also aspects or isolate factors, consist in cognizing reality (*bon shes*), then accepting reality (*bon bzod*), followed by moments of subsequent cognition of reality (*rje shes*) and subsequent acquiescence (*rje bzod*). This is a sequence for the realization of the four truths.

145 The question here seems to be that when one directly perceives the ultimate, does the knowledge of all aspects mean that one knows everything in general or everything in all its details?

146 This is a quote from an unknown scripture.

147 This sentence is particularly unclear. It seems to allude to "blindly" treading the path of vision. *Blar phyin 'jig rten pa'i blar phyin mthong lam la 'das pa rnam khyen min pa la med byas pas / slob pa lam gyi mthar thug la 'dod pa ni.*

148 The five fears (*'jigs pa lnga*) are the fear of a livelihood being cut short (*'tsho ba chad dogs pa'i 'jigs pa*), the fear of death (*'chi dogs pa'i 'jigs pa*), the fear of being deprived of praise and of being blamed (*mi bngags pa ste mi snyan pa sgro dogs pa'i 'jigs pa*), the fear of evil rebirth (*ngan song ltung dogs pa'i 'jigs pa*), and the fear of impediments in cyclic existence (*'khor ba las bag chags ba'i 'jigs pa*). See Tado, *Dictionary*, 785.

149 The five coarse things (*rags pa lnga*) correspond to the five divisions of the general psycho-physiological constituents of a person. These correspond to the five groupings: the aggregates, the four elements, the six sense powers, the five objects of the senses, and the primordial cognition at the time of the base (*gzhi dus kyi ye shes*).

150 For the thirteen strengths of fearlessness (*mi 'jigs pa'i stobs bcu gsum*), see the Glossary and Tado, *Dictionary*, 545; also Achard, "Contribution aux nombrables," 132.

151 This refers to the thirty-three gods monitoring the three realms. It follows the classical Indian model.

152 Gnyö A rin? See Martin, *Unearthing Bon Treasures*, 101.

153 May refer to someone from the Sakya establishment prior to Rongtön Chöjé (Rong ston Chos rje, 1367–1449).

154 "Knowables" (*shes bya*) means "that which can be known" or "that which can be an object of knowing." It can be also translated as "object of knowledge" or "object that can be known." In the Indian Sāṃkhya school of philosophy (known as the "Enumerators," *grangs can pa*, because of their long lists), formally known from the fourth century CE onward, there are twenty-five knowables. They consist in things such as eye, ear, nose, and tongue, and more abstract concepts such as

person, nature, rational mind, etc. See Cabezón, *A Dose of Emptiness*, 51, 127, passim; and Duff, *Illuminator Dictionary*, *shes sgrib*.

155 For the nine stages of the path of meditation, see the next chapter.

156 Is this Zhuchen Yeshé Rinchen, disciple of Matön Söldzin (b. 1092)? See Karmay, *Treasury*, 167.

157 Mindfulness and mindful recollection are used interchangeably according to the context to translate the Tibetan term *dran pa*. It means to recollect in order not to forget essential points, as well as to be mindful of the task at hand, such as awareness during calm abiding meditation, and so on.

158 It seems that there is no response to the fourth point here.

159 *Yang dag pa'i rig pa bdun*; see the Glossary entry, "seven completely pure awarenesses."

160 The term here is *rang rgyud*, which is often used to translate *svatantra*, "that which is self-dependent." The narrative here discusses the notion of independent existence.

161 Specifically characterized phenomenon (*rang mtshan*) is a category used by the Sautrantika school of Buddhism. It is a self-characterized phenomenon that is implied as inherently existent, as opposed to a generally characterized phenomenon (*spyi mtshan*), which is considered a non-existent entity in its own right and merely a concept.

162 *Bon can* is the Bön version of the *chos can*, the *dharmin* or subject that is aware of the phenomenon. This is what is aware of passing phenomena.

163 The five uncertainties (*ma nges pa lnga*) of one's future reincarnations are about the place in the world, the kind of body one will inhabit, one's entourage, the doctrine available, and the times. See Tado, *Dictionary*, 215.

164 The list of these six saintly figures (*'dul ba'i gshen drug*) varies, but to each is attributed a special stream of practical instructions, empowerments, and practices. Achard, "Contribution aux nombrables," 115, for example, gives the following list: Ye gshen gtsug phud, Lce rgyal par ti, Gsang ba 'dus pa, Ti sangs rang zhi, Mu cho ldem drug, and Gsang ba ngang ring.

165 This fivefold division that I have translated as "pristine cognition" is more often translated as "the five primordial wisdoms" or "the five wisdoms" (*ye shes lnga*). These correspond exactly. One reason I have favored the term "pristine cognition" is that in Bön the emphasis is on awareness and cognition, as these constitute the bare basics of all its teachings on the Great Perfection and are present in many of its tantras. I believe that this common use of the five wisdoms in contemporary Bön may rest with the overtly Buddhist approach to this Tibetan tradition that avowedly uses Buddhist doctrine, but that comprises so much more. Exceptions to this will be duly noted below.

166 Despite what was said in the previous note, here the context requires us to translate *ye shes gnyis* as "the two primordial wisdoms," to be consistent with the author's pairing them with the two truths, the conventional and the absolute.

167 Og min (*'og min*), lit. "nothing higher."

168 All the following numbered subheadings have been added by the Tibetan editors of our text. Although most headings and subheadings in Tibetan are traditionally found at the end of the section they are attached to, I have not followed this

practice and have put the subheadings at the beginning of the relevant sections of the text. This is relevant only to this particular book. The other books have either been given subheadings at the beginning of the sections by the Tibetan editors, or I have added them myself to help clarify the various sections. In short, all unnumbered subheadings were added by myself.

169 From this point in this commentary, all words in quotation marks or longer quotes without prior titles are citations from the preceding text in this volume entitled *Lore of the Root Tantra, the Precious Universal Gathering.*

170 The text is unclear as to certain concepts of its divisions. This division in two, mentioned only at first, is in my opinion tentative.

171 Words in bold are keywords first listed above.

172 There are different lists for the three benefits. Tado, *Dictionary*, 57, mentions the three benefits of elimination (*spangs*), realization (*rtogs*), and result (*bras*).

173 In this tantric section, *ye shes* will be mostly rendered as "wisdom" (in contrast with the philosophical texts and those dealing with the Great Perfection, which translate *ye shes* as "pristine cognition"). The tantras are first of all ritual traditions for the propitiation of deities. The philosophical concepts of Bön and Buddhism are transformed into gods, goddesses, and demons who populate the court or mandala of the main tutelary deity that heads the particular tantric cycle. On tantrism as being historically ritual traditions, see Dalton, "How Dharanis."

174 Ruzhi (*ru bzhi*, lit. "the four horns") are the four mountain ranges delimiting Central Tibet. In this case, however, they most likely refer to the four limbs of the body in connection to the aggregates of the body. There is a clear metaphor here for the body politics of Tibet.

175 The protectresses (*ma mo*) are different kinds of fierce female deities that protect the teachings of Bön and its practitioners. The most famous is the Queen of the World (*srid pa'i rgyal mo*) with her many forms. On the *ma mo*, see Blondeau, "*Ma mo*," 293–311.

176 Shinpo (*srin po*) in Bön sources are sometimes rendered as *rag sha*, for the Indian *rākṣasa* (guardian). See the special number of *Revue d'Etudes Tibétaines*, April 2, 2002, on the eight classes of gods and demons (*lha 'dre sde brgyad*). On the *srin mo*, the female version of the shinpo, see Gianotti, "*Srin Mo Demoness*," 69–97.

177 *Mtha' rgya dug dmu dpu*, also *mtha' rgya dug mur phu*.

178 In Bön literature *gnas lugs* often refers to the natural state, the unconditioned state of pristine cognition, and is alluded to even in the discussion on tantric practices. However, in this section of our text, it refers specifically to tantric ritual meditation practices that are used in the process of transformation.

179 The scriptural source of this quote is unknown. It is not from the root tantra commented on here. The same applies to other unreferenced scriptural quotes.

180 *Rnams ldan par byed*, lit. "to do what these are endowed with." This refers to sets of practices that must be performed and that are assigned to the different levels of tantric practice.

181 See the Glossary for the ten non-virtuous actions.

182 This passage is neither from our root text nor from an identifiable scripture, as the editors of the Tibetan text have noted.

183   *Mnar med dmyal ba.*

184   *Sdug bsngal dpag med.*

185   *Mnar med na rag*, the lowest and most extreme of the hells.

186   The Tibetan text here abruptly begins a lengthy poem containing brief bracketed interpretations of the key words. The editors specify in a note that this passage has been made to appear as if it were part of the Tantra of Amrta Kundali, the Golden Tree of Paradise. However, this passage has either been lost to the present version of the scripture or is a misquote. Note that only the first section of this portion contains bracketed interpretations.

187   The *hom kung* is a triangular container that is used in rituals for destroying recalcitrant spirits, demons, and the like. See Snellgrove, *Nine Ways of Bon*, 277, illustration h.

188   *Bya bang*, raven and crow, is also an alternative spelling for bat (*pha wang*).

189   According to the Shin hwa edition of this text, vol. 220, the four continents come forth as the fifth topic. See Tibetan original, 390–91nn28–29.

190   *Dga' bo 'jog po*, lit. "the joyful Takṣaka" or "Nanda Takṣaka," is the name of the king of the water-spirits.

191   The four demons (*bdud bzhi*) are a complex topic, since there are variants in their definitions. For instance, these can refer to the kings of the four classes of demons (*bdud kyi rgyal po sde bzhi*), the four streams of demons (*bdud kyi chu bzhi*), or the four wild gods that subdue the demons (*bdud 'dul lha rgod bzhi*). See Tado, *Dictionary*, 121–22.

192   The *È* vowel that "is the root of the celestial pull" is possibly the *dmu* cord that pulled the ancient kings of Tibet before King Drigum back to their heaven. On this see Bsod-nams-rgyal-mtshan, *Mirror*, 138.

193   *Ting 'dzin gsum*; these three concentrations are used during the generation process of the mandala. They consist in the concentration on suchness (*de bzhin nyid kyi ting nge 'dzin*), the all-illuminating concentration (*kun tu snang ba'i ting nge 'dzin*), and the causal concentration (*rgyu yi ting nge 'dzin*). See Achard, "Contribution aux nombrables," 81.

194   *Bswo Owm Ba ba de na hwum ra sa ya. Na g.yu 'brang bdud rtsi owm hwum bswo tha.*

195   The five desirable qualities pleasing to the five senses (*'dod pa'i yon tan lnga*) are pleasant clothes, food, drink, bedding, and husband and wife. See Tado, *Dictionary*, 197.

196   *Rnam drug* could be a reference to the six kinds of protective talisman (*bsrung 'khor rnam drug*). However, I cannot affirm this with certainty. I believe that these are more likely the six deities of the senses that are common to tantric cycles such as *ma rgyud*.

197   The four holies or the four great roots (*rtsa chen bzhi*) are most likely the four objects of refuge: lamas, yidams, sky-goers, and protectors.

198   These five Shen or priests might be the first five initial Shen of causal Bön and the methods they introduced. See Nima, "Genealogy," 53. This sentence is difficult to understand and is contextual to funerary rites. It runs like this: *de yang gshen lnga'i spur sbyong na zhib bo.*

199   Again, the *Khams chen* is the Bönpo version of the Perfection of Wisdom scrip-

tures. This passage links view (i.e., emptiness) and conduct (i.e., the perfections) to the Bön practices of the secret mantras.

200 This is the process of "vase breathing" where one presses one's abdominal muscle down over the belly while holding one's breath. It would be best to review the technique with a competent lama.

201 Walchen Gekhö (Dbal chen ge khod) is an important tutelary deity of Bön. His cult is associated with Zhangzhung and the area around Mount Kailash. He has a retinue of 360 "brothers" and is part of the Five Perfect Ones of the citadel (*gsas mkhar mchog lnga*). His main ritual text was compiled by Sherab Gyaltsen and is referred to under the general title *Ge khod gsang ba drag chen*. See Kvaerne, *Bon Religion*, 80–84; and Reynolds, *Cult and Practice*.

202 Nyenchen Thanglha (Gnyan chen thang lha) is a local deity associated with the Thangla mountain range located roughly 100 kilometers northwest of Lhasa. The region was conquered by the Yarlung king Namri Löntsen (Gnam ri slon btsan, 570–619) and was epitomized in a poem partly quoted by Karmay. See Karmay, "The Cult of Mountain Deities," 432–50 passim. The deity is found in the Phur pa corpus as a member of Druksé Chempa's entourage. Bellezza has devoted a large part of a monograph on the history, cult, and legends associated with Nyenchen Thanglha. See Bellezza, *Divine Dyads*, chaps. 1–3.

203 Machen Pomra [*pom ra* in our text] is another important local deity associated with the mountain range Anyé Machen (A myes rma chen) in present-day Qinghai Province (Amdo region). This deity, its cult, and its place in Tibetan local religion has been studied extensively. See Buffetrille, "Evolution," "Great Pilgrimage," and "A Bon po Pilgrimage." See also Sehnalova, "Powerful Deity"; Bellezza, *Spirit-Mediums*; and Karmay, "Cult of Mountain Deities," 432–50.

204 This quote is not referenced in the text and does not belong to the root text commented on here.

205 Mapang Yutso (Ma pang g.yu mtso) is the Tibetan name for Manasarovar Lake at the foot of Mount Kailash. It is very important in Bön cosmology and is given an almost cosmic dimension in Bön writings. The deity at the center of the Phurpa mandala mentioned in our text is Druksé Chempa ('Bru gsas chem pa). Its supervising deity is Mapang Lhachen (Ma pang lha chen), or the Great God of Mapang. Bönpos consider the region as part of the ancient kingdom of Zhangzhung conquered during the reign of Trisong Detsen and one of the mythical sources of the Yundrung Bön religion in Tibet. Many scholars consider the Kailash region as the heartland of ancient Zhangzhung, a point of contention among Tibetologists. Mapang is also associated with funerary cults as well as the cult of Phurpa. See, for example, the *Root Ritual of the Sphere of Mapang of the Peaceful Deities* (*Zhi ba ma pang dbyings chen rtsa ba'i sgrub pa*, T244.13), a ritual text used for the general propitiation of Phurpa.

206 As mentioned before, Druksé Chempa is the tutelary deity at the center of the Phurpa mandala. On Phurpa in Bön, see Des Jardins, "Records"; and Mayer and Cantwell, "Neither the Same nor Different."

207 *Ye shes* can be translated as "pristine cognition" or "primordial wisdom," according to the context. I used "pristine cognition" when the context seems to require a more precise translation pointing at an uncontaminated apprehension of the

non-compounded. Because in Bön the tantras are never too far away from the context of the Great Perfection, I sometimes felt that it was better to use "pristine cognition" instead of the more general rendering "primordial wisdom."

208 *Bsnyen pa* has the sense of coming close, going near, approaching. In the context of the tantras, it is often considered as the first part of the practices where one approaches the tutelary deity through mantra recitation. Hence, *bsnyen sgrub* (*bsgrub*), which is also part of this discourse, is the common name for the text used for the recitation of the propitiation rite of the tutelary deity. Here the aspirant recites mantras and the texts that describe the offerings, the appearances of the mandala, its denizens, and so forth. This section analyzes the words, making the various expressions relate to the practice as well as using the multilayered meanings relating to approach, completion, and/or accomplishment, hinting at nearing the final point of the journey and approaching the realization of the unconditioned. The text is full of double meanings and also mixes a standard tantric approach with Great Perfection practices.

209 Magic-wheel (*sgyu 'phrul gyi 'khor lo*), or literally, "wheel of illusion," are imaginary or drawn devices with seed-syllables and mantras circling them. These are used in the various operations of approach and propitiation, the four tantric activities, the wheel of protection, etc. See for instance Cuevas, "Politics," "Illustrations," and "'Calf's Nipple.'" See also Des Jardins, "A Tibetan Bonpo"; and Douglas, *Tibetan Tantric Charms*.

210 Alias Shen Yeshé Lodrö.

211 *Sad gyer spungs la dun gu hrun! Sad gyer* is Zhangzhung for *lha bon*, or Bön priest of the gods. Martin, "Zhangzhung Dictionary," 227. *Spungs* is either teacher or Bön master (63). *Dun gu hrun* is for *gu dun hrun*, to bow, to salute (56). Therefore, I propose this translation in view of what immediately follows that expresses a similar idea: I pay homage to the Bön priest(s) of the gods!

212 This is a general title to a collection of related scriptures, tantras, and commentaries.

213 T193.97.

214 T216.3.

215 T216.

216 The names of categories not italicized refer not to titles but rather to general categories, to which other titles, special instructions, ritual and practice manuals, and so forth may be attached.

217 T113–40.

218 See for example *Zil gnon khyung nag ral chen gyi skong ba*, T229.12, 229.13.

219 T241.61.

220 *'Gu ya*, T230.24, 193.4.

221 *'Od zer 'khyil ba*, T168.

222 *Brnag pa las kyi snying gzer*, T011.61.

223 *Gab pa dgu skor*, K172–73.

224 On these sixty limbs free from extremes, see Tado, *Dictionary*, 562.

225 *Mchong gi 'phrin las* (ritual activities of the agate gem) are rituals of exorcism associated with the agate (*mchong*, sometimes translated as quartz or jade), a stone with demonifuge properties. See for instance Des Jardins, "Rites of the Deity Tamdrin."

226 A part of the Jewel (*nor bu*) tradition is to be found in *Snyan rgyud nor bu lugs*, T222.4.

227 The Rolling of the Mound (*sgang sgril*) are rites of suppression associated with the fierce activities of the Phurpa deities.

228 The modern Tibetan text editor's note on this passage mentions that these two sentences were added later, since they are not found in the original manuscript. See Tibetan text, 393n9.

229 *Owm! A da da de de phyod phyod sa le ha lo seng.*

230 *A dkar A rmad du tri su nag po zhi zhi mal mal swa hwa.*

231 See Karmay, *Treasury*, 54n55.

232 The six topics are (1) the view of the nine trunks combined, (2) the conduct that cuts the spatial droplets, (3) the meditation on the sprout of intrinsic mind, (4) the activities of the completely perfected ones, (5) the collections of commitments, and (6) the accomplishments of the truths, the meaning, and the scriptures. See Tado, *Dictionary*, 252. These correspond to the six classes of teachings and realizations in Bön pertaining to philosophical view, conduct, commitments, enlightened activities, spiritual realizations, and accomplishments. See also Martin, *Mandala Cosmogony*, 26n99.

233 Lit. "of one taste" (*ro snyoms*).

234 *Rag sa* in the Bön context refers to demons, the *rākṣasa*.

235 *Bdud sri* (*sri* is pronounced shee) are demons draining the life force from beings.

236 The three trainings (*bslab gsum*) are ethics, concentration, and wisdom, or refutation, proof, and compatibility.

237 The three precepts (*sdom gsum*) are levels of ordination. See Glossary.

238 The two knowledges (*mkhyen gnyis*) are the knowledge of the nature of things and knowledge of the extent of the knowables.

239 *U ya smar ro* is an expression in the Zhangzhung language whose exact meaning is unclear. *U ya* means secret (*gsang*), accomplishment (*dngos grub*), or offerings (*mchod rdzas*); *maro* (*smar ro*) means virtue, good fortune, auspicious (*dge'o dang bkra shis so*). One can thus derive an approximate meaning, such as the wish, "Accomplishments and good fortune!" Pasar Tshultrim Tenzin et al., *A Lexicon of Zhangzhung*, 297–98 and 199; and Martin, "Zhangzhung Dictionary," 250 and 177.

240 These consist in the five points of Tsewang Rikzin: the shoulders open like the wings of an eagle, the spine straight like a stack of coins, etc.

241 These are the nine perceptions (*shes pa dgu*) associated with the eyes, the ears, the nose, the tongue, tactile sensations (*lus kyi rnam par shes pa*), the mind, the experiences associated with suffering (*nyon smongs pa can gyi rnam par shes pa*), the universal ground (*kun gzhi*), and the end of time (*dus mtha'*). See Tado, *Dictionary*, 384.

242 There are different lists associated with the ten recollections (*dran pa dcu*). This can be a list of objects of refuge to be remembered, such as the Three Jewels, monastic vows, giving, the tutelary deity, etc. See Das, *Tibetan-English Dictionary*, 650. They also refer to exercises in mindfulness, types of mindfulness, etc. The Bönpo dictionary of numbered items (Tado, *Dictionary*, 360) mentions the nine recollections, such as past and future, principal deity and retinue, the

recollection of the plays of Hanudrel (Ha nu sprel rtsed mo), the recollection of the embarrassments of previous lies, etc. Some points need further explanation, but suffice it to say that they all relate to meditating on impermanence and transitoriness.

243   The five inexpiable sins (*mtshams med pa lnga*): killing a master, killing a student, matricide, killing one's son, and patricide. See Tado, *Dictionary*, 220.

244   The five nearly inexpiable sins (*nye ba lnga*): killing a Bön priest (gshen), destroying a reliquary or stupa, abusing the teachings, killing those approaching the teachings, and corrupting pledges for fellow practitioners. See Tado, *Dictionary*, 185.

245   The four heavies (*lji ba bzhi*): disturbing the mind of the lama, teaching wrongdoing to spiritual friends, causing sadness to the faithful, and making false promises. See Tado, *Dictionary*, 110.

246   The eight perverse actions (*log pa brgyad*): throwing things down a mountain, lighting a forest fire, changing the flow of a great river, teaching false spiritual instructions, restraining the peregrination of living animals, stirring up quarrels in the county, causing a targeted killing, and engaging in dominating women. See Tado, *Dictionary*, 338.

247   The nine deceptive minds (*'khrul ba blo dgu*): having a confused mind about (or holding on to a wrong understanding of) past and present, upper and lower positions, long life, counting time, friends and foes, good and evil actions, knowledge from hearing and seeing, limited compassion, and apprehending forms and ideas from signs and symbols. See Tado, *Dictionary*, 346.

248   The ten non-virtuous actions (*mi dge ba bcu*) consist in the three wrongful actions of the body: taking life, taking what was not given, wrongful sexual action; the four wrongful actions of speech: lies, harsh words, mistaken statements, and divisive speech; and the three actions of the mind: cursing thoughts, cruelty, and wrong views. See Tado, *Dictionary*, 408.

249   *Owm na ma a dkar shag sale sang gne swa hwa. A dkar shag* is a common expression in Bön mantras expressing perfect purity. *Sale* means "clear" or "lucid." *Sang nge* means "pure." See Martin, "Zhangzhung Dictionary," 243, 225, 226.

250   *Brwum ri ti gar ma la ho. Bruṃ* is the seed-syllable for the central mountain of the universe; *ti ga* means "first"; *mala* expresses excellence. See Martin, "Zhangzhung Dictionary," 90; and Waldo, *Glossary Compilation, ti ga.*

251   *A yaṃ raṃ maṃ khaṃ bruṃ shag sale sa nge svāhā.* [*A yaṃ raṃ maṃ khaṃ bruṃ!*] The first six syllables are the seed-syllables for the elements and correspond respectively with space, wind, fire, water, earth, and the cosmic central mountain.

252   *Phyod phur sale ha lo seng. Phyod phur* are pegs used for delimiting a consecrated area, which in this case are the delimiting continents and subcontinents imagined as pegs. See also Martin, "Zhangzhung Dictionary," 147–48, and the entries for *Phyo* as well as *Phyod. Ha lo* is the name of a flower, possibly the hollyhock. *Seng* in this case is the verb "to raise."

253   *Stong gsum*: one billion consists in three one-thousandfold universes.

254   *A dkar a rmad du tri su nag po zhi zhi mel mel svāhā!* [White A! Marvelous A! Du Tri Su Black Pacify! Pacify! Mel! Mel! Svāhā!] A very popular mantra recited by all current Bönpo practitioners. *Du tri su* are seed-syllables representing the three poisons: ignorance, anger, and craving. Mal! Mal! Indicate transcendence.

This mantra is recited to purify one's karmic tendencies and imprints. It is part of the nine mantras of the preliminary practices to be recited one hundred thousand times.

255 *Sa le 'od: Āḥ oṃ hūṃ a dkar sa le 'od a yang oṃ duḥ!* [The Limpid Light! (mantra): Āḥ oṃ hūṃ! White A! Limpid light! Windy A! Oṃ! Liquid offering!] This is a free interpretation based on Zhangzhung and Tibetan words contained in the mantra. There are numerous interpretations of this mantra, which is associated with the absolute body of enlightened ones (*bon sku*). It is part of the nine mantras of the preliminary practices to be recited one hundred thousand times. See relevant entries in Martin, "Zhangzhung Dictionary."

256 The three unwholesome activities (*mi dge ba gsum*): killing, stealing, and wrongful sexual practices.

257 The four non-virtuous actions of speech (*ngag gi mi dge ba bzhi*) are lying, rash language, slander, and idle talk.

258 The three non-virtuous unwholesome thoughts (*sems kyi ngan rtog mi dge ba gsum*) are covetous thoughts, malicious thoughts, and wrong views.

259 Although this section deals with open-sky practices and gazing, part of it still provides instructions on dark retreat practices.

260 Sangwa Düpa is the Bönpo miracle worker of the mythical past who is credited as the source of many tantric lineages in Bön.

261 *Tsang ri pur lang* is a Zhangzhung expression for the eye faculty, the vessel of visual senses (*mig gi dbang po snod du ston*); Martin, "Zhangzhung Dictionary," 180.

262 The three spaces (*nam mkha' gsum sbyor*): merging the subtle channels with emptiness (*rtsa khams tong pa*), the emptiness of the sky (*nam mkha' stong pa*), and the emptiness of the mind (*sems stong*). Tado, *Dictionary*, 53.

263 *Mi 'jug pa gsum gyi lag len*; see Tado, *Dictionary*, 68.

264 The original text has *pu shel*; however, the notes from the Sman ri edition correct this to *pu she li*. See the original Tibetan edition, 408n199.

265 Here, "horse" is a traditional medical term meaning the substance on which the medicine "rides" the body.

266 The Tibetan edited volume, 409n228, stipulates that this text, the *A gsal*, has been lost.

267 This appears to be either a citation from a lost source or a reference to a saying in the Revelatory Transmission teachings.

268 In this case, below the right eye and ear, using the fingers and thumb of the right hand. See Lopön Tenzin Namdak, *Main Dzogchen*, 81.

269 *Khyung* is usually rendered as garuda, a mythical Indian horned bird. However, since this is a Tibetan Bön text, I opted for keeping the Tibetan word, or use "horned eagle," so as not to lead the reader into a Buddhist-influenced reading despite the obvious similarities and influences.

270 *Aksho* is unclear here. It could stand for *ākāśa*, the Sanskrit for "ether." Thanks to Marc-Henri Pavot for this suggestion.

271 As mentioned in note 249, *Sale* is a distinctive Bönpo word meaning "clear, lucid" (*gsal ba*). Martin, "Zhangzhung Dictionary," 225.

272 *Sgra bo che gyer po che*; lit. "are widely known and highly reputed."

273 *She thun rtsa 'dzin*; this is the name of a secret place inside the heart where

awareness resides. Achard translates it as "holding the channels of the heart" (*Six Lamps*, 64). *She thun* is a Zhangzhung word denoting the heart (*snying*). See Martin, "Zhangzhung Dictionary," 222.

274   *Spyan drug*; these six glances eventually help develop realization. Once these practices are perfected, these six glances and their accompanying realizations are given the following names: the glance into the reality (*bon gyi spyan*) of pristine cognition (*ye shes kyi spyan*), of awareness (*rig pa'i spyan*), of the enlightened mind (*thugs rje'i spyan*), of emanation (*sprul pa'i spyan*), and of excellent wisdom (*shes rab kyi spyan*). Tado, *Dictionary*, 256.

275   *Phung po lnga*: the five "heaps" are the five aggregates.

276   *Rang 'od lnga*: the five colored lights self-manifesting as part of the three natural manifestations of sound, lights, and rays, and as detailed in this Practice Manual.

277   *'Byung ba'i dbyings lnga*: the five elemental spheres of fire, water, earth, air, and space.

278   *Klong lnga*: the five expanses are those of the sky, earth, air, fire, and water. Achard, "Contribution aux nombrables," 106. See also Tado, *Dictionary*, 178.

279   *Lha lnga*: the peaceful deities, the deities of increase, the deities of power, wrathful deities, and deities of continuous activity (*rgyun*). Achard, "Contribution aux nombrables," 114.

280   *Sku lnga*: the five bodies of reality (*bon sku*), perfection (*rdzogs*), emanations (*sprul sku*), essence (*ngo bo'i sku*), and manifested purity (*mngon par byung byang chub*). Achard, "Contribution aux nombrables," 107. See also Tado, *Dictionary*, 168.

281   *Rigs lnga*: the five enlightened families, or clans, are those represented by the symbols of Suchness: the swastika (*g.yung drung*), the wheel, the lotus, and the jewel. See Achard, "Contribution aux nombrables," 112.

282   *Gzhi lnga*: the five bases are the visible body (*snang ba gzugs*), the primary mind (*gtso bo sems*), mental content (*'khor sems*), the compositional factors of the non-existent one (*ldan pa ma yin pa 'du byed*), and the uncompounded inherent nature (*rang bzhin 'dus ma byas pa*). In Tado, *Dictionary*, 222.

283   *Yan lag lnga*: in the context of the yogic meditations of the present system, these five limbs are the channels emanating from the central wheel in the center of the heart. See Achard, "Contribution aux nombrables," 112.

284   *Mdzod lnga*: there are a number of possibilities here, but most likely the five treasuries refer to the five aggregates or the five main organs of the body (liver, heart, etc.) in their non-contaminated forms.

285   *Zag med dbang po lnga*: five uncontaminated sensory powers.

286   *Dri med kyi ye shes lnga*: the five unobstructed pristine cognitions are the five wisdoms: the wisdom of intrinsic emptiness from the emptiness of the intrinsic essence of the base (*gzhi ngo bo nyid stong cha nas stong nyid*); the mirror-like wisdom from the luminous inherent nature (*rang bzhin gsal cha nas me long ye shes*); the wisdom of equanimity from non-dualistic empty luminosity (*gsal stong gnyis med kyi cha nas mnyam nyid ye shes*); the wisdom realizing discriminating awareness from all phenomena of cyclic existence and transcendence (*'khor 'das kyi bon thams cad so sor rtogs pas sor rtogs ye shes*); and the wisdom of accomplishing enlightened activities, spontaneous from the beginning, where all faults and qualities of cyclic existence and transcendence are without energy (*'khor 'das kyi*

rkyon yon thams cad ma rtsal te ye nas lhun grub tu yod pas bya grub ye shes). In Tado, *Dictionary*, 225.

287 *Rnam par dag pa'i yul lnga*: the five completely pure objects are the objects as perceived by a purified awareness in the domain of the senses of form (*gzugs*), sounds (*sgra*), smell (*dri*), taste (*ro*), and tactile sensations (*reg bya*). In Tado, *Dictionary*, 225.

288 *Rnam par dag pa'i ye shes lnga*: the five completely pure pristine cognitions are similar to the above five unobstructed pristine cognitions.

289 *Nyams nga med pa'i stobs lnga*: the five unimpaired strengths are the strength of love (*byams*), peace (*zhi ba*), expansiveness (*yangs pa*), primordial wisdom (*ye shes*), and giving (*sbyin pa*). There are also alternative lists. See Tado, *Dictionary*, 181. See also Achard, "Contribution aux nombrables," 108, where he lists faith (*dad pa*), zeal (*brtson 'grus*), sublimated knowledge (*shes rab*), intrepidity (*mi 'jigs pa*), and imperishable strength (*mi nyams pa*).

290 *Bla na med pa'i 'bras bu lnga*: I could find no definitive details on these five unsurpassable results, but I believe they are related to the realization of the five wisdoms, above.

291 *Rdzogs pa'i dkyil 'khor lnga*: the five perfected mandalas of the five enlightened families.

292 *Zhing khams lnga*: the five pure realms of the five directions, each headed by a different enlightened being; east is led by Tönpa Salwa Rangyung, south by Gawa Döndrup, west by Jedrag Ngomé, north by Gelha Garchug, and the center by Ökar Nezin. See Tado, *Dictionary*, 222.

293 Indicating that this chapter is the second supplementary text in this Manual.

294 Here the text clearly mentions an unknown source under the abbreviated title of *The Key* (*Lde mig*).

295 In the Tibetan text, *gsung rab*, or the "excellent sermon," is another name for the Bön version of the *Perfection of Wisdom in One Thousand Verses* entitled the *Eight Realms*.

296 *Gzugs sku* means a body endowed with a perceivable form, be it in a material or spiritual sense, such as the emanation and enjoyment bodies.

297 *Kho'i ngang du*, lit. "in the condition of you," is synonymous with the natural state (*rang bzhin*). See Reynolds, *Practice of Dzogchen*, 215n6, who cites Lopön Tenzin Namdak as his source in a personal communication.

298 Tsen (*gcan*, also *gtsan*) are roaming spirits of Tibetan origin. See Nebesky-Wojkowitz, *Oracles and Demons of Tibet*, for an introduction to these various creatures: haughty spirits (*gregs pa*); gods (*lha*); subterranean snakes, usually conflated with the Indic nāga (*klu*); and scent eaters (*dri za*), often conflated with the Indian gandharvas. See also Blondeau, "Le réseau des mille dieux-démons," 199–250 passim.

299 This text did not come with a diagram. However, in Bön there are a number of diagrams describing visions of light nets, dots, and so forth. See, for instance, a body mandala linked to the practices described in Karmay, *Little Luminous Boy*, 86–102. The chart listing the teachings of the Bön Dzogchen approach to religious training with the goal of reaching complete enlightenment is reproduced in Himalayan Art Resources, https://www.himalayanart.org/items/98461.

300 *Gde'o*, lit. "Virtue is!" In Bön texts this is a common expression calling for auspiciousness at the end of discourses.

301 This is the third supplementary text of the Manual.

302 The six collections of consciousness (*tshogs drug*) are associated with each of the five senses and with the sixth, the mind.

303 The *Elucidation* (*gsal byed*, lit. "to elucidate," "to make clear") remains unidentified despite many texts in both the Bön canon and commentaries bearing this word in their titles. I have not been able to identify the quote with the editors of our Tibetan original text (see 423n15).

304 The ten perfections (*phar phyin bcu*) consist in the practices of giving, morality, patience, effort, meditation, wisdom, skillful means, aspirations, strength, and pristine awareness.

305 The text itself cites the *Six Transmissions*. However, the Tibetan editors did not find this quote in the *Six Transmissions* but in the *Coming of the Three Meanings* (see 425n55).

306 *Gsal gdab* means visualizing or clearly imagining. However, since the text stipulates that this is done by someone else (*gzhan gyis*), it probably means that someone else recites these recollections or mentions them to the dying person. In Tibetan religion, the dying process does not stop when the breath ends or the heart stops, but continues until reincarnation or a more felicitous state has been acquired by the deceased.

307 This appears to be the recitation pronounced during the funeral rite. The text does not add any sources other than the lama.

308 At that point, the seed-syllable *A* has reached the aperture of Tshangpa that is the opening of the crown cakra. This cakra must be imagined as opened while the seed-syllable passes through it. It then closes after the seed-syllable begins to hover above the head.

309 *'Od kyi tsi ta*, the place in the heart where awareness abides, is also called "the brown cornelian tent" (*mchong gur smug po*).

310 The text here indicates the reference as the *Outer Tantra* (*Spyi rgyud*). This *Outer Tantra* is either lost, is an unknown source, or is a general title given to a specific scripture at the time of the writer.

311 *Ka ra khyor gzhug* most likely refers to the practice of twisting the torso and alternatively taking short breaths and holding the breath. See the Tibetan text, 432n23. One will soon see lights and droplets due to the effort. This is mentioned again below.

312 *Mi bkyod pa gnyis*, the two imperturbables, immovables, or unshakables, are the practices hereby explained.

313 *'Og min*, lit. "Nothing Higher," is the name of the highest pure land in both Buddhism and Bön. It is often rendered by its Sanskrit name, Akaniṣṭha. I decided to translate it as a proper noun for non-Tibetan readers and non-specialists.

314 The editors of the Tibetan text did not have this last paragraph as part of the quotation. However, the paragraph is so close to the original text of the *Lamp* (216.4) that I included it as part of the original. I believe the Tibetan editors simply missed it. See, for instance, Achard, *Six Lamps*, 82–83.

315 The Tibetan original [341] has "third" here. The topic is, however, the second in

the third section entitled "Direct introduction on the resulting three enlightened bodies." I have taken the liberty of correcting it here.

316 The eight consciousnesses or collections (*tshogs brgyad*) are the five sense consciousnesses, mind consciousness, self-consciousness, and all-ground consciousness.

317 The eight objects (*yul brgyad*) are the objects of the eight consciousnesses: sight, sound, smell, taste, texture, mental objects, the all-ground, and appearance.

318 The five poisons (*dug lnga*) are desire, anger, delusion, pride, and envy.

319 *Dbu zhabs spyan ljags* are all honorific words for head, feet, eyes, and tongue, respectively, and should be understood as belonging to the emanated divine forms.

320 The six types of cause (*rgyu drug*) are the principal cause (*byed pa'i rgyu*), the mutual cause (*lhan cig 'byung ba'i rgyu*), the mature cause (*rnam par smin pa'i rgyu*), the simultaneous cause (*mtshungs par ldan pa'i rgyu*), the cause that affects everything (*kun du 'gro ba'i rgyu*), and the associated cause (*skal pa mnyam pa'i rgyu*).

321 The four times (*dus bzhi*) represent past, present, future, and indefinite time. See Tado, *Dictionary*, 120.

322 Figures and drawings are absent in the text.

323 The threshold or staircase's large mouth joint (*tshigs pa kha chen gyi them pa*) is the junction where all three main channels connect. See Hatchell, *Naked Seeing*, 426n96.

324 *Klu chen ar la gtad*, lit. "fixating on the great serpent," is a meditation position used to generate the inner fire and clear the channels. The hands are in the meditation position, legs crossed, back straight, and shoulders spread out like the wings of an eagle.

325 The ocean is the belly and the excellent mountain is the spine. One presses the belly to the spine.

326 Something similar to these six exercises is described with pictures in Tempa Dukte Lama, *Thrul khor*, 142–49. These instructions, according to tradition, were written during the thirteenth century, and there are diverging interpretations, regional variances, etc. It would be best to learn these from a competent lama and accept discrepancies between the text and the actual practices. This Manual was used only as a mnemonic device for the oral tradition.

327 *Ma ning gi rlung*: the neutral wind is a non-aligned wind that pervades the whole body.

328 Pönsé Gyalpo (Dpon rgyal btsan po, fl. ninth–tenth century) is traditionally named as one of the translators of the Zhangzhung revelatory transmission into Tibetan. See Achard, *Enlightened Rainbows*, 232.

329 See Tempa Dukte Lama, *Thrul khor*, 152–53.

330 Tempa Dukte Lama, *Thrul khor*, 154–55.

331 Tempa Dukte Lama, *Thrul khor*, 156–57.

332 Tempa Dukte Lama, *Thrul khor*, 158–59.

333 *Rkyangs* for *sgyangs*, to square the shoulders, stretching, like when someone is put on a cross for flogging. See Waldo, *Glossary Compilation*, *rkyangs*.

334 Tempa Dukte Lama, *Thrul khor*, 160–61.

335 Tempa Dukte Lama, *Thrul khor*, 162–63.

336 *Gtum mo* is the power of heat generated by yogic practices that enable adepts to

tolerate freezing temperatures. It is personified as the fierce woman (*caṇḍālī*) who dances in fire.

337 *Bying med pa*, lit. "no sinking in water, sand, etc." Could it be synonymous with "no drowning"? The term is unclear but relates to having power over the water element.

338 See Tempa Dukte Lama, *Thrul khor*, 166–67.

339 Tempa Dukte Lama, *Thrul khor*, 168–69.

340 Tempa Dukte Lama, *Thrul khor*, 170–71.

341 Tempa Dukte Lama, *Thrul khor*, 172–73.

342 Tempa Dukte Lama, *Thrul khor*, 174–75.

343 Tempa Dukte Lama, *Thrul khor*, 178–79.

344 Tempa Dukte Lama, *Thrul khor*, 180–81.

345 Tempa Dukte Lama, *Thrul khor*, 182–83.

346 Tempa Dukte Lama, *Thrul khor*, 184–85.

347 Tempa Dukte Lama, *Thrul·khor*, 186–87.

348 This text has r*ma bya chu 'thung*, a variant of *rma bya chu sprug* ("the peacock stirring water"), which is used in other versions of this manual. See Tibetan text 437n3.

349 First written as *en ra* (354, line 16), then as *E na ra* (354, line 22), I suggest this is an inconsistent spelling for the Zhangzhung word *E na ya*, which signifies the black antelope and epitomizes some of the qualities of Shenrab. See Martin, "Zhang-zhung Dictionary," 251–52.

350 Tempa Dukte Lama, *Thrul khor*, 190–91.

351 Tempa Dukte Lama, *Thrul khor*, 192–93.

352 Tempa Dukte Lama, *Thrul khor*, 194–95.

353 Tempa Dukte Lama, *Thrul khor*, 196–97. In Tempa Dukte Lama's book, the exercise is called "ene hopping to the side." Ene renders *E na ya*, the black antelope, as mentioned earlier.

354 *Rgyu zhabs*, lit. "the cause of the foot." Terms are so misleading in this section of the manual that one wonders if this text was not written intentionally to mislead uninitiated readers. The Tibetan editors did very little correction here.

355 Tempa Dukte Lama, *Thrul khor*, 198–99.

356 Again here, *ther khrag* is used with the literal meaning of "bare blood," possibly pointing to the arterial pulse that can be felt at the back of the leg behind the knee or in the groin.

357 Tempa Dukte Lama, *Thrul khor*, 202–3.

358 *Gyi ling* is a type of prized horse in Tibet known for its speed and energy. The term is used as a metaphor for dance and physical exercise.

359 Tempa Dukte Lama, *Thrul khor*, 204–5.

360 Tempa Dukte Lama, *Thrul khor*, 206–7.

361 Tempa Dukte Lama, *Thrul khor*, 208–9.

362 Tempa Dukte Lama, *Thrul khor*, 210–11.

363 'Or sgom kun 'dul (fl. twelfth century). See Karmay, *Treasury*, 111n9.

364 The Tibetan original has "loosening the channels and controlling the heat" (*drod 'dul*, 355), which was a mistake that was corrected later when describing the movements. I have therefore changed it to what appears to be the correct heading.

365 Tempa Dukte Lama, *Thrul khor*, 214–15.
366 Tempa Dukte Lama, *Thrul khor*, 216–17.
367 Tempa Dukte Lama, *Thrul khor*, 218–21.
368 Tempa Dukte Lama, *Thrul khor*, 228–29.
369 *Rgya mo dar 'thag*. This series of movements is also referred to as "the Chinese silk weaver" in the Manual. For illustrations and brief explanations, see Tempa Dukte Lama, *Thrul khor*, 222–27.
370 The text has "left" here, but that is an improbability. It is one of the many mistakes riddling chapter 8. Unlike the other sections, this one contains no editorial notes, which makes the translation extremely problematic.
371 Dampa Bumjé was a disciple of Yangtön Chenpo Sherab Gyaltsen (fl. twelfth century).
372 *Stod*, also called "the Upper Transmission," refers to the place where Dru Gyalwa spent part of his apprenticeship and where he learned these practices. See Achard, "Mesmerizing," 138; and Blezer, "Greatly Perfected," 80.
373 This alludes to the shape of the Tibetan letter *cha* [ཆ] and the two rounds at its base that are imagined as its feet.
374 *Nye lo U* is a Zhangzhung word meaning "concentration." See Martin, "Zhangzhung Dictionary," 82–83.
375 *Bswo*.
376 This indicates, in not so clear terms, that one is to breathe in with the visualizations briefly described, then hold one's breath while continuing with the imaginings and taking seven small incremental breaths, and finally breathe out. These instructions are better verified with a lama who practices the dark retreat.
377 *Khrag rlun* seems to be a mistaken spelling for *khrag rlung*.
378 *Klung chen* refers to holding the breath.
379 *Rgya mtsho ri rab la bcar*, pressing back the stomach into the spine.
380 *Ro 'dzin btson du bzung*, keeping the tongue free inside the mouth.
381 *Gza' chen gyen du ldog*, turning the eyes upward, as described previously.
382 *Snang ma skos*, lit. "entrusted with manifestations."
383 *Klad sprin*, lit. "brain cloud," refers to either the ventricles of the brain (as opposed to its center, where the pineal gland is) or the fascia covering the brain, as Reynolds seems to interpret it. See Reynolds, *Practice of Dzogchen*, 280.
384 *Rtse rgyal du sbyang pa* is another name for the process of the transference of consciousness seen earlier.
385 Nya Lishu Takring (fl. eighth century) was one of those early Bönpo lineage holders whose historical existence is still not ascertained. He is said to have been a contemporary of Padmasambhava and Drenpa Namkha.
386 Those words are attributed to the Zhangzhung language. *A ya* is synonymous with "morality" and is an exclamation of regret. *Ag tham* is synonymous with "keeping secret" and is frequently encountered at the closing of Bön secret teachings and restricted manuals. *Shu* means "impediment." See Martin, "Zhangzhung Dictionary," 244, 246, 221. *Bam* has no clearly stated current meaning. I suspect that it may stand for *śubham*, Sanskrit for "auspicious."

Glossary

THE TERMS THAT HAVE no references were taken directly or derived from our translations of the texts in this volume.

all-knowing sixty-one pristine cognitions (*mkhen pa'i ye shes drug cu rtsa gcig*). Also known as the sixty-one superior wisdoms of knowledge. Tado, *Dictionary*, 565–61.

cause (*rgyu*). *See* six types of causes.

characteristic (*mtshan*). There are characteristics of purity and impurity. The five omni-present mental factors (feeling, discrimination, intention, attention, and mental engagement), the four ambivalent mental events, and the ten virtues (three good actions of the body, four good actions of speech, and three good actions of the mind) are the basis of the characteristics of purity. The eight and the fourteen modes of consciousness, the six roots of suffering, and the twenty approaches are the basis for the characteristics of impurity.

Dutrisu mantra. *A Kar A Med Du Tri Su Nagpo Zhi Zhi Mal Mal So Ha* (*A' A dkar sale 'od A yam om' 'du. A dkar A rmad du tri su nag po zhi zhi mal mal swa ha'*). This mantra is one of the nine sets of the hundred thousand repetitions (*'bum dgu*) that need to be recited as part of the preliminary practices in Bön.

eight consciousnesses (*tshogs brgyad*). These consist in the five sense consciousnesses, mind consciousness, self-consciousness, and all-ground consciousness.

eight enlightened qualities (*yon tan brgyad*). The qualities of an enlightened intelligence, associated with Mawa Sengé (*Smra ba seng ge*), the "lion of eloquence": imperturbable (*blo gros 'gyur med*), unimpeded (*'gags med*), unequaled (*mtshungs med*), unhindered (*thog med*), the intelligence of the sun (*blo gros nyi ma*), the intelligence of kings (*blo gros rgyal po*), the intelligence of influence and destiny (*blo gros rgyal mtshan*, lit. "the intelligence of the victory banner"), and matchless intelligence (*blo gros zla bral*). Tado, *Dictionary*, 335.

eight limbs of Shenrab (*gshen rab kyi yan lag brgyad*) These consist in the extremely pure view (*yang dag pa lta ba*), realization (*rtogs pa*), speech (*ngag*), destiny (*las kyi mtha'*), livelihood (*'tsho ba*), effort (*rtsol ba*), recollection/mindfulness (*dran pa*), and concentration (*ting nge 'dzin*). Tado, *Dictionary*, 338.

eight modes of consciousness (*rnam shes tshogs brgyad*). See eight consciousnesses.

eight non-declining qualities (*mi phyed pa brgyad*). These consist in undivided tireless faith in the lama, undivided clarity on the mantras of the tutelary deity, undivided exertion toward the accomplishment with consort, undivided earnest discipline toward the sacred items, undivided pure pledges toward accomplishments, undivided great love toward spiritual siblings, undivided great compassion toward sentient beings, and undivided good behavior toward everything.

eight objects of the consciousnesses (*yul brgyad*). They are sight, sound, smell, taste, texture, mental objects, the all-ground, and appearances.

eight perverse actions (*log pa brgyad*). These consist in throwing things down a mountain, lighting a forest fire, changing the flow of a great river, teaching false spiritual instructions, restraining the peregrination of living animals, stirring quarrels in the county, being the cause of a targeted killing, and dominating women. Tado, *Dictionary*, 338. See alternative lists in Achard, *Dawn of Awareness*, 30.

eight types of intellectual knowledge (*blo rig/rigs brgyad po*). The eight means of knowledge of the ordinary mind: doubt (*the tshom*), non-ascertainment of meaning (*don du ma nges pa*), wrong consciousness (*log shes*), non-ascertainment of visions (*snang la ma nges pa*), mental assumptions (*yid dpyod*), decisive cognizance (*bcad shes*), direct valid cognition (*dngos sum gyi tshad ma*), and inference by valid cognition (*rjes dpag tshad ma*). Tado, *Dictionary*, 324.

eighteen emptinesses (*stong nyid bco rgyad*). (1) emptiness of the subject (*nang stong pa nyid*), (2) emptiness of the object (*phyi stong pa nyid*), (3) emptiness of both inside and out (*phyi nang stong pa nyid*), (4) emptiness of emptiness (*stong pa nyid stong pa nyid*), (5) great emptiness (*chen po stong pa nyid*), (6) emptiness of ultimate reality (*don dam pa stong pa nyid*), (7) conditioned emptiness (*'dus byas stong pa nyid*), (8) unconditioned emptiness (*'du ma byas stong pa nyid*), (9) infinite emptiness (*mtha' las 'das pa stong pa nyid*), (10) emptiness without beginning or end (*thog ma dang tha ma med pa stong pa nyid*), (11) emptiness of non-repudiation (*dor ba med pa stong pa nyid*), (12) emptiness of inherent nature (*rang bzhin stong pa nyid*), (13) emptiness of all phenomena (*bon thams cad stong pa nyid*), (14) emptiness of defining characteristics (*rang gi mtshan nyid stong pa nyid*), (15) unascertainable emptiness (*mi dmigs pa stong pa nyid*), (16) emptiness of the inherent essence of non-concrete reality (*dngos po med pa'i ngo bo nyid stong pa nyid*), (17) emptiness of non-existence (*dngos po med pa'i stong pa nyid*), and (18) emptiness of inherent essence (*ngo bo nyid stong pa nyid*). Tado, *Dictionary*, 490; Conze, "List of Buddhist Terms."

eighteen sensory bases (*khams bco brgyad*). These are the six bases of the sense-possessing objects, the six bases of the outer objects, and the six bases of consciousness.

fifty-one categories of the aggregate of formation (*'du byed kyi phung po lnga bcu rtsa gcig*). These consist in the six roots of suffering, the twenty secondary afflictions, the four changeable mental factors, the five omnipresent mental factors, the five distinct objects, and the eleven virtues.

five aggregates or heaps (*phung po lnga*). Form (*gzugs*), feelings (*tshor ba*), cognition (*'du shes*), formation (*'du byed*), and consciousness (*rnam shes*).

five coarse things (*rags pa lnga*). The five groupings of the twenty-five coarse things (*rags pa nyer lnga*), which consist in the five aggregates (*phung po lnga*), the four elemental fields (*'byung ba bzhi*), the six sources (*skye mched drug*), the five objects (*yul lnga*), and the pristine cognition of the moment of directly perceiving the base (*gzhi dus ye shes*).

five fears (*'jigs pa lnga*). The fear for one's livelihood being cut short (*'tsho ba chad dogs pa'i 'jigs pa*), the fear of death (*'chi dogs pa'i 'jigs pa*), the fear of being deprived of praise and of being blamed (*mi bngags pa ste mi snyan pa sgro dogs pa'i 'jigs pa*), the fear of evil rebirth (*ngan song ltung dogs pa'i 'jigs pa*), and the fear of impediments in cyclic existence (*'khor ba las bag chag ba'i 'jigs pa*). Tado, *Dictionary*, 185. Azha Lodrö Gyaltsen himself lists the five fears as (1) fears of fire and water, (2) poisons, (3) epidemics, (4) famine, and (5) afflictions."

five inexpiable sins (*mtshams med pa lnga*). These are killing a master, killing a student, matricide, killing one's son, and patricide. Tado, *Dictionary*, 220.

five lights, also **five natural lights** (*rang 'od lnga*). The five colored lights self-manifesting as part of the three natural manifestations of sound, lights, and rays.

five nearly inexpiable sins (*nye ba lnga*). Killing a Bön priest (*gshen*), destroying a reliquary or stupa, abusing the teachings, killing those approaching the teachings, and corrupting pledges for fellow practitioners. Tado, *Dictionary,* 185.

five non-established natures (*rang bzhin ma grub pa lnga*). The non-established object with graspable characteristics; the non-established measure to seize a real body; the non-established circles of listening to manifested form; the scriptures, tantras, and commentaries that are non-established Bön; and the non-established fields of training where there is grasping to a self.

five poisons (*dug lnga*). Ignorance (*gti mug*), craving (*'dod chags*), anger (*zhe sdang*), pride (*nga rgyal*), and jealousy (*phrag dog*). See the lengthy entries in Tado, *Dictionary,* 193.

five powers/strengths (*stobs lnga*). These are faith, diligence, superior knowledge, fearlessness, and imperishable power. Achard, "Contribution aux nombrables," 108.

five sense faculties (*dbang po lnga*). These consist in sight, touch, smell, hearing, and taste.

five spacial elements (*'byung ba'i dbyings lnga*). Fire, water, earth, air, and space.

five uncertainties (*ma nges pa lnga*). Body, entourage, time, place, and difficulties. Tado, *Dictionary*, 214.

five undefined natures (*rang bzhin ma nges pa lnga*). The undefined appearances of the body, the undefined duration of life, the undefined circles of the listeners, the undefined doctrines explained, and the undefined pure fields of training.

foe destroyer (*dgra bcom*). One who destroys afflictive emotions and vanquishes ignorance. A Tibetan rendering of the Sanskrit term "arhat" (i.e., worthy of worship), which denotes a spiritual status just before becoming enlightened. The term also refers obliquely to saintly monks who have achieved enlightenment, for the sake of propriety would defer to one at the level of a Buddha.

four causes to the aggregate of form (*rgyu bzhi gzugs kyi phung po*). These are the four great elements: fire, water, earth, and air.

four heavies, or the four heavy sins (*lji ba bzhi*). Disturbing the mind of the lama, teaching wrongdoings to spiritual friends, causing sadness to the faithful, and making false promises. Tado, *Dictionary,* 110. See alternative lists in Achard, *Dawn of Awareness*, 99.

four miraculous feet, or the four bases of miraculous power (*rdzu 'phrul gyi rkang ba bzhi*). To abandon discursiveness with regard to devotion, to abandon discursiveness with regard to aspiration, to abandon discursiveness with regard to the realization of clarity, and to abandon discursiveness with regard to the state of equanimity. Achard, "Contribution aux nombrables," 103.

four names of the four parts of the aggregates of the mind (*ming bzhi sems kyi phung po bzhi*). These are the aggregate of feelings, the aggregate of distinctive perception, the aggregate of formation, and the aggregate of consciousness.

four natural expressions (*rang bzhin brjod pa bzhi*). The nature of reasoning (*rigs kyi rang bzhin*), the nature of objects (*bya ba'i rang bzhin*), the nature of enlightened qualities (*yon tan rang bzhin*), and the nature of substantial entities (*rdzas kyi rang bzhin*). Tado, *Dictionary*, 154

four non-perceptibles (*dmigs med*). The ground that cannot be apprehended as a place from the very beginning, a visible distance that cannot be apprehended as having an end, the force whose source cannot be apprehended, and intended action that cannot be apprehended.

four non-virtuous actions of speech (*ngag gi mi dge ba bzhi*). Lying, rash language, slander, and idle talk.

four recollections (*dran pa bzhi*): To remind oneself of the opportunity offered by a human body, of death, of the conditioned suffering of cyclic existence, and of karma, the law of cause and effect.

four reversals, or four facets (*ldog pa bzhi*). Aspects or isolate factors that consist in cognizing reality (*bon shes*), then accepting reality (*bon bzod*), followed by moments of subsequent cognition of reality (*rje shes*), and subsequent cognition (*rje bzod*). This is a sequence for the realization of the four truths.

four times (*dus bzhi*). The past, present, future, and indefinite time. Tado, *Dictionary*, 120.

four thorough abandonments/eliminations (*yang dag par spong ba bzhi*). To abandon the conceptual limitations pertaining to existence and non-existence, to abandon nihilism and eternalism, to abandon conceptual limitations such as manifestation and emptiness, and to abandon the conceptual limitations of production and cessation. Achard, "Contribution aux nombrables," 104.

four true distinctions (*nges 'byed bzhi*). The four levels or stages of the path of application that lead to the path of seeing: Heat, Peak, Forbearance, and Highest Bön. Its full name is the four types of things to distinguish (*nges 'byed cha mthun bzhi*). Tado, *Dictionary*, 105.

grounds (*sa*). *See* ten grounds.

Highest Realm (*'og min*). Usually rendered in Sanskrit, Akaniṣṭha is the highest possible level of existence, a pure land where bodhisattvas live.

knowables (*shes bya*). That which can be known, or an object that can be known. There are twenty-five knowables according to the Indian Sāṃkhya school. They include things such as the eye, ear, nose, and tongue, and more abstract concepts such as person, nature, rational mind, etc. Cabezón, *A Dose of Emptiness*, 51, 127 passim; Duff, *Illuminator Dictionary*, *shes sgrib*.

leap-over practices (*thod rgal*). Also known as "direct crossing" or "crossing over" practices: one crosses over (*rgal*) to the top level (*tod*) with advanced practices of the Great Perfection. They succeed the "cutting through" (*khregs chod*) practices, and this is the level at which one becomes a mindful witness to the increasing manifestations of the three dynamisms.

nine concentrations (*ting nge 'dzin dgu*). The nine forms of concentration consist in the concentration of the perfected wisdom of non-perception (*mi migs pa'i shes rab rdzogs pa'i ting nge 'dzin*), the concentration endowed with energy and irreducibility without attachment (*mi rtags pa'i rdul shugs dang ldan pa*), the supreme strength in unevenness (*mi mnyam pa'i stobs mchog*), the pristine cognition of non-conceptuality (*mi rtogs pa'i ye shes*), the concentration of the immovable victory banner (*mi nub pa'i rgyal mtshan*), the concentration of the indestructible citadel (*mi shig pa'i gsas mkhar*), the infallible memory (*mi rjed pa'i gzungs*), the concentration that reaches the height of unmistakability (*mi 'khrul pa'i bla ru phyin pa*), and the guidance of non-distraction (*mi yengs pa'i man ngag*). Tado, *Dictionary*, 356.

nine concepts on objects to be eliminated (*spang bya rtog pa dgu*). These consist in the defilement of predispositions (*bag chags kyi sgrib pa*); the predispositions to disorderliness and worldliness (*'khor dang zang zing gi bag chags*); the predispositions toward the three realms and the nine grounds (*khams gsum sa dgu'i bag chags*); the predispositions toward grasping at concepts as objects of knowledge (*shes bya'i rtog 'dzin gyi bag chags*); the predispositions toward taking on rebirth in suffering (*sdug bsngal skyed len gyi bag chags*); the predispositions toward the four demonic streams (lit. "water," *bdud kyi chu bzhi'i bag chags*: the four "waters" are those of ignorance [*ma rig pa*], desire [*'dod pa*], view [*lta ba*], and craving [*sred pa*]); the predispositions toward forgetfulness (*brjed nges kyi bag chags*); the predispositions toward mistaken perceptions (*'khrul pa'i mtshan ma'i bag chags*); and the predispositions toward being distracted by objects of knowledge (*shes bya rnam par gyeng ba'i bag chags*). Tado, *Dictionary*, 367.

nine deceptions (*'khrul pa dgu*)**, or the nine deceptive minds** (*'khrul ba blo dgu*). These refer to individuals who have a confused mind or who hold on to a wrong understanding about past and present, upper and lower social positions, long life, counting time, friends and foes, good and evil actions, knowledge from hearing and seeing, limited compassion, and apprehending forms and ideas from signs and symbols. Tado, *Dictionary*, 346.

nine expanses (*dbyings dgu*). These consist in the different qualities assigned to infinite expanse: boundlessness (*mu med pa*), universal pervasiveness ('*byams yas pa*), limit-lessness (*rgya ma chad pa*), without top or bottom (*kha gting med pa*), measureless-ness (*dpag tu med pa*), fearlessness (*dogs pa med pa*), infinitely spread (lit., "the great spread," *gdal ba chen po*), inexhaustibility (*zad pa med pa*), and immutability ('*gyur ba med pa*). Tado, *Dictionary*, 272–73.

nine limits, or the nine extremes (*mtha' dgu*). These are: empty appearances (*snang stong*), existence and non-existence (*yod med*), negation and affirmation (*dgag sgrub*), rejection and adoption (*spang blang*), arising and ceasing (*skye 'gag*), eternalism and nihilism (*rtag chad*), wavering and firmness (*g.yo rtsol*), emerging and entering ('*byung 'jug*), and emanation and reabsorption ('*phro 'du*). Tado, *Dictionary*, 348.

nine ordinary deluded minds ('*khrul ba'i blo dgu*). These consist in minds fixated on past and future (*dus snga phyi 'dzin pa*), on high and low places (*gnas mtho dman 'dzin pa*), on long or short life (*tshe ring thung 'dzin pa*), on counting time (*dus grangs su 'dzin pa*), on the duality of friend and foe (*dgra gnyen gnyis su 'dzin pa*), on good and bad deeds (*las bzang ngan 'dzin pa*), awareness fixated on sight and hearing (*mthong thos rig pa 'dzin pa*), on a limited form of compassion (*snying rje phyogs char 'dzin pa*), and on the complexion of mind and body (*brda mtshon yid gzugs 'dzin pa*).

Another classification of the **nine deluded minds** consists in the ordinary deluded mind that is an illusory dream (*rmi lam sgyu ma 'khrul ba'i blo*), the deluded mind that discriminates erroneously (*rnam par rtogs pa*), deceiving one's intellect (*yid kyi bslu ba*), continual distraction (*rgyun gyi g.yengs pa*), the ordinary deluded mind that clings to misconceptions that hinder (*bag chag* [?*bar chad*] *mtshan mar 'dzin pa*), causing mischief for others (*gzhan la 'tshe ba*), the ordinary deluded mind that clings to desired objects that obstruct and torment (*yul gdung bag chag* [?*bar chad*] *chags 'dzin pa*), clinging to cyclic existence and torment ('*khor bar gdung bar 'dzin pa*), and the ordinary mind that is deluded about the actual conditions of actions (*las kyi rkyen dngos 'khrul ba'i blo*). Tado, *Dictionary*, 381; Achard, "Contribution aux nombrables," 346.

nine perceptions (*shes pa dgu*) are associated with the eyes, the ears, the nose, the tongue, tactile sensations (*lus kyi rnam par shes pa*), the mind, the experiences associated with suffering (*nyon smongs pa can gyi rnam par shes pa*), the universal ground (*kun gzhi*), and the end of time (*dus mtha'*). Tado, *Dictionary*, 384.

nine spheres of everlastingness (*g.yung drung gi dbyins dgu*). *See* nine expanses.

path of application (*sbyor lam*). One of the five interconnected paths. Its stages of spir-itual development and achievement consist in Heat (*drod*); Forbearance, zeal, or resilience (*bzod pa*); and Highest Reality or Highest Bön (*bon mchog*).

peak (*rtse mo*). This is one of four aspects of ascertainment of the path of application. *See* above, **path of application.**

self-isolate (*rang ldog*). A self-isolate consists in objects perceived as existing categories. An example would be a pot. *Rang ldog* is also translated as "category differential." It is to be distinguished from what individualizes it, such as a golden pot, which would be its *definiendum* (*mtshon bya*), or characterizing mark.

seven completely pure awarenesses (*yang dag pa'i rig pa bdun*). These consist in the completely pure awareness of the consciousness that transcends the extremes of non-existent duality (*yod med gnyis kyi mtha' las 'das par shes pa'i yang dag pa'i rig pa*), the completely pure awareness of the consciousness that appears like the letter *A* (*yi ge a ltar gsal ba shes pa'i yang dag pa'i rig pa*), the completely pure awareness of pristine cognition that does not forsake characteristics (*mtshan mar mi spong pa'i ye shes yang dag pa'i rig pa*), the completely pure awareness of the consciousness that does not separate or unite (*mi sbyor mi 'byed par shes pa'i yang dag pa'i rig pa*), the completely pure awareness of the consciousness that is empty of true existence of all phenomena (*bon thams cad bden stong du shes pa'i yang dag pa'i rig pa*), the completely pure awareness of the consciousness that compounded phenomena are all in their natural state from the very beginning (*gnas lugs thams cad ye nas 'dus byas su shes pa yang dag pa'i rig pa*), and the completely pure awareness without boundaries in the emptiness of the view of the sky where all is in its natural state (*gnas lugs thams cad nam mkha' lta bu stong la rgya ma chad pa'i yang dag pa'i rig pa*). These are one part of the twenty-one intrinsic characteristics of the body of reality of pristine awareness (*ye shes bon sku*). Tado, *Dictionary*, 290; Achard, "Contribution aux nombrables," 117.

seven enlightened limbs of everlastingness (*g.yung drung gi yan lag bdun*). The limb of the everlasting perfection of mindfulness (*dran pa yang dag g.yung drung gi yan lag*), the limb of the everlasting perfection of the investigation of phenomena (*bon rnam par 'byed pa yang dag g.yung drung gi yan lag*), the limb of the everlasting perfection of diligence (*brtson 'grus yang dag g.yung drung gi yan lag*), the limb of the everlasting perfection of joy (*dga' ba yang dag g.yung drung gi yan lag*), the limb of the everlasting perfection of utter purity (*shin tu sbyang ba yang dag g.yung drung gi yan lag*), the limb of the everlasting perfection of concentration (*ting 'dzin yang dag g.yung drung gi yan lag*), and the limb of the everlasting perfection of equanimity (*stang snyoms yang dag g.yung drung gi yan lag*). Tado, *Dictionary*, 291. Azha Lodrö Gyaltsen writes: "wisdom, mindfulness, joy, diligence, pliancy, concentration, and equanimity are the seven limbs."

seven mental applications (*yid la byed pa bdun*). The awareness of defining characteristics, the arising of the activities of faith, isolation, joy, withdrawal, practice, and mental applications up to the limits of the path of application.

six clairvoyances, or six higher perceptions (*mngon shes drug*). These consist in acquiring the eyes of the gods (*lha'i spyan*), the hearing of the gods (*lha'i snyan*), the ability to read the minds of others (*pha rol gyi sems shes pa*), remembrance of past lives (*sngon gyi gnas rjes su dran pa shes pa*), the ability to perform miraculous transformations (*rdzu 'phrul gyi bya ba zhes pa*), and the ability to destroy all imperfections (*zag pa sad pa shes pa*).

six glances (*spyan drug*). These develop as realization becomes perfected: the glance into reality (*bon gyi spyan*), the glance of pristine cognition (*ye shes kyi spyan*), the glance of awareness (*rig pa'i spyan*), the glance of the enlightened mind (*thugs rje'i spyan*), the glance of emanation (*sprul pa'i spyan*), and the glance of excellent wisdom (*shes rab kyi spyan*). Tado, *Dictionary*, 256.

six recollections (*rjes dran drug*). The recollection of the tutelary deity (*yi dam*), the path, the place of rebirth, the meditative state, the oral instructions of the teacher, and the view.

six types of causes (*rgyu drug*). The principal cause (*byed pa'i rgyu*); the co-occurring or simultaneously arising cause (*lhan cig 'byung ba'i rgyu*); the cause due to maturing or ripening (*rnam par smin pa'i rgyu*); the concomitant cause (*mtshungs par ldan pa'i rgyu*); the omnipresent cause, which effects everything (*kun du 'gro ba'i rgyu*); and the associated cause, or a cause that belongs to the same class (*skal pa mnyam pa'i rgyu*).

sixteen moments of acceptance and cognition of perceived objects in the four truths (*ngo bo bden pa bzhi la dmigs pa'i shes bzod bcu drug*). *See* sixteen facets of the four truths.

sixteen facets of the four truths (*bzhi ldog pa bcu drug*). The same as the four noble truths of Buddhism. The truth of suffering: impermanence, suffering, emptiness, and lack of self. The truth of the origin of suffering: causes, origin, production, and secondary conditions. The truth of the cessation of suffering: cessation, pacification, excellence, and definite emergence. The truth on the path: the path, awareness, achievement, and deliverance. On the path of vision, one goes through each of these in sixteen moments. One first cognizes (*shes*) one of the four aspects of the four truths and then one accepts (*bzod*) it as a moment of realization.

sixteen isolates (*bzhi ldog pa bcu drug*). *See* four reversals and sixteen facets of the four truths.

sixteen reversals (*ldog pa bcu drug*). *See* sixteen facets of the four noble truths.

ten grounds, or ten grounds of everlastingness (*g.yung drung sa bcu*). These are the ten spiritual levels that heroes of everlastingness cross toward the highest form of spiritual realization. To each level are attributed different realizations, practices, and dogmas, and their explanations make much of the discourse of Azha Lodrö in this volume. The ten grounds: Extremely Joyous (*rab tu dga' ba*), Stainless (*dri ma med pa*), Radiant (*'od zer 'phro ba*), Seal of Transformation (*phyag rgya bsgyur ba*), Host of Clouds of Intrinsic Reality (*bon nyid sprin tshogs*), Realization of the Endowment of Bliss (*bde ldan rtogs*), Pure Non-Attachment (*ma chags dag pa*), Wheels of Letters (*yi ge 'khor lo*), and the ground of Unchanging Everlastingness (*mi 'gyur g.yung drung sa*). Tado, *Dictionary*, 513.

ten non-virtuous actions, or wrongdoings (*mi dge ba bcu*). Consist in the three wrongful actions of the body: taking life, taking what was not given, and wrongful sexual behavior; the four wrongful actions of speech: lies, harsh words, mistaken statements, and divisive speech; and the three actions of the mind: cursing thoughts, cruelty, and wrong views. Tado, *Dictionary*, 408.

ten perfections (*phar phyin bcu*). The ten perfections are giving, moral practice, patience, effort, meditation, wisdom, skillful means, aspirations, strength, and pristine awareness.

ten unsurpassed conducts (*bla med spyod pa bcu*): conduct without reifying attachment (*'dzin chags med pa'i spyod pa*), conduct without reproach (*'chal ba med pa'i spyod pa*), conduct without dualistic perception (*byung tshor med pa*), conduct free of negligence (*btang snyoms dang bral ba*), irrevocable conduct ('*gyur ldog med pa*), conduct devoid of downfall (*ltung ba bral ba pa*), conduct without selfishness (*bdag phyogs med pa*), conduct without entertaining hope or worry (*re dogs med pa*), conduct without attachment (*chags pa med pa*), and conduct with the wisdom that seizes non-apprehension (*dmigs pa med pa'i shes rab kyis zin par spyod pa*). Tado, *Dictionary*, 381; Achard, "Contribution aux nombrables," 407–8.

thirty-seven paths, or the thirty-seven collections of Everlasting Bön (*lam so sum cu so bdun/so bdun*). *See* the four recollections, the four thorough abandonments, the four miraculous feet, the five sense faculties, the five powers, the seven enlightened limbs of everlastingness, and the eight limbs of Shenrab. Tado, *Dictionary*, 457.

thirteen strengths of fearlessness (*mi 'jigs pa'i stobs bcu gsum*). These are the thirteen aspects of fearlessness: the strength of pristine cognition (*ye shes chen po'i stobs*), the strength of love (*byams pa'i stobs*), the strength of peace (*zhi ba'i stobs*), the strength of giving (*sbyin pa'i stobs*), the strength of expansiveness (*yangs pa'i stobs*), the strength of compassion (*snying rje'i stobs*), the strength of the view (*lta ba'i stobs*), the strength of forbearance (*brston 'grus kyi stobs*), the strength of concentration (*bsam gtan gyi stobs*), the strength of illusory feats (*rdzu 'phrul gyi stobs*), the strength of patience (*bzod pa'i stobs*), the strength of insight (*shes rab kyi stobs*), and the strength of the cognizance of phenomena (*bon shes kyi stobs*). Tado, *Dictionary*, 545; Achard, "Contribution aux nombrables," 132.

three antidotes (*gnyen po gsum*). Mindfulness, introspection, and equanimity.

three concentrations (*ting 'dzin gsum*). These are used during the generation process of the mandala. They consist in the concentration on Suchness (*de bzhin nyid kyi ting nge 'dzin*), the all-illuminating concentration (*kun tu snang ba'i ting nge 'dzin*), and the causal concentration (*rgyu yi ting nge 'dzin*). Achard, "Contribution aux nombrables," 81.

three defining characteristics (*mtshan nyid gsum*). The three aspects given to any characterized object: the character that constitutes the conceptual label or the character that is all conceptualized (*kun brtags pa'i mtshan nyid*), the character that is an appearance labeled by something else that controls it (*gzhan gyi dbang gi mtshan nyid*), and the character that is thoroughly established or proven (*yongs su grub pa'i mtshan nyid*). Only the last is considered factual, the other two being imputed or fictional. This key doctrine of the Yogācāra school is known as the doctrine of the three inherent natures, *trisvabhāva*. One of the key studies on this doctrine is by Boquist, *Trisvabhāva*. Tado, *Dictionary*, 72.

three distinctions (*khyad par gsum*). The distinction of the essence that is the union of calm abiding and insight, the distinction of the cause that arises from the accumulation of virtue of what is below, and the distinction of the agent that clears away the stains of the faults of meditation.

three excellences (*phun sum tshogs*). This means "perfectly complete" or "perfectly excellent" and is an idiomatic expression pointing to an object endowed with abundance, grace, and glory.

three kinds of conventional truth (*kun rdzob gsum*). The relative truth of the relative truth (*kun rdzob kyi kun rdzob*), the relative truth of the non-existent completely pure (*yang dag pa ma yin pa'i kun rdzob*), and the relative truth of the completely pure (*yang dag pa'i kun rdzob*). Tado, *Dictionary*, 74.

three kinds of feelings (*tshor ba gsum*). Feelings of pleasure, pain, and neutrality.

three modes (*tshul gsum*). Analyzing objects (conceptual or real) using logic to recognize three characteristics: the quality or property of the object under investigation (*phyogs bon/chos*), the forward pervasion (*rjes khyab*) or what is included in the object, and the counterpervasion (*ldog khyab*) or what is excluded in the object. Dreyfus, *Recognizing Reality*, 199–200.

three manifest objects (*snang ba'i yul gsum*). *See* three natural dynamisms.

three natural dynamisms (*rang rtsal gsum*). The manifestation of the natural dynamism or the energy of reality manifest in sound, lights, and rays.

three non-virtuous, unwholesome thoughts (*sems kyi ngan rtog mi dge ba gsum*): Covetous thoughts, malicious thoughts, and wrong views.

three parts of the aggregate of distinctive perception (*'du shes gsum*). The perception of extensiveness, the perception of smallness, and the perception of indeterminate size.

three precepts (*sdom gsum*). The vows of seeking personal liberation (*so sdom*), the vows of the heroes of everlastingness of the mind of perfect purity (*byang sdom*), and tantric vows (*sngags sdom*). Achard, "Contribution aux nombrables," 91.

three trainings (*bslab gsum*). These are trainings in either ethics, concentration, and wisdom, or refutation, proof, and compatibility.

three spaces (*nam mkha' gsum sbyor*): Merging the subtle channels with emptiness (*rtsa khams stong pa*), with the emptiness of the sky (*nam mkha' stong pa*), and with the emptiness of the mind (*sems stong*). Tado, *Dictionary*, 53.

three unwholesome activities (*mi dge ba gsum*): killing, stealing, and wrongful sexual practices.

three vows, or three vowed restraints (*bsdam pa gsum*). Sets of pledges according to the lower, higher, and tantric vehicles.

twelve sensory spheres (*ske mchad bcu gnyis*). The collections of the six senses and their six kinds of objects.

two knowledges (*mkhyen gnyis*). The knowledge of the nature of things and understanding the extent of knowables.

two purities (*dag pa gnyis*). The purity of primordial essence (*ngo bo ye dag*) and the purity of the adventitious (*glo bur 'phral dag*). The latter can be replaced with the purity of clarity in concentration (*ting nge 'dzin gsal dag*). Tado, *Dictionary*, 381.

Vehicle of the Perfections (*phar phyin theg pa*). The path described in the Perfection of Wisdom literature adopted by the followers of the Everlasting Bön tradition.

Bibliography

Works Cited

A few versions of the Bön canonical scriptures (K for *Bka' 'gyur*) and the canon of commentaries (T for *brten* of *Bka' brten*) were used in this volume. All printed editions of the canonical scriptures stem from the original version that was "rediscovered" at Balkhyung Monastery in late 1980s, edited by Möngyal Lhasé and printed in Sichuan in 1999. Möngyal Lhasé (1935–2014), who was its master, had the originals cleaned and rephotographed in order to print clear versions of the texts, which had been one of the main problems of the earlier reprints. This is now the standard edition. Unless otherwise stated, all canonical sources referenced with volume number (K) refer to this edition. The titles are based on the standard indexes and in particular that of Keutzer and O'Neil. "A Handlist of the Bonpo Kangyur and Tengyur." In *Revue d'Etudes Tibétaines* 17 (2009): 63–128.

The other scriptural references are either woodblock prints from Menri Monastery or the Thopsar (*Thob gsar*) prints from New Menri Monastery in India. I have no volume references for the Thopsar woodblock prints. The Shin hwa references come from the *Bön Canon Catalogue* of Yungdrung Tsultrim. The references to the Thob gsar version and the Chamdo version are taken directly from the Tibetan editors of the edited volume used for this translation. No volume numbers are supplied in the references.

The references to the canon of commentaries are from the edition in three hundred volumes printed in Lhasa in 1998 under the late Sokdé Tenpai Nyima (Sog sde Bstan pa'i nyi ma, 1943–2012) with the help and expertise of Yungdrung Tenpai Gyaltsen (1926–97). All references to T come from Nagano and Karmay, *A Catalogue of the New Collection of Bönpo Katen Texts*. On the different versions of both the canonical scriptures and the canon of commentaries, see Martin, "Introduction," and Nagano and Karmay, *Catalogue of the New Collection of Bönpo Katen Texts.*

Canonical Scriptures

The title of the work is followed by the volume number (K), the section (mdo, mdzod, rgyud, sems sde), and the booklets using the Tibetan ordering system of letters (*ka, kha, ga,* etc.). Some titles attributed to this canon are either lost or not yet found. These titles may have missing information, such as the volume number and so forth.

Arcana (Gab pa). Rdzogs pa chen po byang chub sems kyi smyu gu gab pa dgu skor, K172, sems sde, *ka, cha, ja.*

Clearing Away the Limits to the Primordial Throne [the section entitled Moon] *(Ye khri mtha' sel las zla'i bam po). Spyi rgyud chen po nam mkha' dkar po ye khri mtha' sel gyi rgyud las bzla ba'i bam po,* K176, sems sde, *nga.*

Collected Discourse (Mdo sdud). Mdo 'dus pa rin po che'i rgyud thams cad mkhyen pa'i bka' tshad ma, K30, mdo sde.

Collection of the Rising of the Nine Suns. 'Bum nyi ma dgu shar, K125.34, 'bum sde.

Coming of the Three Meanings. Don gsum shog, sems sde.

Commentary on the Nine Mirrors ('Grel me long dgu dkor). Theg pa'i rim pa mngon du bshad pa'i mdo rgyud kyi 'grel ba 'phrul gyi me long dgu skor. Thob gsar edition, no volume reference.

Compendium of the Water-Spirits (Klu 'bum). Bon rin po che 'phrul ngag bden pa gtsang ma'i klu 'bum dkar nag khra bo, K135–36, mdo sde.

Compendium on the Spreading (Bdal 'bum). Bon nyid snying po bdal ba'i 'bum, K105–14, 'bum sde.

Cycle That Clears Away the Ten Thousand Limits to the Primordial. Ye khri mtha' sel, K177, sems sde.

Deity's Instructions on the Revelatory Transmission (Snyan rgyud lha khrid). Kun bzang lha khrid kyi dbu phyogs. Shin hwa 156, sems sde, *cha.*

Determining the Root of the Realms (Khams rtsa rnam nges). Bsdus pa'i 'bring po khams rtsa'am bka' 'dus, K102, 'bum, *ka.*

Discourse on the Stainless Root (Dri med rtsa ba'i mdo). 'Dus pa'i rin po che'i rgyud dri med pa rtsa ba'i mdo sangs rgyas kyi rnam thar rin chen phreng ba, K26, mdo sde.

Eight Realms (Khams brgyad). Khams brgyad gtan la phab pa stong phrag brgya pa rtsa ba'i 'bum, K99, 'bum sde.

Eight Realms (Khams brgyad). Shes rab kyi pha rol tu phyin pa rgyud pa'i khams, K77, 'bum sde, *ga*.

Eight Realms (Khams brgyad). Shes rab kyi pha rol tu phyin pa srid pa'i khams, K75, 'bum sde, *ka*.

Enlightened Ethic of Activities. Mdzad khrims. A lost canonical source.

Eye of the Needle (Mdo dri med gzer mig). 'Dus pa rin po che'i rgyud gzer mig le'u bco brgyad pa, K28–29, mdo sde.

Four Cycles of the Oral Diffusion of the Revelatory Transmission from Zhang-zhung of the Great Perfection. Rdzogs pa chen po zhang zhung snyan rgyud bka' rgyud skor bzhi, K171, sems sde.

Great Realms Scripture. 'Phyong 'bum, K91, 'bum sde.

Hundred Thousand Verses on the Summit of Awareness (Rig pa'i rtse mo'i 'bum). Shes rab kyi bla na med pa phyin par mngon rtogs rig pa'i rtse mo'i 'bum, K115, 'bum sde, *ka*.

Lamp (Sgron ma). Sgron ma drug bzhugs pa'i dbu phyogs, K171, sems sde, *da*.

Lamp of Clear Expression. Rtags tshad gsal ba'i sgron ma, K171, sems sde, *pa*.

Leaping the Grounds of Everlastingness. G.yung drung sa 'phar. Unknown canonical scripture.

Little Nails. Gzer bu, K171, sems sde, *ba*.

Lore for the Accomplishment of the Very Pure. Rnam dag gi sgrub gzhung, K57, mdo sde.

Lore of the Cuckoo of Awareness. Rig pa khu byug gi gzhung, K175, sngags sde, *nga*.

Minute Scriptures (Mdo phran). Mdo phran nyi shu rtsa gcig pa, K41, mdo sde.

Nine Arcana. Rdzogs pa chen po byang chub sems kyi smyu gu gab pa dgu skor and the *Rdzogs pa chen po byang chub sems kyi smyu gu gab pa dgu skor*, K172, sems sde

Nine Arcana Commentary. The first chapter of the cycle of the Nine Arcana, the Tantra: The Commentary on the Arcana of the Heroes of Enlightenment. Rgyud gab pa dgu skor gyi le'u dang po; Byang chub sems kyi gab pa'i 'grel pa, K173, sems sde.

Precious Garland Tantra (Rin chen 'phreng ba'i rgyud). 'Dus pa rin po che'i rgyud dri ma med pa rtsa ba'i mdo sangs rgyas kyi rnam thar rin chen 'phreng ba, K26, mdo sde.

Realms of Awareness. Rig pa'i khams. An unknown canonical scripture mentioned by Azha Lodrö Gyaltsen.

Rising of the Nine Suns in a Hundred Thousand Verses ('Bum nyi ma dgu shar). Bon nyid kyi snying po thugs rje nyi ma dgu shar gyi 'bum, K125–34, 'bum sde.

Roots of the Hundred Thousand (Rtsa 'bum). Khams brgyad gtan la phabs pa stong phrag brgya pa rtsa ba'i 'bum, K99, 'bum sde, *ka.*

Scripture of the Eight Realms (khams brgyad). This is a general reference to a collection of *Eight Realms* scriptures. See the 'bum sde section.

Scripture of the Generation of the Mind of Enlightenment. Sems bskyed mdo. A lost canonical scripture.

Scripture of the Joyful Kunzang. Kun bzang bde ba'i lung. A lost scripture.

Scripture of the Prophecy of the Lord of the Throne. Khri rje lung bstan gyi mdo, K51, mdo sde.

Six Essential Points (Gnad drug). Byang chub sems kyi gnad drug zhes pa'i lag len, K171, sems sde, *tha.*

Six Transmissions (Lung drug, aka *Dgong lung). Rdzogs chen lung drug shes bya ba,* K175, sngags sde, *nga.* Referred throughout the text of the *Phyag khrid* as the *Dgong lung.*

Summary of the Hundred Thousand. 'Bum tig. A lost scripture or a designation that is no longer recognized.

Tantra Explaining the Primordial Throne (Ye khri bshad rgyud). Dgos 'dod gsal byed bshad bzhi'i mchong, K176, sems sde, *cha.*

Tantra of Amrta Kundali, the Golden Tree of Paradise. Gser lo ljon shing bdud rtsi 'khyil ba'i rgyud, K152, sngags sde, *ba.*

Tantra of the Pure Aspects of the Activities of Everlastingness (G.yung drung las dag). G.yung drung las rnam par dag pa'i rgyud, K56, mdo sde.

Tantra of the Secret Empowerment of Everlastingness (G.yung drung gsang ba dbang gi rgyud). G.yung drung gsang ba dbang gi rgyud bar mi yul du bsgrags pa, sems sde.

Tantra of the Secret Everlastingness, the Secret Life-Bearer. 'Gu ya srog 'dzin g.yung drung gsang ba'i rgyud, K148, sngags sde, *nga.*

Tantra of the Wonderful Demonstration of the Universal Gathering of Great Power. Dbang chen kun 'dus ngo mtshar ston pa'i rgyud, sems sde, *ga.*

Tantric Scripture of the Way of Syllogism That Destroys the Heretics. Mu steg tshar gcod gtan tshigs theg pa'i mdo rgyud. In the Chamdo (*Chab mdo*) version of the canon of scriptures, *nga.*

Tantric Scripture That Explains the Real Stages of the Spiritual Way. Theg pa'i rim pa mngon du bshad pa'i mdo rgyud. In the Thopsar woodblock prints.

Transmission of the Boundless Spreading of the Great Perfection. Rdzogs pa chen po mu med bdal pa'i rgyud, K178, sems sde.

Transmission of the Mind (Sems lung). Sems lung gsal ba'i sgron me ma rig mun sel. In the Thopsar version of the canon of scriptures.

Treasury of the World (Mdzod phugs). Srid pa'i mdzod phugs, K2, mdo sde.

Triflings of the Mind. Sems phran. As a separate part of the *Rig pa khu byug gi gzhung,* K172, sems sde, *na.*

Trilogy of the Proclamation of the Great Perfection. Rdzogs chen bsgrags pa skor gsum, K174–75, sems sde.

Very Hidden Heart, the Tantra of the Mother Tugje Nyima. Thugs kyi yang gab ma rgyud thugs rje nyi ma'i rgyud, K154, sngags sde.

Very Pure Tantra (Rgyud rnam dag). G.yung drung las rnam par dag pa'i rgyud, K56, mdo sde.

Victorious Summit of Primordial Wisdom (Ye shes rtse rgyal). Ye shes rtse rgyal lta ba'i 'phyong, K150, sngags sde, *ta.*

White Heaven of the Great General Transmission, the Cycle That Clears Away the Ten Thousand Limits to the Primordial. Ye khri mtha' sel, K177, sems sde.

White Hundred Thousand Water-Spirits (Klu 'bum dkar po). Bon rin po che 'phrul ngag bden pa gtsang ma'i klu 'bum dkar po, K135, 'bum sde, *ka.*

Canonical Treatises

Azha Lodrö Gyaltsen (A zha Blo gros rgyal mtshan). *Concise Explanations on the Actualization of the Peaceful Asel. Zhi ba A gsal gyi mngon rtogs chung ba gsal byed,* T027.6: 45–48.

———. *Elixir of the Precious Lamp Elucidating the Rubrics for the Secret Syzygies. Gsang ba yab yum gyi phyag bzhes gsal ba'i sgron ma rin po che'i bcud,* T048.3: 35–66.

———. *Intention of the New and Old Traditions of the Scripture Category, the General Method to Practice the Recitations for (Transference of) Virtues/Merit. Mdo sde gsar rnying lung gi dgongs pa tshig spyi dril nyams su len thabs,* T207.11: 123–206.

———. *Lamp That Clarifies the Rubrics of the Very Perfected Everlasting Peaceful Deities of the Universal Heap. Spyi spungs zhi ba g.yung drung yongs rdzogs kyi phyag bzhes gsal byed sgron ma*, T230.1: 1–35.

———. *Lamp That Elucidates the Rubrics for the Secret Rite of Drenpa, the Accomplishment of the Great Secret Lama. Gsang ba bla chen sgrub pa dran pa gsang sgrub kyi phyag bzhes gsal byed sgron ma*, T048.4: 67–102.

———. *Magical Key to Elucidating the Practice of the Secret Rite of Tsewang. Tshe dbang gsang sgrub kyi phyag bzhes gsal ba 'phrul gyi lde mig*, T061.37: 635–55.

———. *Method of Entering the Path of the Secret Mantras, the Necklace of Pearl. Gsang sngags lam gyi 'jug chog mu tig 'phreng ba*, T251.1: 1–60.

———. *Mirror That Elucidates the Directives for the Liberation Rite, Ransom Offering, and Thread-Cross Ceremony. Thar glud mdos kyi lag len gsal ba'i me long*, T232.15: 471–77.

———. *Rubric for the Performance of the Outer Rite*, also called the *Precious Lamp for the Supplications (Section) for the Outer Rite. Phyi sgrub phyag bzhes*, T048.7: 123–28.

———. *Rubrics on the Inner Rites. Nang sgrub phyag bzhes*, also known as the *Precious Lamp That Clearly Explains the Inner Rites. Nang sgrub gsal byed sgron ma rin po che*, written at the request of a monk from Upper Dolpo, T048.2: 35–66.

———. *Rubrics for the Oral Transmission. Snyan rgyud kyi phyag bzhes*, T048.24: 443–98.

———. *Summoning Tsewang in India. Tshe dbang rgya gar ma'i skong ba*, T061.50: 798–806.

———. *Treasure Text for Full Confession and Amends of Tsewang. Tshe dbang skong bshags tshangs pa'i gter*, T088.28: 525–47.

———. *Well-Arranged Mountain of Fire, Rubrics for Phurpa. Phur pa'i phyag bzhes me ri bkod legs*, T245.1: 1–95.

Circling of Light Rays. 'Od zer 'khyil ba, T168.

Collection of the Nine Trunks. Sdong po dgu dus lta ba'i rgyud chen, T216.3.

Commentary on the Sun. Nyi khrid. An unknown designation for a canonical treatise.

Cycle of the Nine Arcana (Gab pa dgu skor). Byang sems gab pa dgu skor, T216.

Cycles of the Nine Mirrors. 'Phrul gyi me long dgu skor, T113.40.

Drenpa Namkha (Dran pa gnam mkha', fl. eighth century). *Lamp Dispelling the Darkness of Provisional Meaning. Drang don mun sel sgron ma*, T206, sems sde, *ka*.

Dru Gyalwa Yungdrung (Bru rgyal ba G.yung drung, 1242–90). *Activities of the Mother of Namdak Padma. Rnam dag Padma yum gyi 'phrin las.* Shin hwa, T254.

Great Lineage of Revelation (Snyan rgyud chen mo). Unknown source or possibly a general reference to the Revelatory Transmission teachings.

Great Sword of the Black Long-Maned Suppressing Khyung. Zil gnon khyung nag ral chen gyi skong ba, T229.12.

Gyerpung Nangzher Löpo (Gyer spungs snang bzher lod po, fl. eighth century). *Root Commentary on the Nails (Gzer bu'i rtsa 'grel). Rdzogs pa chen po zhang zhung snyan rgyud las gzer bu nyi shu rtsa gcig gi gzhung.* From woodblocks preserved in the Menri Monastery, sems sde, *ra*.

Instructions of the Gods of Revelation. Snyan rgyud lha khrid, T146, sems sde, cha.

Khepa Mizhi (Mkhas pa mi bzhi). *Commentary on the Arcana (Gab 'grel). Sems lung gab pa dgu skor gyi 'grel pa rgya cher bshad pa. Shin Hwa,* T216, sems sde.

Magical Net (Sgyu 'phrul). Sgyu 'phrul gsang ba'i gtso mchog thugs sgrub kyi lag len gsal byed nam mkha'i nyi zer, T137.

Nine Gates of the Small Gems. Dbal mo las thig gi mchong chung, T241.61.

Realm of Emptiness (Stong khams). Sher phyin rgyan 'grel dang bcas kyi skabs bzhi pa stong khams kyi mtha' dpyod dbyar gyi rnga sgra blo gsal mdongs tha dga' ba'i dgyes glu, T179.3.

Root Ritual of the Sphere of Mapang of the Peaceful Deities. Zhi ba ma pang dbyings chen rtsa ba'i sgrub pa, T244.13.

Shari Uchen (Sha ri dbu chen). *Key Point of Shari (Sha ri'i gal mdo). Bon thams cad kyi yang snying gtan tshigs nges pa'i gal mdo tan tra nyi ma'i 'khor lo.* From woodblocks preserved in the Menri Monastery, sems sde, ra.

Stainless Splendor (Gzi brjid) is the twelve-volume hagiography of the teacher Shenrab. Excerpts have been translated in Snellgrove, *Nine Ways of Bon.*

Tsultrim Palden (Tshul khrims dpal ldan). *Ornament of Clear Realization (Mngon rtogs rgyan). Shes rab kyi bla na med par phyin pa mngon par rtogs pa lam gyi rim pa'i rgyan.* Thopsar, mdo sde.

Twenty-One Nails (Gzer bu nyer gcig). See Gyerpung Nangzher Löpo, *Root Commentary on the Nails (Gzer bu'i rtsa 'grel).*

Walchen Trogyal. *Secret Capable Sen-Demoness of the Universal Heap. Spyi spungs gsang ba bsen thub rtsa ba'i rgyud,* T193.7: 817–1073.

Secondary Sources

Achard, Jean-Luc. "Contribution aux nombrables de la tradition Bon po: L'appendice de bsTan 'dzin Rin chen rgyal mtshan à la *Sphère de Cristal des Dieux et des Démons* de Shar rdza rin po che." *Revue d'Etudes Tibétaines* 4 (2003): 78–146.

———. *The Dawn of Awareness: The Practice Manual for the Special Preliminaries of Dzogchen.* Zhangzhung Nyengyü Studies 2. Munich: Naldjor Institute for Movement, 2006.

———. *Enlightened Rainbows: The Life and Works of Shardza Tashi Gyaltsen.* Brill's Tibetan Studies Library 18. Leiden: Brill, 2008.

———. "A Fourfold Set of Emanations, Variegated Currents and Alien Elements: Contribution to the Origins and Early Development of New Bön and Its Revelations." In *Challenging Paradigms: Buddhism and Nativism: Framing Identity Discourse in Buddhist Environments*, edited by Henk Blezer and Mark Teuwen, 77–122. Leiden: Brill, 2013.

———. *Les instructions sur le A Primordial*, vol. 1, *Histoire de la Lignée.* Sumène: Editions Khyung-Lung, 2007.

———. *La lampe clarifiant les conseils oraux sur la base universelle, traduction du tibétain et commentaire.* Sumène: Editions Khyung-Lung, 2009.

———. "Mesmerizing with the Useless? A Book-Review Inquiry into the Ability to Properly Reprint Older Worthy Material." *Revue d'Etudes Tibétaines* 10 (2010): 133–43.

———. *The Precepts in Eight Chapters, from the Oral Transmission of the Great Perfection in Zhangzhung.* Zhangzhung Nyengyü Studies 4. Munich: Naldjor Institute, 2010.

———. *The Six Lamps: Secret Dzogchen Instructions of the Bön Tradition.* Somerville, MA: Wisdom Publications, 2017.

Achard, Jean-Luc, in collaboration with Lopön Tenzin Namdak Rinpoche. *The Four Lamps.* Zhangzhung Nyengyü Studies 3. Munich: Naldjor Institute, 2007.

———. *The Three Precepts from the Oral Transmission of the Great Perfection in Zhangzhung.* Zhangzhung Nyengyü Studies 1. Munich: Naldjor Institute, 2005.

Baker, Ian A. *Tibetan Yoga: Principles and Practices.* London: Thames & Hudson, 2019.

Bellezza, John Vincent. *Divine Dyads: Ancient Civilization in Tibet.* Dharamsala: Library of Tibetan Works & Archives, 1997.

———. "Notes on Three Series of Unusual Symbols Discovered on the Byang Thang." *East and West* 47.1 (1997): 395–405.

———. *Spirit-Mediums, Sacred Mountains and Related Bon Textual Traditions in Upper Tibet: Calling Down the Gods.* Leiden: Brill, 2005.

Blezer, Henk. "A Brief Bibliographical Key to *Zhang zhung snyan rgyud* Editions with Special Attention for Sources on the Early Lineage." *Revue d'Etudes Tibétaines* 20.6 (2011): 142.

———. "The 'Bon' dBal-mo Nyer-bdun(/brgyad) and the Buddhist dBang-phyug Nyer-brgyad: A brief Comparison." In *New Horizons in Bon Studies*, edited by Samten G. Karmay and Yasuhiko Nagano, 117–78. Senri Ethnological Reports 15. Osaka: Museum of Ethnography, 2000.

———. "Greatly Perfected, in Space and Time: Historicities of the Bon Aural Transmission from Zhang Zhung." *The Tibet Journal* 34 (2009): 3–4.

Blondeau, Anne-Marie. "Analysis of the Biographies of Padmasambhava according to the Tibetan Tradition: Classification of Sources." In *Tibetan Studies in Honour of Hugh Richardson: Proceedings of the International Seminar on Tibetan Studies*, edited by Michael Aris and Aung San Suu Kyi, 45–52. Warminster: Aris & Phillips, Oxford, 1979.

———. "Le Lha-'dre bka'-thañ." In *Etudes tibétaines à la mémoire de Marcelle Lalou*, edited by A. Macdonald, 29–126. Paris, 1971.

———. "Les *Ma mo*: Mythes cosmogoniques et théogoniques dans le *rNying ma'i rgyud 'bum*." In *The Many Canons of Tibetan Buddhism*, edited by H. Eimer and David Germano, 293–311. Leiden: Brill, 2002.

———. "Le réseau des mille dieux-démons: Mythes et classifications." *Revue d'Etudes Tibétaines* 15.11 (2008): 199–250.

Boquist, Åke. *Trisvabhāva: A Study of the Development of the Three-Nature-Theory in Yogācāra Buddhism.* Stockholm: Almqvist & Wiksell International, 1995.

Bru-sgom rGyal-ba G.yung-drung. *The Stages of A-Khrid Meditation: Dzogchen Practice of the Bon Tradition.* Translated by Per Kvaerne and Thupten Rikey. Delhi: Paljor Publications, 2002.

Bsod-nams-rgyal-mtshan (Sa-skya-pa Bla-ma Dam-pa). *The Mirror Illuminating the Royal Genealogies: Tibetan Buddhist Historiography: An Annotated Translation of the XIVth Century Tibetan Chronicle: RGyal-rabs Gsal- Ba'i Me-long.* Wiesbaden: Otto Harrassowitz Verlag, 1994.

Buffetrille, Katia. "A Bon po Pilgrimage Guide to Amnye Machen Mountain." *Lungta* 8 (1994): 20–24.

————. "The Evolution of a Tibetan Pilgrimage to A mnyes rMa chen Mountain in the 21st Century." In *Collected Papers: Symposium on Contemporary Tibetan Studies, 21st Century Tibet Issue,* edited by the Mongolian and Tibetan Affairs Commission, 325–63. Taipei: Mongolian and Tibetan Affairs Commission, 2003.

————. "The Great Pilgrimage of A-myes rMa-chen: Written Traditions, Living Realities." In *Maṇḍala and Landscape,* edited by A. W. Macdonald, 75–132. New Delhi: D. K. Printworld, 1997.

Byang-chub-Rgyal-mtshan and Tshe-brtan-Phun-tshogs (Jangchub Gyaltsen and Tseten Phuntsok). *Rlangs kyi po ti bse ru rgyas pa.* Lhasa: Lha-sa Bod-ljongs Mi-dmangs Dpe-skrun-khang, 1986.

Cabezón, José. *A Dose of Emptiness: An Annotated Translation of the sTong thun chen mo of mKhas grub dGe legs dpal bzang.* Albany: State University of New York Press, 1992.

————, ed. *Tibetan Ritual.* Oxford: Oxford University Press, 2010.

Cech, Krystina. "The History, Teaching and Practice of Dialectics according to the Bon Tradition." *The Tibet Journal* 11.2 (1986): 3–28.

Conze, Edward. "List of Buddhist Terms." In *Tibet Journal* 1.1 (1975): 54–55.

Coseru, Christian. *Perceiving Reality: Consciousness, Intentionality, and Cognition in Buddhist Philosophy.* Oxford: Oxford University Press, 2012.

Cuevas, Bryan. "The 'Calf's Nipple' (Be'u bum) of Ju Mipam ('Ju Mi pham): A Handbook of Tibetan Ritual Magic." In Cabezón, *Tibetan Ritual,* 165–86.

————. "Illustrations of Human Effigies in Tibetan Ritual Texts: With Remarks on Specific Anatomical Figures and Their Possible Iconographic Source." *The Journal of the Royal Asiatic Society* 21.1 (2011): 73–97.

————. "The Politics of Magical Warfare." In *Faith and Empire: Art and Politics in Tibetan Buddhism,* edited by Karl Debreczeny, 171–89. New York: Rubin Museum of Art, 2019.

Dagkar, Namgyal Nyima. "gShen: The Ancestral Clan of Rin then bzang po." In *The Tibet Journal* 24.2 (1999): 45–59.

Dalton, Jacob P. "A Crisis of Doxography: How Tibetans Organized Tantra during the 8th–12th Centuries." In *Journal of the International Association of Buddhist Studies* 28 (2005): 115–81.

————. "How Dharanis WERE Proto-Tantric: Liturgies, Ritual Manuals, and the Origins of the Tantras." In *Tantric Traditions in Transmission and Translation*, edited by David B. Gray and Ryan Richard Overbey, 199–229. Oxford: Oxford University Press, 2016.

Das, Chandra. *A Tibetan-English Dictionary*. Calcutta: Gaurav publishing House, 1985 [1902].

Des Jardins, J. F. Marc. "About the Zhangzhung Master Stag la me 'bar, Was He a *Tājik*?" In *Ancient Civilization of Tibetan Plateau: Proceedings of the First Beijing International Conference on Shang shung Cultural Studies*, vol. 1, edited by Tsering Thar Tongkor and Tsering Dawa Sharshon, 161–84. Lanzhou: Qinghai minzhu chubanshe, 2018.

———. "Notes on the History of Bon and the Ye shes Monastery in Nyag rong, Sichuan." *The Journal of the International Association for Bon Research* 1 (2013): 55–76.

———. "The Records of Tshul khrims mchog rgyal on the Black Phur pa Cycle of the Tibetan Bon pos." *Revue d'Etudes Tibétaines* 23.4 (2012): 169–203.

———. "Rites of the Deity Tamdrin (Rta mgrin) in Contemporary Bön: Transforming Poison and Eliminating Noxious Spirits with Burning Stones." In *Tibetan Rituals*, edited by José Cabezón, 187–205. Oxford: Oxford University Press, 2009.

———. *Le sutra de la Mahāmāyūrī: Ritual et politique dans la Chine des Tang (618–907)*. Québec: Les Presses de l'Université Laval, 2011.

———. "Tantric Ritual Standardization in g.Yung drung Bon: Common Ritual Template underlying the Tantric Cycles of Phur Nag and Ma rgyud." Paper presented at the Bon panel "The Many Faces of Bon: Moving across Center and Periphery," International Association for Tibetan Studies (IATS), Paris, 2019.

———. "A Tibetan Bonpo Priest's Grimoire: An Example of a Collection of Magical Recipes for Daily Use by a Minority Religion Specialist." In *Manuscript Culture*, edited by Charles Ramble and Agnieszka Helman-Wazny, vol. 9, 19–38. Hamburg: Centre of the Study of Manuscript Cultures, Universität Hamburg, 2023.

Doctor, Thomas. *Tibetan Buddhism: Mabja Jangchub Tsöndrü and the Traditions of the Middle Way*. London: Routledge, 2014.

Dotson, Brandon. "Complementarity and Opposition in Early Tibetan Ritual." *Journal of the American Oriental Society* 128.1 (January–March 2008): 41–67.

Douglas, Nik. *Tibetan Tantric Charms and Amulets*. Mineola, NY: Dover Publications, 2002 [1978].

Dreyfus, Georges B. J. *Recognizing Reality: Dharmakīrti's Philosophy and Its Tibetan Interpretations.* Albany: State University of New York Press, 1997.

———. *The Sound of Two Hands Clapping: The Education of a Tibetan Buddhist Monk.* Berkeley: University of California Press, 2003.

Duckworth, Douglas S. "Two Models of the Two Truths: Ontological and Phenomenological Approaches." *Journal of Indian Philosophy* 38 (2010): 519–27.

Duff, Tony. *Illuminator Dictionary: Tibetan-English Encyclopaedic Dictionary.* Kathmandu: Padma Karpo Translation Committee, 2016.

Dunne, John D. *Foundations of Dharmakīrti's Philosophy.* Somerville, MA: Wisdom Publications, 2004.

Geshe Sonam Gurung, and Daniel P. Brown, trans. *Pith Instructions for A Khrid rDzogs Chen by Bru rGyal ba g.Yung drung.* Translated by Geshe Sonam Gurun and Daniel Brown, PhD. San Francisco: Bright Alliance Publications, 2017.

Gianotti, Carla. "The *Srin Mo* Demoness and Her Submission to the Buddhist Tibetan Dharma: Some Different Modes of Her Transformation." *Buddhist Asia* 2. *Papers from the Second Conference of Buddhist Studies Held in Naples in June 2004,* edited by Giacomella Orofina and Silvio Vita, 69–97. Kyoto: Italian School of East Asian Studies, 2010.

Gurung, Kalsang Norbu. "The Emergence of a Myth: In Search of the Origins of the Life Story of Shenrab Miwo, the Founder of Bon." Unpublished PhD dissertation, Institute for Area Studies, Leiden University, 2011.

G.yung drung bon gyi mdo sgnags sems gsum gyi gzhung. New Delhi: Institute of Tibetan Classics, 2010.

G.yung drung tshul khrims dbang drag, fl. 1876–1880 (Yungdrung Tsultrim Wangdrak). *Bon Canon Catalogue. Rgyal ba'i bka' dang bka' rten rmad 'byung dgos 'dod yid bzhin gter gyi bang mdzod la dkar chags blo'i tha ram bkrol byed 'phrul gyi lde mig.* Chengdu: Bod ljongs Shin hwa par 'debs bso grwa, 1998.

Gyermi Nyiö (Gyer mi Nyi 'od, b. 1108). *The Great Commentary. Sgra 'grel chen mo.* In *Bden pa'i mdzod phugs rnam par 'byed pa'i lde mig,* 1–35. Lnga rig bon gyi snying gter 1. Chengdu: Si khron dpe skrun tshogs pa, Si khron mi rigs dpe skrun khang, 2005.

Hatchell, Chris. *Naked Seeing: The Great Perfection, the Wheel of Time, and Visionary Buddhism in Renaissance Tibet.* Oxford: Oxford University Press, 2014.

Hayes, Richard. *Dignāga on the Interpretation of Signs.* Dordrecht: Reidel Publishing, 1982.

Huber, Toni. *Source of Life: Revitalisation Rites and Bon Shamans in Bhutan and the Eastern Himalayas.* Vienna: Verlag der Österreichischen Akademie der Wissenschaften, 2020.

Hugon, Pascale. *Le rTags kyi rnam gźag rigs lam gsal ba'i sgron me de Glo bo mkhan chen bSod nams lhun grub: Un manuel tibétain d'introduction à la logique. Edition et traduction annotée.* Wiener Studien Zur Tibetologie Und Buddhismuskunde 55. Vienna: Arbeitskreis für tibetische und buddhistische Studien, Universität Wien, 2002.

———. *Trésors du raisonnement: Sa skya Paṇḍita et ses prédécesseurs tibétains sur les modes de fonctionnement de la pensée et le fondement de l'inférence. Edition et traduction annotée du quatrième chapitre et d'une section du dixième chapitre du Tshad ma rigs pa'i gter.* Wiener Studien Zur Tibetologie Und Buddhismuskunde 69, vols. 1–2. Vienna: Arbeitskreis für tibetische und buddhistische Studien, Universität Wien, 2008.

Jinpa, Thupten, trans. *The Book of Kadam: The Core Texts.* Library of Tibetan Classics 2. Boston: Wisdom Publications, 2014.

Jurkovic, Ratka. "Prayer to Ta pi hritsa: A Short Exposition of the Base, the Path and the Fruit in Bon Dzogchen Teachings." *Revue d'Etudes Tibétaines* 16 (2009): 5–42.

Karmay, Samten G. *The Arrow and the Spindle: Studies in History, Myths, Rituals and Beliefs in Tibet,* vol. 1. Kathmandu: Mandala Book Point, 1998.

———. "The Cult of Mountain Deities and Political Significance." In Karmay, *Arrow and the Spindle,* 432–50.

———. *The Little Luminous Boy: The Oral Tradition from the Land of Zhangzhung Depicted on Two Tibetan Paintings.* Bangkok: White Orchid Press, 1998.

———. "Tibetan Indigenous Myths and Rituals with Reference to the Ancient Bön Text: The Nyenbum (Gnyan 'bum)." In Cabezón, *Tibetan Ritual,* 53–68.

———. *The Treasury of Good Sayings: A Tibetan History of Bon.* Oxford: Oxford University Press, 1972.

Keutzer, Kurt, and Kevin O'Neil. "A Handlist of the Bonpo Kangyur and Tengyur." In *Revue d'Etudes Tibétaines* 17 (2009): 63–128.

Kumagai, Seiji. *The Two Truths in Bon*. Kathmandu: Vajra Publications, 2011.

Kvaerne, Per. *The Bon Religion of Tibet: The Iconography of a Living Tradition*. London: Serindia, 1995.

———. "Bonpo Studies: The A Khrid System of Meditation." In *Kailash* 1.4 (1973): 19–50, 247–332.

Lalou, Marcelle. "Rituel bon-po des funérailles royales." *Journal Asiatique*, no. 240 (1952): 339–61.

Lhagyal, Dondrup. "Bonpo Family Lineages in Central Tibet." In *New Horizons in Bon Studies*, edited by Samten G. Karmay and Yasuhiko Nagano, 429–505. Senri Ethnological Reports 15. Osaka : National Museum of Ethnology, 2000.

Lopön Tenzin Namdak Rinpoche. *The Main Dzogchen Practices: From the Oral Transmission of the Great Perfection in Zhang Zhung*. Edited by Gerd Manush. Munich: Naljor, 2001.

———. *The Meditation on Clear Light: From the Oral Transmission of the Great Perfection in Zhang Zhung*. Edited by Gerd Manush. Munich: Naljor, 2001.

———. *Nyam Gyü: The Experiential Transmission of Drugyalwa Yungdrung, according to the Teachings and Transmissions of Tenzin Wangyal Rinpoche*, vol. 2, plus *Ngö zhi* Supplement. Compiled, edited, and introduced by Gerd Manush. Munich: Naljor, 2001.

Martin, Dan. "Comparing Treasuries: Mental States and Other *mDzod phug* Lists and Passages with Parallels in Abhidharma Works by Vasubandhu and Asanga, or in Prajñāpāramitā Sūtras: A Progress Report." In *New Horizons in Bon Studies*, edited by Samten G. Karmay and Yasuhiko Nagano, 37–42. Senri Ethnological Reports 15. Osaka: National Museum of Ethnography, 2000.

———. "Introduction." In *A Catalogue of the Bon Kanjur*, compiled and authored by Tseyang Changngoba et al., edited by Dan Martin, Per Kvaerne, and Yashuhiko Ngano. Bon Studies 8. Senri Ethnological Reports 40. Osaka: National Museum of Ethnology, 2003.

———. *Mandala Cosmogony: Human Body, Good Thought and the Revelation of the Secret Mother Tantras of Bon*. Wiesbaden: Harrassowitz Verlag, 1994.

————. *Unearthing Bon Treasures: Life and Contested Legacy of a Tibetan Scripture Revealer, with a General Bibliography of Bon.* Leiden: Brill, 2001.

————. "Zhangzhung Dictionary." In *Revue d'Etudes Tibétaines* 18.4 (2010): 5–254.

Mayer, Robert. "Rethinking Treasure (Part One)." *Revue d'Etudes Tibétaines* 52 (October 2019): 119–84.

————. "A Bon Tantric Approach to the Senses: The Evidence from Khu tsha zla 'od's *Black Pillar* (*Ka ba nag po man ngag rtsa ba'i rgyud*)." *Revue d'Etudes Tibétaines* 50 (2013): 40–55.

Mayer, Robert, and Cathy Cantwell. "Neither the Same nor Different: The Bon Ka ba Nag po in Relation to Contemporaneous rNying ma Phur pa Texts." In *Scribes, Texts, and Rituals in Early Tibet and Dunhuang: Proceedings of the Third Old Tibetan Studies Panel Held at the Seminar of the International Association for Tibetan Studies, Vancouver 2010*, edited by Brandon Dotson, Kazushi Iwao, and Tsuguhito Takeuchi, 87–100. Wiesbaden: Reichert Verlag, 2013.

Nagano, Yasuhiko, and Samten G. Karmay. *A Catalogue of the New Collection of Bönpo Katen Texts*, vols. 1–2. Bon Studies 3–4 (indices), Senri Ethnological Reports 24–25 (indices). Osaka: National Museum of Ethnology, 2001.

Nebesky-Wojkowitz, René de. *Oracles and Demons of Tibet: The Cult and Iconography of the Tibetan Protective Deities.* Kathmandu: Tiwari's Pilgrims Book House, 1993 [1956].

Nima Hojer Lama (Nyima Woser Choekhortshang). "The Genealogy of Ya-ngal Family of Dolpo (Critical Edition of the Text, Translation into English, Analyses of Abbreviations and Introduction to the Dolpo Dialect). Genealogie rodu Ja-ngal z Dolpa (Kritická edice textu, překlad do angličtiny, analýza zkratek a úvod do dialektu Dolpa)." PhD dissertation, Charles University, 2017.

O-thog bsTan-'dzin dbang-rgyal. "An Introduction to the Index of gZi-brjid and gZer-mig." *The Tibet Journal* 11.2 (1986): 29–35.

Obermiller, Eugène, trans. *History of Buddhism (Chos-hbyung), by Bu-ston. Part I, The Jewelry of Scripture.* Materialien zur Kunde des Buddhismus 18. Heidelberg: Harrassowitz, 1931.

Pasar Tsultrim Tenzin, Changru Tritsuk Namdak Nyima, and Gatsa Lodroe Rabsal. *A Lexicon of Zhangzhung and Bonpo Terms.* Edited by Yasuhiko

Nagano and Samten G. Karmay. Bon Studies 11. Osaka: National Museum of Ethnology, 2008.

Perdue, Daniel E. *Debate in Tibetan Buddhism.* Ithaca, NY: Snow Lion, 1992.

Phuntsok Tsering (Phun tshog Tshe ring). *Situation Regarding the History and Views of Tibetan Bon Monasteries. Bod kyi bon dgon khag gi lo rgyus dang lta'i gnas bab.* Beijing: Mi rigs dpe skrun khang, 2002.

Ramble, Charles. "Ston pa Gshen rab: The Bön Buddha." In *Brill's Encyclopedia of Buddhism*, vol 2, *Lives*, edited by Jonathan A. Silk, 1233–38. Leiden: Brill, 2019.

———. "Tsewang Rigdzin. The Bon Tradition of Sacred Geography." In *Bon: The Magic Word. The Indigenous Religion of Tibet*, edited by Samten G. Karmay and Jeff Watt, 125–45. New York: Rubin Museum of Art, 2007.

Reynolds, John Myrdhin. *The Cult and Practice of the Bön po Deity Walchen Gekhöd, also Known as Zhang-Zhung Meri.* Kathmandu: Vajra Publications, 2020.

———, trans. *Oral Tradition from Zhang-Zhung: An Introduction to the Bonpo Dzogchen Teachings of the Oral Tradition from Zhang-Zhung known as the Zhang-zhung snyan-rgyud.* Kathmandu: Vajra Publications, 2005.

———, trans. *The Practice of Dzogchen in the Zhang-Zhung Tradition of Tibet, containing Translations from the Bonpo Dzogchen Practice Manual for the Zhang-zhung Nyan-gyud, Known as the Gyalwa Chaktri of Druchen Yungdrung, and from the Odsal Dunkor, "The Seven-fold Cycle of the Clear Light," Being the Dark Retreat Practice from the Same Tradition, Translated with Commentaries and Notes.* Kathmandu: Vajra Publications, 2011.

Ryavec, Karl E. *A Historical Atlas of Tibet.* Chicago: University of Chicago Press, 2015.

———. "Regional Perspectives on the Origin and Early Spread of the Bon Religion Based on Core Areas of Monastery Construction across the Tibetan Plateau." *Revue d'Etudes Tibétaines*, no. 54 (April 2020): 5–27.

Sehnalova, Anna. "Powerful Deity or National Geopark?: The Pilgrimage to A-myes-rma-chen in 2014/2015, Transformations of Modernisation and State Secularism, and Environmental Change." *Inner Asia* 21 (2019): 216–82.

Sga ston Tshul Khrims rgyal mtshan (Gatön Tsultrim Gyaltsen). *A Treatise with Autocommentary Presenting the Bonpo Abhidharma by Sga-ston Tshul-khrims-rgyal-mtshan*, vol. 1. Delhi: Tashi Dorji, 1974.

Shar rdza bKra' shis rGyal mtshan. "Man ngag rin po che a khrid kyi bla ma brgyud pa'i rnam thar padma dkar po'i phreng ba ces bya ba." In Shar rdza, *Collected Works (Bka' 'bum)*, vol. 13, 1–90. Chamdo, 1990.

———. *Self-Arising Three-Fold Embodiment of Enlightenment of Bon Great Completion Meditation*. Translated by Geshe Sonam Gurung and Daniel P. Brown. San Francisco: Bright Alliance, 2019.

Sherab Gyaltsen (1356–1415). *Bka' 'bum. Rgyal ba gnyis pa sman ri ba mnyam med chen po'i bka' 'bum bzhugs so*, 10 vols., edited by Dpon slob Shes rab g.yung drung gtsug phud. Chengdu: Si khron mi rigs dpe skrun khang, 2015.

Shinya Moriyama. "Ratnākaraśānti's Theory of Cognition with False Mental Images (*alīkākāravāda) and the Neither-One-Nor-Many Argument." *Journal of Indian Philosophy* 42.2/3, Special Issue on Ākāra in Buddhist Philosophical and Soteriological Analysis (June 2014): 339–51.

Snellgrove, David L., ed. and trans. *The Nine Ways of Bon: The Excerpts from gZi-brjid*. Oxford: Oxford University Press, 1967.

Tado Tsering Jam (Rta do Tshe ring byams), ed. *Dictionary: A Compendium of Bön Enumerations (Tshig mdzod: Bon gyi rnam grangs kun btus)*. Beijing: Mi rigs dpe skrun khang, 2016.

Tardar, Sangye, and Richard Guard. "The Twelve Deeds of Shenrab." *The Tibet Journal* 17 (Summer 1992): 28–44.

Tempa Dukte Lama. *Thrul khor: Ancient Tibetan Bon Yoga*. Pittsburg, PA: Olmo Ling Publications, 2019.

Thuken Losang Chökyi Nyima (1737–1802). *The Crystal Mirror of Philosophical Systems: A Tibetan Study of Asian Religious Thought*. Library of Tibetan Classics 25. Somerville, MA: Wisdom Publications, 2017.

Torri, Davide. *Landscape, Ritual and Identity among the Hyolmo of Nepal*. New York: Routledge, 2020.

Tsering Thar, et al. *Gangs ti se bon gzhung rig mdzod*. 25 vols. Beijing: Mi rigs dpe skrun khang, 2010.

Waldo, Ives. "Glossary Compilation." *The Rangjung Yeshe Tibetan-English Dictionary of Buddhist Culture*. Kathmandu: Rangjung Yeshe Publications, 1979–2003.

Yamamoto, Carl S. *Vision and Violence: Lama Zhang and the Politics of Charisma in Twelfth-Century Tibet*. Leiden: Brill. 2012.

Index

elephants, 356, 440
for extensive perfection, 490
farmer forgetting seeds, 116
fire, 322, 331
fire and smoke, 90
four water-demons, 292, 306, 310
gauze covering vase, 284
gold threading jewel necklace, 355, 433
horned-eagle, 515
of illusion, eight, 76, 721n95
infant's clothing, removing, 571
jewel that fulfills all wishes, 366, 413
lamp's light, 14, 15, 223, 286
learned woman teaching her child,
    472
lion pouncing, 519
lotus, 650
magician's illusion, 84, 488
mirages, 525
mirror's reflection, 85, 232, 339, 488
moons, 47, 58, 60, 253, 287, 719n78
peacocks, 356, 435
physician, 63, 489
pillars, 129, 720n81, 720n84
rabbit's horns, 54, 74, 78, 85
rope taken as snake, 507
seed and sprout, 68, 69, 84–85
sky, 48, 411
sky flower, 70
sound, 82, 240–41, 276
sow perceived as woman, 73
sun, 70, 129, 223, 490
teachings on, 358, 473–74
tortoises, 416, 521, 567
waves and ocean, 603
wick nurtured with butter, 639
wild horse, 315
wish-fulfilling tree, 494
See also butter lamps; rainbows;
    sounds
analysis, 36, 57, 264, 474, 596, 724n133
of conventional truth, 226
distinctiveness and, 193
eliminating, 209
example and meaning, 354, 358, 380,
    473–74
final, 55

of finality, 44, 66
of grounds and stages, 49–53
inability to bear, 57, 59, 61, 67, 72
on path of vision, 220, 236
of production, 83–84
purpose of, 513
sacrificial cakes and, 460
of subject and objects, 84–85
subsequent cognition and, 196
transcending, 521
See also reasoning and logic
anger, 246, 247, 249, 489–90, 603, 604,
    647, 673, 675, 737n318
animals, 96, 391, 658
annihilation, 81, 115
antidotes, 300
awareness as, 458
compassion as, 443
elimination and, 280
in meditation, 209–10
merit and, 259
modes of, 250–51, 252
primordial insight as, 457
pristine cognition as, 514
suppression by, 290
symbols of, 659
to three great afflictions emotions, 207
timing, 258, 261–64
variant views, 237, 240–41, 255–57,
    262, 274–75, 311–13, 328–29
vital, 420
Anyé Machen mountain range, 729n203
appearance-only, 84–85
appearances, 86, 87
imputation and, 258
inherent emptiness and, 74–75
limits of, 115
manifest, 322–23
mere, 82, 332, 488
and mind, relationship of, 340
non-ascertainable, absurdity of, 48
as object of negation, 78
of otherness, 328, 329
in relative truth, 331, 332, 334, 343
stopping, 330–31
three bodies and, 337
unascertained, 281

approach, 360, 380, 491, 497–98,
730n208
close, 498
divisions, 494–95
essence and definition, 493
example, 354
White A and, 408
Arcana, 197, 327
on afflictions, 224, 312
on afflictive obstructions, 243
on Bön of transcendence, 334
on defilements, 218, 221, 253, 254
on grasping, 303
on illusions, 76
on intrinsic mind, 48
on intrinsic reality, 233, 342–43
on mind of purity, 249
on realization, 99
on sentient beings, obscurations of, 56
on six bodies, 337
on three times, 333
on ultimate truth, 333–34
arhats, 721n92. *See also* foe destroyers
armor, engaging, 134–35, 136, 137–39,
140, 141, 144
arrogance, 96–97, 246, 411, 699
Asaṅga, 719n74, 724n132
Ascertaining the Root of the World, 661
ascetics and ascetic practices, 272,
439–40, 614. *See also* great ascetics
vehicle
aspiration, 158, 481, 508, 510
in approach, 493
to benefit others, 126, 127
empowerment and, 444
in entering path, 120–21
of heroes, 120
in intermediate states, 645
result of, 322–23, 328, 344
as root, 177, 178
as support, 153, 300, 301
See also mind of enlightenment
asserted proof, 72–73
Atri lineage, 3, 8, 12, 22. *See also* White A
attachment, 50, 246, 522, 560, 674, 675,
700
autonomy, 323–25, 726n160

awareness, 281, 320, 328, 585, 616
accomplished, 194
of applied mind, 510
and clear light, merging, 612
concordant, 324
continuous, 620
dynamism of, 602, 652
emanation of, 326
in Great Perfection, 8
in heart, 586
impure and quintessential, separating,
597, 599, 667, 673
in intermediate states, 639–40
and mind, distinction between,
527–28
natural radiance of, 574, 578
and objects, integrating, 650–51
potentiality of, 491
primordial, 39, 236
primordial purity of, 622
resulting accumulation, 457
rootless, 618
self-luminous, 514, 598
self-manifestation of, 657
of son, 596–97
sound of, 653
stabilizing, 698
at time of death, 637
training, 573, 600
See also knowing awareness; pristine
awareness; self-awareness
Azha clan (aka Tuyuhun), 11
Azha Lodrö Gyaltsen, 3, 4, 11–14, 22,
326–27, 715n40. See also *Magical
Key to the Precious Gradual Path
and Ground of the Greater Vehicle*

Banam Kyölpo, 539
Barnang Kujung, 539
base, path, result, 8, 17, 34–35, 318–82
benefitting others, 124, 125, 156, 198,
344, 365, 497, 657
birth, 309
four kinds, 598
through one's own efforts, 104
refuting, 84–85, 722n102
See also rebirth and reincarnation

masters viewed as, 510
motivation of, 57
qualities of, 133, 143, 366
spontaneous arising of, 619
enlightened qualities, 59, 374, 452, 481,
491
eight, 298
elimination realized by, 319
in empowerments, 563
five, 624
ground of, 294
for one's own benefit, 159
for others' benefit, 160
path of, 585
source of, 363
of ten grounds, 297–99
enlightenment, 100, 701
approaching, 620
attaining, 509–10, 622, 647
cause, 102
death and, 640
dedication to, 637
directly pointing at, 656
manifest, 323, 330
mind of enlightenment needed for,
116
for one's own sake and others', distinction between, 128–29
for others' sake, 119–20, 125
pursuing, purpose of, 611
selflessness and, 319, 335
self-manifestation of, 646
sudden and gradual, variant views,
149–52
three kinds, 655
entailing agent, 48, 61, 71–72, 85
entailing factors, 70, 82, 201, 720n87
in analyzing subject and objects,
84–85
establishing, 60, 72–73
false views on, 74
of five paths, 90
inference and, 70
negation and, 61
in one and many, 80
on path of vision, 210
sphere of absolute and, 289

in two truths, 87
envy, 97, 208, 246, 489–90, 522, 647,
737n318
equanimity, 314, 386, 488, 509, 518
abiding in, 377
as antidote, 178
attaining, 485
empowerment and, 449
in first concentrative state, 209
generating, 105
of heroes, 207–8, 209, 210
of impermanence, 453
limb of, 231
on path of application, 157, 201
as root, 177
times for practicing, 437
eternalism, 68, 70–71, 176, 246, 508
ethical conduct, 279, 296, 302, 388
Ethics of Deeds, 61
Everlasting Bön (Yungdrung Bön), 388
blood sacrifices and, 713n4
Buddhist elements in, 3–4
classificatory schemes, 9–11
curriculum, 4
Great Perfection systems, 8–9
headquarters of, 713n9
on individual existence, 719n75
origins, 1, 729n205
Perfection of Wisdom in, 723n121
scriptural system, 6, 715n26
Sherab Gyaltsen's role in, 21
systematization, 19
tantric systems, 6–8
thirty-seven collections of, 186, 296,
724n135
evil destinies, 93, 104, 141, 350
birth in, 89, 396, 397, 647
causes of, 95
grasping at, 236–37
as non-existent, 68
as object of elimination, 313, 314
path of application and, 230
path of vision and, 251
pledges and, 389, 393
protection from, 316
transcending, 143, 145, 509
wandering in, 513, 519

five poisons and, 417
natural radiance of, 578
non-perception of, 521
spontaneous perfection of, 513
in yogic exercises, 675–76
foe destroyers, 67, 300, 721n92
food and drink, 394, 395, 422–24, 454,
522, 570, 591, 671. *See also* alcohol
forbearance, 161–62, 178, 193, 198, 200,
239, 243
forceful purification, 25
in current life, 627–34
of intermediate state, 639–48
at time of death, 634–39
forgetfulness, 178, 278, 310, 392, 512
form realm, 216, 607
form-bodies, 614, 617, 622, 735n296
formless realm, 206, 216, 607
four activities, 461, 498–99, 529, 619,
659
four activities for accomplishment, 133,
134–39
four causes to aggregate of form, 477
four conceptions, 193, 196, 249–50
*Four Cycles of the Oral Diffusion of
the Revelatory Transmission of
the Great Perfection from Zhangzhung*, 8–9
four demons, 406, 728n191
four elements, 477
balancing, 673
disintegration of, 634–35
dominance in practitioners, 567
impure, stopping, 617–18
reabsorption, 635–37
in yogic exercises, 675–76
four facets, 213–14. *See under* four truths
four flaws of non-observance, 396–98
four heavies, 556, 732n245
four holies, 438, 728n197
four immeasurables, 119, 209, 301, 412,
414, 518
four marks that characterize, 148,
723n123
four miraculous feet, 173, 724n135
four modes of interpretation, 153
four mountain ranges, 367, 727n174

four names of four parts of mind aggregates, 477
four natural expressions, 129, 723n122
four non-perceptibles, 487
four non-virtuous speech actions, 569,
733n257. *See also* ten non-virtuous
actions/wrongdoings
four portals and one treasury, 10–11
four recollections, 173–75, 178, 724n135
four roots, 177–78
four thorough abandonments/elimina-
tions. *See under* elimination
four times, 658, 737n321
four true distinctions, 190, 724n136. *See
also* path of application
four truths, 14, 63, 231, 296, 308
correct perception, 279
distinctiveness and, 286
five paths and, 113
forty objects of, 245
four facets of, 213–14, 216
four recollections and, 173
for kinds of acceptance of cognizance
in, 226
particularities of, 287
path of application and, 154
path of vision and, 152
pristine cognition and, 239
purpose of, 67
union of meditation and post-meditation in, 223
See also sixteen facets of four truths
freedom from elaboration/proliferation,
326–27, 331, 411, 491, 513, 514, 515,
517, 617, 618
freedom from extremes, 302, 507, 514,
515, 517, 521, 523, 545, 594

Garsé/Garsé Tsenpo, 323, 402, 658
Gawa Döndrop, 658, 735n292
Gawo Jokpo, 401, 728n190
gazes
in breathing practices, 589
in dark retreats, 566
in daylight practices, 581–82
in direct introductions, 597, 602
in open sky practices, 572–73, 576, 577

792 *The Tradition of Everlasting Bön*

two purities, 37–38, 286–87, 289
Two Sharpnesses, 505
two truths, 14, 79
　all roots of phenomena in, 37, 38
　awareness of, 72
　concise meaning, 42–44
　different-essence arguments, 52–53
　differentiating, 265
　dispelling objections on, 328–31
　divisions of, 50
　empowerment and, 405
　essences of, 49–50
　five paths and, 113, 122
　logic and reasoning on, 54, 77
　in *Magical Key* tradition, 53–54, 56–58
　object and agent in, 270
　one-essence argument, refutation of,
　　51
　others' traditions, 55
　on path of accumulation, 156
　scriptural proofs, 76
　in scriptures and commentaries, 324,
　　325
　specifically characterized phenomena
　　and, 49
　two primordial wisdoms and, 342,
　　726n166
two views of examination, 91, 722n110
two welfares, 33, 297, 314, 512, 525,
　526–27, 719n71

ultimate truth. *See* absolute truth
unilateral decision, 721n88, 721n90
universal base, 37–39, 570, 595, 650, 654
　arising of, 571
　base, path, result in, 35
　causes from, 129
　covering, 605
　empowerment and, 356
　examples, 354, 374, 380, 596, 600
　in final visions, 620
　in heart, 586
　in intermediate states, 639–40
　mirror-like pristine cognition and, 323
　recognizing, 577, 608
　at time of death, 636, 641
　two truths and, 75

universal ground, 379
　in Great Perfection, 359, 491
　mantras and, 415
　merit and, 456
　path of accumulation and, 451, 452
　secret empowerment and, 445
　seeds in, 290
　two collections on, 480
　See also under mind of enlightenment
Universal Heap cycle, 13, 717n46
universal monarch, 298, 302
universal origination, 62, 63, 64–65
Unsurpassed Moon vehicle, 10, 514
Unsurpassed pure land, 654, 736n313
Uri Sögyal, 542
Utsé Karpo, 20
Utsé Marpo, 20

valid cognition, 149, 195, 196, 251, 315
　direct, 231
　entailing factors and, 72–73
　following faith as, 179–80
　of intrinsic reality, 218
　of ordinary mind, 343
　of others' continuum, 255–56
　pervasive, 249
　of substantial entity, 281
　use of, 88
　yogic, 343
Vase Empowerment, 404, 405
vehicle of compassionate heroes, 73
Vehicle of Prediction, 436
vehicle of self-realization, nine views
　of, 9–10
Vehicle of the Perfections, 126, 373,
　723n121
*Very Hidden Heart, the Tantra of the
　Mother Tukje Nyima*, 448
very pure mind (*thugs*), 435
Very Pure Tantra, 323
Very Pure Transmission, 45, 327, 334,
　338
Victorious Summit, 697, 739n384
Victorious Summit, 94
views, 15, 382, 433–34
　and conduct, relationship between,
　　699, 703

About the Translator

J. F. Marc des Jardins is Associate Professor of East Asian Religions in the Department of Religions and Cultures at Concordia University in Montreal. He teaches the social and cultural history of Chinese and Tibetan religions. His research focuses on the cultural interactions and religions along the former Sino-Tibetan frontiers, where Tibetan and Chinese cultures mixed and nourished each other. Since 1991 he has researched Tibetan indigenous ritual practices and the Bön religion of Tibet. He has published a monograph (*Le sūtra de la Mahāmayūrī: Rituel et politique dans la Chine des Tang*) on the importance of esoteric Buddhism during the Tang dynasty as well as articles on Tibetan indigenous magic, tantric ritual practices, the ritual of exorcism, and others. He is the chief editor of *The Journal of the International Association for Bön Research*.

Institute of Tibetan Classics

THE INSTITUTE OF TIBETAN CLASSICS is a nonprofit, charitable educational organization based in Montreal, Canada. It is dedicated to two primary objectives: (1) to preserve and promote the study and deep appreciation of Tibet's rich intellectual, spiritual, and artistic heritage, especially among the Tibetan-speaking communities worldwide; and (2) to make the classical Tibetan knowledge and literature a truly global heritage, its spiritual and intellectual resources open to all.

To learn more about the Institute of Tibetan Classics and its various projects, please visit www.tibetanclassics.org or write to this address:

Institute of Tibetan Classics
304 Aberdare Road
Montreal (Quebec) H3P 3K3
Canada

The Library of Tibetan Classics

"This new series edited by Thupten Jinpa and published by Wisdom Publications is a landmark in the study of Tibetan culture in general and Tibetan Buddhism in particular. Each volume contains a lucid introduction and outstanding translations that, while aimed at the general public, will benefit those in the field of Tibetan Studies immensely as well."

—Leonard van der Kuijp, Harvard University

"This is an invaluable set of translations by highly competent scholar-practitioners. The series spans the breadth of the history of Tibetan religion, providing entry to a vast culture of spiritual cultivation."

—Jeffrey Hopkins, University of Virginia

"Erudite in all respects, this series is at the same time accessible and engagingly translated. As such, it belongs in all college and university libraries as well as in good public libraries. *The Library of Tibetan Classics* is on its way to becoming a truly extraordinary spiritual and literary accomplishment."

—Janice D. Willis, Wesleyan University

Following is a list of the thirty-two proposed volumes in *The Library of Tibetan Classics*. Some volumes are translations of single texts, while others are compilations of multiple texts, and each volume will be roughly the same length. Except for those volumes already published, the renderings of titles below are tentative and liable to change. The Institute of Tibetan Classics has contracted numerous established translators in its efforts, and work is progressing on all the volumes concurrently.

23. *Ornament of Abhidharma: A Commentary on the "Abhidharmakośa,"* Chim Jampaiyang (thirteenth century). NOW AVAILABLE

24. *Beautiful Adornment of Mount Meru: A Presentation of Classical Indian Philosophies,* Changkya Rölpai Dorjé (1717–86). NOW AVAILABLE

25. *The Crystal Mirror of Philosophical Systems: A Tibetan Study of Asian Religious Thought,* Thuken Losang Chökyi Nyima (1737–1802). NOW AVAILABLE

26. *Gateway for Being Learned and Realized: Selected Texts*

27. *The Tibetan Book of Everyday Wisdom: A Thousand Years of Sage Advice.* NOW AVAILABLE

28. *Mirror of Beryl: A Historical Introduction to Tibetan Medicine,* Desi Sangyé Gyatso (1653–1705). NOW AVAILABLE

29. *Selected Texts on Tibetan Astronomy and Astrology*

30. *Art and Literature: An Anthology*

31. *Tales from the Tibetan Operas.* NOW AVAILABLE

32. *A History of Buddhism in India and Tibet,* Khepa Deu (thirteenth century). NOW AVAILABLE

To receive a brochure describing all the volumes or to stay informed about *The Library of Tibetan Classics,* please write to:

support@wisdompubs.org

or send a request by post to:

Wisdom Publications
Attn: Library of Tibetan Classics
132 Perry Street
New York, NY 10014 USA

The complete catalog containing descriptions of each volume can also be found online at wisdomexperience.org.

Become a Benefactor of the Library of Tibetan Classics

THE LIBRARY OF TIBETAN CLASSICS' scope, importance, and commitment to the finest quality make it a tremendous financial undertaking. We invite you to become a benefactor, joining us in creating this profoundly important human resource. Contributors of two thousand dollars or more will receive a copy of each future volume as it becomes available, and will have their names listed in all subsequent volumes. Larger donations will go even further in supporting *The Library of Tibetan Classics*, preserving the creativity, wisdom, and scholarship of centuries past, so that it may help illuminate the world for future generations.

To contribute, please either visit our website at wisdomexperience.org, call us at (617) 776-7416, or send a check made out to Wisdom Publications or credit card information to the address below.

Library of Tibetan Classics Fund
Wisdom Publications
132 Perry Street
New York, NY 10014 USA

Please note that contributions of lesser amounts are also welcome and are invaluable to the development of the series. Wisdom is a 501(c)(3) nonprofit corporation, and all contributions are tax-deductible to the extent allowed by law.

If you have any questions, please do not hesitate to call us or email us at support@wisdompubs.org.

To keep up to date on the status of *The Library of Tibetan Classics*, visit the series page on our website, and subscribe to our newsletter while you are there.

About Wisdom Publications

Wisdom · Publications is the leading publisher of classic and contemporary Buddhist books and practical works on mindfulness. To learn more about us or to explore our other books, please visit our website at wisdomexperience.org or contact us at the address below.

Wisdom Publications
132 Perry Street
New York, NY 10014 USA

We are a 501(c)(3) organization, and donations in support of our mission are tax deductible.

Wisdom Publications is affiliated with the Foundation for the Preservation of the Mahayana Tradition (FPMT).